Western World Handbook and Price Guide to Avon Bottles

Produced by Western World Publishers and the
Western World Avon Collectors Club

Printed in the United States of America
by Western World Publishers
San Francisco, California U.S.A.

ISSN 0192-4060 * ISBN 0-931864-07-0

FROM THE PUBLISHER'S DESK...

It was an Easterner, Jack Wiseburn, who first made the Avon collecting hobby known to the world. From his shop, Den of Antiquity in Clayton, New Jersey, Jack provided photos and the Avon information for that first and original article on Avon collecting – it appeared in Western World's magazine, then called The Western Collector – the year was 1968.

And from that first article, almost 14 years ago, came the all color books from Western World – Avon-7 is the largest and the latest of that famed series, with some 12,000 Avon items pictured, described and priced to reflect today's economy.

Dorothy Bernard, our Senior Editor, and *Sylvia McCann,* our Art Director, have combined their talents to again bring us this collecting book of noteworthy dimension. Thanks are due to *Bruce Leppanen* who assisted Sylvia in the artwork preparation of the book, and thanks also to *Irene Zabelny* who assisted Dorothy in the editorial function. The sorting, selecting and research to Avon-7 was a monumental task.

To the many who contributed to this new book our sincere gratitude, there are too many to list – but special mention is made of *Doyle and Faye Darch, Shirley Mae Onstot, Jo and Olie Olsen, Joan Huff, Mike and Linda Stone, Lilliebelle Willsey, Maynard Watson, Ray and Ralphie Lintz, Don and Netta Bryant, Bob and Marge Augerson, Cal and Gladys Calvin, Ron and Pat Federico* – and a special thank-you to *George Gaspar* who provided much Avon historical information from his extensive Avon Catalog collection. Ron and George are members of the Board of Directors of the National Association of Avon Collectors. To all who helped, and there were many, our deepest appreciation.

As with all of the Western World Handbooks and Price Guides to Avon Bottles, the Market Price, **MP**, represents the median price from all sections of the country. The Original Price is the Avon Company's first issued price, later prices may vary.

... and now, for you, enjoyable reading and good Avon collecting ..

Joe Weiss

Joe Weiss
Western World Avon Collectors Club

CONTENTS

From a 1902 Catalog . .

THE AVON STORY

by Dorothy Bernard

Mr. David H. McConnell

Our Avon story begins in Oswego, New York in 1878 when a good friend of the McConnell family visited the Oswego farm and persuaded young David McConnell to come to work as a book agent. Young Dave accepted and bid his family a fond farewell, saying to his father, "I'm off to make my fortune," in just those words.

David McConnell had been a farm boy. There's something special about farm work – sometimes you must struggle to get a job done, but when the job's over you can see the fruits of your labor. And that's how Dave McConnell grew up on the family farm in Oswego – continually rewarded by a sense of accomplishment. It made Dave a solid person and he was seldom discouraged.

But his fortunes changed. Young McConnell had started out travelling New England on horseback selling "Pilgrim's Progress" and "The American Book of Home Nursing" in the hope of quickly moving on to larger horizons. Two years passed and Dave was still a travelling salesman. The door-to-door drudgery might have physically tired a lesser lad, but the solid constitution he developed on the farm continued to serve him well.

Young David was not tired in his bones, he was tired in his soul. He was losing his battle with the great enemy of people in his profession – rejection and discouragement.

At the outset Dave consoled himself by rationalizing that his product was a difficult one to sell. He was selling books but there was another factor involved – Dave's farm boy heart was not really into literature.

What could he do? To return home would have been an admission of failure; to remain on the road might be disheartening and financially unsound.

Because books are best sold *inside* the home, Dave tried various means of getting himself *invited* into people's homes so that he would not have to make the sales pitch for his books on the prospect's front porch.

Dave did discover such a way, and on that way built a new business that is still growing the world over. Because Dave's market research showed that most of his door-to-door customers were women, he sought their favor with a small gift – an inexpensive bottle of perfume. It was then that Dave introduced himself as a book seller.

After three successful years Dave was promoted to General Traveling Agent. He traveled almost every state east of the Rockies, appointing Canvassers and General Agents. Later, Dave purchased and managed the business himself.

Although successful in book sales, Dave McConnell's ambition was to manufacture a line of goods that could be sold direct to a consumer at home. Since the perfumes he offered were often in greater demand than his books, he decided that the perfume business was a logical choice for his new venture.

To name his new company, McConnell chose the title *California Perfume Company* from the reports of his former employer who had moved to California and written glowing accounts of the flowers there. The perfume business was started in one small room on the sixth floor of a building at 126 Chambers Street just below Union Square in New York City.

At first only five fragrances were made – *Violet, White Rose, Heliotrope, Lily of the Valley* and *Hyacinth.* These were the natural perfumes of the flower, made the natural way with the process used by French perfumers.

Mr. McConnell had in his employ a widow from New Hampshire, Mrs. Persus Foster Eames Albee (pronounced All-bee). She had worked with him in the book business and it was in her hands that Mr. McConnell placed the first sample case of the new perfumes.

For the first six months Mrs. Albee was the only General Agent (now called *District Manager*) and traveled by train and horse-drawn carriage to make calls on the women of New England. On her trips she recruited other ladies who also made calls in New England and then in the Mid-west. The Depot Agents *(Representatives)* would first visit the Minister and through the parish be introduced to new prospects in the community.

Mrs. P. F. E. Albee

Thus the new concept of women in business, selling in their own neighborhood, offering quality products with a then unique *Money Back Guarantee,* was established. Because Mrs. Albee was first, she has been given the title of *Mother of the California Perfume Company.*

Additional fragrances and products were added to the line. Early additions were *Shampoo Cream, Witch Hazel Cream, Almond Cream Balm, Hair Tonic, Bay Rum, Lait Virginal (a milky bath), Bandoline (to keep waves in place), Facc Powder, Shaving Soap* and *Baby Powder.*

1888 The business had grown and occupied an entire floor. In 1894 the entire building was used for manufacturing.

1895 The first *Branch* distribution office was opened at Luzerne, Pennsylvania. It was phased out in 1934. Temporary manufacturing was set up in Suffern, New York.

1896 Control of manufacturing was put in the hands of Adolph Goetting, a noted perfumer. Additional Branch offices were opened in Davenport, Iowa and Dallas, Texas. The first Company catalog, consisting of text only, was issued on November 2, 1896.

1898 A fourth Branch office was opened in San Francisco, to be rebuilt and reopened after the 1906 earthquake.

1903 There were 48 General Agents and more than 10,000 Depot Agents. A Kansas City, Missouri Branch was opened and consolidated the Davenport and Dallas Branches. A history of the California Perfume Company by David McConnell, *The Great Oak,* was printed and in 1945 it was reprinted and given to employees and Representatives.

1905 The *Outlook,* a magazine for Representatives, was introduced and published continuously until 1974 when the *Avon Calling* publication took its place.

1906 The Company's first advertisement was seen in the Good Housekeeping magazine, featuring Roses Perfume.

1909 The CPC Home Office moved from Chambers Street to 31 Park Place in New York City.
1914 The first CPC International Branch and Laboratory opened in Montreal, Canada.
1915 The Company received a Gold Medal award for its *Quality of Products and Beauty of Packaging* at the Panama-Pacific International Exposition in San Francisco.
1916 The California Perfume Company incorporated in the state of New York.
1920 The first *Perfection* label appeared on *Concentrated Coloring* bottles and a *Coloring Set*.
1926 The CPC Home Office moved to 114 Fifth Avenue and there were more than 25,000 Representatives.
1928 *Avon,* a river in England, reminded Mr. McConnell of Suffern, and was the name chosen for newly introduced products – a toothbrush, household cleaner and talc.
1932 Three week campaigns replaced 4-week campaigns and less-than-regular-price *Specials* were introduced.
1935 *Friends,* a twice-weekly radio show was started.
1936 *Avon Products, Inc.* became a wholly owned subsidiary and Distributor of CPC. The English cottage picture was dropped from packaging in November, 1936 and the *Tulip-A* and the *Good Housekeeping Seal* were added.
1937 The name *California Perfume Company* no longer appeared. Labels read *Avon Products, Inc., Distributor.* The Home Office moved to 30 Rockefeller Plaza in New York. David McConnell died at the age of 79.
1942-45 World War II and the Suffern Plant converted to war effort, manufacturing Insect Repellant, Pharmaceuticals, Paratrooper Kits and Gas Mask Canisters. Plastic containers replaced metal, many products were temporarily discontinued and often an empty tube was required for the purchase of a new Shaving Cream or Toothpaste tube. In 1944 the Lipstick & Rouge Division moved to larger quarters in Middletown, New York and assumed the name of *Allied Products.*
1946 On March 21st the CPC name was legally changed to *Allied Products, Inc.* and to *Avon Allied Products, Inc.* under New York corporation laws. Stock in the corporation was offered over-the-counter to the public.
1947 The Pasadena, California laboratory was opened and marked the last year *Montreal* appeared on labels. Labels were changed to read *New York-Pasadena.*
1950 On December 31st Allied Products, Inc. and Avon Allied Products, Inc. merged and assumed the name *Avon Products, Inc.* The word *Distributor* was dropped from the labels and in 1951 labels read *Avon Products, Inc. New York-Pasadena.* Today, the word *Distributor* appears on labels when the product is made by an outside vendor. A few are *Nail Strengthener, Room Fresheners* and *Decorative Ceramic Gifts.* **Carton Dating**: *Upon opening a carton from the bottom, a number will be found. Transpose the the first two numbers in the un-hyphenated series. If the number was 862429, the first two numbers would read 68, indicating the carton was made in 1968. On some cartons a number like 8-70 may be found. It indicates the carton was made in August of 1970.* **Remember, please!** *This method will date* **cartons only**, *not bottles.*
1953 The first Avon television commercial was seen in Chicago and New York. On TV, in 1954, the *Ding-Dong, Avon Calling* bell was first heard. The first Avon color TV commercial was in 1957; first men's commercial in 1958.
1954 Off-continent operations were started in Venezuela, South America and in Puerto Rico.
1955 *Sales Brochures* were introduced to support the campaign selling effort.
1964 April 2nd, Avon stock was listed and trading started on the New York Stock Exchange.
1968 A new marketing concept started. Representatives in the west and some mid-west states began calling on customers every *two weeks.* As the program proved successful, other Divisions joined the plan. Complete national conversion to the plan came in March, 1969.
1971 Jewelry was first introduced in the U.S. Avon is now the *largest distributor of costume jewelry in the world!*
1972 Avon moved to new World Headquarters at 9 West 57th Street in New York. Sales topped the *one billion dollar* mark. Avon entered the ceramics market in 1972 and in 1973 welcomed a wholly-owned subsidiary — *Family Fashions by Avon,* a company selling wearing apparel by mail from Newport News, Virginia.

1977-78 Avon started sponsoring women's athletic events: in tennis the *Avon Futures Circuit,* in women's running, the *Avon Marathon* and the popular *Avon Championship Tennis.*
1979 Test marketing of Avon Vitamins started in January at the Springdale Branch and Avon's total worldwide sales topped *two billion dollars* for the year. In April of 1979 *Tiffany & Co.,* noted jewelers, was joined to the Avon company. *Roses to the Winners,* created as a tribute to women in sports, was the theme of Avon's first Pasadena Tournament of Roses Parade entry in 1979. The 1980 Parade entry was a tribute to *The World of Music* and featured Frank Sinatra who was Grand Marshal of the Parade. In 1981 the Avon entry, *Autumn Splendor,* was a Grand Prize winner in the Tournament of Roses.

The 1982 Avon entry in the Rose Parade, shown above, will be titled *Beauty of the Orient* and follows the Grand Kubuki of Japan in styling. Six Kubuki dancers and Leslie Kin Kawai, the 1981 Rose Queeen, will appear on the float – which will be dedicated by Avon to the Representatives and Managers in Avon's Japanese market.
1981 New Collectible Products to be introduced include Porcelain Figurines, Decorative Plaques, Keepsake Banks and Christmas Ornaments. Many different materials, such as wood, metal, fabric and fine glassware will be used in the making of new products and many will be signed or initialed by the creator or artist.

Now, in 1981-82, the tiny company that a young man founded, is the world's leading manufacturer and distributor of cosmetics, fragrances and fashion jewelry. Since 1886, Avon products have been sold to customers in their home by independent Representatives – just as David McConnell envisioned they would be –*almost one hundred years ago! A remarkable dream come true!*

And that Company. created by a despairing traveling salesman now offers more than 700 products. Today, there are 1,250,000 Representatives around the world, bringing service to millions of customers in 32 different countries. A lasting tribute to a far-sighted man.

Western World Avon Collectors NEWSLETTER

WESTERN WORLD AVON CLUB • BOX 27587, SAN FRANCISCO, CALIFORNIA 94127 • JULY-AUGUST 1981

Dear Western World Club Member:

AVON 7 As we close this July-August issue of the Newsletter we're putting finishing touches on the bright, new – better than ever – Avon-7. A new larger size, new features, over 33% more material than Avon-6, and of course, every page is in full color. Read Dorothy Bernard's article on this page, see pages 2 and 3, then fill out the enclosed Order Form or use the order form on page 15 – there's a great Avon collectors book in your future! Ready about August 20

Just look at the Ads! If you're wondering where the foremost market place for Avon collectibles is – you're looking at it! Your Western World Newsletter runs more ads more often than any other publication and – best of all – ads are Free to Members! In this issue forty-three of the 50 states are represented and there are over 200 ads to look over for what you want to buy, what you want to sell or what you want to trade. Have you put in your ad? There's a form on page 16!

Did you write for a Pen Pal? If you haven't you've not had the family fun that hundreds of Western Worlders have had – there are Pen Pals in Avon's England, Scotland, Wales and Ireland for the whole family. We've had letters from little helpers ages 6 and 7, all the way up to Busy Bees in their eighties! You can join the fun, just write to me and say, 'OK, Joe, send me a Pen Pal' and I'll do it right away. You and your family will love corresponding with nice people, just like you, half way around the world. Look for some interesting Pen Pal comments in the Letters Section.

They're all Here! Your favorite writers, that is – you'll find Lola Schlining on page 7, Monte Hart is on page 9, Jack Jamieson, the Plant Man, is on page 8, Trevor Hall, our European Connection is on page 5 and Teri Hayden tells us something about Avon-ing in New Zealand on page 6. So read on for the very best in Avon collecting reporting.

Joe Weiss
Western World Publisher

Does your label read LAST ISSUE RENEW TODAY? Use Order Form on page 15, only $8.50 to renew!

AVON 7 NEW LARGER STY... WILL BE READY... PRESSES ABO...

Ads Are FREE To Members

WESTERN WORLD AVON COLLECTOR'S CLUB

WWAC now has more than 5,000 Members in every state of the union, and in many foreign countries, too. The WWAC Newsletter – a big 16 page, professionally prepared bi-monthly – brings Avon facts and late reports in every issue. Editor Dorothy Bernard, a President's Club Member since 1957, knows whereof she speaks and writes! Her column "What's New Avon Lady" has come to be the most respected and informative article of its type – anywhere!

Dorothy Bernard, Western World's Senior Editor of Avon information, is an authority on Avon Company history and Avon collecting. She is a noted writer and long time member of the Avon President's Club.

FREE ADS *to Members! There's never a charge to buy or to sell or to swap or just write. Ads are always FREE to Members! The Market Place for the Avon Collector is the WW Newsletter!*

Only $8.50 *a year for six big issues – join up. Join Today!* **Western World Avon Club, Box 27587, San Francisco, CA 94127**

Lola Schlining

Teri Hayden

Trevor Hall

And there's more – you get top rated Avon reporting, like the "Letter from Lola" by Lola Schlining in Indiana. You get the word on "Avon Around the World" from Teri Hayden and WW's European Connection is Trevor Hall in London, England.

AVON COLLECTING
with Dorothy Bernard

Since 1969, when the first *Western World Handbook* was published, one of our great assets in determining prices has been readers who will quote specific prices for bottles. It is, of course, the buyer and seller of Avon bottles who determine the price. What a buyer is willing to pay for a bottle and what a seller is willing to sell his bottle for– are the determining factors. With information gathered from all corners of the nation, our *Handbook and Price Guide* represents the national median in pricing.

Regular Price (shown preceding the **MP**) reflects Avon's price at original issue date. Later Avon prices may increase or decrease from the original issue price.

MP *(Market Price)* reflects empty containers, except for tubes, and where the product is an integral part of the container–for example, soap dishes and Sunshine Rose Candle. **MP** does not include the box unless it is necessary to the collectible, such as in sets and boxed soaps.

MP followed by an asterisk (*) tells you that the item was still available from Avon at time of publication and the **MP** is the same as you would pay for the full, mint product at Avon's special pricing. Because of generally increasing prices, you will often find that the **MP*** is the same amount, or more, than the original issue price.

If you are a new collector, you may find that *Western World Handbook* prices vary in relationship to current Market Prices. Even an expert cannot keep up with the changing values brought on by the discontinuance or re-introduction of Avon containers or just the effects of inflation. And we must all contend with the variations in value dependant on the condition of the item. Even though Market Prices at times seem puzzling, they give us a good overview of what's happening to the general price picture– *up, up, up!*

Mint, full and boxed items continue to be most in demand and draw the highest price. The *mint condition bottle* is empty, without flaked paint, cracks or chips, has all labels, correct lid and all accessory parts.

Bottles with cracks, chips or missing labels are affected in value. A slight chip on a common bottle would reduce its value about 50%, on a rare bottle about 25%. Badly chipped, or bottles without labels, on the other hand, are very severely penalized–generally, about 75% for the rare bottle and 90% for the common one.

There's always a reason for occasional changes in Market Prices. For example, increased interest in collecting Perfection, paper items, older samples and demonstration aids have caused these items to increase greatly in value, as has appreciation of different packaging issued during wartime or a glass strike, containers issued for only a short time or special Christmas or Anniversary packaging.

Clubs and Chapters are an ideal place to make your Avon wants and needs known. And one of the primary functions of Western World has been to provide Club Members with a Market Place where buyers and sellers of bottles can meet to Buy, Sell or Trade. The WWAC Newsletter offers you Free Ads and the opportunity to do your own Market Survey. Whether at your Club or in the Newsletter, Avon-7 and the Free Ads are a hard combination to beat!

Dorothy Bernard's

CPC/AVON LABEL DATING GUIDE

Until an established CPC/Avon product was re-issued in newly designed packaging, its original catalog picture (called a pick-up) was shown in succeeding catalogs for a period of sometimes several years. This is notably apparent, for example, in the Perfection Line. Because of this, the CPC and Avon Catalogs through the 1950's fail to reveal the many different label changes that took place over the years. Labels serve an important function in helping to date CPC/Avon bottles within a particular time period.

1886-88 CALIFORNIA PERFUME COMPANY
New York

1888-98 As Above
(with Eureka Trademark)

1898-04 CALIFORNIA PERFUME COMPANY
New York-San Francisco-Dallas

1904-11 CALIFORNIA PERFUME COMPANY
New York-San Francisco-Kansas City
(with CP logo circled within Eureka TM)

1911-15 CALIFORNIA PERFUME COMPANY
New York-San Francisco-Kansas City
(with oval CPC logo)

1915-23 CALIFORNIA PERFUME COMPANY
New York-San Francisco-Kansas City-Montreal

1923-27 CALIFORNIA PERFUME COMPANY
New York-Kansas City-Montreal

1927-30 CALIFORNIA PERFUME COMPANY, INC.
New York-Montreal

1930-34 CALIFORNIA PERFUME COMPANY, INC.
New York-Montreal
(with Cottage "A" logo)

1934-36 CALIFORNIA PERFUME COMPANY, INC.
AVON PRODUCTS, INC., DIV.
New York-Montreal

1936-39 AVON PRODUCTS, INC., DIV.
CALIFORNIA PERFUME CO., INC.
New York-Montreal
(with Tulip "A" logo)

1939-47 AVON PRODUCTS, INC., DIST. OR DISTRIBUTOR
New York-Montreal

1947-51 AVON PRODUCTS, INC., DIST.
New York-Pasadena

1951-57 AVON PRODUCTS, INC.
New York-Pasadena

1957-67 AVON PRODUCTS, INC.
New York, N.Y.

1967-72 AVON PRODUCTS, INC.
New York, N.Y. 10020

1972. . . AVON PRODUCTS, INC.
New York, N.Y. 10019

Note: The Home Office location appears on all packaging, either New York, or N.Y., depending upon label space. Very early labels may also carry the 126 Chambers Street address. Occasionally, when space was adequate, a few bottle labels and Perfection containers listed an added Branch office. Luzerne may be seen on 1915-1934 labels and Los Angeles 1939-47. Boxes most always listed all Branch offices.
(See Perfection Guide pg. 26)

1888-1904

1904-1911

1911-1930

1929

1930-1936

1936-53

1940's

1953

1976

1978. . .

Dorothy Bernard's

CPC FRAGRANCE DATING GUIDE

1886 *Heliotrope*
Hyacinth (re-intro 1974)
Lily of the Valley (re-intro 1963)
Violet (re-intro 1972)
White Rose

1890 *Orange Blossom*
Oriental

1890-96 *Bay Rum (for Men & Women)*
Carnation (re-intro 1972)
Crab Apple Blossom
Eau de Cologne
Florida Water
Lavender
Lou Lillie
Sweet Cologne
Sweet Pea
White Heliotrope

1896-98 *L'Odeur de Violette*
Le Parfum des Roses
Musk
Peau d'Espagne
White Lilac

1900-05 *Bouquet Marie*
Frangipani
Golf Club
Golf Violet
Jack Rose
Jockey Club
Marie Stewart
May Blossom
New Mown Hay
Rose Geranium (re-intro 1942)
Stephanotis
Trailing Arbutus
Tube Rose
Venetian Carnation
Ylang, Ylang

1905 *California Bouquet*
Treffle

1906 *Roses*

1907 *American Ideal (re-intro 1941)*

1910 *Honeysuckle (re-intro 1966)*

1914 *Natoma Rose*

1916 *Daphne*

1922 *Mission Garden*

1923 *Vernafleur*

1925 *Lilac Vegetal (renamed Lilac 1936)*
Narcissus

1926 *Jardin d'Amour (renamed Garden of Love 1939)*

(For Avon Fragrance Line dating see: Women's and Girl's pg. 34, Men's pg. 181)

1912 *Depot Agent's Demonstration case. 20 food extracts & colorings* **MP $1900, $200 empty** *(shown closed, above)*
1930 *Order Book* **MP $25**

1911 *Brush Runabout motor car, won by Effie Miller, Oregon Depot Agent for her fine sales record.*

CPC DEPOT AGENT

1898 *Second Sales Catalog, issued in November, 60 pages.* **MP $400 to $500**
1917 *Smaller size of large Sales Catalog, text only, to leave with customers, 40 pages* **MP $300**

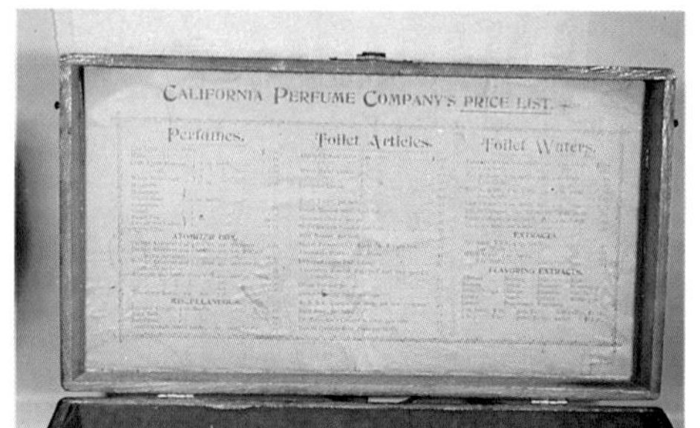

1897 *Demonstration Case holds variety of products* **MP $250**

1900-1910 *Identification Pin given to Depot Agent after first order* **MP $175**

1910 *Identification Pin* **MP $160**
1910 *Honor Pin for reaching sales of $250* **MP $175**
1936 *50th Anniversary Award 24k gold- plated pin* **MP $55**

By 1898 there were 5,000 Depot Agents. In 1911 the number increased to 10,000 and they were called Sales Managers. Today, over 1 million Representatives share Avon's unique earning opportunity.

1915 *Sales Catalog (same cover on catalogs through 1921)* **MP $225 each complete catalog.**

1920's *Depot Agent's Bag with CPC–Avon printed materials* **MP $40 bag only**

1912 *Powder Puff Jar for reaching sales of $50 during December* **MP $200**

1922 *Sales Catalog (same cover on catalogs through 1929)* **MP $200 each complete catalog**

(See also pg. 227 for Avon catalogs)

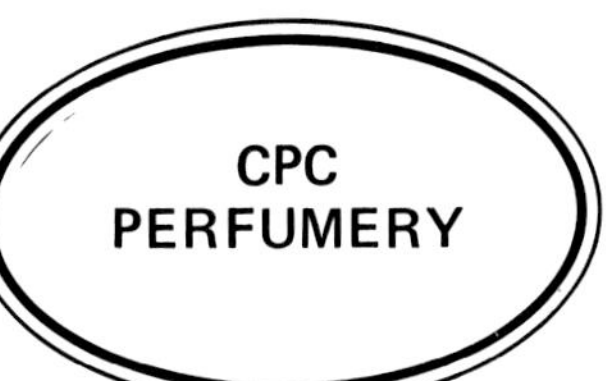

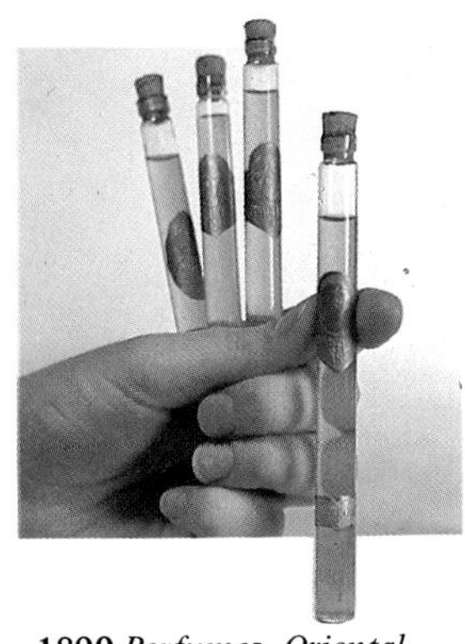

1890 *Perfumes, Oriental, Orange Blossom and two called Parfum, each 15¢* **MP $200 each**

1893 *Extract of White Rose 1oz 40¢* **MP $175**

1906 *Peau D'Espagne French Perfume, trial size 25¢* **MP $140**
1917 *Peau D'Espagne, trial size 50¢* **MP $140**

1917 *Le Parfum des Roses, trial size 50¢* **MP $140**

A 1908 catalog states: "The CP perfumes are without question the standard of excellence in the United States, being even more fragrant and lasting than the most expensive imported perfumes – for which almost double the true value is charged owing to the enormous duty on all imported perfumes and toilet articles."

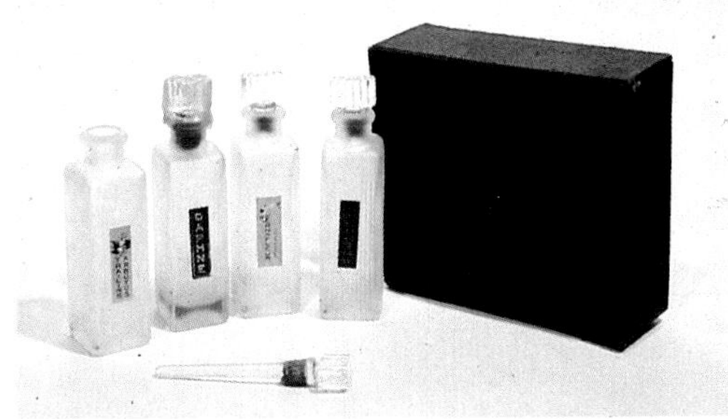

Perfume Demonstrators, 4 bottles per case, 3 drams each.

1923 *Vernafleur, Trailing Arbutus, Daphne & American Ideal* **MP $350 $75 each bottle**

1925 *Vernafleur, Trailing Arbutus, Daphne & Mission Garden* **MP $350, $75 each bottle**

"Moreover, CP Perfumes are natural floral extracts, not chemical compounds as is the case with most other perfumes at equal cost. The regular line of CP Floral extracts consists of thirty odors."

1906 *Extract of Crab Apple Blossom Perfume 1oz 50¢* **MP $155**

1908 *Rose Sachet Powder 25¢* **MP $125**
1910 *Rose Sachet Powder 25¢* **MP $125**

1908 *Heliotrope Sachet Powder 25¢* **MP $125**
1910 *Heliotrope Sachet Powder 25¢* **MP $125**

1908 *Heliotrope Perfume 50¢* **MP $150**

1908 *Extract of Heliotrope Perfume 1oz 40¢* **MP $155**

1915 *Heliotrope Triple Extract Perfume 1oz 90¢* **MP $145, $175 boxed**

1893 *Lavender Salts 35¢* **MP $210**

1906 *Lavender Salts. Label reads: "These. Goods are guaranteed under the Pure Food & Drug Act June 30, 1906." 35¢* **MP $175**
1918 *Lavender Salts 35¢* **MP $130**
1920 *Lavender Salts 35¢* **MP $130**

1925 *Lavender Salts 50¢* **MP $95**

1923 *Lavender Salts 49¢* **MP $110**

1906 *Rose Pomade 25¢* **MP $50**
1906 *Extract of White Rose Perfume, trial size 25¢* **MP $80**

1923 *American Ideal Toilet Water 2oz $1.50* **MP $130**

1915 *Lotus Cream Sample* **MP $85**
1919 *Lily of The Valley Perfume 1oz 50¢* **MP $130**
1924 *Rose Water, Glycerine & Benzoin Sample* **MP $75, $95 boxed**

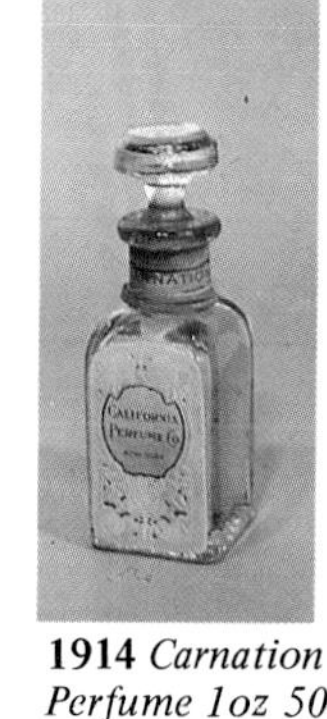

1914 *Carnation Perfume 1oz 50¢* **MP $150**

1908 *Hyacinth Perfume 1oz 50¢* **MP $175**

1917 *Crab Apple Blossom Quadruple Extract Perfume ½oz 90¢* **MP $150, $175 boxed**

1917 *Le Parfum des Roses ½oz $1* **MP $150, $175 boxed**

1915 *Carnation Triple Extract Perfume 1oz 90¢* **MP $150, $175 boxed**

1915 *Lily of The Valley Triple Extract Perfume 1oz 90¢* **MP $150, $175 boxed**

1915 *White Lilac Triple Extract Perfume 1oz 90¢* **MP $150, $175 boxed**

1915 *White Rose Quadruple Extract Perfume 1oz $1.10* **MP $150, $175 boxed**

1917 *Perfume, in choice of 23 fragrances & Perfect Atomizer $1.50 to $3* **MP $185, $215 boxed**
Perfect Atomizer, separate 70¢ **MP $30**

. . . CPC PERFUMERY

1918 *Musk Perfume Atomizer Bottle 1oz* **MP $175**

1909 *White Rose Perfume 50¢* **MP $150**

1918 *White Lilac Perfume. Sold only in Atomizer Set* **MP $150, $180 w/atomizer**

1915 *Perfume 2oz embossed label $2.25* **MP $175**

1915 *Carnation Sachet 25¢* **MP $90**

1915 *California Bouquet Perfume 8oz $3.25* **MP $180**

1908 *Traveler's Bottle, 8 frag. 50¢* **MP $130**

1915 *New Mown Hay Triple Extract Perfume 1oz 90¢* **MP $150, $175 boxed**

1923 *Concentrated Perfume in 9 frag. ½oz Roses shown 59¢* **MP $115, $135 boxed**

1923 *1oz Perfume in 9 frag. Lily of The Valley shown $1.17* **MP $125, $150 boxed**

1925 *1oz Perfume in 6 frag. Crab Apple Blossom shown $1.17* **MP $120**

1928 *Perfume & Atomizer $2.25* **MP $150**

1915 *Perfume, intro size 60¢* **MP $125, $150 boxed**

1915 *Perfume 1oz $2, 2oz $3.75* **MP $135 each**

1915 *Powder Sachet $1* **MP $95**

1914 *Perfume with wooden holder 75¢* **MP $225 complete, $135 Bottle only**

1915 *Toilet Soap 50¢* **MP $95, $60 Soap only**

1915 *Talcum Powder 4oz 35¢* **MP $85**

AMERICAN IDEAL . . . *a highly concentrated perfume, was called the Queen of American Perfumes.*

1917 *Perfume, intro size 75¢* **MP $125, $150 boxed**

1917 *Perfume 1oz $2.50* **MP $135, $160 boxed**

1918 *Sachet Powder $1.25* **MP $90**

1918 *Toilet Water 2oz $1.50* **MP $135, $160 boxed**

1917 *Talcum Powder 3½oz 75¢* **MP $100**

1923 *Talcum Powder 3½oz 72¢* **MP $95**

1918 *Perfume intro size 75¢* **MP $125, $150 boxed**

1918 *Perfume 2oz $4.75* **MP $135**

1928 *Perfume Flaconette $1.10* **MP $95**

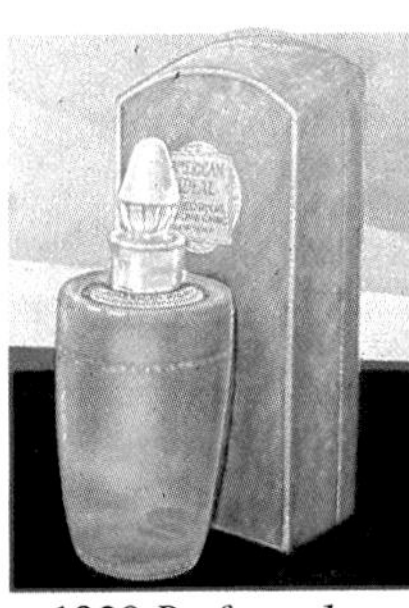
1928 *Perfume 1oz $2.40* **MP $125, $150 boxed**

1941 *Perfume 1oz 20¢ introductory, then 75¢ (sold only 4 months)* **MP $100, $140 boxed**

It was so penetrating, a very small quantity was sufficient to perfume a whole room and a single drop thoroughly perfumed a handkerchief or dress.

1920 *Compact, Compressed Face Powder or Rouge 59¢* **MP $40**

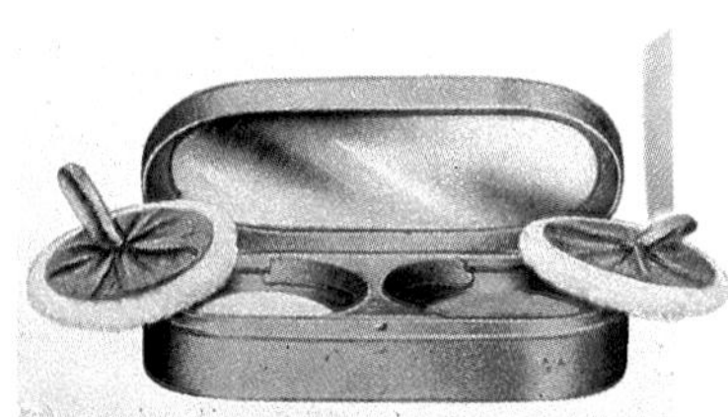
1920 *Double Compact, Face Powder or Rouge $1.17* **MP $60**

1915 *Face Powder, white or flesh colored 75¢* **MP $65**

1923 *Face Powder 96¢* **MP $55**

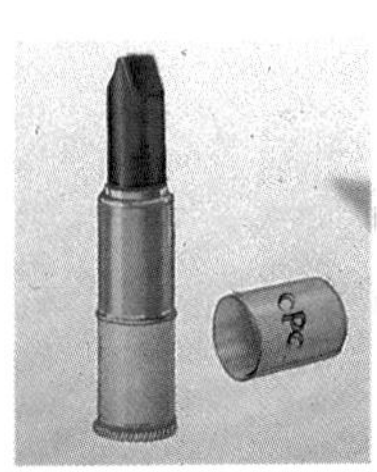
1928 *Lipstick $1* **MP $20**

1919 *Soap 60¢* **MP $70**

1923 *Soap 48¢* **MP $65**

1926 *Boxed Toilet Soaps 96¢* **MP $80**

. . . AMERICAN IDEAL

1918 *Cream Deluxe $1* **MP $60**

1923 *Cream Deluxe 96¢* **MP $50**

1928 *Talcum 75¢* **MP $75**
1928 *Face Powder $1* **MP $40**
1928 *Cream Deluxe $1* **MP $40**

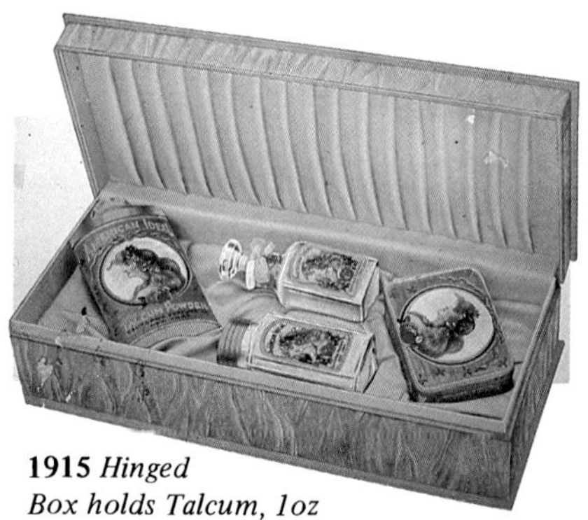

1915 *Hinged Box holds Talcum, 1oz Perfume, Sachet Powder and Soap $4* **MP $425**

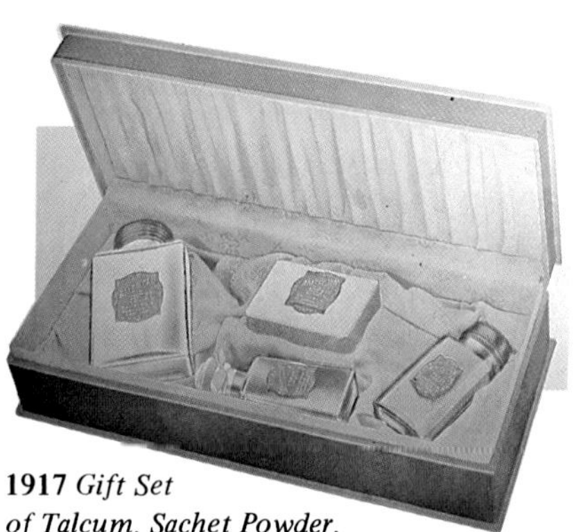

1917 *Gift Set of Talcum, Sachet Powder, Soap and 1oz Perfume in hinged Wooden Box $5.50* **MP $395**

1923 *Threesome Set. Talcum, Sachet Powder and 2oz Toilet Water $3.95* **MP $325**

1926 *Foursome Set. Talcum, Face Powder, Cream Deluxe and 1oz Perfume $6.50* **MP $350**

DAPHNE

1926 *Boxed Soaps 72¢* **MP $70**

1922 *Sachet 96¢* **MP $85**

1920 *Sachet 96¢* **MP $90**

1926 *Sachet $1* **MP $75**

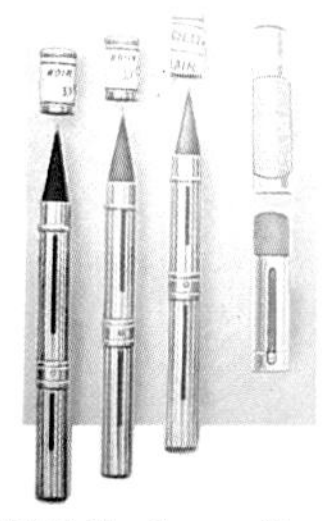

1917 *Eyebrow Pencils, Br, Blk, Blonde 30¢ Lipstick 50¢* **MP $20 each**

1917 *Cerate 75¢* **MP $60**

1917 *Face Powder 75¢* **MP $65**

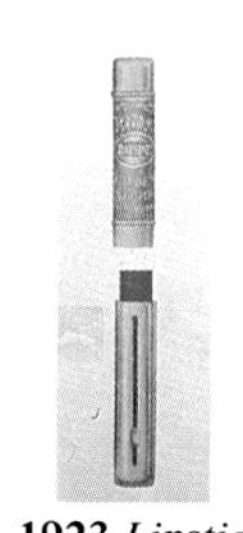

1923 *Lipstick 39¢* **MP $20**

1916 *Perfume 1oz $1.90* **MP $135**
1919 *Perfume 4oz $6.50* **MP $215**

1928 *Perfume Flaconette $1* **MP $95**

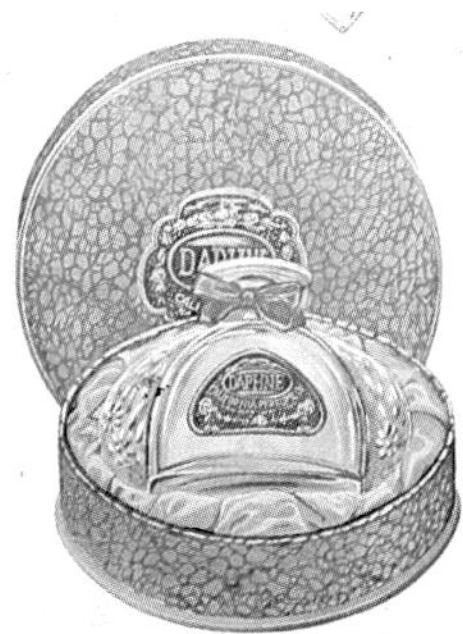

1926 *Perfume 1oz $1.85* **MP $135, $160 boxed**

1923 *Toilet Water 2oz $1.20* **MP $130, $155 boxed**

1926 *Toilet Water 2oz (shown with outer box, left) $1.20* **MP $180 as shown**

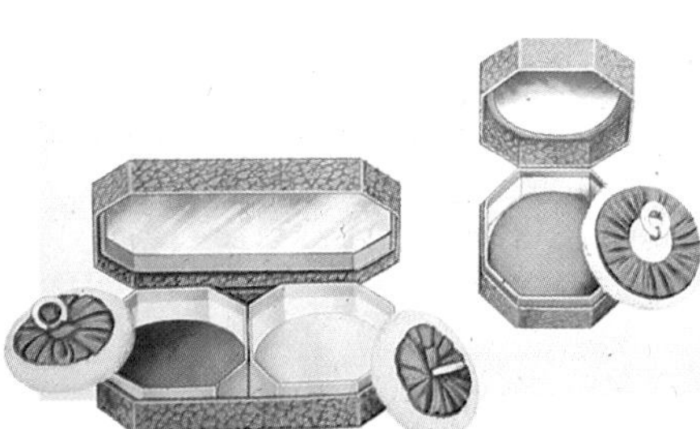

1917 *Double Vanity Box. Face Powder and Rouge Compacts $1* **MP $55**
1917 *Vanity Rouge Compact (also available with powder) 50¢* **MP $40**

1926 *Single Compact, Rouge or Face Powder 39¢* **MP $35**

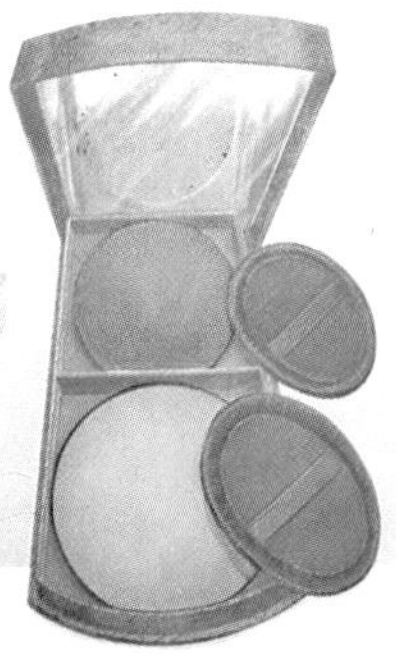

1926 *Duplex Compact, Rouge & Face Powder 98¢* **MP $45**

1920 *Talcum Powder 4oz 48¢* **MP $65**

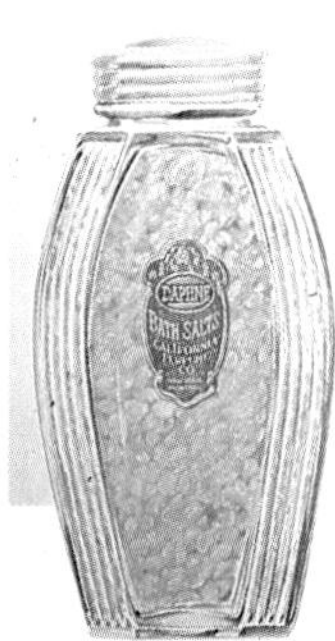

1926 *Bath Salts 98¢* **MP $75**

. . . DAPHNE

1923 *Cerate 72¢* **MP $50**

1923 *Rolling Massage Cream 69¢* **MP $50**

1926 *Cerate (shown) or Derma Cream 75¢* **MP $45**

1926 *Massage Cream 75¢* **MP $45**

1928 *Massage Cream 70¢* **MP $40**

1928 *Cerate (shown) or Derma Cream 75¢* **MP $40**

"CP Massage Cream, being a true skin food, nourishes the tissues of the skin, and quickly fills out sunken cheeks, as well as the bust," claimed the 1908 Catalog.

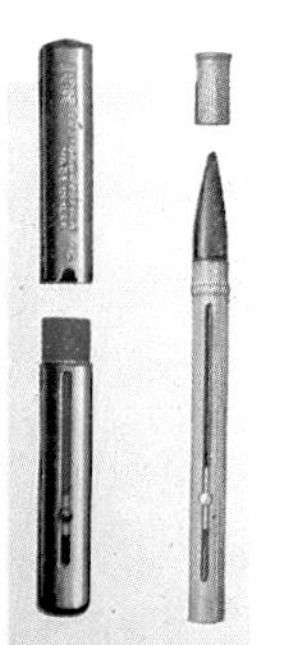

1926 *Lipstick 39¢ Eyebrow Pencil 29¢* **MP $18 each**

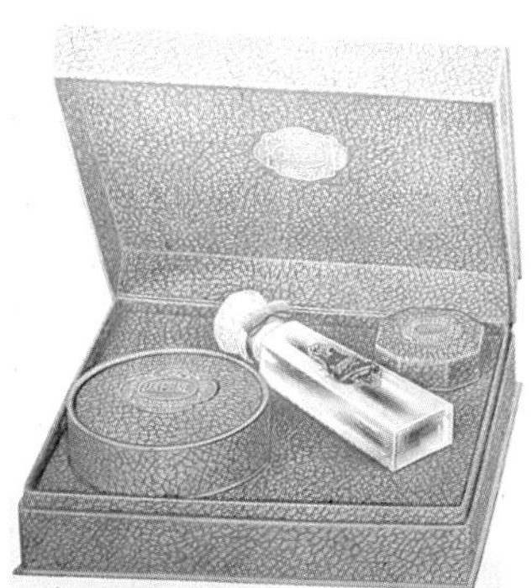

1917 *Daphne Set. Face Powder, Perfume 1oz & Rouge $3.50* **MP $325**

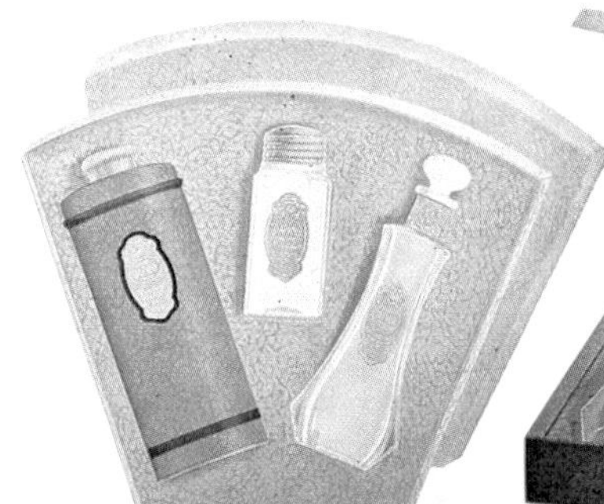

1923 *Daphne Threesome. Talcum & Sachet Powders, Toilet Water 2oz $3.20* **MP $300**

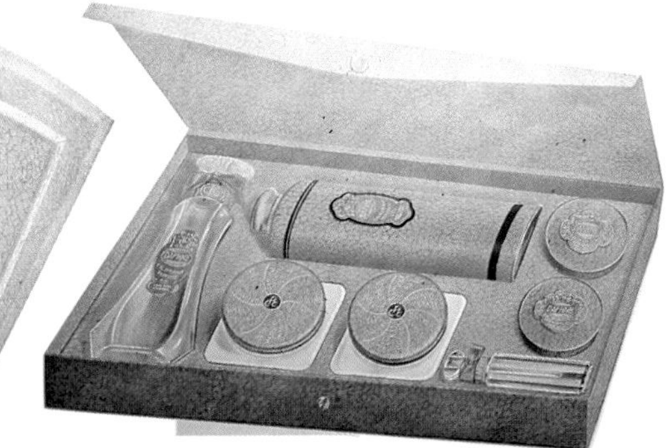

1926 *Septette Gift. Cerate & Derma Creams, Face Powder & Rouge Compacts, Talcum, Toilet Water & Perfume Extract $2.95* **MP $425**

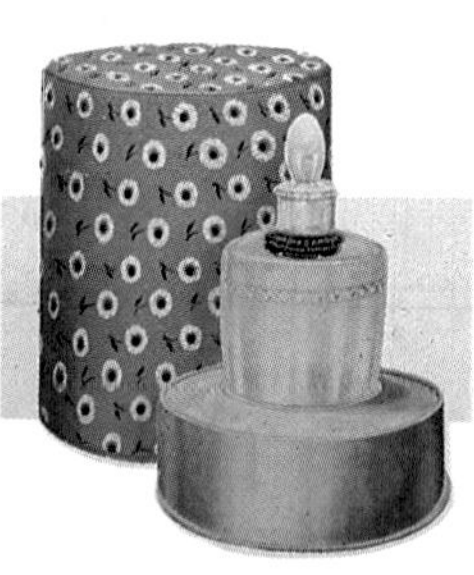

1926 *Perfume 1oz $3.50, 2oz $6.50* **MP $115, $150 boxed**

1926 *Talcum 75¢* **MP $50**

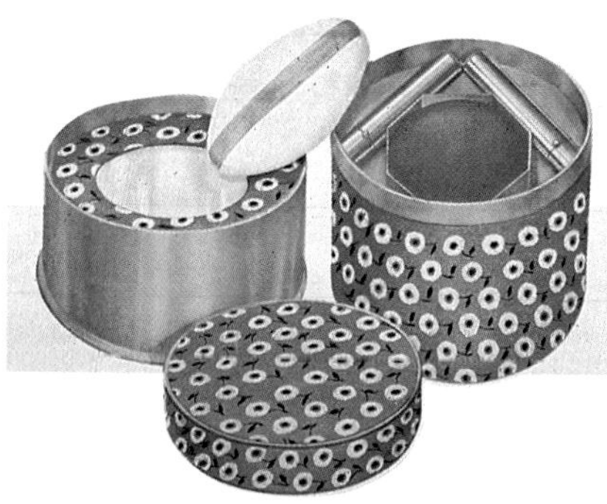

1926 *Ensemble Set. Brow Pencil, Rouge, Face Powder, Lipstick $2.25* **MP $200**

JARDIN D'AMOUR

1926 *Vanity Compact, Rouge & Powder $2.25* **MP $45**

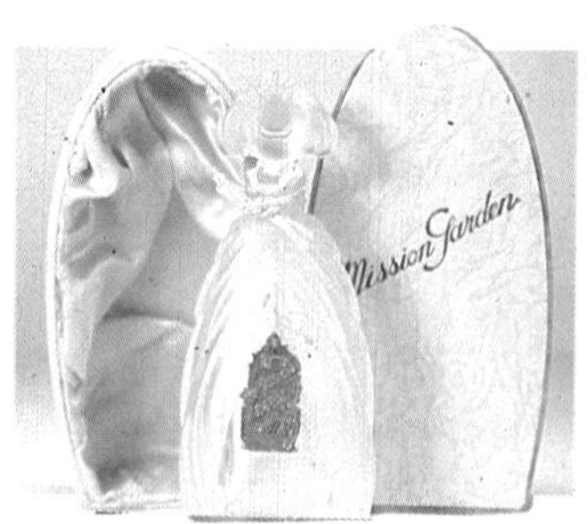

1922 *Perfume 1½oz $4.95* **MP $210, $300 boxed**

1922 *Toilet Water 2oz $2.25* **MP $130, $160 boxed**

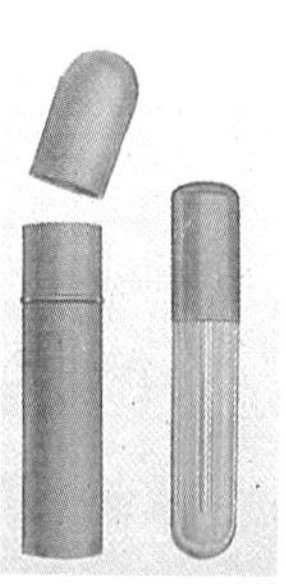

1922 *Flaconette Perfume & Brass Holder 98¢* **MP $100**

1922 *Sachet Powder $1.75* **MP $85**

1923 *Twin Compact $1.48* **MP $45**

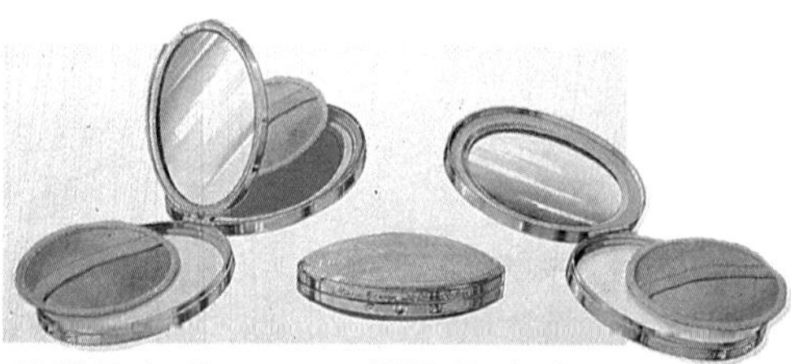

1925 *Twin Compact $1.48* **MP $40**

1925 *Single Compact 98¢* **MP $35**

MISSION GARDEN

1928 *Perfume Flaconette $1.20* **MP $95, $125 boxed**

1925 *Perfume 1oz $2.85* **MP $120**

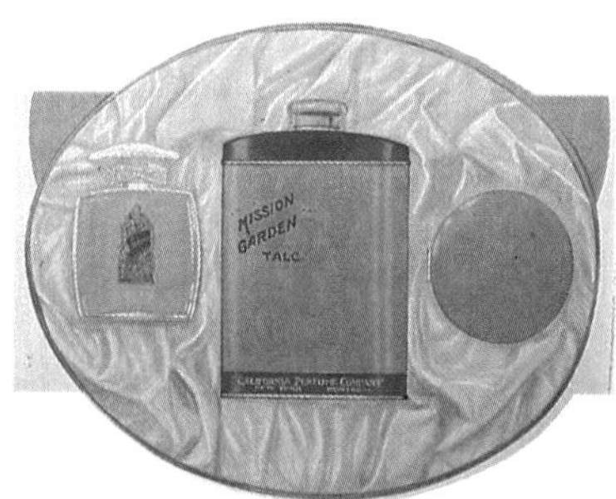

1925 *Threesome Set. Perfume 1oz, Talc & Twin Compact $7* **MP $270**

1925 *Perfume 1oz $2.10* **MP $120**

NARCISSUS

1928 *Perfume Flaconette $1* **MP $95**

1926 *Perfume Flaconette 84¢* **MP $95**

1926 *Perfume 1oz $2.19* **MP $115, $150 boxed**

1918 *Perfume 1oz $1.40* **MP $135**

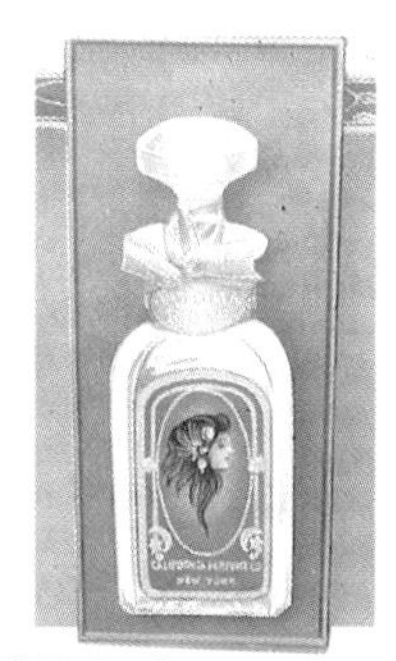
1917 *Perfume 1oz $1.40* **MP $125, $155 boxed**

1915 *Box N, Perfume ½oz 75¢* **MP $140, $170 boxed**

1915 *Perfume 1oz $1.40* **MP $135, $160 boxed**
1916 *Perfume 1oz $1.40* **MP $115, $140 boxed**

NATOMA ROSE

1915 *Rolling Massage Cream 5oz 75¢* **MP $155**

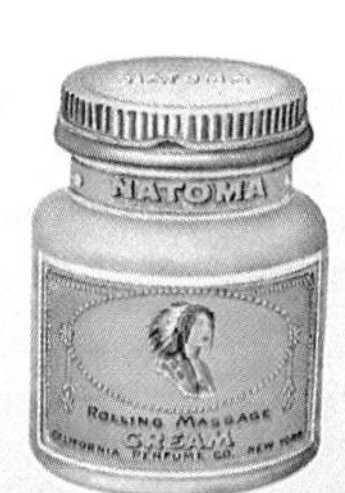
1918 *Rolling Massage Cream 5oz 75¢* **MP $110**

1918 *Talcum 4oz 35¢* **MP $75**
1914 *Talcum 4oz 35¢* **MP $85**
1921 *Talcum 4oz 35¢* **MP $75**

1915 *Perfume 2oz $3.75* **MP $200**
1915 *Toilet Water 2oz 75¢, 4oz $1.50* **MP $130**

1914 *Perfume 1oz $1.10* **MP $135, $185 boxed**

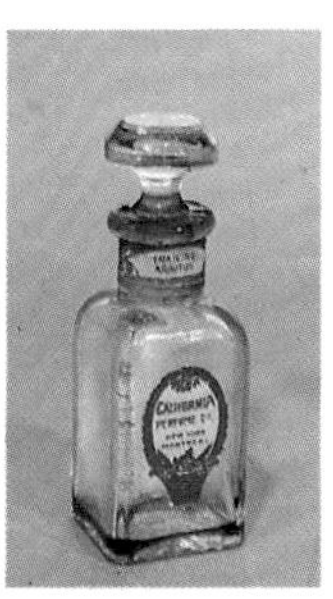
1923 *Perfume 1oz $1.17* **MP $115**

1925 *Perfume 1oz & 2oz $1.17 & $2.10* **MP $125, $160 boxed**

TRAILING ARBUTUS

1917 *Sachet Powder 60¢* **MP $95**

1915 *Sachet Powder 60¢* **MP $95**

1925 *Sachet Powder 72¢* **MP $85**

1923 *Sachet Powder 72¢* **MP $85**

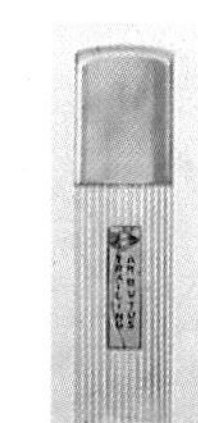
1928 *Perfume Flaconette 59¢* **MP $95**

1914 *Talcum Powder Sample, Eng. & French Label* **MP $100**

1914 *Talcum Powder 4oz 25¢* **MP $100**

1915 *Talcum Powder 4oz 25¢* **MP $75, $100 boxed**

1917 *Talcum Powder 1lb. to refill powder containers 89¢* **MP $125**

1915 *Talcum Powder (Sets only) 4oz* **MP $75**
1923 *Talcum Powder 4oz 35¢* **MP $55**

1925 *Bath Powder 4¾oz 35¢* **MP $60**

1925 *Talcum Powder 1lb. 89¢* **MP $75**

. . . TRAILING ARBUTUS

. . . a fragrance of demure sweetness which awakens tenderness and chivalry.

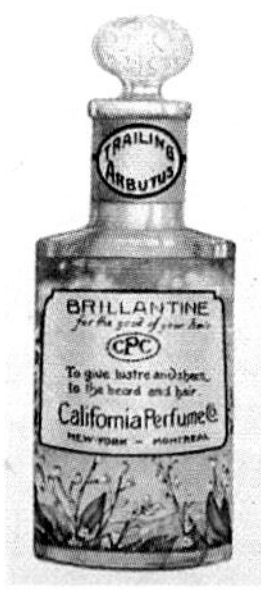

1923 *Brilliantine 2oz 39¢* **MP $115**

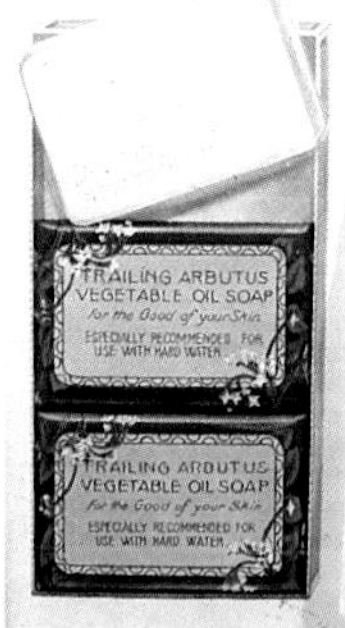

1925 *Vegetable Oil Soap, 3 cakes 39¢* **MP $100**

1925 *Cold Cream tube 23¢* **MP $25**

1928 *Rouge, cardboard 40¢* **MP $25**

1925 *Vanishing Cream, 2 & 4oz size 33¢ & 59¢* **MP $50 each**

1925 *Cold Cream, Reg. & Dbl. size 33¢ & 59¢* **MP $50 each**

1928 *Cold Cream 69¢* **MP $45**

1923 *Face Powder 33¢* **MP $40**

1925 *Face Powder 33¢* **MP $35**

1928 *Face Powder 35¢* **MP $35**

1915 *Set 'T' 4oz Sprinkle-top Toilet Water, Sachet Powder, 4oz Talcum Powder $2.50* **MP $350**

1923 *Threesome Set. 2oz Toilet Water, 4oz Talc & Sachet Powder $1.85* **MP $300**

1925 *Sextette Set. 2 Vegetable Oil Soaps, Cold Cream, Face Powder, Vanishing Cream and Talcum Powder $1.59* **MP $280**

1925 *Toilet Soap, 3 cakes 69¢* **MP $100**

VERNAFLEUR

1923 *Tissue Creme, small 48¢, large 89¢* **MP $50**

1923 *Nutri-Creme, small 48¢, large 89¢* **MP $50**

1928 *Nutri-Creme, regular 50¢, double 90¢* **MP $45 each**

1928 *Tissue Creme, regular 50¢, double 90¢* **MP $45 each**

1920 *Fragrance Sample* **MP $85**
1923 *Fragrance Sample* **MP $85**

1925 *Perfume Flaconette ¼oz 48¢* **MP $100**

1923 *Perfume Flaconette ¼oz 48¢* **MP $90**

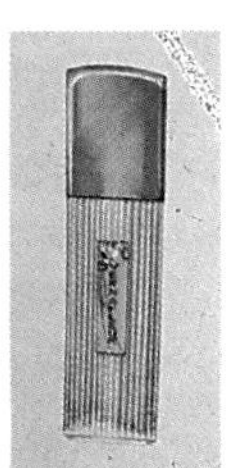

1928 *Perfume Flaconette 69¢* **MP $95**

1923 *Perfume 1oz $1.44* **MP $125**
MP $125, $150 boxed
$150 boxed
1923 *Toilet Water 2oz 74¢*
MP $85

1928 *Perfume 1oz $1.45*
MP $120, $150 boxed

Vernafleur Face Powder was a rich creamy powder of the adherent or "cold cream" type. It was slightly heavier than ordinary face powders and stayed on longer. It was specially suited for oily skins.

1923 *Adherent Face Powder 48¢* **MP $40**

1925 *Adherent Face Powder 48¢* **MP $40**
1925 *Face Powder Sample* **MP $40**

1928 *Toilet Soap, 3 cakes 70¢* **MP $100**

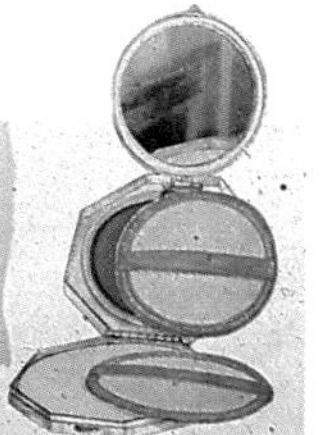

1928 *Double Compact $1.50* **MP $45**

1928 *Single Compact $1* **MP $30**

... VERNAFLEUR

1923 *Vernatalc 4oz 39¢* **MP $60**

1926 *Bath Salts 10oz 75¢* **MP$85**

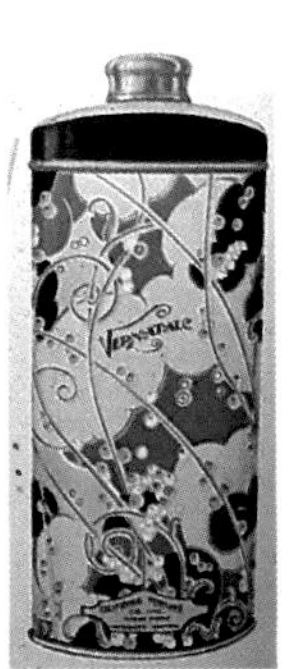

1926 *Vernatalc 4oz 39¢* **MP $55**

1928 *Quintette Set. Tissue Creme, Nutri-Creme, Perfume, Face Powder & Vernatalc $2.25* **MP $300**

1928 *Bath Set. Dusting Powder, Bath Salts 10oz, 2 Toilet Soaps $3.50* **MP $200**

VIOLET

1912 *Sachet Powder 25¢* **MP $125**

1915 *Sachet Powder 25¢* **MP $90**

1923 *Sachet Powder 49¢* **MP $85**

1915 *Almond Meal 8oz 50¢* **MP $100, $130 boxed**
1920 *Almond Meal 3¾oz 50¢* **MP $80**
1923 *Almond Meal 4oz 48¢* **MP $75**
1922 *Almond Meal (not shown) as above with San Francisco on label.* **MP $90**

Almond Meal, made from pure flower of Sweet Almond and scented with Violet perfume, served a dual purpose. When added to water it became a milky wash for the hands and face. It was also a skin 'bleacher' that softened and purified the skin.

1918 *Toilet Water 2oz 75¢*
MP $125
1906 *Violet Water 2oz 75¢*
MP $180

1917 *L'Odeur De Violette 1oz $1.90* **MP $140, $165 boxed**

1915 *Violet Toilet Water 2oz 65¢* **MP $135, $160 boxed**

1908 *Perfume Extract 2oz 75¢* **MP $175**

1917 *Atomizer Set Perfume Bottle* **MP $150**

1915 *Perfume 1oz 90¢* **MP $150 $175 boxed**

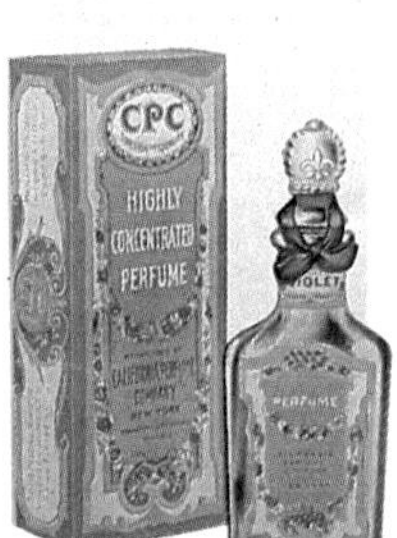

1917 *Perfume ½oz 50¢* **MP $140 $170 boxed**

. . . VIOLET

1915 *Gift Set H. Talcum, Perfume ½oz, Atomizer, Sachet Powder $1.35* **MP $360**

1905 *Talcum Powder 3½oz 25¢* **MP $100**

1923 *Talcum 3½oz 23¢* **MP $75**

1923 *Threesome Set. Talcum, Toilet Water 2oz and Sachet Powder $1.40* **MP $280**

1915 *Nutri-Creme small 50¢* **MP $50**

1915 *Nutri-Creme double size 90¢* **MP $50**

1923 *Nutri-Creme small 49¢* **MP $40**

1923 *Nutri-Creme double size 89¢* **MP $40**

1925 *Nutri-Creme 89¢* **MP $40**

1898 *Bay Rum 1 pint $1.25* **MP $240**

Bay Rum

1915 *Bay Rum 4oz 40¢* **MP $125**

1918 *Bay Rum 4oz 75¢, 8oz $1.50, pint $3.00* **MP $95 each**

1896 *Bay Rum 4oz 40¢* **MP $200**
1908 *Bay Rum 4oz 40¢* **MP $160**
1912 *Bay Rum 4oz 40¢* **MP $140**
1915 *Bay Rum 16oz $1.44* **MP $160**
1927 *Bay Rum 4oz 50¢* **MP $100**

1923 *Bay Rum 4oz 47¢, 8oz 84¢, pint $1.44* **MP $100 each**

1930 *Bay Rum 4oz 52¢* **MP $60**

(See also pg.182)

1915 *White Lilac Toilet Water 2oz 75¢* **MP $135**

1917 *Carnation Toilet Water 2oz 75¢* **MP $135**

1926 *White Rose Toilet Water 2oz 59¢* **MP $90**
1917 *White Rose Toilet Water 2oz 75¢* **MP $135**

1923 *White Rose Toilet Water 2oz 59¢* **MP $100 $120 boxed**

1923 *Crab Apple Blossom Toilet Water 2oz 59¢* **MP $100, $120 boxed**

1926 *Lily of the Valley Toilet Water 2oz 59¢* **MP $90**

CPC TOILETRIES

1915 *Lait Virginal Milk Bath 2oz 65¢* **MP $135**

1918 *Benzoin Lotion 2oz 90¢ and 4oz $1.75* **MP $105 each**

1923 *Benzoin Lotion 2oz 59¢* **MP $100**

1926 *Benzoin Lotion 2oz 59¢* **MP $85**

1928 *Rosewater Glycerin and Benzoin Lotion 4oz 48¢* **MP $75**

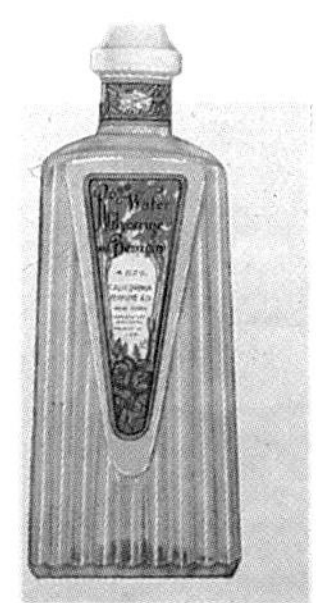
1925 *Rosewater Glycerin and Benzoin Lotion 48¢* **MP $85**

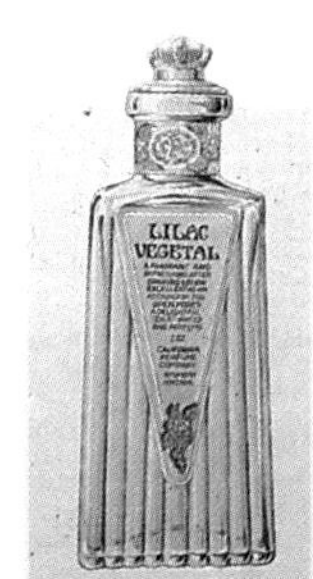
1926 *Lilac Vegetal 2oz 59¢* **MP $90**

1915 *Witch Hazel Extract 4oz 25¢* **MP $100**

1912 *Witch Hazel Extract 4oz 25¢* **MP $110**
1920 *Witch Hazel Extract 4oz 39¢* **MP $90**

1923 *Witch Hazel 4oz 39¢* **MP $85** *8oz 69¢* **MP $85** *32oz $3.25* **MP $100**

1926 *Witch Hazel 4oz 39¢* **MP $80,** *8oz 69¢* **MP $80,** *Pint $1.20* **MP $85**

1912 *Face Lotion, white or pink, 6oz $1* **MP $100**

1917 *Face Lotion, white or pink, 6oz $1* **MP $90**

1923 *Face Lotion, white or pink, 6oz 97¢* **MP $85**

1926 *Liquid Face Powder 97¢* **MP $80**

1917 *Lotus Cream 12oz $1.25* **MP $150**
1917 *Lotus Cream 4oz 50¢* **MP $100**

1925 *Lotus Cream 50¢* **MP $70**

1915 *Eau de Quinine Hair Tonic 65¢* **MP $90**

1923 *Eau de Quinine Hair Tonic 6oz 69¢* **MP $80**

1915 *Liquid Shampoo 35¢* **MP $90**

1923 *Liquid Shampoo 6oz 48¢* **MP $85, $105 boxed**

CPC CREAMS

1908 *Shampoo Cream Sample* **MP $60**

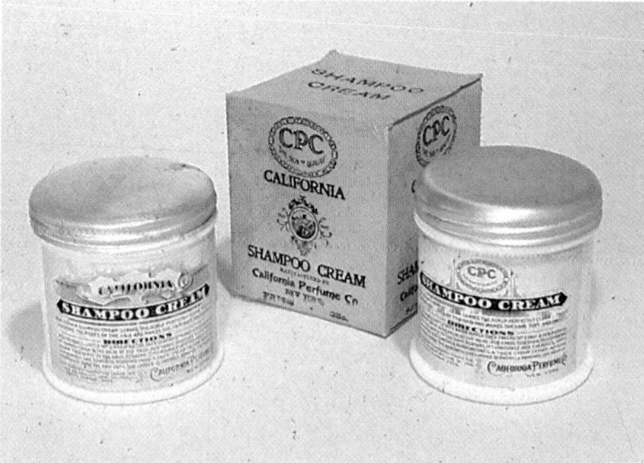

1908 *Shampoo Cream 4oz 35¢* **MP $95**
1915 *Shampoo Cr. 4oz 35¢* **MP $85, $110 boxed**

California Shampoo Cream was used in all first-class shaving parlors in New York City, proving its value by its popularity with barbers.

1915 *Bandoline Hair Dressing 35¢* **MP $85**

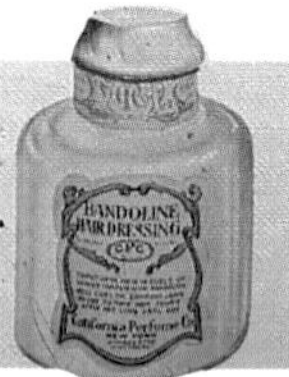

1923 *Bandoline Hair Dressing 4oz 45¢* **MP $75**

1915 *Almond Cream Balm 2oz small 25¢, 4oz 50¢* **MP $50 each**

1918 *Almond Cream Balm 30¢* **MP $50**

1923 *Cold Cream, small 23¢, large 45¢* **MP $50 each**

CP Almond Cream Balm, made from pure almond blossoms, was used for removal of freckles, tan, and other skin discolorations.

1915 *Cold Cream, small 25¢* **MP $80**

1915 *California Cold Cream 45¢* **MP $90**

1917 *Cold Cream, triple size 65¢* **MP $80**

1926 *Rose Cold Cream 63¢* **MP $60**

In 1908 Catalogs stated: "CP Cold Cream, unlike the kind of Cold Cream that is usually sold in drugstores, will positively not promote the growth of hair, nor is it offensively oily."

1908 *Massage Cream 50¢* **MP $110**

1917 *Dermol Massage Cream 75¢* **MP $85**

1923 *Dermol Massage Cream 96¢* **MP $75**

1926 *Lemonol Cleansing Cream 50¢* **MP $60**

MEN'S TOILETRIES

1918 *Shaving Leaves, Pad of 50 sheets 15¢* **MP $30**

Being slightly antiseptic, CP Shaving Soap also healed all minor facial irritations and any abrasion caused by shaving too close.

1915 *Cream Shaving Soap 25¢* **MP $75**

1915 *Shaving Powder 2oz 35¢* **MP $50**

1915 *Cream Shaving Stick in metal container. 35¢* **MP $55**

1918 *Bayberry Shaving Stick 33¢* **MP $45**

The favorite shaving soap of particular self-shavers as well as professional barbers who wanted the best.

1915 *Witch Hazel Cream small 25¢* **MP $50**

1917 *Menthol Witch Hazel Cream (small) 25¢* **MP $50**

1918 *Menthol Witch Hazel Cream 35¢* **MP $50**

1918 *Bayberry Shaving Cream 35¢* **MP $50**

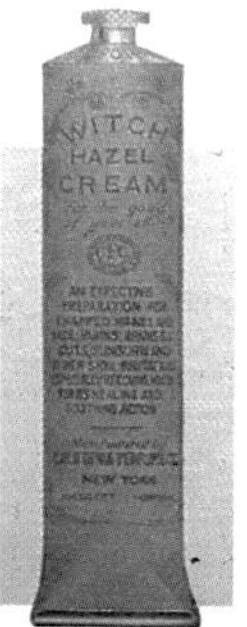

1923 *Witch Hazel Cream, triple size 59¢* **MP $50**

1923 *Witch Hazel Cream, small size 30¢* **MP $50**

1928 *Avon Talc for Men 25¢* **MP $35**

1928 *Avon Shaving Stick 35¢* **MP $40**

1917 *Elite Powder 1lb. to refill powder containers* *89¢* MP $125

1923 *Elite Powder* *24¢* MP $65

1915 *Elite Powder* *25¢* MP $80

1912 *Elite Powder* *25¢* MP $85

1892 *Tooth Tablet, embossed sides* *25¢* MP $100

1906 *Tooth Tablet* *25¢* MP $90

1923 *Tooth Tablet* *24¢* MP $75

CPC ELITE POWDERS

(See also Elite Powders pg. 128)

1915 *Tooth Wash 25¢* MP $100

1918 *Tooth Wash 35¢* MP $100

1923 *Tooth Wash 33¢* MP $85

1915 *Tooth Powder 25¢* MP $70

CPC TOOTH PRODUCTS

In the 1890's the Tooth Tablet was the only dental product offered by the California Perfume Company.

In the early 1900's Tooth Wash was introduced as an antiseptic cleanser of the mouth and teeth. A few drops in a glass of water provided a pleasant tasting mouthwash.

The CPC dentifrice line rapidly expanded to include regular Tooth Powder, Dental Cream and Sen Den Tal Cream. The Sen Den Tal Cream contained a breath fragrance similar to Sen-Sen and was advertised as a mildly abrasive dentifrice and breath purifier. Toothbrushes were added to the line in 1928 and were the first items to carry the 'Avon' name.

1915 *Smoker's Tooth Powder* *50¢* MP $125

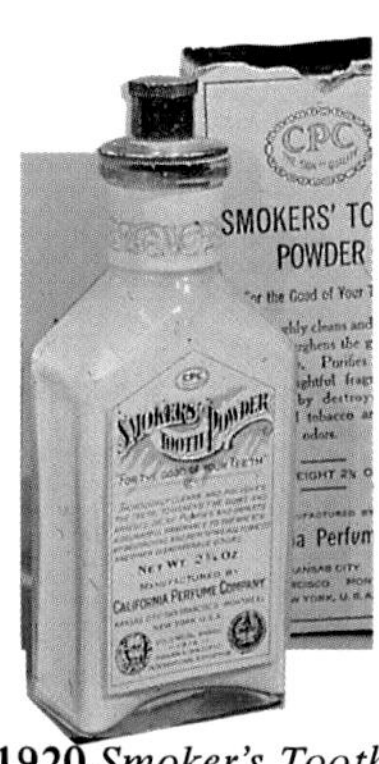
1920 *Smoker's Tooth Powder 2¾oz 25¢* MP $110, $135 boxed

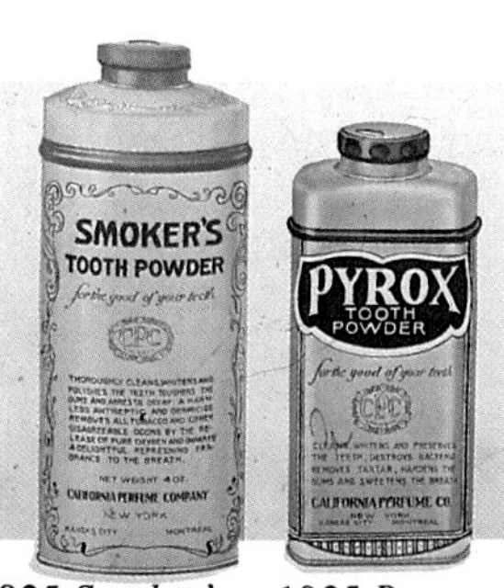
1925 *Smoker's Tooth Powder* *48¢* MP $55

1925 *Pyrox Tooth Powder* *24¢* MP $45

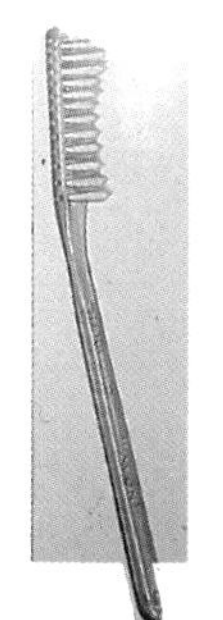
1928 *Avon Toothbrush ass't colors.* *50¢* MP $20

1918 *Sen Den Tal Cream* *50¢* MP $60

1915 *Dental Cream* *25¢* MP $50

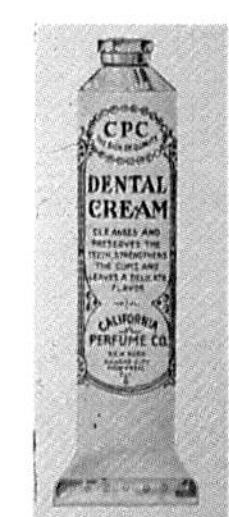
1923 *Dental Cream* *35¢* MP $50

Shaving Cabinet No. 9 *came out for Christmas selling in 1931 and was available for only about one year. The Shaving Cabinet, pictured in black and white, appears on a special insert page that was added to the 1930 Sales Catalog. The white metal cabinet was cleverly constructed to comfortably hold 3 regular size Avon Shaving requisites:*

A bottle of of Toilet Water for the ladies, a Gold Plated Gem Safety Razor and two extra blades. In addition, there was a slot for a shaving brush. Three holes in the top of the cabinet provided ventilation. A mirror was positioned on the outside of the cabinet door. Product copy on the catalog page states, "The Cabinet, complete with fittings is offered at a special price – which is less than the container alone would cost if it could be bought in the stores."

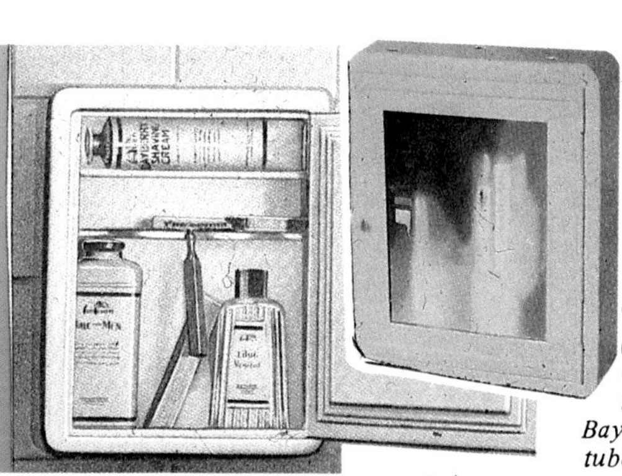
1930 *Shaving Cabinet No. 9 (white enamel 8x6½x2 3/8" deep) sold with contents: Bayberry Shaving Cream, tube 35¢, Talc for Men 35¢, Styptic Pencil 10¢, 2oz White Rose Toilet Water for the ladies 75¢, gold plated Gem Safety Razor and 2 extra blades. $2.50* **MP $250, $100 cabinet only**

CPC FACE & BODY POWDERS

CPC talc was imported from the snow-capped Alps in Northern Italy. This talc produced dusting, body and talcum powders of a soft consistency, that were smoother, whiter, lighter, and more velvety than other brands.

In 1896 the forerunner of Sweet Sixteen Face Powder was introduced. It was called a Toilet Powder and its name was California 'Sweet Sixteen' and Baby Powder

1908 *Rose Talcum Antiseptic Powder 3½oz 25¢* **MP $105**

1915 *Bath Powder 4½oz 25¢* **MP $70, $85 boxed**

1917 *White Lilac Talcum 4oz 25¢* **MP $60**

1918 *White Lilac Talcum 4oz 25¢* **MP $70, $85 boxed**
1920 *White Lilac Talcum 4oz 24¢* **MP $70, $85 boxed**

1912 *Rose Talcum Antiseptic Powder 3½ oz 25¢* **MP $100**
1920 *California Rose Talcum 3½ oz 72¢* **MP $95**

1923 *California Rose Talcum 4oz 33¢* **MP $70**

1925 *Dusting Powder $1* **MP $75**

1926 *Body Powder $1.19* **MP $75**

1911 *Face Powder Leaves. Scented paper with Face Powder on one side in 3 shades. Rose, white or rachel, 72 leaves per book. 20¢* **MP $35**

1915 *Hygiene Face Powder 3 tints 50¢* **MP $65**

1916 *Sweet Sixteen Face Powder 25¢* **MP $70**

1919 *Hygiene Face Powder white, pink or brunette 50¢* **MP $65**

1915 *Rouge Tin De Theatre 25¢* **MP $50**

1915 *Liquid Rouge 25¢* **MP $95**

1915 *Nail Bleach 25¢* **MP $110**

1916 *Nail Powder 25¢* **MP $45**
1923 *Radiant Nail Powder 24¢* **MP $50**

1917 *Depilatory 50¢* **MP $60**

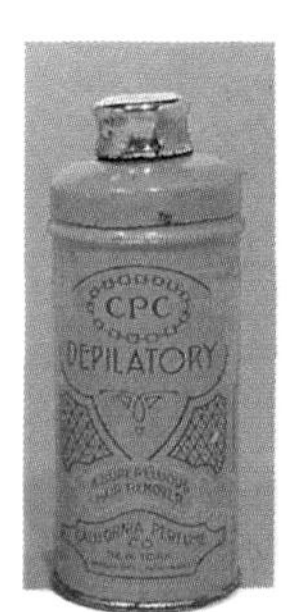

1920 *Depilatory 50¢* **MP $60**

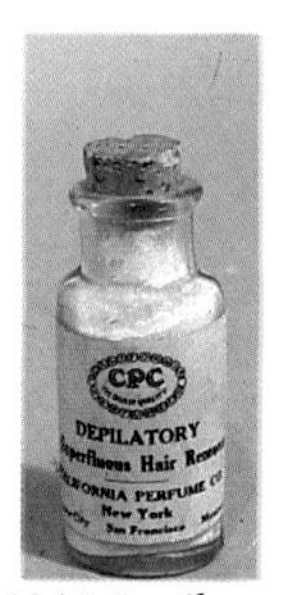

1915 *Depilatory 50¢* **MP $100**

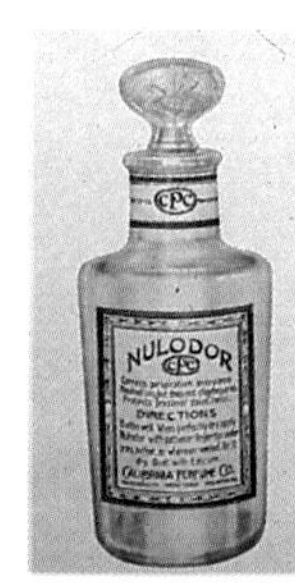

1926 *Nulodor 33¢* **MP $90**

1928 *Nulodor 35¢* **MP $90**

1896 *California Baby Soap 15¢* **MP $80**

BABY SOAP

1915 *California Baby Soap 4oz 15¢* **MP $50**

1915 *Castile Soap 25¢* **MP $50**

1925 *Castile Soap 33¢* **MP $45**

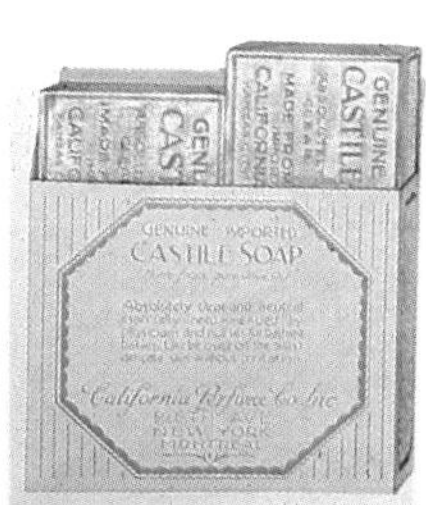

1928 *Castile Soap, 2 cakes 50¢* **MP $50**

Genuine Castile Soap, made in the province of Castile, Spain, from which this neutral soap takes its name. Made of pure olive oil, it is especially recommended for the baby.

Dr. Zabriskie's Cutaneous Soap
1915 *25¢* **MP $50**
1923 *24¢* **MP $45**

1906 *Toilet Almond Meal Soap, 3 cakes 25¢* **MP $100**

1906 *Almond, Buttermilk & Cucumber Soap, 3 cakes 40¢* **MP $125**

1926 *Almond Bouquet Toilet Soap, 3 cakes 30¢* **MP $100**

CPC SOAPS

1920 *Lemonol Toilet & Complexion Soap, 3 cakes 45¢* **MP $100**

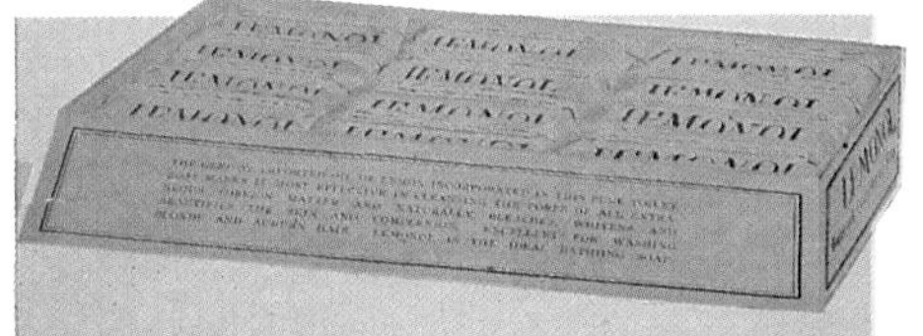

1923 *Lemonol Toilet Soap, 12 per carton $1.65* **MP $125**

1923 *ABC Toilet Soap 6 guest size cakes 48¢* **MP $110**

Lemonol Soap, fragrant with the genuine imported oil of lemon, may also be used as a shampoo to cleanse and lighten blonde and auburn hair instead of a lemon rinse.

Japan Toilet Soap so named because of its pleasing scent from an Oriental perfume.

1915 *Peroxide Hard Water Toilet Soap, 3 cakes 50¢* **MP $100**

1906 *Savona Bouquet Soap, 2 cakes 50¢* **MP $100**

1906 *Japan Toilet Soap, 3 cakes 25¢* **MP $125**

1926 *Apple Blossom Complexion, 3 cakes 69¢* **MP $100**

Peroxide Hard Water Toilet Soap, especially made for localities where water is very hard. Made from the best of refined tallow and cocoanut oil. Peroxide gives the soap an antiseptic quality.

(See also pg. 134, Men's pg. 191, Children's pg. 211)

CPC GIFT SETS

Dainty bottles tied with ribbon to contrast prettily with their contents, then placed in boxes of many different shades and coloring showing a delicate tracery of flowers – all artistically touched with gold trimmings.

1915 *Atomizer Box. Three 3oz Triple Extract Perfumes & Perfect Atomizer. Choice of 11 fragrances. $2.70* **MP $500**

1915 *Gift Box No. 2. Perfume ½oz & Sachet Powder in White Lilac, Violet, Heliotrope or White Rose. 50¢* **MP $260**

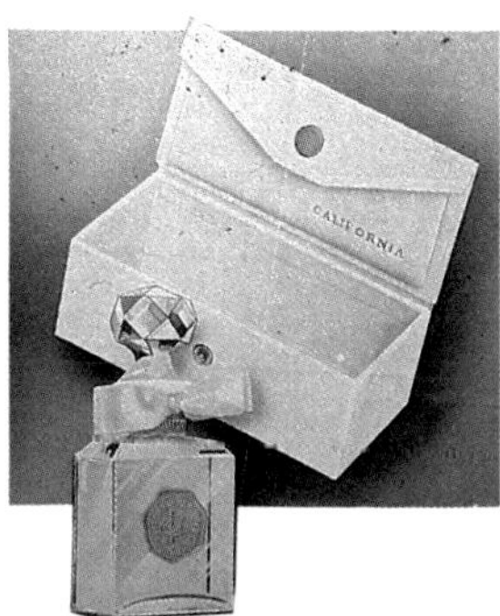

1915 *Gift Box F. Crab Apple Blossom or Trailing Arbutus Perfume 2oz $3.75* **MP $225**

1915 *Gift Box A. Two ½oz Perfumes in a choice of Violet, White Rose, Carnation, White Lilac, Heliotrope and Lily of the Valley. 50¢* **MP $310**

1917 *Gift Box No. 3. Two ½oz Perfumes, choice of fragrances. 95¢* **MP $320, $140 each bottle**

1923 *Gift Box No. 2. Perfume ½oz & Sachet Powder in Violet, Heliotrope or Carnation. 97¢* **MP $245**

1928 *Vanity Set. Lipstick & Compact $2.40* **MP $75**

CPC CHILDREN'S SETS

Lovely gift sets for little ladies contained miniature sized perfumes and toiletries in colorful picture boxes with hinged covers. Not only were they pleasing gifts, but taught little girls to be "little ladies".

1915 *Juvenile Set. Miniatures, Savona Bouquet Soap, Natoma Talcum, Violet Water & Tooth Powder. 50¢* **MP $500**

1926 *Jack & Jill Jungle Jinks. Trailing Arbutus Talcum & Daphne Perfume. Apple Blossom Soap, Cold Cream, Sen Den Tal Cream & Toothbrush. $1.50*
MP $400, $75 box only

LITTLE FOLKS SETS

Combination sets of 4 gem bottles of perfume, packaged especially as a set for children. The same 4 odors are used in each set. Each bottle is coded and ribboned, the box is artistically lithographed in 7 colors and each is gold embossed. The perfumes are regular CPC Triple Extracts.

1906 *Little Folks Set. Violet, White Rose, Carnation & Heliotrope Perfume 40¢* **MP $550, $100 ea. bottle**

1915 *Little Folks Box. Violet White Rose, Carnation & Heliotrope Perfume 90¢* **MP $375, $80 each bottle**

1923 *Little Folks Gift Box. Violet, Carnation, White Lilac & Heliotrope Perfumes 69¢* **MP $350. $75 ea. bottle**

(See also Little Folks pg. 82)

1915 *Manicure Set: Nail Bleach w/Cuticle Stick, Rose Pomade, Nail Powder and Emery Board 65¢* **MP $240 boxed**

1915 *Nail Bleach with Cuticle Stick 25¢* **MP $110**
1915 *Rose Pomade 25¢* **MP $50**
1915 *Nail Powder, paper box 25¢* **MP $45**

1915 *Complete Manicure Set: Buffer, Scissors, File, Nail Bleach, Nail Powder & Rose Pomade, Orange Wood Stick & 6 Emery Boards $4.50* **MP $400 as shown**

1923 *Manicure Set: Nail Bleach w/Orange Stick, Emery Board, Radiant Nail Powder & Rose Pomade 72¢* **MP $240**

Nail Bleach 2oz with Orange Wood Stick 24¢ **MP $110**
4oz 72¢ **MP $130**
8oz $1.23 **MP $150**
16oz $1.95 **MP $200**
Radiant Nail Powder 24¢ **MP $45**
Rose Pomade 24¢ **MP $50**

CPC MANICURE SETS

Complete manicure equipment in plain compact boxes or fancy gift boxes.

Leatherette covered gift boxes had hinged covers, side ribbon straps and were beautifully lined.

1926 *Boudoir Manicure Set: Radiant Nail Powder, Nail White, Cuti-Creme & Cutrane $1.20* **MP $240**

Radiant Nail Powder 24¢ **MP $45**
Nail White 30¢ **MP $35**
Cuti-Creme 30¢ **MP $35**
Cutrane 30¢ **MP $90**

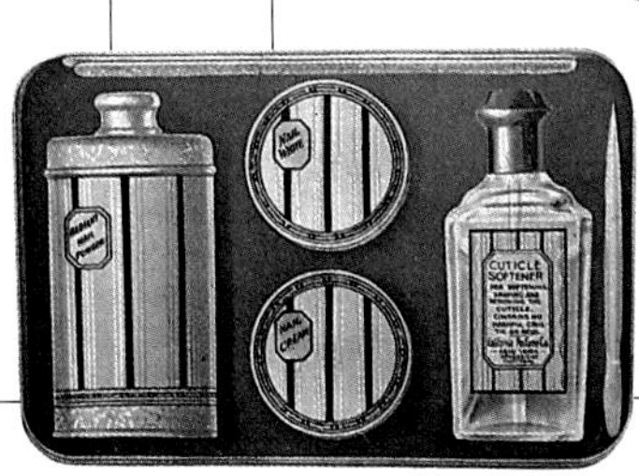

1928 *Boudoir Manicure Set: Radiant Nail Powder, Nail White, Nail Cream & Cuticle Softener $1.20* **MP $225**

Radiant Nail Powder 30¢ **MP $45**
Nail White 30¢ **MP $35**
Nail Cream 30¢ **MP $25**
Cuticle Softener 30¢ **MP $75**

SETS FOR BABY

1915 *Baby Powder 30¢* **MP $70**

1917 *Baby Set. Powder, Soap & Violet Water 2oz $1.30* **MP $295**
Baby Powder 30¢ **MP $65**
Baby Soap 25¢ **MP $80**
Violet Water 75¢ **MP $125**

1922 *Baby Set. Soap, Powder & Violet Toilet Water 2oz 99¢* **MP $250**
Soap 23¢ **MP $70**
Powder 29¢ **MP $55**
Toilet Water 2oz 48¢ **MP $100**

1925 *Baby Set. Supreme Olive Oil 4oz, Baby Powder 4oz, Boric Acid & Castile Soap 5oz $1.78* **MP $350**

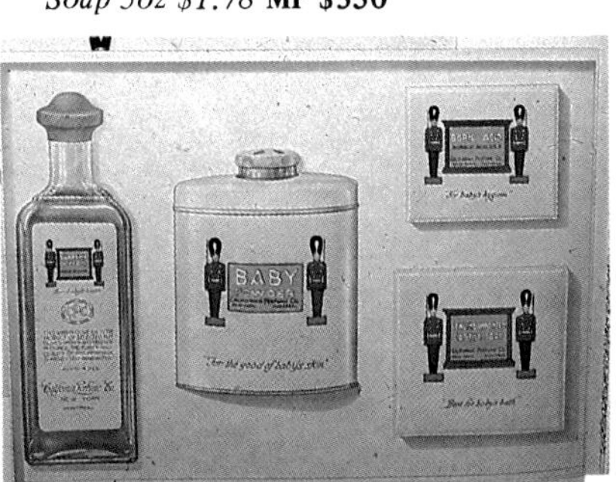

Supreme Olive Oil **MP $115**
Baby Powder 29¢ **MP $55**
Baby Soap 23¢ **MP $70**
Boric Acid 23¢ **MP $75**

PERFECTION

PERFECTION 1920

1941

Throughout the early years, Sales Catalogs encouraged the use of CPC baking products for guaranteed "perfect results" and "perfection in baking." It is not surprising, then, that in 1920 the Company chose the name **Perfection** *for the CPC baking line.* ***Concentrated Colorings*** *and* ***Coloring Set*** *introduced the newly designed Perfection packaging, followed by* ***Flavoring Extracts*** *and* ***Baking Powder*** *in 1923.*

Between 1928 and 1929 two household products, ***Avon Maid Powdered Cleanser*** *and* ***Auto Lustre,*** *were introduced in new Avon packaging. During this transition, it was decided that the household product line have its own name.*

In 1930 the entire baking and household lines were introduced in orange, brown and white Perfection packaging. For ten years the basic packaging remained the same, but each item was issued under **five** *different labels.*

Exceptions were ***Powdered Cleaner,*** *issued with* **four** *different labels, and* ***Auto Polish,*** *(formerly* ***Auto Lustre)*** *discontinued in 1936, issued with only two. These two products did not join the Perfection line until 1933 when their original Avon containers were depleted.*

Sales Catalogs are useless in determining when label changes took place.

During the entire ten year period, the company continued to utilize the 1930 catalog picture of products.

The following guide will tell you when your 1930-1940 Perfection product was issued.

Dorothy Bernard's 1930's PERFECTION LABEL DATING GUIDE

1930-33	An Avon Product Made by California Perfume Co., Inc. New York-Montreal
1933-34	An Avon Product California Perfume Co., Inc. New York-Montreal
1934-36	California Perfume Co., Inc. Avon Products, Inc., Div. New York-Montreal
1936-39	Avon Products, Inc., Div. California Perfume Co., Inc. New York-Montreal
1939-40	Avon Products, Inc. Distributor New-York-Montreal-Kansas City Los Angeles

In 1941 Perfection household items were introduced in newly designed brown, green and white packaging and baking products in brown, red and white. Labels read: **Avon Products, Inc., Distributor, New York-Montreal.** *This packaging remained in the line for* **only** *one year and is extremely difficult to find.*

By late 1942 all Perfection items were issued in wartime cardboard or glass containers. Following the war, products continued in wartime packaging until most were discontinued between 1947-48. The 8 remaining products were re-issued in packaging identical to introductory packaging of 1941, except that **Pasadena** *replaced* **Montreal** *on the label.* ***Baking Powder, Savory Coloring, Mending Cement*** *and* ***Furniture Polish*** *were discontinued in 1953 and* ***Liquid Shoe White, Spots-Out, Powdered Cleaner*** *and* ***Mothicide*** *were discontinued in 1957.*

1915 *Gentlemen's Shaving Set: Menthol Witch Hazel Cream, Violet Talcum Powder, Cream Shaving Stick, Bay Rum, White Lilac Toilet Water, Styptic Pencil & Shaving Pad, 50 sheets $1.50* **MP $515**

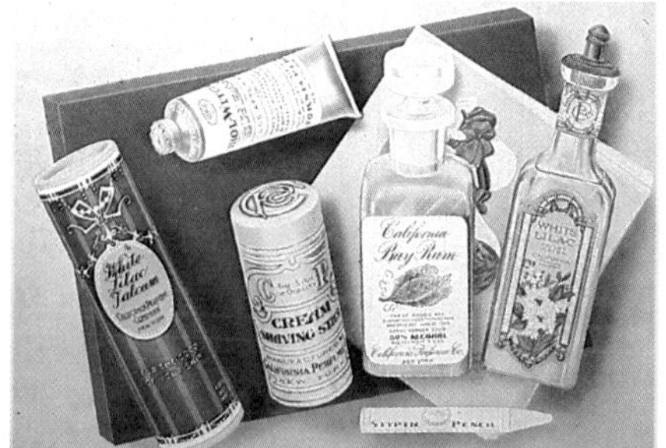

1917 *Gentlemen's Shaving Set: White Lilac Talcum, other items identical to those seen in 1915 set $2.35* **MP $475 complete**

CPC MEN'S SETS

1918 *Gentlemen's Shaving Set: Menthol Witch Hazel Cream, White Lilac Talcum, Cream Shaving Stick, Bay Rum 4oz, White Lilac Toilet Water, Styptic Pencil & Shaving Pad, 50 sheets $2.25* **MP $475 complete**

1923 *Gentlemen's Shaving Set: White Lilac Toilet Water, Bay Rum 4oz, White Lilac Talcum, Menthol Witch Hazel Cream, Bayberry Shaving Cream, Styptic Pencil and Shaving Pad $1.95* **MP $425 complete**

1926 *Humidor Shaving Set: Lilac Vegetal, Bay Rum 4oz, White Lilac Talcum, Menthol Witch Hazel Cream or Trailing Arbutus Cold Cream, Bayberry Shaving Cream & Styptic Pencil $1.95* **MP $390 complete**

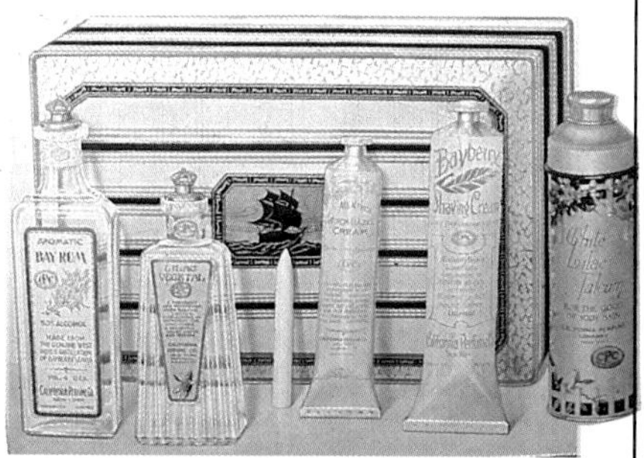

1928 *Humidor Shaving Set: Bay Rum 4oz, Lilac Vegetal, Styptic Pencil, Witch Hazel Cream, Bayberry Shaving Cream, White Lilac Talcum or CPC Talc for Men $2.25* **MP $390 complete**

1930-33 *Flavoring Set. 2oz Vanilla, Tonka & Vanillin, ½oz each Lemon, Wintergreen, Peppermint & Almond Extracts $1* **MP $175 set. Bottles each $25, metal can $25**

FLAVORING SETS

1933-36 *Flavoring Set. Metal can, Recipe Book, 2oz Vanilla, Tonka & Vanillin, ½oz each Lemon, Wintergreen, Peppermint & Almond Extracts $1* **MP $150 set. Bottles each $20, metal can MP $20, Cook book MP $20**

1941-47 *Food Flavorings: Maple, Black Walnut, Vanilla and Lemon 2oz each (Orange, Wintergreen, Peppermint & Almond not shown) 40¢* **MP $12**

1941-47 *Flavoring Set. Recipe Booklet, 2oz Vanilla, ½oz each Lemon, Almond, Black Walnut & Maple $1* **MP $100 set, $12 ea. bottle, $20 Recipe Book, $15 Metal Can**

1930-33 *Coloring Set. 2oz red, ½oz each green, yellow, blue & brown. Cardboard container 85¢* **MP $160 set. Bottles each MP $25, box MP $20**

COLORING SETS

1936-39 *Coloring Set. 2oz red & four ½oz bottles & Recipe Book 85¢* **MP $150 set. Bottles each $20, metal can MP $20, recipe book MP $20**

1936 *Cook Book* **MP $20**
1936 *Colorings 2oz red, yellow 25¢ each* **MP $20**
1941 *Yellow Coloring 2oz 25¢* **MP $12**
1945-46 *Savoury Coloring 4oz (rare spelling) 39¢* **MP $22**

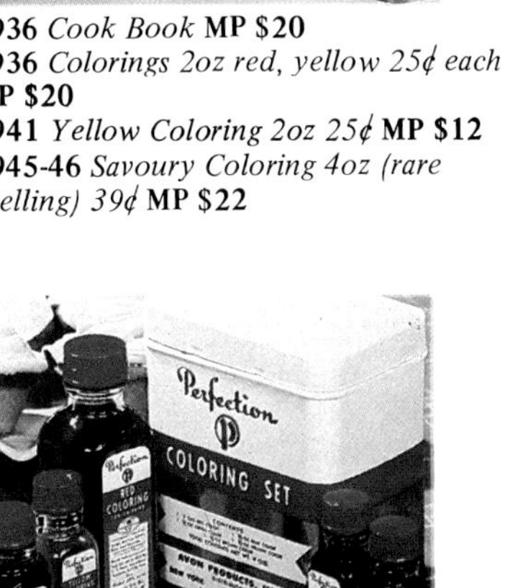

1941-47 *Coloring Set with Recipe Booklet. 2oz red, ½oz each yellow, green, blue and brown 85¢* **MP $100, $12 ea. bottle, $15 metal can, $20 Recipe Book**

1933-36 *Cake Chest contains 1 lb Baking Powder, Coloring Set, 5 Flavorings & Cook Book $3.50* **MP $350 complete and full, $50 Cake Chest only**

CAKE CHESTS

1938 *Cake Chest. Same contents as 1933 Set, but Avon Products, Inc. Div. added to labeling $3.50* **MP $325 complete and full, $40 Cake Chest only**

1941-42 *Cake Chest. Same contents as 1938 above but new package design $3.95* **MP $260 complete, $40 Cake Chest only**

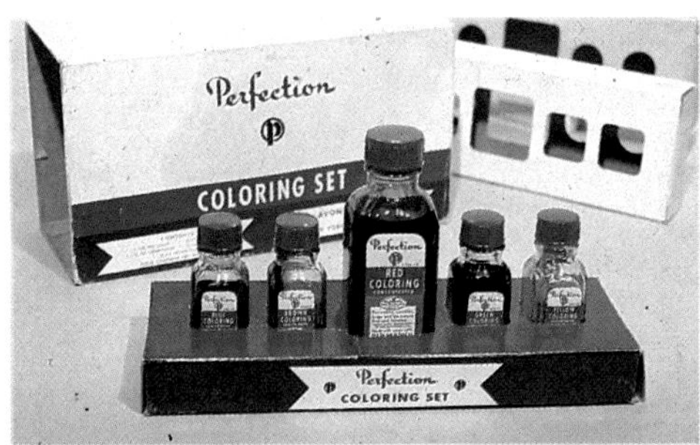

1943-45 *Coloring Set, same bottles as 1941 (left) but issued in cardboard "Victory Packaging" 98¢* **MP $160**

1902-08 *Vegetable Coloring, 8 colors, shown in Lemon Yellow 2oz 25¢, 4oz 45¢* **MP $120**
1908 *Harmless Coloring, 8 colors, shown in Red 2oz 25¢, 4oz 45¢* **MP $90**

1893-1908 *California Extract of Lemon 2oz 25¢, 16oz $1.75, 32oz $3.25* **MP $110, $150 Qt.**
1902-08 *4oz size (shown) 45¢* **MP $110**

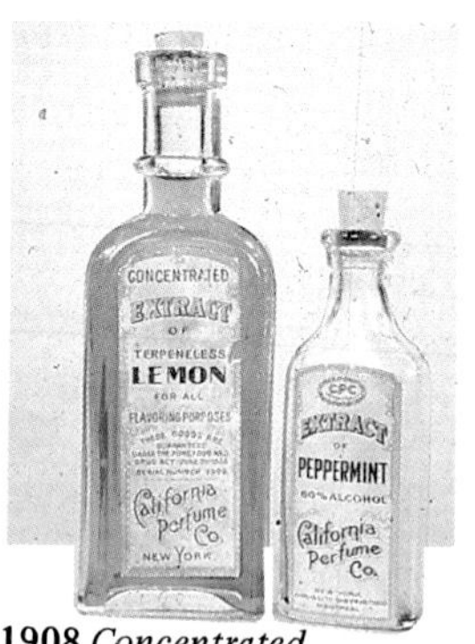

1908 *Concentrated Extract of Terpeneless Lemon Extract 4oz 45¢* **MP $90**
1917 *Extract of Peppermint 2oz 55¢* **MP $60** *(N.Y.-Kansas City, S'Francisco-Montreal)*

1915-17 *Harmless Coloring, 8 colors, shown in Red 1oz 20¢ 2oz 35¢* **MP $50**

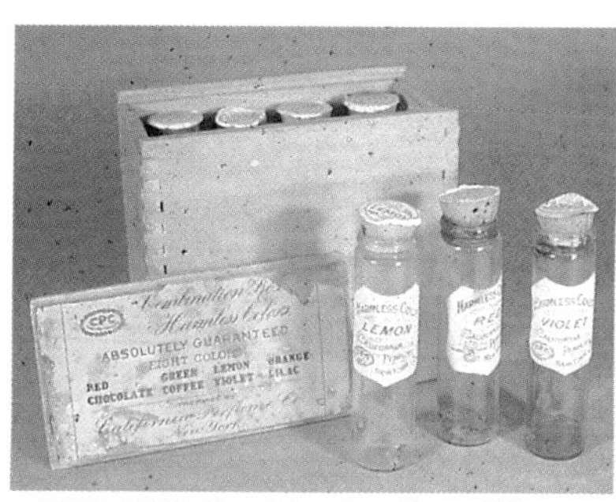

1915-1917 *Combination Box of 8 harmless Food Colorings 50¢* **MP $375 complete, $40 box only, $40 ea. bottle**

1915-17 *Flavoring Extracts, Vanilla, Tonka and Vanillin shown 8oz 90¢* **MP $65 with glass stopper**

1915 *Box X, Flavoring Extract Set: two 2oz bottles and four 1oz bottles $1* **MP $325, $50 each bottle**

FLAVORINGS AND COLORINGS

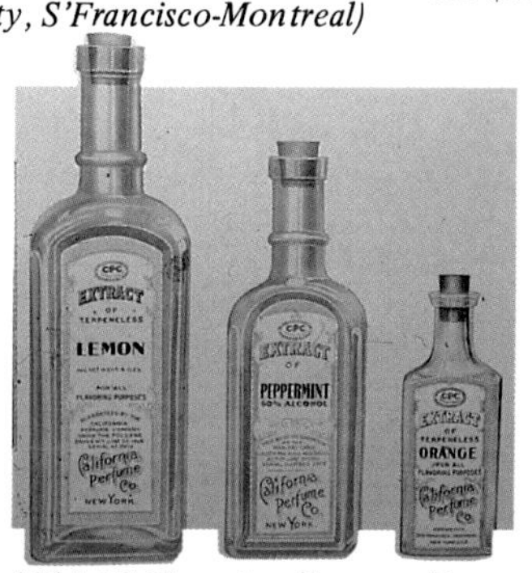
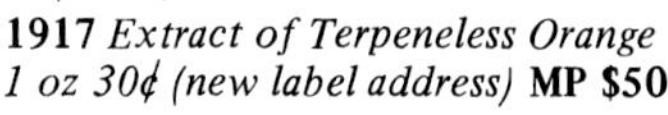

1915-17 *Flavoring Extracts (Lemon & Peppermint shown) 4oz 45¢, 2oz 25¢* **MP $50 each**
1917 *Extract of Terpeneless Orange 1 oz 30¢ (new label address)* **MP $50**

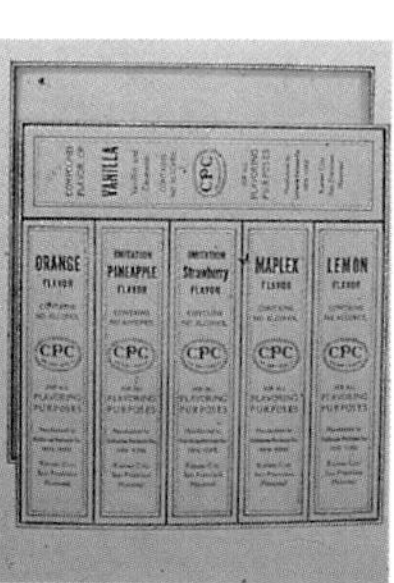

1919 *Box X, No-Alcohol Flavoring Set: 1 large tube Vanilla and 5 small tubes Orange, Strawberry, Maplex, Pineapple and Lemon flavors $2* **MP $400 boxed set. Tubes $50 each**

1917 *No-Alcohol Flavoring, Compound of Vanilla shown. Small tube 30¢, large 55¢* **MP $50 each**

1923 *True Fruit Raspberry Flavor 2oz 39¢, 4oz 74¢, 8oz $1.44* **MP $55**

1923 *No-Alcohol Flavor, Vanilla Compound shown, large 45¢* **MP $30**

1923 *No-Alcohol Flavor, Lemon shown, small 24¢* **MP $25**

1923 *Concentrated Flavoring Extracts: Qt. $6.25, Pt. $3.25 (shown), 8oz $1.75, 4oz 90¢ (shown), 2oz 45¢ (shown), 1oz 25¢* **MP $45 each**

1920 *Perfection Coloring Set. Cardboard box holds 2oz red, ½oz each green, yellow, blue & brown 74¢* **MP $270, $45 each bottle**

1923 *True Fruit Flavors in Lemon, Loganberry, Orange, Grape, Cherry and Raspberry 2oz 39¢, 4oz 74¢, 8oz $1.44* **MP $55 each, $25 Paper Flyer**

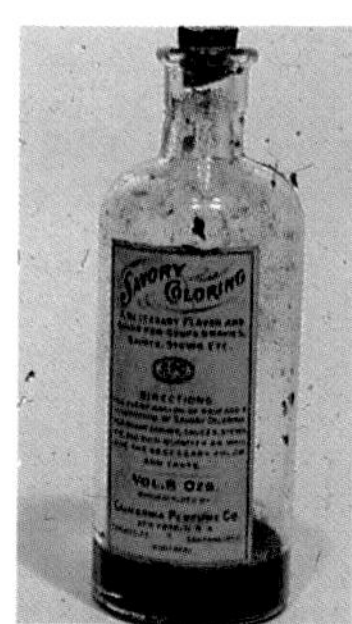

1918-20 *Savory Coloring 8oz (rare) 69¢* **MP $100**

1918-20 *Savory Coloring 3oz (rare) 33¢* **MP $75**

1920 *Savory Coloring 3oz (rare) 35¢* **MP $55, $75 boxed**

1930 *Flavoring Extract, shown in Lemon, 2oz 50¢, 4oz 75¢, 8oz $1.45* **MP $25 ea.**

1930 *Savory Coloring 4oz 50¢* **MP $40**

1934 *Savory Coloring 4oz 35¢* **MP $20, $28 boxed**

1941-47 *Savory Coloring 4oz 35¢* **MP $18**

1915 *Baking Powder 16oz 55¢* **MP $60**

1920 *California Baking Powder 16oz 55¢* **MP $70**

1925 *Baking Powder 8oz 24¢* **MP $50**
1928-29 *Baking Powder 16oz 45¢* **MP $60**

BAKING POWDER

1923 *Baking Powder 16oz 45¢* **MP $50**

1933-34 *Baking Powder Sample* **MP $50**

1936-39 *Baking Powder Sample* **MP $50**

1934-36 *Baking Powder Sample* **MP $50**

1934-36 *Baking Powder 16oz 45¢* **MP $30**

1941-47 *Baking Powder 16oz 45¢* **MP $40** (1947-53 *Same as above with Pasadena label)*

1915 *Olive Oil, table size $1* **MP $85**

1923 *Huile D'Olive, pint $1.35* **MP $50**

OLIVE OIL

1930-33 *Olive Oil, pint $1.35* **MP $40**

1934-36 *Olive Oil 16oz $1.35* **MP $40** *(Avon Products, Inc, Div. added to label)*

1941-42 *Olive Oil, pint $1.35* **MP $50 (rare)**

1915 *Starch Dressing, 25 tablets 25¢* **MP $50**

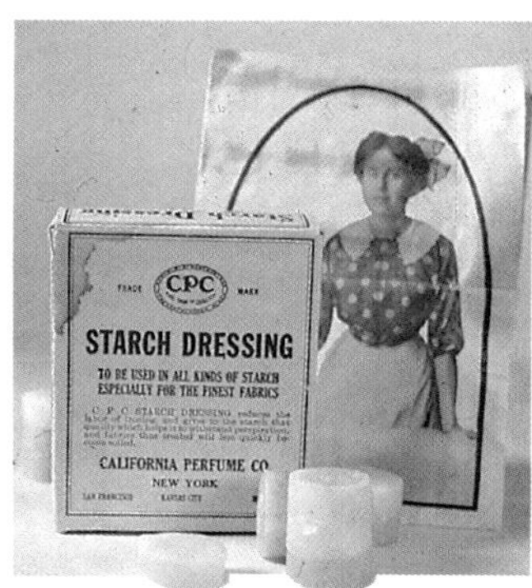

1920 *Starch Dressing 33¢* **MP $40**

1930-33 *Prepared Starch 6oz 35¢* **MP $40**

1941-47 *Prepared Starch 8oz 35¢* **MP $20**

1943-45 *Prepared Starch 8oz, cardboard 39¢* **MP $25**

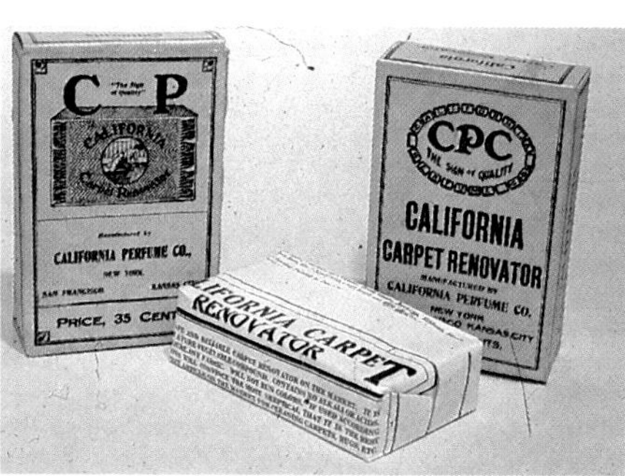

1906 *Carpet Renovator 35¢* **MP $80**
1915 *Carpet Renovator, 1 cake 35¢* **MP $80**

1915 *Naptha Laundry Crystals, 13 per box 25¢* **MP $50**

1930-33 *Laundry Crystals 13 per box 25¢* $45

1934-36 *Laundry Crystals Perfumed 25¢* **MP $30** *(Avon Products, Inc., Div.)*

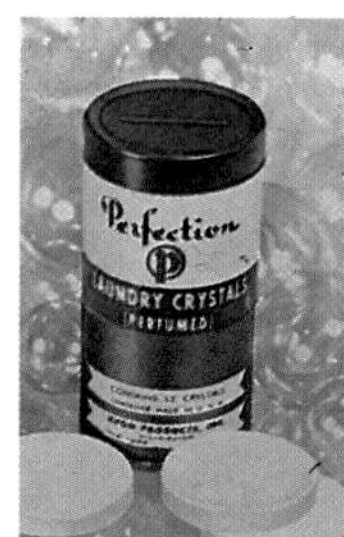

1941-42 *Laundry Crystals (perfumed) 13 per box 25¢* **MP $30**

1943-47 *Laundry Crystals (perfumed) 13 per box 29¢* **MP $30**

In the CPC/Avon line for more than 60 years, this cleaner was the first CPC household product introduced and one of the last Perfection products to be discontinued.

1893 *It was manufactured under the name of* **California Carpet Renovator,** *because that was its original purpose.*
1898 *The catalog relates that* **California Carpet Renovator** *is also an excellent cleaner for curtains, blankets, fine dresses, woodwork, furniture, window shades and patent leather shoes. One cake provides two gallons cleaning solution.*
1908 *The Catalog refers to the product now as* **C P Renovator,** *a preparation for cleaning and brightening many articles. Put up like a cake of soap with directions on the wrapper of each cake (see pg. 29).*
1920 *Because of WWI,* **C P Renovator** *is discontinued, then re-introduced in* **1925** *under the name of* **Easy Cleaner.** *Newly designed packaging, featuring the* **E-Z Maid** *girl, contains two cakes of soap.*
1928 *Both the original product form and name is changed to* **Avon Powdered Cleaner.** *New blue packaging features* **Avon Maid,** *but continues to carry the oval CPC logo.*
1930 *Product is issued in a canister-designed package and the cottage* **Avon** *logo replaced the CPC oval.*
1933 **Avon Powdered Cleaner** *joins the* **Perfection** *line in brown, white and orange packaging.*
1941 *Packaging is again updated as a circled* **P** *logo replaces Avon on the label.* **Perfection Powdered Cleaner** *remained in the line until* **1957** *when it was discontinued.*

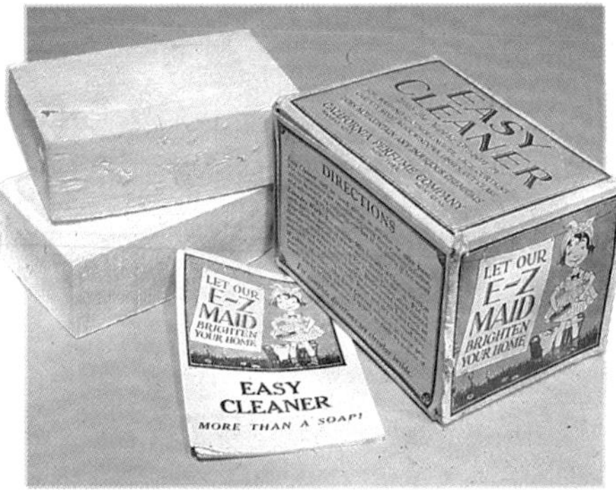

1925 *Easy Cleaner Naptha Bar Soaps 2½ lb 33¢* **MP $100 boxed**
Easy Cleaner Folder **MP $25**

SPOTS OUT

Spots Out was a cleansing paste used to remove dirt, grease and other spots from anything that was washable – especially recommended for cleaning the upholstery of automobiles. It was not harmful to hands because it was free from acids, grit, sand or caustic materials.

1918-21 *Spots-Out ½ lb 35¢, 1 lb 65¢* **MP $75**

1921-29 *Spots-Out ½ lb 33¢, 1 lb 59¢* **MP $50**

1930-33 *Spots-Out ½lb 40¢* **MP $25**

1929 only *Spots-Out Liquid 4oz 50¢* **MP $50**

1930-33 *Liquid Spots-Out 4oz 50¢* **MP $40 (CPC on lid)**

1933-34 *Liquid Spots-Out 4oz 40¢* **MP $50, $60 boxed**

1943-47 *Spots-Out 9½oz 45¢* **MP $30**

1941-42 *Spots-Out (Montreal label) ½lb 40¢* **MP $40**
1947-50 *Spots-Out, as above (Pasadena label)* **MP $20**

1941-42 *Liquid Spots Out (smooth lid) 4oz 40¢* **MP $40**

1943-47 *Liquid Spots Out (Montreal label) 4oz 50¢* **MP $25**

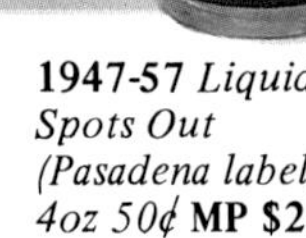

1947-57 *Liquid Spots Out (Pasadena label) 4oz 50¢* **MP $20**

CPC/AVON CLEANERS . . .

1928-30 *Avon Maid Powdered Cleaner (with CPC oval) 12oz 25¢* **MP $75**

1930-33 *Avon Maid Powdered Cleaner 16oz 35¢* **MP $75**

1934 *Powdered Cleaner 16oz 35¢* **MP $45**

1939-41 *Powdered Cleaner (Los Angeles added to label) 16oz 35¢* **MP $50**

. . . PERFECTION CLEANERS

1941-42 *Powdered Cleaner (Montreal label) 16oz 35¢* **MP $40**
1947-57 *As above (Pasadena label)* **MP $20**

1943-47 *Powdered Cleaner, cardboard 16oz 35¢* **MP $25**

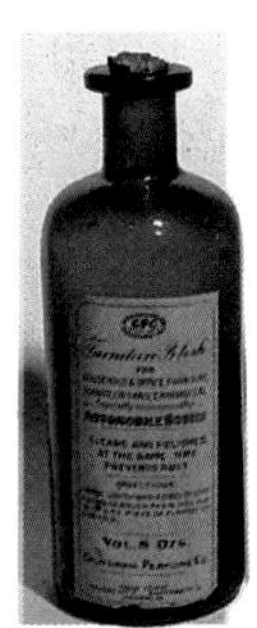

1919 *Furniture Polish, rare amber bottle 8oz 60¢* **MP $160,** **$125** clear glass

1910 *Furniture Polish 8oz 50¢* **MP $160** **$180** boxed
1912 *Furniture Polish 8oz 50¢* **MP $150**
1915 *Furniture Polish 8oz 50¢* **MP $135**

1918-20 *Furniture Polish 8oz 60¢* **MP $125**

1916-17 & 1921-24 *Furniture Polish, lg. 48¢, qt. $1.20* **MP $60,** *½ gal $2.25* **MP $75**

1927 *Furniture Polish 12oz 48¢, qt. $1.20* **MP $50 each**

1930 *Furniture Polish 12oz 75¢, qt. $1.25* **MP $30**

1939 *Furniture Polish 12oz 75¢ (shown)* **MP $30,** *1 qt. $1.15* **MP $45**

FURNITURE POLISH

1929 *Auto Lustre Sample (rare)* **MP $100**

1929-33 *Auto Lustre 16oz 75¢* **MP $75**

1933 *Auto Polish 8oz 75¢* **MP $55** with short issue label

1934-36 *Auto Polish 16oz 75¢* **MP $40**

AUTO POLISH

1941-42 *Furniture Polish 12oz 60¢, qt. $1.15 (rare)* **MP $40**
1948-53 *As above, Pasadena label, 16oz 79¢* **MP $20**

1944-47 *Furniture Polish 12oz 69¢* **MP $45**

1943-44 *Furniture Polish 12oz 69¢* **MP $45**

1920 *Shoe White Dry Cleaner 5oz 25¢* **MP $55**

1926 *Liquid Shoe White 4oz 35¢* **MP $55**

1930 *Liquid Shoe White 4oz 50¢* **MP $40**

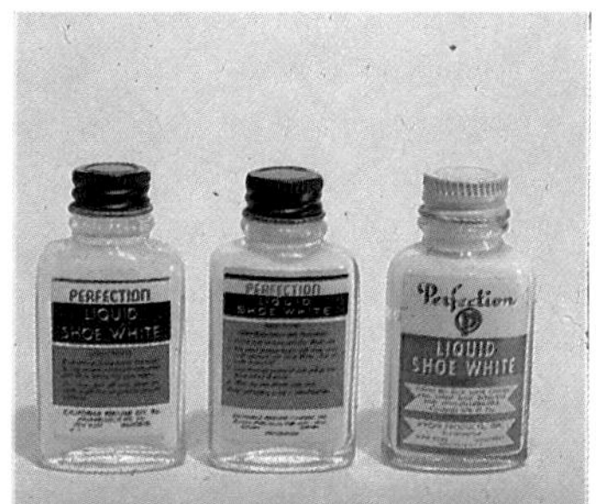

1934-35 *Liquid Shoe White Sample* **MP $40**
1935-36 *Liquid Shoe White Sample* **MP $35**
1941-42 *Liquid Shoe White Sample* **MP $50**

1941-42 *Liquid Shoe White (smooth lid) 4oz 37¢* **MP $20**

SHOE WHITE

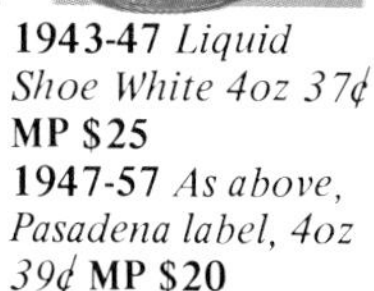

1943-47 *Liquid Shoe White 4oz 37¢* **MP $25**
1947-57 *As above, Pasadena label, 4oz 39¢* **MP $20**

1930 *Machine Oil 3oz 25¢* **MP $25**

1934-36 *Machine Oil 3oz 26¢* **MP $25,** **$32** boxed

1941-42 only *Machine Oil 3oz 26¢* **MP $40**

1943-44 *Machine Oil 3oz 29¢* **MP $40**

1944-48 *Machine Oil 3oz 29¢* **MP $30**

MACHINE OIL

1930 *Mending Cement, large tube 25¢* **MP $20**

1941-47 *Mending Cement, large tube 25¢* **MP $15**
1947-50 *As above, Pasadena label 29¢* **MP $15**

MENDING CEMENT

1922 *Kwick Cleaning Polish ½lb 24¢, 1 lb 45¢* **MP $50**

KWICK METAL

1926-29 *Kwick Metal Polish ½ lb 24¢* **MP $40**

Kwick Metal Polish not only polished but also preserved metal surfaces.

1930 *Kwick Metal Polish ½lb 35¢* **MP $35**

It was recommended as an automobile soap and as a mechanic's hand soap.

1941-42 *Kwick Metal Polish ½lb 35¢* **MP $25**
1943-48 *Glass wartime pkg. (See mothicide far right) 8oz 39¢*
MP $35, rare

1915-18 *California Plate Polish 4oz 35¢* **MP $90**
1902-15 *(not shown) Same container, no oz on front 25¢* **MP $150**

1919 *Silver Cream Polish 30¢* **MP $65**

SILVER POLISH

1922-29 *Silver Cream Polish 8oz 30¢, 16oz 54¢* **MP $50**

Silver Cream Polish was chosen by hotels and other institutions.

1941-42 *Silver Cream Polish ½lb 35¢* **MP $25**
1947-51 *As above, (Pasadena label)* **MP $20**
1951-53 *In glass (not shown)* **MP $25**

1926 *Mothicide ½lb 48¢* **MP $40**

MOTHICIDE

1930 *Mothicide ½lb 50¢* **MP $25**

1930 *Silver Cream Polish ½lb 35¢* **MP $25**

1941-42 *Mothicide ½lb 50¢* **MP $25**

1914-21 *Lavender Fragrance Jar 6¾" high $2.50* **MP $155**

1921-30 *American Beauty Fragrance Jar $2.95* **MP $130**

FRAGRANCE JARS

CPC/Avon Fragrance Jars are among Avon's finest designs. A combination of scented liquid and ammoniated cubes created a pleasing fragrance – they were also used for faintness and dizziness.

In 1943, because of Suffern's heavy war production, the 1934 Fragrance Jar was discontinued. No sales catalogs were issued from 1943 to 1946, instead revised price lists were provided and were added by the Representative to her 1942 catalog.

The 1945 pottery Jar insert page shows the lid with white roses and green leaves. Porosity caused the discontinuance of the Jar in May 1945. It was reissued in 1946 with white roses and white leaves on the lid and was discontinued a short time later. Since few of the 1943-1946 insert pages were kept, pictures of the pink ceramic jars are now quite rare.

A heart-shaped Jar was introduced for Christmas 1948. Because moisture collected in the clear glass stopper – in 1949 a frosted stopper appeared to improve the appearance. The beautiful Rose Fragrance Jar remained in the line until the late 1950s. Although the Fragrance Jar was not pictured in Avon's 1957 catalog, it was sold until 1958 when stock was depleted.

1923 *American Beauty Fragrance Jar Liquid 4oz 96¢* **MP $115, $140 boxed**

1942-46 *Mothicide (wartime pkg.) 8oz 55¢* **MP $30, $45 boxed with folder. $7 folder only**

1943-47 *Silver Cream Polish (wartime pkg.) 10½oz 49¢* **MP $30, $38 boxed**
1946-47 *Mothicide 8½oz 55¢* **MP $25**
1947-48 *Mothicide (Montreal label) 55¢* **MP $25**
1948-58 *Mothicide, as above (Pasadena label)* **MP $20**

1934-42 *American Beauty Fragrance Jar incl. liquid & cubes $2.75* **MP $100**

1945 *Rose Fragrance Jar, rose top, green leaves $2.95* **MP $85**
1946 *Rose Fragrance Jar, pink top, white leaves $2.95* **MP $75**

Klean-Air 12 oz $1.89 (left to right) –
1956 *Mint-scented* **MP $8**
1961 *Pine* **MP $3**
1960 *Meadow Fresh* **MP $3**
1960 *Citrus* **MP $3**
1958 *Bouquet* **MP $4**
1962 *Spice* **MP $3**

1948 *Rose Fragrance Jar, Clear $3.50* **MP $75** *(short issue)*
1949-58 *(shown below right) with frosted stopper $3.50* **MP $35**

1937-53 *Fragrance Jar Liquid 6oz $1.25* **MP $20**
Boxed $25

1954-58 *Rose Fragrance Liquid 6oz $1.39* **MP $18**

AVON ROOM FRESH-ENERS

Klean-Air Concentrate – 3oz
1968 *Sudden Spring $1.49* **MP $2**
1968 *Meadow-Fresh $1.49* **MP $2**
1968 *Citrus $1.49* **MP $2**
1969 *Jamaican Waterfall $1.69* **MP $2**

1937 *American Beauty Fragrance Jar Cubes 3oz 75¢* **MP $25**

1949 *Fragrance Jar Set $3.50* **MP $95**
1949 *Refill Liquid 6oz $1.39* **MP $20**
1949 *Refill Cubes 3oz 85¢* **MP $20**

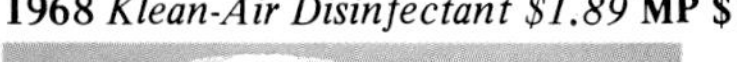

1968 *Klean-Air Disinfectant $1.89* **MP $1**

1965 *Wardrobe Freshener for Men, Sandalwood scented 6oz $2* **MP $3, $6 boxed**

1977 *Wardrobe Freshener 7oz $1.49* **MP $1**
1971 *Lemon Verbena Spray Sachet 6oz $2* **MP $1**
1972 *Floral Fancy Spray Sachet 6oz $2* **MP $1**

Moth Proofer

1956 *Avon moth-proofer 12oz $1.89* **MP $10**
1960 *(same can 11 oz) $1.89* **MP $12**
1961 *Avon moth-proofer 11oz $1.89* **MP $5**
1967 *Avon moth-proofer 11oz $1.89* **MP $4**

Room Fresheners (left to right) all 7oz each –
1973 *Scottish Heather $2* **MP $1**
1977 *Swiss Snowdrops $2* **MP $1**
1975 *French Lavender $1.89* **MP $1**
1976 *Mountain Air $1.89* **MP $1.50***
1975 *Normandy Rose $2.50* **MP $1.50***

Spray Sachets – 6oz
1964 *Carnation $1.50* **MP $2**
1958 *Lavender $1.50* **MP $2**
1960 *Rosiest $1.50* **MP $2**
1963 *Bayberry $1.50* **MP $2**
(add $1 to MP for box)

** Available from Avon at time of publication*

Room Fresheners all 7oz each

1976 *Bayberry $1.89* **MP 50¢**
1977 *Gentle Rain $1.49* **MP $1.50***

1976 *Country Meadow $1.89* **MP $1.50***
1978 *Burst of Spring $1.49* **MP 50¢**
1978 *Lemon $1.49* **MP 50¢**
1978 *Green Apple $1.49* **MP 50¢**
1970 *Green Apple (not shown) with emb. apple on lid $1.69* **MP $1**

1973 *Evergreen $2* **MP 50¢**
1971 *Country Strawberry $2* **MP 50¢**
1979 *Hello Spring $1.49* **MP 50¢**

1979 *Mistletoe & Holly $1.79* **MP 50¢**
1980 *Mistletoe & Holly $2.19* **MP 50¢**
1980 *Bayberry $2.19* **MP 50¢**

**Available from Avon at time of publication*

Dorothy Bernard's
FRAGRANCE DATING GUIDE FOR WOMEN AND GIRLS

All products of the same fragrance and package design are found under the proper name unique to that particular line.

1929 *Ariel*

1930 *391 Perfume (renamed Bolero 1934)*

1934 *Bolero*
Cotillion
Gardenia (re-intro 1972)
Jasmine

1935 *Pine*
Rose (formerly Roses)
Topaze (re-intro 1959)

1936 *Lucy Hays (Mrs. McConnell's maiden name)*
Lilac (re-intro 1963 – formerly Lilac Vegetal)

1937 *Courtship*

1938 *Marionette*

1939 *Ballad*
Garden of Love (formerly Jardin d'Amour)

1940 *Sonnet (re-intro 1972)*

1941 *American Ideal, changed to Apple Blossom same year (re-intro 1974)*

1942 *Attention*
Orchard Blossom
Rose Geranium

1945 *White Moire*

1946 *Crimson Carnation*
Here's My Heart (re-intro 1957)

1947 *Golden Promise*
Swan Lake
Wishing (re-intro 1963)

1948 *Happy Hours*
Quaintance

1949 *Flowertime*

1950 *Luscious*
To A Wild Rose

1951 *Forever Spring*

1952 *Young Hearts (for Girls)*

1954 *Bright Night*

1955 *Nearness*
Merriment (for Girls)

1956 *Elegante*
Persian Wood (first Avon Aerosol Cologne)
Daisies Won't Tell (for Girls)

1957 *Here's My Heart*
Floral

1959 *Topaze*

1960 *Buttons 'n Bows (for Girls)*

1961 *Somewhere*
Skin-So-Soft (Bath line)

1962 *Occur!*

1963 *Wishing*
Lilac
Lily of the Valley

1964 *Pretty Peach (for Girls)*
Rapture

1965 *Hawaiian White Ginger*
Unforgettable

1966 *Honeysuckle*
Regence

1967 *Blue Lotus*
Brocade
Miss Lollypop (for Girls)

1968 *Charisma*
Silk & Honey (Bath line)

1969 *Bird of Paradise*
Elusive
Her Prettiness (for Girls)
Lemon Velvet
Lights and Shadows
Patterns
Strawberry (Bath line)

1970 *Hana Gasa*
Sea Garden (Bath line)
Small World (for Girls)

1971 *Field Flowers*
Moonwind

1972 *Carnation*
Flower Talk (for Girls)
Gardenia
Mineral Springs (Bath line)
Roses, Roses
Sonnet
Violet

1973 *Imperial Garden*
Patchwork
Raining Violets
Sweet Honesty

1974 *Apple Blossom*
Hyacinth
Magnolia
Pink & Pretty (for Girls)
Timeless

1975 *Come Summer*
Queen's Gold
Unspoken

1976 *Emprise*

1977 *Ariane*
Candid
Delicate Daisies (for Girls)

1978 *Blue Tranquility (Bath line)*
Frivolie (Bath line)
Sun Blossoms
Tempo

1979 *Hello Sunshine (for Girls)*
Tasha
Zany

1980 *Country Breeze*
Foxfire
Shower 'Scape (Bath line)
Sportif
Wild Jasmine

1981 *Little Blossom (for Girls)*
Odyssey
Toccaro

(See pg. 7 for CPC Fragrance Guide, pg. 181 for Men's Fragrance Guide)

ARIEL

1929 *Toilet Water 2oz $1.75* **MP $115**

1929 *Perfume 1oz $2.50* **MP $125 $150 boxed**

Ariane

1977 *Cologne Spray 1.8oz marked "First Edition." Sold only at sales meetings. $7.50* **MP $8**
1977 *Cologne Spray 1.8oz $7.50* **MP $7***
1978 *Cologne 2oz $6.50* **MP $6***
1978 *Purse Concentre .33oz $4* **MP $1**
1977 *Cologne .33oz $3* **MP $1**

1978 *Creme Perfume .66oz $4.50* **MP $4***
1978 *Skin Softener 5oz $6* **MP $3***
1978 *Talc 3oz* **MP $2***
1977 *Perfume ¼oz $15* **MP $5**
1977 *Solid Perfume Compact .2oz $3.75* **MP $1**

1979 *Bath Foam 6oz $5.50* **MP $3***
1979 *Light Perfume .5oz $7* **MP $5***
1979 *Soft Body Satin 6oz $5* **MP 50¢**
1979 *Cologne Spray 1oz $7* **MP $5***

1978 *Cologne .33oz $3* **MP $1.50**
1979 *Cologne .33oz $3* **MP $1**
1980 *Cologne .33oz $3.50* **MP $2***
1979 *Powder Mist 4oz $5* **MP $3***

1977 *Beauty Dust 6oz $8.50* **MP $3**
1978 *Boxed Soaps three 3oz cakes $7* **MP $5**

APPLE BLOSSOM

1941 *Toilet Water 2oz $1.04* **MP $50 boxed**
1941 *Cologne 6oz $1* **MP $80**

1941 *Body Powder 5oz 65¢* **MP $26**

1974 *After Bath Freshener 8oz $4* **MP 75¢**
1974 *Powder Mist 7oz $4* **MP $1**
1974 *Cologne Mist 2oz $4.25* **MP $1.25**

1974 *Cologne Gelee 3oz $4* **MP $1**
1978 *Cologne Ice 1oz $3.75* **MP $1**
1974 *DemiStik .19oz $1.75* **MP 50¢**
1975 *Cream Sachet .66oz $3* **MP 50¢**
1974 *Cream Sachet .66oz $2.50* **MP $1.25**

Attention

1943 *Cologne 6oz $1* **MP $80**
1944-45 *Sachet, cardboard 1¼oz $1.15* **MP $20**
1943 only *Sachet 1¼oz $1.15* **MP $28**
1942-47 *Sachet 1¼oz $1.15* **MP $20**

1943 only *Sachet 1¼oz 57¢* **MP $35 in 57th Anniversary box**

1944-46 *Body Powder 5oz 65¢* **MP $25**

1943 only *Body Powder 5oz 65¢* **MP $30**

1947 only *Body Powder 5oz 65¢* **MP $25**

1942 only *Toilet Water 2oz $1.04* **MP $45, $60 in Xmas Box**

**Available from Avon at time of publication*

Bird of Paradise

1969 *Cologne Fluff 3oz $5* **MP $3**
1969 *Emollient Oils 6oz $5* **MP $4**
1969 *Cologne 4oz $5* **MP $3**
1970 *Half-ounce Cologne $1.75* **MP $2**

1970 *Rollette .33oz $3* **MP $1.50**
1970 *Perfume Glace Ring $10* **MP $10**
1970 *Cologne Mist 3oz $6* **MP $1**

1976 *Cologne Spray 2.7oz $7* **MP $2**
1974 *Foaming Bath Oil 6oz $5* **MP $1**
1975 *Soap 3oz $1.25* **MP $1**

1958 *Cologne Mist 3oz $2.75* **MP $24**
1955 *Toilet Water 2oz $2* **MP $22**
1955 *Cologne 4oz $2.50* **MP $22**
1955 *Cologne w/Atomizer 4oz $3.50* **MP $36**

1972 *Boxed Soap, three 3oz cakes with embossed flowers $4* **MP $6**
1970 *Boxed Soap, three 3oz cakes, no flowers $4* **MP $7**
1970 *Bath Brush and 5oz Soap $6* **MP $9**

1971 *Hair Spray 7oz $1.50* **MP $3**
1971 *Powder Mist 7oz $4* **MP $2**
1974 *DemiStik .19oz $2* **MP 50¢**
1969 *Beauty Dust 6oz $5* **MP $5**
1975 *Cream Sachet .66oz $3* **MP $1**

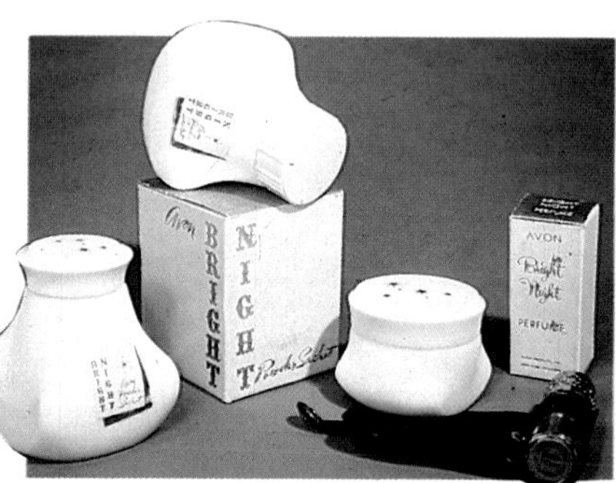

1955 *Powder Sachet .9oz $1.50* **MP $13**
1955 *Rare issue of Powder Sachet with ridged cap $1.50* **MP $22**
1954 *Cream Sachet $1.50* **MP $9**
1955 *One-dram Perfume in suede wrap $2.25* **MP $17**

1971 *Perfumed Talc 3½oz $1.35* **MP 50¢**
1970 *Cream Sachet .66oz $3* **MP $1**
1972 *Emollient Mist 4oz $3* **MP $2**
1971 *Foaming Bath Oil 6oz $4* **MP $1**
1971 *Perfumed Skin Softener 5oz $4* **MP $4**

1974 *Hand & Body Cream Lotion 16oz $5* **MP $1**
1972 *Hand & Body Cream Lotion 8oz $3* **MP $1**
1979 *Creme Perfume .66oz $3.50* **MP $1**
1979 *Purse Concentre .33oz $3* **MP $1**

1957 *Beauty Dust 8oz in hinged box with bow-tied 5/8 dram fragrance $2.50* **MP $35**
1954 *Gift Perfume with crystal stopper and neck tag ½oz $7.50* **MP $90**
1959 *Beauty Dust 6oz $2.95* **MP $14**
1958 *Cologne Mist 3oz $2.75* **MP $21**

1967 *After Bath Freshener 6oz $3* **MP $5**
1970 *Talc 3½oz $1.10* **MP $2**
1969 *Cream Sachet .66oz $2.50* **MP $2**
1969 *Soap 3oz 49¢* **MP $4**
1969 *DemiStik $1.50* **MP $2**
1969 *Cream Lotion 5oz $2* **MP $2**

1978 *Body Freshener 8oz $5* **MP $1**
1978 *Bubble Bath 8oz $5* **MP $1**
1978 *Refreshing Soap on wrist rope 5oz $5* **MP $4**

1955 *Melody Set. Beauty Dust 8oz, Cologne 4oz, Cream Sachet & 1 dram Perfume $8.75* **MP $100**

1956 *Magic Hours Set. 2oz Toilet Water and Cologne Stick $3.50* **MP $50**

BRIGHT NIGHT

1957 *Bright Night Gem Set. Toilet Water 2oz and Cream Sachet $3.50* **MP $45**

1957 *Golden Beauty Set. Contains same items as Melody Set (pg.36) $8.95* **MP $90**

1958 *Golden Glamor Set. 8oz Beauty Dust, 3oz Cologne Mist, Cream Sachet and 1 dram Perfume $8.95* **MP $95**

1968 *Skin Softener 5oz $4* **MP $4**
1968 *Skin Softener 5oz $4* **MP $10**
1968 *Cologne Mist 3oz refillable $6* **MP $4**
1967 *Cologne Mist Refill 3oz $4* **MP $3**

1971 *Beauty Dust 6oz $5* **MP $4**
1968 *Perfume Oil ½oz $6* **MP $9**
1969 *Cologne ½oz $1.75* **MP $4**
1968 *Perfume Glace with Purse$5.50* **MP $10**

BROCADE

1968 *Cologne Silk 3oz $4.50* **MP $5**

1971 *Rollette .33oz, 4-A design on lid, $3* **MP $6**
1967 *Rollette .33oz $3* **MP $3**
1968 *Rollette .33oz, glass strike issue, vertical ribbing, $3* **MP $10**
1968-69 *Rollette .33oz, patterned lid, issued in various Sets* **MP $7**
1967 *Cologne 4oz $6* **MP $7**

1967 *Beauty Dust, plastic 6oz $6* **MP $10**
1968 *Perfumed Skin Softener, glass strike issue 5oz $4* **MP $17**
1968 *Cream Sachet .66oz, label on bottom $3* **MP $6**
1967 *Cream Sachet .66oz, label on lid $3* **MP $7**

1968 *Foaming Bath Oil 6oz $4.50* **MP $2**
1970 *Powder Mist 7oz, different labeling than 1968 issue, $4* **MP $2**
1971 *Hair Spray 7oz $1.50* **MP $4**
1968 only *Talc 2¾oz, Perfumed Pair Set,* **MP $4**
1968 only *Soap 3oz, Perfumed Pair Set,* **MP $4**

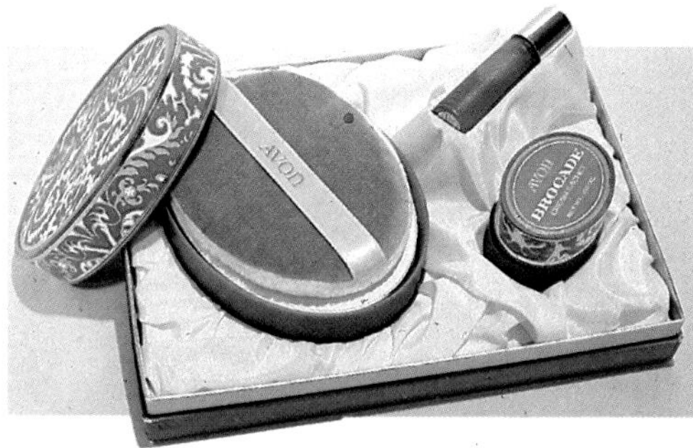

1967 *Deluxe Gift Set. Beauty Dust 6oz, Perfume Rollette .33oz & Cream Sachet .66oz, $12.95* **MP $42**

1960 *Beauty Dust, cdbd. 4oz $2.25* **MP $20**
1962 *Roll-On Deodor. gl. 1¾oz 89¢* **MP $10**
1960 *Cologne Mist 2½oz 89¢* **MP $15**
1961 *Nail Polish 69¢* **MP $7**
1962 *Bubble Bath plastic 4oz $1.35* **MP $9**
1960 *Cream Sachet .66oz $1.35* **MP $11**

1961 *Boxed Soaps $1.35* **MP $27**

Buttons 'n Bows . . .

Charisma

1968 *Rollette .33oz $3* **MP $1**
1968 *Cologne Mist 3oz $4.50* **MP $2**
1969 *Cologne Silk 3oz, frosted $4.50*
MP $5, MP $3 clear glass
1968 *Cream Sachet .66oz $3* **MP $1**

1975 *Powder Sachet 1¼oz $3.50* **MP $1.50**
1969 *Half-ounce Cologne $1.75* **MP $2**
1970-74 *Boxed Soap, 3 3oz cakes $3.50* **MP $7**
1970 *Talc 3½oz $1.35* **MP $1**

1968 *Beauty Dust 6oz $6* **MP $6**
1972 *DemiStik .19oz* **MP $1**
1970 only *Foaming Bath Oil 6oz $3.50* **MP $5**
1971 *As above but no red band on lid.* **MP $2**

1972 *Powder Mist, all metal 7oz $4* **MP $1**
1969 *Powder Mist, paper label 7oz $4* **MP $5**
1970 *Tray 10" dia. $3* **MP $7**
1975-79 *Boxed Soap 3 3oz cakes $6* **MP $6**

1974 *Skin Softener 5oz $4* **MP $4***
1976 *Cologne Spray 2.7oz $8* **MP $7***
1976 *Foaming Bath Oil 6oz $5.50* **MP $1**
1969 *Skin Softener, glass 5oz $4* **MP $4**
1975 *Cream Sachet .66oz $4.50* **MP $1**
1975 *Soap 3oz $1.25* **MP $1***

1975 *Powder Sachet 1¼oz $3.50* **MP $1**
1976 *Rollette .33oz $4.50* **MP $1**
1977 *Cologne Spray 1.8oz $6.50* **MP $2**
1976 *Xmas-wrapped Soap 3oz $2.25* **MP $2**

1979 *Creme Perfume .66oz $3.50* **MP $2.50***
add $1 to MP for 1980 Xmas box
1979 *Purse Concentre .33oz $3* **MP $1**
1979 *Cologne Spray 1.8oz $6* **MP $5***
1979 *Powder Mist 4oz $4.50* **MP 3***

1976 *Bubble Bath Gelee 4oz $3.50* **MP $2**
1975 *Body Splash 12 oz $5* **MP $3**
1975 *Powder Mist 7oz $4.50* **MP $2**
1976 *Talc 3½oz $2* **MP $1**

COME SUMMER

1975 *Cologne Mist 2oz $5* **MP $2**
1975 *Cologne Ice 2¼oz $5* **MP $5**
1976 *Cologne Ice (as above) 2oz $5* **MP $1**
1978 *Cologne Ice 1oz $3.75* **MP $2**
1977 *Touch of Cologne .33oz $1.75* **MP $1**
1977 *Cologne Spray 1.8oz $5* **MP $1**

...Buttons 'n Bows

1960 *Cologne 2oz $1.35* **MP $16**
1961 *Lipstick 89¢* **MP $6**

1962 *Cute as a Button. Pink Nail Polish & Lipstick $1.58* **MP $20**

1962 *Pretty Choice. 2oz Cologne and choice of Cream Lotion or Bubble Bath, 4oz each $2.70* **MP $31**

COUNTRY BREEZE

1980 *Drawer Lining Paper & Powder Sachet 1¼oz $8.50* **MP $4**
1980 *Cologne Spray 1oz $6* **MP $5***
1980 *Powder Mist 4oz $4.50* **MP $3***
1980 *Mini-Spray .33oz $4.50* **MP $4.50***

**Available from Avon at time of publication*

1977 *Boxed Soaps three 3oz $7* **MP $5**
1977 *Skin Softener 5oz $6* **MP $3***
1977 *Solid Perfume Compact .2oz $3.75* **MP $ 1**

1977 *Cologne Spray 1.8oz $7.50* **MP $7***
1977 *Cologne 2oz $6.50* **MP $6***
1977 *Purse Cologne .5oz $3* **MP $2**
1977 *Cologne .33oz $3* **MP $1**
1978 *Pressed Powder Compact $4* **MP $1**

1979 *Purse Concentre .33oz $4* **MP $1**
1979 *Light Perfume .5oz $7* **MP $5***
1979 *Bath Foam $5.50* **MP $3**
1979 *Creme Perfume .66oz $4.50* **MP $4***
1979 *Soft Body Satin 6oz $5* **MP 50¢**

CANDID

1976 *Color Collection $15.25* **MP $7**
Makeup 1.5oz $3.50 **MP $1**
Cheek Color .15oz $3.50 **MP 75¢**
Lip Color $2.25 **MP 75¢**
Eye Color .25oz $3 **MP 75¢**
Mascara .25oz $3 **MP 75¢**

1977 *Under-Makeup Moisturizer 2oz $3.50* **MP $1**
1978 *Face Color 1.5oz $3.50* **MP 50¢**
1977 *Talc 3½oz $3* **MP $2***
1977 *Foaming Body Clnsr. 6oz $4.50* **MP $3.50***

1979 *Powder Mist 4oz $5* **MP $3***
1979 *Cologne Spray 1oz $7* **MP $5***
1980 *Cologne .33oz $3.50* **MP $2***
1978 *Cologne .33oz $3* **MP $1**
1979 *Cologne .33oz $3* **MP $1**

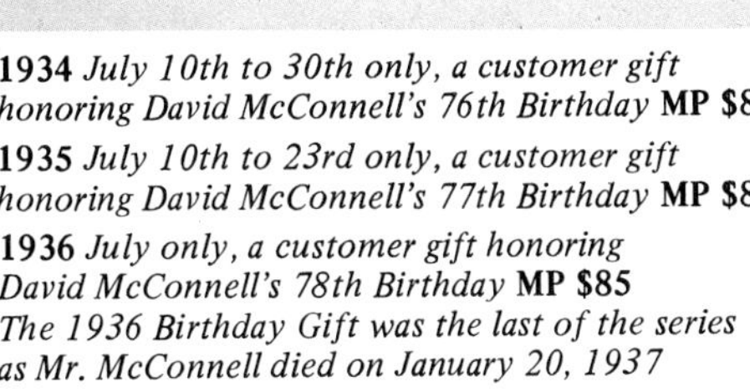

1934 *July 10th to 30th only, a customer gift honoring David McConnell's 76th Birthday* **MP $85**

1935 *July 10th to 23rd only, a customer gift honoring David McConnell's 77th Birthday* **MP $85**

1936 *July only, a customer gift honoring David McConnell's 78th Birthday* **MP $85**
The 1936 Birthday Gift was the last of the series as Mr. McConnell died on January 20, 1937

1937 *Customer gift, with additional purchase 20¢* **MP $85**

1939 *Cusotmer gift, with additional purchase 20¢* **MP $75.**

Add $10 to all MPs if boxed

Mr. David H. McConnell

1948 *Gift Perfume 3 dr. $3* **MP $110**

. . . one of Avon's most popular fragrances ever . . .

Cotillion

1960 *Spray Perfume 2 drams $2.95* **MP $15, $20 boxed**
1960-61 *Spray Perfume 2 drams $2.95* **MP $15**
1961-62 *Spray Perfume $3.50* **MP $10, $14 boxed**
1960-63 *Spray Perfume Refills $1.75 & $2.25* **MP $12 boxed**

1951 *Gift Perfume 3 drams $3.50* **MP $100, $125 boxed**

1957 **only** *Gift Perfume 3 drams and 1 dram Perfume in gold wrapper $6* **MP $130 boxed with ribbon**

1953 *Gift Perfume 3 drams $4.50* **MP $85, $105 boxed**

** Available from Avon at time of publication*

1937 *Powder Sachet $1.04* **MP $26, $45 in Xmas Box**

1937 *Powder Sachet 1½oz $1.04. Sold in special box as "Good Will Gesture" for 20¢* **MP $26, MP $45 boxed**
1939 *Toilet Water 2oz Special packaging sold from May 2 to May 22, 1939 only. 20¢ with another purchase.* **MP $45, $60 boxed**

1939-43 *Talc (metal) 14½oz $1.04* **MP $25**
1943-44 *Talc (cdbd.) 14½oz $1.19* **MP $40**
1944-45 *Talc (cdbd.) 2¾oz 37¢* **MP $30**
1943-44 *Talc (cdbd.) 2¾oz 37¢* **MP $30**
1947 *Talc 2¾oz 39¢* **MP $30**

1936 *Powder Sachet 1½oz $1.04* **MP $26**
1937 *Powder Sachet 1¼oz. $1.04* **MP $20**
1943 *Powder Sachet 1¼oz $1.15* **MP $20**

1943 *Powder Sachet 1¼oz $1.15* **MP $32 boxed**
1946 *Powder Sachet 1¼oz $1.19* **MP $18, $28 boxed**
1946 *Powder Sachet 1¼oz $1.19* **MP $25, $35 boxed**

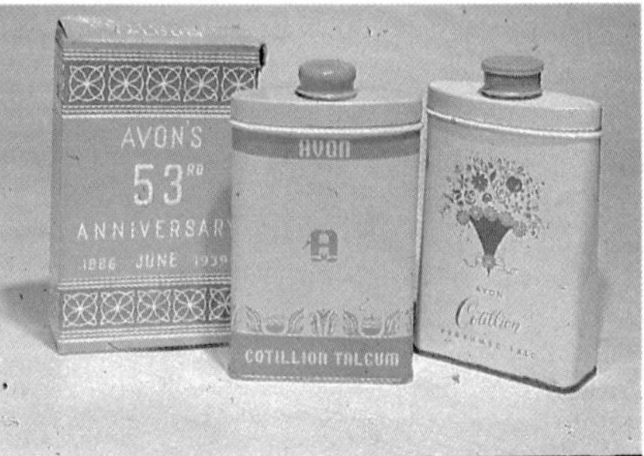

1939 *Talc 2¾oz, 53rd Anniversary Box* **MP $33**
1938-42 *Talc only 37¢* 1943-50 *39¢* **MP $15**
1957 *Talc 2¾oz 69¢* **MP $6**

1946 *Body Powder 5oz 65¢ (rare)* **MP $40**
1947 *Body Powder 4½oz 75¢* **MP $22**
1946 *Cologne 6oz $1.50* **MP $50**
1946 *Toilet Water 2oz $1.19* **MP $38**

1950 *Toilet Water 2oz $1.75* **MP $25, $30 boxe**
1950 *Perfume 1/8oz (rare) $1.50* **MP $80, $100 boxed**
1950 *Cologne 4oz $1.75* **MP $25**

1950 *Powder Sachet 1¼oz $1.25* **MP $20**
1950 *Cream Lotion 6oz 89¢* **MP $30**
1950 *Talc 2¾oz 43¢* **MP $12**
1945 *Powder Sachet, cardboard 1¼oz $1.15* **MP $22**
1944 *Powder Sachet, cardboard 1¼oz $1.15* **MP $22**

1951 *Beauty Dust 6oz $1.75* **MP $23, $30 boxed**

1953 *Beauty Dust 6oz $1.95* **MP $18**
1950 *Body Powder 5oz 75¢* **MP $22**
1951 *Cream Sachet .66oz $1.25* **MP $18**

1950 *Boxed Soaps, three 3oz cakes 79¢* **MP $45**
1954 *Boxed Soaps, three 3oz cakes 89¢* **MP $40**

1956 *Beauty Dust with 5/8 dram bottle of matching fragrance $1.95* **MP $40 complete, $12 bottle only**
1953 *Beauty Dust as above with 5/8 dram square bottle of fragrance $1.75* **MP $45 complete, $17 bottle only**

1953 *Powder Sachet 1¼oz $1.25* **MP $15**
1958 *Powder Sachet 1¼oz $1.50* **MP $12**
1957 *Powder Sachet 1¼oz (white lettering) $1.50* **MP $20**
1953 *Cream Sachet .66oz $1.25* **MP $15**
1958 *Cream Sachet .66oz $1.50* **MP $10**

1954 *Bath Oil 4½oz $1.25* **MP $13**
1954 *Cream Lotion 4½oz 95¢* **MP $13**
1955 *Talc 3oz $1* **MP $15**
1958 *Body Powder 3oz $1* **MP $12**
1956 *Talc 3oz $1* **MP $14**

1959 *Perfumed Bath Oil 8oz $2.50* **MP $20**
1959 *Cologne Mist 3oz $2.95* **MP $23**
1959 *Beauty Dust 6oz $2.95* **MP $15**
1957 *Cologne Mist 3oz $2.50* **MP $25**
1958 only *Cologne Mist 3oz (rare) $2.50* **MP $55**

1959 only *Gift Cologne 4oz (N.Y.-Pasadena label) $2.50* **MP $75**

. . . Cotillion

1961 *Cologne 2oz $1.50* **MP $23**
1953 *Cologne 4oz $2* **MP $20**
1953 *Toilet Water 2oz $1.50* **MP $18**

1961 *Perfumed Bath Oil 6oz $3* **MP $7**
1966 *Foaming Bath Oil 6oz $2.75* **MP $2**
1961 *Cream Lotion 4oz $1.50* **MP $5**
1961 *Body Powder 4oz $2.25* **MP $8**

1961 *Beauty Dust 6oz $4* **MP $7**
1961 *Powder Sachet .9oz $2* **MP $9**
1974 *Talc 3½oz $1.50* **MP 50¢**

1961 *Cologne 4oz $3* **MP $12**
1961 *Cologne 2oz $2* **MP $3**
1963 *Perfume Oil for Bath ½oz $4* **MP $12**
1964 *Perfume Oil ½oz $4* **MP $9**
1969 *Cologne ½oz $1.50* **MP $2**

1961 *Boxed Soaps three 3oz $1.50* **MP $25**

1971-75 *Cologne Mist 3oz $5* **MP $4**
1961 *Cologne Mist 3oz $4* **MP $6**
1975-76 *Cologne Mist 3oz $8* **MP $2**
1976-81 *Cologne Spray 2.7oz $7* **MP $1**

1967 *Cologne Silk 3oz $3.75* **MP $5**
1974 *Talc 3½oz $1.50* **MP 50¢**
1979 *Cologne Spray 1.8oz $6* **MP $1**

1964 *Skin Softener 5oz $3.25* **MP $1**
1966 *Hair Spray 7oz $1.50* **MP $1**
1977 *Foaming Bath Oil 6oz $4.50* **MP $1**
1975 *DemiStik .19oz $2.50* **MP $1**

1975 *Cream Sachet .66oz $3* **MP $1**
1979 *Creme Perfume .66oz $3.50* **MP 50¢**
1968 *Powder Mist 7oz $3.50* **MP $1**
1979 *Purse Concentre .33oz $3* **MP $1**

1940 *Cotillion Classic. Toilet Water 2oz and Talc 2¾oz $1.50* **MP $75**

1939 *Cotillion Enchantment. 1 dram Perfume, Toilet Water 2oz & Powder Sachet $2.95* **MP $180**

1940 *Cotillion Enchantment. Toilet Water 2oz Powder Sachet and 1 dram Perfume $2.85* **MP $125**

1946 *Cotillion Classic. Body Powder 5oz and Cologne 6oz $2.48***MP $120**

1946 *Cotillion Garland. Toilet Water 2oz and Powder Sachet $2.84* **MP $80**

1947 *Cotillion Duet. Toilet Water 2oz and Powder Sachet $2.39* **MP $70**

1948 *Hair Ribbons. Talc, Hand Lotion and 5/8 dram Perfume $1.59* **MP $80**

1949 *Your Charms. Talc, Hand Lotion and 5/8 dram Perfume $1.59* **MP $75**

1951 *Jolly Surprsise. Powder Sachet and 1 dram Perfume $1.99* **MP $50**

1950 *Always Sweet. Talc 2oz, 5/8 dram Perfume, Cream Lotion 2oz and Straw Handbag*

1951 *Always Sweet. Cotillion Talc 2oz, Perfume 5/8 dram, Cream Lotion 2oz and Straw Handbag $2.39* **MP $95**

1950 *Cotillion Garland. Talc and Toilet Water 2oz $1.85* **MP $60**

1950 *The Cotillion. Cream Lotion 6oz and Cologne 4oz $2.39* **MP $75**

1950 *Bath Ensemble. Cream Lotion, Toilet Water, Bath Oil, Talc, Powder and Cream Sachets, 1 dram Perfume and 2 bars Soap $8.25* **MP $200**

. . . Cotillion

1951 *Cotillion Enchantment. Toilet Water 2oz & Cream Sachet $2.50* **MP $60**

1952 *Cotillion Fantasy. Body Powder 5oz and Cream Sachet $1.95* **MP $50**

1953 *Cotillion Duet. Cologne 4oz and Talc 3¼oz $3* **MP $50**

1953-56 *Cotillion Enchantment. 1¼oz Powder Sachet and 1 dram Perfume $3* **MP $40**

1953 *Cotillion Deluxe. Cologne 4oz 1 dram Perfume, Powder Sachet & Talcum $6* **MP $72**

1954 *Cotillion Garland. Cream Lotion & Bath Oil 4½oz each $2.15* **MP $36**

1954 *Special Date. Toilet Water ½oz, Powder-Pak and Fashion Lipstick $1.95* **MP $40**

1956 *Bath Bouquet. Bath Oil, Cologne 2oz each and 1oz cake Soap $2.25* **MP $75**

1956 *Cotillion Carol. Talc & Cream Sachet $2.25* **MP $35**

1956 *Singing Bells. 2 Talcs $1.10* **MP $18**

1956 *Princess. Cologne 4oz and Beauty Dust 6oz $3.95* **MP $68**

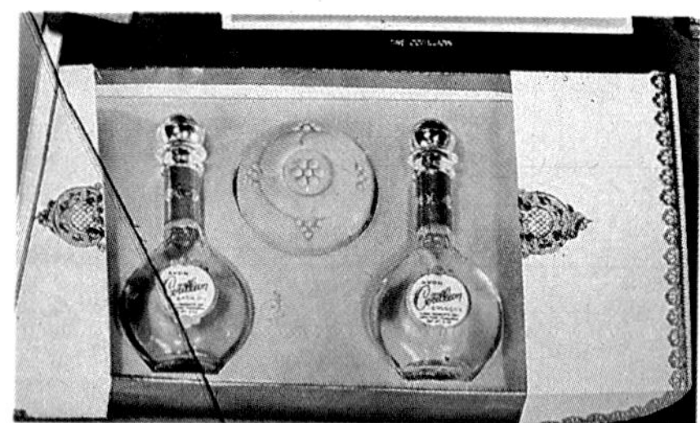
1957 *Cotillion Treasures. Bath Oil, Soap, Cologne $2.75* **MP $75**

1957 *The Cotillion. Beauty Dust, Cream Sachet & Cologne $4.95* **MP $70**

1958 *Cotillion Bouquet. Cologne Mist 3oz & Cream Sachet $3.95* **MP $85**

1961 *With Someone Like You. Cologne 2oz & Cream Sachet $4* **MP $20**

... *Cotillion*

1961 *Cotillion Debut. Beauty Dust, Cream Sachet, Cologne Mist $10* **$MP $30**

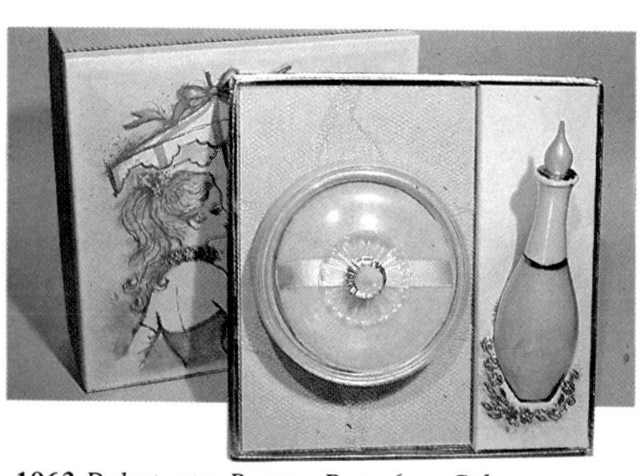
1963 *Debutante. Beauty Dust 6oz, Cologne Mist 3oz $8.50* **MP $25**

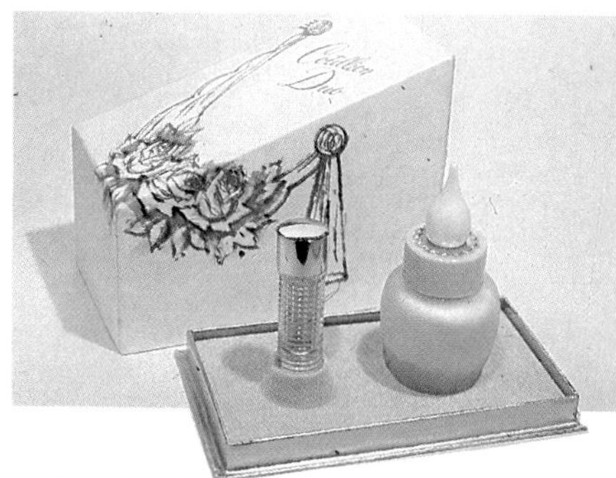
1964 *Cotillion Duo. Powder Sachet & 1 dram Perfume $3.98* **MP $20**

1956 *Cologne 2oz with Atomizer $1.25* **MP $20, $25 boxed**
1956 *Cream Lotion 69¢* **MP $15, $18 boxed**

1958 *Gift Pomade 59¢* **MP $13. Pomade only $4**

Daisies won't tell

1956 *Blossoms Set. Cologne 2oz and Pomade Lipstick $1.59* **MP $22**

1956 *Cologne 2oz (sets only)* **MP $15**
1962 *Pomade Lipstick 59¢* **MP $4**
1961 *Cologne 2oz $1.19* **MP $9**

1958 *Spray Cologne 1½oz $1.59* **MP $17**
1956 *Bubble Bath 4oz $1.10* **MP $12**
1957 *Beauty Dust $1.29* **MP $23**

1956 *Beauty Dust 3.5oz $1.19* **MP $25**
1958 *Beauty Dust 4oz $1.49* **MP $20**

1959 *Fluff-On 4oz powder & puff $1.98* **MP $15**
1957 *Spray Cologne 1.5oz $1.59* **MP $16**

1959 *Daisy Soap $1.19*
MP $20, $25 boxed

1960 *First Waltz Set. Pomade and Nail Polish $1.25* **MP $22**
1960 *Nail Polish 69¢* **MP $8**
1962 *Soap $1.19* **MP $19, $24 boxed**

1959 *Cream Sachet .66oz $1.19* **MP $15**
1963 *Cream Sachet .66oz $1.10* **MP $11**
1962 *Cream Lotion 4oz $1.19* **MP $7, $10 boxed**
1962 *Cologne 2oz $1.19* **MP $7, $10 boxed**
1963 *Cologne Mist 2oz $2.25* **MP $10, $13 boxed**

1958 *Hand Cream 1¾oz 49¢*
MP $8, $10 boxed

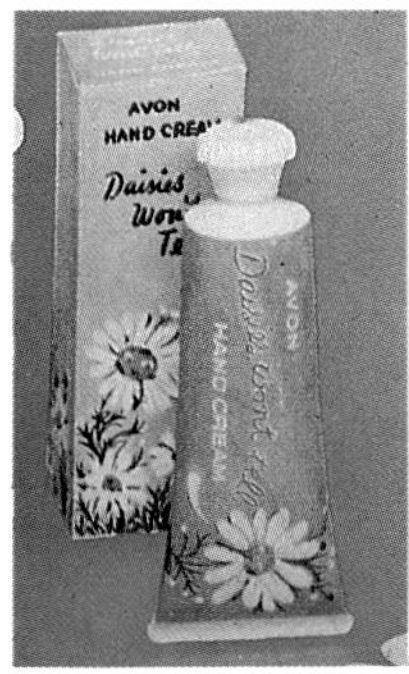

1962 *Hand Cream 1¾oz 59¢*
MP $8, $10 boxed

1956 *Hand Cream 1¾oz. Sets only.*
MP $10, $15 boxed
1957 *Dainty Hands. 2 Hand Cream 1¾oz 79¢* **MP $20, $8 each tube**

1958 *Cream Lotion 4oz $1.19* **MP $10, $15 boxed**
1958 *Bubble Bath 4oz $1.19* **MP $10, $15 boxed**
1958 *Daisy Dust 2oz $1.19* **MP $10, $15 boxed**

1957 *Daisy Petals. Pomade Lipstick and Cologne 2oz $1.59* **MP $27**

1958 *Fairy Touch. Two Hand Cream 79¢*
MP $20, $8 each tube

1956 *Playmate Cologne, Cream Lotion 2oz each, Pomade Lipstick and Doll $3.95* **MP $90, Doll MP $40**

1957 *My Dolly. Cream Lotion, Cologne 2oz each, Pomade Lipstick & Doll $3.95*
MP $85 complete, $40 Doll only

... Daisies won't tell

1956 *Daisies Won't Tell Set. Cologne, Bubble Bath 2oz each, Talc 3¼oz $2.25*
MP $70, Talc MP $25

1956 *Miss Daisy. Cologne 2oz Beauty Dust $2.35* **MP $50**

1956 *Little Charmer. Plastic Handbag. Hand Cream, Pomade Lipstick and Cologne 2oz $3.50* **MP $60**

1957 *Daisies Won't Tell Set. Cologne and Bubble Bath 2oz each, Talc 3¼oz $2.25*
MP $65, Talc MP $25

1957 *One I Love. Cologne, Cream Lotion and Bubble Bath 2oz each $2.49* **MP $57**

1957 *Daisy Bouquet. Cologne 2oz Beauty Dust and Pomade Lipstick $2.95* **MP $50**

1958 *Hearts 'N Daisies. Cologne 2oz and Pomade Lipstick $1.59* **MP $25**

... Daisies won't tell

1958 *Field of Daisies. Bubble Bath, Cream Lotion with red ribbon and Cologne 2oz each $2.19* **MP $48**

1958 *Daisy Darling. Spray Cologne 1½oz and Beauty Dust 4oz $2.98* **MP $45**

1959 *Daisy Bouquet. Cream Lotion, Bubble Bath 4oz each & Daisy Dust 2oz $3.50* **MP $37**

1959 *Daisy Treasure Set. 5 Manicure items $2.75* **MP $57**

1961 *Pretty Beginner. Cologne 2oz and choice of Lotion, Bubble Bath, Shampoo, Daisy Dust or Soap $2.38* **MP $30, $40 with Soap**

1960 *Gay Daisies. Soap and choice of Bubble Bath, Cream Lotion or Shampoo 4oz each or Daisy Dust 2oz $2.35* **MP $37**

1962 *First Recital. Soap and Choice of Cream Lotion, Bubble Bath 4oz ea. or Daisy Dust 2oz $2.38* **MP $35**

1963 *Pick A Daisy. Soap & Cream Sachet $2.38* **MP $36**

1963 *Daisy Chain. Hand Cream 1¾oz, Cologne 2oz $1.78* **MP $24**

DELICATE DAISIES

1977 *Cologne 2oz $3.50* **MP $1**
1977 *Hand Cream 1.5oz $2* **MP 50¢**
1977 *Talc 2oz $2* **MP 50¢**
1977 *Hairbrush 7" long $5.50* **MP $4**

Elusive

1970 *Boxed Soaps, three 3oz cakes $3.50* **MP $6**
1969 *Rollette .33oz $3* **MP $1**
1969 *Half-ounce Cologne $1.75* **MP $3**

1970 *Tray $4* **MP $10**
1970 *Foaming Bath Oil 6oz $3.50* **MP $2**
1969 *Cream Sachet .66oz $3* **MP $1**
1969 *Cologne Mist 3oz $6* **MP $1**
1970 *DemiStik .19oz $1.75* **MP $1**
1969 *Beauty Dust 6oz $6* **MP $5**

1970 *Hair Spray 7oz $1.50* **MP $3**
1970 *Powder Mist 7oz $4* **MP $2**
1971 *Talc 3½oz $1.35* **MP 50¢**
1970 *Skin Softener 5oz $4* **MP $2**
1972 *Powder Mist 7oz $4* **MP $1**

Elégante

An elegant collection of truly regal packaging and superb craftsmanship in glass . . . .

1957 *Powder Sachet .9oz $1.50* **MP $19**
1956 *Cream Sachet .66oz $1.50* **MP $13**
1956 *Perfume 1 dram in suedene wrapper $2.25* **MP $18**
1956 *Cologne 4oz $2.50* **MP $25, $40 boxed**

1956 *Gift Perfume ½oz $7.50* **MP $130, $85 bottle only**

1957 *Sparkling Burgundy. Beauty Dust 6oz, Cream Sachet, Cologne 4oz & 1 dram Perfume $8.95* **MP $120**

1957 *Snow Dreams. Toilet Water 2oz, Cream Sachet & 1 dram Perfume in suedene wrapper $5.50* **MP $80**

1957 *Toilet Water 2oz $2* **MP $25, $40 boxed**
1956 *Beauty Dust 6oz $2.25* **MP $22**

1957 *Beauty Dust 6oz & 5/8 dram Fragrance $2.25* **MP $35 complete**

1976 *Boxed Soaps, three 3oz cakes $6* **MP $6**
1977 *Skin Softener 5oz $6* **MP $3***
1977 *Creme Perfume .66oz $5* **MP $4***

emprise . . .

1976 *Spray Cologne 1.8oz $7.50* **MP $7***
1976 *Perfume ¼oz $15* **MP $8, $10 boxed**
1977 *Cologne 2oz $6.50* **MP $1**
1977 *Cologne .33oz $3* **MP $1.50**
1976 *Purse Concentre .33oz $5* **MP $3***

1977 *Powder Mist 7oz $5* **MP $2**
1977 *Foaming Bath Oil 6oz $5.50* **MP $1**
1977 *Talc 3½oz $4* **MP $2***

** Available from Avon at time of publication*

FLOWER TALK

1972 *Talc 3½oz $1.50* **MP $3**
1972 *Cologne Mist 3oz $5* **MP $5**
1973 *Rollette .33oz $1.75* **MP $5**
1972 *DemiStik .19oz $2* **MP $3**
1972 *Cream Sachet .66oz $2.50* **MP $4**

Field Flowers

1980 *Cologne Spray 1.5oz $6.50* **MP $4.50***
1980 *Talc 3.5oz $2.50* **MP $1.50***
1980 *Soap 3oz $1.75* **MP $1***

1971 *Foaming Bath Oil 6oz $4* **MP $2**
1972 *After Bath Freshener 8oz $4* **MP $2**
1971 *Cologne Mist 3oz $6* **MP $1**
1971 *Cologne Gelee 3oz $4* **MP $3**
1971 *Cream Sachet .66oz $3* **MP $2**

1976 *Body Splash 8oz $5* **MP $1**
1975 *Cream Sachet .66oz $3* **MP $1**
1971 *Powder Mist 7oz $4* **MP $1**
1978 *Cologne Ice 1oz $3.75* **MP $2**
1975 *Soap 3oz $1.25* **MP $1**

1979 *Cologne Spray 1oz $7* **MP $5***
1979 *Powder Mist 4oz $5* **MP $3***
1979 *Body Satin 6oz $5* **MP 50¢**
1979 *Light Perfume .5oz $7* **MP $5***

1971 *Bath Brush & 5oz Soap $6* **MP $10**
1971 *Boxed Soaps, three 3oz cakes $3.50* **MP $8**

(See also awards pg. 246)

1971 *Talc 3½oz $1.35* **MP 75¢**
1973 *Skin Softener 5oz $4* **MP $1**
1972 *Cream Lotion 8oz $3* **MP $1**
1973 *DemiStik .19oz $2* **MP 50¢**
1971 *Skin Softener 5oz $4* **MP $2.50**

... emprise

1979 *Bath Foam 6oz $5.50* **MP $3***
1978 *Cologne .33oz $3* **MP $1**
1979 *Cologne .33oz $3* **MP $1**
1980 *Cologne .33oz $3.50* **MP $2***

1977 *Gift Set. Cologne Spray 1.8oz and Purse Concentre .33oz $11.50* **MP $10**
Box MP $2

(See also Awards pg. 246)

FLOWERTIME

1949 *Powder Sachet, pink cap 1¼oz $1.19* **MP $15**
1950 *Powder Sachet, blue cap 1¼oz $1.19* **MP $20**
1949 *Talc 3¾oz metal shaker 89¢* **MP $25**
1949 *Cologne 4oz $1.75* **MP $23**
1949 *Toilet Water 2oz $1.25* **MP $30**

1949 *Flowertime Set. Cologne 4oz, Talc 3¾oz $2.75* **MP $62**

1950 *Flowers In the Wind. Talc, Powder Sachet, Cologne 1 dram Perfume $5.50* **MP $90**

1951 *Fragrant Mist. Toilet Water 2oz with Atomizer.* **MP $60.**
Atomizer only $15

** Available from Avon at time of publication*

1951 *Perfume 3 dram $5* **MP $95, $110 boxed**
1956 *Perfume ½oz $5* **MP $90, $105 boxed**

1951 *Cologne 4oz $2* **MP $21**
1951 *Toilet Water 2oz $1.50* **MP $20**
1951 *Body Powder 5oz 85¢* **MP $18**

1951 *Spring Corsage. Cologne 4oz and 1 dram Perfume $4.50* **MP $50**

1951 *Spring Song. Cologne 4oz and 1 dram Perfume $3.50* **MP $50**

1952 *Forever Spring Set. Body Powder 5oz, Cream Sachet and 1 dram Perfume $3.95* **MP $60**

1952 *Spring Melody. Body Powder 5oz & Cream Sachet $1.95* **MP $38**

1953 *Spring Creation. Cream Sachet .66oz & 1 dram Perfume $2.75* **MP $40**

1956 *Cream Sachet .66oz $1.25* **MP $12**
1951 *Powder Sachet 1¼oz $1.25* **MP $15**
1951 *One dram Perfume in suedene wrapper $1.75* **MP $20**
1951 *Cream Sachet .66oz $1.25* **MP $14**

Forever Spring

1951 *Beauty Dust 6oz $1.75* **MP $25**
1956 *Beauty Dust 6oz $1.95* **MP $20**

1956 *Cologne 4oz $2* **MP $19**
1956 *Toilet Water 2oz $1.50* **MP $18**

1956 *Spring Mood. Cream Lotion 4oz and Body Powder 4oz $1.95* **MP $50**

1956 *Body Powder 4oz $1* **MP $18**
1956 *Cream Lotion 4oz 95¢* **MP $21**
1958 *Talc 2¾oz 69¢* **MP $13**
1956 *Powder Sachet .9oz $1.25* **MP $13**

1956 *Springtime. Cologne 4oz & Beauty Dust 6oz $3.95* **MP $50**

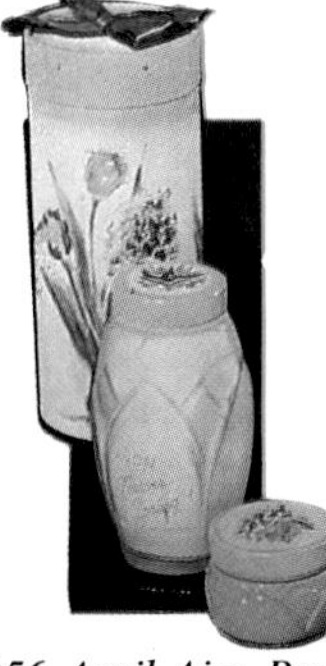
1956 *April Airs. Body Powder 4oz & Cream Sachet $2.25* **MP $40**

1956 *Merry, Merry Spring. Toilet Water 2oz and Cream Sachet $2.75* **MP $40**

1957 *Spring Goddess. Beauty Dust 6oz, Cream Sachet & Cologne 4oz $4.95* **MP $60**

1980 *(2 campaigns only) Gift Soap with Case 3oz $6.50* **MP $5**
1980 *Cologne 2oz $8* **MP $6***
1980 *Light Perfume .5oz $7* **MP $5***
1981 *Cologne .33oz $4* **MP $2***

1980 *Bath Foam 6oz $5* **MP $4***
1981 *Powder Mist 4oz $5* **MP $3***
1980 *Cologne Spray 1.8oz $9.50* **MP $7***

1952 *Powder Sachet 1¼oz $1.25* **MP $16, $20 boxed**
1948 *Powder Sachet 1¼oz $1.19 (sold to customers for 1 campaign in honor of 62nd Anniversary)* **MP $18, $35 boxed**

1954 *Perfume ½oz $3.95* **MP $100, $130 boxed**

1947 *Perfume gift given to Pasadena Branch employees. Both bottle & box state "with best wishes of Avon Products, Inc., Pasadena, Cal."* **MP $100, $125 boxed**
1947 *Perfume ½oz $5* **MP $100, $175 boxed**
1950 *Perfume 3 dram $4* **MP $125, $160 boxed**

1947 *Beauty Dust 6oz $1.50* **MP $22, $27 boxed**
1953 *Cream Sachet .66oz $1* **MP $14**

1947 *Cologne 4oz $2.25* **MP $23, $28 boxed**
1952 *Toilet Water 2oz $1.50* **MP $23, $28 boxed**

GOLDEN PROMISE

1947 *Body Powder 4½oz 75¢* **MP $20**
1949 *Golden Duet. Lipstick & 1 dram Perfumette (glass) in gold metal case and gold pursette $2.50* **MP $50, Perfumette MP $25**

1947 *Golden Promise 3 piece Set. Beauty Dust 6oz, Cologne 4oz and 1 dram Perfume $4.95* **MP $95**

1947 *Golden Promise 2 piece Set. Body Powder 4½oz & Cologne 4oz $2.95* **MP $60**

1950 *Golden Promise Set. Beauty Dust 6oz and Cologne 4oz $3.95* **MP $60**
1951 *Powder Sachet 1¼oz $1.25* **MP $20**

1952 *Deluxe Set. Cologne 4oz, Powder Sachet 1¼oz, Body Powder 4½oz and 1 dram Perfume $6.25* **MP $105**

1953 *Golden Jewel Set. Toilet Water 2oz and 1 dram Perfume $2.75* **MP $45**

* *Available from Avon at time of publication*

Frivole

1978 *Bubble Bath 8oz $4.50* **MP $1**
1978 *Body Splash 8oz $4.50* **MP $1**
1978 *Talc 3.5oz $2* **MP 50¢**
1978 *Cologne Ice 1oz $3.75* **MP $1**

1973 *Cologne Mist 2oz $4.25* **MP $1**
1972 *Bath Freshener 8oz $3.50* **MP $1**
1970 *DemiStik .19oz $1.75* **MP $1**
1972 *Rollette .33oz $2.50* **MP $1**
1973 *Cream Sachet .66oz $2.50* **MP $1**

HAWAIIAN WHITE GINGER

1968 *Foaming Bath Oil 8oz $3* **MP $1**
1975 *Cream Sachet .66oz $3* **MP $1**
1978 *Cologne Ice 1oz $3.75* **MP $1**

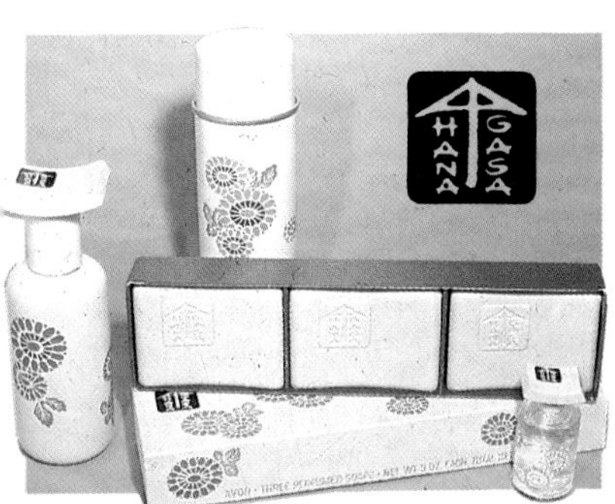

1970 *Cologne Mist 3oz $6* **MP $2**
1971 *Hair Spray 7oz $1.50* **MP $2**
1971 *Boxed Soaps, three 3oz cakes $3.50* **MP $7**
1970 *Half-ounce Cologne $1.75* **MP $3**

1970 *Beauty Dust 6oz $6* **MP $3**
1971 *Foaming Bath Oil 6oz $3.50* **MP $4**
1971 *Foaming Bath Oil 6oz (clear) $4* **MP $3**
1970 *Cream Sachet .66oz $3* **MP $2**
1970 *Rollette .33oz $3* **MP $2**

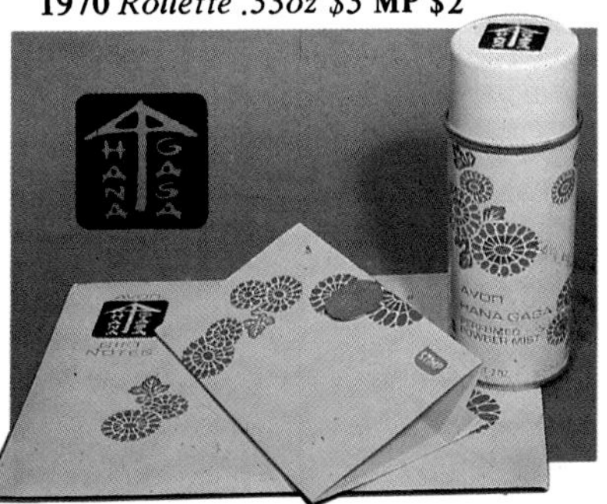

1970 *Gift Notes, 15 with 18 seals $2* **MP $7**
1971 *Powder Mist 7oz $4* **MP $2**

1948 *Star Bouquet Set. Talc 2¾oz and Cologne 1oz $1.25* **MP $80, $30 each Talc or Cologne**

1948 *Happy Hours Set. Cologne 1oz, Talc 2¾oz and Perfume $2* **MP $185**

happy hours

1948 *Memento Set. Cologne 1oz and 3 drams Perfume $1.50* **MP $150, $100 Perfume only**

1965 *After Bath Freshener 5oz $2* **MP $8**
1967 *After Bath Freshener 6oz $2.50* **MP $3**
1969 *Kwickettes, box of 14 $1.35* **MP $3**
1970 *Soap 3oz 60¢* **MP $1**
1970 *Talc 3½oz $1.10* **MP $1**

1967 *Beauty Dust 6oz $3* **MP $5**
1968 *Cream Sachet .66oz $2* **MP $2**
1969 *Cream Lotion 5oz $2* **MP $2**
1969 *Cream Sachet .66oz $2.50* **MP $9**
1971 *Cologne Mist 2oz $4.25* **MP $3**

1972 *Floral Duet. Rollette .33oz and Soap 3oz $3.25* **MP $13**

1980 *Cologne Spray 1.5oz. $6* **MP $4.50***
1980 *Talc 3.5oz $2.50* **MP $1.50***
1980 *Soap 3oz $1.75* **MP $1***

** Available from Avon at time of publication*

Her Prettiness

1969 *Pretty Me Doll. Bubble Bath 5oz and 3 colored pencils for Doll's makeup $6* **MP $12**

1969 *Enchanted Tree. Cologne Mist 3oz $5* **MP $8**

1969 *Art Reproduction (frame not included) 14x18. Free with any Her Prettiness purchase* **MP $9**

1969 *Brush and Comb Set. Brush 6½" long & Comb 5" long. $3.50* **MP $7**

1969 *Bunny Puff & Talc 3½oz $3.75* **MP $6**
1969 *Secret Tower Rollette .33oz $1.75* **MP $4**
1970 *Talc 3½oz $1* **MP $3**

1969 *Love Locket Fragrance Glace $4.50* **MP $12, $14 boxed**

1969 *Flower Belle Cologne Mist 2oz $3.50* **MP $4**
1969 *Lip Kiss Pomades in Cherry, Peppermint and Chocolate $1.95* **MP $4**
1969 *Magic Mushroom Cream Sachet $3* **MP $4**

1970 *Royal Fountain Cream Sachet .66oz $3* **MP $6, $7 boxed**
1969 *Ladybug Solid Perfume Glace $3* **MP $5**

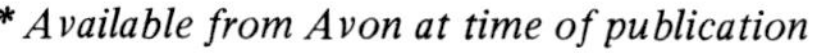

* *Available from Avon at time of publication*

HELLO SUNSHINE

1979 *Cologne 2.5oz $3.50* **MP $3.50***
1979 *Hand Cream 1.5oz $2* **MP $1***
1979 *Nail Tint .5oz $2* **MP 75¢**
1979 *Lipkin Lip Balm .15oz $2* **MP $1***
1979 *Hairbrush 6½" long $5.50* **MP $4**
1980 *Solid Perfume Compact .25oz $3.50* **MP $1**

Here's my Heart

1946 *Gift Perfume ½oz $7.50* **MP $125, $160 boxed**

1958 *Lotion Sachet 1oz (rare) $2* **MP $19**
1958 *Lotion Sachet 1oz $2* **MP $13**
1959 *Lotion Sachet 1oz $2* **MP $7**
1958 *Powder Sachet 1oz $1.75* **MP $12**
1962 *Powder Sachet .9oz $1.75* **MP $10**

1958 *Talc 2¾oz 79¢* **MP $5**
1959 *Toilet Water 2oz $2.50* **MP $12**
1962 *Talc 2¾oz 79¢* **MP $2**
1969 *Half-ounce Cologne $1.50* **MP $2**
1975 *DemiStik .19oz $2* **MP $1**

1958 *Lotion Sachet (rare) 1oz $2* **MP $19**
1958 *Spray Perfume 2 drams $3* **MP $15**
1963 *Perfume Mist 2 drams $3* **MP $7**

1957 *Cologne Mist 3oz $3* **MP $20, $30 boxed**
1958 *Cologne Mist 3oz $3* **MP $3**
1958 *Powder Sachet 1oz $1.75* **MP $12, MP $25 in 1959 "Butterfly Christmas box.** *(Also in 5 other fragrances.)*
1966 *Soaps (box not shown) three 3oz $1.75* **MP $22 boxed**

1966 *Hair Spray 7oz $1.50* **MP $5**
1961 *Body Powder 4oz $1.95* **MP $12**
1958 *Cream Lotion 4oz $1.10* **MP $8**
1960 *Perfumed Bath Oil 6oz $2.25* **MP $8**
1966 *Foaming Bath Oil 6oz $2.50* **MP $7**

1961 *Cologne 2oz $1.75* **MP $4**
1960 *Cologne 4oz $3* **MP $10, $20 boxed**
1964 *Soap 3oz 39¢* **MP $5**
1975 *Cream Sachet .66oz $3* **MP $1**

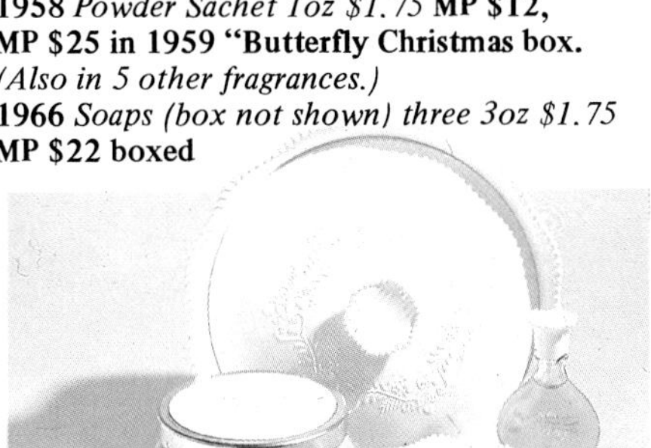

1958 *Beauty Dust 6oz $3* **MP $8**
1964 *Skin Softener 5oz $3* **MP $3**
1959 *Cream Sachet .66oz $2.50* **MP $2**
1964 *Perfume Oil ½oz $3.50* **MP $9**

1962 *Left: two 4oz Boxed Soaps $1.29* **MP $23**
1960 *Boxed Soaps. Two 4oz cakes $1.29* **MP $25**

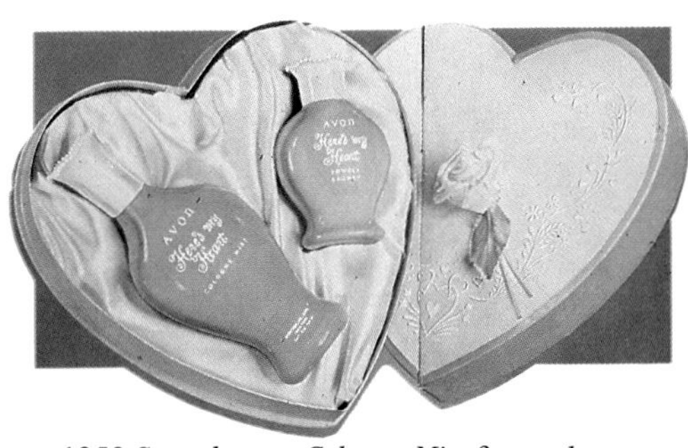

1979 *Purse Concentre .33oz $3* **MP $1**
1979 *Cologne Spray 1.8oz $6* **MP $1, $1.50 in 1980 Xmas Box**

1958 *Sweethearts. Cologne Mist 3oz and choice of Lotion or Powder Sachet $5* **MP $45**

1959 *Heart O' Mine Set. Beauty Dust, Spray Perfume, Cream Sachet & Cologne Mist $11.95* **MP $50**

1960 *Romantic Mood. Cologne Mist, Cream Sachet & Beauty Dust $8.25* **MP $35**

1961 *Two Hearts Set. Cologne 2oz and Cream Sachet $3.50* **MP $26**

1963 *Remembrance Set. Beauty Dust 6oz & Cologne Mist 3oz $6.95* **MP $30**

1964 *Heartfelt Set. Cologne 2oz and Cream Sachet $3.50* **MP $25**

...Here's my Heart

1964 *Hearts in Bloom. Cologne Mist 3oz, Cream Lotion 4oz and Cream Sachet $6.50* **MP $30**

1966 *Bath Freshener 8oz (glass) $3* **MP $2**
1972 *Bath Freshener 8oz (plastic) $3.50* **MP $1**
1973 *Cologne Mist 2oz $4.25* **MP $1**
1972 *Rollette .33oz $2.50* **MP $1**

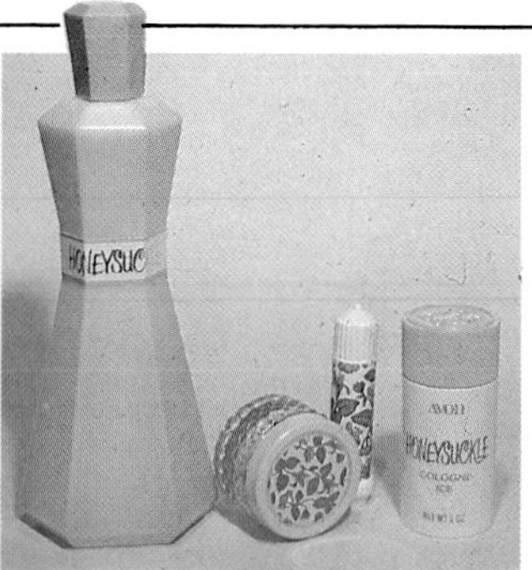

1966 *Foaming Bath Oil 8oz $3* **MP $1**
1973 *Cream Sachet .66oz $2.50* **MP $1**
1970 *DemiStik .19oz $1.50* **MP $1**
1978 *Cologne Ice 1oz $3.75* **MP $2**

1980 *Spray Cologne 1.5oz $6* **MP $4.50***
1980 *Talc 3.5oz $2.50* **MP $1.50***
1980 *Soap 3oz $1.75* **MP $1***

HONEYSUCKLE

1971 *Cologne Mist 2oz $4.25* **MP $2**
1966 *Soap 3oz 49¢* **MP $1**
1969 *Cream Lotion 5oz $2* **MP $1**

1968 *Boxed Soaps, 3 in box $3* **MP $10**
1968 *DemiStik $1.50* **MP $1**
1967 *Cream Sachet .66oz $2.50* **MP $2**
1966 *Talc 3½oz 98¢* **MP $1**

IMPERIAL GARDEN

1973 *Cologne Mist 3oz $7.50* **MP $8 (short issue)**
1973 *Cologne Mist 3oz $7.50* **MP $3**

1973 *Beauty Dust 6oz $7.50* **MP $6**
1974 *Skin Softener 5oz $5* **MP $1**
1974 *Powder Mist 7oz $5* **MP $1**

1975 *Talc 3½oz $2* **MP $1**
1974 *Emollient Mist 4oz $3.50* **MP $1**
1974 *Boxed Soap, three 3oz $4.50* **MP $7**
1973 *Rollette .33oz $4* **MP $2**
1973 *Cream Sachet .66oz $4* **MP $1**

1973 *Ceramic Vase with 18oz peach-colored bath crystals $18* **MP $20**

JASMINE

1934-36 *Jasmine Bath Soaps, 3 cakes $1.02* **MP $60**

1937 *Jasmine Boxed Soaps, 3 cakes $1.02* **MP $55**

1939 *Fantasy in Jasmine. Bath Salts 9oz and 2 cakes Soap $1.35* **MP $90, $40 Bath Salts only**

* *Available from Avon at time of publication*

1940 *Fantasy in Jasmine. Bath Salts 9oz and 2 cakes Soap $1.35* **MP $90**

1950 *Toilet Water 2oz $1.25* **MP $38, $45 boxed**
1948-49 *Toilet Water 2oz $1.19* **MP $40, $50 boxed**

1946 *Powder Sachet 1¼oz $1.15* **MP $23, $28 boxed**
1949 *Powder Sachet 1¼oz $1.19* **MP $35, $42 boxed**
1954 *Bath Salts 8oz 89¢* **MP $30**

1945 *Bath Salts 9oz 69¢* **MP $45**
1948 *Boxed Soaps, 3 cakes $1.59* **MP $40**

1947 *Dusting Powder 13oz $1.50* **MP $35**

1946 *Jasmine Soaps, 3 cakes $1.85* **MP $45**

JASMINE. . . *later named Royal Jasmine and then Wild Jasmine .*

1945 *Fantasy in Jasmine. Bath Salts 9oz and 2 cakes Soap $1.60* **MP $100**

1948 *Fantasy in Jasmine. Toilet Water 2oz and 3 cakes Soap $2.39* **MP $85**

1946 *Fantasy in Jasmine. Bath Salts 9oz (left) & 2 cakes Soap $1.60* **MP $90**
1947 *Fantasy in Jasmine. Bath Salts (right) & 2 cakes Soap $2.25* **MP $90**

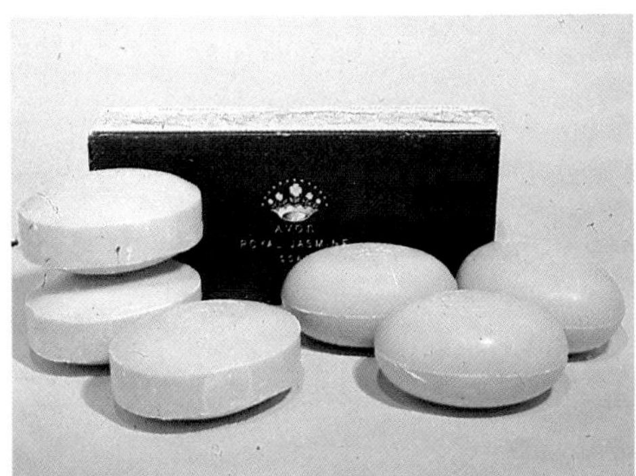

1954 *Royal Jasmine Boxed Soaps, 3 cakes, flat edges $1.69* **MP $30. With Round edges $40**

1954 *Royal Jasmine Set. Bath Salts 8oz and 1 cake Soap $1.39* **MP $50**

1955 *Fantasy in Jasmine. Bath Oil and 2 cakes Soap $1.95* **MP $50**

... JASMINE

1966 *Foaming Bath Oil 8oz $2.50* MP $3
1964 *Talc 3½oz 89¢* MP $2
1964 *Bath Freshener 8oz $2.50* MP $7
1967 *Cream Sachet .66oz $2* MP $2

1966 *Fragrance Kwickettes, 14 per box $1.25* MP $3
1966 *Gift Soaps, three 2oz cakes $2* MP $23

... WILD JASMINE

1980 *Soap 3oz $1.75* MP $1*
1980 *Talc 3.5oz $2.50* MP $1.50*
1980 *Spray Cologne 1.5oz $6* MP $4.50*
1980 *Scented Book Mark. Free with Cologne Spray purchase, only C-17* MP $1

Lemon Velvet

1971 *Bath Mitt $1.50* MP $2
1972 *Powder Mist 7oz $4* MP $1
1971 *DemiStik .19 $1.75* MP 75¢
1972 *Rollette .33oz $2.50* MP $2

(rear)
1969 *Beauty Dust 6oz $3.50* MP $4
1972 *Cologne Mist 2oz $4.25* MP $1
1971 *Moisturized Friction Lotion (emb. flower on lid) 10oz $3* MP $1
(1969 *not shown. As above w/plain lid* MP $4)

(front) 1971 *Cream Sachet .66oz $3* MP $2
1969 *Skin Softener 5oz $3.50* MP $2
1973 *Cream Sachet .66oz $2.50* MP $1

1969 *Boxed Soaps, three 3oz cakes $3* MP $6.50
1971 *Cleansing Gel 6oz $3* MP $1

1934-37 *Lavender Blossoms 50¢ per bag* MP $50, $60 boxed

1934-37 *Lavender Ensemble. Toilet Water 4oz, 2 cakes Soap & Lavender Blossoms Sachet $1.50* MP $155
1934-37 *Toilet Water 4oz 78¢* MP $50

1938 only *Lavender Ensemble. Toilet Water 4oz, 2 cakes Soap and 2 Sachet cakes $1.50* MP $125
1938 only *Toilet Water 4oz 78¢* MP $65
1938 only *Sachet Cakes, 6 per pkg. (not shown) 50¢* MP $75

1939 only *Lavender Ensemble. Toilet Water 4oz, 2 cakes Soap & 2 Sachet Cakes $1.50* MP $125
1939-43 *Toilet Water 4oz 78¢* MP $45
1939-43 *Sachet Cakes, 6 per pkg. 50¢* MP $45

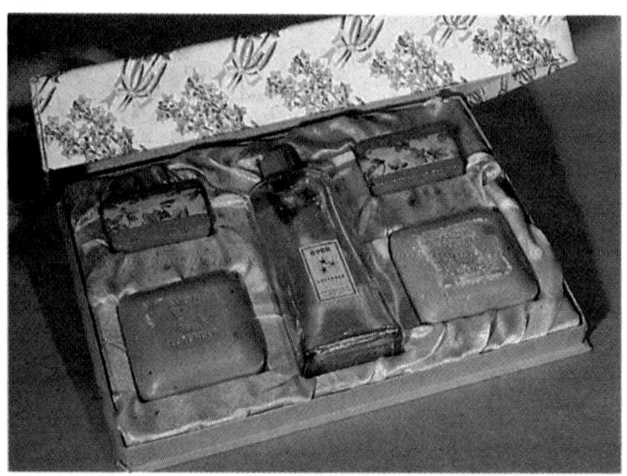

1940-43 *Lavender Ensemble. Toilet Water 4oz, 2 cakes Soap & Sachet Cakes $1.75* MP $120 *Toilet Water 78¢* MP $95

1946 *Sachet Cakes 2 wrapped 57¢* MP $30

1944-45 *Toilet Water 4oz 89¢* MP $50

* *Available from Avon at time of publication*

1963 *Perfumed Talc 3½oz 89¢* **MP $1**
1963 *Bath Freshener 8oz $2.50* **MP $7**
1966 *Foaming Bath Oil 8oz $2.50* **MP $3**
1967 *Cream Sachet .66oz $2* **MP $2**
1973 *Cream Sachet .66oz $2.50* **MP $1**
1970 *Perfumed Demi-Stik $1.75* **MP 75¢**
1968 *Perfumed Demi-Stik $1.50* **MP $2**

LILAC

1968 *Boxed Soaps, three 3oz cakes $3* **MP $6.50**
1966 *Gift Soap, three 3oz cakes $2.50* **MP $18**
1966 *Kwickettes (not shown) 14 per box $1.25* **MP $3**

1934-39 *Toilet Water 2oz 78¢* **MP $40, $50 boxed**

1949 *Toilet Water 2oz $1.19* **MP $30, $40 boxed**

1979 *Fabric Scented Pillow w/spray of Lily of the Valley flowers 10 x 10" $15* **MP $11**

1963 *Bath Freshener 8oz $2.50* **MP $7**
1966 *Boxed Soaps, two 3oz cakes $2* **MP $20**
1967 *Cream Sachet .66oz $2* **MP $2**
1974 *Cream Sachet .66oz $2.50* **MP $2**
1974 *DemiStik .19oz $2* **MP $75¢**

LILY OF THE VALLEY

1979 *Chateau of Flowers, a Harlequin novel exclusively for Avon. $1.99 with $7.50 purchase. U.S. only.* **MP $4**

1934-43 *Lavender Soap, (left) 3 cakes 67¢* **MP $90**
1946 only *Lavender Soap, (right) 3 cakes 85¢* **MP $90**

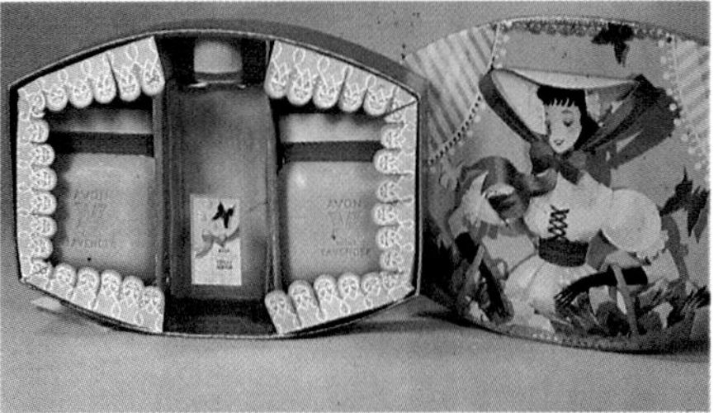

1945 only *Lavender ensemble. Toilet Water 4oz, 2 cakes Soap and 2 Sachet Cakes $1.95* **MP $100**
1944-45 *Sachet Cakes, 2 per pkg. 57¢* **MP $40**

1946 *Lavender Ensemble. Toilet Water 4oz, 2 Cakes Soap & 2 Sachet Cakes $1.95* **MP $95**

Lavender

1946 only *Toilet Water 4oz 89¢* **MP $50, $60 boxed**

1961 *Powder Sachet .9oz (4-A design label) $2* **MP $10**
1965 *Above bottle with Xmas Carton, as shown* **MP $17**
1961 *Powder Sachet with .9oz on front label $2* **MP $14**

1970 *Lavender and Lace. Cologne 1.7oz and Lace-edged handkerchief $4.50* **MP $7. Bottle only MP $4.50**

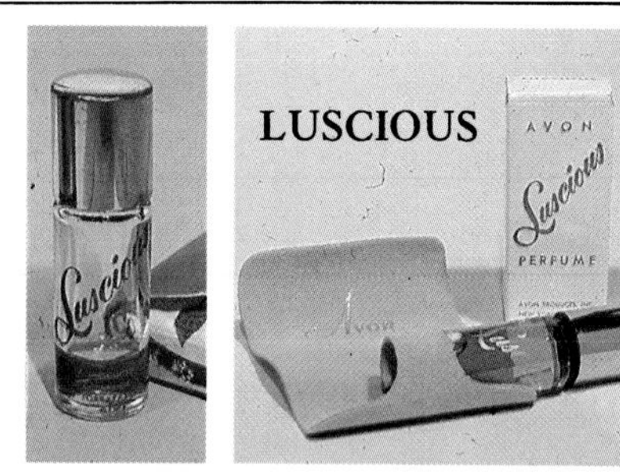

1950 *Luscious Perfume, the only 1 dram bottle issued with silk-screened label $1.75* **MP $15**

1950 *Luscious Perfume 1 dram. Issued with smooth gold cap in Leatherette wrapper $1.75* **MP $22 in wrapper, $25 boxed**

1972 *Boxed Soap, three 3oz cakes $4* **MP $7**
1971 *Cologne Mist 3oz $7.50* **MP $3**
1971 *Rollette .33oz $4* **MP $1**
1972 *Bath Pearls, 75 capsules $5* **MP $6**

1971 *Beauty Dust 6oz $7.50* **MP $6**
1972 *Skin Softener 5oz $5* **MP $3**
1973 *DemiStik .19oz $2.50* **MP $1**
1975 *Powder Sachet 1¼oz $3.50* **MP $2**

1938 *Marionette Toilet Water 2oz. Pre-introduction customer gift offered in C-16* **MP $45, $60 in gift box**

1972-73 *Moonwind Pin/ Scarf Holder $7* **MP $10**

1971 *Cream Sachet .66oz $4* **MP $1**
1973 *Talc 3½oz $1.75* **MP $2***
1975 *Emollient Mist 4oz $4.50* **MP $2**

1972 *Powder Mist 7oz $5* **MP $1**
1975 *Boxed Soap, three 3oz cakes $6* **MP $6**
1976 *Rollette .33oz $4.50* **MP $1**
1975 *Soap 3oz $1.25* **MP $1**

1955 *Merriment Cologne 4oz (shown) or Bubble Bath 4oz in Jolly Surprise Box $1.50* **MP $50, $65 boxed**

1976 *Cologne Mist 3oz $8* **MP $1**
1975 *Cream Sachet .66oz $4.50* **MP $1**
1973 *Skin Softener 5oz $5* **MP $4***
1972 *Foaming Bath Oil 6oz $5* **MP $2**

1979 *Powder Mist 4oz $4.50* **MP $3***
1979 *Cologne Spray 1.8oz $6* **MP $5***
1977 *Cologne Spray 1.8oz $6.50* **MP $1**
1976 *Cologne Spray 2.7oz $8* **MP $7***

Mineral Spring

1972 *Bath Crystals 12oz $6* **MP $2**
1972 *Sparkling Freshener 8oz $4* **MP $1**
1972 *Body Rub 8oz $4* **MP $1**
1973 *Bathfoam 8oz $4* **MP $1**
1972 *Powder Mist 7oz $4* **MP $1**
1976 *Bath Crystals 12oz $5.50* **MP $2**
1972 *Boxed Soaps, two 4oz cakes $3.50* **MP $5**

1977 *Foaming Bath Oil 6oz $5.50* **MP $1**
1980 *Bath Foam 6oz $5* **MP $3***
1979 *Purse Concentre .33oz $3* **MP $2***
1979 *Creme Perfume .66oz $3.50* **MP $2.50***

* *Available from Avon at time of publication*

1968 *Miss Pretty Me. Lip Pop and Rollette $3.25* **MP $13**
1968 *Talc 3½oz $1* **MP $5**
1968 *Hand Cream (black boots) 2oz 75¢* **MP $5**
1967 *Cream Sachet .66oz $2* **MP $5**
1968 *Ice Cream Talc 3½oz $3* **MP $7**

Lip Pops: 1967 *Cherry.* 1968 *Peppermint & Raspberry.* 1969 *Cola. $1.50 ea.* **MP $4 ea.**
1968 *Rollette .33oz $1.50* **MP $5**
1969 *Pretty Touch Switch Plate Cover 29¢* **MP $10**

1967 *Sponge and Soap 4oz $2.50* **MP $13**
1968 *Hand Cream (white boots) 2oz 75¢* **MP $7**

1968 *Bath Powder Mitt $2.50* **MP $7**
1968 *Double Dip Bubble Bath 5oz $2* **MP $6**
1967 *Talc 3½oz and Puff $2.50* **MP $12**
1967 *Boot Cologne 2oz $2* **MP $8**
1967 *Cologne Mist 3oz $3* **MP $8**

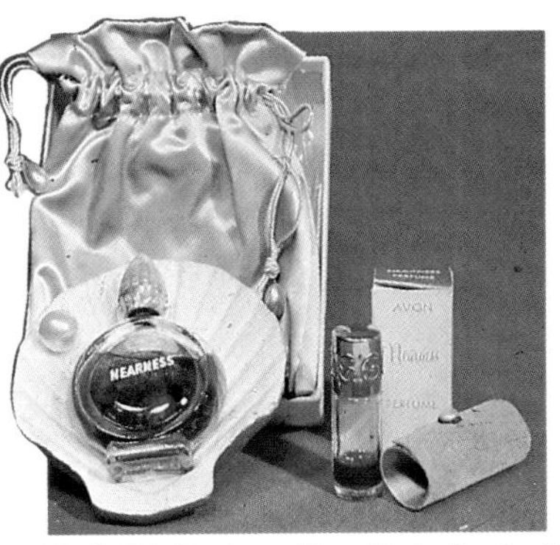
1955 *Gift Perfume ½oz. Satin Bag is gift wrap. $7.50* **MP $100 bottle only, $135 complete**
1955 *One dram Perfume in suedene wrapper $2.25* **MP $10, $17, $20 boxed**

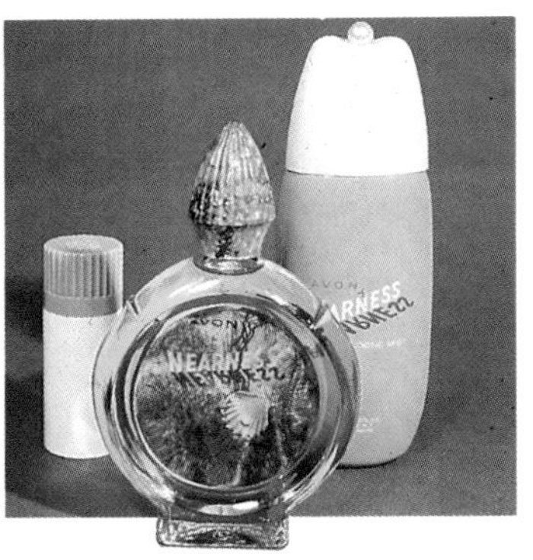
1956 *Cologne Stick $1.50* **MP $10**
1955 *Cologne 4oz $2.50* **MP $20**
1959 *Cologne Mist 3oz $2.95* **MP $23**

1956 *Two Pearls. Body Powder and Cream Sachet $2.50* **MP $45**

1957 *Circle of Pearls. Toilet Water 2oz, Cream Sachet and Pearls $5.95* **MP $65**

1955 *Cream Sachet .66oz $1.50* **MP $11**
1956 *Toilet Water 2oz $2* **MP $20**
1956 *Powder Sachet $1.50* **MP $12**
1957 *Cologne Mist 3oz $2.75* **MP $25**

1956 *Beauty Dust $2.25* **MP $22**
1959 *Beauty Dust $2.95* **MP $20**
1957 *Talc in metal container 69¢* **MP $10**
1956 *Body Powder $1* **MP $16**

1956 *Always Near. Toilet Water 2oz, 1 dram Perfume & Shell Pendant $5.95* **MP $85, $35 Shell Pendant only**

NEARNESS

1958 *Sea Mist. Cologne Mist 3oz and Cream Sachet $3.95* **MP $55**

1964 *Perfumed Bath Oil 6oz $2.75* **MP $8**
1966 *Foaming Bath Oil 6oz $3* **MP $2**
1965 *Skin Softener (glass) 5oz $3.50* **MP $7**
1964 *Cologne 2oz $2.50* **MP $2**
1966 *Hair Spray (not shown) $1.50* **MP $3**

1963 *Cologne Mist 2oz $3* **MP $7**
1964 *Cream Lotion 4oz $1.75* **MP $6**
1967 *Spray Essence 1¼oz $4* **MP $3**
1966-68 *Cologne Silk 3oz $4* **MP $4**
1964 *Perfume Mist 2 drams $3.75* **MP $7**

1963 *Powder Sachet .9oz $2.50* **MP $10**
1964 *Talc, metal, 2¾oz $1* **MP $1**
1964 *Perfume Oil ½oz $5* **MP $10**
1963 *Cologne Mist 3oz $5* **MP $3**
1969 *Cologne ½oz $1.50* **MP $2**

1965 *Boxed Soap, 3 cakes $2.25* **MP $18**
1963 *Cream Sachet .66oz $2.50* **MP $4**
1966 *Cream Sachet .66oz $2.50* **MP $1**
1975 *Cream Sachet .66oz $3* **MP $1**

Occur!

1963 *Beauty Dust 6oz $5* **MP $8**
1971 *Beauty Dust 6oz $4.50* **MP $7**
1975 *Talc 3½oz $2* **MP $2***

1976 *Cologne Spray 2.7oz $7* **MP $7***
1976 *Foaming Bath Oil 6oz $4.50* **MP $1**
1980 *Bath Foam 6oz $5* **MP $3***
1979 *Cologne Spray 1.8oz $6* **MP $5***
1965 *Soap 3oz 49¢* **MP $4**

1979 *Powder Mist 4oz $4.50* **MP $3***
1979 *Perfume Concentre .33oz $3* **MP $1***
1979 *Creme Perfume .66oz $3* **MP $1***

1963 *Sophisticate Set. Cologne Mist, Creme Rollette and Beauty Dust $12.95* **MP $35**

1964 *Fragrance Fortune Set. Perfume Oil ½oz and Cologne 2oz $6.25* **MP $25**

1964 *Elegance Set. Cream Lotion, Cologne 2oz and Talc $5.75* **MP $35**

1965 *Deluxe Set. Beauty Dust, Skin Softener and Cologne Mist $13.95* **MP $38**

ODYSSEY

1981 *Cologne Spray 1.8oz $10.50* **MP $7***
1981 *Powder Mist 4oz $5* **MP $3***
1981 *Bath Foam 6oz $5.50* **MP $3***
1981 *Soap 3oz $2.25* **MP $1***
(See also Awards pg. 247)

* *Available from Avon at time of publication*

1973 *Eye Shadow Collection with applicator $5* **MP $8, $11 boxed**

1973 *Lotion 8oz $3.50* **MP $1**
1973 *Foaming Bath Oil 6oz $5* **MP $2**

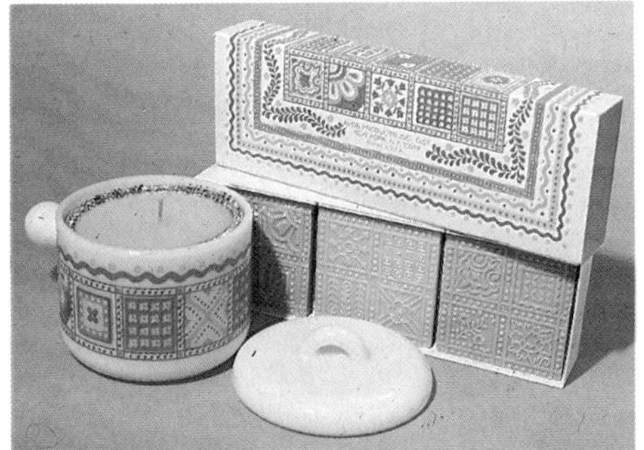

1973 *Perfumed Candle $7* **MP $7**
1973 *Soaps, three 3oz cakes $4.50* **MP $8**

PATCHWORK

(See also Awards pg. 249)

1973 *Cream Sachet .66oz $4* **MP $2**
1973 *Rollette .33oz $4* **MP $2**
1973 *Cologne Mist 3oz $5* **MP $3**
1973 *Cologne Gelee 3oz $5* **MP $3**

1969 *Perfume Glace Ring $6* **MP $12**
1969 *Cream Sachet .66oz $3* **MP $2**
1969 *Lipstick, 3 shades $1.50* **MP $3**

1969 *Tray, 10" plastic $3* **MP $10**

(See also Awards pg. 245)

1969 *Cologne Mist 3oz $6* **MP $3**
1969 *Rollette .33oz $3* **MP $3**
1969 *Shadow Collection $5* **MP $6, $9 boxed**

1957 *Beauty Dust, glass $3* **MP $20**
1956 *Cologne Mist 3oz $3* **MP $15**
1958 *Powder Sachet, plastic 1¼oz $2* **MP $10**
1958 *Lotion Sachet 1oz $2* **MP $11**
1959 *Cream Sachet .66oz $1.75* **MP $10**

1959 *Toilet Water 2oz $2.50* **MP $12**
1961 *Cologne 2oz $1.75* **MP $4**
1960 *Cologne Mist 3oz $3.25* **MP $6**
1960 *Gift Cologne 4oz $3* **MP $10, $20 boxed**

1959 *Cream Sachet .66oz $1.75* **MP $4**
1961 *Cream Lotion 4oz $1.25* **MP $8**
1961 *Beauty Dust, plastic 6oz $3.25* **MP $14**
1961 *Body Powder 4oz $1.95* **MP $12**

1963 *Perfumed Oil for the Bath ½oz $3.50* **MP $12**
1963 *Perfume Mist 2 drams $3.25* **MP $7**
1964 *Perfume Oil ½oz $3.50* **MP $9**
1957 *Spray Perfume 2 drams $3.25* **MP $15**

1964 *Skin Softener 5oz $3* **MP $5**
1960 *Perfumed Bath Oil, plastic 6oz $2.25* **MP $8**
1960 *Skin Softener 5oz $3* **MP $7**
1962 *Bath Oil 6oz (from Bath Bouquet Set) $2.79* **MP $10 Bottle only**

1958 *Talc 2¾oz (gold cap) 79¢* **MP $5**
1962 *Talc 2¾oz (white cap) 79¢* **MP $3**
1975 *Cream Sachet .66oz $3* **MP $1**
1976 *Cologne Mist 3oz (smooth cap) $7* **MP $4**

1958 *Persian Fancy. Cologne Mist and choice of Powder or Lotion Sachet $5* **MP $42**

1959 *Persian Treasures. Cologne Mist, Cream Sachet, Spray Perfume & Toilet Water 2oz $10.75* **MP $60**

... Persian Wood

1961 *Persian Magic. Cologne 2oz & Cream Sachet $3.50* **MP $25**

1961 *Persian Legend. Beauty Dust and Cologne Mist $6.50* **MP $38**

1963 *Persian Intrigue. .3oz Cologne Mist, 4oz Cream Lotion and Perfumed Cream Rollette $6.50* **MP $33**

1964 *Persian Mood. One dram Perfume and Cream Sachet $4* **MP $28**

1940-51 *Bath Oil 6oz 85¢* **MP $30, $35 boxed**

1941 only *Bath Oil 6oz 95¢* **MP $38, $43 boxed**

1957-60 *Royal Pine Bath Oil 8oz $1.95* **MP $25, $30 boxed**

1961 *Original Royal Pine Bath Oil 8oz $2* **MP $8**

Pine

1939-58 *Boxed Soaps, 3 cakes 69¢* **MP $65**
1940 only *Boxed Soaps, 3 cakes (right) 69¢* **MP $80**

1959 *Royal Pine Soaps, 3 cakes $1.25* **MP $30**

1939-42 *Breath of Pine. 2 cakes Soap & Bath Salts $1.25* **MP $70**

1941-42 *Towering Pine. Apple Blossom Body Powder, Pine Bath Oil 6oz & Soap $1.65* **MP $75**

1941-43 *Royal Pine Set. Bath Oil 6oz and 2 Soaps $1.50* **MP $65**

. . . Pine

1943 *Royal Pine Set. Bath Oil 6oz and 2 Soaps $1.60* **MP $65**
1945 *Same set as above, but issued in shorter box (shown closed) $1.60* **MP $65**

1954 *Royal Pine Set. Bath Salts 8oz and Soap $1.25* **MP $50** *(Shown with both issues of Bath Salts offered in Set)* **Either Bath Salts MP $35**

1957 *Bath Salts 8oz 89¢* **MP $25**

1956 *Pinehurst Set. Bath Oil 4oz and 2 cakes Soap $1.75* **MP $55**
Bath Oil **MP $38**

1964 *Cologne Mist (shown with both issues of holder) 2oz $2.50* **MP $16, Holder MP $4, Straws MP $2 each**
1964 *Bubble Bath 4oz $1.35* **MP $10**
1964 *Talc 2½oz 79¢* **MP $10**

1964 *Beauty Dust 4oz $2.50* **MP $15**
1964 *Lotion 4oz $1.35* **MP $10**
1964 *Cologne 2oz $1.50* **MP $10**
1964 *Cream Sachet .66oz $1.50* **MP $7**

1965 *Powder Mitt, peach-shaped, holds 2½oz Talc $1.50* **MP $9, $12 boxed**
1964 *Cream Sachet Sample, peach-shaped foil* **MP $2**
1966 *Peachy-Kleen sponge Bath Mitt and Soap 3oz $2.25* **MP $15, $18 boxed**

1965 *Peach Delight Set. Beauty Dust and Cologne 2oz & enameled "Peach" Necklace $5.95* **MP $60, $25 necklace only**

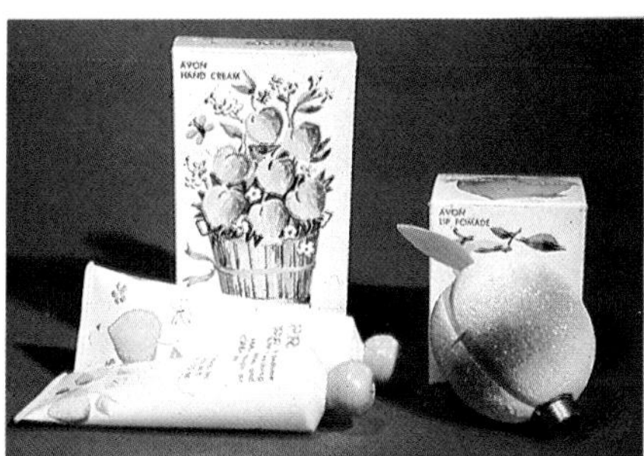

1964 *Peach Smooth Set. 2 tubes Hand Cream 1¾oz each $1.35* **MP $20**
1964 *Lip Pomade encased in styrofoam peach $1* **MP $20, $23 boxed**

1964 *Just Peachy. Peach Soap-On-a-Rope and Lip Pomade $2.35* **MP $40**

PRETTY PEACH

1964 *Soap, 2 halves and pit $1.50* **MP $18, $24 boxed**
1964 *Soap-On-a-Rope $1.35* **MP $12, $18 boxed**

1964 *Peach Surprise. Cologne 2oz, choice of 4oz Bubble Bath or Cream Lotion $2.35* **MP $26**

1965 *Pretty Peach Princess. Talc and Cream Sachet $2.25* **MP $23**

1964-65 *Miss Avon Set. Bubble Bath 4oz, Cologne 2oz, packages of Lip Dew Samples & Talc Samples (10 ea), descriptive product letter to "Miss Avon" & Case $7.50* **MP $95 complete, $115 boxed. Lip Dew Samples MP $10, Talc Samples MP $10, "Miss Avon" Letter MP $25, Case MP $20**

1948 *Beauty Dust 6oz $1.50* **MP $16**
1953 *Toilet Water 2oz $1.25* **MP $18**
1948 *Cologne 4oz $1.75* **MP $14**

1948 *Cologne 2oz (sets only)* **MP $22**

1948 *Powder Sachet .9oz $1.19* **MP $12, $15 boxed**
1948 *Body Powder 4½oz 75¢* **MP $16**
1952 *Cream Sachet .66oz $1.25* **MP $12**
1949 *Powder Sachet, 63rd Anniversary Issue .9oz 63¢* **MP $30, $40 boxed**

1948 *Perfume 1 dram $1.50* **MP $75, $85 boxed**
1950 *Perfume 3 drams $4* **MP $130, $160 boxed**

1948 *Cream Lotion 4oz 89¢* **MP $13**
1949 *Bath Oil 4oz $1.50* **MP $18**

1950 *Cream Sachet, metal lid (rare)* **MP $40**

1949 *Rosegay Set. Body Powder and Cream Lotion $1.75* **MP $60**

1949 *Bowknot Set. Cologne 2oz & Powder Sachet 1¼oz $2.25* **MP $60**

1948 *Quaintance Set. Cologne 2oz and Powder Sachet 1¼oz $2.39* **MP $60**

1948 *Gay Bonnet. Hat-shaped box holds Perfume 1/8oz & Lipstick $2.35* **MP $110**

1954 *Boxed Soap, 3 cakes $1.59* **MP $50**

Quaintance

1950 *Harmony Set. Body Powder and Cologne 2oz $2.85* **MP $60**

1952 *Quaintaince Harmony. Cologne and Cream Lotion 4oz each $2.75* **MP $55, $25 Cologne only**

1952 *Miss Quaintance. Body Powder and Cream Lotion 4oz $1.95* **MP $55**

1954 *Leisure Hours. Bath Oil and Cream Lotion 4oz each $2.15* **MP $55**

(See also Awards pg. 244)

1954 *Harmony Set. Cologne 2oz and Cream Lotion $2.25* **MP $55**

1954 *Rosegay Set. Body Powder and Cream Lotion $1.95* **MP $55**

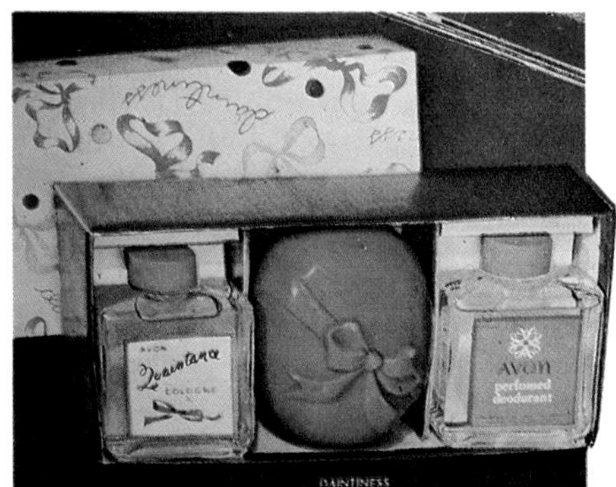

1955 *Daintiness Set. Cologne and Perfumed Deodorant 2oz each, and Soap $1.95* **MP $55**

1956 *Daintiness Set. Cologne and Cream Lotion $1.95* **MP $55**

1973 *Powder Mist 7oz* **MP $1**
1974 *DemiStik .19oz $1.75* **MP $1**
1975 *Cream Sachet .66oz $3* **MP $1**

1973 *Cleansing Gel 6oz $3* **MP $2**
1973 *Emollient Mist 4oz $3* **MP $1**
1973 *Moisturizing Bath Oil 6oz $4* **MP $1**
1974 *Cologne Mist 2oz $4.25* **MP $2**
1973 *Cologne Gelee 3oz $4* **MP $2**
1974 *Cream Sachet .66oz $2.50* **MP $1**

QUEEN'S GOLD

1975 ***Fragrance Sample*** **MP $1.50**

1975 *Powder Mist 7oz $4.50* **MP $5**
1975 *Foaming Bath Oil 10oz $7* **MP $8**
1975 *Cream Sachet .66oz $3* **MP $4**
1975 *Cologne Mist 3oz $7* **MP $5**
1975 *DemiStik .19oz $2* **MP $3**

(See Bath Oil Gift pg. 246)

1965 *Perfumed Bath Oil 6oz $2.75* **MP $7**
1964 *Perfume Mist 2 drams $3.75* **MP $7**

1965 *Cream Lotion 4oz $1.75* **MP $4**
1964 *Powder Sachet .9oz $2.50* **MP $10**
1964 *Beauty Dust 6oz $5* **MP $12**

1966 *Scented Hair Spray 7oz $1.50* **MP $3**
1965 *Talc 2¾oz $1* **MP $1**
1966 *Foaming Bath Oil 6oz $3* **MP $2**

1965 *Skin Softener 5oz $3.50* **MP $3**
1964 *Cologne 2oz $2.50* **MP $3**
1964 *Cologne Mist 3oz $5* **MP $2**

1964 *Rapture Rhapsody. Powder Sachet, Cologne 2oz and 1 dram Perfume $10.95* **MP $52**

See also Awards pg. 245

1966 *Boxed Soap, 4 cakes $2.25* **MP $25**
1964 *Talc 3½oz 89¢* **MP $5**
1957 *Bath Oil 8oz $1.95* **MP $22**

1966 *Perfume 1oz $30* **MP $40. $55 boxed**
1966 *Perfume ½oz $15* **MP $25. $40 boxed**

1966 *Cologne Mist 3oz in Presentation Box* **MP $35**

1966 *Gift Set. Cologne Mist, Cream Sachet & Purse Mirror $12.50* **MP $45, mirror only $12**

RÉGENCE

(Say, "Ray-JAUNCE")
Packaging inspired by malachite, a rare stone treasured by European royal families for centuries

See also Awards pg. 238

1964 *Cream Sachet .66oz $2.50* **MP $1**
1966 *Cologne Mist 2oz $3* **MP $9**
1966 *Cologne Mist 2oz $3* **MP $8**
1965 *Cologne Mist 2oz $3* **MP $7**
1969 *Half-ounce Cologne $1.50* **MP $3**
1964 *Perfume Oil ½oz $5* **MP $9**

1966 *Cologne Mist Refill 3oz $4* **MP $5**
1966 *Cologne Mist 3oz $6* **MP $5**
1968 *Hair Spray 7oz $1.50* **MP $3**
1967 *Powder Mist 7oz $4* **MP $2**
1968 *Talc $1.25* **MP $1.50**

1965 *Deluxe Set. Beauty Dust, Skin Softener 5oz and Cologne Mist 3oz $13.95* **MP $38**

1968 *Perfumed Candle Container 10½" $10* **MP $18**
1967 *Perfumed Candle Container $6* **MP $20**

1966 *Beauty Dust with Malachite band 6oz $6* **MP $10**
1966 *Beauty Dust, paper band (not shown) $6* **MP $13**
1967 *Skin-So-Soft Bath Oil 6oz $5* **MP $6**
1968 *Cream Sachet .66oz $3* **MP $3**
1966 *Cream Sachet .66oz (Malachite band) $3* **MP $8**

Rapture

1971 *Beauty Dust non-refillable 6oz $4.50* **MP $9**
1965 *Boxed Soaps, 3 cakes $2* **MP $20**

1967 *Skin Softener 5oz $4* **MP $7**
1968 *Skin Softener 5oz $4* **MP $5**
1967 *Perfumed Oil ½oz $6* **MP $9**
1967 *Rollette .33oz $3* **MP $2**
1971 *Skin Softener 5oz $4* **MP $3**

1967 *Cologne 2oz $3* **MP $3**
1968 *Cologne Silk 3oz $4.50* **MP $4**
1969 *Cologne 4oz $6* **MP $3**
1967 *Perfume Glace .6oz $5.50* **MP $7**
1969 *Foaming Bath Oil 6oz $3.50* **MP $2**
1969 *Cologne ½oz $1.75* **MP $3**

1973 *Cream Lotion 8oz $3* **MP $1**
1972 *Bath Freshener 8oz $4* **MP $1**
1972 *Powder Mist 7oz $4* **MP $1**

1980 *Cologne Spray 1.5oz $6* **MP $4.50***
1980 *Talc 3.5oz $2.50* **MP $1.50***
1980 *Soap 3oz $1.75* **MP $1***

1972 *Foam of Roses Bath Foam 5oz $4* **MP $1**
1972 *Cologne Mist 3oz $6* **MP $3**
1977 *Cream Sachet .66oz $3* **MP $1**
1978 *Cologne Ice 1oz $3.75* **MP $2**

1964 *Emollient Bath Oil 8oz $4* **MP $2**
1961 *Emollient Bath Oil 4oz $2.25* **MP $2**

ROSES, ROSES

1972 *Cologne Gelee 3oz $4* **MP $2**
1972 *Cream Sachet .66oz $3* **MP $1**
1972 *Boxed Soap, three 3oz cakes $3.50* **MP $6**
1973 *Skin Softener 5oz $4* **MP $3**

1972 *Kwickettes, 14 per box $1.35* **MP $3**
1974 *Talc 3½oz $1.50* **MP $1**
1975 *Cream Sachet .66oz $3* **MP 75¢**
1974 & 75 *Xmas wrap Soap 3oz $1.25* **MP $2**

(See Bubble Bath Gelee pg. 133, Glow of Roses Candle pg. 163, Awards pg. 248)

1970 *Powder Mist 7oz $3.75* **MP $1**
1970 *Emollient Mist 4oz $3* **MP $1**
1970 *Shower Soap 6oz $2* **MP $6**
1970 *Emollient Bath Foam 5oz $4* **MP $3**

1980 *Soft Bristle Shower Brush $13* **MP $10***
1980 *Shower Gel 6oz $5* **MP $4***
1980 *Moisture Mist 2.8oz $4* **MP $4***
1980 *Smooth Talc 5oz $4* **MP $2***

1964 *Soap 3oz 49¢* **MP $1***
1976 *Bath Soap 5oz $1.75* **MP $1.50**
1966 *Gift Soap 5¾oz in covered plastic Soap Dish $1.50* **MP $10. Dish only $5**

1968-76 *Talc 3oz $1.25* **MP 50¢**
1969 *After Shower Smoother 4oz $2.50* **MP 50¢**
1973-79 *Skin Softener 5oz $4* **MP 50¢**
1973 *Powder Spray 7oz $4* **MP 75¢**
1975 *Emollient Mist 4oz $4* **MP $2**

Silk & Honey

1969 *Silk & Honey Bath Gelee with golden ladle 4½oz $6* **MP $10 boxed. Ladle MP $4**

1970 *Soap 3oz 60¢* **MP $2**
1968 *Cream Lotion 6oz $2.50* **MP $2**

1968 *Bath Foam 6oz $3* **MP $2**
1969 *Creamy Masque 3oz $2.50* **MP $2**
1968 *Softalc 3oz $1.50* **MP $2**

1970 *Milk Bath 6oz $5* **MP $5, $7 boxed**
1970 *Powder Mist 7oz $3.75* **MP $3**

** Available from Avon at time of publication*

1972 *Bath Oil (clear) 16oz $7.50* **MP $4***
1972 *Bath Oil (frosted) 16oz $7.50* **MP $6**
1969 *Bath Oil 8oz $4* **MP $4***
1969 *Bath Oil 4oz $2.25* **MP 50¢**
1977 *Bath Oil 1oz trial size 25¢ with another purchase* **MP $1**
(as above, with aqua lid **MP 25¢)**

1978 *Light Bouquet SSS Bath Oil 8oz $5* **MP $4***
1979 *As above, 16oz $8.50* **MP $6***
1980 *Skin Softener 5oz $5.50* **MP $3***

Scented SSS Miniatures (left to right)
1969 *1oz 8 fragrances $1.50* **MP $5**
1969 *2oz 9 fragrances $2.50* **MP $6**
1970 *2oz 8 fragrances $2.50* **MP $3**
1974 *2oz 5 fragrances $4* **MP $3**
1971 *2oz 5 fragrances $2.50* **MP $3**

1970 *Coloring Book sold only to Representatives and given to customer's children.* **MP $5**

1966 *Fragrance Trio. Set of three 1oz miniatures in 9 fragrances* **MP $19 complete with sleeve (not shown). Each bottle MP $5**

1966 *Bath Luxury. Sponge and SSS Bath Oil 4oz $4.50* **MP $12**

1964 *Bath Mates. SSS Bath Oil 4oz and two 3oz Soaps $3.23* **MP $10**

1971 *Fragrance Watch Glace .02oz $3.50* **MP $9**
1970 *Love Dove Cream Sachet .66oz $3* **MP $5**
1970 *Ali Barbara DemiStik $1.50* **MP $3**

. . . SKIN-SO-SOFT

1967 *Skin-So-Soft Complements. Talc 3oz and two 3oz Soaps $2.50* **MP $10**

1965 *Shower Mates. After Shower Foam 4oz and two 3oz Soaps $3.20* **MP $12**

1968 *Skin-So-Soft Smoothies. SSS Bath Oil 4oz and Satin Talc 3oz $2.50* **MP $6**

1970 *Love Cakes, three 2oz Soaps $2* **MP $10**
1971 *Talc 3½oz $1.25* **MP $4**
1971 *Cream Sachet .66oz $2.50* **MP $4**

SMALL WORLD

1970 *Heidi Cologne Mist 3oz $5* **MP $8**
1970 *Bubbly O'Bath Bubble Bath 5oz $3.50* **MP $8**
1970 *Splashu Cologne 2oz $3.50* **MP $8**
1970 *Poolu Non-tear Shampoo 5oz $3.50* **MP $8**

1971 *Wendy Cowgirl Cream Lotion 5oz $5* **MP $8**
1971 *English Girl Bubble Bath 5oz $3.50* **MP $8**
1971 *Senorita Non-tear Shampoo 5oz $3.50* **MP $8**
1971 *Gigi Cologne Mist 3oz $5* **MP $8**

1970 *Lollipop given to Small World customers by Representatives* **MP $17**
1970 *Lipkin, Tropical Fruit $1.75* **MP $4**
1970 *Lipkin, Dutch Chocolate $1.75* **MP $4**
1971 *Rollette $1.75* **MP $4**
1970 *Lipkin, French Mint $1.75* **MP $4**
1970 *Polynesian Pin Pal, .02oz $2.50* **MP $6**
1971 *Scandinavian Pin Pal .02oz $2.50* **MP $6**

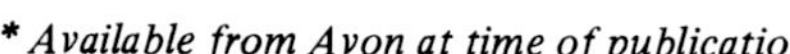
** Available from Avon at time of publication*

1961 *Perfume 1oz $20* **MP $65. $85 boxed**

1961 *Cologne Mist 3oz $4* **MP $6**
1962 *Bath Oil, plastic 6oz $2.50* **MP $6**
1963 *Perfume Oil for Bath ½oz $4* **MP $12**
1962 *Cream Lotion 4oz $1.50* **MP $6**

1961 *Beauty Dust 6oz $4* **MP $12**
1962 *Cream Sachet .66oz $2* **MP $5**
1961 *Cologne 2oz $2* **MP $6**
1962 *Powder Sachet .9oz $2* **MP $8**

Somewhere

1963 *Perfume Mist 2 drams $3.25* **MP $7**
1964 *Perfume Oil ½oz $4* **MP $11**
1962 *Talc 2¾oz 89¢* **MP $4**
1962 *Perfume 1 dram $2.50* **MP $9**

1962 *Unforgettable Set. Cologne Mist 3oz Cream Sachet .66oz and Beauty Dust 6oz $10.95* **MP $40**

1962 *Boxed Soap, three 3oz cakes $1.50* **MP $24**

1964 *Dream Castle. Cologne 2oz and Cream Sachet $4* **MP $32**

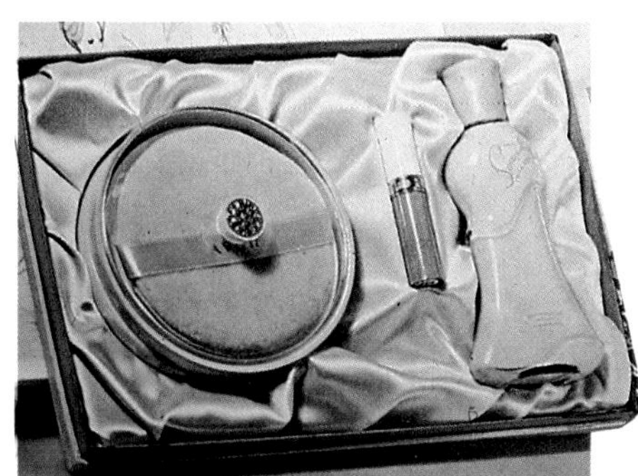

1964 *Dreams of Somewhere. Beauty Dust, Perfume Mist, Cream Lotion 4oz $9.25* **MP $40**

1966 *Beauty Dust 6oz $4* **MP $13**
1967 *Powder Sachet (rare) .9oz $2* **MP $26**
1966 *Cream Lotion 4oz $1.50* **MP $7**
1966 *Cream Sachet .66oz $2* **MP $2**
1966 *Powder Sachet .9oz $2* **MP $22**

1966 *Cologne Mist 3oz $4* **MP $3**
1966 *Perfume Oil ½oz $4* **MP $8**
1966 *Cologne 2oz $2* **MP $3**
1969 *Cologne ½oz $1.50* **MP $3**
1966 *Skin Softener 5oz $3.25* **MP $2**

1966 *Bath Oil 6oz $2.75* **MP $3**
1966 *Soap 3oz 49¢* **MP $4**
1966 *Boxed Soap, three 3oz cakes $2* **MP $14**

1966 *Talc 2¾oz $1* **MP $1**
1975 *DemiStik .19oz $2* **MP $1**
1974 *Talc 3½oz $1.50* **MP 75¢**

(See also Awards pg. 244)

1940 *Toilet Water 2oz in "yellow dress" introductory bottle $1.19* **MP $40, $55 boxed**
1941 *Toilet water 2oz in "green dress", Founder's Day customer offer in July 1941 only. 20¢* **MP $40, $55 boxed**

1941 *Sonnet Set. Toilet Water 2oz and Body Powder 5oz $2* **MP $75**

Sonnet

. . . as eloquent as a love poem . . .

See also Awards pg. 246

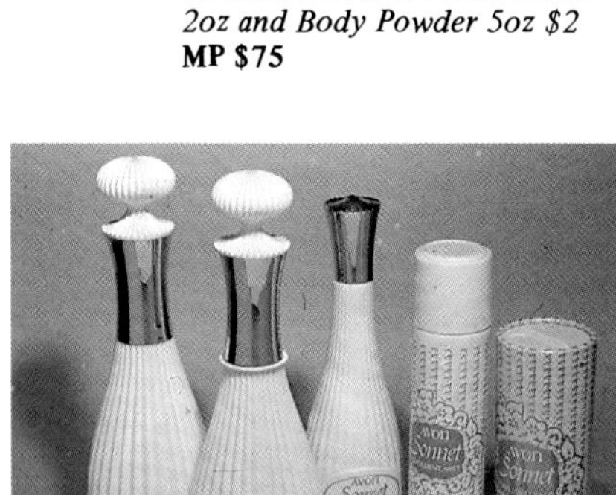

1972 *Cologne Mist 3oz $7.50* **MP $5**
1972 *Cologne Mist 3oz (with ring below neck) $7.50* **MP $1**
1973 *Foaming Bath Oil 6oz $5* **MP $2**
1975 *Emollient Mist 4oz $4.50* **MP $1**
1973 *Talc 3½oz $1.75* **MP 50¢**

1973 *Beauty Dust 6oz $7.50* **MP $5**
1973 *DemiStik .19oz $2.50* **MP $1**
1973 *Skin Softener 5oz $5* **MP $1**

1972 *Boxed Soaps, three 3oz $5* **MP $10**
1977 *Cologne Spray 2.7oz $7.50* **MP $1**
1972 *Rollette .33oz $4* **MP $1**
1977 *Foaming Bath Oil 6oz $4.50* **MP $1**
1972 *Cream Sachet .66oz $4* **MP $1**

1975 *Powder Sachet 1¼oz $3.50* **MP $1**
1973 *Powder Mist 7oz $5* **MP $1**
1973 *Cream Lotion 8oz $3.50* **MP $1**
1973 *Boxed Soap, three 3oz $5* **MP $8**

1975 *Cologne 2oz $5* **MP $1**

1979 *Powder Mist 4oz $4.50* **MP $1**
1974 *Cologne Mist 2oz $6* **MP $2**
1976 *Rollette .33oz $4.50* **MP $2**
1979 *Purse Concentre .33oz $3* **MP $1**
1975 *Soap 3oz $1.25* **MP $1**

1980 *Cologne Spray 1.8oz $6.50* **$6***
1980 *Talc 3.5oz $3* **MP 50¢**
1980 *Moisturizing Body Splash 8oz $5* **MP 75¢**
1980 *Roll-On Deodorant 2oz $1.89* **MP $1***
1980 *Fresh & Foaming Body Cleanser 6oz $5.50* **MP 75¢**

Sportif

See also Awards pg. 262

Strawberry

. . . for a delicious, fragrance-filled experience . . .

1968 *Milk Bath strawberry scented 6oz $4* **MP $6**

1969 *Strawberries and Cream. Strawberry scented Bathfoam 4oz $3.50* **MP $7**
1971 *Bath Gelee 4½oz with golden ladle $7* **MP $9**
1971 *Bath Foam Pitcher 4oz $4* **MP $7**
1973 *Big Berry Strawberry Bathfoam 10oz $5* **MP $5**

1971 *Strawberry Guest Soap, 3 in box, 2oz each $3* **MP $15 boxed (box not shown)**
1969 *Strawberry Fair. Plastic Soap Dish holds cellophane 'straw' and 5oz strawberry scented soap $3* **MP $8, $11 boxed**

** Available from Avon at time of publication*

1978 *Strawberry Porcelain Plate, hand decorated with 22k gold trim. Six 1oz strawberry scented soaps $17.50* **MP $16**
Plate MP $13

Sunny, bright and lively . . . SUN BLOSSOMS

1978 *Cologne .5oz $2* **MP $1**
1978 *Cologne Spray 1.8oz $5* **MP $1**
1978 *Talc 3.5oz $2* **MP $1**
1978 *Body Splash 8oz $5* **MP $1**
1978 *Cologne Ice 1oz $3.75* **MP $2**

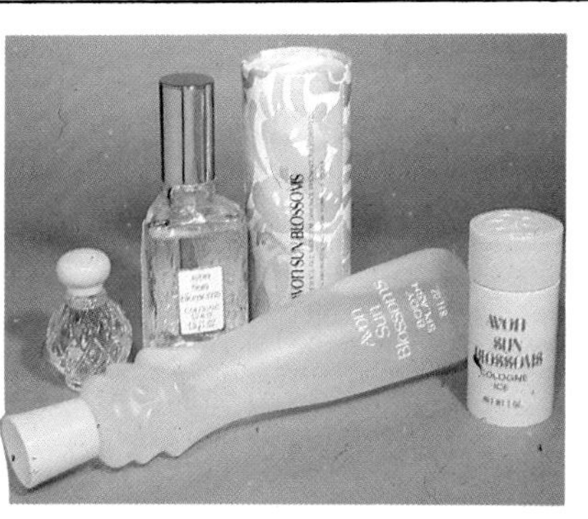

1978 *Strawberry Porcelain Napkin Rings, each 2" diam. and one strawberry scented 5oz soap $11* **MP $10**
1978 *Strawberry Porcelain Demi-Cup Fragrance Candlette, strawberry scent. Saucer 4" diam. $15* **MP $10**
1979 *Strawberry Porcelain Sugar Shaker and Talc 3.5oz $16* **MP $10, Talc MP $1**

1979 *Strawberry Fair Body Lotion 6oz $4.50* **MP $1**
1979 *Strawberry Fair Talc 3.5oz $2.50* **MP $1**
1979 *Strawberry Fair Shower Soap $5.50* **MP $5**
1979 *Bubble Bath 8oz $4.50* **MP $1**

1974 *Pick-A-Berry plastic soap container holds six 1oz strawberry scented soaps $6* **MP $7**

1947 *Body Powder 9oz 85¢* **MP $38**
1947 *Cologne 4oz $1.35* **MP $55, $70 boxed**

1947 *Three Piece Set. Body Powder 9oz, Cologne 4oz and Bath Salts $3.25* **MP $150**
1947 *Bath Salts 85¢* **MP $38**

Swan Lake

1947 *Two Piece Set. Bath Oil 6oz and Body Powder 9oz $2.29* **MP $120**
1947 *Bath Oil $1.25* **MP $55**

1975 *Tennis Hat. White with green lettering. $4.98* **MP $7**
1975 *T-Shirt. Choice of 4 colors. $4.98* **MP $7**

1973 *Cologne Mist 2oz $4.50* **MP $1**
1974 *Powder Mist 7oz $3.75* **MP $1**
1976 *Bubble Bath 10oz $4.50* **MP 50¢**
1976 *Body Splash 10oz $5* **MP 50¢**

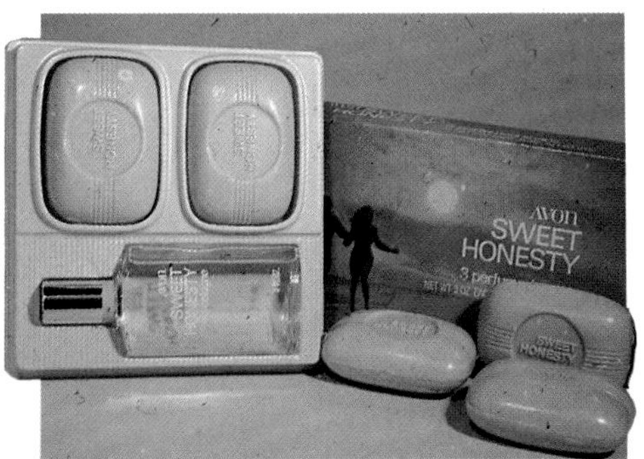

1977 *Gift Set. Two cakes Soap, 3oz each and Cologne 2oz $9* **MP $4**
1978 *Boxed Soap, three 3oz cakes $6.50* **MP $4**

1973 *Cream Sachet .66oz $3* **MP $1**
1973 *Rollette .33oz $3* **MP $1**
1974 *Cologne Gelee 1.5oz $2.50* **MP $1**
1974 *DemiStik .19oz $2* **MP $1**
1974 *Talc 3½oz $1.50* **MP $1**

1977 *Cologne Spray 1.8oz $5.50* **MP $1**
1977 *Cologne Ice 1oz $3.75* **MP $2**
1977 *Cologne 2oz $5* **MP $1**
1973 *Translucent Powder Compact .5oz $$3.50* **MP $1**
1978 *Scarf, with Avon purchase $1. Value $3.50* **MP $4**

1979 *Christmas Cannister Talc 3.5oz $2.50* **MP $1.50**
1979 *Powder Mist 4oz $4.50*
MP $2, short issue
1976 *Cologne Spray 1.8oz $5.50* **MP $1**

1973 *Just Enough Color Foundation 1.5oz $2* **MP 50¢**

1973 *Bright & Shining Eye Shadow .25oz $1.50* **MP 50¢**
1974 *Lip Color .2oz 4 shades $1.75* **MP 50¢**
1973 *Very Real Blush ¼oz $1.75* **MP 50¢**
1974 *Face Beamer 1.5oz $2* **MP 50¢**
1973 *Wide Eyes Mascara .15oz $2* **MP 50¢**

1974 *Cologne Mist 2oz $7.50* **MP $1**
1977 *Cologne 2oz $6.50* **MP $6***
1974 *Rollette .33oz $5* **MP $1**
1976 *Cologne Spray 1.8oz $7.50* **MP 7***
1974 *Creme Perfume .66oz $5* **MP $4***

1976 *Foaming Bath Oil 6oz $5.50* **MP $1**
1975 *Talc 3½oz $2.50* **MP $2***
1975 *Foaming Bath Oil 6oz $5.50* **MP $1**, *12oz, not shown, $8.50* **MP $2**
1975 *Powder Mist 7oz $5* **MP $1**
1976 *Powder Sachet 1¼oz $3.50* **MP $1**

1975 *Boxed Soaps, three 3oz cakes $6* **MP $5**
1977 *Beauty Dust 6oz $9.50* **MP $3**

1975 *Skin Softener 5oz $5.50* **MP $3***
1977 *Cologne .33oz $3* **MP $1**
1976 *Soap 3oz $1.25* **MP 1***
1978 *Solid Perf. Compact .2oz $3.75* **MP $1**

Timeless *... for all your Timeless tomorrows*

1976 *Gift Set. Cologne Spray and Rollette $12.50* **MP $10**
1975 *Gift Set. Cologne Mist 2oz and Creme Perfume $13.50* **MP $8**

1977 *Gift Set. Cologne Spray 1.8oz and Purse Concentre $11.50* **MP $10 (same set as 1976 but with different box cover)**

1979 *Powder Mist 4oz $5* **MP $3***
1979 *Bath Foam 6oz $5.50* **MP $3***
1978 *Cologne .33oz $3* **MP $1**
1979 *Cologne .33oz $3* **MP $1**

1980 *Cologne .33oz $3.50* **MP $2***
1979 *Cologne Spray 1oz $7* **MP $5***
1979 *Body Satin 6oz $5* **MP 50¢**
1979 *Light Perfume .5oz $7* **MP $5***

**Available from Avon at time of publication*

See also Awards pg. 246

Tasha

1980 *Purse Concentre .33oz $4* **MP $3***
1980 *Creme Perfume .66oz $4.50* **MP $4***
1979 *Cologne 2oz $7* **MP $6***
1980 *Soap 3oz $1.75* **MP $1***

See also Awards pg. 247

1980 *Skin Softener 5oz $6* **MP $3***
1980 *Powder Mist 4oz $5* **MP $3***
1979 *Cologne Spray 1.8oz $8* **MP $7***
1979 *Cologne 2oz $7* **MP $6***

1979 *Cologne .33oz $3* **MP $1**
1980 *Cologne .33oz $3.50* **MP $2***
1980 *Bath Foam 6oz $5.50* **MP $3***
1979 *Light Perfume .5oz $7* **MP $5***
1980 *Talc 3.5oz $3.50* **MP $2***

Tempo

1979 *Skin Softener 5oz $6* **MP $3***
1979 *Body Satin 6oz $5* **MP 50¢**
1978 *Solid Perfume Compact .2oz $3.75* **MP $1**
1979 *Creme Perfume .66oz $4.50* **MP $4***

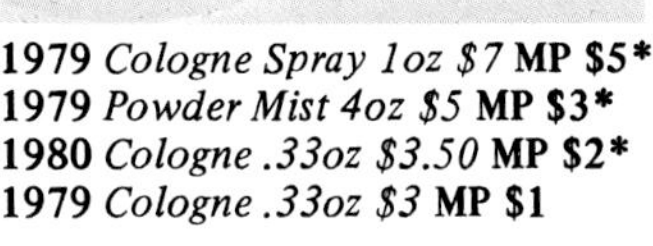

1978 *Cologne Spray 1.8oz $7.50* **MP $7***
1978 *Cologne 2oz $6.50* **MP $6***
1979 *Purse Concentre .33oz $4* **MP $3***
1978 *Ultra Cologne .33oz $3* **MP $1**

1979 *Cologne Spray 1oz $7* **MP $5***
1979 *Powder Mist 4oz $5* **MP $3***
1980 *Cologne .33oz $3.50* **MP $2***
1979 *Cologne .33oz $3* **MP $1**

See also Awards pg. 247

1979 *Bath Foam 6oz $5.50* **MP $3***
1979 *Talc 3.5oz $3* **MP $2**
1979 *Light Perfume .5oz $7* **MP $5***
1980 *Light Spray Cologne, sold only to Reps. Bottle and carton have special labels. 1.8oz $2.75* **MP $4, $6 boxed**

To a Wild Rose

1950 *Gift Perfume. 2 dram $4.50* **MP $85, $120 boxed**

1953 *Cream Lotion 4oz 89¢* **MP $23**
1953 *Bath Oil 4oz $1.25* **MP $23**
1950 *Toilet Water 2oz $1.50* **MP $23**

Rare embossed Rose Lids: Powder Sachet 1¼oz, Cologne 4oz, Toilet Water 2oz, Cream Lotion 4oz and Bath Oil 4oz. For embossed lid add **$5** *to bottle* **MP**

1954 *Talc 2¾oz 49¢* **MP $11**
1950 *Body Powder 5oz 85¢* **MP $20**
1950 *Cologne 4oz $2* **MP $23**

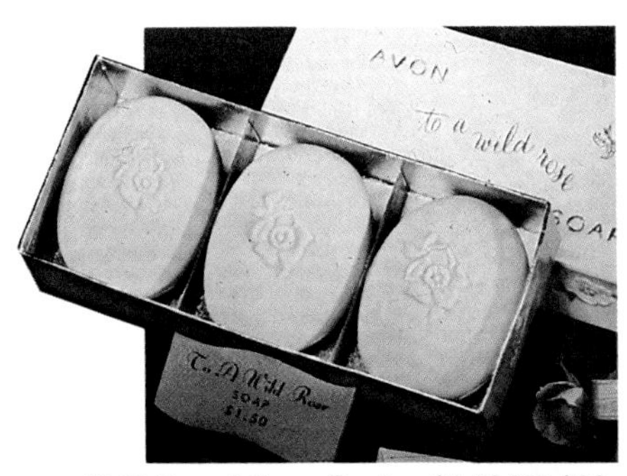

1952 *Boxed Soap, 3 cakes $1.50* **MP $30**

1950 *Cream Sachet $1.25* **MP $13**
1951 *Powder Sachet 1¼oz $1.19* **MP $17**
1963 *Perfume Mist, 2 drams $3* **MP $7**
1960 *Spray Perfume 2 drams $2.95* **MP $12, $16 boxed**

**Available from Avon at time of publication*

1950 *Gift Set. Body Powder 5oz and Cologne 4oz $2.85* **MP $52**

1953 *Rose Petals. Cream Lotion and Bath Oil 4oz each $2.15* **MP $53**

1950 *Pearl of Beauty. Cologne and Beauty Dust. Drawstring silk bag $5.25* **MP 75, bag only $25**

1952 *Wild Roses. Body Powder & Cream Sachet $1.95* **MP $47**

1953 *Wild Roses. Body Powder and Cream Sachet $1.95* **MP $45**

1954 *Petal of Beauty. Beauty Dust and Cologne $3.75* **MP $58**

1960 *Boxed Soap, 3 cakes $1.98* **MP $20**
1954 *Talc 3oz 59¢* **MP $7** *As shown with 1960 Christmas carton 69¢* **MP $13**
1950 *Beauty Dust $1.75* **MP $23**

1956 *Beauty Dust 6oz $1.95* **MP $20, with bottle and ribbon MP $40**

1956 *Cream Lotion 4oz 95¢* **MP $18**
1957 *Cologne 2oz (sets only)* **MP $18**
1955 *Toilet Water 2oz $1.50* **MP $15**
1955 *Powder Sachet 1¼oz $1.25* **MP $12**

...To a Wild Rose

1956 *Gift Perfume ½oz $5* **MP $75, $110 boxed**

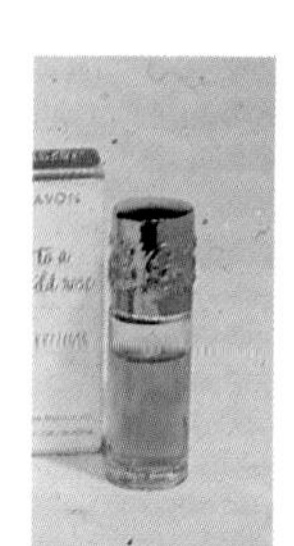

1950 *One Dram Perfume $1.50* **MP $12, $15 boxed**

1956 *Bath Oil 4oz $1.35* **MP $13**
1959 *Bath Oil 8oz $2.25* **MP $9**
1965 *Cream Lotion 4oz $1.25* **MP $9**

1966 *Foaming Bath Oil 6oz $2.50* **MP $5**

1963 *Perfume Oil for the Bath ½oz $3.50* **MP $12**
1964 *Perfume Oil ½oz $3.50* **MP $9**
1958 *Cologne Mist 3oz $2.50* **MP $25**
1969 *Cologne ½oz $1.50* **MP $3**
1955 *Cologne 4oz $2* **MP $20**

1960 *Gift Cologne 4oz $2.50* **MP $28**

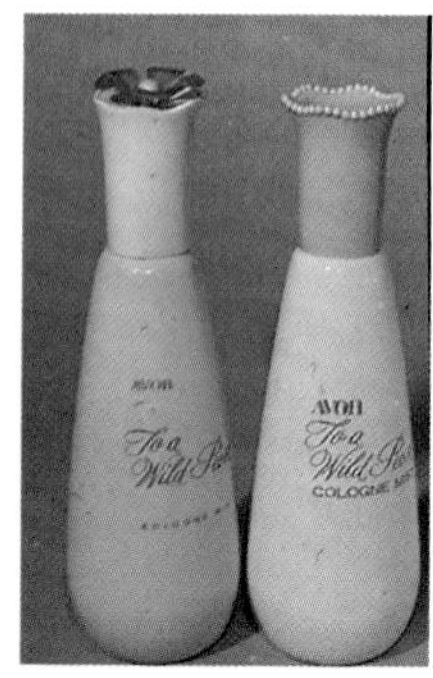

1959 *Cologne Mist 3oz $2.95* **MP $2** *(w/o oz on front)*
1975 *Cologne Mist 3oz $7* **MP $3** *(lid change)*

1966 *Cologne Mist 3oz $3.25* **MP $3** *(with oz on front)*

1964 *Beauty Dust 6oz $3.25* **MP $10**
1955 *Body Powder (paper band) $1* **MP $17**
1961 *Body Powder 4oz (plastic) $1.79* **MP $12**
1962 *Talc 2¾oz $1* **MP $2**

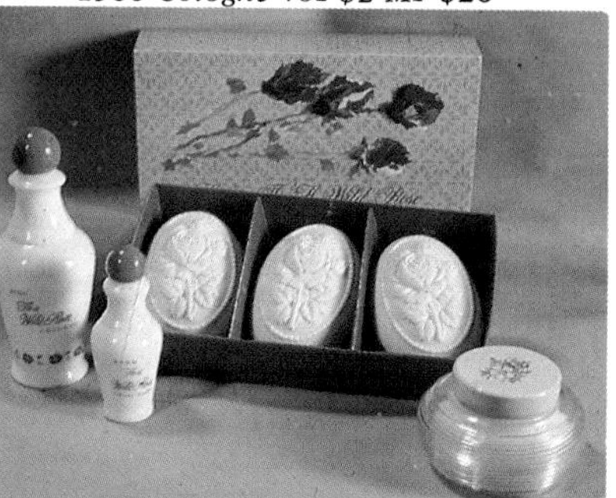

1961 *Cologne 2oz $1.50* **MP $3**
1956 *Toilet Water ½oz from Special Date Set* **MP $25**
1968 *Boxed Soaps three 3oz $3* **MP $7**
1960 *Cream Sachet .66oz $1.25* **MP $3**
Above shown in 1960 Plastic Holder, special purchase 50¢ **MP $9**

1951 *Miss Coed. Cream Lotion, Bath Oil and Cologne 2oz each $2.35* **MP $80 complete. Each bottle $20**

1954 *Bath Bouquet. Cologne, Cream Lotion 2oz each and Soap $1.95* **MP $55. Each bottle MP $18**

1955 *Bath Bouquet. Cologne and Cream Lotion 2oz each and 1 cake Soap $1.95* **MP $55. Each bottle MP $18**

1955 *Pink Bells. 2 Talc 2¾oz each $1* **MP $30**

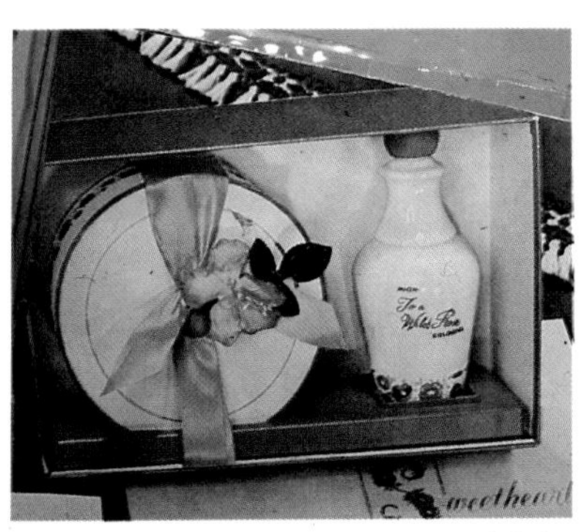

1955 *Sweethearts. Beauty Dust and Cologne $3.95* **MP $50**

1956 *Bath Bouquet. Cologne, Bath Oil 2oz each and 1 cake Soap $2.25* **MP $55. Each bottle MP $18**

To a ... Wild Rose

1955 *Adorable Set (left) Body Powder and Cream Sachet $2.25* **MP $35**
1956 *Adorable Set (right) Body Powder and Cream Sachet $2.25* **MP $35**

1956 *Special Date. Fashion Lipstick, Powder Pak and Toilet Water ½oz $2.50* **MP $50**

1956 *Sweethearts. Beauty Dust and Cologne $3.95* **MP $50**

1957 *Trilogy. Cologne, Cream Lotion, Bath Oil 2oz each $2.95* **MP $65**

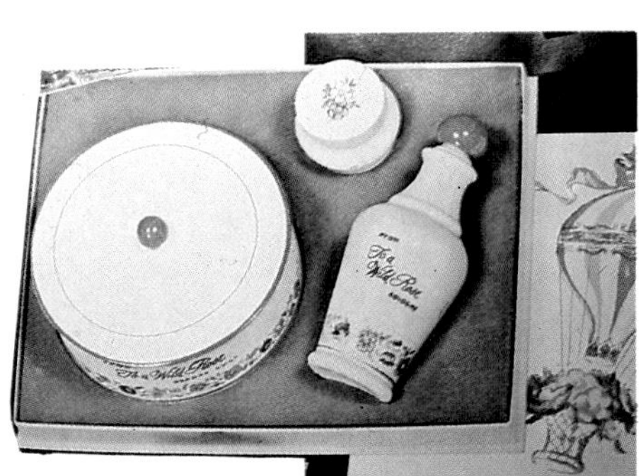

1957 *Roses Adrift. Beauty Dust, Cream Sachet and Cologne $4.95* **MP $55**

1958 *A Spray of Roses. Cologne Mist 3oz & Cream Sachet $3.95* **MP $40**

To a Wild Rose

1961 *Lovely As A Rose. Cologne 2oz and Cream Sachet $3* **MP $30**

1961 *Spray of Roses. Beauty Dust and Cologne Mist 3oz $5.90* **MP $25**

1963 *Holiday Roses Beauty Dust, Cream Lotion 4oz and Cologne 2oz $6.50* **MP $55**

1964 *Wild Roses. Cologne 2oz and Cream Sachet $3.50* **MP $25**

1965 *Bath Flower 3oz Soap and Bath Sponge $2.50* **MP $20**

1971 *Skin Softener* **(lid change)** *5oz $3.50* **MP $3**
1971 *Powder Mist 7oz $3.75* **MP $4 (label change)**
1975 *Cream Sachet .66oz $3* **MP $1**

1935 *Customer Gift, March 5-25*

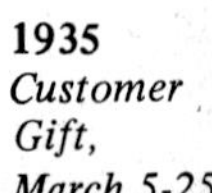

honoring the McConnells' Golden Anniversary **MP $80**

1959 *Cologne 4oz $3.75* **MP $15, $25 boxed**
1960 *Cologne 2oz $2* **MP $2, $3 boxed**
1960 *Temple of Love Holder for .75oz Topaze Cream Sachet 75¢* **MP $16, $20 boxed.** *Cream Sachet .75oz $2* **MP $8**

1969 *Cologne ½oz $1.50* **MP $3**
1959 *Perfume 1oz $20* **MP $105, $140 boxed**
1963 *Perfume Oil for the Bath ½oz $4* **MP $50, $60 boxed**
1964 *Perfume Oil ½oz $4* **MP $9, $10 boxed**

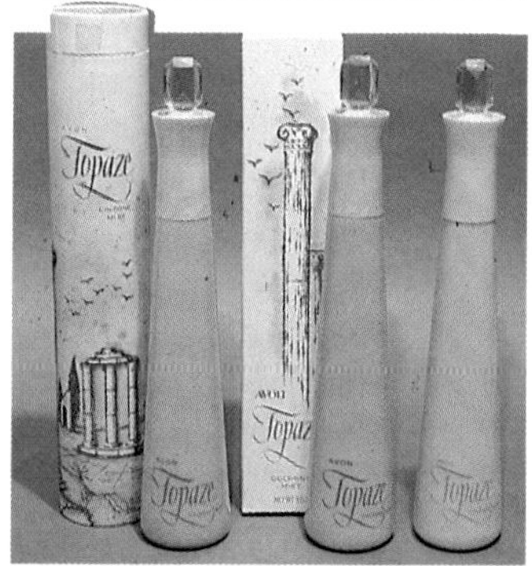

1959 *Cologne Mist 3oz $4* **MP $1**
$5 in round box
1969 *Cologne Mist, as above, boxed* **MP $3**
1971 *Cologne Mist, 3oz $5* **MP $1**

1961 *Body Powder 4oz $2.25* **MP $12**
1959 *Powder Sachet .9oz $2* **MP $6**
1961 *Powder Sachet .9oz (right) $2* **MP $10**
1959 *Spray Perfume 2 dram $3.75* **MP $12**
1962 *Talc 2¾oz $1* **MP $2**

1959 *Cream Lotion 4oz (rare jeweled closure) $1.50* **MP $12**
1961 *Talc, tin 2¾oz $1* **MP $10**
1960 *Cream Lotion 4oz $1.50* **MP $3**
1965 *Cream Sachet .66oz $2.50* **MP $1**
1966 *Foaming Bath Oil 6oz $2.75* **MP $1**

Topaze

1961 *Boxed Soap, 2 cakes $1.50* **MP $25**
1965 *Column of 3 Soaps $1.75* **MP $30**
1964 *Skin Softener 5oz $3.25* **MP $3**

(See also Awards pps. 242 & 244)

1961 *Beauty Dust 6oz $4* **MP $4**
1960 *Beauty Dust as above but with yellow lamb's wool puff $4* **MP $15**
1964 *Soap 3oz 39¢* **MP $4**
1966 *Hair Spray 7oz $1.50* **MP $3**

1974 *Talc 3½oz $1.50* **MP $1**
1975 *Cream Sachet .66oz $3* **MP $1**
1975 *DemiStik .19oz $2* **MP $1**
1977 *Purse Concentre .33oz $3* **MP $1**
1967 *Spray Essence 1¼oz $3.50* **MP $3**
1977 *Cologne Spray 1.8oz $5.50* **MP $1**

1960 *Topaze Treasure. Cologne 2oz and Beauty Dust 6oz $5.95* **MP $32**

. . . Topaze

1960 *Golden Topaze. Beauty Dust, Cologne Mist 3oz and Cream Sachet .75oz $9.95* **MP $38**

1961 *Topaze Jewel. Cream Lotion 4oz and Cologne Mist $4.95* **MP $30**

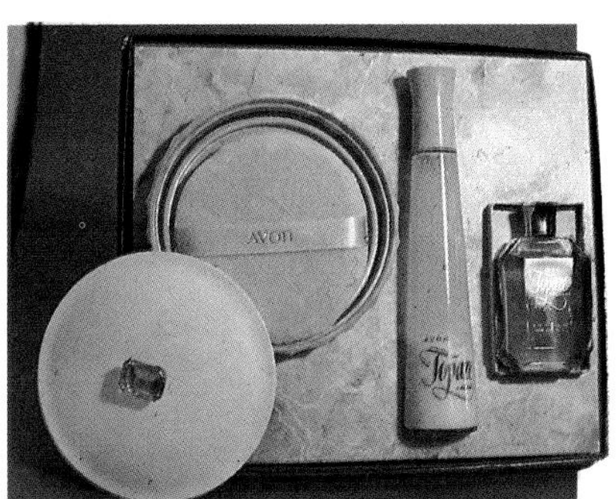

1963 *Topaze Elegance. Cream Lotion 4oz, Cologne 2oz and Beauty Dust 6oz $7.95* **MP $35**

1964 *Topaze Princess. Cologne Mist and Cream Lotion $5.95* **MP $25**

1964 *Topaze Setting. Cologne 2oz and Powder Sachet $4* **MP $25**

1977 *Foaming Bath Oil 6oz $5.50* **MP $1**
1977 *Powder Mist 7oz $5* **MP $1**
1977 *Skin Softener 5oz $5.50* **MP $3***
1977 *Talc 3½oz $2.50* **MP $2***

1979 *Creme Perfume .66oz $3.50* **MP $2.50***
1979 *Cologne Spray 1.8oz $6* **MP $5**
1979 *Purse Concentre .33oz $3* **MP $2***
1979 *Powder Mist 4oz $4.50* **MP $3***
1980 *Bath Foam 6oz $5* **MP $3***

1975 *Cologne 2oz $4* **MP $1 with Christmas carton MP $3**
1976 *Cologne Spray 2.7oz $8* **MP $7***
1977 *Cream Sachet .66oz $4.50* **MP $1**
1963 *Perfume Mist 2 drams $3.25* **MP $7**
1977 *DemiStik .19oz $2.50* **MP $1**

1946 *French Milled Soap 8½oz bar $1.15* **MP $55**
1946 *Body Powder, plastic sifter 65¢* **MP $26**
1946 *Cologne 6oz $1.75* **MP $85**
1949 *Powder Sachet 1¼oz $1.19* **MP $21**
1947 *Powder Sachet 1¼oz $1.19* **MP $25**
1946 *Powder Sachet, white cap 1¼oz $1.15* **MP $30, in 60th Anniversary Box (not shown) MP $45**

White Moiré

1945 *White Moire Set. Body Powder 5oz and Cologne 6oz $2.50* **MP $145**

Unforgettable

1966 *Cologne 2oz $2.50* **MP $3**
1965 *Perfume Mist 2 drams $3.75* **MP $7**
1975 *Cream Sachet .66oz $3* **MP $1**
1975 *DemiStik .19oz $2* **MP $1**

1968 *Powder Mist 7oz $3.75* **MP $1**
1965 *Boxed Soap, three 3oz cakes $2* **MP $20**
1975 *DemiStik .19oz $2* **MP $1**
1969 *Cologne ½oz $1.50* **MP $3**
1965 *Perfume Oil ½oz* **MP $8**

1965 *Beauty Dust 6oz $5* **MP $6**
1966 *Cream Lotion 4oz $1.75* **MP $6**
1966 *Foaming Bath Oil 6oz $3* **MP $3**
1966 *Cream Sachet .66oz $2.50* **MP $1**

1965-76 *Cologne Mist 3oz with open filigree trim, $5* **MP $1.** *With solid filigree trim 3oz $5* **MP $6**
1965 only *Powder Sachet .9oz $2.50* **MP $15**
1966-67 *Powder Sachet .9oz $2.50* **MP $3**
1965 *Powder Sachet .9oz $2.50* **MP $2**
1968-69 *Powder Sachet .9oz $2.50* **MP $2**

1965 *Skin Softener 5oz $3.50* **MP $1**
1966 *Talc 2¾oz $1* **MP $2**
1971 *Beauty Dust, cardboard, 6oz $4.50* **MP $7**

1974 *Talc 3½oz $1.50* **MP 50¢**
1976 *Cologne Spray 2.7oz $7* **MP $1**
1979 *Purse Concentre .33oz $3* **MP $1**
1979 *Creme Perfume .66oz $3.50* **MP $1**

1965 *Deluxe Set. Beauty Dust 6oz, Cream Sachet .66oz and Cologne Mist 3oz $12.95* **MP $38**

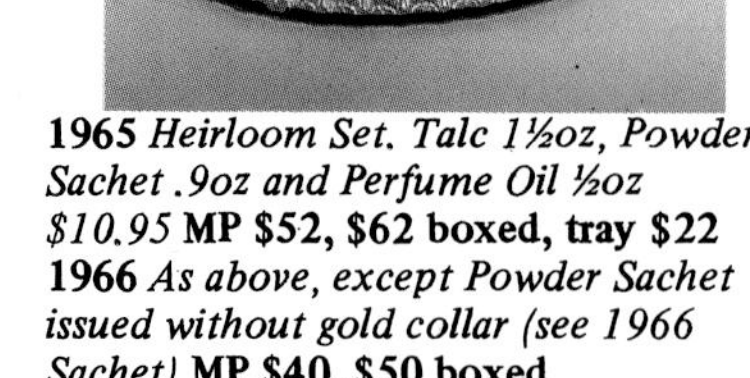

1965 *Heirloom Set. Talc 1½oz, Powder Sachet .9oz and Perfume Oil ½oz $10.95* **MP $52, $62 boxed, tray $22**
1966 *As above, except Powder Sachet issued without gold collar (see 1966 Sachet)* **MP $40, $50 boxed**

* *Available from Avon at time of publication*

For those moments that go beyond words

Unspoken

See also Awards pg. 246

1975 *Cologne Spray 1.8oz $7.50* **MP $7***
1977 *Cologne 2oz $6.50* **MP $2**
1975 *Rollette .33oz $5* **MP $1** *(name changed to Purse Concentre in 1979* **MP $3****)*
1977 *Cologne .33oz $3* **MP $1**

1975 *Boxed Soap, three 3oz cakes $6* **MP $50**
1975 *Creme Perfume .66oz $5* **MP $1**
1976 *Skin Softener 5oz $5.50* **MP $3**

1976 *Talc 3½oz $2.50* **MP $2***
1976 *Foaming Bath Oil 6oz $5.50* **MP $1**
1976 *Foaming Bath Oil 12oz $8.50* **MP $2**
1977 *Powder Mist 7oz $5* **MP $1**

1976 *Gift Set. Cologne Spray 1.8oz and Rollette .33oz $12.50* **MP $10**

1977 *Gift Set. Cologne 2oz and Rollette .33oz $10.50* **MP $7**

...Unspoken

1979 *Cologne .33oz $3* **MP $1**
1978 *Cologne .33oz $3* **MP $1**
1980 *Cologne .33oz $3.50* **MP $2***
1979 *Body Satin 6oz $5* **MP 50¢**

1979 *Bath Foam 6oz $5.50* **MP $3***
1979 *Powder Mist 4oz $5* **MP $3***
1979 *Light Perfume .5oz $7* **MP $5***
1979 *Cologne Spray 1oz $7* **MP $5***

1947 *Toilet Water 2oz $1.19* **MP $40**

1947 *Toilet Water 2oz 61¢ for one campaign honoring 61st Anniversary.* **MP $60 in Anniversary Box**

1947 *Toilet Water 2oz $1.19* **MP $40**

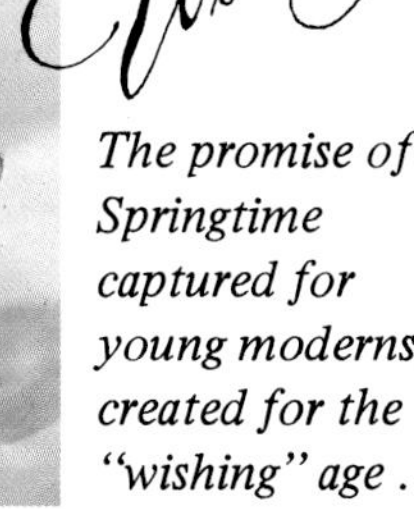

Wishing

The promise of Springtime captured for young moderns, created for the "wishing" age . . .

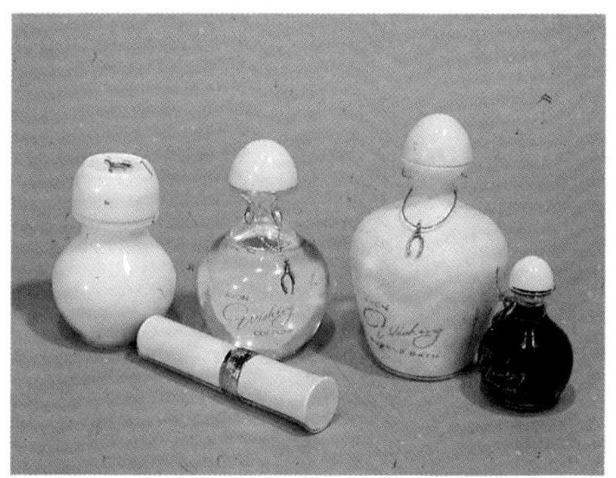

1964 *Powder Sachet .9oz $1.75* **MP $10**
1963 *Cologne 2oz with wishbone $1.78* **MP $9**
1963 *Bubble Bath 4oz $1.35* **MP $6**
1964 *Perfume Oil ½oz w/wishbone $3.50* **MP $12**
1965 *Perfume Mist 2 dram $3* **MP $7**

1965 *Skin Softener 5oz $3* **MP $4**
1963 *Cream Lotion, plastic 4oz $1.35* **MP $6**
1963 *Talc 2¾oz 79¢* **MP $4**
1963 *Cream Sachet .66oz $1.75* **MP $2**

1963 *Cologne Mist 2½oz $2.95* **MP $4**
1968 *Cologne Mist 2½oz $3.50* **MP $6**

1964 *Bath Oil 6oz $2.25* **MP $12 with wishbone**

1963 *Beauty Dust 4oz $2.95* **MP $13**
1963 *Boxed Soap, 3 cakes $1.35* **MP $25**

1963 *Wish Come True. Cologne 2oz and Bubble Bath 4oz $3.10* **MP $27**

1963 *Secret Wish. Cream Lotion 4oz and Talc 2¾oz $2.14* **MP $20**

** Available from Avon at time of publication*

(See also Awards pg. 244)

1964 *Wishing Duette. Creme Rollette and Cream Sachet .66oz $3.50* **MP $20**

...*Wishing*

1964 *Charm of Wishing. Beauty Dust, Cologne Mist and Wishbone Charm Necklace $8.50* **MP $65. Necklace $20, $30 boxed**

1964 *Perfumed Pair. Talc and Soap 3oz $1.18* **MP $20**

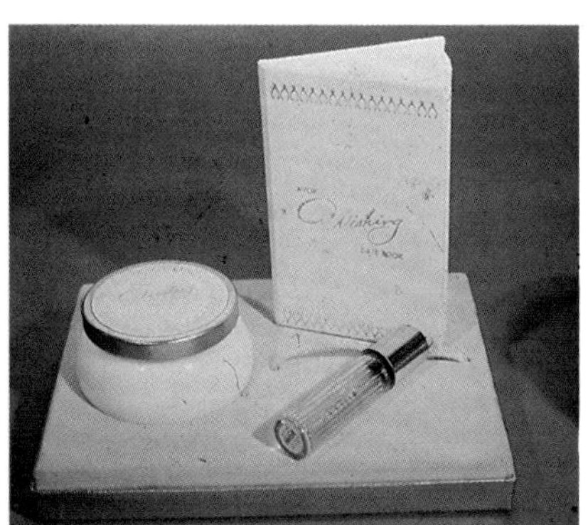

1965 *Wishing Date Set. Rollette, Skin Softener and Date Book $6* **MP $35**
Date Book MP $15

1952 *Perfume (sets only) 1 dr* **MP $65 Bottle**

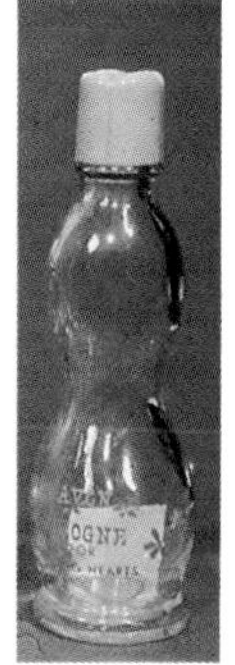

1952 *Cologne (sets only) 2oz* **MP $35 Bottle**

1954 *Cologne (sets only) 1oz* **MP $30 Bottle**

Young Hearts

... it was only the Young Hearts packaging that was exclusive to little girls, the fragrance was Cotillion.

1952 *Young Hearts Set. Bubble Bath, Cologne and Talc $1.65* **MP $90**
Bubble Bath and Talc MP $20 each

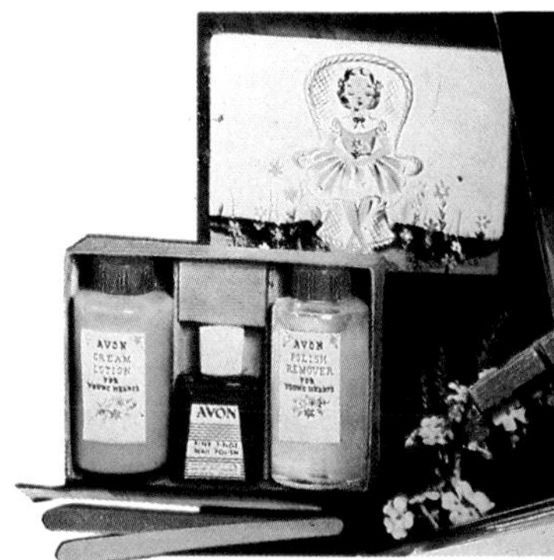

1952 *'N Everything Nice. Cream Lotion, Nail Polish, Polish Remover, Orange Stick and 2 Emery Boards $1.50* **MP $70**
Polish Remover MP $25

1953 *Young Hearts Set. Cologne, Talc and Bubble Bath $1.75* **MP $110**

1953 *'N Everything Nice. Cream Lotion 2oz, Nail Polish .5oz, Polish Remover 2oz, Orange Stick and 2 Emery Boards $1.50* **MP $70**

1952 *Bubble Bath 2oz $1.10* **MP $50 with head, $65 boxed**
1952 *Cologne 2oz $1.25* **MP $50 with head, $65 boxed**

1953 *Honey Bun. Toilet Water ½oz and Pomade Lipstick $1.19* **MP $55**
1954 *Honey Bun. Cologne 1oz and Pomade Lipstick $1.19* **MP $52**

1952 *Rain Drops. Umbrella Handbag holds Cream Lotion, 1 dram Perfume and 2oz Cologne $2.95* **MP $160, $25 Cream Lotion, $35 Handbag only**

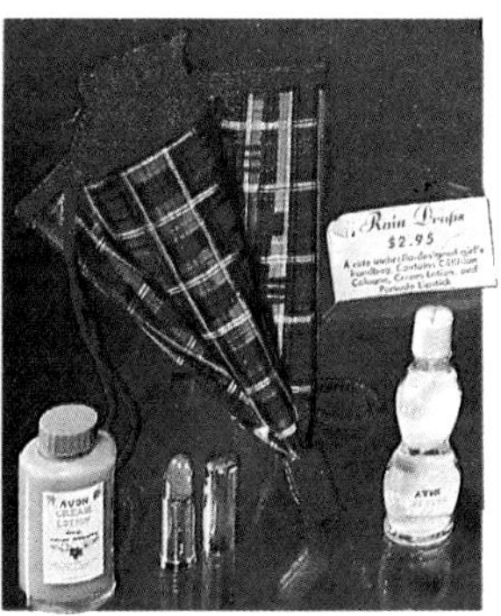

1953 *Rain Drops. Cream Lotion, Pomade Lipstick and Cologne $2.95* **MP $110, $7 Pomade, $35 Umbrella Handbag**

1954 *Rain Drops. Umbrella Handbag holds Cologne 1oz, Pomade Lipstick and Cream Lotion $3.25* **MP $110, $35 Umbrella Handbag**

1952 *Honey Bun. Toilet Water ½oz and Pomade Lipstick $1.19* **MP $55, $35 Toilet Water**

1954 *Kiddie Kologne $1.25* **MP $45 with head, $55 boxed**
1954 *Kiddie Bubble Bath $1.10* **MP $45 with head, $55 boxed**

1954 *Cream Lotion 50¢* **MP $20, $25 boxed**

... Young Hearts

1954 *Miss Fluffy Puff. Cologne and Beauty Dust $2.35* **MP $70**

1954 *Beauty Dust $1.19* **MP $25**

1954 *Young hearts Set. Cologne 1oz, Talc and Bubble Bath $1.95* **MP $100, $25 Talc, $30 each bottle**

1954 *Little Doll Set. Cologne, Pomade Lipstick and Cream Lotion $2.95* **MP $125, $40 Doll**

1955 *Neat and Sweet. Cologne with Atomizer, Cream Lotion and heart shaped Soap $2.50* **MP $95**
1954 *Neat and Sweet (not shown) Same as above, but without atomizer $2.10* **MP $85**

** Available from Avon at time of publication*

a fragrance for fun, created just for teens.

(The Zany Radio and Disco Bag, a prize in the Zany Sweepstakes, is shown on page 247)

1979 *Cologne Ice 1oz $4* **MP $1.50**
1979 *Creme Perfume .66oz $3.50* **MP $3***
1979 *Cologne Spray 1.8oz $5.50* **MP $5***
1979 *Try-It Size Cologne .33oz 75¢ in C-17 & C-18 only* **MP $1.50, $2 boxed**

1979 *Powder Mist 4oz $2.25* **MP $3***
1979 *Body Splash 10oz $5* **MP $4***
1979 *Bubble Bath 10oz $4.50* **MP $4***

1979 *Jug of Shampoo 10oz $6* **MP $2**
1979 *Jug of Bubble Bath 10oz $6* **MP $2**
1979 *Xmas Canister Talc $2.50* **MP $1**
1979 *Talc 3.5oz $2.50* **MP $1.50***
1979 *Purse Concentre (not shown) .33oz $3* **MP $1**

1927-29 *Gertrude Recordon Introductory Facial Set, trial-size containers of Peach Lotion, Cleansing Cream, Skin Food and Astringent and roll of Facial Tissues. $1* **MP $325 complete set, $85 each bottle, $55 each jar**

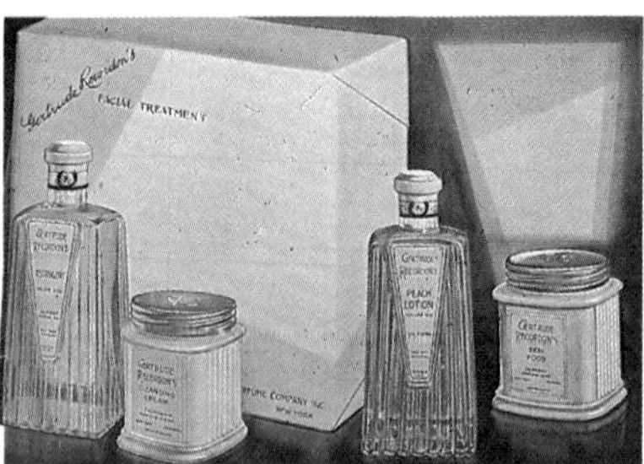

1927-29 *Gertrude Recordon Facial Set. Peach Lotion, Astringent, Cleansing Cream and Skin Food $4* **MP $280 complete set, $80 each bottle, $50 each jar**

1928 *Christmas Cheer Set. Four boxes of Sachet Powder with Greeting Card and Mailing Carton $1.40* **MP $175 complete, $35 each box**

1931 *Little Folks Gift Box. Vernfleur, "391", Trailing Arbutus and Ariel Perfumes 90¢* **MP $240, $45 each bottle**

LITTLE FOLKS SETS

1932 *Little Folks Gift Box. Vernafleur, "391", Arbutus and Ariel Perfumes 90¢* **MP $230, $45 each bottle**

1936 *Little Folks Gift Box. Cotillion, Gardenia, Narcissus and Trailing Arbutus Perfumes 94¢* **MP $155, $30 each bottle**

1930-31 *Atomizer Set No. 6A. Atomizer Bottle and Ariel Perfume 1oz $1.75* **MP $160** *Set 6B issued with Vernafleur Perfume $2* **MP $155, $85 atomizer bottle only**

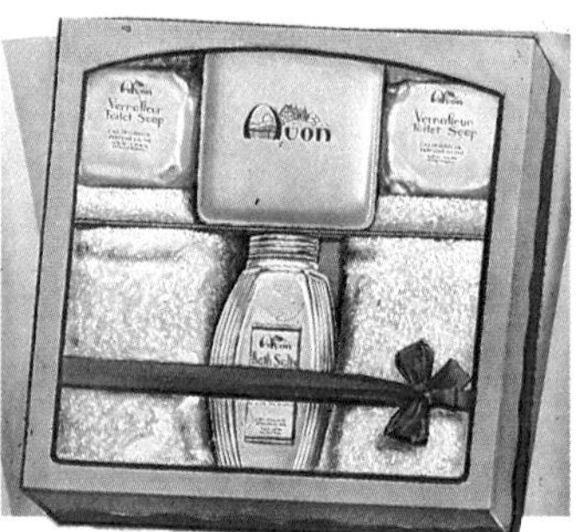

1931-33 *Assortment No. 8. Dusting Powder, Bath Salts, 2 Vernafleur Toilet Soaps, Cannon Bath Towel 45x22½, 2 Washcloths $3.50* **MP $160**

1935 *Facial Set. Cleansing Cream, Tissue Cream, Astringent, Ariel Face Powder and Cleansing Tissues $1.68* **MP $145**

GIFT SETS OF THE 1930's

1934 *Facial Set. Cleansing Cream, Astringent, Tissue Cream, Ariel Face Powder and Cleansing Tissues $1.68* **MP $150**

1934 *Avon Trio. Trailing Arbutus Toilet Water, Daphne Talcum and Ariel Sachet Powder $1.60* **MP $140**

1935 *Gift Set D. Ariel Perfume Flaconette and Sachet, Ariel or Vernafleur Face Powder $2.34* **MP $135**

1931-35 *Hair Treatment Set for Women. Liquid Shampoo 6oz, Pre-Shampoo Oil 2oz, Wave Set 4oz and Hair Tonic Eau de Quinine 6oz for dry or oily hair $3* **MP $185**

1935 *Bath Ensemble. Jasmine Bath Salts and 2 Cakes Soap, Dusting Powder 13oz and Trailing Arbutus Toilet Water 2oz $3.50* **MP $180**

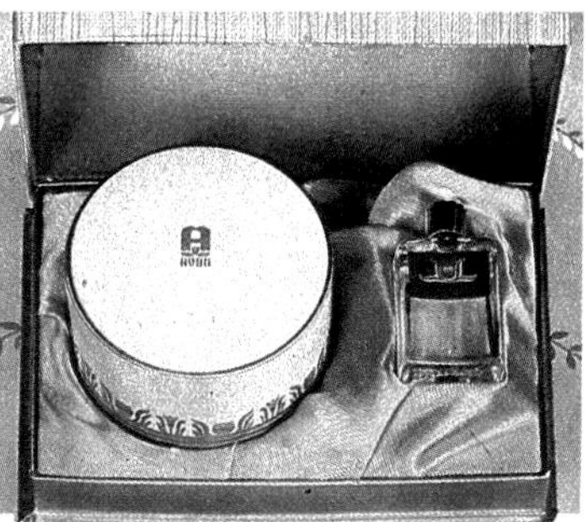

1936 *Gift Set A. Face Powder and Gardenia Perfume Flaconette $1.30* **MP $95**

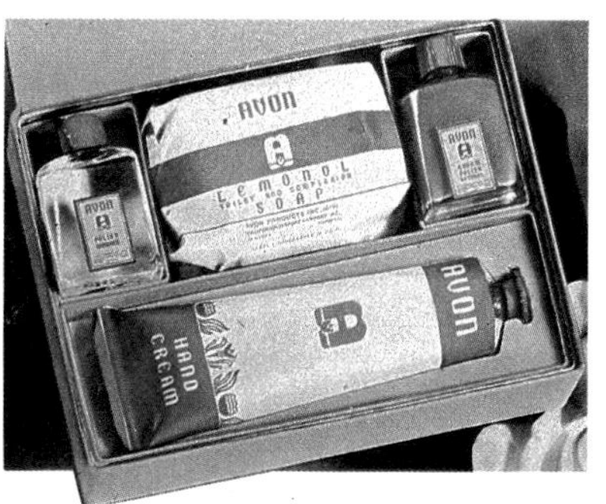

1938-39 *Beauty Kit for Fingers. Nail Polish, Polish Remover, Lemonol Soap, Hand Cream $1.35* **MP $90**

1939 *Bath Duet. Daphne Talc and Bath Salts in choice of Pine, Vernafleur, Ariel or Jasmine $1* **MP $60**

1939 *Facial Set for Dry or Oily Skin. Lotus Cream, Skin Freshener or Astringent, Tissue Cream, Cleansing Cream, Face Powder & Tissue $1.89* **MP $95**

1939 *Colonial Set. Gardenia Perfume 1 dram and Face Powder $1.30* **MP $95**

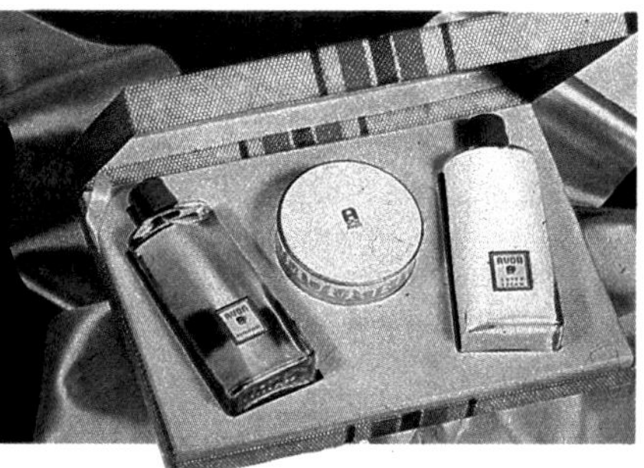

1939 *Wings to Beauty. Skin Freshener and Lotus Cream 2oz and Face Powder $1* **MP $65**

1934 *Vanity Book. Double Compact and Lipstick $2.27* **MP $65**

1931-32 *Vanity Book. Double Fan Compact and Lipstick $2.50* **MP $75**

1933-35 *Gift Set No. 21. Face Powder, Dressing Table Rouge and Lipstick $1.56* **MP $75**

1934-45 *Avon Threesome. Double Compact, Face Powder and Bolero Perfume Flaconette $3.57* **MP $150**

COSMETIC SETS OF THE 1930's . . .

1935 *Gift Set F. Double Compact, Ariel or Vernafleur Face Powder and Lipstick $2.80* **MP $90**

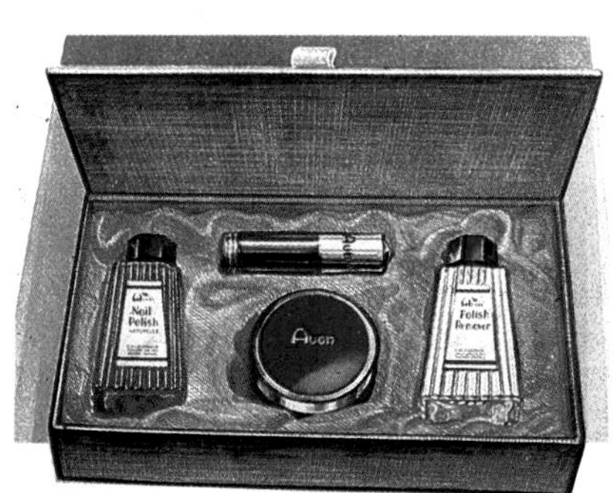

1935 *Gift Set W. Nail Polish, Polish Remover, Rouge Compact and Lipstick $1.67* **MP $100**

1935 *Gift Set B. Lipstick, Rouge Compact and Trailing Arbutus Perfume Flaconette $1.56* **MP $115**

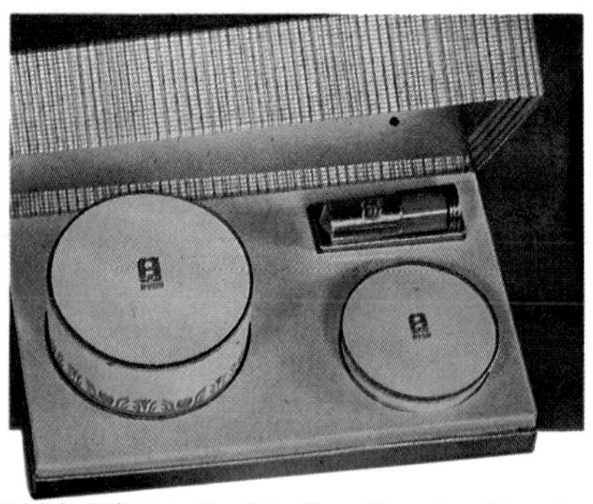

1936 *Gift Set No. 21. Face Powder, Dressing Table Rouge and Lipstick $1.56* **MP $50**

1936 *Powder-Compact Set (named Aristocrat in 1938) Face Powder and Double Compact $2.50* **MP $55**

1936 *Gift Set F (named Mastercraft in 1938) Double Compact, Face Powder and Lipstick $3.05* **MP $65**

. . . COSMETIC SETS OF THE 1930's

1936 *Gift Set K (named Empress in 1938) Lipstick, Double Compact and Gardenia Perfume $2.79* **MP $125**

1936 *Vanity Book (named The Sportwise in 1939) Double Compact and Lipstick $2.27* **MP $50**

1936 *Threesome Set (named Mayfair in 1939) Double Compact, Face Powder and Bolero Perfume Flaconette $3.57* **MP $140**

1936 *Gift Set B. Lipstick, Rouge Compact and Trailing Arbutus Perfume Flaconette $1.56* **MP $110**

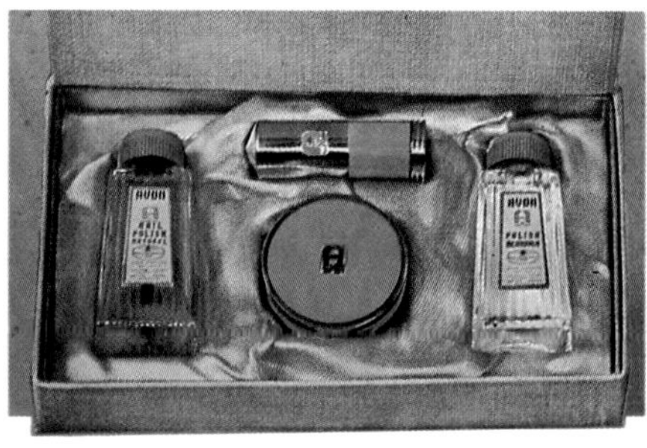

1936 *Gift Set W. (named Cosmopolitan in 1938) Nail Polish, Polish Remover, Rouge Compact and Lipstick $1.67* **MP $90**

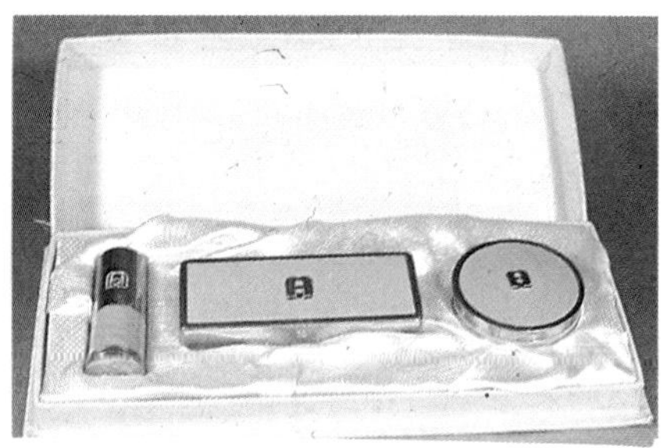

1938 *Charmer Set. Lipstick, Mascara and Rouge Compact $2.15* **MP $60**

1939 *Spectator Set. Rouge Compact, Trailing Arbutus Flaconette and Lipstick $1.56* **MP $110**

1939 *Orchid Set. Lipstick, Rouge Compact and Cream Polish $1.50* **MP $55**

1939-41 *Makeup Ensemble. Face Powder, Lipstick and Dressing Table Rouge $1.56* **MP $50**

1934 *Perfume Handkerchief Set. 4 Handkerchiefs, Ariel and Bolero Perfumes 1/8oz 89¢* **MP $125, $45 each bottle**

1933 *Vernafleur, Ariel and "391" Perfumes $1.40* **MP $165, $45 each bottle**

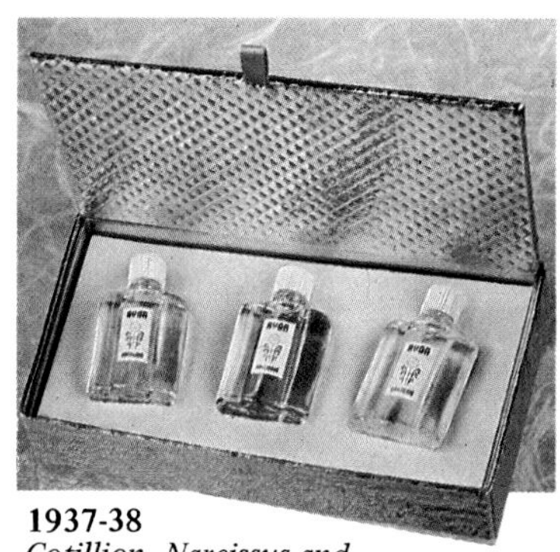

1937-38 *Cotillion, Narcissus and Gardenia Perfumes 1/8oz $1.25* **MP $100, $25 each bottle**

1936 *Perfume Handkerchief Set. 4 Handkerchiefs, Cotillion and Gardenia Perfumes 1/8oz $1* **MP $85, $20 each bottle**

1939-40 *Cotillion, Gardenia and Trailing Arbutus Perfumes $1.25* **MP $95, $25 ea. bottle (label change)**

1940-43 *Gardenia, Cotillion and Trailing Arbutus Perfumes $1.35* **MP $95 $25 each bottle**

1939 *Perfume Handkerchief Set. Four Handkerchiefs, Cotillion and Gardenia Perfumes 1/8oz $1* **MP $80, $20 ea. bottle**

PERFUME HANDKERCHIEF SETS

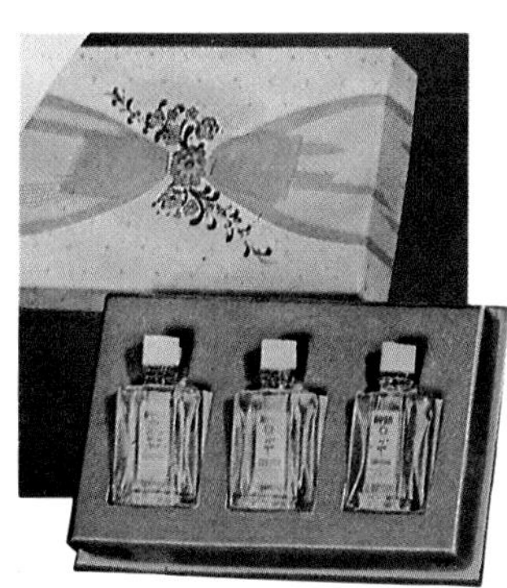

1944 *Gardenia, Cotillion and Trailing Arbutus Perfumes $1.50* **MP $90, $22 each bottle**

GOLD BOX SETS

1945 *Gardenia, Cotillion and Trailing Arbutus Perfume $1.50* **MP $90, $22 each bottle**

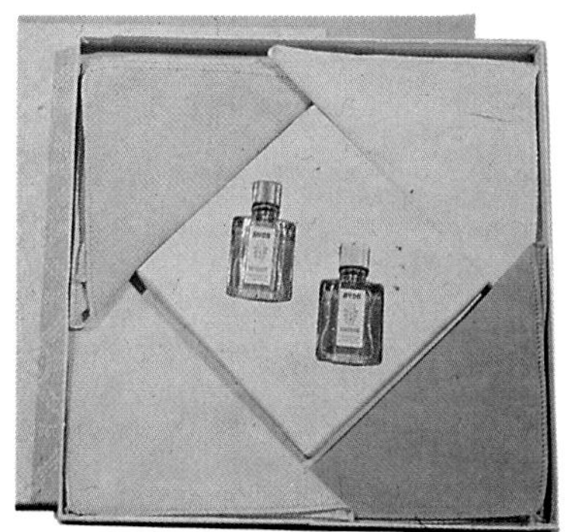

1940-42 *Perfume Handkerchief Set. 4 Handkerchiefs, Cotillion and Gardenia Perfumes 1/8oz $1* **MP $75, $18 each bottle**

1947 *Gold Box Set. Cotillion, Ballad and Garden of Love Perfumes 1 dram $2.50* **MP $85, $20 each bottle**

1949 *Gold Box Set. Cotillion, Flowertime and Golden Promise Perfumes 1 dram $2.25* **MP $85, $20 each bottle**

1940-42 *Facial Set for dry, normal or oily skin. Cleansing Cream 1¾oz, Night Cream 7/8oz, Foundation Cream 7/8oz or Finishing Lotion, Skin Freshener or Astringent 2oz, Face Powder, Facial Tissues and Folder $1.89* **MP $80**

1943-44 *Facial Sets. Same contents 1940-1942 Sets (see left) except for Wartime packaging of substitute lids. $1.98 each set.* **MP $100 w/Wartime packaging**

1940-43 *Bath Ensemble. Jasmine Bath Salts and 2 Bath Soaps, Dusting Powder and Jasmine Toilet Water $3.50* **MP $140**

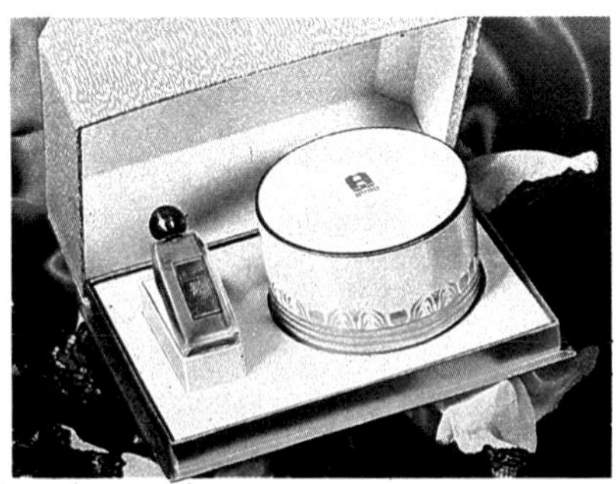

1940 *Colonial Set. Face Powder and 1 dram Garden of Love Perfume $1.25* **MP $65**

1940-42 *Fair Lady. Sweet Pea, Cotillion, Gardenia & Trailing Arbutus Perfume 1/8oz each 94¢* **MP $125, $25 each bottle**

1940-41 *Bath Duet. Daphne Talcum and Bath Salts in choice of Jasmine, Pine, Ariel or Vernafleur $1* **MP $55**

GIFT SETS OF THE 1940's

1940-42 *Mr. and Mrs. Smoker's Tooth Powder, After Shaving Lotion, Cotillion Toilet Water 2oz and Cotillion Talcum $2.50* **MP $125**

1941-42 *Fragrant Mist. Toilet Water in Marionette, Sonnet, Jasmine, Cotillion or Apple Blossom $1.50* **MP $60**

1941 *Wings to Beauty. Skin Freshener and Lotus Cream, 2oz each and Face Powder (also issued with cardboard Feather Face Powder) $1* **MP $55**

1942 *Flower Time. Apple Blossom Body Powder and Cologne 6oz $1.65* **MP $110**

1942-44 *Rainbow Wings. Cream Lotion and Rose Geranium Bath Oil 6oz each $2* **MP $75**

1942 *Colonial Days. Sonnet Body Powder 5oz and Cream Lotion 6oz $1.60* **MP $65**

1943 *Flower Time. Attention Body Powder 5oz and Attention Cologne 6oz $1.65* **MP $110**

1943 *Scentiments Set. 2 Pillow Sachets and Attention Toilet Water 2oz (Set did not include atomizer as shown $1.85* **MP $70**

1945 *Fair Lady. 4 Perfumes 1/8oz each $1* **MP $125, $25 each bottle**

1946 *Fair Lady. Lily of the Valley, Gardenia, Cotillion & Garden of Love Perfume 1/8oz $1.50* **MP $115, each bottle MP $22**

1948 *Fair Lady. 4 Perfumes 1/8oz each $1.50* **MP $115, $22 each bottle**

1943 *Petal of Beauty. Orchard Blossoms Cologne 6oz and Beauty Dust $2.20* **MP $110**

1943 only *Pink Ribbon Set. Attention Bath Salts 9oz and Attention Body Powder 5oz $1.61* **MP $75, each item MP $25**

1944-45 *Pink Ribbon Set. Attention Bath Salts 9oz and Attention Body Powder 5oz in wartime fold-out box $1.61* **MP $75, $25 each item**

1945 *Scentiments. Attention Cologne 6oz and 2 Sachet Pillows $2.50* **MP $125**

1945 *Flower Time. Attention Body Powder 5oz and Attention Cologne 6oz $1.65* **MP $105**

1945 *Rainbow Wings. Rose Geranium Bath Oil and Cream Lotion 6oz each $2* **MP $75**

1945 *Petal of Beauty. Apple Blossom Beauty Dust and Orchard Blossoms Cologne 6oz $2.20* **MP $125**

1944 *Little Jewels. Cotillion, Garden of Love & Attention Powder Sachet $3.25* **MP $80, $22 each Sachet**

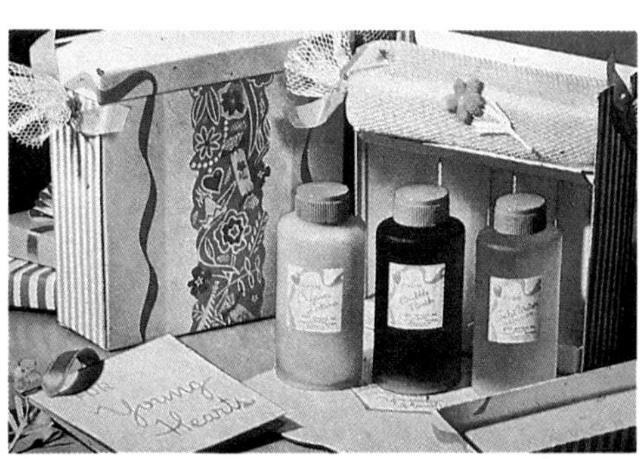

1945 *Young Hearts Set. Cream Lotion, Toilet Water and Bubble Bath, all 2oz, Cotillion Fragrance $3.75* **MP $80, $20 each bottle**

1949 *Perfumed Deodorant Set 98¢* **MP $22**

1940 *Mayfair Set. Double Compact, Face Powder and 1 dram Cotillion Perfume $3.35* **MP $95**

1940 *Spectator Set. Rouge Compact, Lipstick and Garden of Love Perfume, 1 dram $1.56* **MP $80**

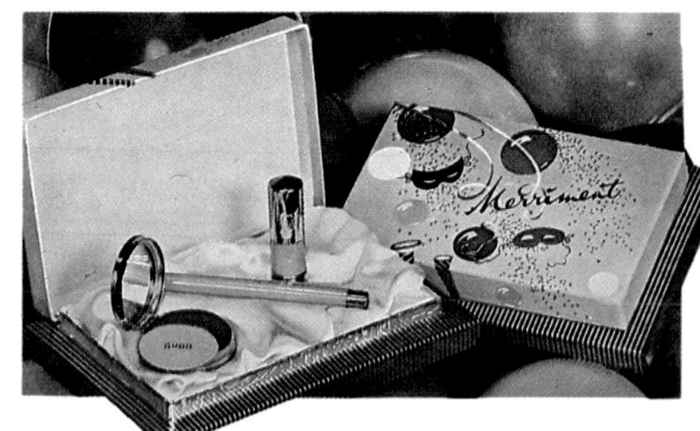

1940-41 *Merriment. Rouge Compact, Eyebrow Pencil and Lipstick $1.50* **MP $50**
1942 *(not shown) As above, except Lipstick Case is gold Bamboo $1.60* **MP $50**

COSMETIC SETS OF THE 1940'S

1941 *Colonial Set. Apple Blossom Perfume 1 dram and Face Powder $1.25* **MP $65**

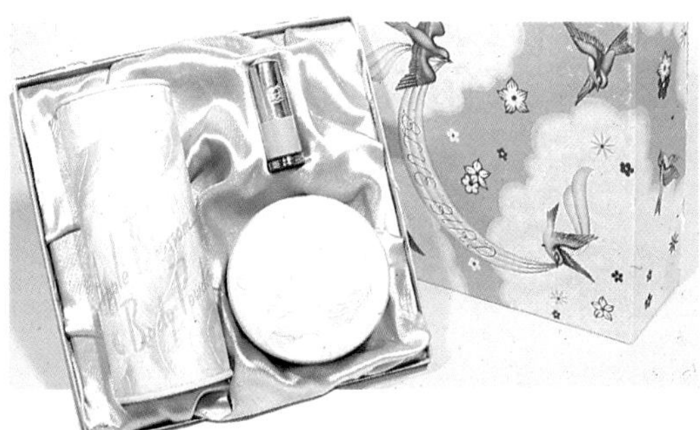
1941 *Blue Bird Set. Apple Blossom Body Powder, Face Powder and Lipstick $2.25* **MP $65**

1942 *Make-Up Ensemble. Face Powder, Rouge and Lipstick, plastic $1.75* **MP $50**

1942 *Minuet. Powder Compact, Rouge, Lipstick & Face Powder $2.95* **MP $65**

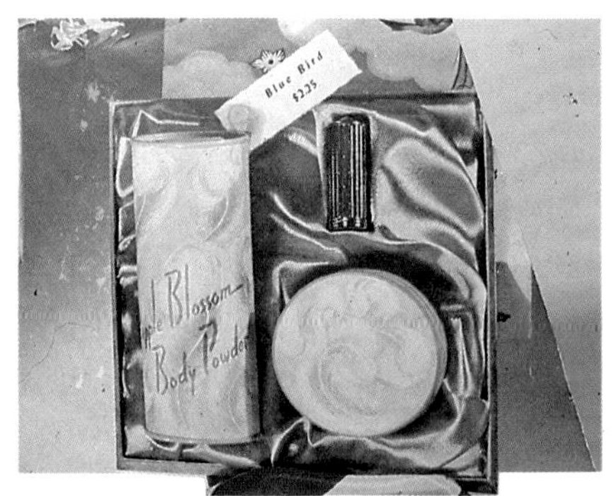

1942 *Blue Bird. Apple Blossom Body Powder, Face Powder and Lipstick $2.25* **MP $75**
1943 *(not shown) same as above, except Lipstick case is blue plastic.* **MP $80**

1941-42 *Reception Set. Face Powder, Compact and Cotillion Perfume 1 dram $2.95* **MP $75**

1942-43 *Peek-a-Boo Set. Lipstick, Rouge and Face Powder, all cardboard $2.50* **MP $65**

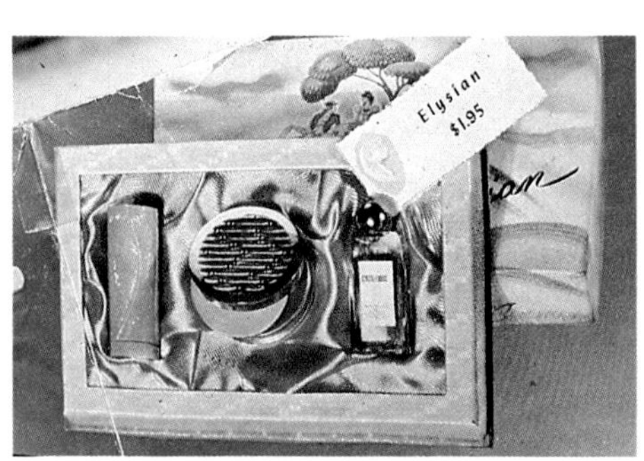

1942 *Elysian Set. Lipstick, Rouge Compact and Cotillion Perfume 1 dram $1.95* **MP $75**

1942 *Tandem Set. Lipstick and Single Compact $1.95* **MP $50**

1943 *Make-Up Ensemble. Face Powder, Rouge and Lipstick $1.75* **MP $50**

1944 *Peek-a-Boo Set. Lipstick, Rouge and Sachet Pillow $2.50* **MP $75**

1944 *Minuet Set. Rouge, Lipstick, Cotillion Perfume and Sachet Pillow $3.95* **MP $95**

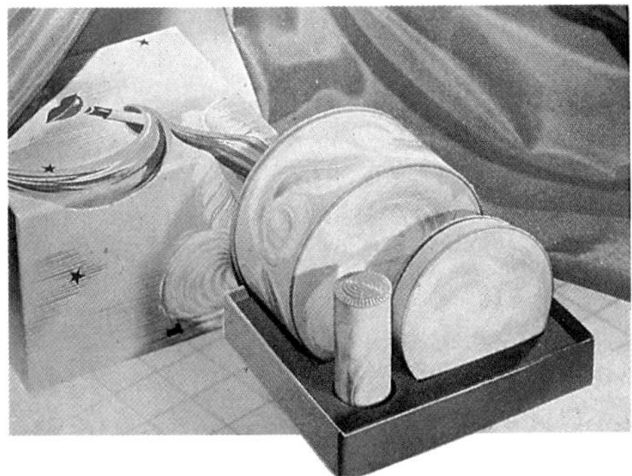

1945 *Make-Up Ensemble. Face Powder, Rouge and Lipstick $1.75* **MP $45**

1947 *Make-Up Ensemble. Face Powder, Rouge Compact and Lipstick $2.35* **MP $50**

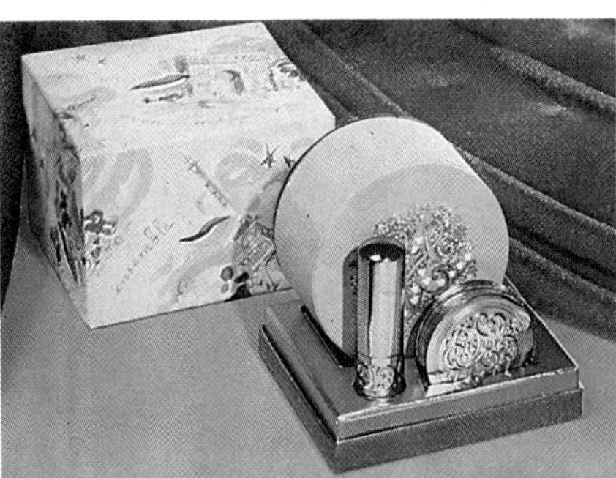

1949 *Make-Up Ensemble. Face Powder, Rouge and Lipstick $2.35* **MP $40**

1946 *Color Cluster. Lipstick, Rouge Compact and ½oz Nail Polish $2* **MP $45**

1947 *Color Cluster. Lipstick Rouge Compact and ½oz Nail Polish $2* **MP $45**

1948 *Color Cluster. Lipstick, Rouge Compact and ½oz Nail Polish $2* **MP $45**

1948 *Beauty Mark. Lipstick and ½oz Nail Polish $1.35* **MP $35**

1946 *Double Dare Set. Double Dare Nail Polish ½oz and Lipstick $2.95* **MP $50**

1947 *That's For Me. Cake Make-Up, Nail Polish and Lipstick $2* **MP $40**

1949 *That's For Me. Cake Make-Up, Nail Polish and Lipstick $2* **MP $35**

1949 *Flower Cluster. Face Powder, Lipstick & 1 dram Perfume $3* **MP $50**

1949 *Color Magic. Nail Polish and Lipstick $1.35* **MP $32**

1949 *Color Magic Threesome. Nail Polish, Lipstick and Purse Rouge $2.19* **MP $45, $55 boxed**

1950 *Color Magic. Nail Polish, Lipstick and Purse Rouge $2.15* **MP $40**

. . . COSMETS SETS OF THE 1940's

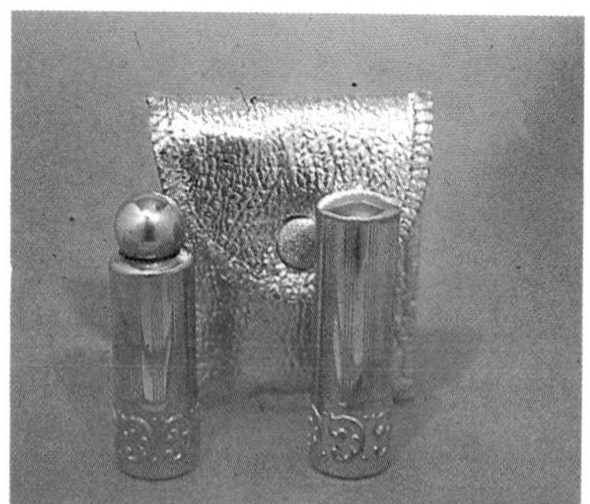

1949 *Golden Duet. Purse holds 1 dram Golden Promise Perfumette and Lipstick $2.50* **MP $50**

1949 *Beauty Muff Set. Muff holds 1 dram Quaintance Perfume and Lipstick $2.35* **MP $115**
1950 *Beauty Muff Set. Muff holds choice of 1 dram Perfume and Lipstick $2.39* **MP $100**

1949 *Gay Look. Taffeta Snap-Case holds Deluxe Lipstick and Compact $5* **MP $30**

1950 *Adorable Set. Powder Pak 7/8oz and Lipstick $2.15* **MP $50**

1951 *Adorable Set. Powder Pak 7/8oz, Lipstick and Sachet Packet $2.95* **MP $60, $65 boxed**

1950 *Gay Look. Taffeta Snap-Case holds Deluxe Lipstick and Compact $5.75* **MP $30**
1953 *Gay Look. Faille covered case holds Deluxe Lipstick and Compact $5.75* **MP $30**

COSMETIC SETS OF THE 1950's . . .

1950 *High Fashion. Black faille box holds 1 dram Perfume, Deluxe Compact and Lipstick, Compact Rouge $10* **MP $60**

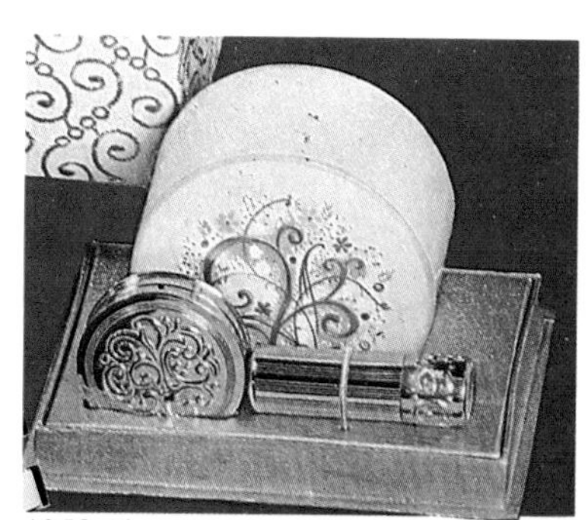

1952-53 *Make-Up Ensemble. Face Powder, Purse Rouge and Lipstick $2.75* **MP $35**

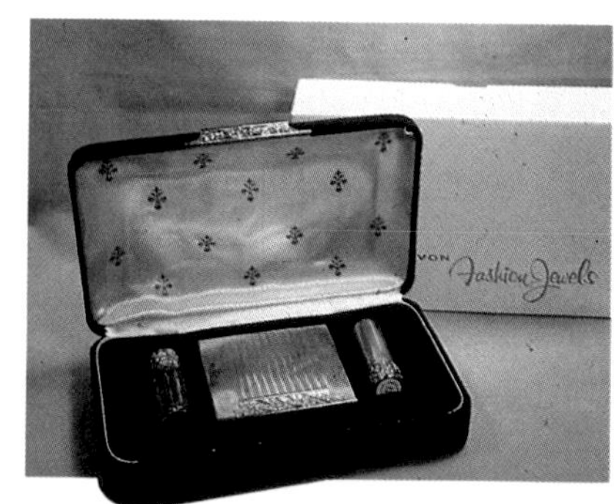

1954 *Fashion Jewels. Gold Compact, jeweled Lipstick and Perfume 1 dram $10.50* **MP $45, $50 boxed**

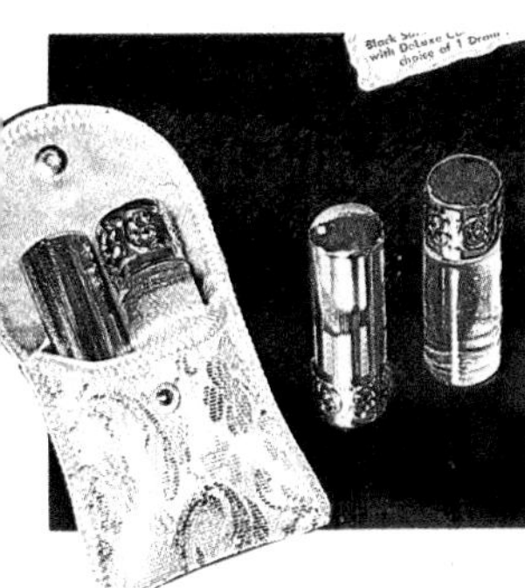

1950 *Avonette. Lipstick and 1 dram Perfume $2.50* **MP $50**

1950 *Lady Fair. Nail Polish and Lipstick $1.65* **MP $30**

1952 *Time For Beauty. Nail Polish and Lipstick $1.65* **MP $30**

1954 *Beauty Pair. Deluxe Lipstick and Nail Polish $1.50* **MP $25**

1956 *Top Style. Liquid Rouge, Nail Polish and Deluxe Lipstick $1.95* **MP $30**

COSMETIC SETS OF THE 1950's

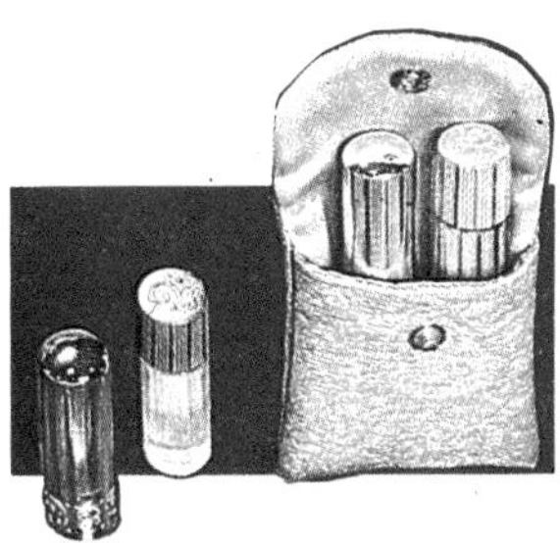

1952 *Avonette. Lipstick and 1 dram Perfume $2.65* **MP $45**

1953 *Avonette. Lipstick and 1 dram Perfume $2.65* **MP $45**

1953 *Holiday Fashion. 2 brass Lipsticks $1.10* **MP $30**
1954 *Charmer. Brocade Case holds jeweled Lipstick and 1 dram Perfume $3* **MP $38**

1953 *Gadabouts. Compact and Cologne Stick $2.25* **MP $28**

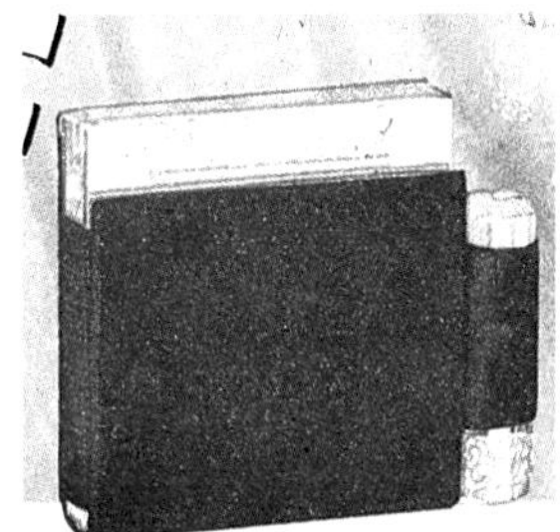

1955 *Gay Look. Faille Case holds Deluxe Lipstick and Compact $5.75* **MP $30**

1955 *Color Corsage. Face Powder and Lipstick $1.89* **MP $25**

1956 *Beauty Bound Powder Compact and jeweled Lipstick $2.50* **MP $22**

1954 *Gadabouts. Compact and Deluxe Lipstick $2.10* **MP $26**

1958 *Makeup Mates. Face Powder and Lipstick $1.98* **MP $20**

1958 *Touch of Paris. Powder Compact and Lipstick $2.10* **MP $20**

1958 *Classic Style. Deluxe Lipstick and Compact $5* **MP $25**

1959 *Pearl Favorites. Powder-Pak Compact and Lipstick $2.19* **MP $20**

1952 *Sunny Hours. White net umbrella holds 1 dram Perfume and gold Lipstick $2.50* **MP $40, $48 boxed**

1953-55 *Christmas Angels. Cream Sachet .66oz in choice of Forever Spring (shown), To A Wild Rose, Quaintance, Cotillion and Golden Promise and Deluxe Lipstick $2* **MP $32**

1950 *Doubly Yours. Cotillion and Flower Time Colognes 2oz each $2.10* **MP $75**

GIFT SETS OF THE 1950's . . .

1955 *Two Loves. 2 gold Lipsticks $1.10* **MP $35**

1956 *Two Loves. 2 Fashion Lipsticks $1.49* **MP $35**

1957 *Beauty Pair. 2 Fashion Lipsticks $1.49* **MP $35**

1958 *Fashion First. Two Fashion Lipsticks $1.69* **MP $25**

1951 *Fragrant Mist. Toilet Water 2oz and 1 dram Perfume in 4 fragrances $2.35* **MP $55**

. . . COSMETIC SETS OF THE 1950's

1954 *Lady Belle. Two 1 dram Perfumes in choice of Cotillion, To A Wild Rose, Golden Promise, Quaintance and Forever Spring $3* **MP $85**

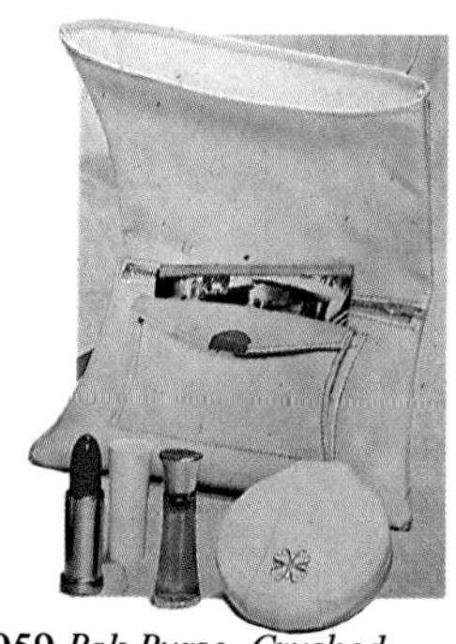

1959 *Pak-Purse. Crushed Leather purse holds Fashion Lipstick, 1 dram Top-Style Perfume and Powder-Pak Compact $8.95* **MP $40**

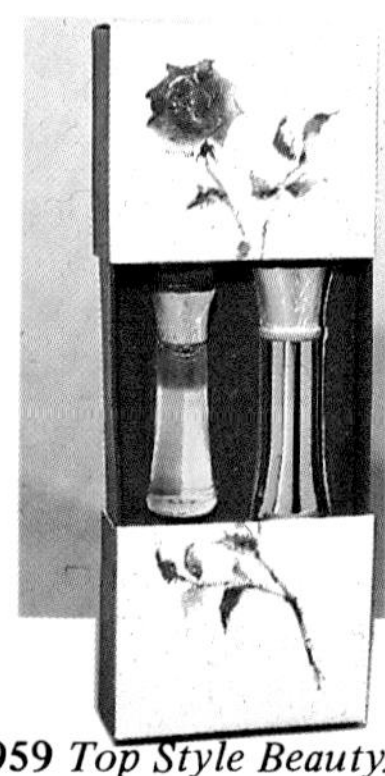

1959 *Top Style Beauty. Top Style Lipstick and 1 dram Perfume $2.95* **MP $28**

1950 *Avon Blossoms. Cotillion, Quaintance, Golden Promise & Luscious Perfumes 5/8oz ea. $2* **MP $100, $120 boxed, $18 each bottle**

1956 *LadyFair. Genuine Leather Wallet, choice of Long Life or Deluxe Lipstick and any 1 dram Perfume $5.95* **MP $55**

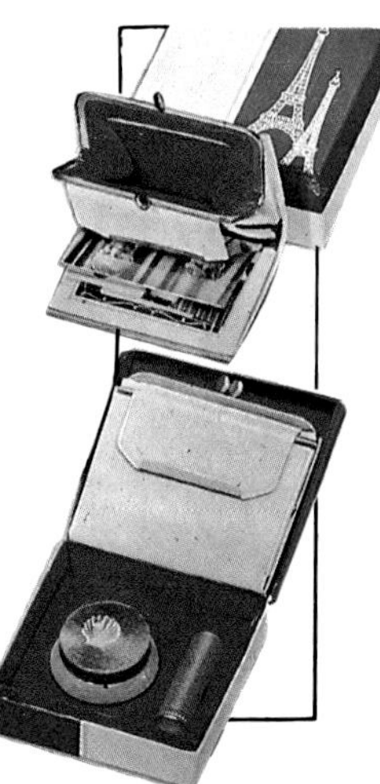

1957 *Avon Tri-Color. Top-grain cowhide French Purse, choice of Cream Sachet and Satin Sheen Lipstick. $7.75* **MP $55**

1959 *Two Lips. 2 Fashion Lipsticks $1.69* **MP $24**

1952 *Silver Wings. Body Powder and Cream Sachet in Forever Spring, To A Wild Rose, Quaintance or Golden Promise $2.10* **MP $45**

1951 *Sweet as Honey. Foam beehive holds Quaintance, Golden Promise, Luscious and Cotillion Perfumes $2.50* **MP $95, $120 boxed**

1952 *House of Charm. Lily of the Valley, Cotillion, Golden Promise and Quaintance 5/8oz each. $1.95* **MP $115, $18 each bottle**

1954 *House of Charm. Same fragrances as 1952 Set (left) 5/8oz each. $1.95* **MP $115, $18 each bottle**

1953 *Fragrance Tie-Ins. Four ½oz bottles of Fragrance: Forever Spring, Quaintance, Cotillion and To A Wild Rose $2.50* **MP $75**

1954 *Fragrance Rainbow. Four ½oz bottles of Fragrance: Cotillion, To A Wild Rose, Forever Spring, Quaintance $2.50* **MP $75**

1954 *Perfume Set. 1½oz & 1 dram $15* **MP $200 complete**

1955 *Cupid's Bow. Four ½oz bottles of Fragrance: Bright Night, Quaintance, Cotillion and To A Wild Rose $2.50* **MP $75**

1956 *Fragrance Rainbow. Four 3 dram bottles of Fragrance: Nearness, Bright Night, Cotillion and To A Wild Rose $2.75* **MP $75**

1957 *Gems in Crystal. Four ½oz bottles of Bright Night, Cotillion, To A Wild Rose and Nearness (Two different bottles used) $2.95* **MP $75 either set**

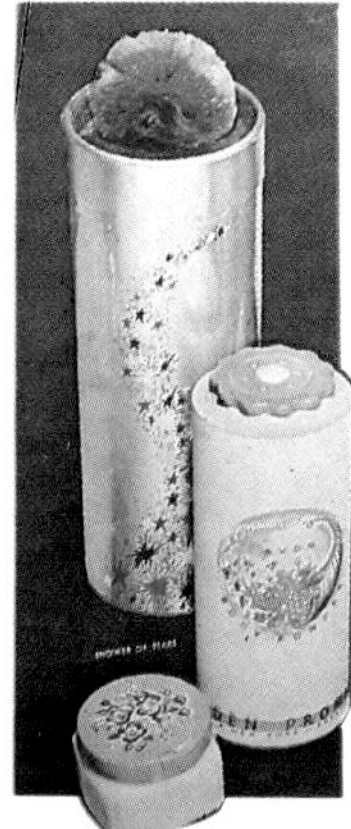

... GIFT SETS OF THE 1950's ...

1955 *Shower of Stars. Body Powder 4½oz and Cream Sachet .66oz in Golden Promise, Quaintance or Forever Spring $2.10* **MP $40**

1956 *Cream Sachet Petites. 4 individually colored plastic jars hold Cream Sachet in Cotillion (pink), Bright Night (white), Nearness (blue) and To A Wild Rose (rose). Each separately boxed and issued in gold Gift Box $3.25* **MP $60, $10 each boxed jar**

1957 *Somewhere Over the Rainbow. Four .3oz Cream Sachets in To A Wild Rose, Cotillion, Bright Night and Nearness $3.25* **MP $60 complete, $10 each jar**

1958 *Wishing Set. ½oz Cologne, Lotion Sachet and jar of Cream Sachet in choice of fragrances. Any combination of 3 $2.50* **MP $55 complete, $15 each item boxed**

1958 *Dramatic Moments Set. Essence de Fleurs Spray 1oz and Beauty Dust in 6 fragrances $5 to $5.50* **MP $45**

1959 *Paris Mood Set. Spray Essence 1oz, Beauty Dust 6oz and Cream Sachet. Choice of 6 fragrances $7.95* **MP $48**

1952 *Twin Pak. Two 4oz Hand Lotion $1.10* **MP $40**

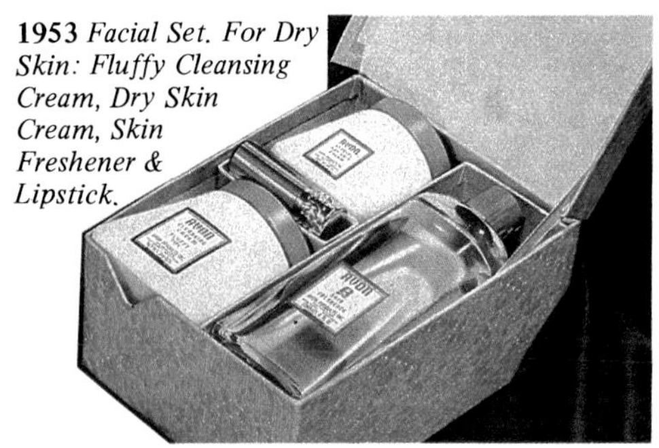

1953 *Facial Set. For Dry Skin: Fluffy Cleansing Cream, Dry Skin Cream, Skin Freshener & Lipstick.*

For Normal Skin: Fluffy Cleansing Cream, Skin Freshener, Super Rich or Ozonized Night Cream & Lipstick. . .
For Oily Skin: Cleansing Cream, Ozonized Night Cream, Astringent & Lipstick Each Set $3.39
MP $50 each Set

1954 *For Your Loveliness. Rich Moisture Cream 3½oz & choice of Skin Freshener or Hand Lotion 4oz $2.75* **MP $22**

1954 *Hand Beauty. Two 4oz Hand Lotion $1.10* **MP $20**

1955 *Hand Beauty. Two 4oz Hand Lotion $1.18* **MP $20**

1956 *Doubly Yours. Two 4oz Hand Lotion $1.19* **MP $20**

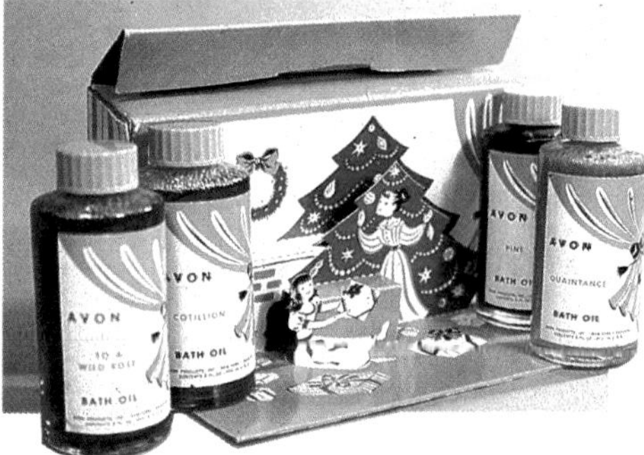

1956 *That's For Me. Four 2oz Bath Oils: To A Wild Rose, Cotillion, Pine and Quaintance $1.95* **MP $90, $18 each bottle**

BATH AND SKIN CARE SETS OF THE 1950's . . .

1953 *Hand Cream Duo. Two 2½oz Hand Cream $1.10* **MP $18 boxed**

1954 *For Beautiful Hands. 2 Hand Creams with Lanolin added 2½oz each $1.10* **MP $25 boxed**

1953 *Two Hand Cream 2½oz each in 67th Anniversary Box $1.10* **MP $25 boxed**

1953 *Hand Cream Duo. Two 2½oz Hand Cream $1.10* **MP $25 Xmas boxed**

1954 *Hand Cream Duo. Two 2½oz Hand Cream $1.10* **MP $25 Xmas boxed**

1955 *Doubly Yours. 2 tubes Hand Cream $1.18* **MP $25 Xmas boxed**

1956 *Hair Beauty. Two tubes Creme Shampoo $1* **MP $20 Xmas boxed**

1955 *Bath Delights. Bubble Bath 4oz and Body Powder 4½oz in Golden Promise, Quaintance, Forever Spring $2.10* **MP $40 Xmas boxed**

1954 *Happy Traveler. Rich Moisture Cream, Cleansing Cream, Hand Cream, Skin Freshener, Deodorant, Pack of Tissues and empty plastic jar $5.95* **MP $60 complete**

1956 *Women's Travel Kit. Zippered bag holds tube of Hand Cream and Cream Deodorant, Skin-So-Soft 4oz, Cleansing Cream and choice of one Night Cream $12.95* **MP $60 complete**

1957 *Modern Mood. Two Talc in a choice of 4 fragrances $1.29* **MP $18 Xmas boxed**

1955 *Foam 'N Spray. Creme Lotion Shampoo 6oz and Hair Spray $2.19* **MP $30 Xmas boxed**

1955-56 *Happy Traveler. Cleansing Cream, Hand Cream, Rich Moisture Cream, Skin Freshener, Deodorant and empty plastic jar $5.95* **MP $60 complete**

AVON TRAVEL KITS

1958 *Shower of Freshness. Two 2oz Perfumed Deodorant $1.38* **MP $20 Xmas boxed**
1957 *Bouquet of Freshness. Two 2oz Perfumed Deodorant $1.38* **MP $20 Xmas boxed**

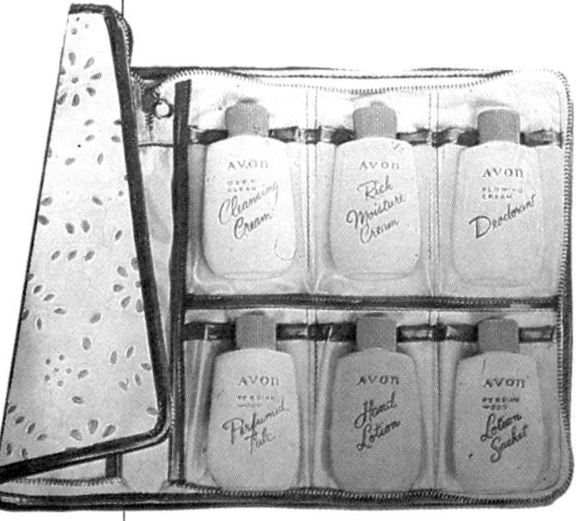

1958 *Safe Journey. Zippered bag holds Cleansing Cream, Rich Moisture Cream, Flowing Cream Deodorant, Persian Wood Talc, Lotion Sachet and Hand Lotion $6.95* **MP $70, $8 each bottle**

1957 *Beautiful Journey. Plastic zipper bag holds refillable containers of Cleansing Lotion, Rich Moisture Cream, Cotillion Cologne, Perfumed Deodorant, Hand Lotion and Skin Freshener $5.95* **MP $85, $15 Cotillion Cologne, $10 each container**

1956 *For Your Beauty. Deep Clean Cleansing Cream, Skin Freshener & Rich Moisture Cream $2.95* **MP $30**

1957 *A Thing of Beauty. Deep Clean Cleansing Cream, Rich Moisture Cream & Skin Freshener $3.50* **MP $25**

1958 *Beautiful You. Skin Freshener, Rich Moisture Cream & choice of Deep Clean Cleansing Cream or Rich Moisture Suds $3.50* **MP $25**

1959 *Gift of Beauty. Deep Clean Cleansing Cream & choice of Vita Moist or Rich Moisture Cream $3.50 & $3.95* **MP $20**

1959 *On The Wing. Skin Freshener and Cleansing Lotion 2oz each, Talc 2¾oz and choice of Rich Moisture or Vita Moist Cream 1½oz $6.25* **MP $45**

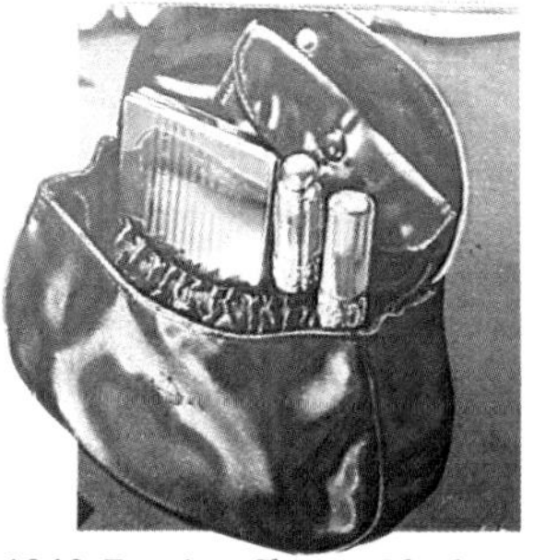

1949 *Evening Charm. Black Satin Evening Bag with Coin Purse, Deluxe Compact and Lipstick and 1 dram Perfume $10* **MP $65**

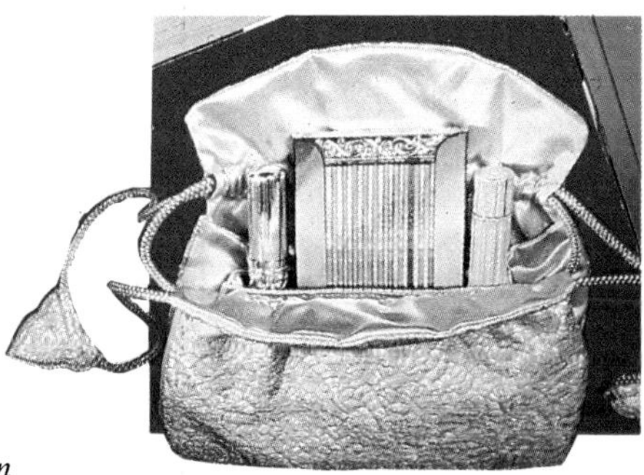

1952 *Evening Charm. Evening Bag contains Deluxe Compact, Lipstick and 1 dram Perfume $10.95* **MP $60**

1962 *Tote Along. Tapestry design bag with Cream Lotion 4oz, Cologne 4oz, Cream Sachet .66oz. Choice of 6 fragrances (Somewhere issued with two 2oz Colognes) $12.95* **MP $40**

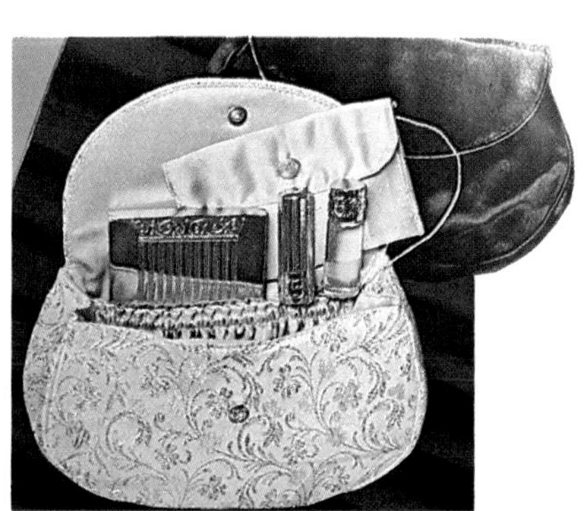

1950 *Evening Charm. Brocade Evening Bag with coin purse contains Deluxe Compact, Lipstick and 1 dram Perfume $10.95* **MP $60**

1950 *Evening Charm. Black Satin Evening Bag contains Deluxe Compact, Lipstick, 1 dram Perfume and Coin Purse $10.95* **MP $60**

1963 *Women's Travel Kit. Choice of Night Cream, Moisturized Hand Cream, Talc, Perfumed Deodorant and Skin-So-Soft 4oz $11.95* **MP $40**

1953 *Evening Charm. Brocade Evening Bag contains Deluxe Compact, Lipstick and 1 dram Perfume $10.95* **MP $50**

1953 *Evening Charm. Black Velvet Bag with Deluxe Compact and Lipstick and 1 dram Perfume $10.95* **MP $50**

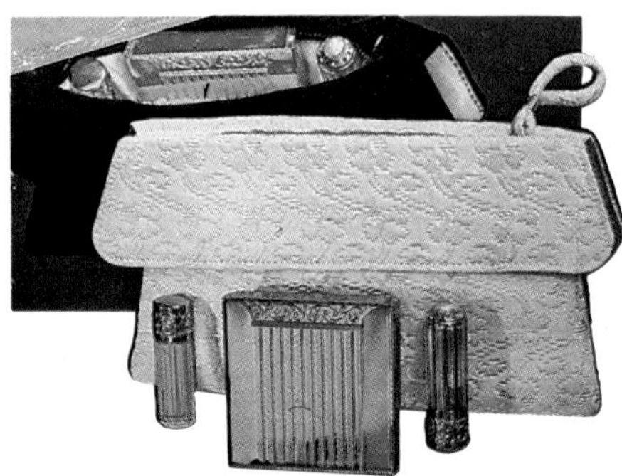

1954 *Evening Charm. Brocade Evening Bag (shown) or Black Velvet Bag contains Deluxe Compact, jeweled Lipstick and 1 dram Perfume $12.50* **MP $50**

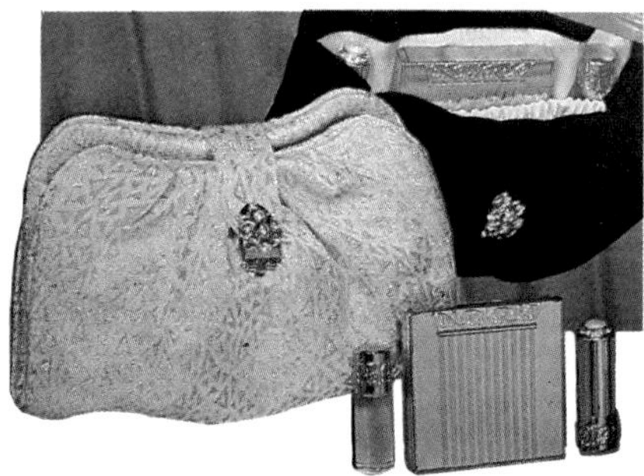

1955 *Evening Charm. Brocade or Black Satin Evening Bag contains Deluxe Compact, jeweled Lipstick and 1 dram Perfume $12.50* **MP $50**

1955 *Dress-Up. Black Faille bag contains Deluxe Compact, jeweled Lipstick and 1 dram Perfume $10.95* **MP $50**

1956 *Dress-Up. Reversible Bag contains Deluxe Compact, jeweled Lipstick and 1 dram Perfume $12.50* **MP $50**

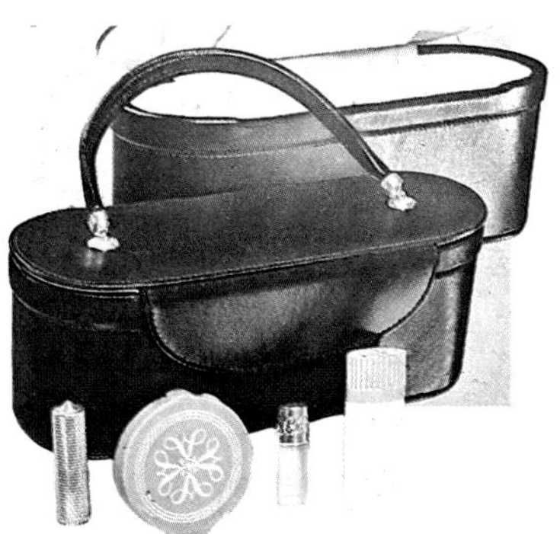

1956 *Around Town. Polished calf leather Bag contains Cologne Stick and 1 dram Perfume (choice of frag.) Long Life Lipstick and Powder-Pak Compact $12.50* **MP $50**

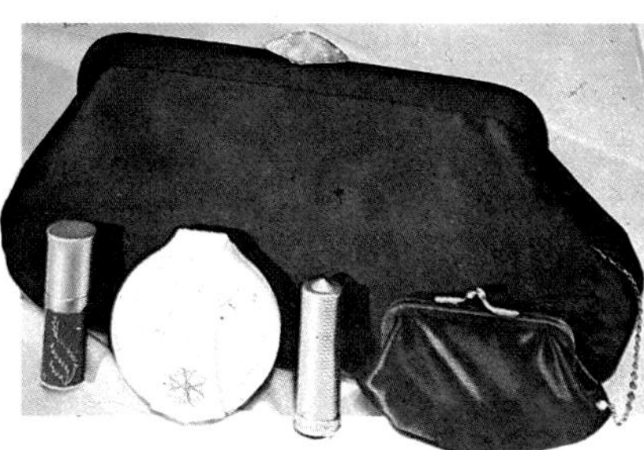

1957 *In Style. Brushed Satin Bag with attached coin purse contains Persian Wood Spray Perfume, Powder Pak Compact and Satin Sheen Lipstick $12.95* **MP $50**

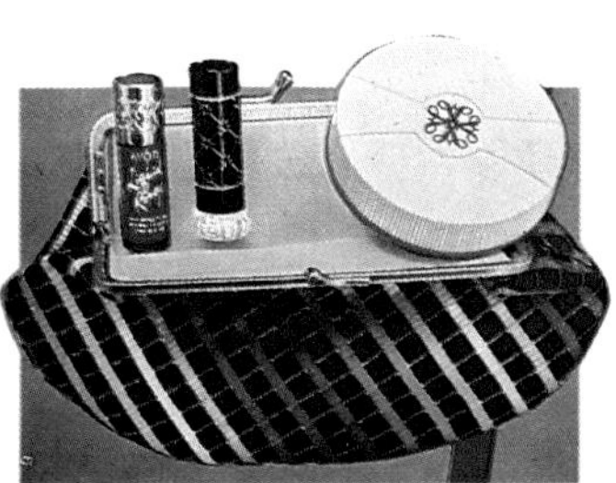

1957 *Make-Up Tuck-In. Cosmetic purse contains Liquid Rouge, Fashion Lipstick and Powder-Pak $3.50* **MP $35**

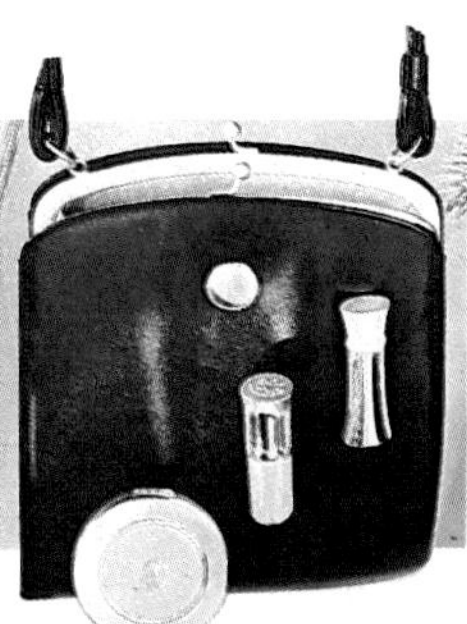

1958 *On The Avenue. Leather Bag contains Top Style Compact and Lipstick and Persian Wood Spray Perfume $12.95* **MP $50**

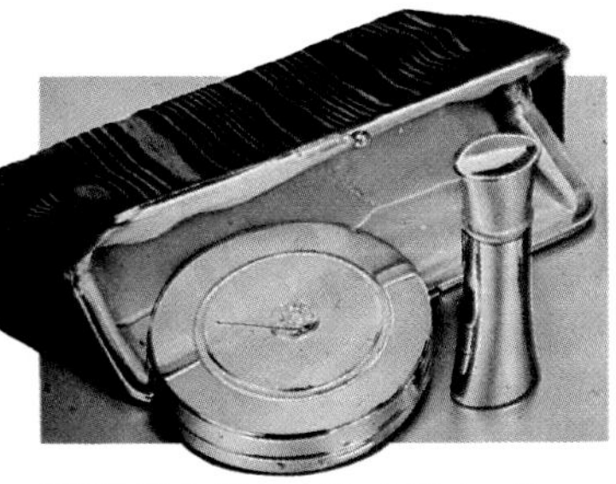

1960 *High Style. Black Moire Cosmetic Purse contains Top Style Compact and Lipstick $5.95* **MP $30**

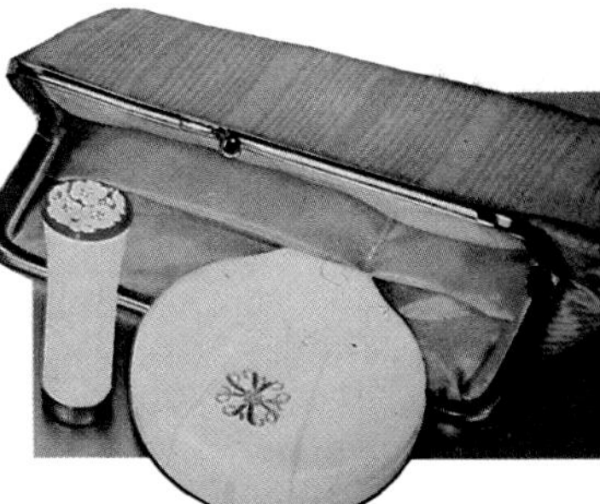

1960 *Going Steady. Grey Moire Cosmetic Purse contains Pearlescent Compact and Fashion Lipstick $3.50* **MP $25**

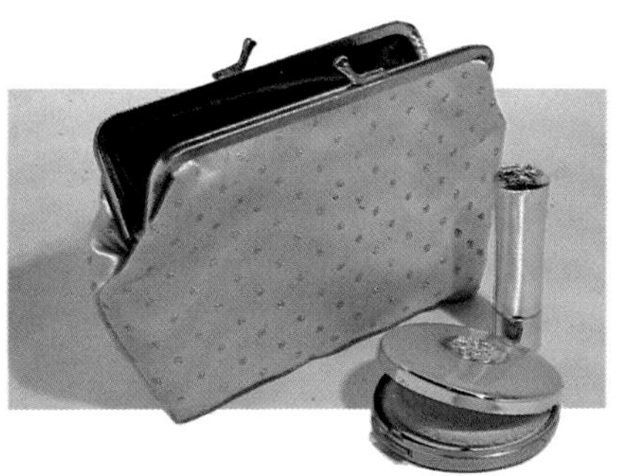

1961 *Champagne Mood. Satin Bag contains Compact Deluxe and Lipstick Deluxe $6.50* **MP $25**

1961 *Fashion First. Cosmetic Bag contains Pearlescent Compact and Fashion Lipstick $3.95* **MP $20**

1962 *Fashion First. Cosmetic Bag contains Fashion Compact and Lipstick $3.95* **MP $25, $28 boxed**

1963 *Modern Mood. Acetate Satin Cosmetic Bag with pockets to hold Compact Deluxe and Lipstick $7* **MP $23**

1963 *Modern Mood. Acetate Satin Cosmetic Bag with pockets to hold Pink Pearl Compact and Fashion Lipstick $4.50* **MP $20**

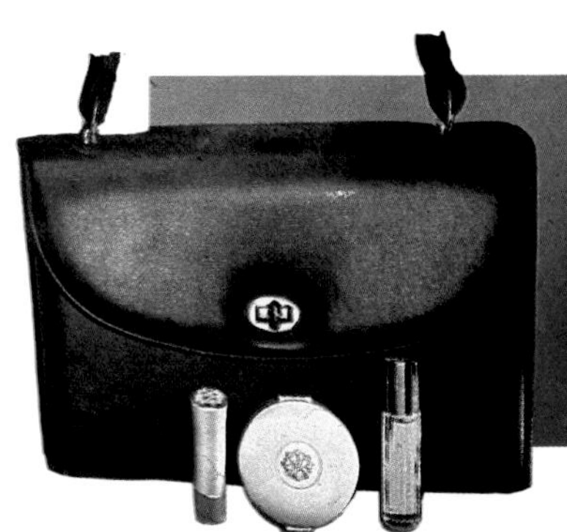

1964 *Beauty Bound. Simulated Calfskin Handbag contains Compact Deluxe, Lipstick Deluxe, Creme Rollette in choice of 9 frag. $14.95* **MP $45**

1964 *Purse Companions. Cameo Compact and Fashion Lipstick $6.50* **MP $25**

. . . EVENING BAG AND PURSE SETS

1965 *Purse Companions. Brocade Purse with Cameo Compact and Lipstick $6.50* **MP $25**

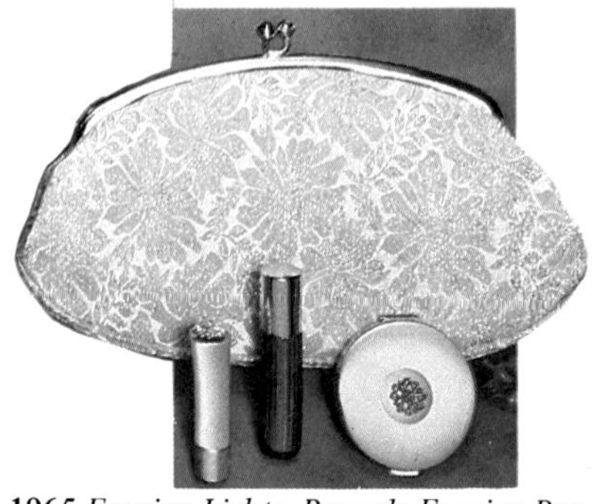

1965 *Evening Lights. Brocade Evening Bag contains Compact Deluxe, Lipstick Deluxe, Creme Rollette, choice of 9 frag. $14.95* **MP $30**

1978 *Evening Bag. Gold leather-like 10 x 6" $6.50 with $15 purchase* **MP retail value $15**

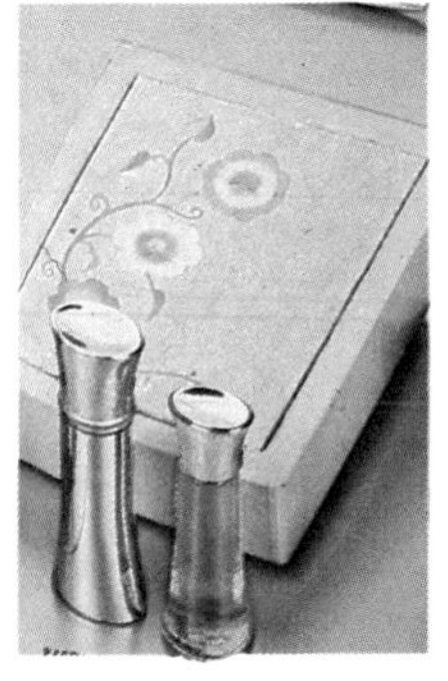

1960 *Party Fun. Top Style Lipstick and 1 dram Perfume $3.75* **MP $25**

1960 *Classic Harmony. Lipstick, Compact and 1 dram Perfume, all Top Style $6.95* **MP $35**

1962 *Color Trick. Two Fashion Lipsticks $1.96* **MP $25**

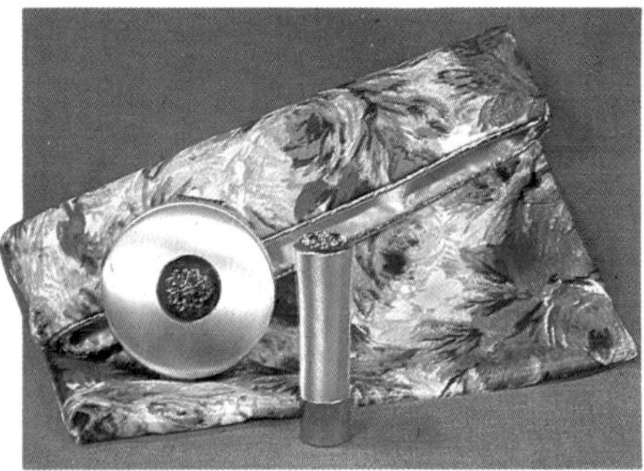

1962 *Deluxe Twin Set. Taffeta Clutch Bag, Compact Deluxe and Lipstick Deluxe $7.50* **MP $20, $7 bag only**

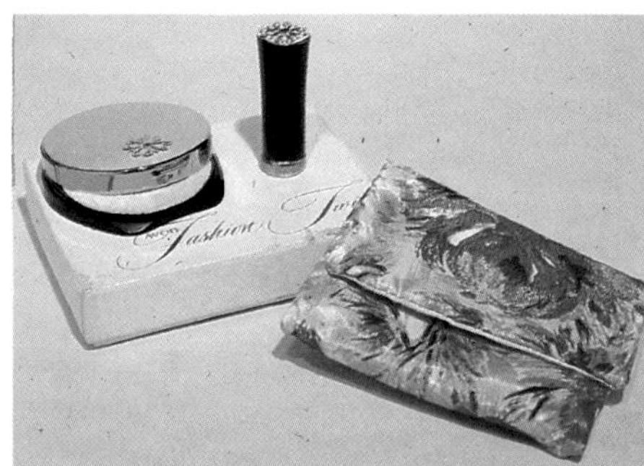

1962 *Fashion Twin Set. Fashion Compact and Lipstick $3.50* **MP $30, $7 bag only**

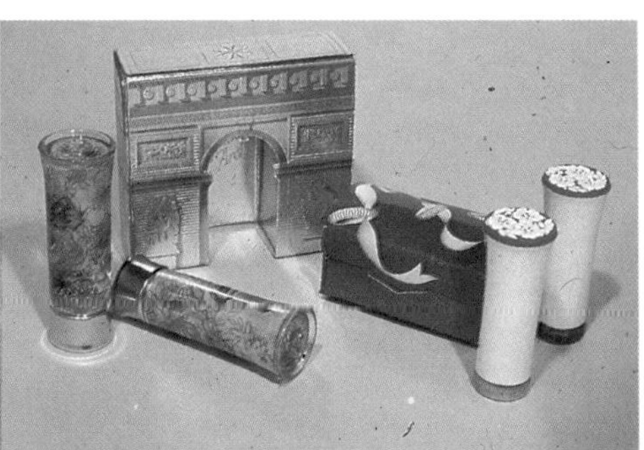

1964 *Golden Arch. 2 floral Fashion Lipsticks $1.96* **MP $26**
1960 *Golden Rings. 2 Fashion Lipsticks $1.79* **MP $26**

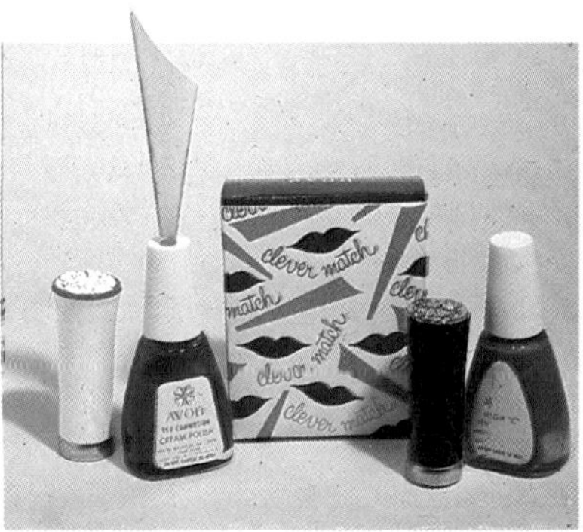

1961 *Clever Match (left) Lipstick and Cream or Pearl Nail Polish $1.67 & $1.83* **MP $18 boxed**
1962 *Clever Match (right) Lipstick and Cream or Pearl Nail Polish $1.67 & $1.83* **MP $18 boxed**

1963 *Color Note. Fashion Lipstick and Cream or Silver Notes Nail Polish $1.67 and $1.83* **MP $18**

1963 *Fashion Star. 2 Fashion Lipsticks $1.69* **MP $25**

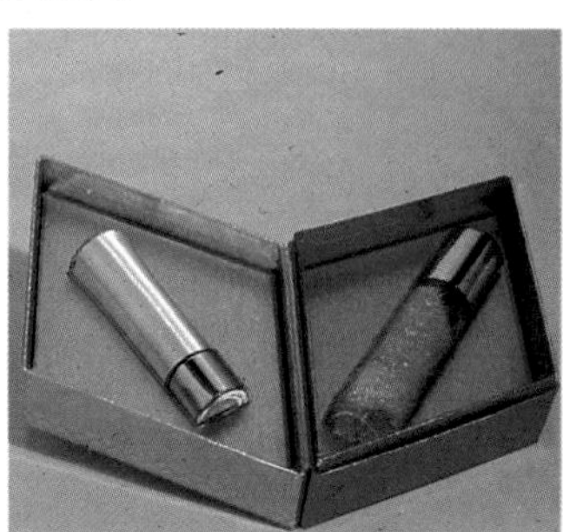

1963 *Touch-Up Twins. Lipstick Deluxe and Creme Rollette in a choice of Here's My Heart, Persian Wood, To A Wild Rose $3.10. Somewhere, Topaze, Cotillion $3.35 Occur! $3.85* **MP $23**

1965 *Cameo Set. Compact, Lipstick and Brooch $6.50* **MP $45, Brooch MP $18**

1964 *Pair Tree. Nail Polish and Fashion Lipstick $1.83* **MP $18**
1965 *Fashion Twins. 2 Cameo Lipsticks $1.65* **MP $22**

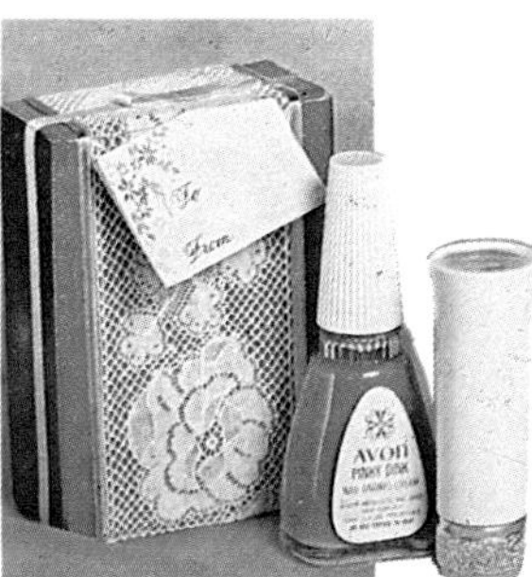

1965 *Color Compliments. Cameo Lipstick and Pearl or Satin Nail Polish $1.80 with Cream Nail Polish $1.65* **MP $18**

1965 *Touch-Up Twins. Cameo Lipstick and Rollette in choice of Here's My Heart, Persian Wood, Wishing, To A Wild Rose $2.70. Somewhere, Topaze, Cotillion $2.95. Occur!, Rapture $3.45* **MP $15**

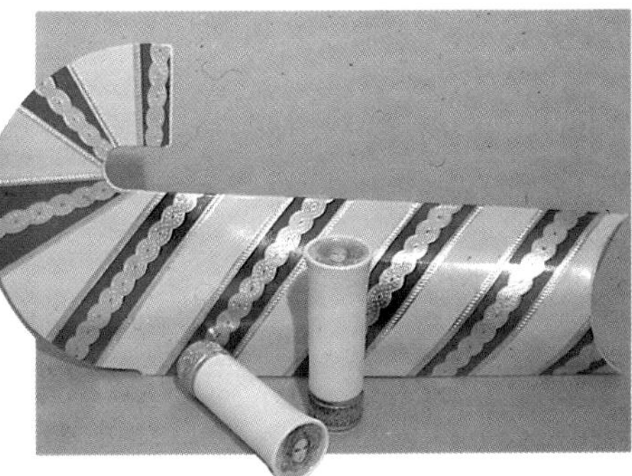

1966 *Candy Cane Twins. 2 Fashion Cameo Lipsticks $1.96* **MP $23**

1965 *Pretty Notions. Vinyl Case holds Fashion Award Compact, Cameo Lipstick $4.50* **MP $25**

1965 *Star Attractions. Lipstick Deluxe and Cologne ½oz in 9 frag. $2.50* **MP $18**

. . . COSMETIC SETS OF THE 1960's

1966 *Sleigh Mates. Cameo Lipstick and Satin Nail Enamel $1.83, with Pearl Nail Enamel $1.93* **MP $20**

1966 *Avon Blushmates. Telescopic make-up brush, Avon Blush or Sparkling Blush $5.50 and $6* **MP $16**

1966 *Golden Vanity holds 5" Mirror, Lipstick and Rollette $10* **MP $33 complete, $18 holder only, $5 mirror only**
1964 *Vanity Showcase, 3" h. Lipstick Deluxe and 1 dram Perfume $5* **MP $25, $10 holder only**

1967 *Merry Fingertips. 2 Nail Enamels in velvetized Gift boxes $1.70* **MP $10**
1967 *Merry Liptints. 2 Encore Lipsticks in velvetized Gift boxes $2.20* **MP $10 boxed and with sleeve**

1968 *Vanity Tray. Fashion Lipstick and Perfumed Rollette .33oz $6* **MP $18 complete, tray only MP $8**

1968 *Golden Heirloom Jewel Box. Deluxe Lipstick and Rollette $15* **MP $40, $30 box only**

1960 *Modern Simplicity. Bath Oil 4oz, Beauty Dust 3oz and Soap in Cotillion, To A Wild Rose or Here's My Heart $3.98* **MP $45**

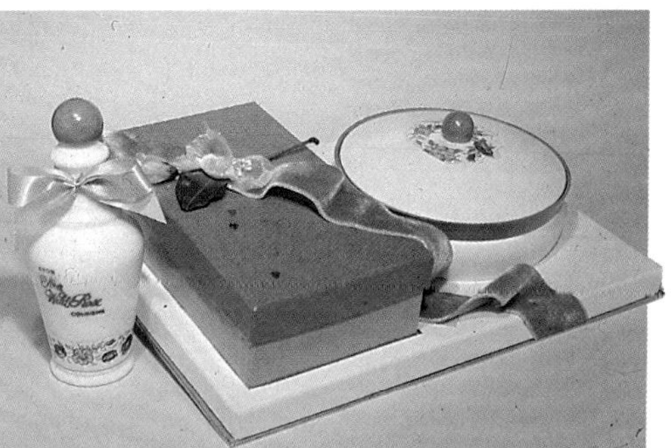

1960 *A Lady's Choice. Beauty Dust and Splash Cologne 4oz in To A Wild Rose (shown), Here's My Heart, Cotillion and Persian Wood $5.45* **MP $42**

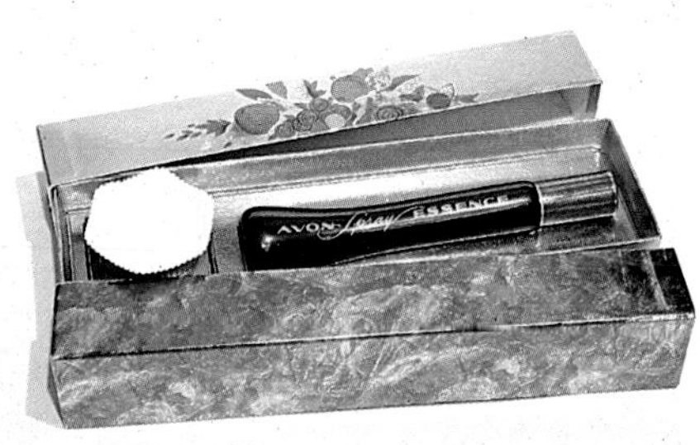

1960 *Beguiling. Cream Sachet and Spray Essence in Bright Night, Nearness, To A Wild Rose, Cotillion $4.50 Here's My Heart and Persian Wood $5* **MP $25**

1962 *Refreshing Hours. Talc 2¾oz and Cologne 2½oz in To A Wild Rose $2.25, Here's My Heart and Persian Wood $2.50, Somewhere, Topaze and Cotillion $2.75* **MP $30**

1962 *Bath Bouquet. Bath Oil 6oz and Soap 3oz in 10 fragrances $2.79 & $2.98* **MP $20, bottle only MP $10**

1963 *Floral Enchantment. Cologne Mist 2oz and Cream Sachet .66oz in 7 frag. $4 to $5.50* **MP $18**

1962 *Bath Classic. Cologne 1½oz and Bath Powder 5oz in 6 frag. $4.50 to $5* **MP $36**

GIFTS SETS OF THE 1960's . . .

1963 *Flower Fantasy. Cream Sachet .66oz and Creme Rollette .33oz in Here's My Heart, Persian Wood, To A Wild Rose $3.50 and Cotillion, Somewhere, Topaze $4 and Occur! (shown) $5* **MP $18**

1964 *Fragrance Fortune. Cologne 2oz and Perfume Oil ½oz To A Wild Rose, Persian Wood, Here's My Heart $5.50 and Topaze (shown) Cotillion, Somewhere $6.25* **MP $27**

1964 *Bath Bouquet. Bath Oil 6oz and Soap 3oz in 6 fragrances $2.64 & $2.89* **MP $18**

1962 *Fragrance Gems. Cream Lotion 4oz and Cream Sachet .66oz in 6 frag. $2.60 to $3.50* **MP $16**

1964 *Fragrance Gold. Three ½oz Colognes in 9 frag. $3.50* **MP $25 with sleeve, each bottle $5, $6 boxed**

1965 *Fragrance Gold Duet. Two ½oz Colognes in a choice of 9 frag. $2.30* **MP $18 with sleeve, each bottle $5, $6 boxed**

1965 *Fragrance Favorites. Three ½oz Colognes in 10 frag. $3.50* **MP $23 with sleeve**

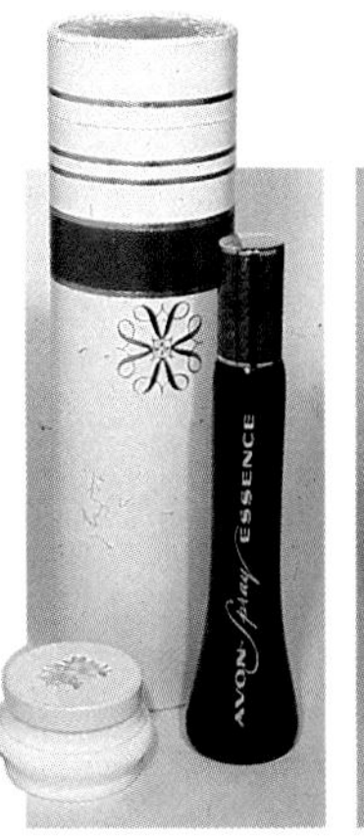

1964 *Decoration Set. Spray Essence 1oz and Cream Sachet .66oz in Here's My Heart, Persian Wood, To A Wild Rose $5.50; Topaze, Cotillion Somewhere, $6* **MP $20**

1964 *Flower Bath Set. Talc 3½oz and two 3oz Soaps in Lily of the Valley, Lilac, Jasmine or Rose Geranium $1.67* **MP $20**

1963 *Bath Bouquet. Perfumed Bath Oil 8oz & 3oz Soap Lilac or Lily of the Valley $2.39* **MP $18**

1965 *Bath Sparklers. Powdered Bubble Bath, set of 3 frag. 5oz each in tubes $2.50* **MP $30, $7 each tube**

1964 *Beauty Scents. Skin Softener 5oz and Creme Rollette in 6 frag. $4.75 to $5.25* **MP $15**

1965 *Floral Talc Trio: Lily of the Valley, Lilac and Jasmine 3½oz each $2.65* **MP $18**

Xmas 1965 *Double Paks –*
2 Moisturized Hand Cream 3¾oz each, $1.75 **MP $12**
2 Avon Hand Cream 3oz each, $1.35 **MP $12**
2 Hand Lotion 4oz each, $1.55 **MP $12**
2 Silicone Glove 2¼oz each, $1.55 **MP $12**

1965 *Bath Bouquet. Cologne ½oz Bath Oil 2oz and Talc 1½oz in Here's My Heart, To A Wild Rose, Wishing $4; Somewhere, Cotillion, Topaze $4.25; Rapture & Occur! $4.50* **MP $38**

1964 *Jewel Collection. Six 5/8 dram flacons of Perfume Oil: Somewhere, Topaze, Cotillion, Persian Wood, Here's My Heart and To A Wild Rose $5.95*
MP $62, $8 each bottle

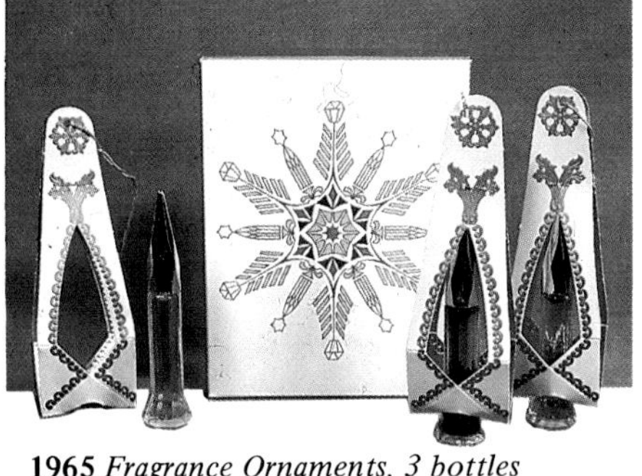

1965 *Fragrance Ornaments. 3 bottles Perfume Oil 5/8 dram: Set A, Wishing, Somewhere & Occur!; Set B, Rapture, To A Wild Rose & Topaze; Set C, Unforgettable, Here's My Heart & Cotillion $4.50 set*
MP $60 boxed set of 3, $15 each bottle in cut-out tree ornament, $11 each bottle only

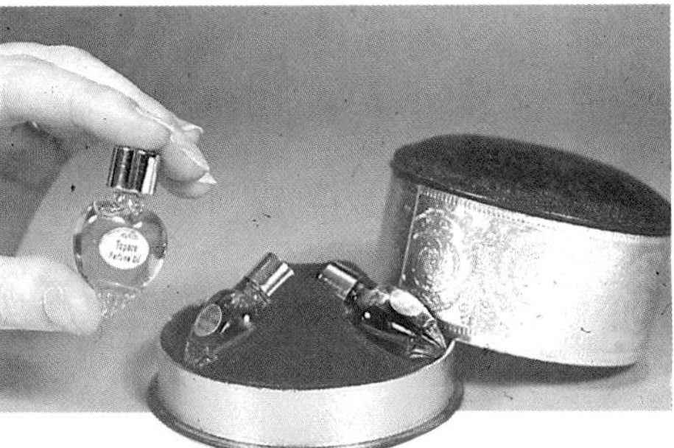

1966 *Perfume Oil Petites. Three 5/8 dram bottles in Set A, B and C (same frag. as those in 1965 Fragrance Ornaments) $4.50*
MP $55 in re-usable pin-cushion box. MP $13 each bottle

1966 *Colognes ½oz (sold individually) in 10 frag. $1.25* **MP $5, $6 boxed**
1966 *Fragrance Vanity Tray (glass) $1.25* **MP $9, $15 boxed**

1966 *Renaissance Trio. ½oz Colognes in a choice of 9 frag. $1.75 each or 3/$3.50*
MP $5 each, $19 boxed set of 3 in sleeve

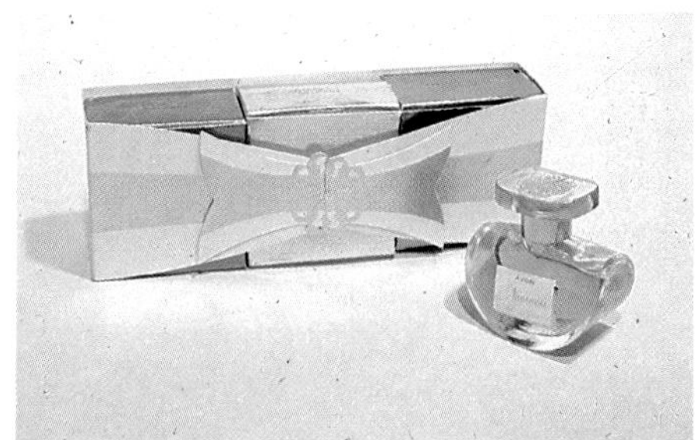

1960 *Gift Magic Set. 3½oz Colognes in choice of Topaze, Persian Wood, Here's My Heart, To A Wild Rose, Cotillion, Nearness & Bright Night, each in a different colored foil box. $2.98* **MP each $8 boxed, $30 boxed set of 3 in sleeve**

1966 *Fragrance Duette. Cologne 2oz and Rollette in Rapture, Unforgettable and Occur! $5* **MP $16**

. . . SETS OF THE 1960's

1966 *Fragrance Chimes. Talc 2¾oz and Cream Sachet in Here's My Heart, Wishing and To A Wild Rose $2.54; Somewhere, Topaze, Cotillion $2.89; Unforgettable, Rapture and Occur! $3.50* **MP $13**

1967 *Floral Medley. Cream Sachet & Talc Honeysuckle (shown), Jasmine, Lily of the Valley $3.48* **MP $13**

1967 *Keepsakes. Cologne Mist 3oz and Rollette in Occur!, Rapture and Unforgettable $8.50* **MP $15**

1967 *Cologne Gems in 8 frag. Choice of 2, 1oz each. $3.50* **MP $15 complete, $5 each bottle, $6 each boxed**

1967 *Two Loves. Cream Sachet and Rollette in 8 frag. (Rapture shown) $3.50 $4 & $5* **MP $14**

1968 *Fragrance Fling Trio. Cologne in 3 frag. ½oz $4* **MP $14 with sleeve, $3 each bottle, $3.50 boxed**

1968 *Scentiments Set. Cream Sachet & Rollette Somewhere, Topaze, Cotillion $4; Rapture, Unforgettable, Occur! $5; Brocade & Regence $6* **MP $14**

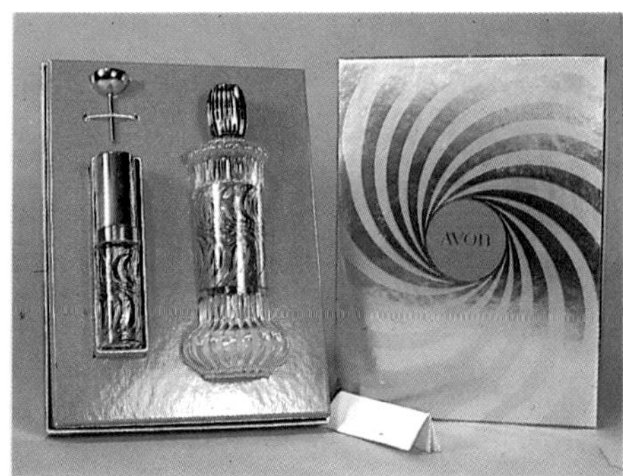

1968 *Splash 'N' Spray Set. Cologne in 5 frag. 2½oz Purse Spray bottle and funnel $6.50 to $7* **MP $32, $6 funnel only**

1969 *Pyramid of Fragrance. Cream Sachet .66oz, Cologne 2oz and Perfume 1/8oz in 3 frag. $12.50* **MP $25 boxed, $9 Perfume, $6 Sachet and Cologne**

1969 *Scentiments. Cream Sachet ½oz and Soap 3oz in Occur!, Rapture, Topaze, Unforgettable, Somewhere and Cotillion $3.50* **MP $13**

1969 *Two Loves Set. Rollette .33oz and Cream Sachet .66oz in Brocade (shown), Charisma and Regence $6* **MP $13**

1969 *Lights and Shadows. Lights Cologne in clear bottle, Shadows Cologne in shadowed bottle, each 2oz. Set $4* **MP $6**

1962 *To A Wild Rose $1.08; Here's My Heart, Persian Wood $1.18; Somewhere, Topaze, Cotillion $1.28* **MP $20**

1963 *Persian Wood, Here's My Heart, To A Wild Rose $1.18; Somewhere, Topaze, Cotillion $1.28* **MP $18**

1964 *Here's My Heart, Persian Wood, To A Wild Rose $1.18; Somewhere, Topaze, Cotillion $1.28* **MP $16**

1964 *Wishing* **MP $20** *(left)*
1966 *Here's My Heart, To A Wild Rose, Wishing $1.28; Cotillion, Somewhere, Topaze $1.38; Unforgettable, Rapture, Occur! $1.49* **MP $14**

1967 *(left) Here's My Heart, To A Wild Rose $1.39; Somewhere, Topaze, Cotillion $1.49; Unforgettable, Rapture, Occur! $1.59* **MP $12**
1968 *(right) Honeysuckle, Hawaiian White Ginger, Unforgettable, To A Wild Rose $1.79; Brocade, Regence $1.98* **MP $10**

PERFUMED PAIRS

Each set contains one Talc 2¾oz and one matched Soap 3oz

(See 1974 Perfumed Pair pg. 104)

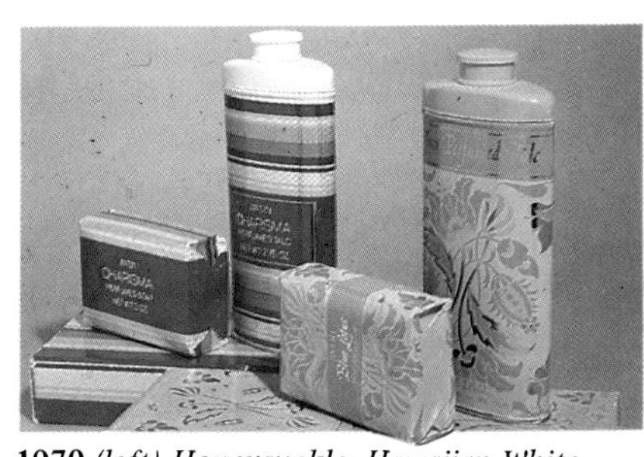

1970 *(left) Honeysuckle, Hawaiian White Ginger, Elusive, Blue Lotus, Bird of Paradise, Charisma $2.25* **MP $8**
1969 *(right) Honeysuckle, Hawaiian White Ginger, Blue Lotus, To A Wild Rose $2; Brocade, Charisma $2.25* **MP $10**

1969 *Fluff Puff and two Beauty Dust 3½oz each in Regence, To A Wild Rose, Cotillion and Unforgettable $5.50* **MP $22**
1967 *Fluff Puff, long-handled (not shown) and one 3½oz Talc. Carton design and fragrances same as above. White with pink puff only.* **MP $20**

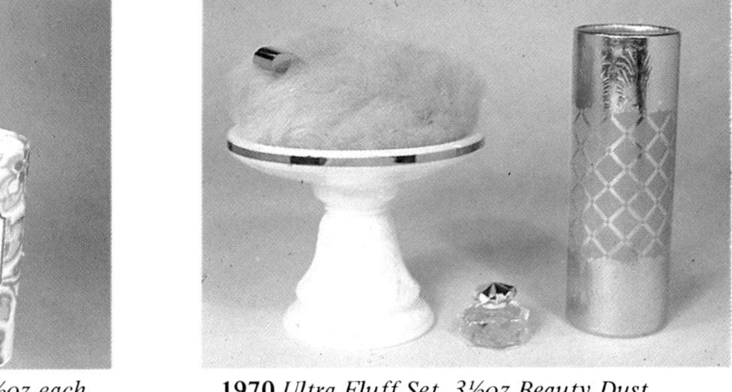

1970 *Ultra Fluff Set. 3½oz Beauty Dust, Lamb's Wool Puff and 1/8oz Perfume in Charisma, Brocade and Regence $10* **MP $16**

1969 *Fluff Puff and Talc 3½oz Occur! (shown), Unforgettable and Rapture $6* **MP $13**

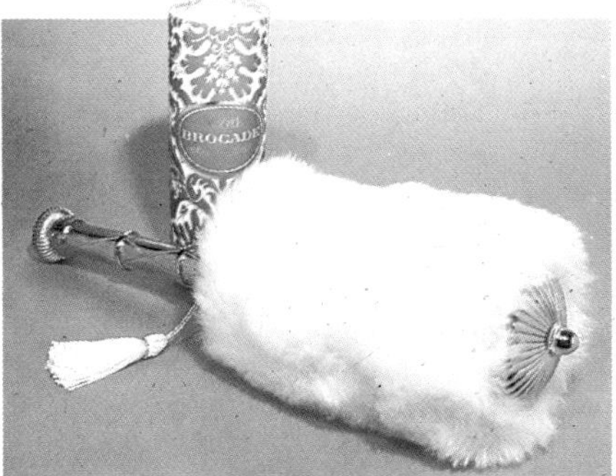

1969 *Roll-A-Fluff. Roll-on dispenser and Talc 3½oz. Brocade in white; Charisma, red; Regence, green $13.50* **MP $20**

1976 *Fluff Puff and 2oz Talc (left) in Sonnet or Roses, Roses $7.50* **MP $5**

1968 *Fluff Puff and Talc (center) 3½oz. Shown in Somewhere. Also in Here's My Heart (blue), Honeysuckle (yellow) and To A Wild Rose (pink) $6* **MP $15**
1970 *Powder Puffery Beauty Dust (right) 5oz in Charisma, Brocade, Cotillion and To A Wild Rose $5* **MP $7**

1970 *Two Loves Set. Rollette .33oz and Cream Sachet .66oz in Bird of Paradise, Elusive and Charisma $6* **MP $13**

1972 *Floral Duet. Rollette .33oz and Soap 3oz in Hawaiian White Ginger (shown) and Honeysuckle $3.25* **MP $13**

1971 *Sheer Companions. Vinyl carrying case holds Ultra Sheer Pressed Powder Compact ½oz and Lipstick $6* **MP $9**

1972 *Fragrance and Frills. Perfume 1/8oz and four 1½oz Soaps in Field Flowers or Bird of Paradise $6.75* **MP $8 boxed**

1971 *Precious Pair. Cologne ½oz and Talc 1½oz in 7 frag. $4* **MP $5**
1972 *Fragrance Fancy. Talc 1.5oz and Rollette .33oz in 7 frag. $4* **MP $5**

1973 *Minuette Duet. Cologne ½oz and Talc 1½oz in 6 frag. $4* **MP $5**

1974 *Fragrance Treasures. Cream Sachet .66oz and Soap 3oz in Sonnet, Charisma or Moonwind $5* **MP $6**
1974 *Perfumed Pair. Cologne ½oz and Talc 1½oz in choice of 6 frag. $4* **MP $5**

SETS OF THE 1970's

1973 *Treasure Chest. Cologne 4oz, Skin-So-Soft 4oz and Soap 5oz all in Sonnet or Moonwind $25* **MP $42**

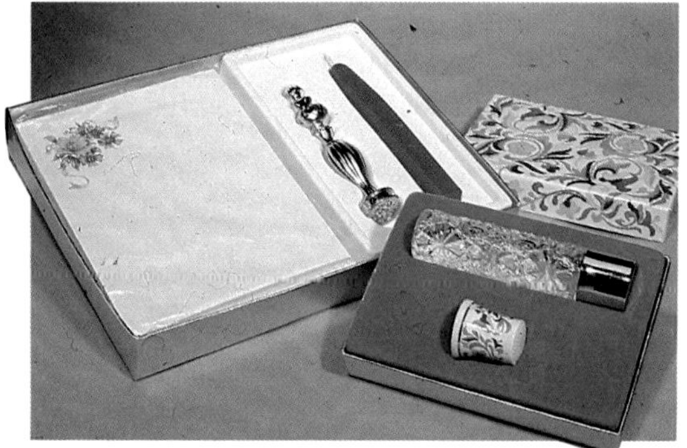

1977 *Fragrance Notes. 18 Earthflowers scented Notes and Seal w/Sealing Wax $9* **MP $8**
1978 *Frugrant Notions. Needle Holder bottle with .33oz Ariane or Timeless Cologne and Porcelain Thimble $8.50* **MP $8**

1974 *Care Deeply Hand Cream Set. Two 4oz tubes $3* **MP $3 Xmas boxed**

SETS OF THE 1980's

1980 *Silken Scents Scarf & Cologne. Vanity bottle of Candid or Timeless Cologne 1.75oz & Polyester Scarf 25 x 25" $15* **MP $13***

1980 *Scent With Love. 15 Fragranced Postalettes, 15 gummed Seals and packet of Unforgettable Sachet .18oz $6.50* **MP $5 complete**

1980 *The Duo. Colorcreme Lipstick and Ultra Wear Creme or Pearl Nail Polish $6* **MP $2 boxed**

** Available from Avon at time of publication*

MANICURE SETS

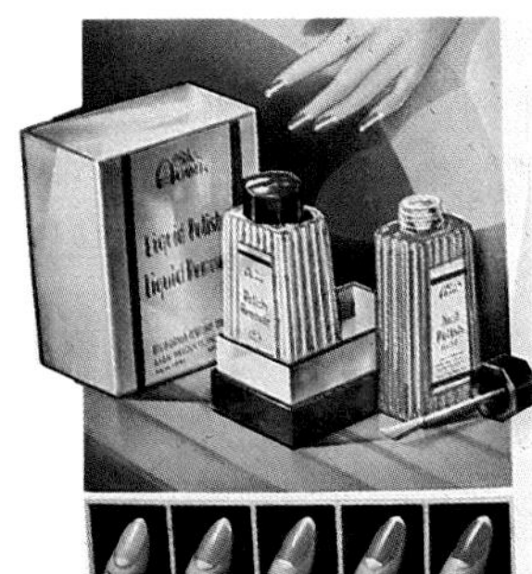

1930-36 *Manicure Set No. 1. Nail Polish and Polish Remover, booklet "What Story Do Your Hands Tell?" $1* **MP $75, $10 booklet**

1930-36 *Manicure Set No. 2. Polish Remover, Nail White, Nail Polish, Nail Cream and Cuticle Softener, Orangewood Stock, Cotton, Emery Boards $2.50* **MP $120**

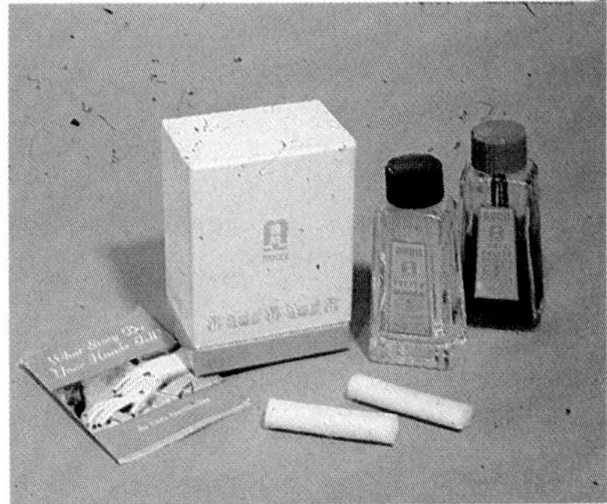

1937 *Manicure Set No. 1. Polish Remover, Nail Polish, 2 Cotton Rolls and Booklet "What Story Do Your Hands Tell?" 52¢* **MP $70**

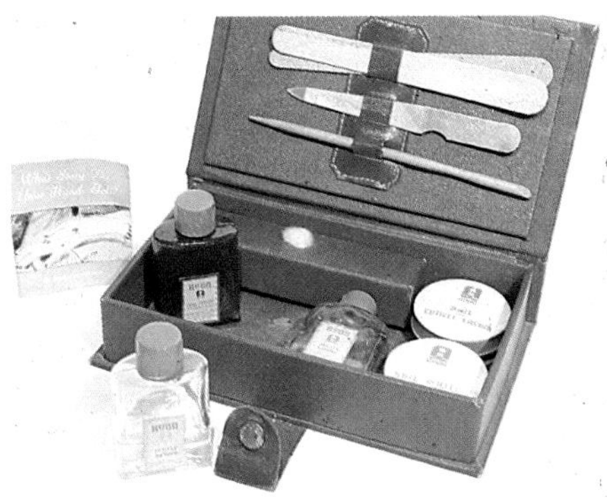

1938 *Manicure Set No. 2. Nail Polish, Cuticle Softener, Oily Remover, Nail Cream, Nail White, Orange Stick, Nail File, 2 Emery Boards, Cotton and Booklet $1.89* **MP $85**
1939 *Manicure Set No. 2. As above, except Nail & Cuticle Cream replaces Nail Cream $1.89* **MP $75**

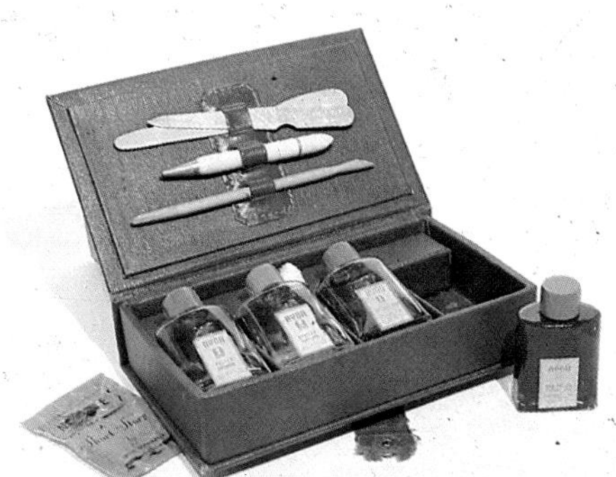

1940-42 *Manicure Set Deluxe. (with Aqua lids) Nail Polish, Oily Remover, Cuticle Softener, Cuticle Oil, Nail White Pencil, 5" Orangewood Stick, 2 Emery Boards, Cotton and Booklet $2.25* **MP $65**
1943 *As above, with Black lids $2.35* **MP $75**

1941-43 *Combination Set. Nail Base and choice of Nail Polish (shown in Royal Windsor shade) 52¢* **MP $35**
1944-45 *Combination Set. Nail Polish and choice of Base or Top Coat 59¢* **MP $37**

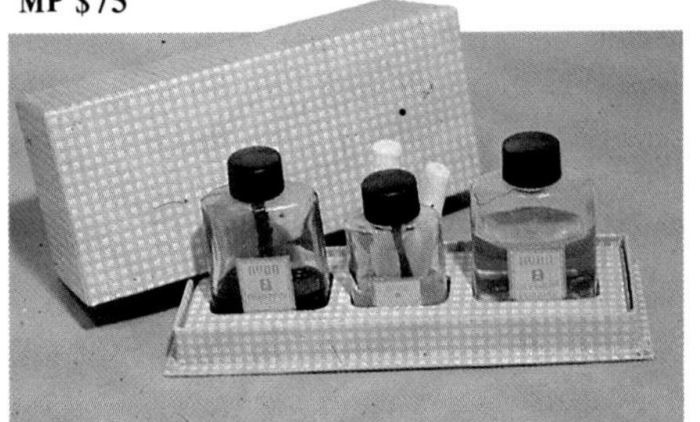

1942 *Nail Polish Threesome. Nail Polish, Nail Base, Oily Remover and Booklet 85¢* **MP $42**

1943 *Nail Polish Threesome. Nail Polish, Oily Remover, Nail Base, 2 rolls Cotton and Booklet 85¢* **MP $45, $10 Booklet**

1943 *Nail Polish Twosome. Nail Polish, Oily Remover, 2 rolls Cotton and Booklet 59¢* **MP $30**

1944 *Nail Polish Twosome. Nail Polish and Cuticle Softener ½oz each, 2 rolls Cotton and Booklet 59¢* **MP $30**

1944 *Deluxe Manicure Set. Nail Polish, Nail Base, Top Coat, Cuticle Softener, Oily Remover and Nail White Pencil $3.25* **MP $60**
1945 *Manicure Set Deluxe. As above, except bottles have Aqua lids $3.25* **MP $55**

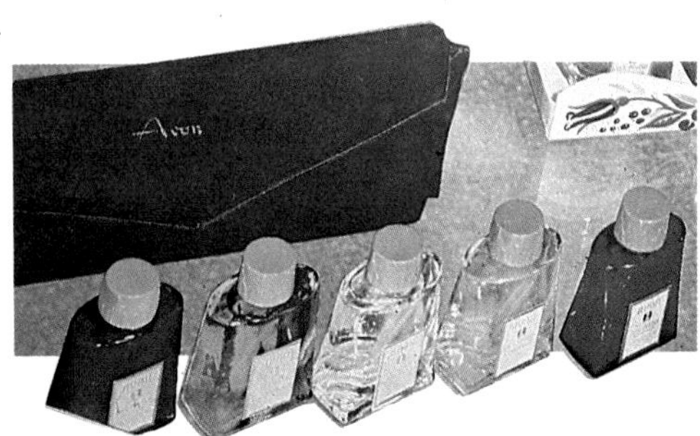

1947 *Deluxe Manicure Set. 2 bottles Nail Polish, Cling-Tite, Oily Remover, Cuticle Softener, Nail White Pencil, Orange Stick and 2 Emery Boards $3.50* **MP $50**

1948 *Deluxe Manicure Set. Nail Polish, Cling-Tite, Oily Remover, Cuticle Softener, Orange Stick and 2 Emery Boards $3.50* **MP $45**

1947-49 *Manicure Threesome. Nail Polish, Cling-Tite, Oily Remover $1* **MP $25**

1950 *Deluxe Manicure Set. Cuticle Softener, Cling-Tite, Nail Polish, Oily Remover, Orange Stick and 2 Emery Boards $2.50* **MP $35**

1950 *Nail Polish Twosome. Nail Polish and Oily Remover 98¢* **MP $15**

1950 *Manicure Threesome. Oily Remover. Nail Polish, Cling-Tite $1.29* **MP $25**

. . . MANICURE SETS

1953 *Deluxe Manicure Set. Cuticle Softener, Double Cote, Nail Polish, Oily Remover 2oz, Orange Stick and 2 Emery Boards $2.50* **MP $35**

1954 *Deluxe Manicure Set. Oily Remover 2oz, Cuticle Softener, Nail Polish, Double Cote, Orange Stick and 2 Emery Boards $2.65* **MP $35**

1955 *Little Favorite. Nail Polish, Oily Remover, Cuticle Softener $1.50* **MP $20**

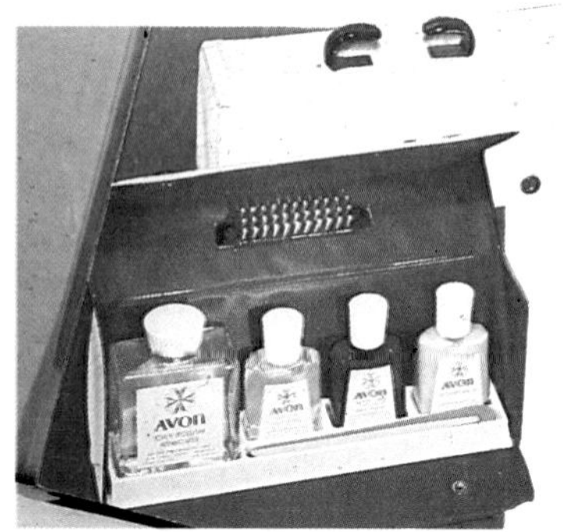

1955 *Deluxe Manicure Set. Oily Remover, Cuticle Softener, Nail Polish, Silvery Base Coat, Nail Brush & Emery Boards $2.95* **MP $30**

1956 *Deluxe Manicure Set. Removable tray holds Polish, Polish Remover, Cuticle Softener, Silvery Base, Top Coat, Emery Boards, Nail Brush. Handle seen through top of case. $3.25* **MP $33**

1957 *Color Changes. Oily Remover 2oz, Top Coat ½oz and Nail Enamel ½oz $1.95* **MP $20**

1956 *Polka Dot. Nail Polish, Oily Remover 2oz and Top Coat $1.69* **MP $20**

1958 *Color Bar. Set of 4: Nail Polish, Silvery Base, Top Coat and Cuticle Softener $3* **MP $20, $8 Tray only**

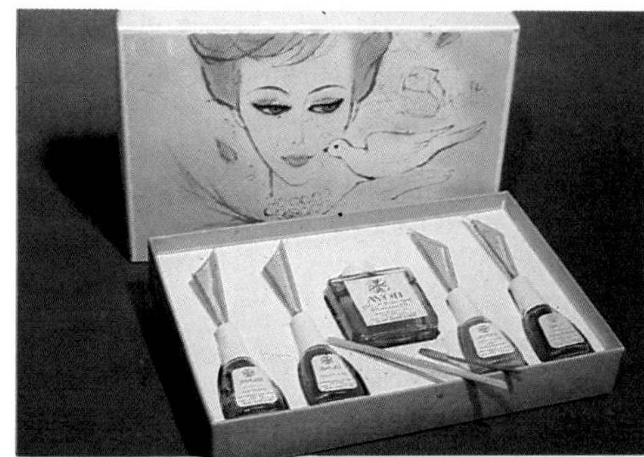
1959 *Manicure DeLuxe. Cuticle Softener, Silvery Base, Top Coat, Cream Polish, Oily Remover 2oz, Emery Board & Orangewood Stick $3.95* **MP $22**

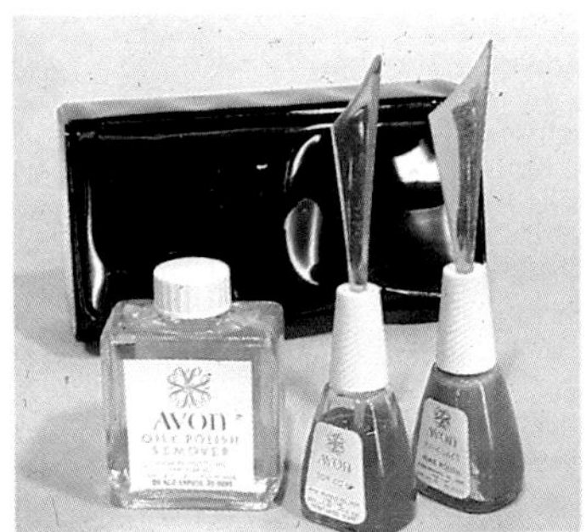

1960 *Manicure Petite. Oily Remover, Nail Enamel, Top Coat $2.98* **MP $16**

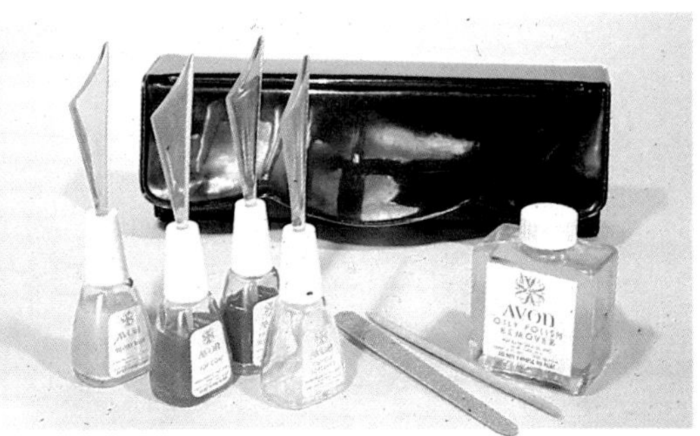

1960 *De Luxe Manicure Set. All vinyl Case holds Oily Remover, Silvery Base, Top Coat, Nail Enamel, Cuticle Softener, Orangewood Stick and Emery Board $4.98* **MP $25**

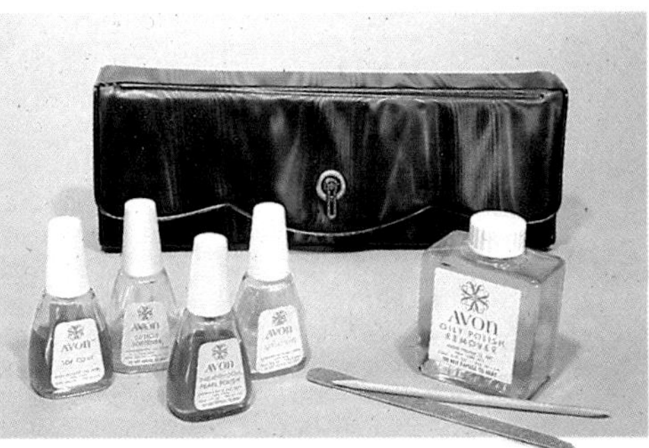

1961 *Deluxe Manicure Set. Moire plastic Case holds Silvery Base, Cuticle Softener, Nail Enamel, Top Coat, Oily Remover, Orange Stick and Emery Board $4.98* **MP $25**

1962 *Hawaiian Delights. 4 bottles Nail Polish. Aqua, Pink, Shell and Gold $2.98* **MP $20, $4 each bottle**

1962 *Manicure Complete. Nail Beauty, Cuticle Remover, Oily Remover, Double Coat, Nail Polish, Orange Stick and Emery Board $3.98* **MP $25 boxed, $10 Tray only**

1964 *Color Garden. 4 bottles Nail Polish. Cream $2.76, Pearl $3.40* **MP $17**

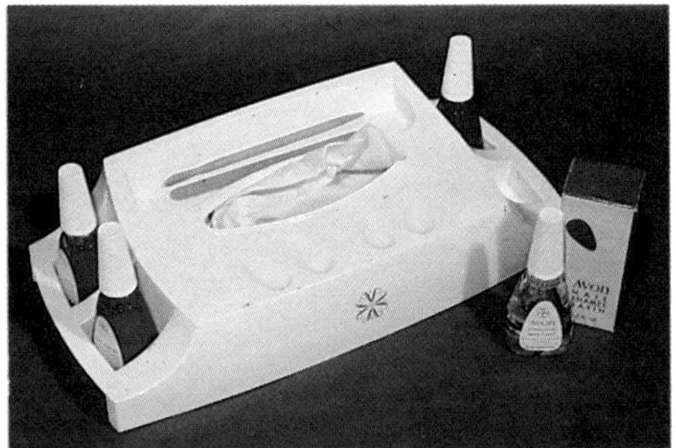

1965 *Manicure Tray. Long-Last Base Coat, 3 Nail Enamels, Orange Stick, Emery Board and Tissues $5* **MP $18, $9 Tray only**

1966 *Manicure Kit. Nail Enamel, Nail Beauty, Cuticle Remover, Base Coat, Enamel Set, 10 Remover Pads, Orange Stick, Emery Board $8.50* **MP $22 boxed, $8 Case only**

1967 *Manicure Complete. Tray 10¼" long, Nail Polish, Double Coat, Cuticle Cream, Nail Beauty, 10 Remover Pads, Emery Board and Orange Stick $5* **MP $18, $8 Tray only**

1968 *Manicure Beauti-Kit. Long-Last Top Coat, Enamel Set, Cuticle Conditioner, Enamel Remover Pads (10), Cuticle Remover, 2 Nail Enamels and Emery Board $12* **MP $22, $8 Case only**

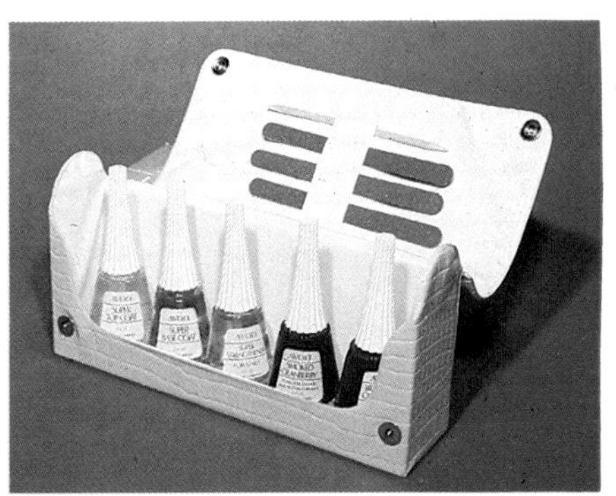

1978 *Nail Care Kit. Simulated alligator Kit, sold only in U.S., holds .5oz Super Strengthener, Base Coat, Top Coat and 2 Nail Enamels, 3 Emery Boards and Cuticle Stick $10* **MP $7**

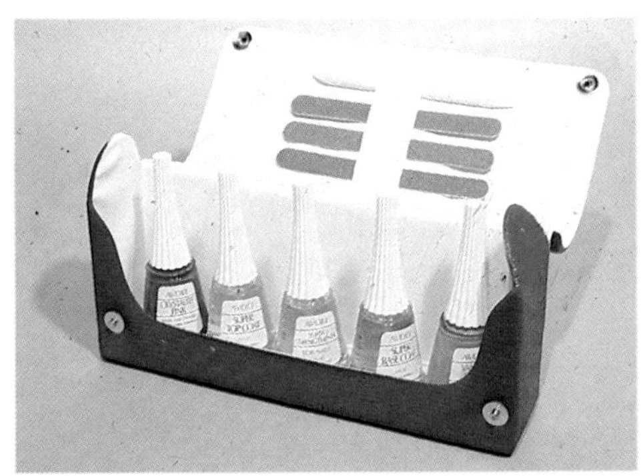

1979 *Nail Care Kit. Simulated alligator Kit, sold only in U.S. Issued with same items as 1978 Kit (left) Retail value $12* **MP $6**

1930 *Polish Remover 50¢* **MP $25, $30 boxed**

MANI-CURE ITEMS BY AVON

1936-37 *Oily Polish Remover 2oz 43¢* **MP $25**

1940-49 *Nail and Cuticle Cream 1oz jar 37¢* **MP $8, $10 boxed**
1939 *Nail & Cuticle Cream (top) 26¢* **MP $10**
1937 *Nail White 26¢* **MP $4, $9 boxed**
1937-39 *Nail Cream 26¢* **MP $4, $9 boxed**
1941 *Nail White Pencil 52¢* **MP $4, $8 boxed**

1950-54 *Oily Remover 2oz 49¢* **MP $8, $12 boxed**
1950 *Nail Polish 49¢* **MP $6, $8 boxed**
1950 *Double-Cote 49¢* **MP $6, $8 boxed**
1950 *Nail & Cuticle Cream 49¢* **MP $7, $10 boxed**

1955 *Oily Remover 2oz 49¢* **MP $4, $6 boxed**
1954 *Long-Last or Pearlescent Nail Polish 59¢ & 75¢* **MP $4, $6 boxed**

1957 *Nail Beauty 1oz tube 59¢* **MP $5, $6 boxed**
1967 *Enamel Remover Pads, 10 per box 90¢* **MP $7 boxed**

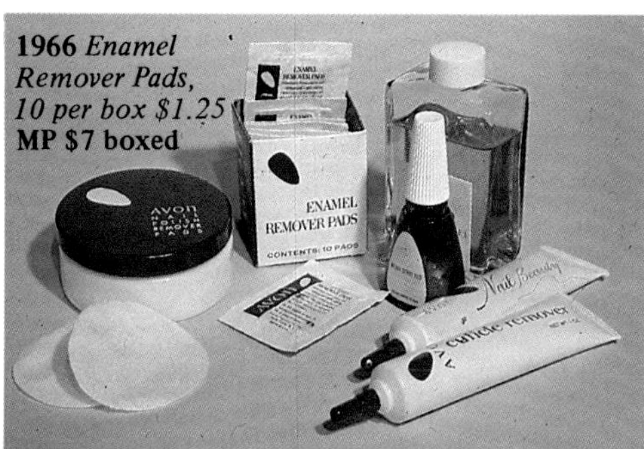

1966 *Enamel Remover Pads, 10 per box $1.25* **MP $7 boxed**

1963-66 *Nail Polish Remover, 20 Pads 98¢* **MP $11**
1962 *Nail Polish 85¢* **MP $3**
1962 *Oily Remover 3oz 69¢* **MP $3.50**
1962 *Nail Beauty 69¢* **MP $4**
1962 *Cuticle Remover 69¢* **MP $4**

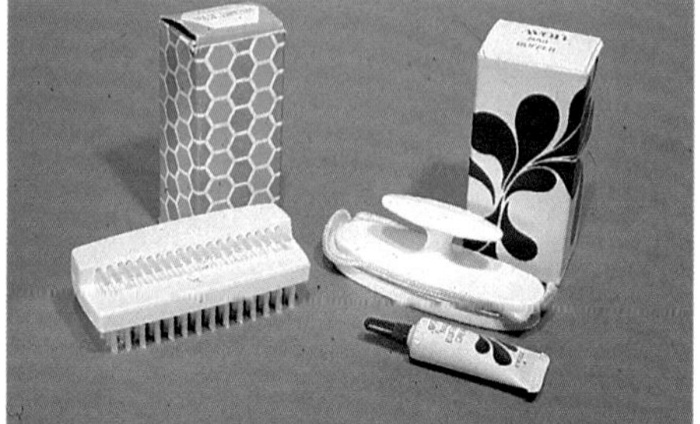

1970 *Nail Brush $2.50* **MP $2, $3 boxed**
1973 *Nail Buffer 3½" long $2.50* **MP $3, $4 boxed**
1973 *Nail Buffing Cream ¼oz $1.25* **MP $2**

1975 *Super Top Coat .5oz $1.75* **MP 50¢**
1977 *Super Top Coat .5oz $1.29* **MP 50¢**
1975 *Super Base Coat .5oz $1.75* **MP 50¢**
1977 *Super Base Coat .5oz $1.29* **MP $50¢**
1977 *Nail Strengthener .5oz $1.39* **MP 50¢**

1977 *Nail Enamel .5oz Cremes & Pearls, 32 shades $2.25* **MP 50¢**
1974 *Nail Enamel .5oz Cremes, Satins & Pearls $1.10 & $1.20* **MP 50¢**
1968 *Oily Enamel Remover 3oz 90¢* **MP 75¢**
1971 *Enamel Set Spray 7oz $2* **MP $2**
1977 *Oily Enamel Remover 4oz $1.19* **MP $1.50***

1969 *Enamel Fling Nail Enamel in Mauvelous or Sunspin .5oz $1.25* **MP $3 each**

1968 *Tinsel Topping Nail Enamel, Silver or Copper .5oz $1.25* **MP $4 each**
1971 *Skylighters Nail Enamel, 3 shades .5oz $1.25* **MP $4 each, $6 boxed**
1966 *Iced Cream Nail Enamel, 6 shades .5oz $1.25* **MP $4 each, $6 boxed**
1966 *Sugar Frost Matte Overlay .5oz $1.25* **MP $4**
1966 *Chic Sparklers Nail Enamel .5oz $1.25* **MP $4 each, $6 boxed**

1980 *Super Nail Mend & Wrap Kit. Mending Liquid ½oz, Mending Tissues & Cuticle Stick $4.75* **MP $3***
1980 *Super Strengthener for Nails ½oz $1.65* **MP $1***
1980 *Super Nail Dry ½oz $2* **MP $1***

1980 *Ultra Wear Creme or Pearl Enamel ½oz $2.75* **MP $2***
1980 *Ultra Wear Base Coat ½oz $1.65* **MP $1***
1980 *Ultra Wear Top Coat ½oz $1.65* **MP $1***

* *Available from Avon at time of publication*

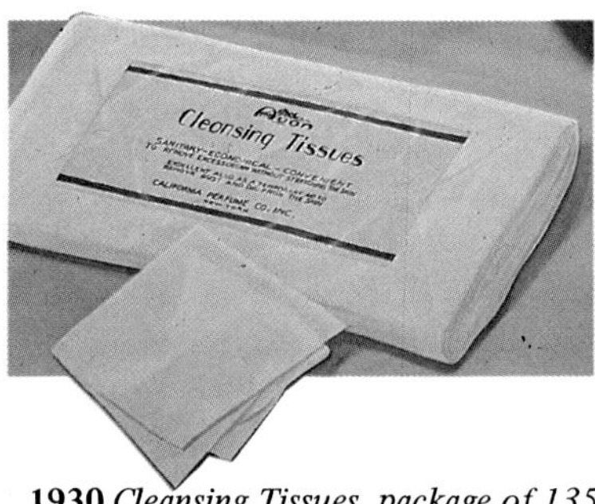

1930 *Cleansing Tissues, package of 135 wrapped in Cellophane 50¢* **MP $65**

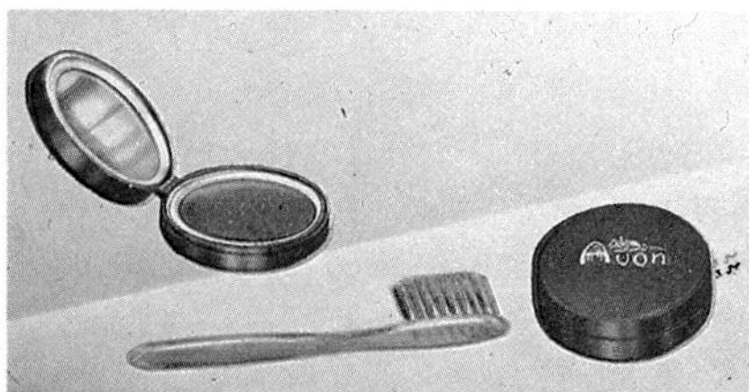

1931-33 *Eyelash Cream, Brown or Blue-Gray $1* **MP $25**

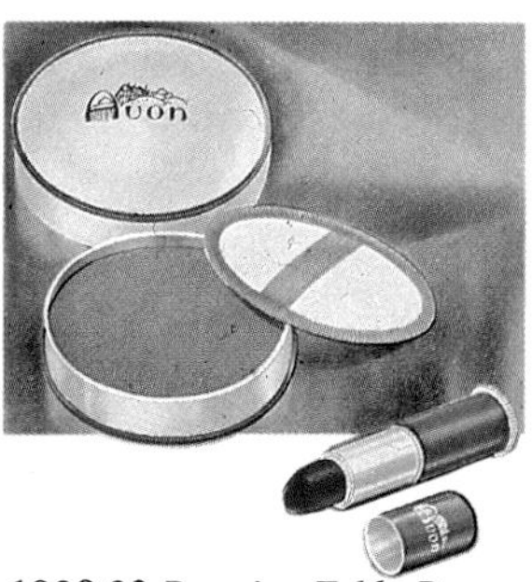

1930-33 *Dressing Table Rouge 45¢* **MP $30**
1931-32 *Lipstick 65¢* **MP $15**

1930 *Face Powder, Ariel or Vernafleur, 8 shades 75¢* **MP $25, $37 boxed**

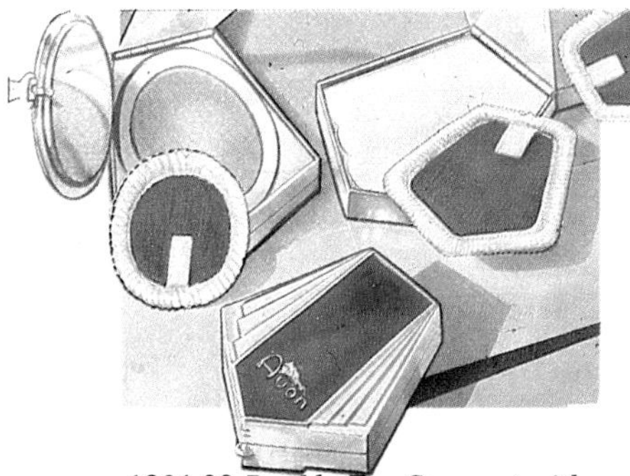

1931-32 *Double Fan Compact with Mirror, Powder and Rouge, refillable $1.50* **MP $40**

1933-35 *Dressing Table Rouge (redesigned puff), 3 shades 47¢* **MP $30**
1933-34 *Lipstick, push-up mechanism, 3 shades 52¢* **MP $15**
1934-36 *Lipstick (not shown) See 1935 Gift Sets B, F & W pg. 83 52¢* **MP $15**

1933-36 *Mascara Compact, brown or black shades $1.04* **MP $35**

1936-41 *Lipstick 52¢* **MP $12, $15 boxed**
1936-41 *Mascara Compact, brown or black $1.04* **MP $18**
1940 *Eyebrow Pencil in brown or black, Metal Case 35¢* **MP $10**
1936-41 *Cream Rouge Compact 78¢* **MP $18**

1936-41 *Double Compact for Loose Powder and Rouge $1.75* **MP $20**
1936-41 *Single Compact for Loose Powder $1.25* **MP $18**

1936-41 *Dressing Table Rouge 47¢* **MP $10, $12 boxed**

1936-41 *Face Powder, Ariel or Vernafleur 78¢* **MP $15, $20 boxed**

1937 *Facial Tissues, 360 per box 50¢* **MP $45**
1965 *Facial Tissues, issued with 1965 Manicure Tray (see pg. 107)* **MP $8**

1946-49 *Heavenlight Face Powder, one texture 89¢* **MP $10 (must say Heavenlight on packaging), $15 boxed, $20 with sleeve**

(rear)
1944-45 *Lipstick Refill 40¢* **MP $20 boxed**
1941-46 *Avon Face Powder 2½oz, two textures 89¢* **MP $10**
1943-44 *Lipstick 59¢* **MP $12**
1942 *Lipstick 59¢* **MP $12**

(front) **1943** *Mascara 69¢* **MP $20**
1941-47 *Dressing Table Rouge 47¢* **MP $10**
1943-45 *Rouge Compact, single feather 59¢* **MP $15**
1946-48 *Above Compact issued with Eye Shadow 79¢* **MP $15**

1949 *Dressing Table Rouge ½oz 59¢* **MP $5**
1949 *Powder-Pak 89¢* **MP $5**
1949 *Face Powder 2½oz 89¢* **MP $8**

1955 *Powder-Pak 95¢* **MP $4**
1955 *Face Powder 2½oz 95¢* **MP $7, $10 boxed**

1958 *Sheer Mist Face Powder 2½oz $1.10* **MP $7**
1960 *Fashion Finish Face Powder 2½oz $1.25* **MP $5, $7 boxed**

. . . MAKEUP BY AVON

1954-56 *Powder-Pak Compact w/Mirror $1.10* **MP $6**
1954 *Powder-Pak Plaque 69¢* **MP $5, $7 boxed**
1958 *Powder-Pak Plaque 79¢* **MP $4, $6 boxed**

Compacts –
1957 *Powder-Pak $1.25* **MP $3, $5 boxed**
1957 *Dressing Table Powder-Pak .7oz 95¢* **MP $3, $5 boxed**
1958 *Cake or Cream Rouge w/Mirror $1* **MP $3**
1965 *Dressing Table Powder-Pak .7oz $1.25* **MP $3**

Compact Puff Refills –
1960's *Compact and Powder-Pak 2/20c* **MP $2 each, $5 envelope of 2**
1960's *Foam 2/20¢* **MP $2, $5 envelope of 2**
1940's *For Double Compacts 2/5¢* **MP $3 each**
1950's *For Deluxe Compact 10¢ ea.* **MP $3 in env.**
1940's-50's *Rouge Compacts 2/10¢* **MP $2, $5 in env**

Bamboo-design Makeup–

1941-42, then 46-48 *Single Compact $1.25* **MP $18**
1941-42, 1946-48 *Double Compact $1.75* **MP $25**
1942, 1946-48 *Lipstick 59¢* **MP $11**
1942, 1946-48 *Cake Rouge Compact 59¢* **MP $9**
1941-42, 1946-48 *Cream Rouge Compact 78¢* **MP $9**

1949-57 *Cream Rouge Compact 69¢* **MP $6**
1949-57 *Cake Rouge Compact 79¢* **MP $6**
1949-57 *Deluxe Compact $3.50* **MP $12**
1954 *Jeweled Lipstick (right) 95¢* **MP $12**
1949-57 *Jewel-Etched Deluxe Lipstick (front) 89¢* **MP $8**

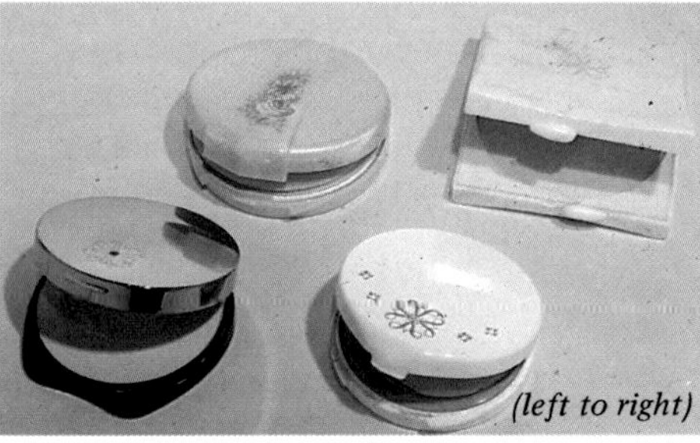
(left to right)

1962-63 *Powder-Pak Fashion Compact .5oz $2* **MP $6**
1963 *Pink Pearl Compact .7oz $2.50* **MP $4**
1963 *Petti-Pat Compact, non refillable .5oz $1.10* **MP $5**
1965 *Fashion Award Compact (square) .7oz $1.75* **MP $6**

1958-61 *Top Style Compact .5oz $3.50* **MP $9, $11 boxed**
1958-61 *Top Style Lipstick $1.50* **MP $8**
1961-65 *Compact Deluxe .5oz $3.50* **MP $7**
1961-65 *Lipstick Deluxe $1.35* **MP $6**

1965-67 *Imperial Jewel Compact .5oz $6* **MP $8**
1966 *Competite Compact .25oz $4.50* **MP $8**
1967 *Imperial Deluxe Compact .5oz $7* **MP $8**

1967 *Deluxe Oval Compact .5oz $5.50* **MP $7**
1967 *Deluxe Lipstick $2* **MP $5**
1968 *Jeweled Lipstick, refillable $6* **MP $6**
1968 *Jeweled Compact .5oz $10* **MP $10**

COMPACTS AND LIP MAKEUP

1965 *Fashion Cameo Lipstick 98¢* **MP $5**
1964 *Cameo Compact .5oz $2.50* **MP $6**
1967 *Fashion Compact .7oz $2.25* **MP $3**
1967 *Fashion Glace Compact, 8 fragrances, $2.50 & $3* **MP $3**
1967 *Fashion Lipstick $1.35* **MP $2**

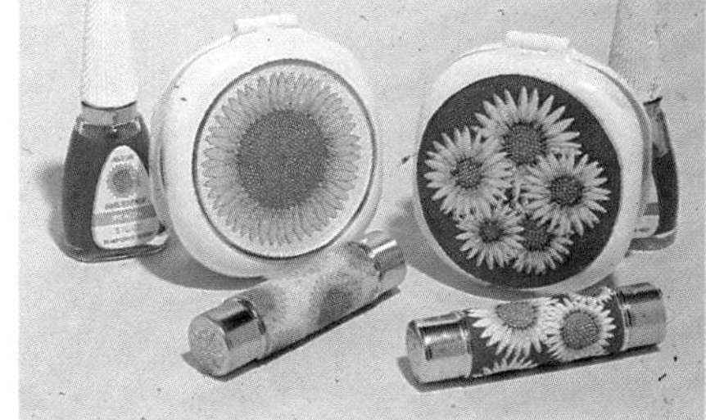

1967-68 *Flower Prints Coordinates in flowered Fabric Cases–*
Lipsticks *and* **Nail Enamels** *issued in shades of Pink in Poppy design, Red in Daisy design, Mauve in Carnation design and Peach in Sunflower design. Compacts, issued in a choice of Flower design and Powder-Pak shade.*
–Compacts .5oz $2.50 **MP $5** *–Lipsticks $1.50* **MP $4** *–Nail Enamels .5oz $1.25 each* **MP $4**

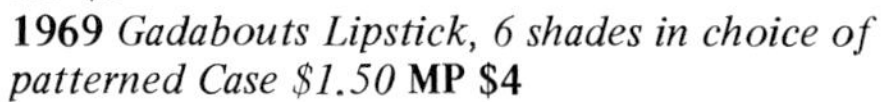

1969 *Gadabouts Compact .5oz in black and white or yellow and white checked pattern $2.50* **MP $5**
1969 *Gadabouts Lipstick, 6 shades in choice of patterned Case $1.50* **MP $4**

1968 *Festive Fancy Oval Compact .5oz $3* **MP $4**
1968 *Festive Fancy Lipstick, 6 shades $1.75* **MP $3**
1968 *Festive Fancy Demistik (not shown) in Rapture, Occur! or Unforgettable $2.50* **MP $3**
1968 *Encore Lipstick $1.25* **MP $2**
1969 *Encore Compact .5oz $2* **MP $3**

1969 *Empress Compact, oval .5oz $7.50* **MP $6**
1969 *Empress Lipstick $3* **MP $3**
1969 *Deluxe Compact "Carved Ivory" .5oz $4* **MP $4**
1969 *Deluxe Lipstick "Carved Ivory" Refillable $2.50* **MP $4**

1969 *Captivator Lipsticks–$1.75 each* **MP $3 each, $4 boxed**
Tiger with Jungle Red or Instant Mocha
Zebra with Sultry Coral or Desert Dawn
Leopard with Wild Amber or Persimmon
1969 *Captivator Compacts, Tiger, Zebra or Leopard design in choice of powder shades $3.50* **MP $4 each, $5 boxed**

(left to right)
1967 *Simplicity Compact .5oz $1.75* **MP $3**
1971 *Simplicity Compact .5oz $2.75* **MP $4**
1973 *Designers Accent-in-Mauve Compact .5oz. Sold empty $1.50* **MP $2**
1973 *Designers Accent-in-Yellow Compact .5oz. Sold empty $1.50* **MP $2**

1969 *Lip Twins.*
Mirrored Case with 2 Lipsticks $4 **MP $5**
1969 *Blushmaker Compact. Highlighter, Blush .3oz each and 2" long Brush in mirrored Case with drawer. $5* **MP $6**
1974 *Looking Pretty Mirrored Lipstick, 4 shades $3* **MP $4**
1970 *Powder Shadow Duet .06oz $2.25* **MP $1**

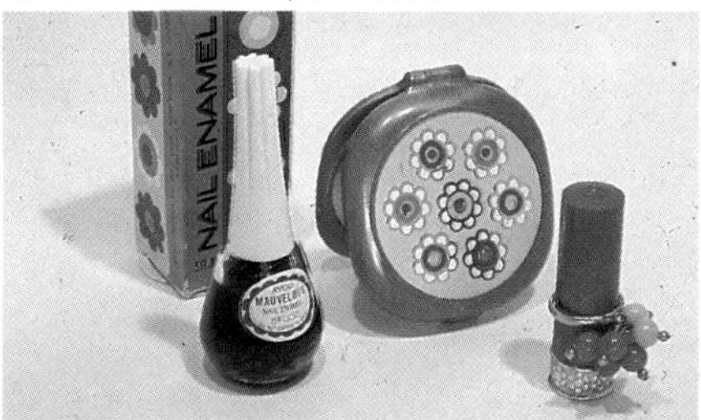

1969 *Enamel Fling in Mauvelous and Sunspin .5oz $1.25* **MP $3 each**
1969 *Swing Fling Compact .5oz $3* **MP $4**
1969 *Ring Fling Lipstick in Jazzberry with pale and dark pink adjustable Ring. $3* **MP $9, $5 Ring only (see also pg. 112)**

1971 *Encore Compact .5oz $3.50* **MP $3**
1971 *Encore Lipstick .13 oz $1.35* **MP $2**
1972 *Fashion Lace Compact .5oz $3.50* **MP $3**
1972 *Fashion Lace Lipstick .13oz $1.50* **MP $1**

1974 *About Town Compact .5oz $3.50* **MP $2, $3 boxed**
1974 *About Town Lipstick .13oz $1.50* **MP $1**
1976 *About Town Compact .5oz Translucent only $3.75* **MP $2**
(1977 Available in 7 shades $3.50 **MP $2***)*

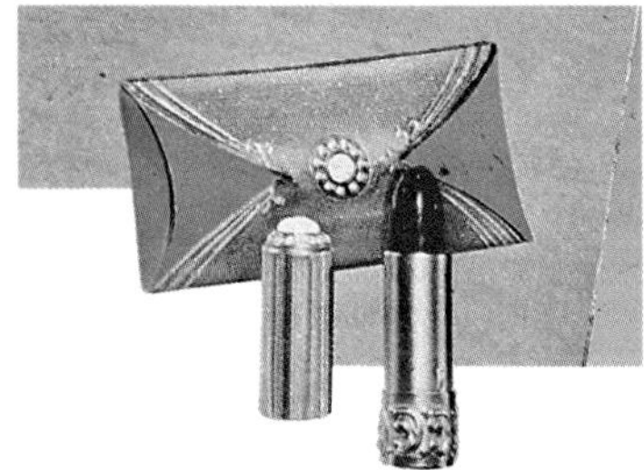

1956 *Jewelled Deluxe Lipstick in Christmas Wrap $1.50*
MP $18, $12 Lipstick only

1954 *Fashion Lipstick 95¢* **MP $12, $17 boxed**
1956 *Long Life Lipstick $1.10* **MP $10**
(1958 *Above Lipstick called Satin Sheen $1.10* **MP $10**)
1956 *Fashion Lipstick 79¢* **MP $12**
1957 *Fashion Lipstick 79¢* **MP $12**
1957 *Fashion Lipstick 89¢* **MP $12**
1958 *Fashion Lipstick, honey beige cap 89¢* **MP $11**

1960-61 *Fashion Lipstick 98¢* **MP $10, $13 boxed**
1962 *Fashion Lipstick 98¢* **MP $10**
1963 *Fashion Lipstick 98¢* **MP $9**
1966 *Ultra Sheer Lipstick $1.75* **MP $1**
1966 *Lipstick Refillable $2* **MP $8, $10 boxed**

1962 *Lip Dew $1.25* **MP $3**
1966 *Lip Toner in Mocha, Plum and Lime $1.25* **MP $3**
1969 *Lipmaker in Warm Tone or Cool Tone $1.50* **MP $3, $5 boxed**
1969 *Lip Dew $1.50* **MP $2, $3 boxed**
1971 *Lip Foundation in Fair or Deep .15oz $1.50* **MP $1, $1.50 boxed**

1966 *Nail Enamel in Yum Plum, Comin' Up Rose, Polk-A-Lily and Peach-A-Boo (shown) $1.25* **MP $4, $6 boxed**
1966 *Yum Plum Lipstick $1.25* **MP $4**
1966 *Peach-A-Boo Lipstick design shown on box $1.25* **MP $4, $6 boxed**
1966 *Polk-A-Lily Lipstick $1.25* **MP $4**
1966 *Comin' Up Rose Lipstick $1.25* **MP $4**

1969 *Ring Fling Lipsticks with Adjustable Ring $3 each* **MP $9, $5 Ring only, $12 boxed**
Glazed Copper with White & Black Ring
Iced Cantaloupe with Coral & Orange Ring
Iced Watermelon with Aqua & Navy Ring
Put-On Pink with Lime & Green Ring
Nectar (not shown) in yellow Case with Yellow & Orange Ring (see Jazzberry pg. 111)

1967 *Applique Lipstick with snap-open Mirror $3.50* **MP $8**
1966-67 *Encore Lipstick, also used as refill $1.10* **MP $6, $8 boxed**
1967-68 *Encore Lipstick, also used as refill $1.10* **MP $6**
1970 *Sunseekers Lipstick in 4 shades $2* **MP $3**
1972 *Encore Lipstick $1.35* **MP $1**

1971 *Lipstick a la Mode .13oz. Flip-open lid on top holds .02oz Perfume Glace in choice of 5 fragrances. Both refillable. $4.50* **MP $7**
1972 *Pop-Top Lipstick .13oz, $2* **MP $3, $4 boxed**
1973 *Pop-Top Lipstick .13oz, 4 shades $2* **MP $2**
1974 *Color Magic Lipstick .13oz of blue or green turns to pink or peach on lips $2* **MP $4, $6 boxed**
1975 *Windsor Lipstick $2* **MP 50¢**

1978 *Colorcrème Lipstick $2.25* **MP $2.50***
1978 *Lipstick Case, with any Avon purchase C-16 only 99¢ (2 styles, round or square ends)* **MP $4**

(See Patterns pg. 61, Petit Point pg. 153)

1973 *Ultra Sheer Lip Gloss Pot .10oz, 2 shades $2.25* **MP $1**
1973 *Lip Glosser .10oz $2* **MP $1**
1978 *Lip Lustre .30oz, $3.50* **MP 50¢**
1978 *Good and Glossy Roll-On Lip Gloss .33oz in Natural, Mint & Strawberry flavors $3* **MP $1**

* *Available from Avon at time of publication*

1974 *Sweet Lips, cookie shaped, 2 shades $4* **MP $4**
1976 *Lucky Penny .14oz, 2 shades $4* **MP $2**
1976 *Kiss 'N Makeup .20oz, 2 shades $4* **MP $2**
1978 *Sunnyshine Up .14oz, 2 shades $5* **MP $2**
1978 *Tasti-Mint .14oz 2 shades $5* **MP $1**
1977 *Funburger .20oz 2 shades $4.50* **MP $2**

1980 *Nestle Crunch Lip Gloss Compact .14oz $5.50* **MP $1**
1979 *Chocolate Chiplick Lip Gloss Compact .15oz $5.50* **MP $1.50**
1980 *Reflector Protector Lip Gloss Compact .14oz $6* **MP $5***
1979 *Berry Nice Lip Gloss Compact .14oz $5.50* **MP $1.50**

1960 *Making Eyes. Curl 'n Color Mascara, Eyebrow Pencil and Eye Shadow Stick $3.95* **MP $20**

1965 *Eye Shadow Wand on Xmas Card $1.35* **MP $5 on card**

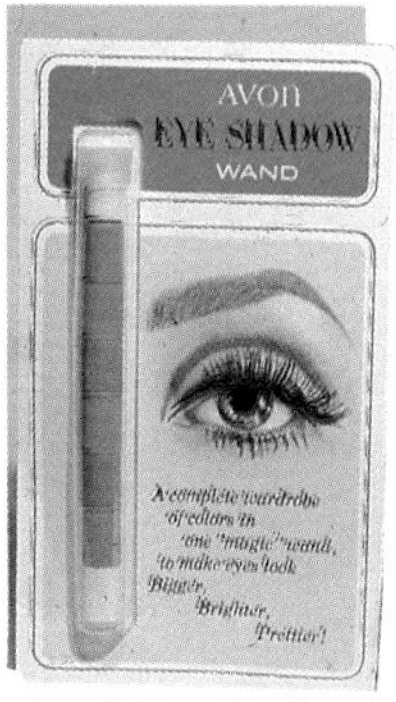

1964 *Eye Shadow Wand in plastic holder, 7 shades $1.35* **MP $2, $4 on card**

EYE MAKEUP BY AVON

1963-66 *Cream Eye Shadow, 7 shades $1.25* **MP $1, $3 on card**
1963-66 *Luminous Cream Eye Shadow, 5 shades $1.25* **MP $1, $3 on card**

1959-63 *Curl 'n Color Mascara, 6 shades $2* **MP $4, $6 on card** *(below left)*

1962-66 *Eyebrow Pencil, 5 shades $1* **MP $2, $3 on card** *(below left)*

1963-70 *Making Eyes Mascara, 5 shades $1.35* **MP $1, $2 on card**
1959-66 *Cake Mascara with Brush, 2 shades $1* **MP $2, $4 boxed**
1959-66 *Cream Mascara with Brush in plastic case 69¢* **MP $4, $6 boxed**

1960-62 *Eyebrow Pencil, 4 shades $1* **MP $3, $5 on card**
1967-74 *Cake Eyeliner, 7 shades $1.50* **MP $1 boxed**
1972 *Flow-On Automatic Eyeliner, 4 shades $4.50* **MP $2 boxed**

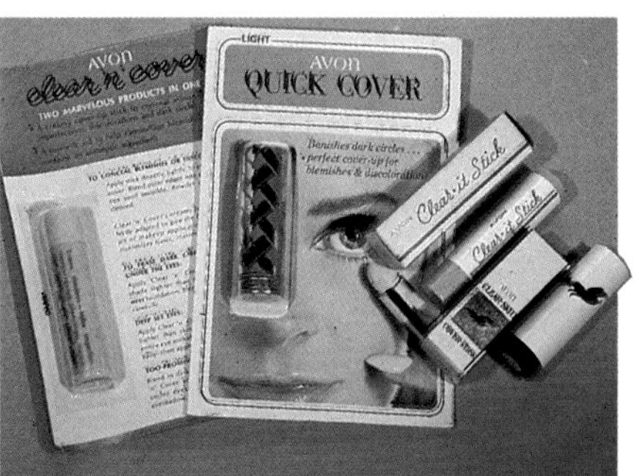

1963-66 *Clear 'n' Cover Stick 89¢* **MP $3, $6 on card**
1968-73 *Quick Cover, 3 shades $1.50* **MP $3, $5 on card**
1959-63 *Clear-it Stick 89¢* **MP $5, $8 boxed**
1970-72 *Clear Skin Cover Stick $1.75* **MP $1, $2 boxed**

1965-66 *Gold Satin Eye Highlight Brush $1.50* **MP $5, $7 in plastic case on card**
1962-67 *Eye Makeup Brush $1* **MP $5 as shown**
1965-68 *Makeup Brush in gold Telescopic Case $2.25* **MP $7 on card, $5 brush only**

1970-75 *Crystal Shadows .07oz, 4 shades $2* **MP $1**
1957-66 *Eye Shadow Stick, 5 shades $1* **MP $4**
1968 *Sparkling Cream Eye Shadow, 4 shades $1.75* **MP $1 boxed**
1970 *Eye Gleam .06oz $1.50* **MP $1, $2 boxed**

1977 *Colorstick Twin Sharpener $1.25* **MP $1**

1972 *Certain Look Eye Shine $1.50* **MP 25¢**
1969 *Flatter Eyes Compact, 2 Eye Shadows, Eyeliner & Brush $4.50* **MP $1**
1977 *Colorstick for Lips .05oz, 7 shades $3.50* **MP $2***
1977 *Colorstick for Eyes .06oz, 7 shades $3.50* **MP $2***

1973 *Lash Supreme .15oz $2* **MP $1**
1971 *Shine Down Stick .6oz $2.50* **MP $4**
1977 *Cover-All Concealing Stick $3.25* **MP $2.50***
1978 *Lash Supreme .25oz $2.75* **MP $2***
1977 *Lash Supreme .5oz $2.75* **MP $1**

1970 *Butterfly Collection. Lipstick and 4 Eye Shadows $7.50* **MP $7**
1972 *Owl Collection. Lip Gloss, Lip Conditioner and 3 Powder Eye Shadows $8* **MP $6**
1973 *Honey Cat Makeup Collection. Lip Gloss, Lip Conditioner, 4 Eye Shadows $8* **MP $6**

1980 *Blue-Eyed Susan, Green-Eyed Susan and Brown-Eyed Susan Eye Shadow Compacts .15oz $6* **MP $3**

* *Available from Avon at time of publication*

1971 *Eye Makeup Sealer .5 oz $1.50* **MP 50¢**

1969-75 *Cleaner and Conditioner for False Eyelashes .75oz $1.50* **MP 50¢**
1969-73 *Eyelash Applicator $1.50* **MP $1, $1.50 boxed**
1970 *Natural Full Lashes $6.50 or Fluffy Lashes $7 and Adhesive* **MP each $6, $7 boxed**
1969 *Demi-Lashes and Adhesive $6* **MP $5, $6 boxed**

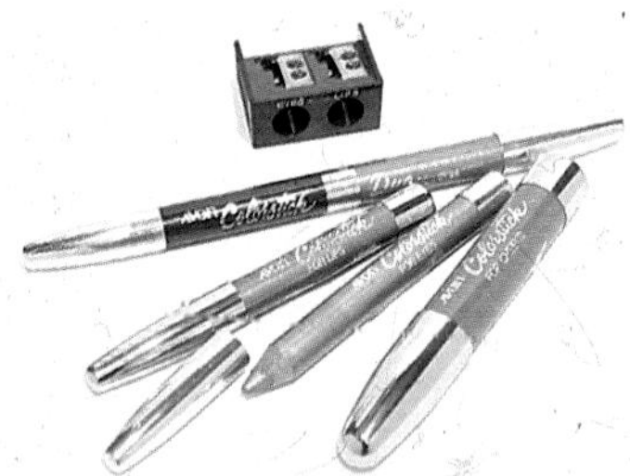
Colorsticks (top to bottom) –
1979 *Sharpener for Lip and Eye Lining $1.25* **MP $1***
1979 *Duo for Eyes .10oz $5* **MP $4***
1979 *Lip Lining .03oz $3* **MP $2***
1979 *Eye Lining .03oz $3* **MP $2***
1979 *Cheeks .15oz $4.50* **MP $5***

1980-81 *Soft Powder Eye Lustre 5 shades .13oz $4.50* **MP 50¢**
1980 *Lots O'Lash Mascara 2 shades .33oz $4* **MP $3.50***
1980 *Paint Box Brights for Eyes 3 shades .30oz $2* **MP 50¢**
1980 *Paint Box Brights for Lips 3 shades .25oz $2* **MP 50¢**

1980-81 *Sensational Eyes Collection. Five eye shadows in reuseable container .15oz $11* **MP $6**

1963-66 *Platinum Rose –*
Complexion Highlight .07oz $1.35 **MP $4**
Fingertip Highlight .5oz $1.35 **MP $4**
Lip Highlight $1.35 **MP $7**
Eye Highlight $1.35 **MP $4**

WOMEN'S MAKEUP BY AVON

1969 *Cover Perfect Foundation 2oz $1.50* **MP $1**
1969 *Liquid Eyeliner ¼oz $2* **MP $1**
1965 *Gold Satin Lip Highlight $1.75* **MP $7, $9 boxed**
1965 *Gold Satin Complexion Highlight .8oz $1.75* **MP $5**

1971 *Go Togethers. Foundation Stick ½oz and Blush Stick .3oz $6* **MP $3**
1972 *Creme Stick Foundation .85oz $3.50* **MP $2**

1961-67 *Cream Rouge $1* **MP 75¢, $1 boxed**
1959-66 *Liquid Rouge 2 dram 89¢* **MP $3, $5 boxed**
1956-59 *Liquid Rouge No. 1 through No. 5, ¼oz 69¢* **MP $5, $8 boxed**

1967-69 *Finishing Face Powder 2.5oz $1.50* **MP $4, $6 boxed**
1968-70 *Blushing Cream 3 shades ¼oz $2* **MP $4, $6 boxed**
1970-75 *Blushing Cream 3 shades ¼oz $1.50* **MP $1, $2 boxed**

1975-76 *The Glisteners Cheek Color .25oz Coral or Pink $1.75* **MP 50¢**
1975-76 *The Glisteners Lip Color .25oz Coral or Pink $1.75* **MP 50¢**
1976 *Real Rouge Liqui-Tint .25oz $2* **MP 25¢**
1976 *Real Rouge Creme Fluff .25oz $2.50* **MP 25¢**

Great Blush –
1976-79 *Powder Compact .40oz & Brush, 4 shades $4.50* **MP $2**
1978-79 *Creme Cheek Pot .25oz $3* **MP 50¢**
1976-78 *Soft Creme 3 shades .25oz $2.50* **MP 50¢**
1976-79 *Frost Stick .85oz $4.50* **MP 50¢**

1979-80 *All-Over Face Color 1oz $3.50* **MP $1**

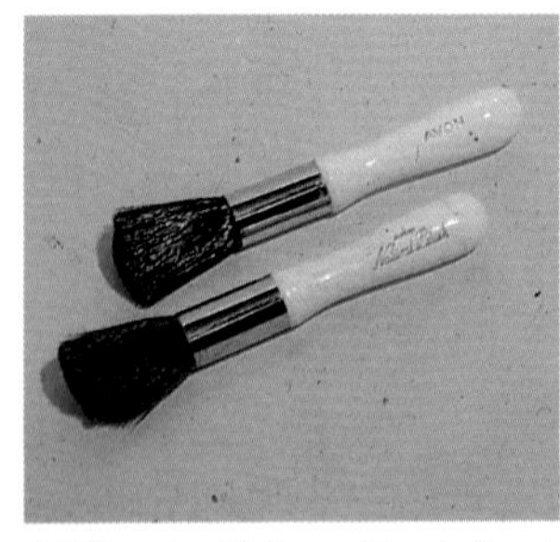
1965 only *Makeup Brush (top) $2* **MP $8**
1965 only *Brush for Natural Blush $2* **MP $10**

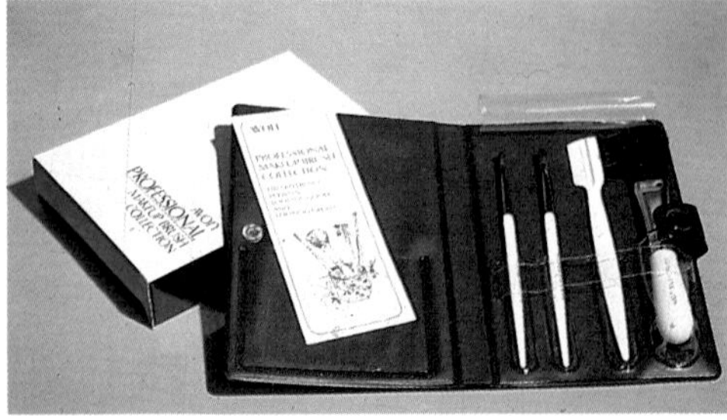
1980 *Professional Makeup Collection. Vinyl Kit holds Lip Brush, Eye Shadow Brush, Brow/Lash Brush, Blush Brush and instruction booklet $15* **MP $12***

**Available from Avon at time of publication*

Tinted lotion, specially designed for the oily skin, was Liquid Powder in the 1930's, renamed Finishing Lotion in the 1940's and then Foundation Lotion in the 1950's.

1931-36 *Liquid Powder 4oz $1* **MP $50**

1944 *Finishing Lotion 2oz 59¢* **MP $20 with black lid, $26 boxed**

1938-50 *Finishing Lotion 2oz 52¢* **MP $15**

FOUNDATIONS AND MAKEUP

1950-52 *Foundation Lotion 2oz 59¢* **MP $22**

1943-46 *Twin-Tone Makeup 1-7/8oz 89¢* **MP $12**

1946-52 *Color Pick-Up Cream 1-7/8oz 89¢* **MP $10**
1952-53 *As above, except smaller size 1oz 75¢* **MP $15**

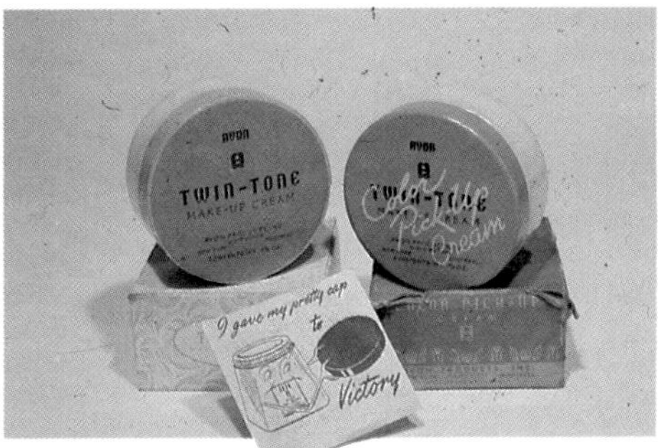

1944-45 *Twin-Tone Makeup with wartime cardboard lid 89¢* **MP $20**
1946 *Color Pick-Up Cream stamped over Twin-Tone Makeup lid, issued during name change period* **MP $14 as shown**

1946-48 *Color Pick-Up Liquid 1oz 59¢* **MP $10**

1952-53 *Fashion Film Liquid 1oz 75¢* **MP $9, $12 boxed**
1954-58 *Fashion Film Liquid 1oz 95¢* **MP $8**

1946-54 *Cake Make-Up, 5 shades 1¾oz $1.25* **MP $5, $8 boxed**
1948-54 *Cream Cake, 6 shades .6oz 89¢* **MP $5, $8 boxed**

1954-56 *Cake Make-Up, 8 shades 1¾oz $1* **MP $6**
1954-56 *Cream Cake, 8 shades .6oz 95¢* **MP $6**
1961-65 *Color Cake 2oz $1.25* **MP $4, $5 boxed**

1953-54 *Fashion Film 1oz 75¢ (smooth lid)* **MP $9, $12 boxed**
1958-61 *Fashion Film 1oz $1.10* **MP $8**
1957-64 *French Frosting 1oz $1.25* **MP $7**

1963-67 *Tone 'N' Tint 2oz 10 shades $1.35* **MP $3**
1965-67 *Ultra Cover, 11 shades 2oz $1.35* **MP $3**
1965-67 *Foundation Supreme, 11 shades 1½oz $1.35* **MP $3**
1967 only *Foundation Supreme* **(gold lid)** *8 shades 1.9oz $1.50* **MP $5**
1967-68 *Foundation Supreme, 8 shades 1.9oz $1.50* **MP $3**

1967 only *Ultra Cover, 8 shades 2.1oz $1.75* **MP $5 with gold lid**
1967-69 *Ultra Cover, 8 shades 2.1oz $1.75* **MP $2**
1967 only *Tone 'N' Tint, 8 shades 2oz $1.50* **MP $5 with gold lid**
1967-76 *Tone 'N' Tint, 8 shades 2oz $1.50* **MP 50¢**

1970-73 *Satin Supreme, 8 shades 1½oz $1.50* **MP $1**
1968-70 *Satin Supreme 1-1/8oz $1.50* **MP $1**
1966-68 *Hide 'N' Lite .75oz $1.50* **MP $2 with gold lid**
1968-69 *Hide 'N' Lite .75oz $1.50* **MP $1**

1971 *Mirror, Mirror $3.50* **MP $5, $7 boxed**

MAKEUP LINES

Polished Gold

1978 *Creamy Eye Shadow .12oz, 2 shades $3* **MP $1.50**
1978 *Lipstick .13oz 3 shades $4* **MP $1.50**
1978 *Nail Enamel .5oz 3 shades $2.25* **MP $1.50** *(See Evening Bag pg. 98)*

Crystal Lights –

1979 *Moisture Lipstick, 3 shades .13oz $3* **MP $1, $1.50 boxed**
1979 *Eye Shadow, 4 shades .10oz $4* **MP $1, $1.50 boxed**
1979 *Pearl Nail Enamel, 3 shades .5oz $2.50* **MP $1, $1.50 boxed**

1975 *Shades of Beauty Liquid Foundation 1.5oz $2* **MP 50¢**
1975 *Shades of Beauty Creamy Blush .25oz $2* **MP 25¢**

1979 *Fresh Look Makeup, Oil-control 1.5oz or Moisturizing $2.50* **MP $3***

Eventone

1976 *Ultra Cover Dewy or Matte 2oz $2.75* **MP Dewy $3*, Matte 50¢**
1976 *Medium Cover Matte 2oz $2.25* **MP 50¢**
1976 *Light Cover Dewy 2oz $2.25* **MP 50¢**
1976 *Fin. Face Powder & Puff 1.5oz $3* **MP $5***
1976 *Medium Cover Dewy 1.5oz $2.25* **MP 50¢**
1970 *Liquid Foundation 1.5oz $1.50* **MP 50¢**

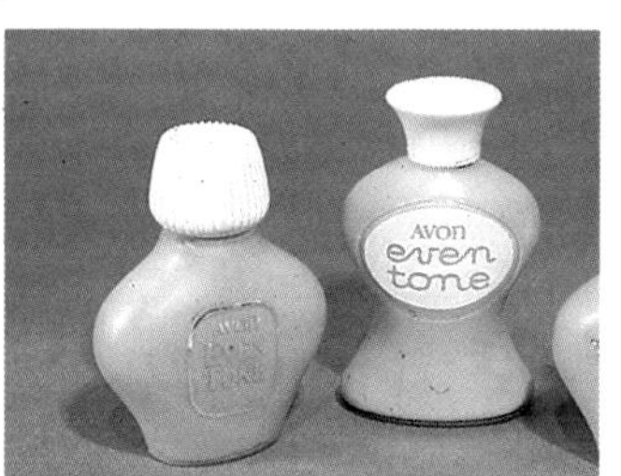

1966-70 *Foundation 1½oz $1.50* **MP $1**
1962-66 *Foundation 1½oz $1.35* **MP $1**
(1961 *not shown, as above, with gold lid $1.35* **MP $4)**

Beautiful Reflections –

1980 *Reflective Nail Glaze, 2 shades .5oz $3* **MP $1**
1980 *Reflective Lipstick .13oz $3.50* **MP $1**
1980 *Soft Reflections Body Glow, 2 shades 1½oz $6.50* **MP $1**
1980 *Dazzle Dust Highlighting Powder, 3 shades .05oz $6.50* **MP $1**

1976 *Flow-On Eyeliner .10oz 3 shades $4.50* **MP 50¢**

1976 *Powder Brow Makeup .10oz 3 shades $3* **MP 75¢**
1976 *Cream Eye Shadow .25oz 5 shades $2* **MP 50¢**
1976 *Brow & Liner Pencil, 3 shades $2.50* **MP 50¢**

Making Eyes

1976 *Creamy Powder Eye Shadow, Velvet .10oz $2.25 Frosted .12oz $2.50* **MP 50¢**

1977 *Waterproof Mascara .43oz 2 shades $2.75* **MP $2**
(1976 *Waterproof Mascara .12oz not shown $2.50* **MP $2)**
1978 *Waterproof Mascara .20oz 2 shades $2.75* **MP 50¢**
1976 *Frosted or Velvet Eye Shadow Wand. 5 colors .05oz ea. $2.75* **MP 75¢**

Ultra Sheer –

1967-68 *Nail Tints, 3 shades .5oz $1.50* **MP $3**

1968-74 *Nail Tints, not shown, new issue with gold lid* **MP 50¢**
1969-74 *Under-Makeup Moisturizer, 3 shades 2oz $3.50* **MP 75¢**
1971-74 *Transparent Face Tint, 4 shades 1.5oz $2.50* **MP 50¢**
1974-76 *Under-Makeup Moisturizer, 3 shades 2oz $3.50* **MP $1**

1976 *Blush Compact .4oz $5* **MP 50¢** *Delicate Beauty –*

1974 *Pressed Powder Compact ½oz $3.50* **MP $1**
1976 *Powder Eye Shadow .1oz $3.50* **MP 50¢**
1975 *Automatic Mascara .15oz $3.50* **MP 50¢**
1975 *Automatic Eyeliner .1oz $5* **MP 50¢**
1974 *Under-Makeup Moisturizer 2oz $5* **MP 50¢**
1974 *Lipstick .13oz $2.25* **MP 25¢**
1974 *Cream Foundation 2oz $5* **MP 50¢**
1975 *Powder Shadow Duet (not shown) $3.50* **MP $1**
1977 *Gentle Liquid Makeup (not shown) 2oz 3 shades $5* **MP 75¢**

1966-75 *Lipstick $1.75* **MP 25¢**
1966-75 *Face Powder 1 shade 1¾oz $2.50* **MP $1**
1966-75 *Natural Veil 2 shades 1oz $2.25* **MP 50¢**
1967-74 *Finishing Glo ¾oz $2.50* **MP 50¢**
1966-74 *Pressed Powder with Puff .5oz $3* **MP $2**
(See Lip Gloss Pot, p. 112)

** Available from Avon at time of publication*

A Certain Look –

1972-75 *Dew Glow 2¼oz $3.50* **MP $2, $3.50 boxed**
1970-74 *Lipstick .13oz $1.50* **MP $1**
1972-75 *Lash-Long Mascara .15oz $2* **MP $1**
1970-74 *Blushpetite and Brush .19oz $3* **MP $2**
(See Eye Shine pg. 113)

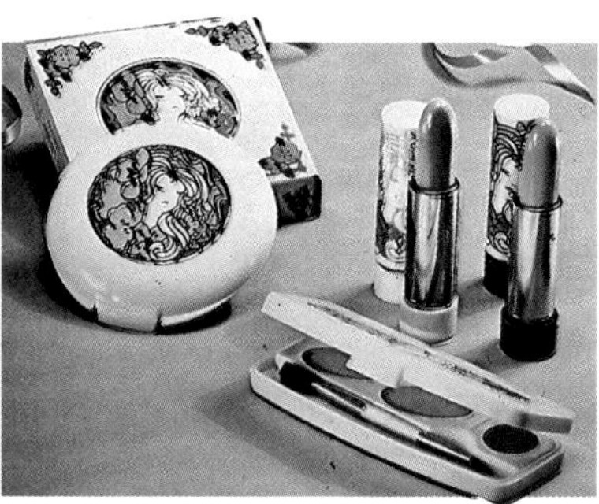

1970-74 *Blushpetite.19oz $3* **MP $3 boxed**
1970-74 *Lipstick $1.50* **MP $1**
1970-74 *Lip Beamer .13oz $1.50* **MP $1**
1970-74 *Shadow and Liner Trio. Cake Eyeliner .02oz, 2 Eye Shadows .08oz and double-tipped Brush $4.50* **MP $3**

Spunsilks –
1980 *Spunfinish Cream Makeup 1oz $6.50* **MP $6***
1980 *Spunpowder Eye Shadow Duo .20oz $8* **MP $7***
1980 *Spuncolor Lipstick .13oz $4.50* **MP $4***
1980 *Spuncolor Nail Enamel .5oz $4* **MP $4***
1980 *Spuncolor Blush .20oz $8* **MP $7***

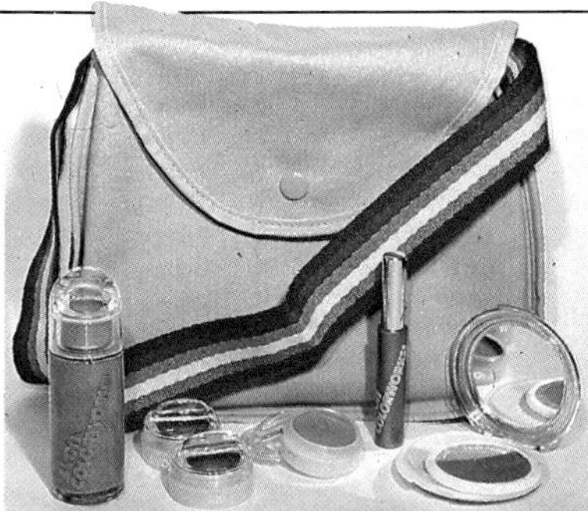

1977 *Colorworks –*
Oil-Free Makeup 1.5oz $3 **MP $4***
Supershine Lip Gloss .15oz $2.50 **MP $2***
Oil-Free Cheekblush .20oz $3 **MP $2.50***
Lasting Color Eye Shadow .15oz $2.50 **MP $2.50***
Lashes, Lashes Mascara .25oz $2.75 **MP $3***
1978 *Oil-Absorbing Pressed Powder Compact .5oz $3.75* **MP $5***
1977 *Canvas Bag. Free with purchase* **MP $12**

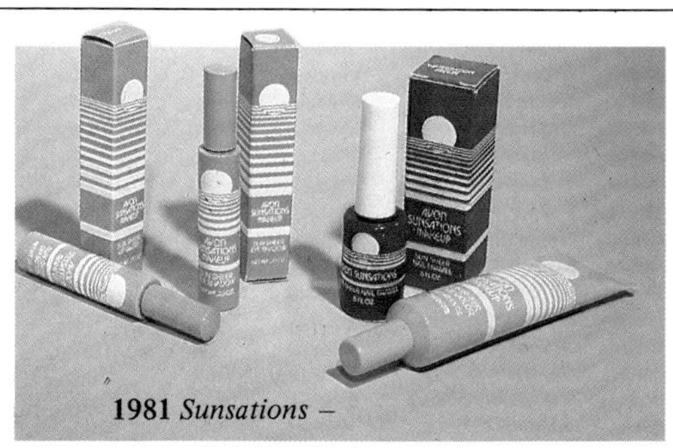
1981 *Sunsations –*

Sun Sheer Eye Shadow .20oz $5 **MP $4***
Sun Sheer Lip Gloss .25oz $5 **MP $4***
Sun Sheer Nail Enamel .5oz $3.50 **MP $3***
Sun Sheer Face Color 1.5oz $4 **MP $3***

(See Candid, Patterns & Sweet Honesty in Fragrance Line section)

1980 *Colorcreme*

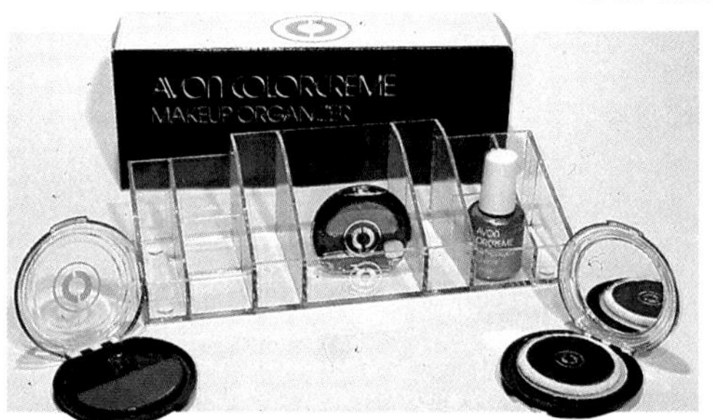

Makeup Organizer 10x3½" with purchase, U.S. only $3.99 **MP $6**
Creamy Powder Blush .25oz and Brush $5 **MP $4***
Creamy Powder Eye Shadow .10oz $4 **MP $4***
All-Over Face Color 1oz $3.50 **MP $3***
Colorsetter Powder Compact .5oz $5 **MP $4***

Moisturizing Blushing Cream .25oz $3.50 **MP $3*** *(left)*

Cream Eye Shadow .25oz $3.50 **MP $3.50***
Blush-Up Stick .25oz $5 **MP $4.50***
Moisture Lipstick .13oz $2.50 **MP $3***
Waterproof Mascara .20oz $3.50 with silver lid **MP $3**
Waterproof Mascara .20oz $3.50 (white lid) **MP $3***

1979 *Envira –*
Pure Color Blush .33oz $4 **MP $4***
Conditioning Makeup 1oz $4 **MP $4***
Soft Eye Definer .25oz $4.50 **MP $4***
Gentle Eye Color .25oz $4 **MP $5***
Conditioning Mascara .25oz $4 **MP $4***
Pure Color Lipstick .13oz $2.75 **MP $3***

Fashion Makeup Group

1977 *Cremelucent Collection $16* **MP $20 set**
Under-Makeup Moisturizer 2oz $5 **MP $1**
Cremelucent Lipstick .13oz $2.50 **MP $3***
Powder Eye Shadow .10oz $3.50 **MP $4***
Cremelucent Foundation 2oz $5 **MP $4.50***
1971 *Blushing Stick .75oz $4* **MP $5***

* *Available from Avon at time of publication*

1975 *Liqui-lucent Foundation 2oz 1 shade $4* **MP $1**
1976 *Pressed Powder Compact 5oz, Translucent $5.50* **MP $1**
1978 *Cremelucent Moisture Blush .5oz $3.75* **MP $1**
1971 *Under-Makeup Moisture Veil 2oz Aerosol $5* **MP $1**

1974 *Automatic Eyeshadow .15oz $4.50* **MP 50¢**

1975 *Creamy Rouge Compact .20oz $4* **MP $1**
1971 *Brushstick for Lips .05oz $4.50* **MP $1**
1975 *Eye Color Creme .25oz (white cap) $2.50* **MP $25¢**
1973 *Eye Color Creme .25oz (gold cap) $2.50* **MP $1**
1973 *Moisture Droplets 2oz $4* **MP 50¢**

1980 *Avon Number One Packaging –*

Colorcreme Cream Eye Shadow .25oz $4.50 **MP $3, $4 boxed**
Colorcreme Lipstick .13oz $3.50 **MP $2, $3 boxed**
Colorcreme Mascara .20oz $4 **MP $2, $3 boxed**
Ultra Wear Nail Enamel .25oz $2.75 **MP $2, $3 boxed**

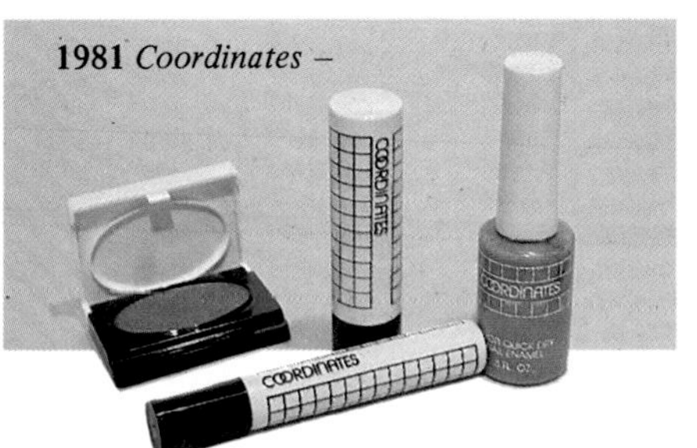

1981 *Coordinates –*

Smooth Touch Powder Eye Shadow .08oz $4.50 **MP $3***
Full Color Lipstick .13oz $3 **MP $2***
Quick Dry Nail Enamel .5oz $2.50 **MP $2***
Roll-On Lash Color .15oz $3.50 **MP $3***

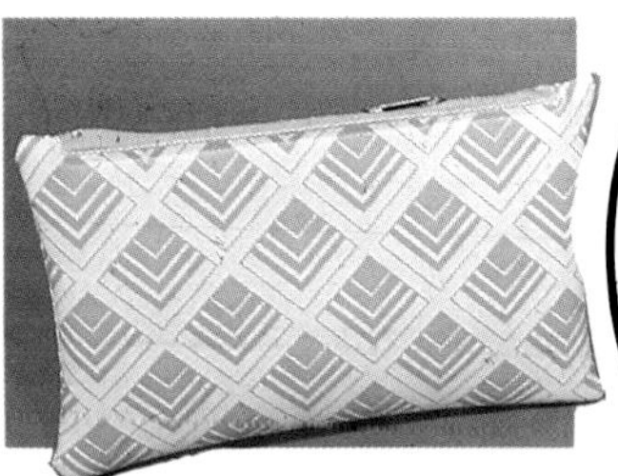

SKIN CARE LINES BY AVON

1977 *Zippered Cosmetic Case $1 with specified purchase. Designed exclusively for Avon, the Deco-inspired vinyl case is approximately 8x5". Included, a pamphlet of makeup tips from Sunny Griffin on how to make yourself more beautiful. One campaign only. Retail value over $3* **MP $5**
(See matching mirror pg. 262)

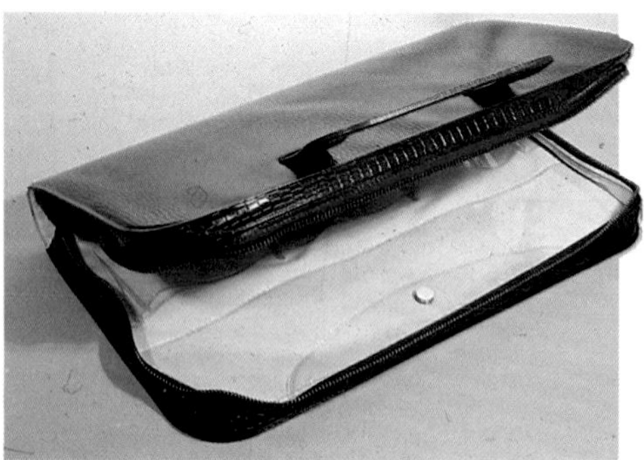
1976 *Sunny Griffin Makeup Case. First a Sales Prize and then sold to Representatives* **MP $13 with Award Certificate, $8 without**

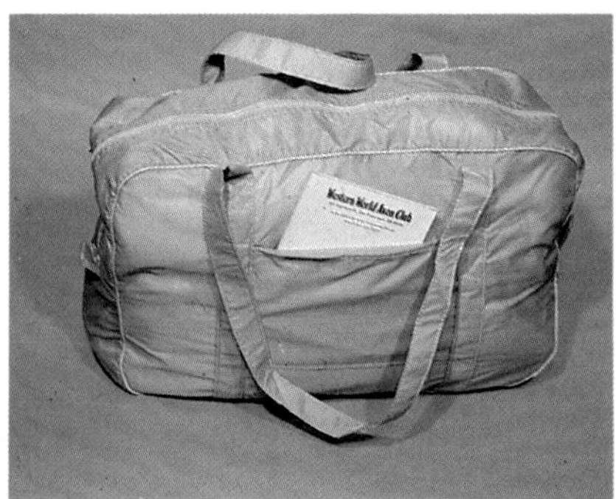
1980 *Sportin' Tote. Nylon bag with $5 purchase in C-17 only $6.99* **MP $8**

1981 *Spring Beauty Bag, 7¼x5" fabric with $8.50 purchase in C-6 only. Take-Along Hand Cream inc. free $1.99* **MP $5, $6 boxed (U.S. only)**

Rich Moisture

1953-54 only *Cream, embossed lid, 2oz $1.50* **MP $15**
1954-57 *Cream 2oz (shown) & 3½oz $1.50 & $2.50* **MP $6 each**
1957-61 *Cream 2oz $1.50* **MP $3**
1957-61 *Cream 3½oz $2.50* **MP $4**
1961-72 *Cream 2oz $1.50* **MP $1, $1.50 boxed**

(below left)
1977-80 *Cream (lid change) 3.5oz $3.50* **MP 75¢**

1973-77 *Cream 3.5oz $3* **MP 50¢**
1965 *Lotion 8oz $3* **MP $1**
1969-75 *Hand Cream 3.75oz 89¢* **MP 50¢**
1974-75 *Hand Cream 6oz $2* **MP $2**
1972-78 *Bath Bar 5oz $1.50* **MP $2.50**

1979 *Trial Size Hand Cream .5oz with purchase 35¢* **MP 50¢**
1980 *Face Cream 3.5oz $3.50* **MP $3***
1980 *Hand Cream 3.75oz $2* **MP $1***
1980 *Facial Lotion 4oz $3.75* **MP $3***
1980 *Body Lotion 8oz $3.50* **MP $2***

Vita-Moist

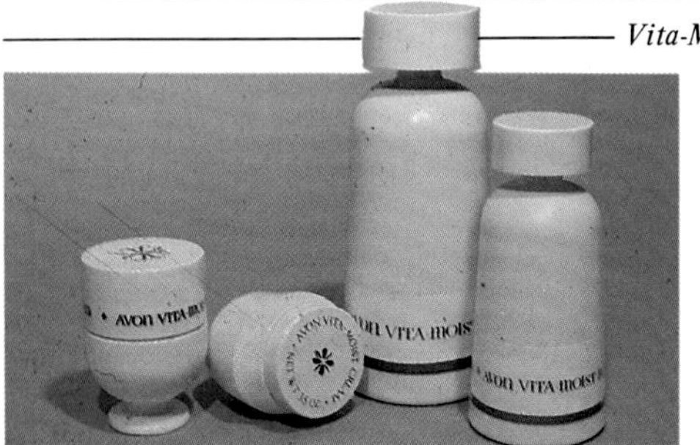

1959 *Cream 2oz $3* **MP $2**
1961 *Cream 1oz (not shown) $1.75* **MP $4**
1974-80 *Cream 3.5oz $3.50* **MP 50¢**
1974-80 *Lotion 16oz $5.50* **MP 75¢**
1969-80 *Lotion 8oz (new design) $3* **MP 25¢**

1980 *Body Lotion 8oz $3.50* **MP $2***
1980 *Hand Cream 3.75oz $2* **MP $1***
1980 *Face Cream 3.5oz $3.50* **MP $3***

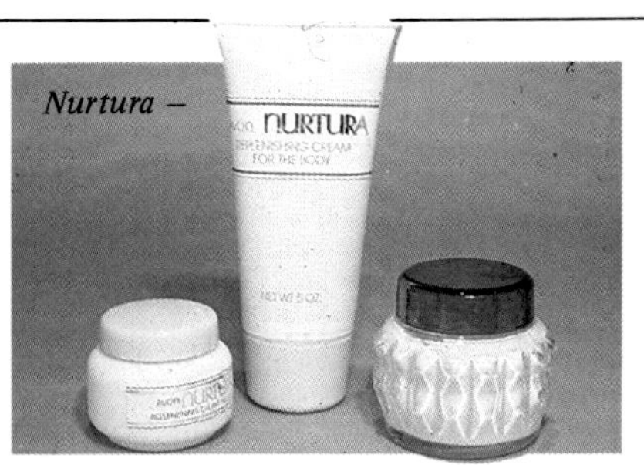

Nurtura –

1979 *Replenishing Cream 2oz $5.50* **MP $5***
1980 *Replenishing Cream for the Body 5oz $5.50* **MP $5***
1980 *Vanity Jar 4oz $8* **MP $4**

* *Available from Avon at time of publication*

SKIN CARE LINES

Perfect Balance, Dry Skin –

1974 *Tissue-Off Cleansing Cream 4oz $3* **MP 50¢**
1974 *Night Cream 2½oz $4* **MP 50¢**
1974 *Toning Freshener 6oz $3* **MP 50¢**
1974 *Eye Cream ¾oz $3.50* **MP 50¢**

Perfect Balance, Oily Skin –

1974 *Toning Astringent 6oz $3* **MP 50¢**
1974 *Night Time Moisturizer 3oz $4* **MP 50¢**
1974 *Wash-Off Cleansing Lotion 4oz $3* **MP 50¢**

Summer Dew –
1973 *Moisturizing Body Fluff 4oz $5* **MP $4**
1973 *Moisturizing Body Creme 5oz $5* **MP $4**

Dew Kiss

1975 *Dew Kiss 5oz $4.50* **MP 75¢**

1972 *Dew Kiss 1.5oz $1.50* **MP 25¢**

1966 *Dew Kiss (left) 1½oz $1.25* **MP $3**
(1967 *As above, 3½oz $2.50* **MP $3)**
1960 *Dew Kiss 1½oz $1.25* **MP $5 with Tag**

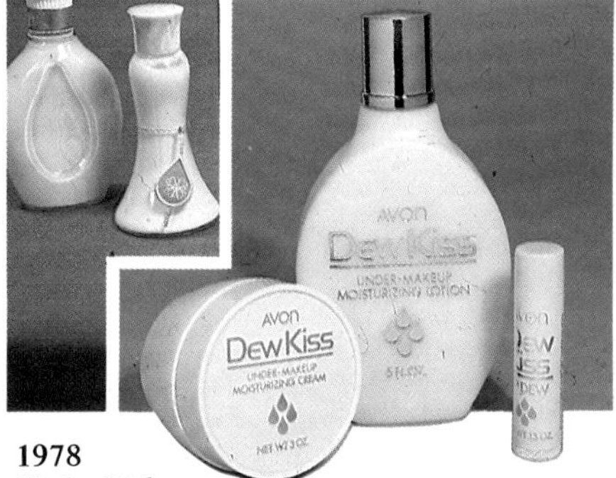

1978
Under-Makeup Moisturizing Cream 3oz $3.50 **MP $4***
1978 *Under-Makeup Moisturizing Lotion 5oz (shown) $4.50* **MP $2.30*,**
1.5oz $2 **MP $2*,** *3.5oz $3.50* **MP $1**
1978 *Lip Dew .15oz $1.75* **MP $1***

1973 *Vanity Decanter 4oz $4* **MP $5**
1974 *Vanity Decanter 4oz $5* **MP $4**
1974 *Vanity Decanter 4oz $5* **MP $3**

* *Available from Avon at time of publication*

Prima Natura

1971 *Thermal Facial and Mask 3oz $6.50* **MP $7 complete**
1971 *Cleansing Formula 4oz $5.50* **MP $6**
1971 *Moisturizing Freshener 4oz $3.50* **MP $5**

1971 *Toning Freshener 4oz $3.50* **MP $5**
1971 *Creme of Soap 5oz $4.50* **MP $5**
1971 *Night Veil Concentrate 2½oz $6* **MP $5**
1971 *Eye Cream Concentrate ¾oz $4* **MP $5**

Delicate Beauty

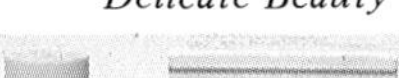

1976 *Gentle Freshener 5oz $4* **MP 50¢**
1976 *Whipped Nightcreme 3oz $5* **MP 50¢**
1976 *Lotion Cleanser 4oz $4* **MP 50¢**

1980 *Pure Essentials –*
Cold Cream 3oz $1.89 **MP $1.75***
Petroleum Jelly Plus 4oz $1.89 **MP $1.75***
All-Purpose Cream 3oz $1.89 **MP $1.75***

Skinplicity –

1978 *Tote Bag. Free with purchase of 3 Skinplicity items in C-12* **MP $6.50**
1978 *Complexion Bar 3oz $1.50* **MP $1**
1978 *Facial Toner 6oz $3* **MP 50¢**
1978 *Cream Cleanser 4oz $3* **MP 50¢**
1978 *Moisturizer AM/PM 3oz $4* **MP 50¢**

Moisture Secret

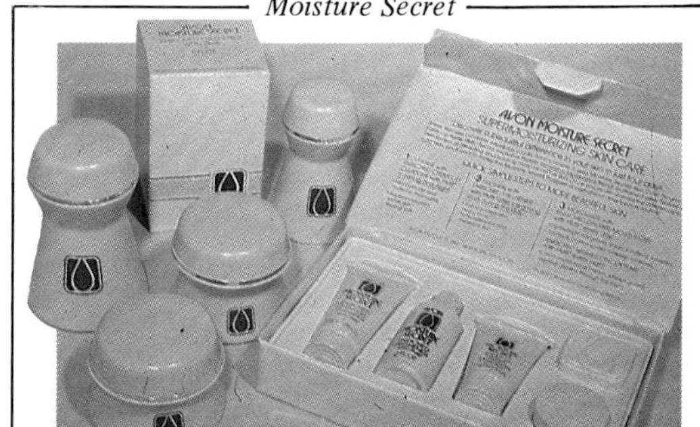

1975 *Enriched Freshener 5oz $5* **MP 50¢**
1977 *Daytime Moisturizer 3oz $5* **MP 50¢**
1975 *Cremegel Cleanser 4oz $5* **MP 50¢**
1975 *Night Concentrate 3oz $6* **MP 50¢**
1978 *4-Day Difference Kit: $2.50* **MP $6 boxed**

CLEAR SKIN

1957 *Soap 3¼oz 49¢* **MP $9 boxed**

1957 *Lotion 6oz $1* **MP $10**
1963 *Lotion 3oz 79¢* **MP $1**

1959 *Clear-It Shampoo 6oz $1.25* **MP $5**
1961 *Clear-It Suds 6oz $1.25* **MP $5**

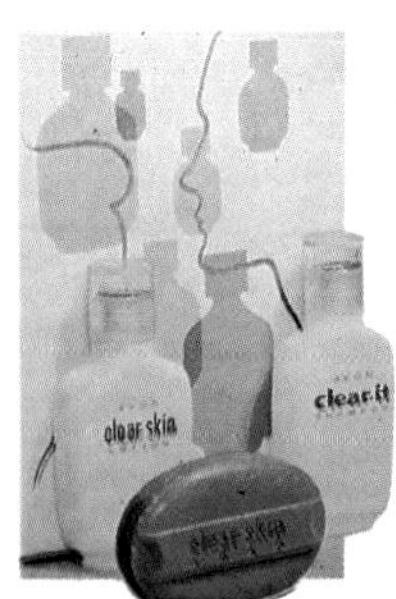

1959 *Clear-It Skin Care Kit. Soap, Lotion, Clear-It Shampoo $2.50* **MP $28**

1973 *Liquid Cleanser 5oz $2* **MP 50¢**
1970 *Lotion 4oz $1.50* **MP $1**
1970 *Liquid Makeup 2oz $1.75* **MP $1**

. . . SKIN CARE LINE

(rear)
1978 *Med. Astringent 12oz $2.99* **MP $3.50***
1978 *Medicated Liquid Cleanser 10oz $2.99* **MP $3***

1970 *Cleansing Grains 4½oz $1.75* **MP 75¢**

1974 *Liquid Cleanser 10oz $3.50* **MP 50¢**
1973 *Astringent 12oz $3* **MP 50¢,** *6oz $1.75* **MP 50¢**

1973 *Cleansing Gel 6oz $3* **MP $1**
1970 *Soap 3oz 70¢* **MP $2**

1976 *Cleanser Plus 3oz $1.79* **MP 50¢**
1977 *Blemish Cream 1oz $1.29* **MP 75¢**

1970 *Cream Cleanser 5oz jar $1.50* **MP $1**
1978 *Medicated Lotion 4oz $1.89* **MP $2.75***
1978 *Medicated Soap 3oz 99¢* **MP $1***
1978 *Medicated Cleanser Plus 3oz $1.99* **MP $2.50***

Care Deeply –

1973 *Hand Cream 4oz $1.35* **MP $1.50*,** *6oz $1.79* **MP $2***
1974 *Lotion 16oz shown $2.99* **MP $3*,** *8oz $1.99* **MP $2***
1975 *Lip Balm .15oz $1.10* **MP 25¢**
1977 *Lip Balm with Sunscreen .15oz 79¢* **MP 60¢***

Moisture Garden

1979 *Pump Dispenser, free with Body Lotion in C-3 only* **MP $1.50 boxed**
1979 *Hand Cream 4oz $1.59* **MP $1.75***
1979 *Body Lotion 10oz $2.99* **MP 50¢**
1979 *Facial Lotion 4oz $2.59* **MP 50¢**
1979 *Rosea Vinca Collection Seed Starter Kit $1 with purchase in C-3 only* **MP $2**

1980 *Envira –*
Conditioning Cleansing Cream 3.75oz $5 **MP $5***
Clarifying Toner 5oz $5 **MP $5***
Protective Moisturizing Lotion 2oz $5 **MP $5***
All-Night Conditioning Cream 3.75oz $6 **MP $6***

1970 *American Sportster –*
Super Stick 1/3oz $2.50 **MP $4**
Showering Soap/Shampoo 8oz $2.50 **MP $4**
Skin Comfort Gel 3oz $2.50 **MP $4**
Outdoor Shield .9oz $2.50 **MP $4**

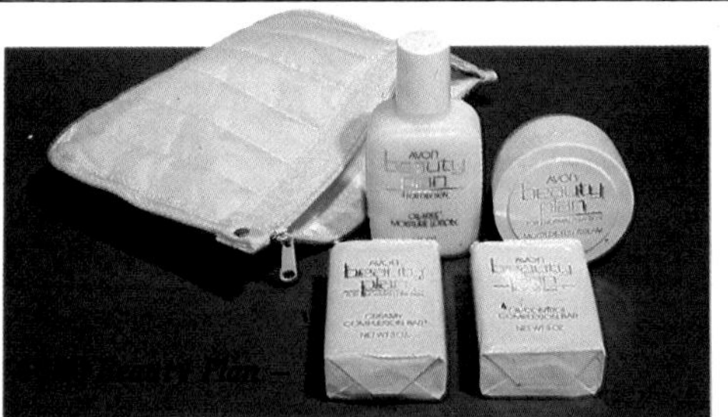

Beauty Plan Bag with purchase only in C-13 $2.99 **MP $3.50**
Oil-Free Moisture Lotion 3oz $4 **MP $3***
Moisture-Full Cream 3oz $4 **MP $3***
Creamy Complexion Bar 3oz $1.75 **MP $1.25***
Oil-Control Complexion Bar 3oz $1.75 **MP $1.25***

1981 *Accolade –*

Facial Toning Rinse 4oz $7.50 **MP $6***
Complete Cleansing Complex 3oz $7.50 **MP $6***
Daytime Moisture Support 3oz $7.50 **MP $6***
Night Treatment 1.75oz $8.50 **MP $7***

** Available from Avon at time of publication*

1930-34 *Bleach Cream 3oz 75¢* **MP $45**

1930-34 *Tissue Cream 2oz 75¢* **MP $45**

1932-34 *Rose Cold Cream 2oz 52¢* **MP $45**
1930-32 only *Rose Cold Cream (not shown) 4oz 75¢* **MP $55**

1930-32 *Violet Nutri-Cream 4oz $1* **MP $55**
1932-34 *As above (not shown) 2oz 65¢* **MP $45**

1931-34 *Cleansing Cream 4oz $1* **MP $55**
1934-35 *Bleach Cream 2oz 52¢* **MP $38**

CREAMS AND LOTIONS

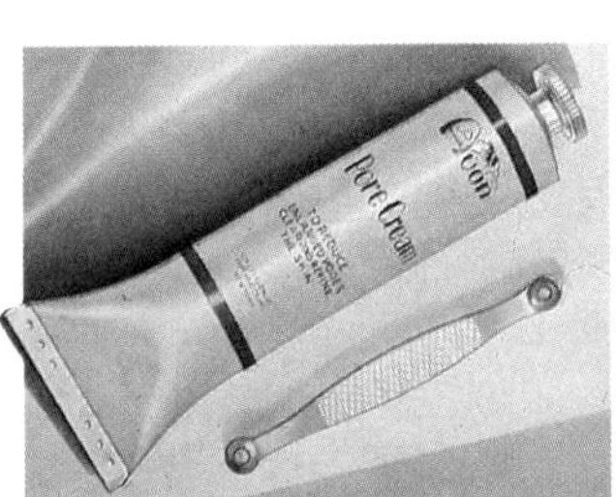

1930-34 *Pore Cream 75¢* **MP $25**
1930 *Blackhead Remover 15¢* **MP $10**

1932-34 *Vanishing Cream 2oz 52¢* **MP $45**

1930-32 *Vanishing Cream 4oz 75¢* **MP $55**

1934-36 *Rose Cold Cream 4oz 78¢* **MP $40**

1934 *Violet Nutri-Cream 2oz 52¢* **MP $38** *(left)*

1934-36 *Cleansing Cream 4oz 78¢* **MP $40**
1934-36 *Tissue Cream 2oz 52¢* **MP $38**
1934-36 *Vanishing Cream 2oz 52¢* **MP $38**
Above jars, boxed, MP add $8

1934-36 *Pore Cream 78¢* **MP $22, $30 boxed**
1936 *Pore Cream 1¼oz 78¢* **MP $12, $18 boxed**

1940 *Special Formula Cream 1¼oz 78¢* **MP $10**

1956 only *Cleansing Cream 2½oz 59¢* **MP $9, $12 boxed**

1941 *Rose Cold Cream in gift box 1¾oz 52¢* **MP $18 as shown**
1940 *Rose Cold Cream in gift box 2oz 52¢* **MP $20 as shown**

1951 *Cleansing and Night Cream Set. 2 large jars, 1 medium size $1.78* **MP $35 set**

Witch Hazel

1930-34 *Witch Hazel Extract 4oz (shown) 8oz & 16oz 50¢, 85¢ and $1.45* **MP $45, $55 & $75**

1934-36 *Witch Hazel Extract 4, 8 and 16oz 33¢, 57¢ and $1.04* **MP $40, $50 & $70**

1930-34 *Witch Hazel Cream 75¢* **MP $25**

1930-34 *Menthol Witch Hazel Cream 50¢* **MP $25**

1936-39 *Witch Hazel Cream 52¢* **MP $12, $18 boxed**

1937 *Witch Hazel Extract 4oz 37¢, 8oz 63¢ 16oz $1.04* **MP $25**
1939-41 *Witch Hazel Cream, tube 52¢* **MP $11, $15 boxed**

Night Cream 1¾oz each (add $4 to MP for box) –

1944-45 *For Normal skin 89¢* **MP $10 w/black lid**
1951-54 *Ozonized 89¢* **MP $9, $20 ("Distributor")**
1941-51 *Normal Skin 78¢* **MP $8**
1944-45 *Dry Skin 89¢* **MP $10 w/black or white lid**
1941-46 *Dry Skin 78¢* **MP $8**
(1940-41 *Dry, Normal or Oily, not shown,*
2oz *78¢* **MP $10)**

Cleansing Creams 3½oz (add $4 to MP for box) –

1944-45 *Dry Skin 89¢* **MP $10 w/ metal lid**
1941-46 *Oily Skin 78¢* **MP $8**
1944-45 *Oily Skin 89¢* **MP $10 w/metal lid**
1941-46 *Dry Skin 78¢* **MP $8**
1944-45 *Dry Skin 89¢* **MP $10 w/white lid**
(1937-41 *Dry, Normal or Oily, not shown, 4oz 78¢* **MP $10)**

1937-41 *Violet Nutri Cream 2oz 52¢ (shown) & 4oz 78¢* **MP $12**
1941-45 *Violet Protective (formerly Nutri) Cream 3½oz 78¢* **MP $9**
1944-45 *Violet Protective 3½oz 89¢* **MP $11 w/metal lid**
1941-45 *Violet Protective 1¾oz 52¢* **MP $9**
1944-45 *Violet Protective 1¾oz 59¢* **MP $11 w/black lid** *(add $4 to MP for box)*

DATING GUIDE FOR JARS FROM 1937 THROUGH 1954

Catalogs often did not reflect the changes in labels. Original product pictures were often seen in subsequent catalogs. Jar size, contents and label information all aid in dating these Cream Jars.
1937-38 *Jar labels appeared with name of product, tulip-A and Avon.*
1939 *Avon Products, Inc., Div. N.Y.-Montreal was added to the labels.*
1939-47 *Labels were changed to read Avon Products, Inc., Dist. N.Y. -Montreal.*
1947-51 *Labels were changed to Avon Products, Inc., Dist. N.Y.-Pasadena and the tulip-A was dropped from the label.*
1951-54 *Labels were changed to read Avon Products, Inc., N.Y.-Pasadena (Dist. was dropped).*
Jar Sizes: 1937-41 *Shown in catalogs as: Medium (2oz) and Large (4oz)*
1941-54 *Medium (1¾oz) and Large (3½oz). Smaller jar sizes were issued in sets only.*
1939-46 *Makeup creams were issued only in 7/8oz size jars – Foundation Cream, Color Pick-Up and Twin-Tone.*
Regular Pricing:
1937-42 *52¢ (Medium) and 78¢ (Large).*
1942-54 *59¢ (Medium) and 89¢ (Large).*
Name Changes:
1940 *Tissue Cream re-named Complexion Cream, discontinued in* **1949**
1941 *Viloet Nutri-Creme re-named Violet Protective, discontinued* **1945**
1943 *Foundation Cream re-named Twin-Tone, changed in* **1946** *to Color Pick-Up.*
1947 *Night Cream for Dry Skin re-named Special Dry Skin, changed in* **1950** *to Super Rich.*
1951 *Night Cream for Normal Skin re-named Ozonized Night Cream.*
1953 *Rose Cold Cream re-named All-Purpose Cream, discontinued in* **1954** *in this jar design.*

Cleansing Creams 3½oz (add $4 to MP for box) –
1941-46 *Normal Skin 78¢* **MP $8**
1944-45 *Normal Skin 89¢* **MP $11 with metal lid and Victory folder**
1947-54 *Fluffy type 89¢* **MP $8**
1947-54 *Fluffy type 89¢* **MP $8**
(1937-41 *For Dry, Normal or Oily, not shown,* **4oz** *78¢* **MP $10)**

1946 only *Color Pick-Up Cream 7/8oz 89¢* **MP $20**
1939-43 *Foundation Cream 7/8oz 52¢* **MP $10**
1943 *Foundation Cream 7/8oz 59¢* **MP $12**
1937-40 only *Tissue Cream 2oz 78¢* **MP $13**
1936-39 *Tissue Cream 7/8oz (in Facial sets only)* **MP $15**
(add $4 to MP for box)

1943 *Complexion Cream (formerly Tissue) 1¾oz 59¢* **MP $12**
1940-49 *Complexion Cream 2oz 52¢* **MP $8**
1941-45 *Vanishing Cream 1¾oz 59¢* **MP $9**
1937-41 *Vanishing Cream 2oz 52¢* **MP $12**
1951-54 *Super-Rich Cream (formerly Special Dry Skin Cream) 1¾oz 89¢* **MP $9**
$20 ("Distributor" on label)
(add $4 to MP for box)

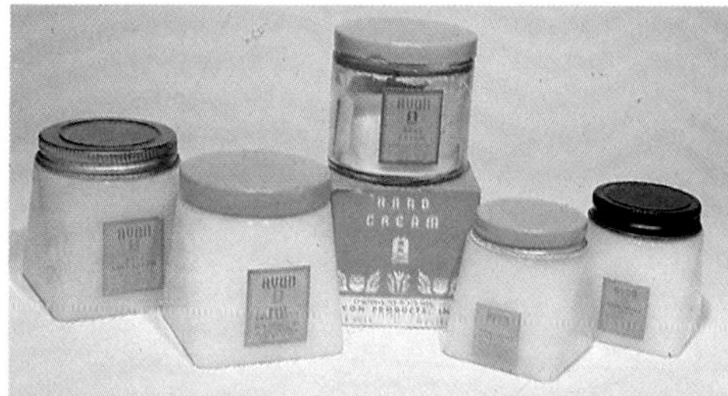

1944-45 *Rose Cold Cream 3½oz 89¢* **MP $10 w/metal lid**
1941-53 *Rose Cold Cream 3½oz 78¢* **MP $8**
1943-45 *Hand Cream 3-1/3oz $1.78* **MP $20 in wartime pkg., Boxed $25**
1946-51 *Special Formula Cream 1¾oz 89¢* **MP $9**
1945 *As above w/black lid* **MP $11**

1957-61 *Strawberry Cooler 3¾oz $1.50* **MP $6**
1961-69 *Creme Supreme 2¼oz $3* **MP $3**
1969-74 *Creme Supreme 2¼oz $3* **MP $1**
1968-69 *Super Rich Cream 2¼oz $3* **MP $4**
1965-68 *Super Rich (not shown) as above but lid label in script and 4-A gold design* **MP $3**

1954-61 *Hormone Cream 1¾oz $2* **MP $4**
1965-74 *Hormone Cream 2¼oz $3* **MP $1**
1969-74 *Stepping Out Foot Care Cream 4oz $2* **MP 50¢**
1976-80 *Cold Cream 3.1oz $1.39* **MP 25¢**

1980 *Time Control .75oz $7.50* **MP $6***
1980 *Beauty Fluid 3oz $5* **MP $4***
1981 *Banishing Cream 3oz $6.50* **MP $5***

** Available from Avon at time of publication*

1935-36 *Skin Freshener 2oz 45¢* **MP $50**
1930-36 *Skin Freshener 4oz 75¢* **MP $45**
1935-36 *Astringent 2oz 45¢* **MP $50**
1930-36 *Astringent 4oz 75¢* **MP $45**

1930-36 *Lotus Cream 4oz 75¢* **MP $45**
1936-44 *Lotus Cream 4oz 52¢* **MP $18**
1936-54 *Skin Freshener 4oz 78¢* **MP $15**
1936-54 *Astringent 4oz 78¢* **MP $15**

1954-58 *Skin Freshener 2oz (sets only)* **MP $5**
1965-66 *Skin Freshener for Dry or Normal Skin 4oz $1.25* **MP $7**
1957-65 *Skin Freshener or Astringent, Moisturized 4oz $1* **MP $4**
1954-57 *Astringent (shown) or Skin Freshener (pink lotion) 4oz $1* **MP $5**

1966-69 *Deep Clean Wash-Off Cleanser for Normal Skin 6oz $1.25* **MP $3**
1966-69 *Deep Clean Cleansing Lotion for Dry Skin 6oz $1.25* **MP $3**
1966-69 *Deep Clean Wash-Off Cleanser for Oily Skin 6oz $1.25* **MP $3**

1968-69 *Skin Freshener, Moisturized, for Dry Skin 4oz $1.25* **MP $2**

1968-69 *Skin Freshener, Moisturized, for Normal Skin 4oz $1.25* **MP $2**
1968-69 *Astringent Freshener, Moisturized, for Oily Skin 4oz $1.25* **MP $2, $3 boxed**
(1966-68 *As above, except labels read: For Dry, Normal or Oily Skin* **followed** *by the word Moisturized* **MP $4)**

1969-73 *Skin Freshener 4oz $1.25* **MP $1**
1969-73 *Astringent 4oz $1.25* **MP $1**
1970-73 *Cleansing Lotion 6oz $1.50* **MP $1**

1945-49 *Leg Makeup 4oz 49¢* **MP $20, $25 boxed**
1945-47 *Sun Cream 4oz 85¢* **MP $20**

1943-45 *Sun Cream 4oz (black lid) 85¢* **MP $20**
1943-45 *Leg Makeup 4oz (black lid) 69¢* **MP $20**

1966 *Lady Shave 4oz (blue cap) $1.25* **MP $2**
1971 *Lady Shave 4oz (pink cap) $1.25* **MP 50¢**
1971 *Fashion Legs Leg Makeup Trial 1oz 50¢ with purchase* **MP 75¢**
1968 *Fashion Legs Leg Makeup 6oz $3* **MP 50¢**

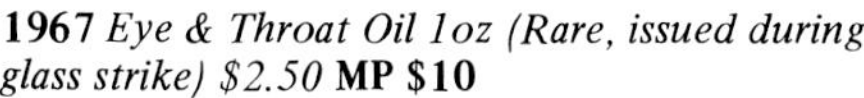
1967 *Eye & Throat Oil 1oz (Rare, issued during glass strike) $2.50* **MP $10**

1965 *Eye & Throat Oil 1oz $2.50* **MP $3**
1960 *Eye Cream .58oz $1.75* **MP $2**

Insect Repellant –

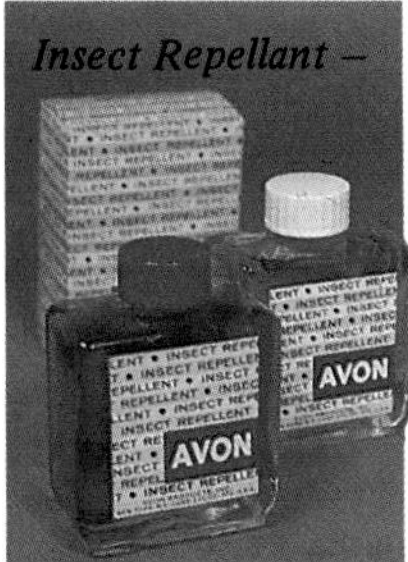

1959 *(red cap) 2oz 59¢* **MP $8**
1960 *(white cap) 2oz 59¢* **MP $7**

1949-57 *Sun Lotion 4oz 98¢* **MP $12**

1958 *Tan Moisturized Suntan Lotion 4oz 98¢* **MP $3**
1962 *Kwick Tan for Quickest Tan 4oz $1.10* **MP $1**

Bronze Glory –

1975 *Tanning Lotion 6oz $3* **MP 25¢**
1977 *Tanning Butter 1.75oz $1.49* **MP 25¢**
1975 *Kwick Tan 5.5oz tube $3* **MP 25¢**
1975 *Sun Safe 5.5oz tube $3* **MP 25¢**
1973 *Sun Safe Stick .15oz 89¢* **MP $25**

1979 *Sun Seekers – (rear) Tanning Oil 4oz $2.29* **MP $3***
Sunsafe Lotion 4oz $2.29 **MP $3***
Tanning Lotion 4oz $2.29 **MP $3**

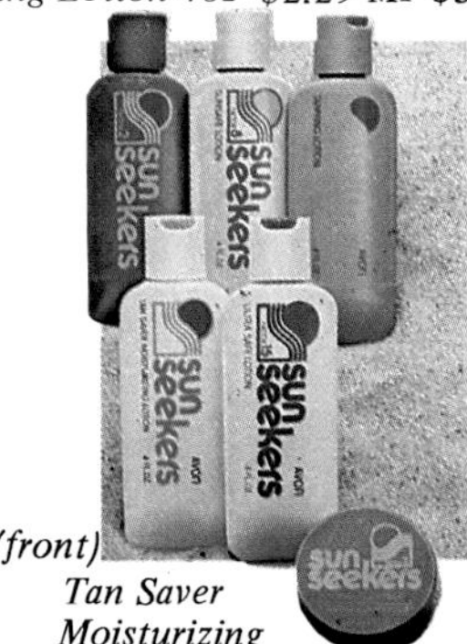

(front) Tan Saver Moisturizing Lotion 4oz $2.29 **MP $3***
1980 *Ultra Sunsafe Lotion 4oz $3.75* **MP $4***
1980 *Tanning Butter 1.75oz $3* **MP $3***

** Available from Avon at time of publication*

1934-35 *Hand Cream 52¢*
MP $22

1938-54 *Hand Creams 2½oz 52¢*
MP $8, $12 boxed

1939 *Hand Cream 52¢* **MP $20 boxed**
1941 *Hand Cream 52¢* **MP $17 boxed**

1940 *Hand Cream 52¢* **MP $18 boxed**

1942 *Hand Cream 59¢* **MP $17 boxed**

1955-57 *Hand Cream 59¢* **MP $6 (Pasadena)**
1957-59 *Hand Cream 59¢* **MP $5 (Pasadena)**
1958-62 *Moisturized Hand Cream 79¢* **MP $4**
1962-68 *Moisturized Hand Cream 3¾oz 89¢* **MP $3**

1957 *Hand Cream, Xmas boxed 59¢*
MP $8

HAND CREAMS AND FACIALS

1959 *Hand Cream, Xmas boxed 59¢* **MP $7**
1962 *Silicone Glove, Xmas boxed 2¼oz 79¢*
MP $5

1963
Moisturized Hand Cream, Xmas boxed 3¾oz **MP $5**

1960 *Hand Cream, Xmas boxed 69¢* **MP $6**
1960 *Moisturized Hand Cream, Xmas boxed 89¢* **MP $6**

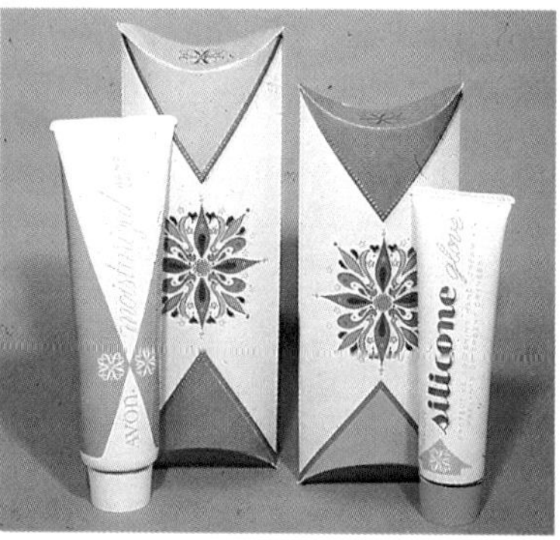

1964 *Moisturized Hand Cream, Xmas boxed 89¢* **MP $5**
1964 *Silicone Glove, Xmas boxed 79¢*
MP $4

1980 *Take-Along Hand Cream in Vita-Moist (red) or Rich Moisture (blue) 1oz $1.29 each* **MP 75¢**

Facial Masks

1967 *New You Peel-Off Masque 2oz $2.50* **MP $2, $3 boxed** *(left)*

1977 *Moistureworks Creamy 3oz $3*
MP 50¢
1978 *Fresh Strawberry Peel-Off 3oz $3*
MP $2*
1973 *Peach Supreme Creamy 3oz $2* **MP 75¢**
1977 *Natural Earth 3oz $3* **MP $2***

1979 *Ripe Avocado Cond. 3oz $3*
MP $2* *(left)*

1976 *Cucumber Cooler Peel-Off 3oz $3*
MP $2*
1977 *Lemon Peel-Off 3oz $3* **MP $2***
1975 *Essence of Camomile 4oz $2* **MP 50¢**
1978 *Milk Frost 3oz $3* **MP 50¢**
1971 *Matter of Minits, Aerosol 3.75oz $2.50* **MP $2**

1962 *Rosemint 3oz $1.25* **MP $3, $5 boxed**
1980 *Aloe Smooth Peel-Off 3oz $3*
MP $2*
1981 *Egg White Firmer Peel-Off 3oz $3.50* **MP $2***

1978 *Cucumber Cooler Facial Freshener 8oz $3.50* **MP 75¢**
1978 *Cucumber Cooler Splash-Off Cleanser 6oz $3.50* **MP 75¢**

** Available from Avon at time of publication*

1930-36 *Rose Water, Glycerine & Benzoin 4oz 75¢* **MP $45**

1936 *Rose Water, Glycerin & Benzoin 4oz Xmas boxed 78¢* **MP $60**
1937-41 *Rose Water, Glycerin & Benzoin 4oz 78¢* **MP $20, $25 boxed**

1941-47 *Hand Lotion, Rose Water, Glycerine & Benzoin 4oz 52¢* **MP $17, $21 boxed**

Hand Lotion –
1948-50 *4oz 59¢* **MP $17**
1950-53 *4oz 59¢* **MP $16**
1953-58 *4oz 69¢* **MP $6**

. . . AND LOTIONS

1958-62 *White Pearl Hand Lotion 6oz 98¢* **MP $4**
1966-70 *Hand Lotion 10oz $1.50* **MP $3, $6 as shown in 1966 Xmas box**
1970-74 *Moisturized Hand Lotion 10oz $1.50* **MP $2**
1969-74 *Protective Hand Lotion with Silicone 7.75oz $1.50* **MP $2**

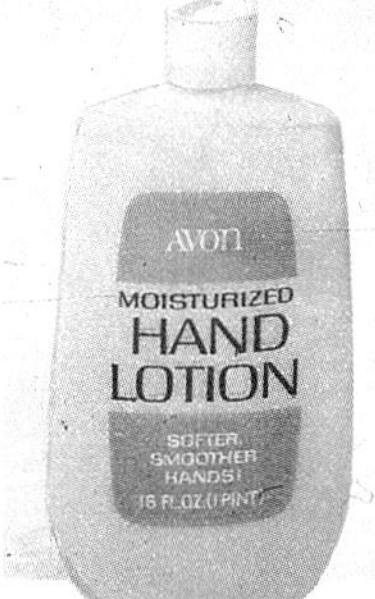

1979 *Moisturized Hand Lotion 16oz $2.99* **MP 50¢**

1975 *Perfect Care Body Lotion for Dry Ashy Skin 6oz $3* **MP 50¢**
1970 *Silicone Glove 2.25oz 79¢* **MP $1.25***, *4.5oz $1.35* **MP $2***
1976 *Moisturized Hand Lotion 16oz $2.69* **MP 75¢**

1956 *Hand Lotion 8oz $1.39* **MP $15, $22 as shown in 1957 Xmas box**

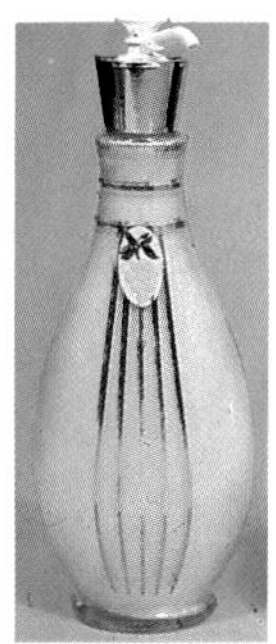

1963 *Gift Hand Lotion 8oz $2.50* **MP $11**

1965 *Gift Body Lotion. Rich Moisture or Vita Moist Lotion 8oz $3.50* **MP $8**

1973 *Pineapple Decanter with Moisturized Hand Lotion 10oz $6* **MP $9**

1974 *Country Pump with Rich Moisture or Vita Moist Lotion 10oz $6* **MP $6**
1977 *Golden Harvest Moisturized Hand Lotion 10oz $8.50* **MP $6**

1971 *Lovely Touch with Rich Moisture or Vita Moist Lotion 12oz $6* **MP $7**
1972 *Lovely Touch with Rich Moisture or Vita Moist Lotion 12oz $6* **MP $8**

LOTION DISPENSERS

Country Style Coffee Pots, Moisturized 10oz Hand Lotion – **1975** *Blue $7.50* **MP $7**
1978 *Yellow $8.50* **MP $6**
1979 *Red $9.50* **MP $6**
1979 *Green $9.50* **MP $6**

1976 *Country Jug Moisturized Hand Lotion 10oz $8* **MP $5**
1978 *Country Creamery, 10oz Moisturized Hand Lotion $8.50* **MP $5**
1979 *Garden Fresh Moisturized Hand Lotion 10oz $9.50* **MP $7***

DEODORANTS . . .

1929-30 *Deodorant 2oz 50¢* **MP $75**

1930-36 *Deodorant 2oz 50¢* **MP $45, $55 boxed**
1944-47 *Liquid Deodorant with Applicator 2oz 59¢* **MP $22, $30 boxed**

1937-44 *Deodorant 2oz 52¢* **MP $20**

1938-44 *Cream 37¢* **MP $8, $12 boxed**

** Available from Avon at time of publication*

1947-48 only *Perfumed 2oz 59¢* **MP $10 with N.Y.–Montreal label, $14 boxed**

1948-54 *Perfumed 2oz 59¢* **MP $6 (Pasadena), $8 boxed**
1967-76 *Perfumed 2oz 79¢* **MP $1**
1967-68 *As above 4oz (not shown) $1.25* **MP $4**
1976 *Perfumed 2oz $1.49* **MP $1.50***

1955-67 *Perfumed 2oz 69¢* **MP $2**
1963-66 *Flow-On (glass) 1¾oz 89¢* **MP $6**
1960-63 *As above, plastic (not shown)* **MP $4**
1963-66 *Cream 1¾oz 79¢* **MP $3**

1960-63 *Cream 1¾oz 79¢* **MP $4**

1966 *Cream 1¾oz 79¢* **MP $4***
1967-70 *Cream 1¾oz 79¢* **MP $2**
1970-71 *Cream* **1.75oz** *(not shown) 98¢* **MP $4**
1971-76 *Cream 2oz 98¢* **MP 50¢**

1958-60 *Flow-On 2oz 98¢* **MP $5**
1954-60 *Cream 1oz 49¢* **MP $5**

. . .DEODORANTS

1956-60 *Stick 1.8oz 79¢* **MP $8**
1960 only *Stick 1.8oz 79¢* **MP (4-A on lid) $15**
1972-76 *Habit 1.5oz $1.50* **MP $1**
1970-72 *As above 1¼oz (not shown) $1.25* **MP $3**

1960-63 *Habit 1¼oz $1* **MP $3**
1963-65 *Habit, Normal 1¼oz $1* **MP $3**
1967-70 *Habit 1¼oz $1.25* **MP $2**
1970 only *Habit 1¼oz $1.25* **MP $4**

1965-67 *Habit 1¼oz $1.25* **MP $3**
1965-66 *Aerosol 3oz $1.25* **MP $4**
1965-66 *Touch-On 1¾oz $1.25* **MP $5**
1965-68 *Stick 2¾oz $1.25* **MP $3**

1960-63 *Stick 1¾oz 89¢* **MP $7**

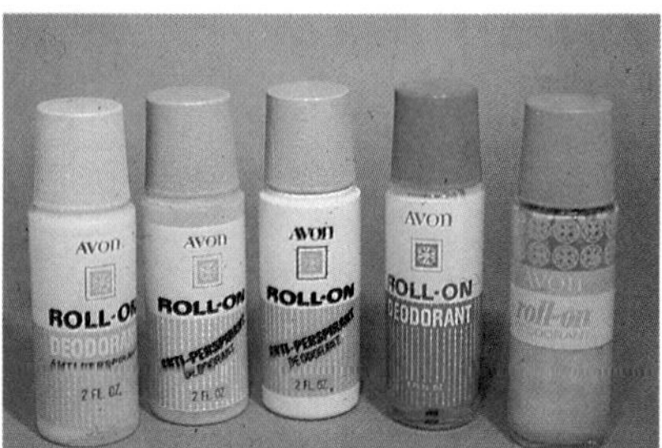

1969-71 *Roll-On 2oz 98¢* **MP $3**
1972-76 *Roll-On 2oz $1.35* **MP 50¢**
1971-72 *Roll-On 2oz 98¢* **MP $1**
1968-69 *Roll-On 1¾oz 98¢* **MP $3**
1966-67 *Roll-On 1¾oz 98¢* **MP $4**

1966-67 *Spray 3oz (squeeze bottle) 98¢* **MP $3**
1968-76 *Aerosol Perfumed 4oz $1.25* **MP $1**
1970-76 *Aerosol Family 7oz $1.79* **MP 50¢**
1971-76 *Unscented Ultra-Dry 7oz $1.89* **MP 50¢**
1970-75 *Ultra-Dry 7oz $1.25* **MP 50¢**

On Duty –
1977 *Soap 3oz (special only)* **MP 50¢**
1975 *Aerosol 7oz $2.75* **MP 50¢**
1977 *Spray 4oz $2.29* **MP 50¢**
1976 *Roll-On 2oz $1.49* **MP $1.25**

Feelin' Fresh – **1978-81** *Body Powder 8oz $1.99* **MP 50¢**
1978-81 *Body Splash 8oz $2.29* **MP 50¢**

Dri-N-Delicate –
1976 *Swivel-Up Cream 1.5oz $1.69* **MP 50¢**
1976 *Roll-On 2oz $1.49* **MP $1.25***
1976 *Cream 2oz $1.49* **MP 50¢**

1978 *Deodorant Soap 3oz shown in Bonus wrapper, free to customers in introduction campaign* **MP $2**
1978 *Roll-On Deo. 2oz $1.49* **MP $1.25***
1978 *Aerosol Deo. 4oz $2.59* **MP $2***
1978-81 *Foot Comfort Spray 3oz $2.59* **MP 50¢**

1970 *Assura Spray 3oz $1.75* **MP $1.50**
1972 *Assura Spray Powder 3oz $1.75* **MP $1.50**

ANTISEPTICS

1930-37 *Antiseptic 6oz 35¢* **MP $35**
1933-37 *12oz (not shown) 62¢* **MP $40**
1936-41 *Antiseptic 6oz 36¢* **MP $18**
1936-41 *12oz (not shown) 62¢* **MP $23**
1941-54 *Antiseptic 6oz 36¢* **MP $10**
1941-54 *12oz (not shown) 62¢* **MP $14**
1954-61 *Antiseptic 7oz 49¢* **MP $5**

* *Available from Avon at time of publication*

(See Men's Deodorants pgs. 188-189)

1931-37 *Dental Cream 25¢* **MP $30**

1931-37 *Sen Den Tal 40¢* **MP $30**

1931-37 *Dental Cream No. 2, 40¢* **MP $30**

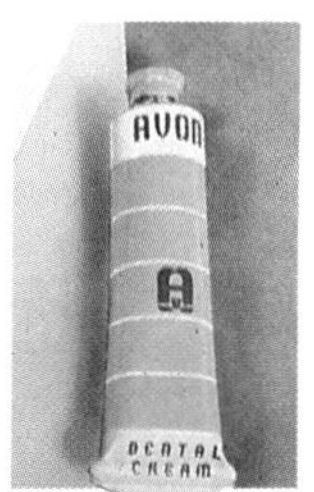

1937-47 *Dental Cream 26¢* **MP $22**

1937-40 *Sen Den Tal 36¢* **MP $26**

1937-49 *Tooth Paste 23¢* **MP $22**

1941-50 *Tooth Paste No. 2, 25¢* **MP $20**

1953-56 *Tooth Paste (white) 49¢* **MP $15**
1953-56 *Tooth Paste (green) with Chlorophyll 49¢* **MP $15**

Dental Cream was a foamy dentifrice, containing no abrasives or strong chemicals.

Sen Den Tal was a mildly abrasive cleanser, especially designed for hard to clean teeth.

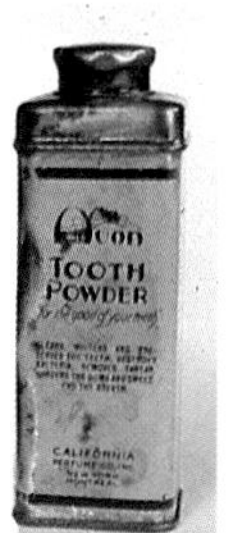
1932-37 *Tooth Powder 35¢* **MP $35**

1930-31 *Tooth Powder 35¢* **MP $40**

1930-31 *Smoker's Tooth Powder 50¢* **MP $45**

1950-54 *Smoker's Tooth Powder 57¢* **MP $18** *(left)*

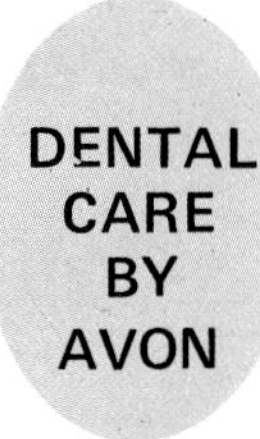

Smoker's Tooth Powder cleaned teeth and also destroyed mouth odors, especially those of tobacco.

1931-36 *Smoker's Tooth Powder 50¢* **MP $38**
1938-42 *Smoker's Tooth Powder 51¢* **MP $30**
1944-45 *Smoker's Tooth Powder 51¢* **MP $20**
1942-43 *Smoker's Tooth Powder 51¢* **MP $25**

1943-44 *Smoker's Tooth Powder 51¢* **MP $25**

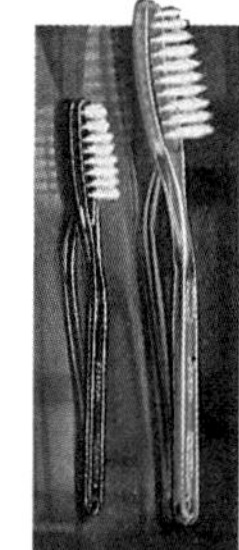
1932-47 *Tooth Brushes, Amber, Red or Green. Adult 50¢, Youth 35¢* **MP $5 each**

1936-38 *Smoker's Tooth Powder 50¢* **MP $35**
1946-50 *Smoker's Tooth Powder 51¢* **MP $18**
1936 *Smoker's Tooth Powder Samples (CPC label)* **MP $50**
1937 *Smoker's Tooth Powder Sample* **MP $40**

1943-44 *Tooth Powder 26¢* **MP $25**
1940 only *Tooth Paste No. 2 25¢* **MP $35 (see 1941-50 above)**
1936-49 *Tooth Powder 36¢* **MP $20**
1949-55 *Ammoniated Tooth Powder 49¢* **MP $15**

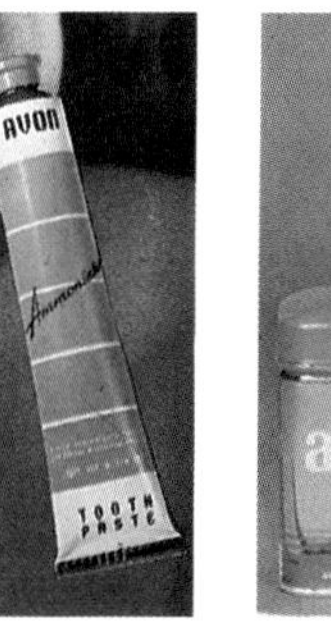

1949-55 *Ammoniated Tooth Paste 49¢* **MP $15**

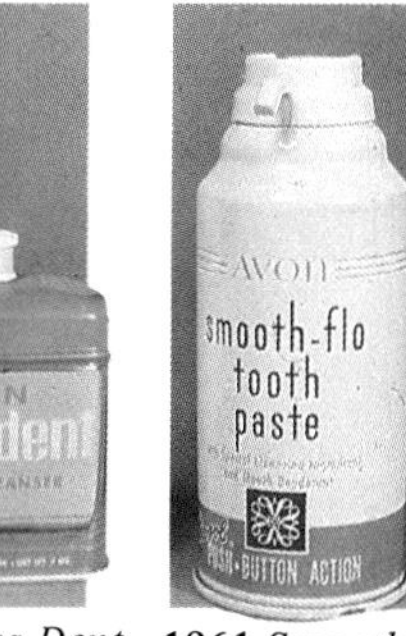

1958 *Aqua-Dent 7oz 99¢* **MP $8**

1961 *Smooth-Flo Tooth Paste 5½oz 89¢* **MP $5**
1958 *As above, with red cap (not shown)* **MP $8**

Breath Fresh –

1971 *Spray-Peppermint .5oz $1.50* **MP $1**
1968 *Spray .5oz $1.25* **MP $1**
1970 *Concentrated Mouth Wash 1oz $1.75* **MP $2**
1969 *Tooth Paste 4.75oz 89¢* **MP $2**

1976 *Flavor Fresh Mouthwash 14oz $1.59* **MP 50¢**

1976 *Plaque Control Toothbrush, blue only 98¢* **MP $1 boxed**
1978 *Plaque Control Toothbrush in blue, red or green $1.09* **MP $1 boxed**
1969 *Smoker's Toothpaste 4.75oz 89¢* **MP $1 (new size, labeling)**

1974-75 *Twice Bright Tooth Polish 2¾oz $1.89* **MP $2**
1981 *Twice Bright Toothpaste 5oz $1.89* **MP $1.50***
1981 *Twice Fresh Mouthwash 10oz $2.49* **MP $2***
1981 *Twice Clean Toothbrushes. Blue and green in 1 box $2.49* **MP $2***

** Available from Avon at time of publication*

Elite and Antiseptic Powders

A body talcum containing a mild deodorant, a baby powder, a foot powder and a powder to relieve skin irritations were benefits provided by Elite. Because of World War II, it was necessary to replace the metal containers with cardboard packaging in 1943. Discontinued in 1955, Elite was followed with its counterpart, Avon Antiseptic Powder.

1932-36 *Elite Powder 3oz 35¢* **MP $45**
1932-36 *16oz (not shown) $1* **MP $55**
1936-49 *16oz $1.04* **MP $30**
1936-54 *Elite Powder 37¢* **MP $19**
1944-45 *Elite Powder, cardboard 43¢* **MP $25**

1943-44 *Elite Powder, cardboard 43¢* **MP $25**

1955-62 *Antiseptic Powder 3oz 59¢* **MP $6**
1962-68 *Antiseptic Powder 2¾oz 69¢* **MP $3**

1968-72 *Antiseptic Powder 3.5oz 89¢* **MP $1**

(See also Elite Powders pg. 21)

1930-36 *Dusting Powder 8oz $1.35* **MP $50**

1930-31 *Talcum 35¢* **MP $45**

1932-36 *Daphne Talcum 35¢* **MP $40**
1932-36 *14½oz $1* **MP $50**

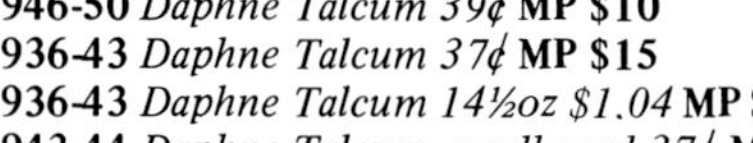

1930-32 *Daphne Talcum 35¢* **MP $45**
1946-50 *Daphne Talcum 39¢* **MP $10**
1936-43 *Daphne Talcum 37¢* **MP $15**
1936-43 *Daphne Talcum 14½oz $1.04* **MP $45**
1943-44 *Daphne Talcum, cardboard 37¢* **MP $25**
1944-45 *Daphne Talcum, cardboard 37¢* **MP $25**

1940 only *Daphne Talc, customer gift with purchase, 10¢* **MP $30 as shown**

TALCS AND DUSTING POWDERS

1936-49 *Dusting Powder 13oz $1.20* **MP $35**

1942-48 *Beauty Dust 6oz $1.10* **MP $38**

1943-44 *Beauty Dust in gift box $1.10* **MP $45, $55 boxed**

1937-46 *Cotillion Talcum 2¾oz 35¢* **MP $15, $18 boxed**

1946-50 *Cotillion Talcum 2¾oz 37¢* **MP $10, $13 boxed**
1946-50 *Daphne Talcum 14½oz $1.04* **MP $30**

1958-61 *Floral Talc 59¢* **MP $12**

1978 *Talc 3.5oz in Burst of Spring box in 6 grag. $2* **MP $1***

1974 *Perfumed Talcs 3.5oz in 4 Xmas scene gift boxes. 7 frag. $1.50 and $2* **MP $2.50 each with box**

1979 *Ultra Perfumed Talcs 3.5oz in Xmas Gift wrap, 6 fragrances $3* **MP $2**
1979 *Perfumed Talcs in Xmas Gift wrap, 10 frag. $2.50* **MP $1.50**

1980 *Perfumed Talc 3.5oz in Xmas Gift wrap (red) 6 frag. $3* **MP $1**
1980 *Ultra Perfumed Talc 3.5oz in Xmas wrap (silver) 7 frag. $3.50* **MP $1.50**
1979-80 *Lady Skater Talc in Sweet Honesty or Ariane 3.75oz $5.50* **MP $3**

BEAUTY DUST CONTAINERS

1971 *Crystalique Beauty Dust (plastic) in Hana Gasa, Elusive, Charisma, Regence, Unforgettable, Rapture, Somewhere, Here's My Heart, Topaze, Cotillion, To A Wild Rose and Occur! $8* **MP $7**

1972 *Crystalique Beauty Dust (glass). Same fragrances as 1971 except Hana Gasa and To A Wild Rose, add Moonwind. $8* **MP $11**

1973 *Cameo Beauty Dust Container 5½" diam. Sold empty for $5* **MP $7**

1975 *Beauty Dust Crystalique Container, sold empty $6* **MP $7***

1966 *Beauty Dust Demonstrator. Box pictures one of 8 containers to fill with choice of 8 Beauty Dust fragrances* **MP $10 box only**

1981 *Sweet Sentiments Valentine Candy in Tin dated "Valentine's Day 1981". Two campaigns only 9oz $7.99* **MP $5 container only**

1966 *Pat 'N' Powder Mitt and Beauty Dust in Occur!, Rapture or Unforgettable 2½oz $2.50* **MP $7, $9 boxed**

1980 *Pamper-Puff Powder Mitt with zippered compartment to hold talc. Sold empty $9* **MP $7, $8 boxed**

Powder Mitts

1957 *Beauty Dust 6oz with ribboned 5/8 dram bottle of matching fragrance in Cotillion, Forever Spring, To A Wild Rose, Nearness, Elegante & Bright Night $1.95-$2.50* **MP $35, $45 Xmas boxed**

1958 *Beauty Dust 6oz with ribboned 5/8 dram bottle of matching fragrance same as 1957 fragrances (above) $1.95-$2.50* **MP $35, $45 Xmas boxed**

1953 *Beauty Dust 6oz with ribboned 5/8 dram bottle of matching fragrance in Cotillion, Forever Spring, Golden Promise, To A Wild Rose and Quaintance $1.75* **MP $45**

BEAUTY DUST GIFTS

1956 *Beauty Dust 6oz with ribboned 5/8 dram bottle of matching fragrance. Same fragrances as 1957, except Quaintance replaces Elegante $1.95* **MP $40, $50 Xmas boxed**

** Available from Avon at time of publication*

More than 80 years ago, a lady used Bandoline for graceful, wavy hair.

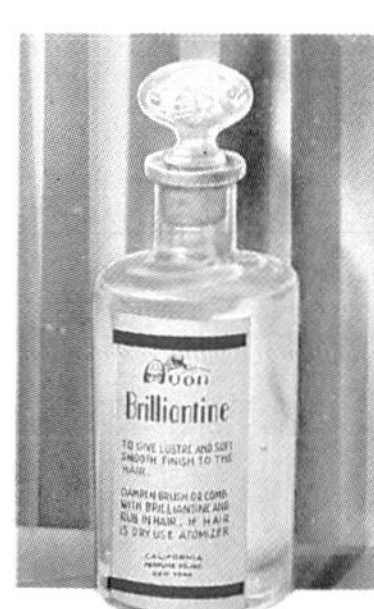

1929-30 *Brilliantine 2oz 50¢* **MP $75**

1930-36 *Hair Tonic Eau de Quinine for Oily Hair 6oz 90¢* **MP $45,** *16oz $1.75* **MP $60**

1930-36 *Hair Tonic Eau de Quinine for Dry Hair 6oz 90¢* **MP $45,** *16oz $1.75* **MP $60**

1930-36 *Pre-Shampoo Oil 2oz 75¢* **MP $45**

1930-36 *Liquid Shampoo 6oz 75¢* **MP $45,** *16oz $1.50* **MP $60**

1930-36 *Wave Set 4oz 75¢* **MP $45**

Eau de Quinine, a delicately scented hair tonic, was used to help prevent dandruff, stop falling hair and retard the graying of the hair.

1930-36 *Brilliantine 2oz 50¢* **MP $45**

1930-36 *Bandoline Hair Dressing and Wave Lotion 35¢* **MP $45**

1936-43 *Wave Set 4oz 52¢* **MP $18**

1936-47 *Brilliantine 2oz 52¢* **MP $15 (Montreal label), $18 boxed**
1944-45 *Brilliantine 2oz 59¢* **MP $18 black lid (Montreal label)**
1943 *Brilliantine 2oz 59¢ (different lid)* **MP $18 (Montreal label)**

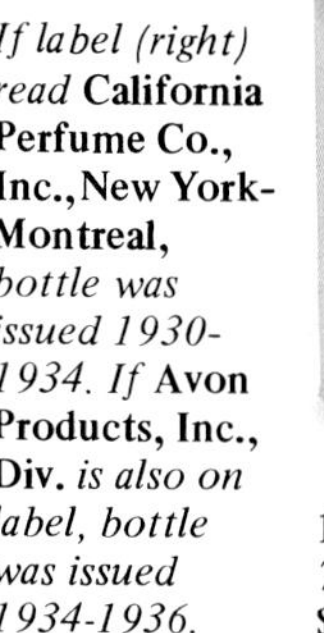

If label (right) read **California Perfume Co., Inc.,New York-Montreal,** *bottle was issued 1930-1934. If* **Avon Products, Inc., Div.** *is also on label, bottle was issued 1934-1936. (See right)*

1934-36 *Wave Set 4oz 78¢* **MP $45, $55 boxed**

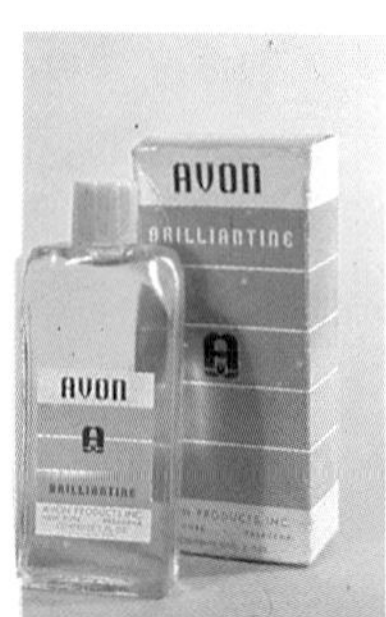

1950-54 *Brilliantine 2oz 59¢* **MP $15, $18 boxed with Pasadena label**

1937-51 *Liquid Shampoo 6oz 51¢* **MP $15, $35 Pasadena label without Dist.**
1937-50 *Liquid Shampoo 16oz $1.02* **MP $20, $45 with Pasadena label.**
1950-54 *Cocoanut Oil Shampoo (formerly Liquid Shampoo) 6oz 59¢* **MP $18,** *16oz* **MP $30**

1953-54 *Creme Hair Rinse 6oz 89¢* **MP $20**
1953-54 *Creme Lotion Shampoo 6oz $1* **MP $20, $25 boxed**

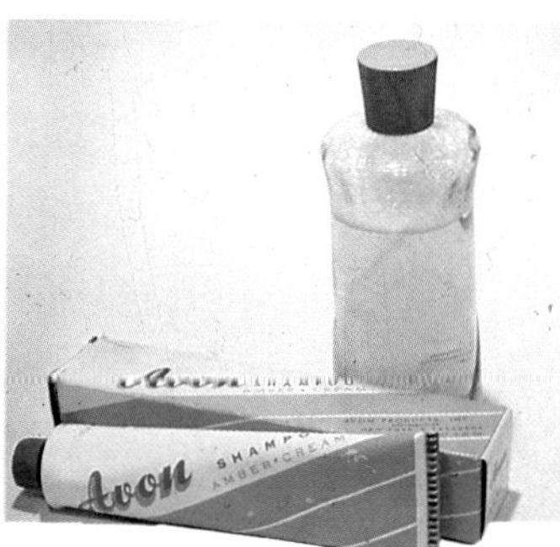

1947-49 *Amber Cream Shampoo 59¢* **MP $22, $30 boxed**
1954-57 *Liquid Cocoanut Oil Shampoo 6oz 79¢* **MP $15,** *16oz $1.59* **MP $25**

1954-56 *Creme Lotion Shampoo 6oz $1* **MP $18**
1954-60 *Creme Shampoo (tube) 6oz 59¢* **MP $8**
1952-53 *Creme Shampoo (jar) $1* **MP $20, $25 boxed**

1960-64 *Sheen-Glo Shampoo 6oz $1.19* **MP $6**
1959-62 *Hi-Light Shampoo for Normal (shown), Dry or Oily Hair 6oz $1.19* **MP $5**
1960-62 *Creme Shampoo 2¼oz 69¢* **MP $8**
1961-65 *Cream Pomade 1¾oz 89¢* **MP $4**

1956-65 *Hair Cosmetic 3oz $1* **MP $3**
1956-64 *Creme Hair Rinse 6oz $1* **MP $3**
1958-64 *AVONnet Regular (shown) or Fine Hair Spray 5oz $1.25* **MP $6**
1961-63 *Sheer-Touch Hair Spray 7oz $1.50* **MP $5**

(See Men's on pgs. 188-190)

1971 *Aerosol Hair Conditioner 2oz $3* **MP 59¢ (label change)**
1966 *Sheen Hair Dressing 2oz $1* **MP $2**

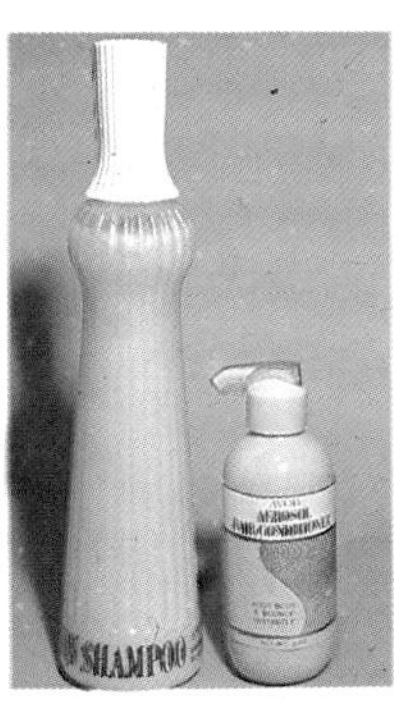
1969 *Gentle Lotion Shampoo 8oz $1.50* **MP $1**
1967-71 *Aerosol Hair Cond. 2oz $3* **MP $2**

hi-light

1963 *Shampoo 12oz $1.50* **MP 50¢**

Gel Shampoo, 3oz 79¢:
1963 *Oily hair* **MP $1** 1963 *Dry hair* **MP $1**
1965 *Tinted, bleached, damaged hair* **MP $1**
1963 *Normal hair* **MP $1**
1968 *Dry, bleached or damaged hair* **MP 50¢**

1975 *Shampoo for normal, oily and dry hair 6.5oz each $1.49* **MP 50¢**
1976 *Creme Rinse 6oz $1.49* **MP 50¢**
1975 *60-second Hair Cond. 6oz $1.49* **MP 50¢**
1975 *Hair Setting Gel $1.49* **MP 50¢**

1969-70 *Hair Color (Test areas only). Cream Developer, Hair Colorant 2oz each and plastic gloves $2.50* **MP $25 complete**

1971-74 *Color Perfect Hair Color. Cream Developer, Hair Colorant 2oz each and plastic gloves $2.50* **MP $4 complete**

1978 *Shampoo for normal, dry or oily hair, extra-size bottle 8.7oz (1 Campaign only) $1.49* **MP $2**

1979 *Shampoo for oily, normal and dry hair 6¼oz each $1.49* **MP $1.75***
1979 *Creme Rinse 6¼oz $1.49* **MP 50¢**

1974 *Spray Creme Rinse 8oz $1.89* **MP 50¢**

Naturally Gentle –
1976 *Shampoo 8oz $1.79* **MP $2**
1976 *Shampoo Trial Size 2oz 25¢ with other purchase* **MP 25¢**
1976 *One Step Creme Hair Rinse 8oz $1.39* **MP 25¢**

1972 *Resilient –*
Hair Spray 7oz $2 **MP 50¢**
Shampoo 8oz $3 **MP 50¢**
Hair Texturizer 4oz $2.50 **MP 50¢**

Keep Clear –
1978 *Anti-Dandruff Shampoo 7oz $2.29* **MP $$2.75***
1979 *Anti-Dandruff Cream Shampoo 7oz $2.49* **MP 50¢**
1973 *Essence of Balsam Conditioner 8oz $3* **MP 50¢**
1977 *Trial Size 2oz 25¢* **MP 50¢**

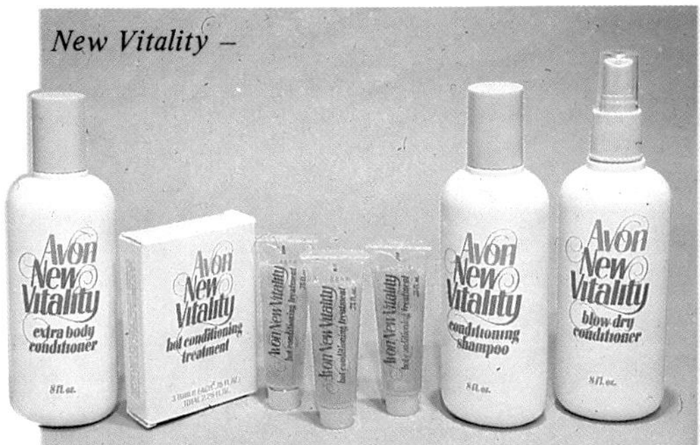

New Vitality –
1978 *Extra Body Conditioner 8oz $2.49* **MP $2.75***
1978 *Hot Conditioning Treatment. Box of three .75oz tubes $2.49* **MP $2.75 ***
1978 *Conditioning Shampoo 8oz $2.49* **MP $2.75***
1979 *Blow-Dry Conditioner 8oz $2.49* **MP $2.75***

Curl Set –
1968 *Setting Lotion 8oz $1.50* **MP 50¢**
1964 *As above, but 7oz $1.50* **MP $2**
1966 *Concentrate 6oz $1.50* **MP 50¢**

1976 *Natural Sheen Hair Dress and Conditioner 3oz $2* **MP 50¢**
1975 *Curl Set Setting Lotion 8oz $1.98* **MP 25¢**
1977 *Firm and Natural Hair Spray 6oz $2.29* **MP $2.50***
1978 *Full Control Natural Pump Hair Spray 6oz $2.29* **MP $2.50***

1980 *Clean & Lively Oil-Free Conditioner 7oz $2.59* **MP $2***
1980 *Clean & Lively Oil-Control Shampoo 7oz $2.59* **MP $2***
1980 *Body Bonus Conditioner 7oz $2.99* **MP $2.50***
1980 *Body Bonus Shampoo 7oz $2.99* **MP $2.50***

1981 *Hair Lights Color Accents in Moonlight Copper, Sunlight Gold, Starlight Ash ½oz $6* **MP $5***

. . . HAIR CARE

* *Available from Avon at time of publication*

Protem

1974 *Dandruff Shampoo 3oz $2.50* **MP 50¢, 1973** *(not shown) $2* **MP $1**
1975 *Super Rich Hair Conditioner 3oz $2.50* **MP 50¢**
1972 *Conditioning Hair Set 6oz $2* **MP 50¢, 1969** *(different lid)* **MP $1**
1975 *Creme Rinse 6oz $3* **MP 50¢**

1971 *Lotion Shampoo 8oz $3* **MP 50¢**
1974 *Hair Contitioner 12oz $5* **MP 50¢**
1975 *Super Rich Hair Conditioner 1oz Trial Size 69¢* **MP 50¢**

Sunny Morn, 8oz $2.29 each:

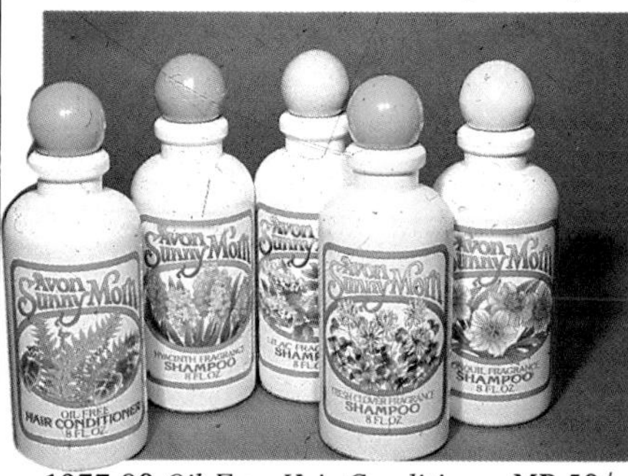

1977-80 *Oil-Free Hair Conditioner* **MP 50¢**
1977-81 *Hyacinth Fragrance Shampoo* **MP 50¢**
1977-80 *Lilac Fragrance Shampoo* **MP 50¢**
1978-80 *Fresh Clover Fragrance Shampoo* **MP 50¢**
1977-81 *Jonquil Fragrance Shampoo* **MP $50¢**

1979-80 *Strawberry Fragrance Shampoo* **MP 50¢**

HAIR CARE

1967-71 *Stay Hair Groom for Men 7oz $1.50* **MP $1**
1968-70 *Unscented Hair Spray 7oz $1.50* **MP $2**
1973-77 *Essence of Balsam Spray Hair Set for Curlers & Heated Rollers 7oz $2.50* **MP 50¢**
1979-80 *Firm & Natural Herbal Scented Aerosol Hair Spray $2.39* **MP $1**

1981 *Salon System $4.50 each:*
Balanced Conditioner 7oz **MP $4***
Freshening Shampoo 7oz **MP $4***
Balanced Shampoo 7oz **MP $4***

Moisture Rich Shampoo 7oz **MP $4***
Moisture Rich Conditioner 7oz **MP $4***
Moisture Rich Pack Intense Conditioning Treatment 5oz **MP $4***
Trial Size 1oz 69¢ **MP 75¢**

1972 *Past and Present Brush and Comb Set $6* **MP $8**

1973 *Cameo Brush and Comb Set. Brush 8" long, comb 7" long $7* **MP $7**
1973 *Cameo Dresser Vanity Mirror, 10" long $5* **MP $7**

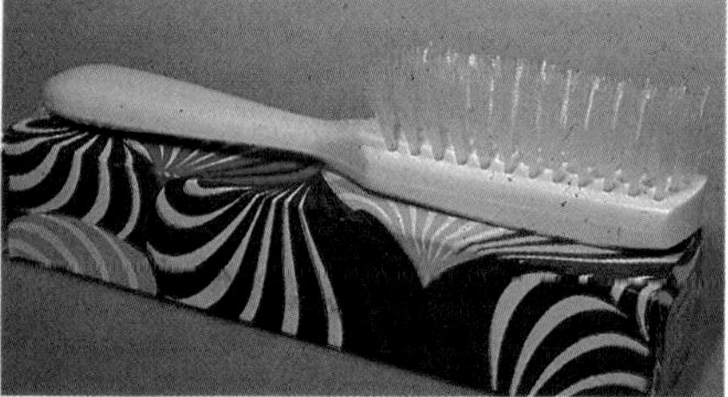

1967 *Professional Style Hairbrush in Ivory or Pink (shown in Xmas box) with purchase of another Hair product $1.50. Value $3* **MP $6, $8 in Xmas box**

Brushes and Brush & Comb Sets

Hairbrushes –

1971 *Flair, 8" long $3* **MP $3***
1975 *Full Round, 8" long $5* **MP $3**
1971 *Natural Bristle, 8" long $9* **MP $6**
1975 *Brush and Comb for Long Wet Hair, both 8" $4* **MP $3***

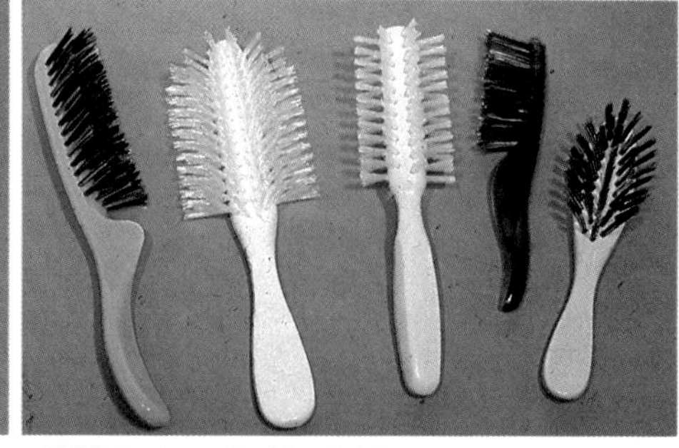

1970 *Styling, 8" $3* **MP $2**
1970 *Half Round, 8" $3* **MP $3***
1977 *Full Round Brush Petite, 7" $4* **MP $3***
1969 *Mini-Brush, 6" $1.50* **MP $2***
1978 *Flair Mini-Brush 5½" $3.50* **MP $2**

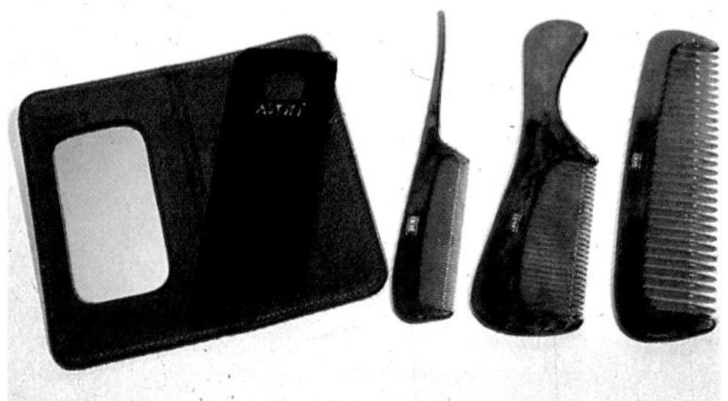

1980 *Pursemates Mirror and Comb. U.S. only $4.99 with a $5 purchase* **MP $9 retail**
1981 *Cambridge Collection. Rattail Comb, Handled Comb and Wide-Tooth Comb $3 each* **MP $2.50 ea.***

* *Available from Avon at time of publication*

1929-30 *Bath Salts 10oz 75¢* **MP $75**

1930-33 *Bath Salts 10oz 75¢* **MP $55**
1933-36 *(not shown) As above, Ariel, green & Vernafleur, pink 8½oz 63¢* **MP $50**

1936-43 *Bath Salts in Ariel and Pine (green), Vernafleur (pink), Jasmine (yellow) 8½oz 63¢* **MP $30**
1946-50 *As above, 9oz 69¢* **MP $25**
1950-53 *Pine only (Pasadena label) 69¢* **MP $25**

1944-45 *Bubble Bath 8oz $2.25* **MP $40, $50 boxed**

1951 *Bubble Bath 4oz $1.29* **MP $18, $23 boxed**

1959 *Bubble Bath 8oz $1.69* **MP $4**

BATH OILS, BUBBLES AND SALTS

1964 *Bubble Bath 8oz $1.98* **MP $4**
1967 *Bubble Bath 8oz $2* **MP $2**
1975 *Bubble Blossom Bubble Bath 14oz $7* **MP $3**

1968 *Santa's Helper. Bubble Bath 8oz $2* **MP $6 with Xmas box**

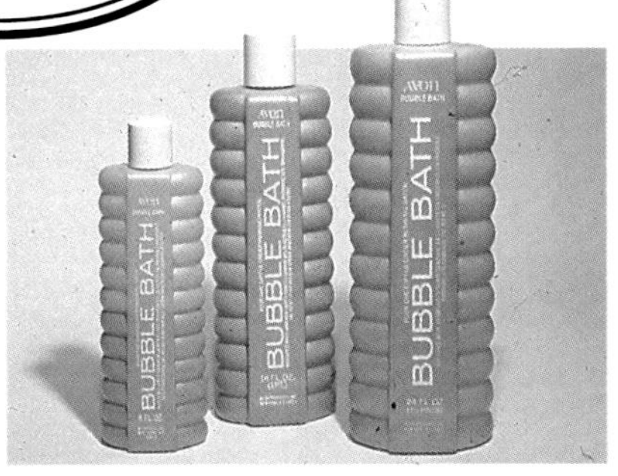

1976 *Bubble Bath 8oz and 16oz with ingredients listed on front $3 & $5.50* **MP $2*** *and* **$4***
1980 *Bubble Bath 24oz $8* **MP $7***

Bubble Bath Gelee:
1972 *Strawberry 4oz $3* **MP $1**
1975 *Roses, Roses 4oz $3.50* **MP 50¢**
1977 *Apple Blossom 4oz $3.50* **MP 50¢**
1977 *Honeysuckle 4oz $3.50* **MP 50¢**

1972 *Eau De Cool 6oz $5* **MP $4**

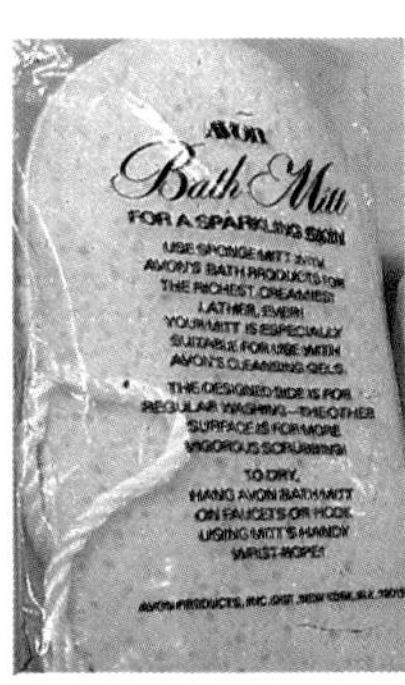

1972 *Avon Bath Mitt $1.50* **MP $3**

1973 *Emollient Freshener for After Bath 6oz Sonnet or Moonwind $5* **MP $4, $5 boxed**
1974 *Imperial Garden and Charisma* **MP $4, $5 boxed**

1975 *Foaming Bath Oil, tinted colors, 6oz in 8 frag. Sold in 1 Campaign only $6* **MP $10 with Bath Oil label, $12 boxed**

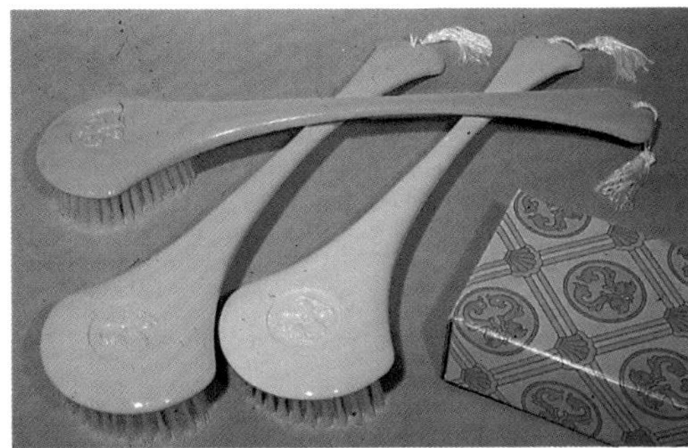

Avon Bath Brushes – 15½" long:
1977 *Blue $8.50* **MP $9***
1978 *Yellow and Ivory $8.50* **MP $9***

Trial Sizes –

1978 *Smooth as Silk Bath Oil 1oz & "29¢ off" coupon. 29¢ with purchase* **MP 40¢**
1976 *Naturally Gentle Shampoo 2oz 25¢ with purchase* **MP 25¢**
1977 *Skin-So-Soft 1oz 25¢ with purchase* **MP 40¢ (blue cap), $1 (white cap)**
1977 *Bubble Bath 1oz 25¢ with purchase* **MP 25¢**

1978 *Smooth as Silk Bath Oil 8oz $5* **MP $5***
1978 *Smooth as Silk Bath Oil 16oz $8.50* **MP $8***
1980 *Smooth as Silk Skin Softener 5oz $5.50* **MP $4***

1980 *Luscious Bubbles Super Bubble Bath 7oz $5* **MP $5***
1980 *Luscious Bubbles Foaming Creamy Cleanser 7oz $5* **MP $4***

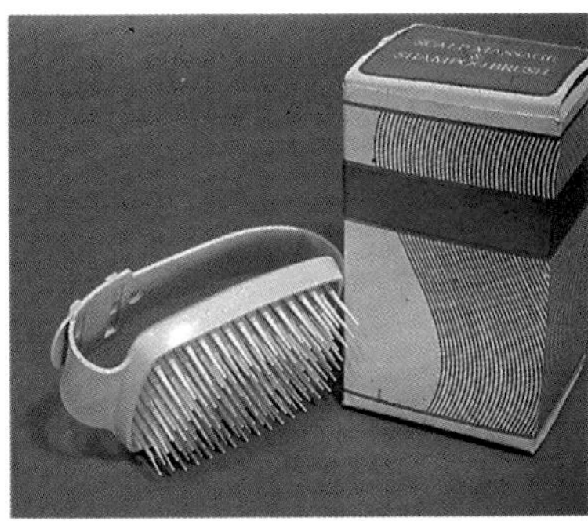

1973-75 *Scalp Massage and Shampoo Brush $1.75* **MP $1.75, $2 boxed**

** Available from Avon at time of publication*

1929-30 *Castile Soap 2 cakes 60¢* **MP $50**

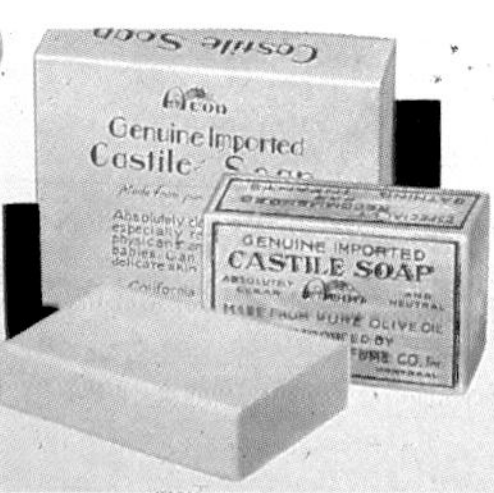

1930-37 *Castile Soap 2 cakes 62¢* **MP $40**

1937-40 *Castile Soap 2 cakes 62¢* **MP $35**
1941-43 *(not shown)* **Genuine Imported** *dropped from wrapper* **MP $40**

1930-36 *Savona Bouquet Toilet Soap. Six 4½oz cakes 50¢* **MP $100**

1930-36 *Vegetable Oil Soap, 3 cakes 45¢* **MP $75**

"Vegetable Oil Soap contains soothing vegetable oils to prevent dry, taut or chapped skin when hard water must be used."

INDIVIDUAL AND BOXED SOAPS

1936-43 *Savona Bouquet Toilet Soap. Box of 6 cakes 51¢* **MP $75**

1942-46 *Dr. Zabriskie's Soap 3oz 33¢* **MP $25 boxed**

Dr. Zabriskie's Cutaneous Soap was a popular skin and complexion soap for over 60 years. It was recommended for all facial blemishes and for treatment of eczema.

1936-42 *Dr. Zabriskie's Soap 3oz 26¢* **MP $35**
1936 only *With CPC label on box* **MP $40 boxed**
1947-54 *Dr. Zabriskie's Soap (Pasadena label) 3oz 43¢* **MP $12 boxed**

1954-62 *Dr. Zabriskie's Soap 3oz in 4-A designed box 43¢* **MP $15**

1963 only *Perfumed Deo. Soap boxed 3oz 39¢* **MP $12**
1964 only *Perf. Deo. Soap, wrapped (not shown) 39¢* **MP $12**

1966 *Complexion Bar 4oz $1.25* **MP $4**
1969 *Special Complexion Bar 3oz 75¢* **MP $3**

XMAS WRAPPED SOAPS

1978 *Perfumed Soaps (top) in 8 frag., red, blue or green Xmas pkg. 3oz each $1.25* **MP $3**
1977 *Perfumed Soaps (bottom) in 6 frag., red, blue or green Xmas pkg. 3oz each $1.25* **MP $3**

1974-75 *Perfumed Soaps, Xmas pkg. 3oz each: Field Flowers, Sonnet, Roses, Roses, Moonwind, Bird of Paradise, (Charisma not shown) $1.25* **MP $4**

1979 *Ultra Perfumed Soaps in gold, red and blue Xmas wrap 3oz $1.50* **MP $2**

1979 *Perfumed Soap, 8 fragrances in red, blue or green foil (center) $1.50* **MP $2**
1980 *Perfumed Soap in Moonwind or Charisma in red Xmas wrap $2.25* **MP $2.25**
1980 *Bar Soap for Men in 3 fragrances in brown & white Xmas wrap $1.75* **MP $1.75**
1980 *Ultra Perfumed Soap in silver Xmas wrap 3oz $2.25* **MP $2.25**

1963 *Soap Treasures with choice of Soaps, 13 frag. available. Only Lilac and Lily of the Valley issued with floral wraps; all others in solid color wraps with white 4-A design band. (Incorrect assortment shown – see pg. 135) $1.95* **MP $30**

1966 *Lemonol Soap Slices. Six 1½oz cakes $2.25* **MP $25**
1954-66 *Lemonol Soap. Three cakes $1.00* **MP $23**

1966 *Butterfly Soap Set. Four 1½oz cakes $2* **MP $24**
1965 *Lady Slippers Gift Soap. Four 1½oz cakes $2.25* **MP $26**

1930-36 *Vernafleur Cold Cream Toilet Soap. Box of 3 cakes 75¢* **MP $80**

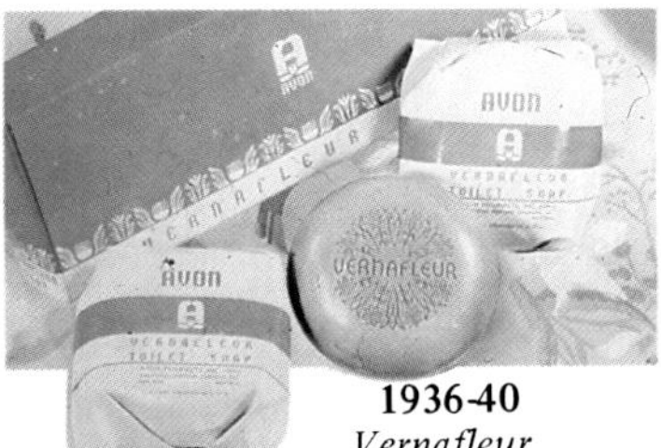
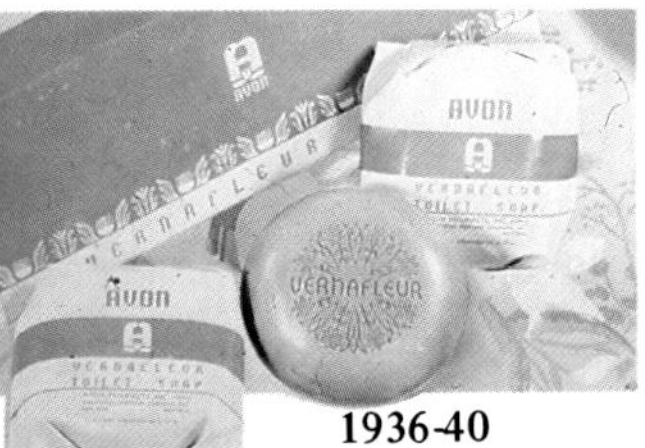

1936-40 *Vernafleur Cold Cream Toilet Soap. Box of 3 cakes 77¢* **MP $75**

1930-36 *Lemonol Toilet Soap. Box of 3 cakes 50¢* **MP $70,** *Carton of 12 cakes (not shown) $1.75* **MP $125**

1936-40 *Lemonol Toilet Soap. Box of 3 cakes 51¢* **MP $60,** *Carton of 12 cakes $1.79* **MP $100**

Vernafleur Toilet Soap, a floral-scented soap containing basic cold cream, was especially suited for skin constantly exposed to the outdoors.

Lemonol Soap was also used as a shampoo to cleanse and lighten blonde and auburn hair instead of a lemon rinse.

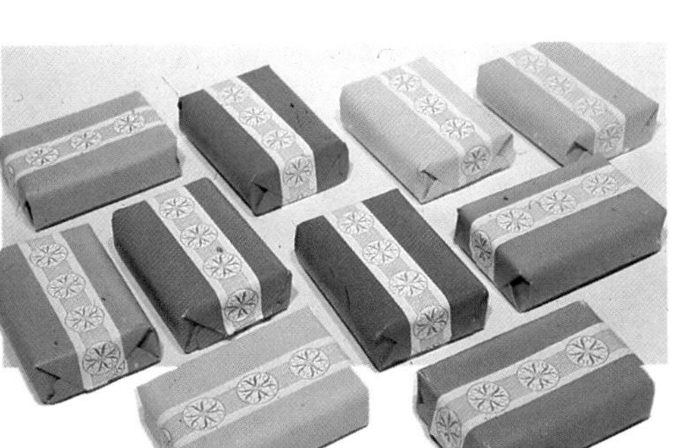

1961-64 *Assortment of Soaps, all 3oz each, 39¢ each* **MP $5 each**
Floral in violet wrap
Lemonol in yellow wrap
Cotillion in pink wrap
Here's My Heart in blue
Persian Wood in red wrap
Royal Jasmine in chartreuse
Somewhere in lilac wrap
Royal Pine in green wrap
Topaze in yellow wrap
Rose Geranium and To A Wild Rose in rose wrap

Assortment of Soaps, all 3oz each:
1964 *Wishing 39¢* **MP $5**
1963 *Lily of the Valley 39¢* **MP $5**
1961 *Topaze 39¢* **MP $5**
1965 *Occur! 49¢* **MP $5**
1964 *Persian Wood 39¢* **MP $5**
1966 *Somewhere 49¢* **MP $5**
1964 *To a Wild Rose 39¢* **MP $5**

1971 *Country Store Scented Soaps 3oz Papaya, Mint, Camomile, Avocado, Pine Tar, Almond 75¢* **MP $2**

1981 *Hearts and Lace Glycerine Soap in Roses, Roses (pink), Special Occasion (red) and Lilac (lavender) 3oz $2* **MP $2**

1945 *Facial Soap, 2 cakes with "Personal Note" 59¢* **MP $30**
1955 *Facial Soap, 2 cakes 89¢* **MP $20**

1962 *Gift Bows. Six cakes $2.25* **MP $30**
1967 *Bayberry Gift Soaps. Caddy Holder contains three 3oz Bayberry scented soaps $3* **MP $25 complete**

1964 *Hostess Soap Sampler. 12 molded cakes $2.50* **MP $23**

1966 *Cherub Soap Set. Two 3oz cakes $2* **MP $23**

1968 *Whipped Creams. Four 1½oz each soaps $3* **MP $10**
1968 *Partridge and Two Pear Soaps 2oz each $3* **MP $9**

(See Men's pg. 191, Children's pg. 214)

1969 *Cameo Soap with rope 4oz $1.75* **MP $6**
1966 *Cameo Soaps. Four 1½oz cakes $2* **MP $20**

1969 *Fruit Bouquet Perfumed Soaps 2oz each $3* **MP $11**

1970 *Spring Tulips. Six cakes boxed $3.50* **MP $12**

. . . BOXED SOAPS

1972 *Hostess Bouquet. Three 2oz cakes $3.50* **MP $8**
1971 *Cupcake Soap Set. Three 2oz cakes $3* **MP $8**

1972 *Lacery Hostess Bath Soaps, 2 cakes 5oz each $4* **MP $7**
1969 *Decorator Gift Soaps. Three 2oz cakes $3* **MP $11**

1971 *Grade Avon Hostess Soaps, 4 cakes 2oz each $4.50* **MP $12**

1974 *Partridge 'N Pear Hostess Fragranced Soaps $4* **MP $7**
1974 *Golden Beauties Hostess Soaps. Three 2oz Soaps $3* **MP $7**

1972 *Hidden Treasure. Bird of Paradise Perfume "pearl" 1/8oz and two Soaps $6* **MP $13**
1978 *A Token of Love. Pink decal Soap holds red heart-shaped Soap 6oz total $6* **MP $7**

1975 *Bayberry Wreaths. Three 1½oz Bayberry scented Soaps $5* **MP $6**
1970 *Pine Cone Soaps (box not shown) Three Pine scented 2oz Soaps $3* **MP $10**

1973 *Soap For All Seasons, 4 cakes 1½oz each $3.50* **MP $6**

1975 *Touch of Love. Three 2oz Spring Lavender fragranced Soaps $5* **MP $7**

1975 *Tidings of Love. Three 2oz Hostess fragranced Soaps $4* **MP $7**

1973 *Avonshire Blue Hostess Soaps. Three 2oz cakes $3* **MP $6**
1973 *Soap Savers. Six spearmint scented 1½oz Soaps $4.50* **MP $8, $1 each soap**

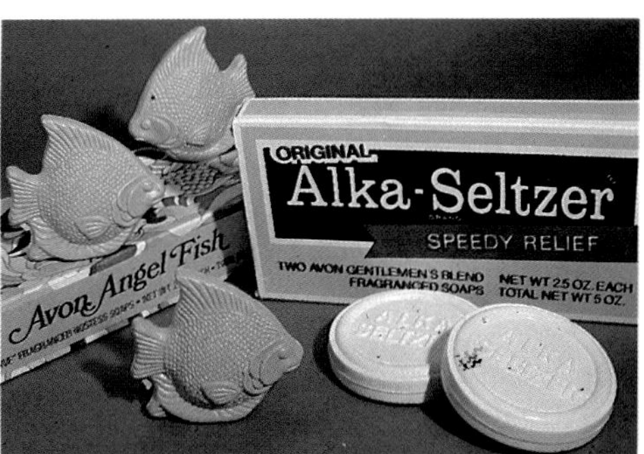

1978 *Angel Fish. Three 2oz Soaps $5.50* **MP $6**
1978 *Alka-Seltzer Soaps. Two 2½oz cakes in Special Occasion fragrance for her and Gentlemen's Blend for him $5* **MP $5**

1978 *Country Garden Hostess Soaps. Two 3oz Special Occasion fragranced decal Soaps $6* **MP $6***
1978 *Beauty in Motion Ballet Picture and Soaps. Two 3½oz Special Occasion fragranced decal Soaps. Lid serves as framed ballet picture to hang $10* **MP $10**

1959 *Hostess Bouquet Soaps. Four guest-size cakes $1.39* **MP $25**
1978 *Royal Hearts Hostess Soap. Two 3oz Festive fragranced decal Soaps $6* **MP $6**

1976 *Bouquet of Pansies. Two 3oz Special Occasion fragranced decal Soaps $5.50* **MP $6**
1977 *Butterflies Hostess Soaps. Two 3oz Special Occasion fragranced decal Soaps $5.50* **MP $6**

1977 *Winter Frolics. Two 3oz decal Soaps $5.50* **MP $5**
1976 *Winterscape Boxed Soaps, two 3oz Special Occasion fragranced decal Soaps $5.50* **MP $6**

1975 *Angel Lace Hostess fragranced Soaps. Three 2oz cakes $4* **MP $6 boxed**
1976 *Little Choir Boys Hostess Soaps. Three 2oz cakes $5* **MP $6 boxed**

1977 *Merry Elfkins Guest Soaps. Three 2oz Festive fragranced cakes $5.50* **MP $6**
1978 *Christmas Carollers. Two 3oz Special Occasion fragranced Soaps $5.50* **MP $6**

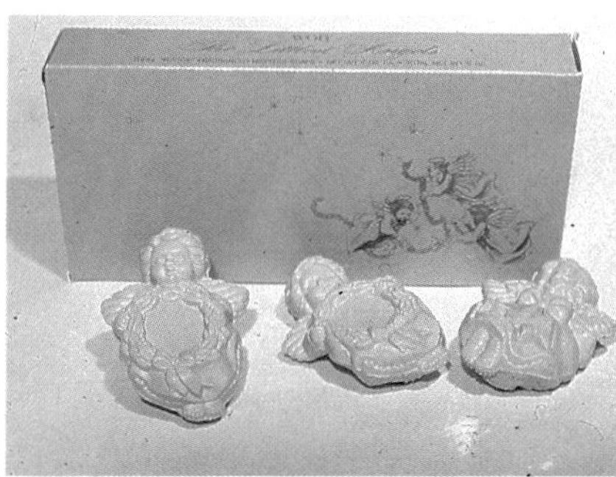

1980 *Littlest Angels Hostess Soaps, 3 cakes 2oz each $5.50* **MP $5.50**

1975 *Petit Fours. Eight 1oz Soaps in 3 shapes $6* **MP $8**

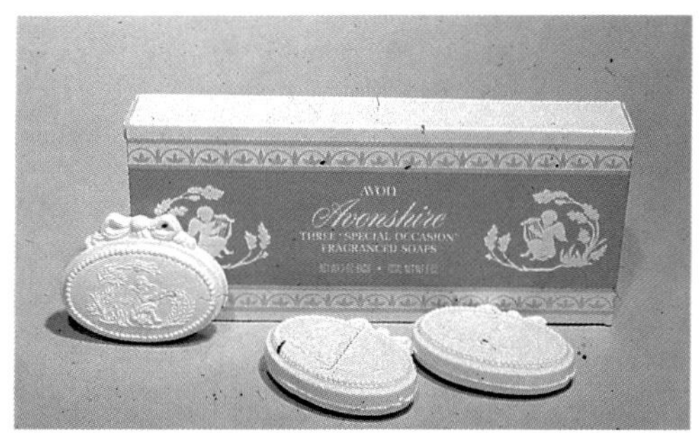

1979 *Avonshire Hostess Soaps. Three 2oz Special Occasion fragranced Soaps $6* **MP $6**

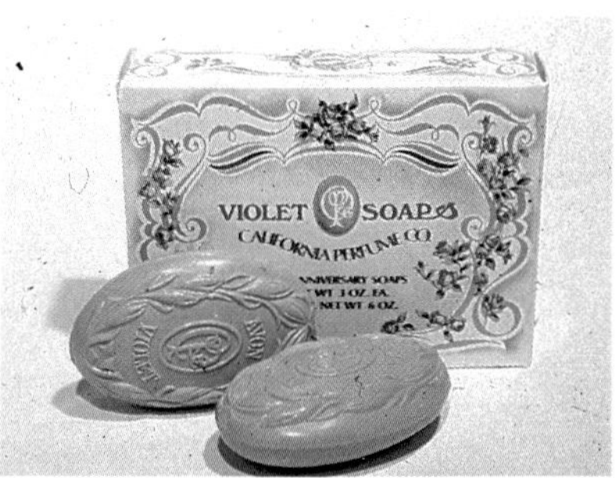

1980 *California Perfume Co. 1980 Anniversary Soaps. Two 3oz Violet scented Soaps $5.50* **MP $5.50**

**Available from Avon at time of publication*

1970 *Dolphin Soap Dish and 4½oz Soaps $8* **MP $12, $15 boxed**

1965 *Bath Flower Set. Flowered sponge and 3oz cake To A Wild Rose Soap $2.50* **MP $15 boxed**

1969 *Bath Blossoms. Flower-shaped Sponge with loop to hang up and 3oz Soap $3.50* **MP $9**
1979 *Bath Blossoms Sponge serves as soap holder for 3oz Special Occasion Soap $8* **MP $8**

1965 *Decorator Soap Miniatures. 12 cakes 9¾" high $4.50* **MP $20, $25 boxed**

SOAP DISHES AND CONTAINERS

1970 *Lady Slipper Soap 5oz with Glass Bow Perfume 1/8oz Charisma or Cotillion $5* **MP $15 Soap and Perfume MP $6 each**
1972 *Fragrance and Frills. Perfume 1/8oz and four 1½oz Soaps in Field Flowers or Bird of Paradise $6.75* **MP $9**

1970 *Heavenly Soap Dish, milkglass. Two 2oz Soaps $5* **MP $10**
1971 *Owl Soap Dish, two 2oz owl Soaps $4.50* **MP $9**

1972 *Gift of the Sea. Siz 1oz seashell Soaps and dish $6* **MP $10**
1971 *Decorator Soap Dish and two 2oz Soaps $7* **MP $8**

1972 *Flower Basket, five 1oz Hostess fragranced Soaps $6* **MP $8**
1978 *Treasure Basket. Handwoven aluminum basket and four 1½oz Soaps $13.50* **MP $11**

1973 *Melon Ball Guest Soaps. Plastic "melon" with six 1oz melon scented soap balls $4.50* **MP $8 complete, $4 container only**

1973 *Butter Dish and three 3oz Hostess scented Soaps $8.50* **MP $12**

1973 *Nesting Hen Soap Dish and four 2oz Soaps $8.50* **MP $10**

1969 *Touch of Beauty Soap Dish (made in Mexico) and two dark pink and two light pink Soaps $5* **MP $12**
1973 *Sittin' Kittens Soap Dish, three 2oz Hostess scented molded Soaps $5* **MP $6**

1973 *Love Nest Soap Dish, three 1oz Soaps $4* **MP $6**
1978 *Love Nest Soap Dish (green) three 1½oz Special Occasion scented Soaps $6.50* **MP $6**

1974 *Recipe Treasures. Metal recipe box holds five 1½oz orange scented balls of Soap $6* **MP $7**
1974 *Lovebirds Soap Dish and two 4oz Hostess scented Soaps $8* **MP $9**

1974 *Beauty Buds Soap Dish, four 1oz Hostess scented Soaps $7.50* **MP $8**
1974 *Hostess Blossoms Flower Arranger Soap Dish and Hostess Fragrance Soap 4oz Adaptable plastic lid serves as flower holder $8* **MP $9**

1975 *Wings of Beauty Soap Dish and two 2oz Hostess scented Soaps $7.50* **MP $8**

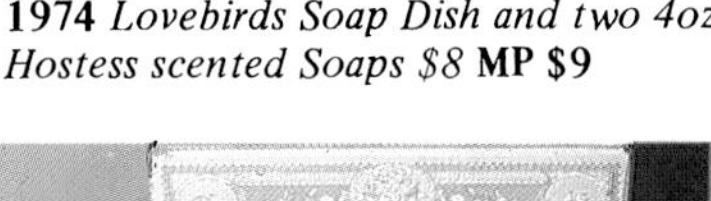

1974 *Hostess Fancy Soap Dish and five 1oz fan-shaped Soaps $7.50* **MP $8**

1975 *Nutty Soap. Plastic shell dish with two 3oz peanut-scented Soaps $6* **MP $6**

1975 *Bicentennial Plate and two 3oz Special Occasion scented Soaps $9* **MP $10**

1975 *Sunny Lemon Soap Dish and three 2oz lemon scented Soaps $6* **MP $7**

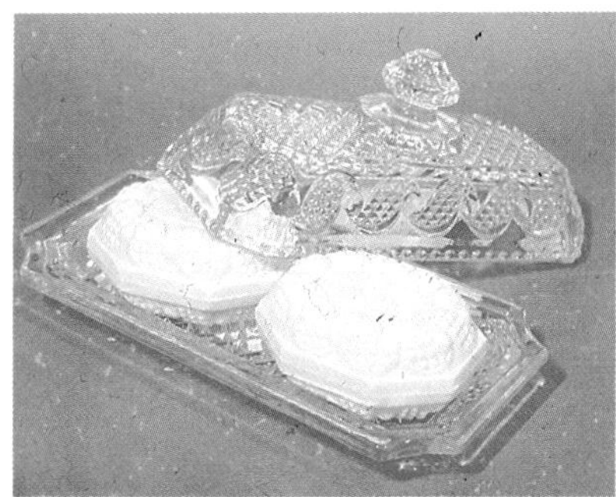

1975 *Crystalucent Covered Butter Dish and two 3oz Soaps $11* **MP $11**

1976 *Nature Bountiful Ceramic Plate, edged in 22k gold and two 5oz Special Occasion scented decal Soaps $25*
MP $25, $15 plate only

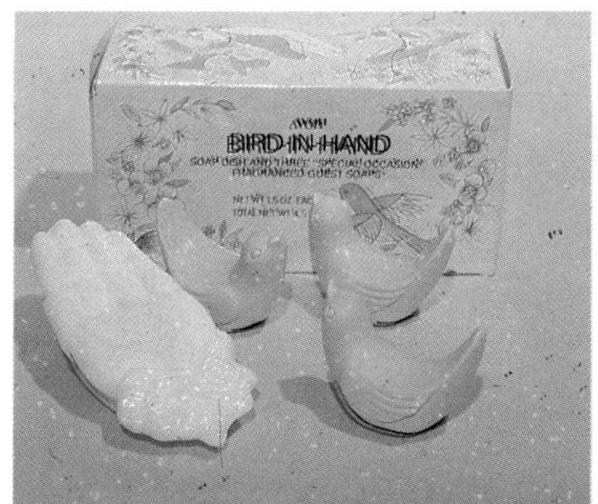

1979 *Bird-In-Hand Soap Dish and three 1.5oz Special Occasion scented Soaps $8.50* **MP $8.50 boxed**

1980 *Orchard Fresh Guest Soaps, six 1oz Peach, Orange or Lemon scented Soaps per carton $6* **MP $6**

1977 *Button, Button Guest Soaps, five 1oz Special Occasion scented Soaps in cardboard "spool" $6* **MP $6**
1977 *Country Peaches Soap Jar, six 1oz peach scented Soaps $8.50* **MP $7**

(See also Fragrance Lines and Collections, pg. 150)

Christmas Cards

left, top –
#4 Ornamental Reindeer $8 **MP $1**
#15 Winter Wonderland $8 **MP $1**
#11 Dove of Peace $9 **MP $1.25**
#22 Wake Up, Comet $6 **MP 75¢**
center –
#36 Snoozing Santa $7 **MP $1**
#16 Bringing Home Tree $5 **MP 75¢**
right, top –
#12 Christmas Tree Cherubs $10 **MP $1.50**
#31 Christmas Eve $7 **MP $1**
#30 Stack of Good Wishes $6 **MP 75¢**
#29 The Christmas Angel $8 **MP $1**

bottom – #34 Little Angel $4 **MP 75¢**
#20 Christmas Wreath $4 **MP 75¢**
#28 Merry Christmas $5 **MP 75¢**

bottom – #9 Christmas Wreath Cherubs $10 **MP $1.50**
#13 The Three Kings $7 **MP $1**
#35 Christmas Centerpiece $7 **MP $1**

1971 *Christmas Greeting Cards, designed exclusively for Avon, were sold in a Test Market area by a limited number of Representatives in the Newark Branch. There were 36 different designs, 25 cards of one design in a box.* **MP** *is for 1 card w/env.*

Vitamins

In 1979 Proper Balance Vitamins were offered in test markets, in 8 Divisions, Springdale Branch. Due to results over the last three years, Avon has made the decision not to expand its Vitamin business further at this time.

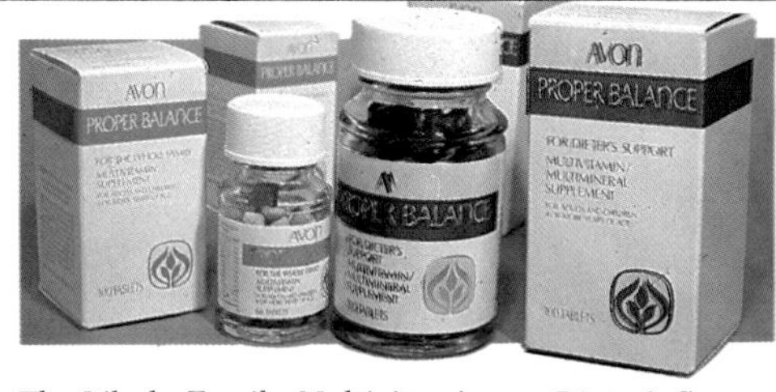

The Whole Family Multivitamin Supplement, 60-tablet size $3.49 **MP $3*** *100 size $4.99* **MP $4***

Dieter's Support Multivitamin Multimineral Supplement, 60-tablet size $4.49 **MP $4*** *100 size $6.49* **MP $5.50***

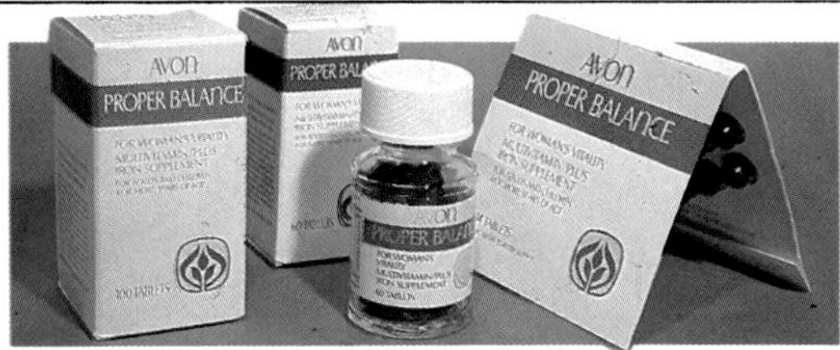

Woman's Vitality Multi vitamin/Plus Iron Suppt. 60-tablet $3.99 **MP $3.50*** *100 size $5.99* **MP $5.49***

14-day trial size Woman's Vitality Vitamins, 1 per customer during C-14 & 15, 1979 49¢ **MP $1**

Avon Books

1980 *The Active Woman's Cookbook, U.S. only, with purchase $2.50* **MP $3**
1981 *Winter Fun Guide, U.S. only, one campaign with purchase $2.99* **MP $4**
1980 *Beautiful Holiday Ideas, U.S. only, one campaign with purchase $2.99* **MP $4**
1981 *Looking Good, Feeling Beautiful. Abridged paperback version of hardcover book. Sold with purchase in C-12 only 50¢* **MP $2**

1981 *Love Notes. Exclusively designed. 4 notes w/eps. Free with purchase in C-2, U.S. only* **MP $1.50** *set of 4*

Cologne and Toilet Water Atomizers –

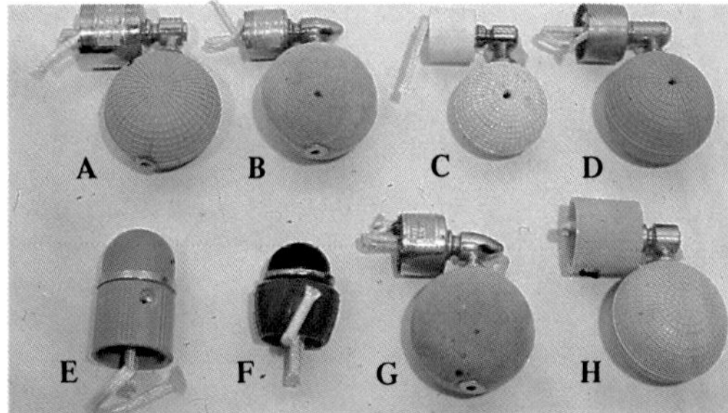

24-karat gold-plated with rubber bulbs –
1955 A. *Fits Golden Promise Cologne and Toilet Water $1* **MP $7**
1950 B. *Toilet Water Atomizer fits Flowertime, Lily of the Valley, Cotillion and To A Wild Rose 89¢* **MP $8**
1955 C. *Fits Cotillion and Bright Night Cologne and Cotillion, Forever Spring, Nearness and To A Wild Rose Toilet Water $1* **MP $7**
1954 D. *Young Hearts Cologne Atomizer from Neat and Sweet Set* **MP $7**
1950 E. *Fits Perfumed Deodorant only 49¢* **MP $4**
1950 F. *Fits Deodorant for Men only 49¢* **MP $4**
1955 G. *Fits Nearness, Forever Spring, Quaintance, To A Wild Rose Cologne and Quaintance Toilet Water $1* **MP $7**
1942 H. *Fragrant Mist Set Atomizer (wartime issue)* **MP $10**

1973 *House Mouse Doll-Making Kit, 11" high $7* **MP $10**
1973 *Calico Kate Doll-Making Kit, 11" high $7* **MP $10**

Needlecraft Kits

Market Prices *are for Kit complete with pattern, needle, yarn and accessories*

top: **1974** *Pals on Parade Picture 6 x 8" $6* **MP $8**
1973 *Owl Mates Pillow 14 x 14" $9* **MP $12**
1974 *Bushel of Strawberries Pillow 14 x 14" $10* **MP $12**
1974 *Thirteen Original Colonies Pillow 14 x 14" $10* **MP $12**
1975 *Tree Owls Wall Hanging 40 x 6" $12* **MP $13**

center: **1973** *Myrtle Turtle Picture 8 x 10" $5* **MP $7**
1975 *First Prize at the County Fair, 3 pictures 4 x 5" $8* **MP $10**
1974 *Vintage Cars Wall Hanging 40 x 6" $12* **MP $13**
1974 *Spring Violets Pillow 14 x 14" $9* **MP $11**

bottom: **1972** *Lakescape Picture 18 x 24" $12* **MP $14**
1974 *Floral Sentiments Pillow 14 x 14" $10* **MP $11**
1974 *Love 'n Stuff Pillow-Making Kit $8* **MP $10**
1975 *Spinning Wheel & Wild Roses 14 x 14" $12* **MP $13**

*****Available from Avon at time of publication

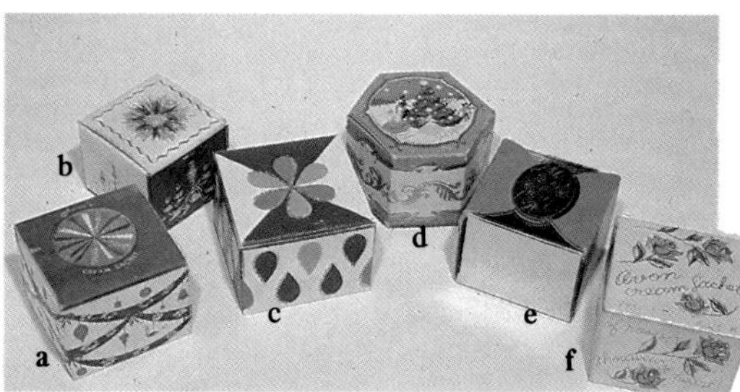

a-1954 *Issued with Cotillion, To A Wild Rose, Forever Spring, Golden Promise & Quaintance* **MP $9**
b-1955 *Issued with above fragrances* **MP $8**
c-1956 *Issued with Cotillion, To A Wild Rose, Forever Spring, Quaintance, Nearness & Bright Night* **MP $8**
d-1957 *Issued with Cotillion, To A Wild Rose, Forever Spring, Nearness, Bright Night & Elegante* **MP $8**
e-1958 *Issued with above fragrances* **MP $8**
f-1958 *72nd Anniversary Box issued with 1957 fragrances* **MP $9**

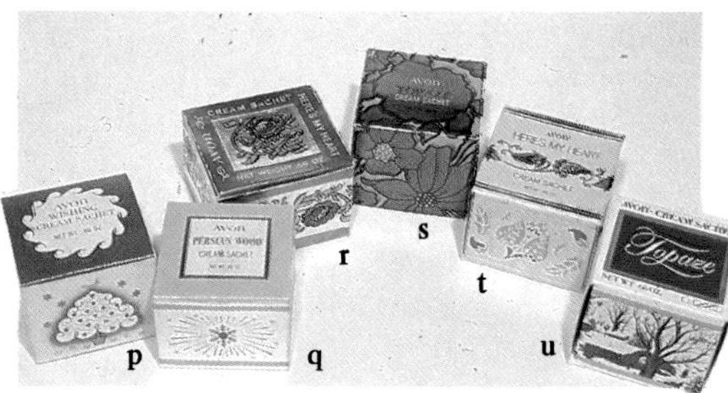

p-1965 *Issued with To A Wild Rose, Somewhere, Unforgettable, Here's My Heart, Persian Wood, Wishing Rapture, Occur!, Cotillion, Topaze* **MP $7**
q-1966 *Issued with above fragrances* **MP $7**
r-1968 *Issued with 1965 fragrances* **MP $7**
s-1969 *Issued with 1965 fragrances, add Charisma, Brocade & Regence* **MP $6**
t-1970 *Issued with above fragrances, add Hana Gasa and Elusive* **MP $6**
u-1973 *Issued with above fragrances, delete Wishing, add Bird of Paradise, Sonnet, Roses & Moonwind* **MP $5**

v-1974 *Issued in 16 in-line fragrances and 12 floral fragrances* **MP $4**
w-1977 *Issued in 10 fragrances in red, blue or green boxes* **MP $2**
x-1978 *Issued in 10 fragrances in red, blue or green boxes* **MP $2**

(below left)
g-1959 *Issued with Cotillion, To A Wild Rose, Nearness, Bright Night, Persian Wood, Here's My Heart* **MP $8**

CREAM SACHET GIFT BOXES

h-1959 *73rd Anniversary Box issued with above fragrances* **MP $9**
j-1960 *Issued with Cotillion, To A Wild Rose, Nearness, Bright Night, Persian Wood, Here's My Heart & Topaze* **MP $8**
k-1961 *Issued with Cotillion, To A Wild Rose, Persian Wood, Here's My Heart & Topaze* **MP $8**
m1962 *Issued with above fragrances, add Somewhere* **MP $8**
n-1964 *Issued with above fragrances* **MP $7**

Market Prices *are for* **Gift Box only.** *(See Fragrance Lines for correct Cream Sachet Jar.)*

Floral Cream Sachets, .66oz $3 each:

1972 *Violet, Carnation and Gardenia* **MP $1**
1974 *Hyacinth and Magnolia* **MP $2**
(1975 Lily of the Valley not shown **MP $2.50***)*

Market Prices *are for* **Gift Box only** *(See Fragrance Lines for correct Powder Sachet Jar. See* **1937** *Gift Box Sachet pg. 40,* **1959** *Gift Box Sachet pg. 53)*

POWDER SACHET GIFT BOXES

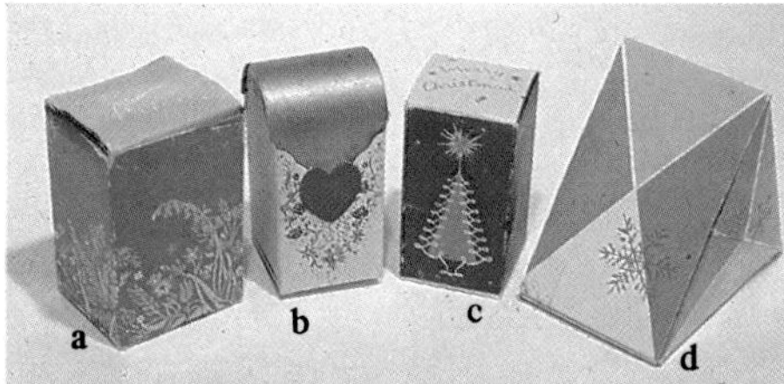

a-1943 *57th Anniversary Box issued with Attention* **MP $15**
b-1952 *Valentine Box issued with Flower Time, Cotillion, Golden Promise & Quaintance* **MP $10**

c-1952 *Issued with* **b-1952** *fragrances* **MP $10**
d-1957 *Issued with Cotillion, To A Wild Rose, Quaintance, Nearness, Forever Spring & Bright Night* **MP $8**
e-1958 *Issued with Cotillion, To A Wild Rose, Nearness, Forever Spring, Bright Night & Elegante* **MP $8**
f-1960 *Issued with Cotillion, To A Wild Rose, Persian Wood, Here's My Heart & Topaze* **MP $8**
g-1963 *Issued with above fragrances, add Somewhere* **MP $8**

h-1964 *Issued with Cotillion, To A Wild Rose, Persian Wood, Here's My Heart, Somewhere, Topaze & Lavender* **MP $7**
j-1965 *Issued in above fragrances, add Wishing, Rapture & Occur!* **MP $7**

1936-39 *Cotillion, Jardin d'Amour, Marionette $1.04; Ariel 78¢* **MP $26**
1939-42 *Cotillion, Garden of Love (formerly Jardin d'Amour), Marionette $1.04; Ariel 78¢*
1942 *Above frag. and Attention $1.15* **MP $20 each**
1943 *(ribbed cap) Above frag. $1.15, Ariel 89¢* **MP $8 each**
1946 *Garden of Love $1.19* **MP $20**

1965 *Perfumed Pillowettes, two Powder Sachet Pillows and Powder Sachet, 9 frag. .9oz $3 to $3.75* **MP $22 complete, $14 bottle only**

POWDER SACHETS

1961 *Sachet Pillows, 6 tissue envelopes in package 50¢* **MP $11**
1977 *Lavender Bouquet Sachet Pillows, 6/$7.50* **MP $1 each, $7 boxed**
1978 *French Ribbon Sachet Pillows, 6 fabric sachets with Garlandia frag. $7.50* **MP $6**

1930 *Perfume "391" 1oz $2.50* **MP $130, $160 boxed** (**1931** *Flaconette 1 dram, not shown, $1.25* **MP $75**) *Note: Because of the Excise Tax, imposed in 1932, above prices were increased to $2.60 and $1.30*

By reversing the numbers, it appears that "391" perfume introduced the beginning of a new decade, "1930".

1934-38 *7 dram Bouquet Perfumes. Jardin d'Amour, Bolero, Cotillion $2.60* **MP $100, $130 boxed**
1936 *Add "Lucy Hays" and Topaze* **MP $110**
1938 *Add Courtship and Marionette* **MP $125**

1934 *2 dram Perfume Flaconette in Cotillion, Bolero or Jardin d'Amour (shown with 1936 Xmas box) $1.04* **MP $90, $100 boxed, $135 Xmas boxed**
1936 *Add "Lucy Hays" and Topaze* **MP $100**
1938 *Add Courtship and Marionette* **MP $115**

1934 *2 dram Floral Perfume Flaconette, plastic gold lid. Lily of the Valley, Trailing Arbutus, Gardenia, Sweet Pea, 52¢, Rose, Narcissus & Ariel 78¢* **MP $75, $90 boxed**
1934 *7 dram Floral Perfumes. Lily of the Valley, Trailing Arbutus, Gardenia, Sweet Pea $1.56, Rose, Narcissus & Ariel $2.34* **MP $100, $130 boxed**

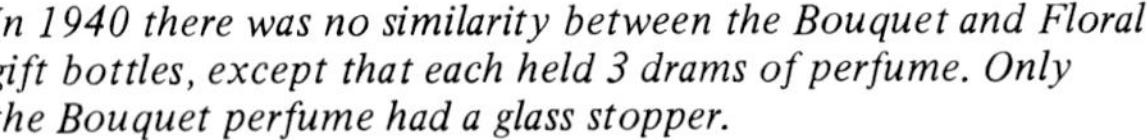
In 1940 there was no similarity between the Bouquet and Floral gift bottles, except that each held 3 drams of perfume. Only the Bouquet perfume had a glass stopper.

1940-42 *Ballad Perfume Flaconette 1 dram $1.25* **MP $40**

1940 *3 dram Bouquet Perfumes in Cotillion, Courtship, Marionette and Garden of Love $2.25* **MP $95, $120 boxed**

1940 *3 dram Floral Perfumes (gold lid) in Trailing Arbutus, Gardenia, Sweet Pea and Lily of the Valley $1.50* **MP $65, $80 boxed**
1945 *3 dram Floral Perfumes (white lid) with same fragrances as 1940 $1.50* **MP $65, $80 boxed**
1946 *Add Crimson Carnation* **MP $70, $85 boxed**

1945 *Gardenia Perfume 3 dram $2.50* **MP $65, $85 boxed as shown**

The magic of real flowers is caught in Avon's floral perfumes. Warm, exotic, fresh and sweet as those precious scents.

1942 *One dram Apple Blossom Flaconette shown in gift box 75¢* **MP $65 boxed**
1940 *One dram Perfume Flaconette (shown in Apple Blossom, issued in 1941) several frag. 52¢ & 75¢* **MP $40**
1943-44 *One dram Perfume Flaconette several frag. 59¢ & 85¢* **MP $40**
(**1945** *Bottle as above, but white plastic lid, not shown* **MP $35**)

AVON Fragrance Names

No other fragrance house anywhere in the world sells more fragrance products than Avon does. Along with choosing new fragrances, new fragrance names also must be found. Avon maintains a treasury of names which they have been gathering for years. From this protected list, which they own by copyright, new names are uncovered.

On occasion, names from the past are recalled and used again. For example, Here's My Heart, *issued in 1946, was re-introduced in 1957;* Sonnet, *issued in 1940, was re-introduced in 1972 and* Topaze, *issued in 1935, was re-introduced in 1959. It is questionable whether it was the original fragrance, or only the fragrance name, that was chosen for re-introduction.*

Especially interesting are two introductions of American Ideal Perfume. *Originally introduced in 1907, CPC catalogs describe* American Ideal *as the most intense, concentrated and lasting odor ever manufactured. Powerful and penetrating, subtle but elusive, it was called the "Queen of American Perfumes". After 28 years in the CPC line, it was discontinued in 1935.*

In June, 1941 American Ideal *was re introduced in honor of Avon's 55th Anniversary. For one campaign a flaconette of* American Ideal Perfume *was offered as a customer gift for only 20¢. The fragrance was described as "gay and summery, having the distinctive odor of apple blossoms".* *(See flaconette pg. 11)*

Because many customers and Representatives referred to the new perfume as "Apple Blossom" instead of American Ideal, *Avon decided to change its name. In C-13-41, only 3 months after introduction,* American Ideal *was re-named* Apple Blossom. *(See flaconette above.)*

In comparing the American Ideal *fragrance description of 1907 with that of 1941, it would appear that only the* American Ideal *name was shared, and not the scent.*

Apple Blossom *was discontinued in 1943, re-introduced in 1974 and has since been discontinued.*

1939 *3 dram Ballad Perfume $3.50* **MP $125, $155 boxed**

1945 *3 dram Ballad Perfume $3.50* **MP $125, $160 boxed (1947** *Golden Promise issued in same bottle and box $5* **MP $135, $160 boxed)**

1948 *3 dram Floral Perfume in Gardenia or Lily of the Valley $2.50* **MP $60, $80 boxed**

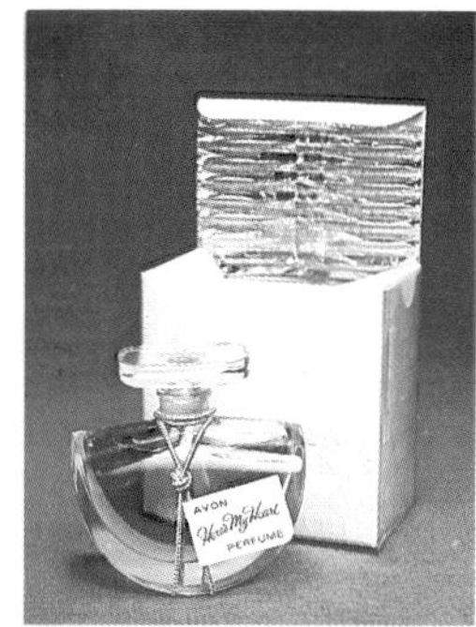

1959 *One-ounce Gift Perfume, Cotillion, To A Wild Rose, Bright Night, Nearness $15; Persian Wood and Here's My Heart $17.50* **MP $65, $80 boxed**

1966 *Half-Ounce Perfume in 9 frag. $10 to $12.50* **MP $12, $17 boxed**

1963 *One-ounce Gift Perfume, Crystal imported from France. Glass 4-A embossed stopper. 7 frag. $17.50 to $25* **MP $50, $70 boxed**

1969 *Half-Ounce Perfume in 10 frag. $11 to $15* **MP $10, $16 boxed**

1950 *One dram Perfume bottle shown in 1954 Xmas box, 6 frag. $1.75* **MP $12, $25 as shown**

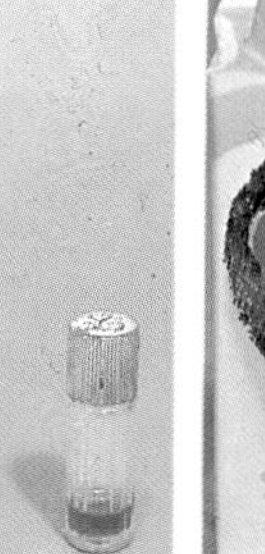

1951 *One Dram Perfume (left) in 9 frag. $1.75* **MP $13**
1951 *With Love Valentine Perfume, 1 dram, in 9 frag. $1.75* **MP $35 boxed**

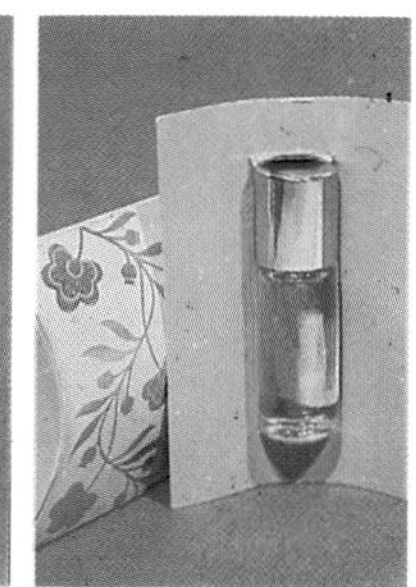

1953 *One dram Perfume (shown in Luscious), several frag. in Xmas box $1.75*
MP $15 boxed

Two dram Perfume Flaconettes –
1936 *"Lucy Hays" (Mrs. McConnell's maiden name). During March only given as a customer gift, with purchase, in honor of Mrs. McConnell's 51st Wedding Anniversary* **MP $75**
1937 *Courtship, gift to Representatives to try before intro and use as a demo* **MP $85**

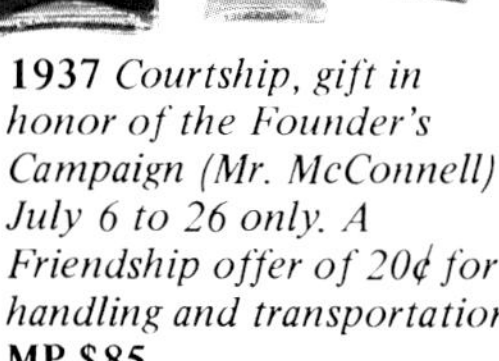

1937 *Courtship, gift in honor of the Founder's Campaign (Mr. McConnell) July 6 to 26 only. A Friendship offer of 20¢ for handling and transportation* **MP $85**
1943-44 *Courtship Perfume Flaconette 1 dram 85¢* **MP $40, $55 boxed**

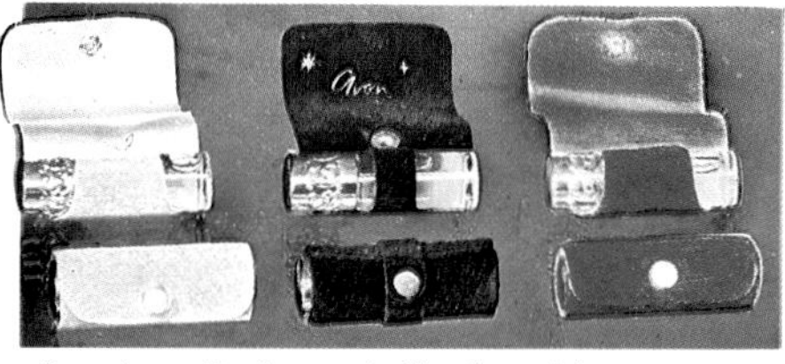

One dram Perfumes in Suedene Wrappers –
1955 *Nearness (blue) $2.25* **MP $17**
1955 *Bright Night (black) $2.25* **MP $17**
1956 *Elegante (burgundy) $2.25* **MP $18**

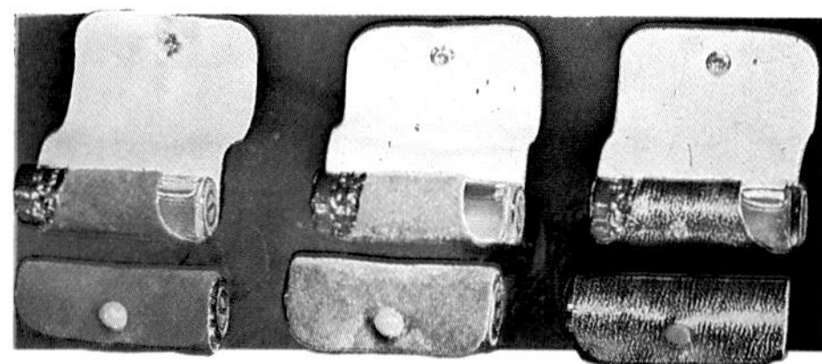

1956 *To A Wild Rose (rose) $2* **MP $17**
1956 *Forever Spring (green) $2* **MP $17**
1956 *Cotillion (simulated gold kid) $2* **MP $18**

Luscious was the first one-dram perfume issued in a wrap-around case. (See pg. 58). Long after Luscious was discontinued, all one-dram perfumes were offered in satin lined wraps with iridescent, pearl-like closures.

PERFUMES BY THE DRAM

A collection of boutique-designed portables to take with you wherever you go.

1959-62 *Top Style One Dram Perfume in 8 frag. $2 to $2.50* **MP $10**
1962-66 *One Dram Perfume in 10 frag. $2.50 to $3.25* **MP $9, $10 boxed**
1966-67 *One Dram Perfume in 9 frag. $2.50 to $3.25* **MP $12**
1974-76 *One Dram Perfume in 6 frag. $3.75 to $4.25* **MP $5**

1961 *Top Style Perfume Xmas boxed $2 to $2.50*
MP $16 Xmas boxed

1969-74 *One Dram Perfume in 15 frag. $2.75 to $3.75* **MP $3**

(See Cotillion customer gift perfumes pg. 39, Topaze pg. 76)

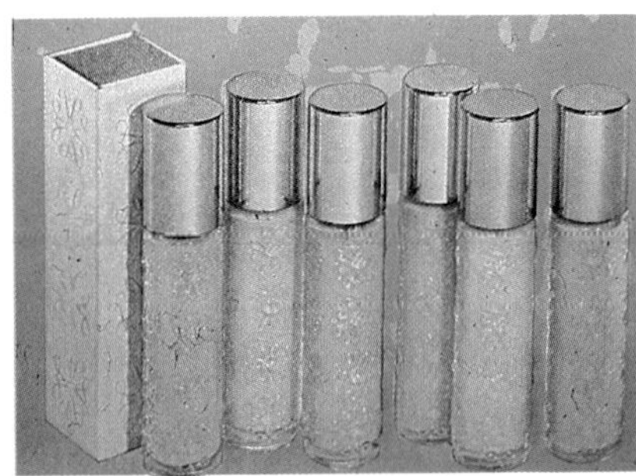

1963 *Perfume Creme Rollette. Somewhere, Topaze, Cotillion $2; Here's My Heart, Persian Wood, To A Wild Rose .33oz $1.75* **MP $6 each, $8 boxed**

1965 *Perfumed Rollettes in 9 frag. Clear formula, tinted glass .33oz $1.75, $2 and $2.50* **MP $9**

1967 *Keynote Perfume in 8 frag. ¼oz $5 to $6.50* **MP $15, $18 boxed**
1971 *Scent With Love Perfume in 5 frag. ¼oz $6 to $7.50* **MP $9, $12 boxed**
1974 *Strawberry Fair in Sonnet or Moonwind 1/8oz $5 & $6* **MP $7, $9 boxed**
1973 *Precious Slipper Perfume in 3 frag. ¼oz $5 & $6* **MP $7, $9 boxed**

PERFUME ROLLETTES

1969 *Perfume Rollette in 8 frag. .33oz $2 & $2.50* **MP 50¢** *(left)*

1975 *Perfume Rollette in Moonwind, Charisma & Sonnet .33oz $4.50 ea.* **MP $1**
1975 *Perfume Rollette in 8 frag. .33oz $3 ea.* **MP 50¢**

SPRAY ESSENCE

An Avon creation of special fragrance oils with lasting powers similar to perfume. The "perfume" women can afford to wear every day.

1973 *Scentiment Perfume Rollette in 3 frag. .33oz $5* **MP $7** *(left)*

1974 *Scentiment Purse Spray Essence in 3 frag. ¼oz $5* **MP $7** *(right)*

1957 *Essence de Fleurs in 6 frag. 1oz $3* **MP $9, $14 boxed**
1959 *Spray Essence in 6 frag. 1oz $3 to $3.25* **MP $5, $10 boxed**

1962 *Crystal Glory Spray Essence in 6 frag. 1oz $4.50 to $5* **MP $17** *(refills, not shown, $2.50 to $3* **MP $7)** *(left)*

1966-67 *Spray Essence in 9 frag. 1¼oz $3.50 to $4* **MP $10**
1967 *Spray Essence in 8 frag. Color coded labels $3.50 to $4* **MP $4**
1969 *Spray Essence in Charisma, Brocade & Regence 1¼oz $4.50* **MP $5**
1979 *Spray Essence in 10 frag. ¼oz $3.50* **MP $3**

PERFUME PETITE FIGURALS

1972 *Perfume Petite (Piglet) in 4 frag. ¼oz $6* **MP $7, $8 boxed**
1974 *Precious Swans Perfume in 3 frag. 1/8oz $6* **MP $7, $9 boxed**
1969 *Love Bird Perfume in 7 frag. ¼oz $6.25 to $7.50* **MP $10, $12 boxed**
1975 *Ladybug Perfume in 3 frag. 1/8oz $6* **MP $5, $6 boxed**

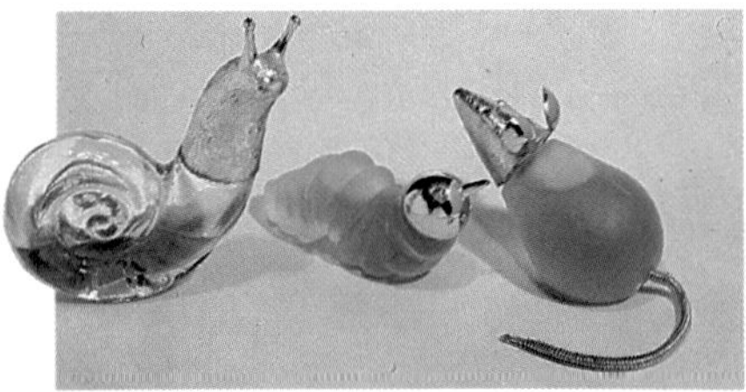

1968 *Perfume Petite (Snail) in 6 frag. ¼oz $6.25 to $7.50* **MP $11, $13 boxed**
1972 *Small Wonder Perfume 1/8oz in 3 frag. $5* **MP $8, $10 boxed**
1970 *Perfume Petite Mouse in 7 frag. ¼oz $6.25 to $7.50* **MP $13, $17 boxed**

1978 *Dapper Snowman Cologne in Sweet Honesty or Moonwind 1oz $5* **MP $3, $4 boxed**

1973 *Snowman Petite Perfume in 3 frag. ¼oz $6* **MP $7, $8 boxed**
1974 *Evening Glow Perfume in 3 frag. .33oz $7* **MP $7, $8 boxed**
1974 *Parisian Garden Perfume in 3 frag. .33oz $7.50* **MP $7, $8 boxed**
1967 *Perfume Flaconette (Icicle) in 9 frag. 1 dram $2.50 to $3.75* **MP $7, $9 boxed**

Perfume Jewelry a la Glace

Table Top Jewelry a la glace. Each refillable gold-toned miniature contains .02oz of Perfume Glace in Moonwind, Elusive, Charisma, Brocade, Regence or Bird of Paradise. Oval refills $1.35 & $2

1971 *Baby Grand $10* **MP $12, $16 boxed**
1971 *Tortoise $9* **MP $10, $14 boxed**
1971 *Memory Book $7* **MP $9, $12 boxed**
1971 *Mandolin $9* **MP $12, $16 boxed**

(See pg. 205 for Glace Jewelry)

PERFUME OILS

1969-73 *Perfume Oil in 9 fragrances ½oz $5 to $7.50* **MP $5** *Hana Gasa & Moonwind* **MP $6**
1971-72 *Fragrance Splendor Perfume Oil in 5 fragrances ½oz $6* **MP $8**
1974-76 *Perfume Concentre in 5 fragrances 1oz $6 to $7.50* **MP $4**

TOILET WATER

1934-39 *Toilet Water 2oz in Vernafleur $1.04, Trailing Arbutus, Lily of The Valley, White Rose, Lilac Vegetal for Men (re-named Lilac in 1936) 78¢* **MP $40, $50 boxed**

1940-47 *Toilet Water 2oz in Jasmine, Trailing Arbutus, Apple Blossom, Lily of The Valley, Lilac ea. 89¢ and Marionette, Cotillion and Sonnet ea. $1.19* **MP $30, $40 boxed; 1942** *Attention* **MP $30; 1946** *Crimson Carnation,* **1947** *Wishing ea. $1.19* **MP $35, $45 boxed**

1946 *Crimson Carnation 2oz $1.19* **MP $40, $55 boxed**

1959 *Gift Magic Cologne. Rocker bottle with flat cap ½oz $1* **MP $10**
1962 *Gift Fancy Cologne. Sea shell bottle with gold cord ½oz $1* **MP $8**
1967 *Half-ounce Cologne. Rocker bottle with round gold cap. 12 frag. $1.25* **MP $5**

1964 *Half-ounce Cologne in 9 frag. $1.25* **MP $6**

1969 *Minuette Cologne in 10 frag. ½oz $1.50* **MP $3**
1970 *Minuette Cologne in 13 frag. ½oz $1.50* **MP $2**
1972 *Fragrance Facets Cologne in 11 frag. ½oz $1.75* **MP $2**

1972 *Pineapple Petite Cologne in 5 frag. 1oz $3.50* **MP $3.50**
1975 *Ultra Cologne, Timeless or Unspoken 1oz $4* **MP $3**
1978 *Cologne Rondelle in 10 frag. ½oz $2.50* **MP $1.25***

1973 *Demi-Cologne in 12 frag. ½oz $1.75* **MP $1**
1975 *Demi-Cologne in choice of 9 frag. ½oz $2* **MP $1**
1976 *Cologne Petite. Choice of 8 frag. ½oz $2* **MP $1**

1972 *Cologne Royale in 6 frag. 1oz $3.50* **MP $4**
1974 *Fragrance Gem Cologne in 11 frag. ½oz $2* **MP $2**
1977 *Floral Half-Ounce Cologne in a choice of 6 floral frag. $2* **MP $1**

1979 *Anniversary Cologne Petite in Regence, Persian Wood, Rapture and Brocade ½oz $2.50* **MP $2, $3 boxed**

COLOGNE MINIATURES

1979 *Cologne Classique in 11 fragrances .5oz $2.50* **MP $1**
1980 *Precious Hearts Cologne in 6 fragrances .5oz $3.50* **MP $1, $2 boxed**
1980 *Cologne-Go-Round in Field Flowers, Hawaiian White Ginger, Honeysuckle or Roses, Roses .5oz $3.50* **MP $1, $2 boxed**

1980 *Crystal Drop Cologne in 8 fragrances .5oz $3* **MP $2***
1981 *Lovechimes Cologne in Roses, Roses, Charisma, Moonwind or Sweet Honesty .5oz $3.50* **MP $1, $2 boxed**

1981 *Floral Colognes in Field Flowers, Hawaiian White Ginger, Roses, Roses, Honeysuckle .5oz $3* **MP $2***

**Available from Avon at time of publication*

1952 Cologne Stick in Xmas Wrap $1.25 **MP $25**
1955 *Cologne Stick in Xmas Wrap $1.25* **MP $25**

COLOGNE STICKS

1952-56 *Cologne Stick in Golden Promise, Quaintance, Cotillion, Forever Spring and To A Wild Rose $1.25* **MP $15 each**
1953-54 *Cologne Stick in Xmas Wrap $1.25* **MP $22**

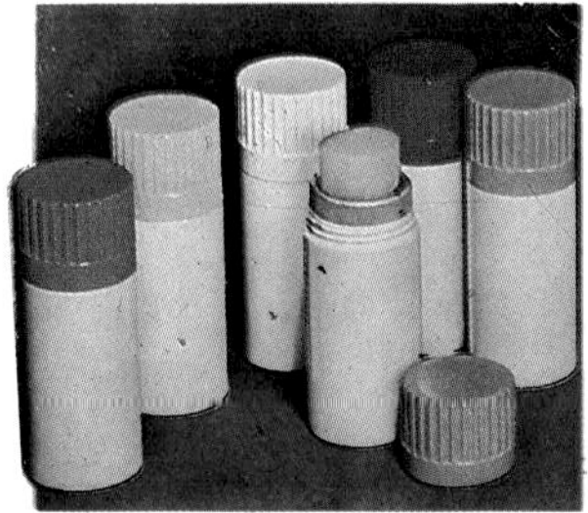

1956-59 *Cologne Stick in Cotillion, To A Wild Rose, Quaintance, Forever Spring $1.25 each; Nearness, Bright Night, Elegante $1.50; Quaintance & Elegante* **MP $10, all others MP $8**

1957 *Cologne Stick in Paper Lantern: Nearness, Bright Night $1.50; Cotillion, To A Wild Rose, Forever Spring and Quaintance $1.25* **Quaintance MP $17, $15 all others**
1956 *See above for fragrances and regular selling price.* **Quaintance MP $17, all others $15**

COLOGNES AND COLOGNE MISTS

HEADACHE COLOGNE

Headache Colognes, *re-named* **Inhalant,** *and then called* **Refreshing Cologne,** *were never intended as fragrances.*

These toiletry Colognes were sprinkled on a handkerchief and then inhaled, providing a soothing treatment for tired nerves, car sickness, fatigue, headache and insomnia. Also refreshing in hot or close atmosphere.

1931-36 *Headache Cologne 4oz 75¢* **MP $50, $65 boxed**
1940-45 *Refreshing Cologne 4oz 52¢* **MP $30** *(1944 issued with black lid, as shown)*
1936-40 *Inhalant Cologne 4oz 52¢* **MP $40, $48 boxed**

Orchard Blossoms Cologne–
1942 *Cologne 6oz (short neck bottle and cap) from Petal of Beauty Set* **MP $70**
1944-45 *Cologne 6oz $1* **MP $70**
1945 *Cologne 6oz (different label) sold in Petal of Beauty Set only* **MP $70**

1969 *Cologne Mist 2oz Charisma, Brocade, Regence & (1970 Elusive) $4.25 each* **MP $4**
1971 *Cologne Mist 2oz in 6 frag. $4.25* **MP $2**
1975 *Cologne Mist 1oz in 6 frag. $3.50* **MP $4**

1962 *Occur! Cologne Mist (black label) 2oz $2.50* **MP $7**

1963 *Cologne Mist 2oz in Cotillion, Somewhere, Topaze, Persian Wood, To A Wild Rose & Here's My Heart $2.25 & $2.50* **MP $6**
1968 *Cologne Mist 2oz in 8 frag. $2.50 & $3* **MP $3**

1976 *Cologne Spray in 6 frag. 1.8oz $5* **MP $1**
1977 *Cologne Spray w/neck label in Topaze, Moonwind, Charisma 1.8oz $6.50* **MP $1**
*(***1974** *Above bottle w/o neck label, Cologne Mist in 10 frag. 2oz $5* **MP $1***)*
1975 *Cologne Mist in 10 frag. 2oz $5* **MP $1.50**
*(***1977** *Above bottle with Cologne Spray in 6 frag. 1.8oz $5* **MP $1***)*

1973 *Cologne Elegante Atomizer in Imperial Garden, Patchwork, Moonwind & Sonnet 3oz $7.50* **MP $8**
1975 *Topalene Cologne Spray Roses, Roses, Moonwind or Patchwork 2½oz $6.50* **MP $4**
1980 *Ultra Mist Atomizer Cologne in Tasha, Timeless, Ariane, Candid 1.5oz $13* **MP $6**

Cologne Silk

– the creamy, translucent cologne that smooths on like silk.

1966-68 *Cologne Silk. Occur!, Unforgettable (shown), Rapture 3oz $4* **MP $4**
1967-68 *Here's My Heart, To A Wild Rose $3.50: Somewhere, Topaze & Cotillion $3.75* **MP $5 ea.**
1968 only *Brocade & Regence $4.50* **MP $6 ea.**

1974 *Winter Garden Cologne Decanter in Topaze, Occur! and Here's My Heart 6oz $6* **MP $5**

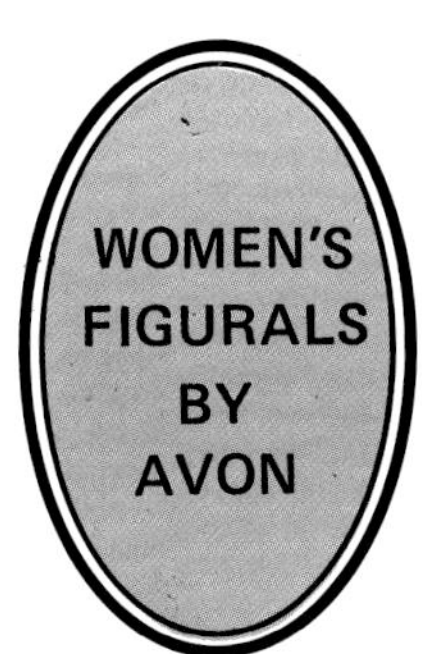

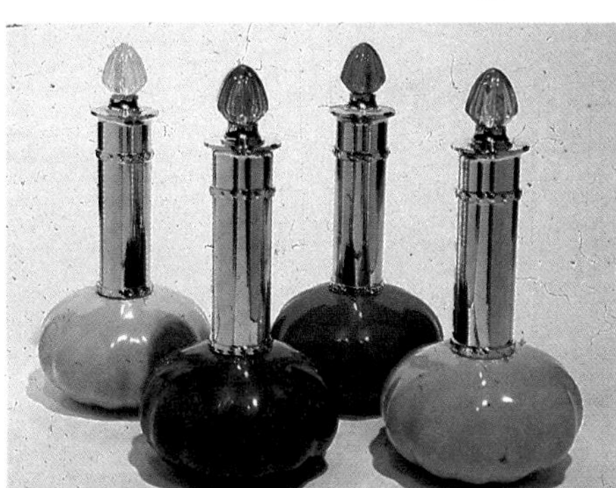

1968 *Gift Cologne 4oz in Cotillion, To A Wild Rose, Somewhere, Topaze & Here's My Heart $4* **MP $5**
1975 *Cologne Crystalique Decanter. Moonwind, Sonnet or Imperial Garden 4oz $8* **MP $8**

1972 *Decorator Cologne Mist in Field Flowers (green), Charisma (red), Bird of Paradise (lt. blue) $7 & $8.50* **MP $12,** *Moonwind (dk. blue)* **MP $15**

1974 *Song of Love Cologne Mist in Bird of Paradise, Charisma or Sweet Honesty 2oz $6* **MP $5**
1976 *Song of Love Cologne Mist 2oz Here's My Heart or Moonwind $7* **MP $5**

1978 *Scentiments Cologne in Sweet Honesty and Here's My Heart 2oz with Mother's Day Greeting Card on front of bottle $6* **MP $5**

1979 *Springsong Cologne in Lily of The Valley or Sweet Honesty 1½oz $8* **MP $3**

1978 *Heavenly Music Cologne in Charisma or Topaze 1oz $4.50* **MP $2**

1970 *Looking Glass Cologne in 13 frag. 1½oz $3.50* **MP $8**
1971 *Purse Petite Cologne in 5 frag. 1½oz $4* **MP $7**

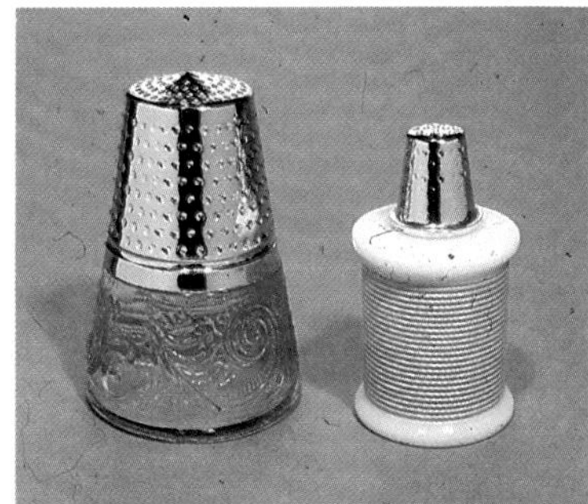

1972 *Golden Thimble Cologne in 4 frag. 2oz $4* **MP $5**
1975 *Sewing Notions Cologne in Sweet Honesty, To A Wild Rose or Cotillion 1oz $4* **MP $4**

1974 *Dovecote Cologne in 4 frag. 4oz $6* **MP $6**

1970 *Picture Frame Cologne in 4 frag. Easel, 6"h. 4oz $10* **MP $11**

1970 *Eiffel Tower Cologne in 6 frag. 3oz $5* **MP $7, $8 boxed**
1972 *Fashion Boot Pin Cushion Cologne in 4 frag. 5½"h. 4oz $6 to $7* **MP $7**
1975 *High-Buttoned Shoe Cologne 2oz Unforgettable or Occur! $4.50* **MP $4**

1972 *Armoire Decanter. Foaming Bath Oil in 4 frag. 5oz $5* **MP $5**
1972 *Secretaire Decanter. Foaming Bath Oil in 5 frag. 5oz $6 to $7.50* **MP $7**
1972 *Victorian Manor Cologne in 4 frag. 5oz $6* **MP $8**

1972 *Royal Coach Foaming Bath Oil in 4 frag. 5oz $6 to $7* **MP $6, $7 boxed**
1973 *Courting Carriage Cologne in Moonwind or Flowertalk 1oz $3.50* **MP $4**
1976 *Magic Pumpkin Coach 1oz Cologne in Bird of Paradise or Occur! $4.50* **MP $3**

1971 *Fragrance Hours (left) Cologne in Bird of Paradise, Charisma, Elusive or Field Flowers 6oz $6* **MP $7**

1972 *Enchanted Hours Cologne in Charisma, Unforgettable, Somewhere or Roses, Roses 5oz $6* **MP $6**
1973 *Beautiful Awakening Cologne in Roses, Roses, Elusive or Topaze 3oz $6* **MP $5**

1970 *Leisure Hours Bath Oil Decanter Foaming Bath Oil in 6 frag. 5oz* **MP $5, $6 boxed**
1974 *Leisure Hours Miniature Cologne in Field Flowers, Bird of Paradise or Charisma 1½oz $4* **MP $4, $5 boxed**

1971 *French Telephone 6oz Foaming Bath Oil and ¼oz Perfume in 4 frag. $20 to $22* **MP $25**
1974 *LaBelle Telephone Perfume Concentre in Sonnet, Moonwind or Charisma 1oz $9* **MP $7, $8 boxed**

1971 *Cornucopia SSS Bath Oil 6oz $6* **MP $6**
1972 *Country Store Coffee Mill Cologne in 4 frag. 5oz $7 to $8* **MP $8**
1972 *Compote Cologne in 4 frag. 5oz $6 to $7* **MP $7**

1973 *Victorian Washstand Foaming Bath Oil in 3 frag. 4oz $6* **MP $6**
1973 *Remember When School Desk Cologne in 4 frag. $6* **MP $8**

18th Century Classic figurines. Cologne or Foaming Bath Oil in Moonwind or Sonnet 4oz – **1974** *Young Girl $7.50* **MP $8**
1974 *Young Boy $7.50* **MP $8**

1971 *Sea Treasure Foaming Bath Oil in 4 frag. 5oz $6* **MP $7, $8 boxed**
1973 *Love Song Decanter 6oz SSS Bath Oil $6* **MP $7**
1974 *Sea Legend Decanter of flint glass. Moonwind or Sonnet Foaming Bath Oil or Roses, Roses Bath Foam 6oz $6* **MP $6**

1972 *Royal Apple Cologne in 4 frag. 3oz $5* **MP $5**

1977 *Silver Pear .66oz Sweet Honesty or Charisma Cream Sachet $6* **MP $4**
1974 *Pear Lumiere Cologne Mist in Roses, Roses, Bird of Paradise or Charisma 2oz $6* **MP $4**
1976 *Enchanted Apple .66oz Charisma or Sonnet Cream Sachet $5.50* **MP $4**

1981 *Spring Bouquet Fragranced Vase, glass coated with Jade Blossom scent 6½" high $12* **MP $10***

1977 *Bath Garden. Hanging Planter and 6 Packets of Mineral Springs Bath Crystals 1oz each $12* **MP $10 complete, $5 Planter only**

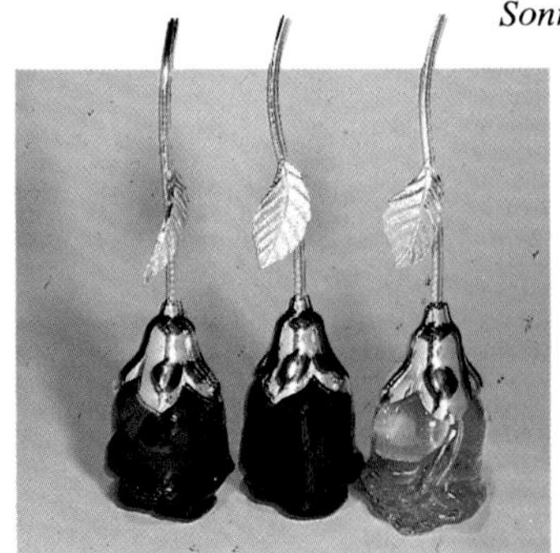
1974 *Courting Rose Cologne in 3 frag. 1½oz $6* **MP $6**
1974 *Same as left, Red Glass* **MP $10**
1977 *Courting Rose Cologne 1½oz Moonwind or Roses, Roses Cologne $6* **MP $4**

1980 *Flower Mouse Cologne in Zany or Cotillion .75oz $6* **MP $2**
1979 *Flower Fancy Cologne in Roses, Roses and Field Flowers 1.25oz $5* **MP $2**

1980 *Crystal Clear Hostess Decanter with Stainless Steel Spoon, Strawberry Bubble Bath Gelee 5.5oz $14* **MP $6**

**Available from Avon at time of publication*

1961 *Dressing Table Cameo Cream Sachet in 6 frag. 1½oz $2.75 to $3.25* **MP $10, $12 boxed**

FOR THE VANITY

1973 *Rich Moisture Cream (silver lid) 5oz $5* **MP $5**
1973 *Skin-So-Soft Skin Softener (gold lid) 5oz $5* **MP $5**
1975 *Vanity Jar. Rich Moisture Cream or SSS Skin Softener 5oz $6* **MP $4**

1973 *Sapphire Swirl. Perfumed Skin Softener in Bird of Paradise or Charisma 5oz $5.50* **MP $6**
1974 *Flight to Beauty in Vita Moist, Rich Moisture or Skin-So-Soft Cream 5oz $6* **MP $6**
1974 *Victorian Sewing Basket. Perfumed Skin Softener in Roses, Roses, Bird of Paradise or Charisma 5oz $6* **MP $6**

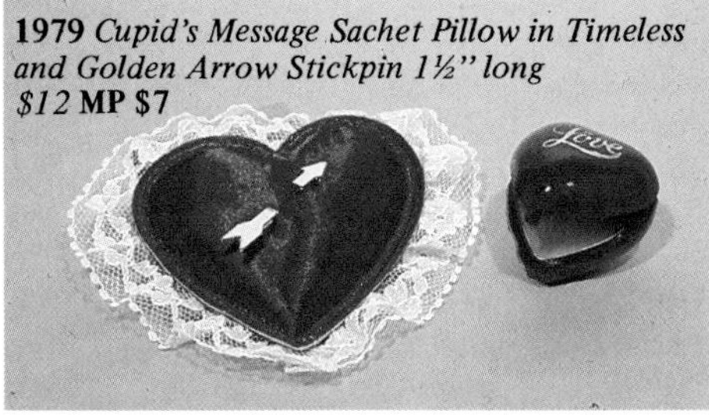

1979 *Cupid's Message Sachet Pillow in Timeless and Golden Arrow Stickpin 1½" long $12* **MP $7**

1979 *Scent with Love Solid Perfume Compact in Sweet Honesty or Here's My Heart .12oz $5* **MP $2**

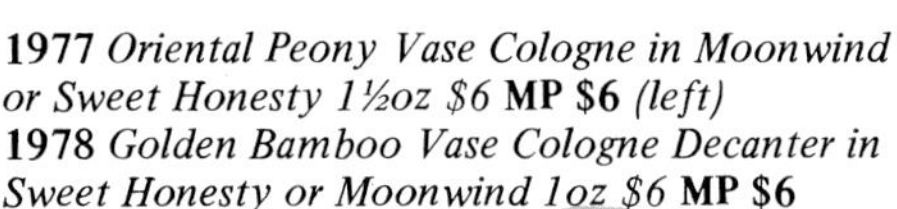

1977 *Oriental Peony Vase Cologne in Moonwind or Sweet Honesty 1½oz $6* **MP $6** *(left)*
1978 *Golden Bamboo Vase Cologne Decanter in Sweet Honesty or Moonwind 1oz $6* **MP $6**

1974 *Scent with Love Cream Sachet in 3 frag. .66oz $5* **MP $5**
1975 *Emeraldesque Cream Sachet in Occur!, Here's My Heart or Sweet Honesty 1oz $4.50* **MP $4**
1976 *Heartscent Cream Sachet in Charisma, Occur! or Roses, Roses .66oz $5.50* **MP $4**

1969 *Powder Sachet (Cranberry) in Charisma, Unforgettable, Cotillion or To A Wild Rose 1½oz $4.50* **MP $10**
1972 *Powder Sachet in 4 frag. 1¼oz $4 to $5* **MP $5**
1973 *Turn-of-Century Powder Sachet Shaker in Charisma or Roses, Roses ¼oz $4.50* **MP $6**

Vases –

Eggs –

1974 *Peach Orchard. Perfume Concentre in Imperial Garden, Moonwind or Sonnet 1oz $7.50* **MP $9**
1975 *Chinese Pheasant. Cologne in Imperial Garden, Charisma or Bird of Paradise 1oz $6.50* **MP $8**
1975 *Delicate Blossoms. Cologne in Patchwork, Sonnet or Charisma 1oz $7.50* **MP $6**

Cream Sachets –

1973 *Vanity Jar in Field Flowers, Charisma or Topaze 1oz $4* **MP $4**
1975 *Gather A Garden in 4 frag. .66oz $5* **MP $3**
1974 *Baroque Cream Sachet in 3 frag. 2oz $7.50* **MP $6**
1975 *Cameo Decanter in 4 frag. .66oz $5* **MP $5**

1970 *Keepsake Sachet. Cream Sachet in 5 frag. .66oz $4.50* **MP $6**
1971 *Keepsake Cream Sachet in 5 frag. .66oz $4 to $5* **MP $5**

1972 *Period Piece Decanter. Skin Softener in 4 frag. 5oz $7 to $8* **MP $7**
1974 *Venetian Blue Emollient Bath Pearls. Frosted jar with 75 "pearls" in Moonwind, Sonnet or Imperial Garden $7.50* **MP $8**

1969 *Petti-Fleur. Elusive, Charisma, Brocade or Regence Cologne 1oz $2.50* **MP $8**
1978 *Dogwood Demi-Decanter Cologne in Moonwind, Apple Blossom ¾oz $4* **MP $1**
1978 *Autumn Aster Demi-Decanter Cologne in Topaze or Sun Blossoms ¾oz $4* **MP $1**

1975 *Crystalier Decanter Cologne in Field Flowers, Roses, Roses or Bird of Paradise 2oz $5* **MP $5**
1973 *Crystal Facets Cologne Gelee in Roses, Roses or Field Flowers 3oz $5* **MP $6**

1975 *California Perfume Co. Anniversary Keepsake. Charisma or Sweet Honesty Cologne. (Limited edition bottle—"1975" embossed on back) 1.7oz $6* **MP $7, $9 boxed** *(See also Manager's Award, page 246)*

1976 *California Perfume Co. Anniversary Keepsake. 1.7oz Moonwind or Cotillion Cologne. (Limited edition bottle—embossed with "1976") $6* **MP $6, $8 boxed**

COLLECTIONS BY AVON

Anniversary Keepsakes
Avonshire
Bristol Blue
Burst of Spring
Buttercup
Butterfly Fantasy
Cape Cod
Castleford
Country Cupboard
Country Garden
Country Kitchen
Crystal
Delft Blue
English Provincial
Flower Fair
Flowerfrost
Fostoria
Hudson Manor
Mount Vernon
Pennsylvania Dutch
Petit Point
Tender Blossoms
Ultra Crystal
Ultra Vanity
Victoriana
Whisper of Flowers

1977 *California Perfume Co. 1977 Anniversary Keepsake (embossed on bottom—"Avon 1977") 3¾oz Trailing Arbutus or Roses, Roses Talc $4* **MP $4, $5 boxed** *(Reps only edition embossed "Anniversary Celebration Talc 1977"* **MP $7***)*

1978 *California Perfume Co. Anniversary Keepsake (embossed on bottom—"Avon 1978") 1.5oz Eau de Cologne in Somewhere, Trailing Arbutus & Sweet Honesty $6.50* **MP $5, $6 boxed**

Avonshire Blue —
1973 *Avonshire Blue Decanter with Foaming Bath Oil or Skin-So-Soft 6oz $7* **MP $9**
1973 *Perfumed Candle Holder. 9 frag. $9* **MP $11**

1971 *Cologne in 4 frag. 6oz $6* **MP $7**
1972 *Soap Dish and oval Soap 5oz $4.50* **MP $7** *(Note: Rare round soaps, demos only* **MP $26***)*
1975 *Glace Compact. Moonwind, Elusive, Charisma .10oz $5* **MP $5**

1979 *California Perfume Co. Anniversary Keepsake Eau de Toilette in Trailing Arbutus. (Limited edition "Avon 1979" embossed on bottom) 8oz $12* **MP $10, $12 boxed**

1979 *California Perfume Co. Anniversary Keepsake Cologne Flacon in Trailing Arbutus or Sweet Honesty. (Limited edition "1979" embossed on lid) ¾oz $6.50* **MP $5, $6 boxed**

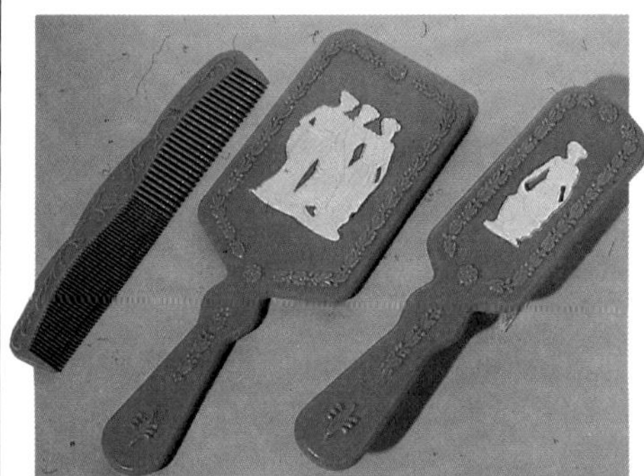
1974 *Vanity Mirror. Plastic with embossed cameo design. 9½" long $6* **MP $8**
1974 *Brush and Comb Set $7* **MP $8**

1979 *SSS Decanter ("May 1979") 6oz $13.50* **MP $8**
1979 *Cologne ("May 1979") 6oz in Somewhere or Charisma $13.50* **MP $8**

1980 *California Perfume Co. Anniversary Keepsake Violet Soap. Two 3oz violet-scented cakes $5.50* **MP $6**

1981 *California Perfume Co. Keepsake Cologne in White Lilac and After Shave in Bay Rum (Dated "1981") All glass bottle is a 1908 replica. 3oz $9.50* **MP $7* boxed**

ANNIVERSARY KEEPSAKES

Beginning in 1975, Avon has commemorated each anniversary with a "Special Edition" Keepsake recalling earlier days. 95 years ago, when Avon was the California Perfume Co., similar creations graced many a Victorian lady's dressing table.

Bristol Blue Collection —
(Imperial Garden, Sonnet or Moonwind)
1974 *Cologne Decanter 5oz $9* **MP $10**
1974 *SSS Bath Oil 5oz $9* **MP $10**
1974 *Soap Dish and Soap 5oz $7* **MP $10**

** Available from Avon at time of publication*

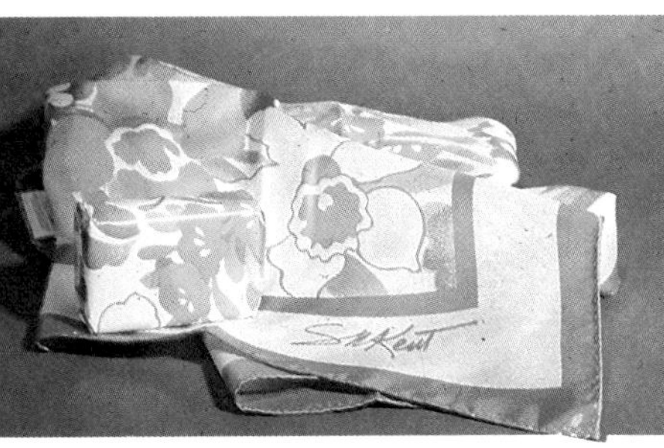

Burst of Spring –

1978 *Beauty Dust Container. Made of tin, sold empty. $6.50* **MP $5**
1978 *Room Freshener 7oz $1.49* **MP 50¢**

1978 *Design -wrapped Soap 3oz $1.25* **MP $1**
1978 *Scarf sold for $2.50 with $8.50 purchase C-7, value $9* **MP $9**

Buttercup –

1974 *Flower Holder perfumed Skin Softener in Moonwind, Sonnet or Imperial Garden 5oz $5* **MP $5**
1974 *Candlestick Cologne in 3 frag. 6oz $7* **MP $8**
1974 *Salt Shaker Cream Sachet in 3 frag. 1½oz $5* **MP $4**
1974 *Candlestick Cologne, later issue with different closure* **MP $7**

Butterfly Fantasy Treasure Porcelain, 22k gold trimmed

1980 *Fan ("1980") $15* **MP $13***
1974 *Egg ("1974") only 110,000 produced. $14.50* **MP $30**
1978 *Egg with "R" (re-issue) on bottom $24.50* **MP $22***

1979 *Two 4" diam. Dishes and Special Occasion Scented Hostess Soap 3oz $16* **MP $16**

Castleford Collection –

1974 *Emollient Bath Pearls holds 60 "pearls" in Moonwind, Sonnet or Imperial Garden 5"h. $10* **MP $10**
1974 *Cologne Gelee in Apple Blossom, Raining Violets or Roses, Roses 4oz $10* **MP $10**

Cape Cod Collection

1977 *Wine Decanter 10" high. Bubble Bath 10oz $20* **MP $22***

1977 *Water Goblet Candle Holder Floral Medley $11* **MP $15***
1976 *Wine Goblet Candlette, Bayberry fragrance $8* **MP $8***
1975 *Candlestick Cologne in Charisma, Bird of Paradise or Patchwork 5oz $11* **MP $8**

1978 *Dessert Bowl and Guest Soap. Three 2oz Special Occasion scented soaps $11* **MP $11***
1978 *Salt Shaker Cologne. Charisma or Topaze 1½oz $6* **MP $5***
1975 *Cruet Decanter with SSS 5oz $11* **MP $8**

1981 *Cream Pitcher Candle Holder, Meadow Morn fragrance $12* **MP $9***
1981 *Sugar Bowl with 3 Timeless Sachet tablets in paper packets $12* **MP $10***

1980 *Dessert Plates, two 7½" diam. $14* **MP $11***
1979 *Hostess Bell, dated "1979" 6½" high with clear glass clapper $15* **MP $15**

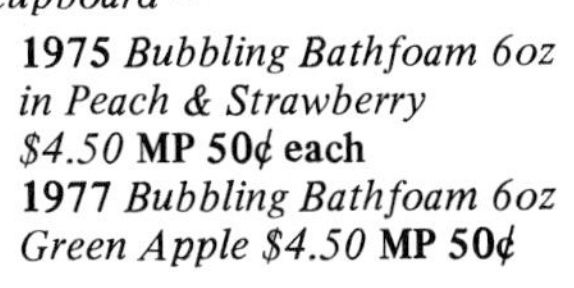

Country Cupboard –

1975 *Talc 5oz in Peach & Strawberry $2.50* **MP 50¢ ea.**
1977 *Talc 5oz Green Apple $2.50* **MP 50¢**

1975 *Bubbling Bathfoam 6oz in Peach & Strawberry $4.50* **MP 50¢ each**
1977 *Bubbling Bathfoam 6oz Green Apple $4.50* **MP 50¢**

Country Garden –
(in Charisma, Elusive or Bird of Paradise)
1971 *Bath Oil 6oz $5.50* **MP $6**
1971 *Beauty Dust 5oz $6* **MP $6**
1971 *Powder Sachet 1¼oz $4.50* **MP $6**
1971 *Soap Dish and Soap $4.50* **MP $6**

Country Kitchen –
1974 *Hand Lotion 10oz $7* **MP $6**
1974 *Soap Dish plastic "scoop" and 5 apple scented 1oz Soaps $7.50* **MP $7.50**

** Available from Avon at time of publication*

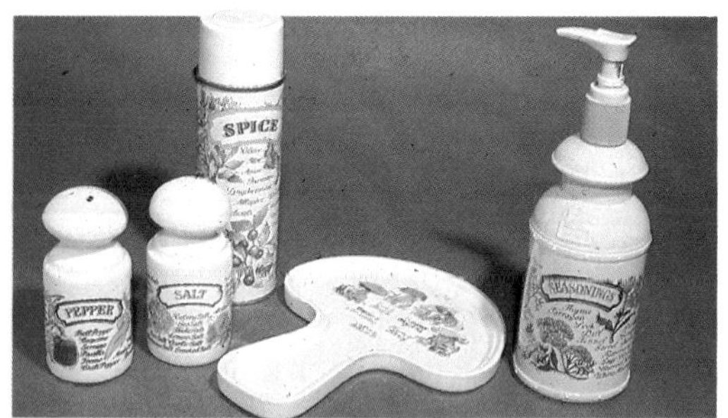

Country Kitchen –
1980 *Ceramic Salt & Pepper Shakers 4" high $12 the set* **MP $10***
1980 *Spice Room Scent 7oz $1.99* **MP $1.50***
1980 *Ceramic Trivet $12* **MP $10***
1980 *Hand Lotion with Pump Dispenser 10oz $9.50* **MP $9***

Crystal –
1966 *Cologne in 8 frag. 4oz $3.50 to $5* **MP $6**
1966 *Beauty Dust in 8 frag. 6oz $4.50 to $6* **MP $17**
1970 *Powder Sachet in 4 frag. 1¼oz $4* **MP $6**

Delft Blue –
1972 *SSS Skin Softener 5oz $5* **MP $6**
1972 *Soap Dish and SSS Soap 3oz $4.50* **MP $6**
1973 *Delft Blue Foaming Bath Oil in Sonnet or Patchwork 5oz $7* **MP $7**
1972 *Pitcher and Bowl, SSS Bath Oil 5oz $8.50* **MP $11**

English Provincial –
(in Bird of Paradise or Charisma)
1972 *Powder Sachet 1¼oz $4.75* **MP $6**
1972 *Foaming Bath Oil 8oz $6* **MP $6**
1972 *Soap Dish and 5oz Soap $4.50* **MP $6**
1973 *Cologne 5oz $6* **MP $6**

Flower Fair –
1974 *Cologne Decanter in Roses, Roses, Sonnet or Moonwind 3oz $7.50* **MP $7**
1974 *Skin Softener Decanter in Skin-So-Soft 5oz $6* **MP $5**

Flowerfrost (Sunny Lemon scent) –
1980 *Crescent Plate and three 2oz scented Guest Soaps $15* **MP $13**
1979 *Goblet and Candlette $14* **MP $12**
1979 *Sherbet Glass and six 1oz Soaps $15* **MP $13**

1979 *Fostoria Crystal Pool Floating Candle $15.50* **MP $13**

Fostoria –
1977 *Heart and Diamond Soap Dish and 5oz Special Occasion scented Soap $9* **MP $9**
1978 *Heart and Diamond Fostoria Loving Cup Candle Holder, Floral Medley $15* **MP $10**
1979 *Heart and Diamond Candlestick with Candlette and Taper $15* **MP $12***

1969 *Fostoria Salt Cellar and silver Spoon, Bayberry Candle, non-refillable $6* **MP $7.50**
1973 *Fostoria Perfumed Candle Holder in 9 frag. $10* **MP $10**
1975 *Fostoria Candlelight Basket in 9 frag. $11.50* **MP $10**

1974 *Fostoria Compote holds 12 SSS Bath Oil Capsules $10* **MP $11**
1977 *Fostoria Egg Soap Dish and 6oz Spring Lilacs scented Soap $15* **MP $10** *("Mother's Day 1977" embossed issue, 2 campaigns only* **MP $15)**

1980 *Fostoria Ring Holder, 3½" wide x 2½" high $10* **MP $9***
1980 *Fostoria Crystal Bud Vase dated "Avon 1980", with pink fabric carnation and fragrance pellet $15.50* **MP $13**

**Available from Avon at time of publication*

Hudson Manor Silverplate

1978 *Hostess Bell 5½" high $22.50* **MP $20**
1978 *Saltcellar and Spoon with Ariane scented Red Candle 2" high, Spoon 3" long $22.50* **MP $20**

1978 *Dish and Satin Sachet, Ariane scent $22.50* **MP $20**

1978 *Bud Vase and Scented Rose. 14" Fabric Flower with 2 Tablets Roses, Roses scent. Vase 8" $22.50* **MP $20**

Pennsylvania Dutch –
(Patchwork, Sonnet or Moonwind)
1973 *Hand and Body Cream Lotion 10oz $6* **MP $6** *(N. A. in Moonwind)*
1973 *Foaming Bath Oil 6oz $6* **MP $6**
1973 *Cologne Decanter 4oz $6* **MP $6**
1973 *Perfumed Skin Softener 5oz $5* **MP $5**
1973 *Powder Sachet Shaker 1¼oz $6* **MP $6**

Petit Point –
(Field Flowers, Bird of Paradise or Charisma)
1974 *Cream Sachet 2"h. 1oz $5* **MP $5**
1970 *Petit Pink Lipstick $2* **MP $4**
1974 *Perf. Skin Softener 3"h. 5oz $5* **MP $5**
1974 *Perfume 2"h. ¼oz $7.50* **MP $7**
1967 *Glace Compact $4.50* **MP $11**

1976 *George and Martha Washington Candle Holders by Fostoria. Floral Medley fragrance. Each $12.50* **MP $10 each**
1977 *Mount Vernon Sauce Pitcher Fostoria Candle Holder, Floral Medley $15.50* **MP $12**

Tender Blossoms –
1977 *Beauty Dust Container. Made of tin, sold empty. $6.50* **MP $6**
1977 *Tender Blossoms Fragrance Candle, Floral Medley scent, non-refillable $6.50* **MP $6**
1977 *Guest Towels and Soaps. 12 Paper Towels and three 2oz Special Occasion fragranced Soaps $6.50* **MP $7**

1979 *Mount Vernon Plate and two 3oz Special Occasion scented Soaps $13* **MP $12**

. . . COLLECTIONS BY AVON

Ultra Crystal –
1981 *Soap Dish and 4oz Soap in Foxfire, Ariane, Tasha or Timeless $12* **MP $10***
1981 *Cologne Decanter in choice of above fragrances 2oz $12* **MP $10***
1981 *Fragrance Candle Holder and Candlette in above fragrances $12* **MP $10***

Ultra Vanity – (Ariane, Candid or Timeless)
1980 *Beauty Dust with Puff in above fragrances 6oz $3.50* **MP $9**
1980 *Soft Body Satin with Pump Dispenser in above fragrances 10oz $12.50* **MP $8**
1980 *Vanity Tray, 12" x 10" metal $10* **MP $10**
1980 *Cologne in above fragrances 2oz $9* **MP $7**
1980 *Luxury Bathfoam in above fragrances 6.75oz $8* **MP $6**

Victoriana –
1972 *Powder Sachet in 2 frag. 1½oz $6* **MP $8**
1971 *Pitcher and Bowl. SSS Bath Oil 6oz $7.50* **MP $12**
1972 *As above with Foaming Bath Oil in 2 frag. $7.50 and $8.50* **MP $11**
1972 *Soap Dish/Soap, 2 frag. $4.50* **MP $7**
1978 *Pitcher and Bowl. Limited edition, embossed "May 1978". Bubble Bath 6oz $13.50* **MP $13**
1978 *Soap Dish and 5oz Special Occasion scented Soap. Dated May 1978 $8.50* **MP $10**

Whisper of Flowers –
1980 *Sachet Pillows in Garlandia fragrance. Set of 5 $9.50* **MP $8**
1980 *Closet Pomander with Garlandia fragranced wax chips $5.50* **MP $5.50 complete, $3 container only**

** Available from Avon at time of publication*

Demi Cups –

1968 *Foaming Bath Oil 3oz $3.50* **MP $8**
1969 *Charisma Foaming Bath Oil 3oz $3.50* **MP $8**
1969 *Regence Foaming Bath Oil 3oz $3.50* **MP $8**
1969 *To A Wild Rose Foaming Bath Oil 3oz $3.50* **MP $9**

1971 *Dutch Treat Demi Cups 3 frag. Cream Lotion 3oz $3.50* **MP $8**

1971 *Koffee Klatch Foaming Bath Oil or Bath Foam 5oz $6* **MP $6**
1973 *Little Dutch Kettle Foaming Bath Oil in 2 frag. or Lemon Bathfoam 5oz $6* **MP $6**
1976 *Hearthside Decanter .66oz Sweet Honesty or Occur! Cream Sachet $5* **MP $5**

KITCHEN FIGURALS

(See also pgs. 151-53)

1968 *Bath Seasons Foaming Bath Oil in Honeysuckle, Lilac & Hawaiian White Ginger 3oz $2.50* **MP $8**

1967 *Bath Seasons Foaming Bath Oil in Lily of The Valley, Honeysuckle, Lilac & Jasmine 3oz $2.50* **MP $10**

1974 *Sweet Treat Cologne, Pink and Pretty 1oz $3.35* **MP $4**
1979 *Bon-Bon Cologne in Sweet Honesty (pink) or Cotillion (yellow) .75oz $6* **MP $2**

1973 *Country Store Mineral Springs Bath Crystals 12oz $7.50* **MP $7**

1974 *Liquid Milk Bath in Moonwind, Sonnet or Imperial Garden 6oz $6* **MP $7**
1973 *Creamery Decanter with Hand and Body Lotion in Roses, Roses or Field Flowers 8oz $6* **MP $6**

1969 *Bath Seasons Foaming Bath Oil in Charisma or Brocade 3oz $3.50* **MP $7 each, $8 boxed**

1976 *Crystalpoint Salt Shaker Cologne in Sonnet or Cotillion 1½oz $4* **MP $3**
1977 *Silver Swirls Salt Shaker Cologne in Sweet Honesty or Topaze 3oz $7.50* **MP $6**
1977 *Country Talc Shaker (metal) Sweet Honesty or Charisma 3oz $7.50* **MP $5**

1973 *Country Charm Cologne in 4 frag. 1½oz $4* **MP $5**

1974 *Teatime Powder Sachet in Moonwind, Roses, Roses or Sonnet 1¼oz $6* **MP $6**
1972 *Dream Garden Perfume Oil in 5 frag. ½oz $6* **MP $12**
1972 *Sweet Shoppe Pin Cushion Cream Sachet in 6 frag. 1oz $5 to $6* **MP $8**

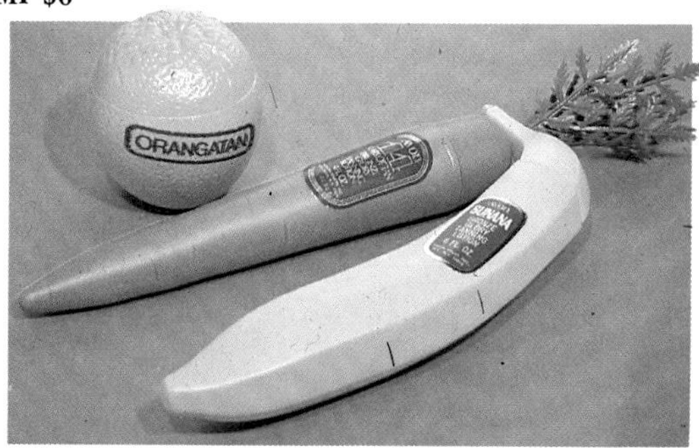

1976 *Orangatan. 6oz Bronze Glory Tanning Lotion $4* **MP $2**
1978 *Karrot Tan. 9" plastic carrot holds 4oz Bronze Glory Tanning Lotion $7.50* **MP $3**
1974 *Sunana Bronze Glory Tanning Lotion 6oz $3.50* **MP $3**

By the Jug –
1974 *Astringent 10oz $4* **MP $3**
1974 *Essence of Balsam Lotion Shampoo 10oz $4* **MP $3**
1974 *Strawberry Bath Foam 10oz $4* **MP $3**
1976 *Sweet Honesty Bubble Bath 10oz $5* **MP $2**

1962 *Skin-So-Soft Bath Oil 10¼"h. $3.50*
MP $14 with card/label, $18 boxed

1963 *Bath Urn opal glass. Perf. Bath Oil 6 frag. $3.50/$3.75*
MP $15 with label

1968 *Riviera Cologne in Brocade or Regence 4oz $6*
MP $9 *(Shown also with reversed base)*

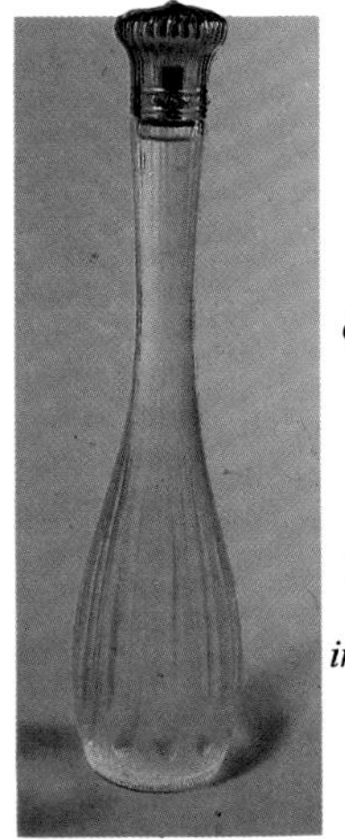

1964 *Deluxe Bath Decanter, Skin-So-Soft 6oz $3.50*
MP $12 with neck tag *(not shown)*

1970 *Ruby Bud Vase in 6 frag. 3oz $5* **MP $10**

1972 *Seagreen Bud Vase Foaming Bath Oil in 3 frag. 5oz $5* **MP $5**

1971 *Emerald Bud Vase Cologne in 5 frag. 3oz $5* **MP $4**

1974 *Empire Green Bud Vase Cologne in 3 frag. 3oz $8.50* **MP $7**

VASES, CRUETS AND URNS

1974 *Regency Skin-So-Soft Bath Oil 6oz $6.50* **MP $6**
1975 *Golden Flamingo Foaming Bath Oil in Bird of Paradise, Charisma or Field Flowers 6oz $7.50* **MP $5**

1974 *Persian Pitcher (left) Foaming Bath Oil in 3 frag. 6oz $7.50* **MP $7**

1972 *Nile Blue Bath Urn, Skin-So-Soft Bath Oil 6oz $7.50* **MP $8**

1974 *Nile Green Bath Urn Foaming Bath Oil in Field Flowers, Bird of Paradise or Charisma $7.50* **MP $8**

1973 *Cruet Cologne Set, 4 frag. 8oz $15* **MP $16**

1966 *Skin-So-Soft Decanter (Cruet) 10oz $5* **MP $10**

1978 *Sea Fantasy Bud Vase, SSS 6oz $10.50* **MP $7**
1979 *Sea Fantasy Bud Vase (reissue) Light Bouquet SSS, Smooth As Silk Bath Oil or Bubble Bath 6oz $11* **MP $7**

1964 *Lotion Lovely Body Lotion in 7 frag. 8oz $3 to $4* **MP $8**

1967 *Cologne Classic in 8 frag. 4oz $3.50 to $5* **MP $6**

1972 *Classic Beauty Decanter Hand & Body Lotion in 2 frag. 10oz $5* **MP $6**

1967 *Bath Urn, Skin-So-Soft 8oz $5* **MP $9**

1965 *Skin-So-Soft Urn 10oz $5* **MP $9**

1974 *Athena Bath Urn (right) Foaming Bath Oil in 3 frag. 6oz $8.50* **MP $7**

1973 *Venetian Pitcher Cologne Mist in 4 frag. 3oz $8* **MP $7**
1974 *Marblesque Cologne Mist in Imperial Garden, Moonwind or Sonnet 3oz $8.50* **MP $6**

1975 *Butterfly Garden Vase Cologne in Roses, Roses, Bird of Paradise or Topaze 6oz $8* **MP $8**

1973 *Garnet Bud Vase Cologne in 4 frag. 3oz $6* **MP $5**
1973 *Hobnail Bud Vase Cologne in 2 frag. 4¾oz $7* **MP $7**
1973 *Grape Bud Vase. Skin-So-Soft Bath Oil 6oz $6.50* **MP $6**

1969 *Fragrance Touch Cologne in Elusive, Charisma, Brocade or Regence 3oz $5* **MP $8**
1970 *Royal Vase Decanter Cologne in 4 frag. 3oz $5* **MP $7**
1973 *Amber Cruet Foaming Bath Oil in Charisma, Bird of Paradise or Field Flowers 6oz $6* **MP $5**

1968 *Bud Vase (left) Cologne in 8 frag. 4oz $4 to $5* **MP $8**

1973 *Floral Bud Vase. Foam of Roses Bathfoam or Field Flowers Foaming Bath Oil 5oz $6* **MP $6**

1971 *Cologne Elegante in 5 frag. 4oz $8.50 to $10* **MP $15**

1972 *Victorian Lady Foaming Bath Oil in 4 frag. 5oz $6* **MP $7**

1969 *Classic Decanter SSS Bath Oil 6oz $6* **MP $10**

1971 *Sea Maiden Skin-So-Soft Bath Oil 6oz $6* **MP $8**

1972 *Grecian Pitcher Skin-So-Soft Bath Oil 5oz $6* **MP $7**
1971 *Bath Urn Foaming Bath Oil or Bath Foam 5oz $5* **MP $7**
1972 *Hobnail Decanter Foaming Bath Oil or Bathfoam in 4 frag. 5oz $7 to $8* **MP $7**

1971 *Aladdin's Lamp Foaming Bath Oil in 5 frag. 6oz $7.50* **MP $11**

1971 *Parlor Lamp Cologne 3oz & Perfumed Talc ¼oz in 5 frag. $7.50 to $9* **MP $10**

1970 *Courting Lamp Cologne in 5 frag. 5oz $7* **MP $12**

1976 *Country Charm Cologne in Field Flowers or Sonnet 4.8oz $10* **MP $7**

1973 *Hearth Lamp Cologne in 3 frag. 8oz $8.50* **MP $8**

1973 *Tiffany Lamp Cologne in 4 frag. 5oz $8 to $9* **MP $10**

1974 *Ming Blue Lamp Foaming Bath Oil in 3 frag. 5oz $7.50* **MP $6**

LAMPS BY AVON

1973 *Chimney Lamp (left) Cologne Mist in 3 frag. 2oz $6.50* **MP $6**

1976 *Library Lamp Cologne in Charisma or Topaze 4oz $9* **MP $6** *(center)*

1975 *Charmlight Decanter Cream Sachet and 2oz Cologne in Imperial Garden, Moonwind or Sonnet $8* **MP $6**

1976 *Mansion Lamp Cologne in Bird of Paradise or Moonwind 6oz $11* **MP $8**

1973 *Hurricane Lamp Cologne in 4 frag. 6oz $9.50* **MP $10**

1976 *Precious Doe Cologne in Field Flowers or Sweet Honesty ½oz $4* **MP $3**
1978 *Silver Fawn Cologne in Sweet Honesty or Charisma ½oz $4* **MP $3**
1977 *Little Lamb Cologne in Sweet Honesty or Topaze ¾oz $5* **MP $3**

A GLASS MENAGERIE

1978 *Sniffy Cologne Decanter in Sweet Honesty or Topaze 1¼oz $7* **MP $5***
1978 *Little Burro Cologne, straw-like hat and flower. Charisma or Sweet Honesty 1oz $6* **MP $5**
1979 *Gentle Foal Cologne in Charisma or Sun Blossoms 1.5oz $7* **MP $3**

1976 *Teddy Bear. ¾oz Topaze or Sweet Honesty Cologne $4.50* **MP $3**
1978 *Honey Bee Cologne in Moonwind or Honeysuckle 1¼oz $6* **MP $3**
1977 *Fuzzy Bear Cologne in Sweet Honesty or Occur! $6.50* **MP $5**

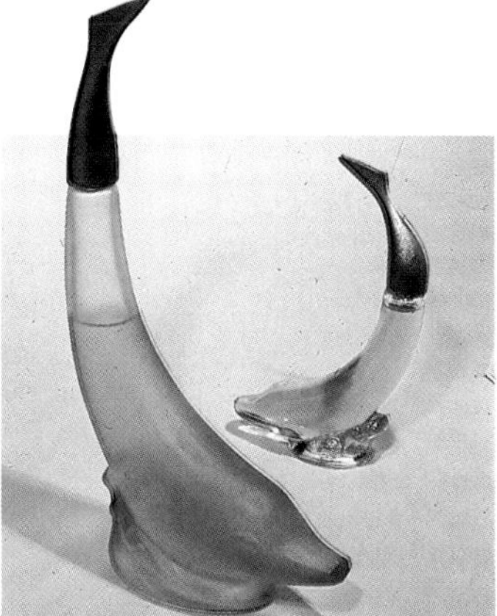

1968 *Dolphin, Skin-So-Soft Bath Oil $5* **MP $9**
1973 *Dolphin Miniature Cologne in Charisma or Field Flowers 1½oz $4* **MP $4**

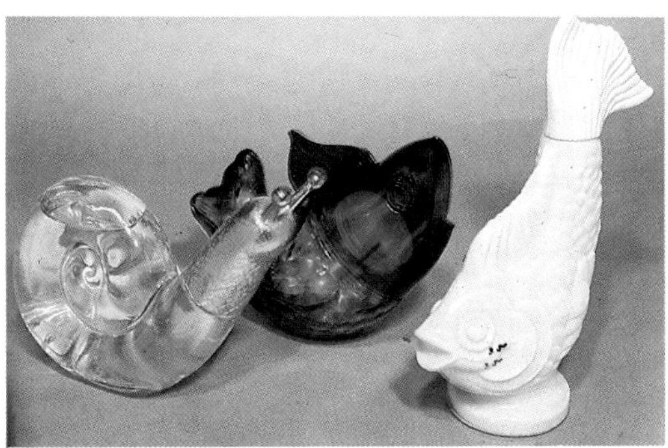

1973 *Bath Treasure (Snail) Skin-So-Soft Decanter 6oz $7.50* **MP $8**
1974 *Song of the Sea, 80 bath "pearls" in 3 frag. $8.50* **MP $8.50**
1973 *Sea Spirit Foaming Bath Oil, 3 frag. 5oz $6* **MP $6**

1970 *Sea Horse Decanter, Skin-So-Soft Bath Oil 6oz $6* **MP $8**
1973 *Sea Horse Miniature Cologne in Unforgettable or Here's My Heart 1½oz $4* **MP $4**
1980 *Seahorse Miniature Cologne in Charisma, Sweet Honesty, Moonwind and Occur! .5oz $3.50* **MP $3***

1974 *Unicorn Cologne Decanter in 4 frag. 2oz $5* **MP $4**
1977 *Baby Hippo Cologne in Sweet Honesty or Topaze 1oz $5* **MP $3**
1976 *Lovable Seal Cologne in Here's My Heart or Cotillion 1oz $4* **MP $2**

1971 *Treasure Turtle Cologne in 14 frag. 1oz $3.50* **MP $4**
1977 *Treasure Turtle Cologne (clear) in Sweet Honesty or Charisma 1oz $4.50* **MP $3**
1975 *Precious Turtle Cream Sachet in Roses, Roses or Patchwork .66oz $5.50* **MP $4**
1978 *Golden Turtle Solid Perfume Compact in Sweet Honesty or Candid .07oz $7* **MP $4**

1977 *Emerald Prince Cologne in Sweet Honesty or Moonwind 1oz $5* **MP $4**
1976 *Fairytale Frog Cologne, Sweet Honesty or Sonnet 1oz $4.50* **MP $2**
1973 *Enchanted Frog Cream Sachet Decanter in Sonnet or Moonwind 1½oz $5* **MP $4**

1974 *Good Luck Elephant Cologne in Sonnet, Imperial Garden or Patchwork 1½oz $5* **MP $4**
1977 *Royal Elephant Cologne in Topaze, Charisma 1½oz $6* **MP $4**
1975 *Graceful Giraffe Cologne in Topaze or To A Wild Rose 1½oz $5.50* **MP $3**

1979 *Snug Cub Cologne in Sweet Honesty or Occur! 1oz $6* **MP $3**
1979 *Merry Mouse Cologne in Cotillion or Zany .75oz $6* **MP $3**

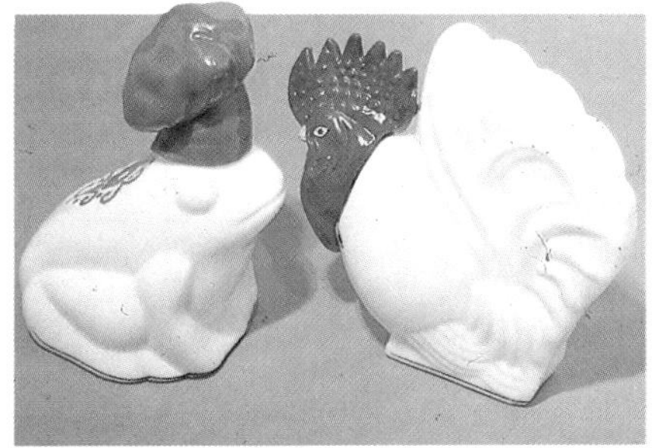

1975 *Handy Frog Decanter with Moisturized Hand Lotion 8oz $7.50* **MP $7**
1973 *Country Kitchen Hand Lotion 6oz $6* **MP $8**

. . . A GLASS MENAGERIE . . .

1974 *Swiss Mouse Cologne in Roses, Roses, Field Flowers or Bird of Paradise 3oz $6* **MP $5**
1977 *Tree Mouse Cream Sachet in Charisma or Sweet Honesty .66oz $6* **MP $3**

1979 *Fuzzy Bunny Cologne in Sweet Honesty or Honeysuckle 1oz $7.50* **MP $7***
1979 *Charming Chipmunk Cologne in Sweet Honesty or Field Flowers .5oz $5.50* **MP $4***
1979 *Monkey Shines Cologne in Sonnet or Moonwind 1oz $7.50* **MP $4**

1972 *Butterfly Cologne in 5 frag. 1½oz $4* **MP $5**
1974 *Snow Bunny Cologne in 4 frag. 3oz $6* **MP $5**
1980 *Fluttering Fancy Cologne in Charisma or Sweet Honesty 1oz $7.50* **MP $5**

**Available from Avon at time of publication*

1973 *Regal Peacock Decanter Cologne in Moonwind, Patchwork or Sonnet 4oz $7* **MP $9**

BIRDS of AVON

1977 *Island Parakeet Cologne in Charisma or Moonwind 1½oz $6* **MP $4**
1979 *Golden Notes Cologne in Moonwind or Charisma 1¾oz $6* **MP $3**

1970 *Bird of Paradise Cologne Decanter 8"h. 5oz $6* **MP $8**
1972 *Swan Lake Cologne in 4 frag. 3oz $5 to $6* **MP $6**
1971 *Flamingo Decanter Cologne in 4 frag. 5oz $5.50* **MP $8**

1971 *Royal Swan Cologne in 6 frag. 1oz $3.50* **MP $6**
1974 *Royal Swan Cologne in 4 frag. 1oz $3.50* **MP $4**
1975 *Pert Penguin Cologne in Cotillion or Field Flowers 1oz $4* **MP $2**
1973 *Snow Bird Cream Sachet Decanter in 3 frag. 1½oz $5* **MP $3**

1973 *Partridge Cologne in Topaze, Unforgettable, Occur! and Somewhere 5oz $6.50* **MP $7**
1974 *Robin Red-Breast Cologne in Roses, Roses, Bird of Paradise and Charisma 2oz $5* **MP $5**

1979 *Precious Chickadee Cologne in Here's My Heart and Sun Blossoms 1oz $6* **MP $3**
1979 *Red Cardinal Cologne in Bird of Paradise or Charisma 2oz $6.50* **MP $3**

1971 *Song Bird Cologne in 5 frag. 1½oz $4* **MP $5**
1972 *Precious Owl Cream Sachet in 4 frag. 1½oz $4 to $5* **MP $5**
1974 *Owl Fancy Cologne Gelee, Raining Violets or Roses, Roses 4oz $6* **MP $6**

1975 *Dr. Hoot Cologne 4oz Sweet Honesty or Wild Country $7.50* **MP $5**
1977 *Dr. Hoot Cologne (blue hat) 4oz Sweet Honesty or Wild Country $7.50* **MP $4**

1977 *Song of Spring. 1oz Sweet Honesty or Topaze Cologne $6* **MP $4**
1978 *Love Bird Cologne in Charisma or Moonwind 1½oz $6* **MP $3**
1980 *Owl Miniature Cologne in Ariane, Timeless, Candid and Tasha .6oz $4* **MP $1**

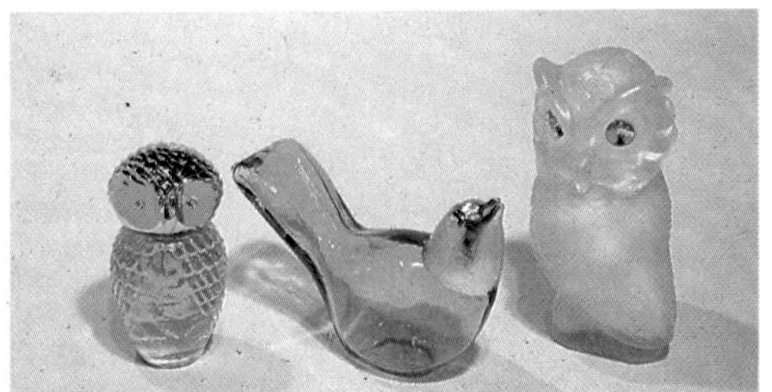

1974 *Baby Owl Cologne. 1oz Occur! or Sweet Honesty $4* **MP $1.50**
1975 *Bird of Happiness Cologne in 4 frag. 1½oz $5* **MP $4**
1976 *Snow Owl. 1¼oz Moonwind or Sonnet Powder Sachet $7* **MP $4**

STUFFED ANIMALS OF AVON

1978 *Kangaroo Two Stuffed Calico Animal and Cologne in Topaze or Sweet Honesty ¾oz $12.50* **MP $10**

1980 *Autograph Hound Stuffed Animal with mortarboard and tassel. Diploma contains .15oz Care Deeply Lip Balm $13.50* **MP $10***
1979 *Ella Elephant Stuffed Animal scented with Garlandia Sachet $9.50* **MP $9**

** Available from Avon at time of publication*

1971 *Ming Cat Cologne in 4 frag. $6.50 to $8* **MP $10**
1975 *Tabatha Spray Cologne in Imperial Garden Bird of Paradise, Cotillion 3oz $7.50* **MP $7**
1978 *Royal Siamese Cologne in Cotillion or Moonwind 4.5oz $8.50* **MP $7**

1973 *Suzette Foaming Bath Oil Decanter in 5 frag. 5oz $6* **MP $5**
1972 *Bon Bon Cologne in 5 frag. 1oz $3.50* **MP $4**
1973 *Bon Bon (black) Cologne in 4 frag. 1oz $3.50* **MP $5**

1973 *Kitten Petite Cologne in Moonwind or Sonnet 1½oz $4* **MP $4**
1972 *Kitten Little Cologne in 5 frag. 1½oz $4* **MP $4**
1975 *Kitten Little (black) Cologne in Bird of Paradise, Roses, Roses or Sweet Honesty 1½oz $3.50* **MP $4**

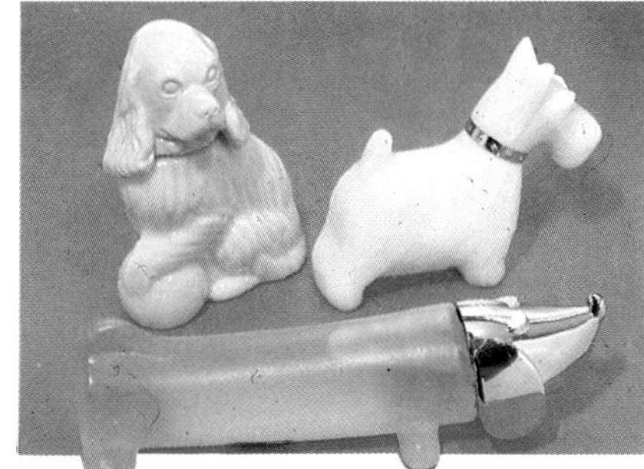

1974 *Lady Spaniel Cologne in Moonwind, Sonnet or Patchwork 1½oz $4.50* **MP $5**
1973 *Queen of Scots Cologne in 5 frag. 1oz $4* **MP $3**
1973 *Dachshund Cologne in 4 frag. 1½oz $4* **MP $4**

1974 *Kitten's Hideaway Cream Sachet in Field Flowers, Bird of Paradise or Charisma 1oz $5* **MP $5**
1975 *Blue Eyes Cologne in Topaze or Sweet Honesty 1½oz $6* **MP $4**
1976 *Sitting Pretty Cologne in Charisma or Topaze 1½oz $6* **MP $4**

1976 *Princess of Yorkshire Cologne in Topaze or Sweet Honesty 1oz $6* **MP $3**
1974 *Royal Pekingese Cologne in Topaze, Unforgettable and Somewhere 1½oz $4* **MP $3**
1978 *Baby Bassett Cologne in Sweet Honesty or Topaze 1¼oz $5* **MP $3**

1979 *Curious Kitty Cologne in Sweet Honesty or Here's My Heart 2.5oz $7.50* **MP $4, $5 boxed**

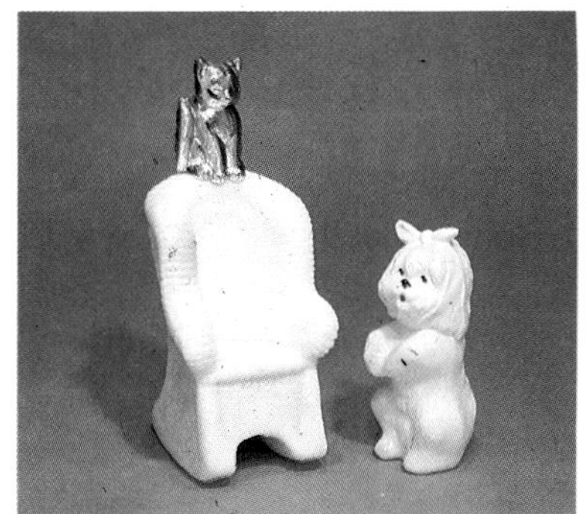

1971 *Sitting Pretty Cologne in 5 frag. 4oz $6* **MP $7**
1979 *Sweet Tooth Terrier Cologne in Cotillion or Topaze 1oz $6* **MP $3**

1972 *Little Girl Blue Cologne in Brocade, Unforgettable, Cotillion and Somewhere 3oz $6* **MP $9**
1974 *Pretty Girl Pink Cologne in Unforgettable, Somewhere, Occur! and Topaze 3oz $6* **MP $12**

1972 *Roaring 20's Fashion Figurine Cologne in Unforgettable, Topaze, Somewhere and Cotillion 3oz $6* **MP $11**
1972 *Elizabethan Fashion Figurine Cologne 4oz in Charisma, Field Flowers, Bird of Paradise $6 and Moonwind $7* **MP $12**

1971 *Victorian Fashion Figurine (left) Cologne in Field Flowers, Elusive, Bird of Paradise or Brocade 4oz $6* **MP $13**
1973 *Victorian Fashion Figurine Cologne in Field Flowers, Charisma, Bird of Paradise 4oz $6* **MP $40**

1974 *Gay Nineties Fashion Figurine in Topaze, Unforgettable or Somewhere 3oz $6* **MP $10**
1979 *On The Avenue Figurine Cologne in Unforgettable or Topaze 2oz $9* **MP $8**
1979 *Adorable Abigail Cologne in Regence or Sweet Honesty 4.5oz $13* **MP $10**

1973 *Dutch Girl Cologne in Topaze, Unforgettable or Somewhere 3oz $6* **MP $9**
1977 *Skater's Waltz Cologne in Charisma or Moonwind 4oz $8.50* **MP $7**
1979 *Skater's Waltz Cologne (blue) in Charisma or Cotillion 4oz $10* **MP $7**

1976 *Bridal Moments Cologne in Sweet Honesty or Unforgettable 5oz $9* **MP $8***
1979 *Wedding Flower Maiden Cologne in Sweet Honesty or Unforgettable 1.75oz $7* **MP $6**
1978 *Proud Groom Cologne in Unforgettable or Sweet Honesty 2oz $9* **MP $8***

1976 *Betsy Ross Cologne in Sonnet or Topaze 4oz $6.99 dated July 4, 1976* **MP $11 Available 2 campaigns only.** *In milk glass* **MP $25**
1974 *Flower Maiden Cologne in Somewhere, Topaze and Cotillion 4oz $6* **MP $8**

1975 *Scottish Lass in Sweet Honesty, Cotillion, Bird of Paradise, Roses, Roses 4oz $7.50* **MP $9**
1975 *Spanish Senorita Cologne in Moonwind, Topaze, To A Wild Rose 4oz $7.50* **MP $9**

1976 *American Belle in Sonnet or Cotillion Cologne 4oz $7.50* **MP $6**
1977 *Dutch Maid Cologne in Sonnet or Moonwind 4oz $7.50* **MP $6**

1978 *Garden Girl (Pink) Cologne in Charisma or Sweet Honesty Cologne 4oz $7* **MP $5**
1975 *Garden Girl Cologne in Sweet Honesty, Somewhere, Cotillion, To A Wild Rose 4oz $7* **MP $6**

1973 *Dear Friends Cologne in Field Flowers, Bird of Paradise, Roses, Roses 4oz $6* **MP $12**
1973 *Little Kate Cologne in Charisma, Bird of Paradise or Unforgettable 3oz $5* **MP $9**
1974 *Sweet Dreams Cologne in Sweet Honesty or Pink & Pretty 3oz $6* **MP $15**

1979 *Sweet Dreams Cologne in Somewhere or Zany 1.25oz $7.50* **MP $5**
1980 *Little Dream Girl Cologne in Sweet Honesty or Occur! 1.25oz $7.50* **MP $5**

. . . THE AVON FIGURINES

1978 *Little Miss Muffet Cologne in Topaze or Sweet Honesty 2oz $7* **MP $6**
1979 *Little Jack Horner Cologne in Topaze or Roses, Roses 1.5oz $7.50* **MP $6***

1976 *Little Bo-Peep Cologne in Sweet Honesty or Unforgettable 2oz $7* **MP $6**
1977 *Mary, Mary Cologne in Sweet Honesty or Topaze 2oz $7* **MP $6**

1981 *Prima Ballerina Cologne in Sweet Honesty or Zany 1oz $7.50* **MP $6**
1981 *First Prayer Cologne in Charisma, Topaze or Occur! 1.5oz $8.50* **MP $7***

** Available from Avon at time of publication*

1977 *Roll-A-Hoop Cologne in Field Flowers or Cotillion 3¾oz $10* **MP $10**

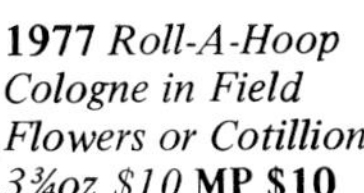

1975 *Fly-A-Balloon (right) Cologne in Moonwind or Bird of Paradise 3oz $9.50* **MP $10**

1975 *Skip-A-Rope Cologne in Sweet Honesty, Bird of Paradise or Roses, Roses 4oz $9.50* **MP $10**

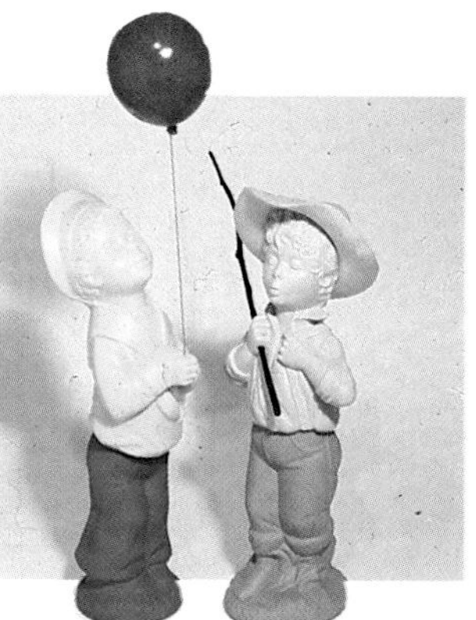

1976 *Catch-A-Fish Cologne in Field Flowers or Sonnet 3oz $9.50* **MP $6.50**

1980 *Marching Proud Cologne in Sweet Honesty or Topaze 2oz $14.50* **MP $12* (Last Figurine in the Motion series)**
1979 *Tug-A-'Brella Cologne in Moonwind or Cotillion 2.5oz $12.50* **MP $10**

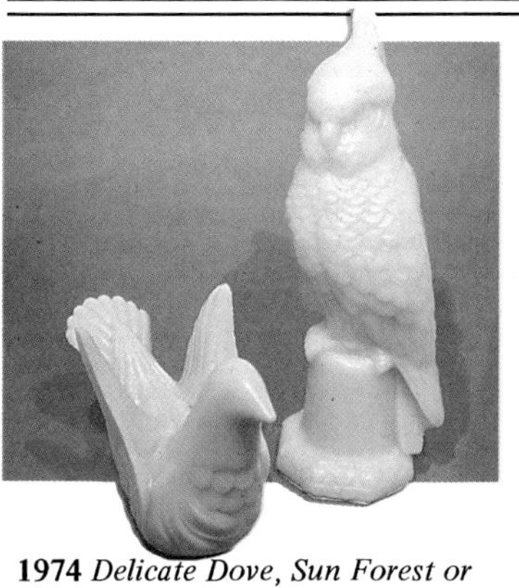

1974 *Delicate Dove, Sun Forest or Summer Breeze scent $6* **MP $7**
1972 *Cockatoo, Floral Medley scent $6* **MP $8**

1974 *Sign of Spring, Fernerie scent $6* **MP $7**
1978 *The Nestlings, Garlandia scent $8* **MP $6**

1979 *Two Turtledoves, Potpourri scent $11* **MP $10**
1980 *Tender Love, Potpourri scent $12* **MP $11**

DECORATIVE POMANDERS

1979 *Honey Bears, Floral Medley scent $9* **MP $8**
1975 *Meadow Bird, Fernerie scent $7.50* **MP $8**

1974 *Pampered Persians, Floral Medley frag. $6* **MP $6**
1977 *Royal Pekingese, Fernerie scent $7.50* **MP $7**

1974 *Duck Decoy, Wild Country or Deep Woods scent $8* **MP $9**
1980 *Peaceful Partners, Fragrant Seasons scent $13* **MP $11***
1980 *Pine Cone Cluster Hanging Pomander, Mountain Pine scent $5.50* **MP $4**

1978 *Bountiful Harvest, Spiced Apple scent $9.50* **MP $9**
1979 *Autumn Harvest Hanging Pomander, Garlandia scent $10.50* **MP $9**

1981 *Heralds of Spring Mini-Pomanders, Potpourri scent. Mouse, Chick, Chipmunk and Owl each 3" high $6* **MP $5***

1979 *Model T Car Pomander, Country Morning scent $3.50* **MP $2**
1980 *Traffic Stopper Car Pomander, Country Morning scent $4* **MP $3**
1980 *Wild Game Car Pomander, Meadow Morn scent $5.50* **MP $4**
1981 *Keep On Truckin' Car Pomander, Fernerie scent $5* **MP $4***

**Available from Avon at time of publication*

1975 *Coral Empress, Fragrant Seasons scent $6* **MP $8**

1972 *Oriental Figurine, Potpourri scent $6* **MP $10**

1973 *Oriental Figurine, Potpourri scent 10"high $6* **MP $9**

1976 *Parisian Mode, Garlandia scent $7.50* **MP $6**

1975 *Florentine Cherub, Fragrant Seasons scent $7.50* **MP $7**

1977 *Florentine Lady, Fragrant Seasons scent $8* **MP $6**

1978 *Viennese Waltz, Potpourri scent $9* **MP $7**

1978 *Christmas Carollers, Festival Garlands scent $7.50* **MP $7**

1979 *Under the Mistletoe, Potpourri scent $12.50* **MP $11**

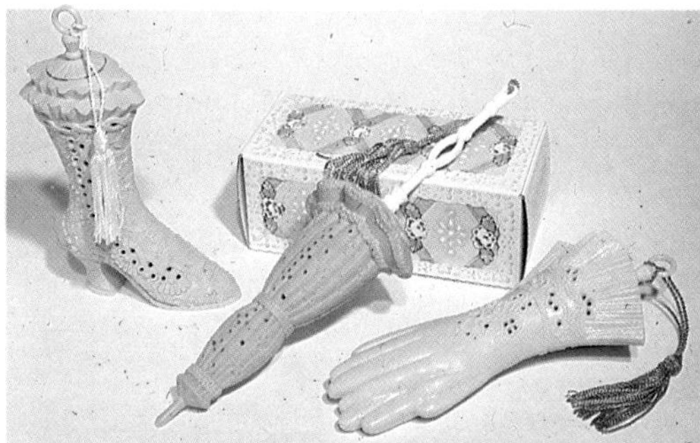

1978 *Frilly Boot Closet Pomander, Poupourri wax chips $6* **MP $3**
1976 *Parasol Closet Pomander, Potpourri $5* **MP $3**
1979 *Lacy Gloves Closet Pomander, Garlandia scent $6* **MP $5***

. . . DECORATIVE POMANDERS

1967 *Lavender Closet Pomander, refillable $5* **MP $7**
1970 *Potpourri Closet Pomander, refillable $5* **MP $7**
1978 *Pampered Piglet Ceramic Pomander, Meadow Morn $10* **MP $8**

1974 *Wise Eyes Closet Pomander, Fernerie scent $4* **MP $5**

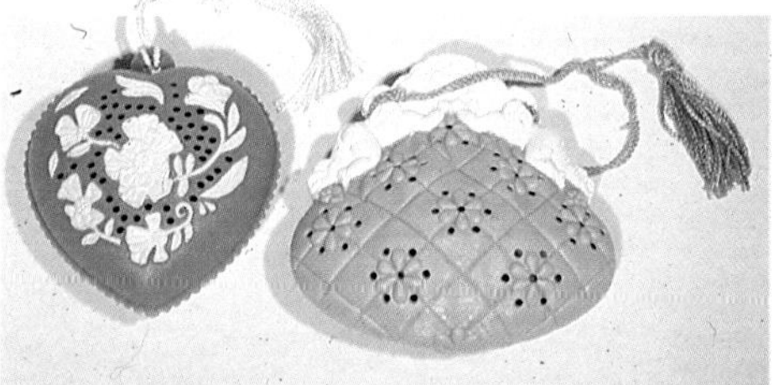

1973 *Heartscent Closet Pomander, Potpourri scent $4* **MP $5**
1977 *Sweet Cherubs Closet Pomander, Potpourri scent $5* **MP $4**

1979 *Fresh Flight Pomander, Potpourri scent $6* **MP $5**

1975 *Picture Hat Pomander, Potpourri scent $5* **MP $5**
1980 *Cameo Closet Pomander, Potpourri scent $6* **MP $5**
1980 *Flirtatious Frog Ceramic Pomander, Fernerie scent $11* **MP $10**

1981 *Basket of Violets Pomander in white opal glass holds fabric violets, Violet scented chips $13* **MP $11***

1981 *Tropical Splendor Hanging Window Pomander $12* **MP $10***

1980 *Fragrant Flight Window Pomander, Flowerburst scent $12* **MP $10***

1981 *Cuckoo Clock Hanging Wall Pomander, Spiced Apple scented chips $12* **MP $10***

* *Available from Avon at time of publication*

(See "Whisper of Flowers" pg. 153)

Perfumed Pedestal Candle Containers:
1965 *Red $4* **MP $17**
1964 *White $3.50* **MP $14**
1965 *Amber $4* **MP $17**

CANDLES BY AVON

1967 *First Christmas Candle, Frankincense and Myrrh, non-refillable $5* **MP $14**
1969 *Perfumed Candle and pedestal-snuffer lid in 9 frag. $7.50 and $8* **MP $10**
1974 *Golden Pine Cone Fragrance Candlette, Bayberry fragrance $6* **MP $6**

1966 *Perfumed Candle (white) in 9 frag. $4.25 to $5* **MP $15**
1967 *Perfumed Candle (frosted) in 8 frag. each in a different colored aluminum cup that shows through the glass $4.50* **MP $16**
1970 *Nesting Dove in 7 frag $7.50* **MP $10**

1972 *Mushroom Candle, Garden Spice (non-refillable) $5* **MP $8**
1972 *Turtle Candle, Garden Spice (non-refillable) $5* **MP $8**

1971 *Floral Medley Perfumed Candles 1.3oz (non-refillable) $5.50* **MP $10**
1972 *Glow of Roses Perfumed Candle and Container $7* **MP $8**

1968 *Golden Apple in 9 frag. $5.75 to $6.50* **MP $14**
1969 *Wassail Bowl Candle Holder with silver ladle $8* **MP $13**

1972 *China Teapot, genuine china, 2 cup size with Perfumed Candle (available one campaign only) $12.50* **MP $20**
1976 *Terra Cotta Bird Fragrance Candlette Holder $8* **MP $7**

1972 *Potpourri Fragrance Candle (non-refillable) $5* **MP $6**

1973 *Hearts and Flowers Candle, Floral Medley scent $5* **MP $5**
1974 *Kitchen Crock Candlette, Meadow Morn fragrance $5* **MP $6**

1979 *Bunny Ceramic Planter Perfumed Candle Holder in Floral Medley or Spice Garden $18* **MP $15**

1971 *Dynasty Perfumed Candle Holder in 7 frag. $7.50* **MP $10**
1974 *Lotus Blossoms Perfumed Candle and Holder in 9 frag. $10* **MP $10**

1977 *Bunny Ceramic Planter Candle Holder in 5 frag., hand-painted and "Handcrafted in Brazil" on bottom. Did not appear in brochure, sold only during C-15-77 at $10.99* **MP $11**
1978 *Bunny Planter-Candle Holder made in U.S. in Roses, Roses or Floral Medley $15* **MP $13**

1980 *Bunny Bright Ceramic Candle Holder, Spiced Apple fragrance Candlette $14* **MP $12***
1981 *Sunny Bunny Ceramic Candle Holder, dated Avon 1981. Floral Medley fragrance Candlette $16.50* **MP $14***

1979 *Revolutionary Soldier Fresh Aroma Smoker's Candle, non-refillable $8* **MP $9**
1979 *As above, issued in amber glass $9* **MP $7***

* *Available from Avon at time of publication*

1979 *Crystalglow Clearfire Transparent Candle, Softscent fragranced Amethyst candle $13.50* **MP $10**
1974 *Ovalique Perfumed Candle Holder in 9 frag. $10* **MP $8**
1978 *Winter Lights Candlette, Moonwind fragrance $10* **MP $8**
1980 *Starbright Candle with Bayberry (red) or Floral Medley (white) scent $11* **MP $8**

1975 *Facets of Light Candlette, Bayberry scent $6* **MP $5**

1980 *Sparkling Swirl Clearfire Transparent Candle, Softscent fragrance $14.50* **MP $12***
1980 *Sherbet Dessert Candle, Spiced Apple scent (pink), Strawberry scent (red), Lemon scent (yellow) $10* **MP $7**

1969 *Crystal Candelier, Frankincense and Myrrh scented candle chips and wick 6½"h. $7* **MP $12 complete**
1979 *Country Spice Candle, Spiced Apple scent $10.50* **MP $7**

1972 *Crystal Glow Candle Holder $10* **MP $11**
1979 *Clearfire Transparent Candle, Softscent fragrance $12* **MP $9***
1980 *Personally Yours Candle, Meadow Morn scent, issued with 26 gold foil alphabet letters $14* **MP $10**

1980 *Floral Light Candle, Floral Medley scent in choice of yellow, lavender or green candle $9* **MP $7**

. . . CANDLES BY AVON

1978 *Bright Chipmunk Candlette, Spice Garden fragrance $9.50* **MP $7**
1977 *Dove in Flight Candlette, Meadow Morn $9.50* **MP $7**
1978 *Sparkling Turtle, Meadow Morn $9.50* **MP $6**

1979 *Shimmering Peacock Clearfire Candle, Softscent fragrance $12.50* **MP $10**
1981 *Snug 'N Cozy Fragrance Candle, Spice Garden scent $12* **MP $10**

1975 *Enchanted Mushroom, Meadow Morn scent, non-refillable, $6* **MP $7**
1975 *Catnip Fragrance Candle, Floral Medley scent, non-refillable, $5* **MP $8**

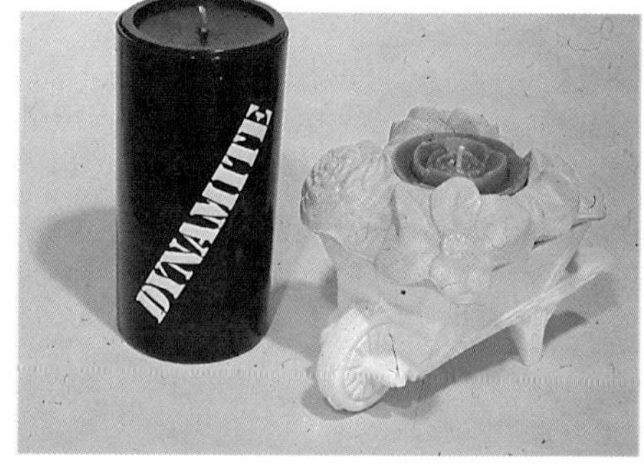

1975 *Dynamite Fragrance Candlette, reusable as pencil holder $6.50* **MP $6**
1979 *Garden Bounty, Meadow Morn scent $9.50* **MP $7**

CANDLESTICKS BY AVON

1970 *Candlestick Cologne in 5 frag. 4oz $6* **MP $11**
1974 *Cologne and Candlelight in Imperial Garden, Roses, Roses or Charisma 2oz $5* **MP $5**

1973 *Hurricane Lamp Cologne in 4 frag., candle not included $9.50* **MP $10**
1973 *Hobnail Patio Candle Holder in 8 frag. $9* **MP $9**

1970 *Crystallite Candlestick Cologne in 6 frag. 4oz $5.50* **MP $6**
1973 *Regency Candlestick Cologne in 4 frag. 4oz $8* **MP $8**
1976 *Opalique Candlestick Cologne in 2 frag. 5oz $12* **MP $8**

1972 *Candlestick Cologne in 4 frag. $7 & $8.50* **MP $8**
1970 *Danish Modern Set. Scented Taper 9"h. $4.50* **MP $8**
1966 *Candlestick Cologne in 3 fragrances 3oz $3.75* **MP $12**

**Available from Avon at time of publication*

1973 *Sunshine Rose Fragrance Candle, Rose scent $8.50* **MP $9**
1973 *Flaming Tulip Candle, Floral Medley scent $8.50* **MP $9**
1971 *Floral Fragrance Candle, Floral Medley fragrance $8.50* **MP $10**

1972 *Water Lily Fragrance Candle, non-refillable, $5* **MP $6**
1974 *Greatfruit Fragrance Candle, Grapefruit scented $5* **MP $5**
1975 *Black-Eyed Susan Candle, Wild Flowers fragrance, non-refillable $6* **MP $5**

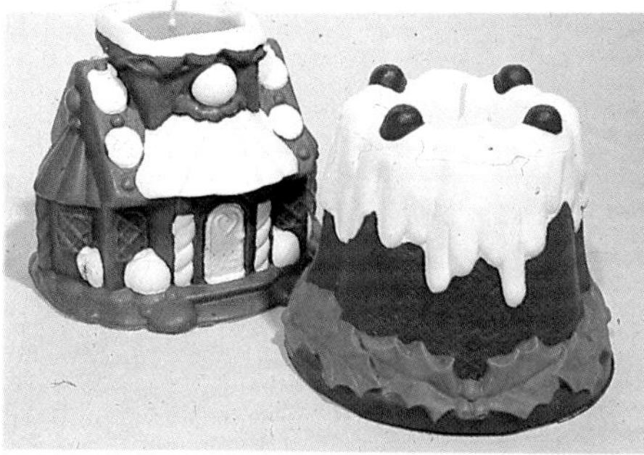

1977 *Gingerbread House Candle, Frankincense and Myrrh scented, non-refillable $7* **MP $6**
1978 *Plum Pudding Candle, Frankincense and Myrrh scented, non-refillable $9* **MP $8**

1979 *Winter Wonderland Candle in glass holder, Bayberry scent $19* **MP $17**
1979 *Mrs. Snowlight Candle, Bayberry scented, non-refillable $9* **MP $8**

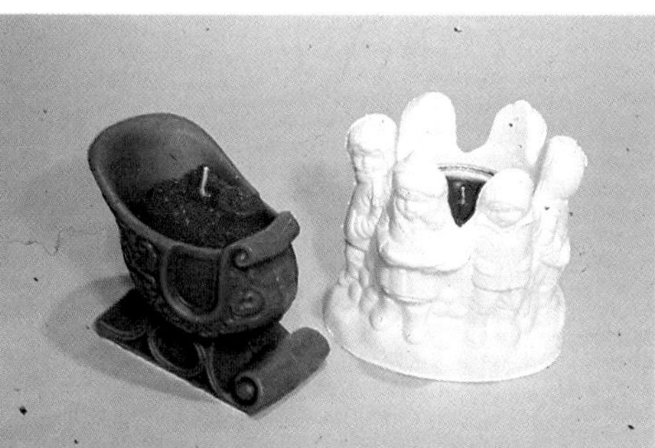

1975 *Sleigh Light Candle, Bayberry scent, non-refillable $7* **MP $6**
1980 *Glow of Christmas Candle in glass holder, Floral Medley scent $12* **MP $10**

1979 *Fresh Aroma Smoker's Candle, non-refillable $9* **MP $8**
1980 *Harvest Time Candle in glass holder, Spice Garden scent $12* **MP $11**

1980 *Holiday Candle Dish with Wreath and 8" Taper Candle. Red in Floral Medley scent, Off-white in Spice Garden and Green in Bayberry $11* **MP $10**

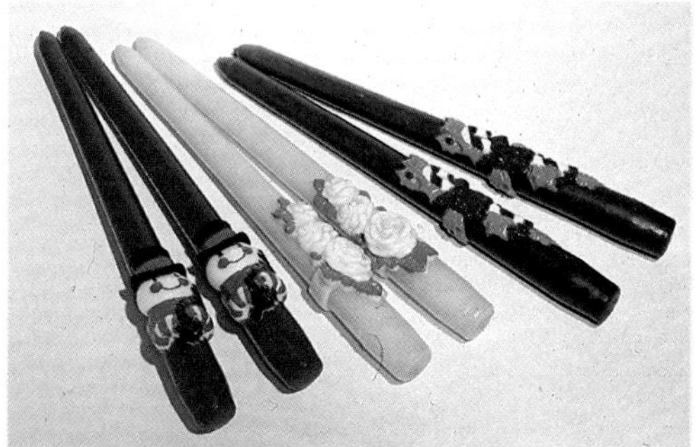

1980 *Fragranced Decorated 10" Taper Candles, Set of two, Bayberry scented $7* **MP $7**
Dapper Snowman in Red, Winter Rose in Off-white, Candy Cane and Holly in Green

1973 *Jennifer Ceramic Figurine $9.99* **MP $45**
1973 *My Pet Ceramic Figurine $9.99* **MP $40**

1980 *Porcelain Floral Bouquet. Hand-painted Bisque, dated 1980 on bottom $19* **MP $18***
1980 *Christmas Ceramic Wreath with golden metallic cord, dated 1980 in 14k gold $10* **MP $10**

1979 *Merry Xmas Tree Hostess Set. Ceramic Pomander Centerpiece and Rag Doll and Teddy Bear Shakers. Only 1 or 2 sets were sold to Representatives $29* **MP $29**

CERAMICS

1974 *Blue Blossoms Cup/Saucer $11.50* **MP $16**
1974 *Pink Roses Cup/Saucer $11.50* **MP $16**
(Both made in England with 22k gold trim.)

**Available from Avon at time of publication*

1974 *Cardinal Plate 10" diam. Cardinal decal designed and painted by Don Eckelberry. $18* **MP $27**

1973 *Betsy Ross Plate 9" diam. $15* **MP $25**
1974 *Freedom Plate 9" diam. $15* **MP $25**
Both Plates produced by Enoch Wedgwood [Tunstall] Ltd., England

1974 *Tenderness Plate 9" diam. Created exclusively for Avon by Alvarez of Spain $15* **MP $22**
(Representative's Commemorative edition with inscription on back **MP $27**
1975 *Gentle Moments Plate 9" diam. Made in England by Wedgwood $17* **MP $22**

1981 *Mother's Day Plate "Cherished Moments" 5" diam. with display easel. Dated and trimmed in 22k gold $12* **MP $10**

1973 *Christmas Plate "Christmas on the Farm", 9" diam. Produced by Wedgwood $15* **MP $85**

1974 *Christmas Plate "Country Church", 9" diam. Produced by Wedgwood $16* **MP $50**

1975 *Christmas Plate "Skaters on the Pond", 9" diam. Produced by Wedgwood $18* **MP $30**

1976 *Christmas Plate "Bringing Home The Tree", 9" diam. Produced by Wedgwood $18* **MP $30**

CHRISTMAS PLATES

1977 *Christmas Plate "Carollers in The Snow", 9" diam. Produced by Wedgwood $19.50* **MP $30**

1978 *Christmas Plate "Trimming The Tree", 9" diam. Produced by Wedgwood $21.50* **MP $27**

1979 *Christmas Plate "Dashing Through the Snow", 9" diam. Produced by Wedgwood $24* **MP $25**

1980 *Christmas Plate "Country Christmas", 9" diam. Produced by Wedgwood and last in this design series $25* **MP $25**

1968 *Christmas Trees Bubble Bath 4oz Silver, gold, red and green, each $2.50* **MP $9**

1974 *Christmas Bells Cologne in 4 frag. 1oz $4.50* **MP $4**
1978 *Peek-A-Mouse Cologne in Sweet Honesty or Unforgettable 1oz in red cloth stocking $7* **MP $6 complete**
1972 *Crystaltree Cologne in Moonwind or Sonnet 3oz $7.50* **MP $5**

1978 *Angel Song (Lyre) Cologne in Here's My Heart or Charisma 1oz $5* **MP $3**
1979 *Angel Song (Mandolin) Cologne in Unforgettable or Moonwind $5.50* **MP $3.50**

1968 *Golden Angel Foaming Bath Oil in 4 frag. 4oz $3.50* **MP $11 with wings**

1976 *Golden Angel Cologne in Sweet Honesty or Occur! 1oz $5* **MP $4**
1974 *Heavenly Angel Cologne in Unforgettable, Sweet Honesty or Occur! 2oz $5* **MP $6**

CHRISTMAS FIGURALS

1967 *Christmas Ornament Bubble Bath 4oz green, silver, gold and red, each $1.75* **MP $10**

1968 *Christmas Sparkler Bubble Bath 4oz gold, blue, silver, red, each $2.50* **MP $9, Purple MP $35**

1969 *Christmas Cologne in 4 fragrances – red: Unforgettable, gold: Topaze, blue: Occur!, green: Somewhere 3oz each $3.50* **MP $8**

1970 *Christmas Ornament (plastic) Bubble Bath 5oz each $2.50* **MP $6**

1979 *Festive Facets Cologne in Charisma (red), Sweet Honesty (green) and Here's My Heart (blue), 1oz $4.50* **MP $3**

1976 *Silver Dove Ornament dated "Christmas 1976" holds ½oz bottle of Bird of Paradise or Occur! Cologne $7* **MP $8**
1979 *Rocking Horse Tree Ornament in Sweet Honesty or Moonwind Cologne .75oz $6.50* **MP $5**

1974 *Yuletree Cologne in Sonnet, Moonwind or Field Flowers 3oz $6* **MP $4**

1975 *Touch of Christmas Cologne in Unforgettable or Imperial Garden Cologne 1oz $4* **MP $3**
1976 *Christmas Surprise Cologne in Sweet Honesty, Moonwind, Charisma or Topaze 1oz $4* **MP $2 Red cap, $3 Silver cap**

1977 *Christmas Candle (left) Cologne in 4 frag. 1oz $4* **MP $2**

1978 *Jolly Santa Cologne in Topaze or Here's My Heart 1oz $1.49 with purchase* **MP $1**
1980 *Christmas Soldier Cologne in 4 fragrances .75oz $3.50* **MP $2**
1980 *Song of Christmas Cologne in 3 fragrances .75oz $5.50* **MP $2**

1980 *Fragrant Tree Trimmings. Set of 3 Mountain Pine scented fabric ornaments with a different design on each side. Cords included $9 a set* **MP $9**

1965 *Fragrance Belle Cologne in 8 frag. 4oz $3.50 to $5* **MP $20 with tag**
1973 *Bell Jar Cologne in 4 frag. 5oz $6* **MP $8**

BELLS BY AVON

1978 *Joyous Bell Cologne in Charisma or Topaze 1oz $5* **MP $2**
1973 *Hobnail Bell Cologne in 5 frag. 2oz $5* **MP $5**
1968 *Fragrance Bell Cologne in 9 frag. 1oz $2* **MP $7**

1975 *Crystalsong Cologne in Sonnet $7.50 or Timeless 4oz $8.50* **MP $6**
1976 *Hospitality Bell Cologne in Moonwind, or Roses, Roses 3¾oz $8* **MP $7 ("Avon '76")**
1977 *Rosepoint Bell Cologne in Charisma or Roses, Roses 4oz $8.50* **MP $6 ("Avon '77") embossed on base)**

1980 *Crystal Snowflake Christmas Bell Cologne in 4 fragrances 3.75oz $10* **MP $8**
1979 *Cherub Hostess Bell Cologne in Bird of Paradise or Topaze 3.75oz ("1979") $9* **MP $7**
1978 *Emerald Bell Cologne in Sweet Honesty, Roses, Roses 3¾oz $8.50* **MP $6 ("Avon-78")**

** Available from Avon at time of publication*

1965 *Just Two. Tribute After Shave Lotion, black and Rapture Cologne, clear 3oz each $5.50* **MP $85, $32 black, $36 clear**

FIGURALS FOR MEN, WOMEN AND TEENS

1980 *Huggable Hippo and sheet of decals in Light Musk After Shave or Zany Cologne 1.75oz $6* **MP $4**
1980 *Rollin' Great in Lover Boy or Zany Cologne 2oz $6* **MP $4***

1975 *Tennis Anyone? in Spicy After Shave or Sweet Honesty After Bath Freshener 5oz $5* **MP $3**
1977 *Mixed Doubles in Spicy After Shave or Sweet Honesty Body Splash 3oz $6* **MP $4**
1978 *On The Run in Wild Country After Shave or Sweet Honesty Body Splash 6oz $6* **MP $4**

1978 *Get The Message in Clint After Shave or Sweet Honesty Cologne 3oz $9.50* **MP $7**
1975 *Stop! Decanter in Wild Country After Shave or Sweet Honesty Bath Freshener 4oz $5.50* **MP $3**
1978 *Strike! Decanter in Wild Country A/Shave or Sweet Honesty Cologne 4oz $5.50* **MP $3**

1976 *Wilderness Classic in Deep Woods After Shave or Sweet Honesty Cologne 6oz $10* **MP $8**
1977 *Just a Twist in Deep Woods After Shave or Sweet Honesty Cologne 2oz $5* **MP $3**

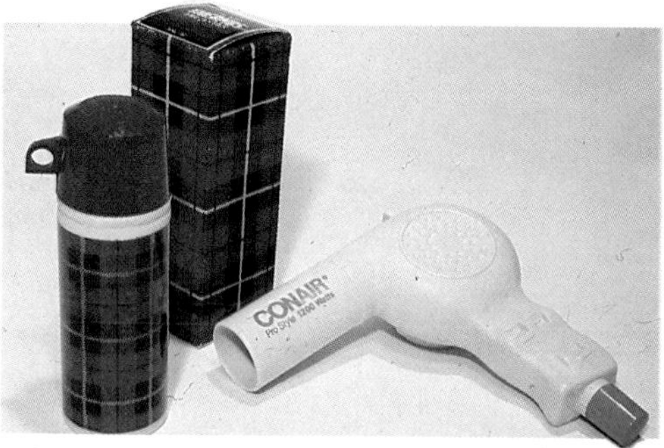

1978 *Plaid Thermos Brand Decanter in Wild Country After Shave or Sweet Honesty Body Splash 3oz $6* **MP $4**
1978 *Conair 1200 Blow Dryer with Naturally Gentle Shampoo 6oz $6* **MP $4**

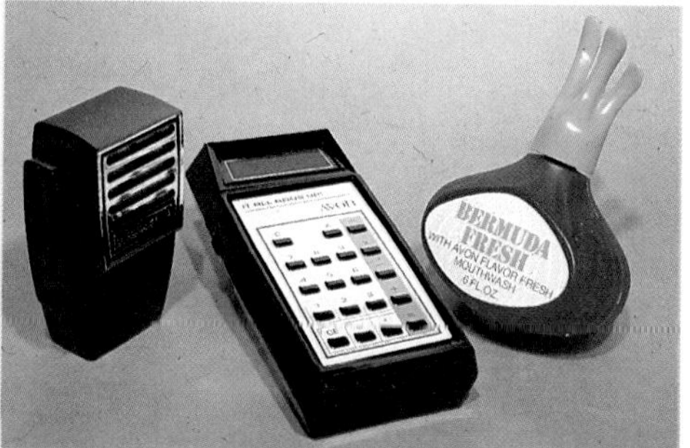

1977 *Breaker 19 with Wild Country After Shave or Sweet Honesty Cologne 2oz $5* **MP $3**
1978 *It All Adds Up! in Deep Woods After Shave or Sweet Honesty Body Splash 4oz $8.50* **MP $6**
1978 *Bermuda Fresh Mouthwash, plastic onion holds 6oz $4.50* **MP $2**

1977 *Juke Box with Wild Country After Shave or Sweet Honesty Cologne 4.5oz $6.50* **MP $4**
1977 *Locker Time with Wild Country After Shave or Sweet Honesty Body Splash 6oz $5.50* **MP $3**
1979 *Dingo Boot with Wild Country After Shave or Sweet Honesty Body Splash 6oz $5.50* **MP $4**

1975 *Star Signs Decanter in Wild Country After Shave or Sweet Honesty Cologne 4oz and embossed personalized Star Sign decal $7*
MP $5 black glass *(left)*
MP $10 painted glass *(right)*

1974 *Breath Fresh Mouthwash 8oz $4* **MP $3**
1976 *Flavor Fresh Mouthwash 6oz $4* **MP $2**

1978 *Vintage Year in Wild Country or Sweet Honesty Cologne 2oz $6* **MP $5***
1979 *Paul Revere Bell in Clint After Shave or Sweet Honesty Body Splash 4oz $9* **MP $8**

Apothecary Decanters:
1972 *Breath Fresh Mouthwash 8oz $3.50* **MP $4**
1973 *Spicy After Shave 8oz $4* **MP $4**
1973 *lemon Velvet Moisturizing Friction Lotion 8oz $4* **MP $4**

1964 *Captain's Choice, After Shave Lotion in 3 frag. or After Shower Cologne 8oz each $2.50 & $2.75* **MP $16**
1965 *Spicy Pre-Electric Shave* **MP $17**
1965 *Royal Orb in Spicy or Original After Shave Lotion 8oz $3.50* **MP $25**

1966 *Viking Horn in Spicy, Original or Blue Blazer After Shave 7oz $7* **MP $22**

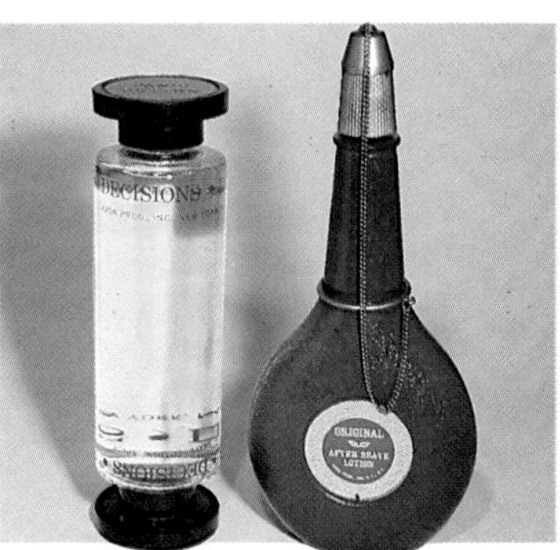

1965 *Decisions, Spicy After Shave Lotion 8oz $2.50* **MP $27**
1966 *Alpine Flask in Spicy, Blue Blazer or Original After Shave 8oz $4* **MP $56**

1967 *First Edition in Bay Rum, Wild Country or Leather After Shave 6oz $3.50* **MP $8 each, $10 boxed**

1969 *A Man's World. Windjammer or Tribute After Shave Lotion 6oz $5* **MP $8 with stand, boxed**

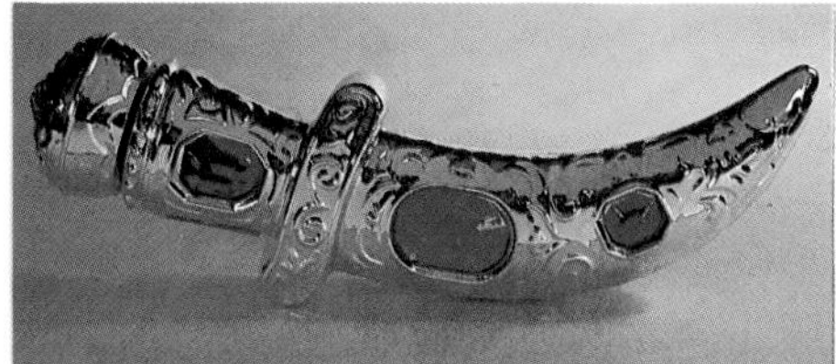

1968 *Scimitar in Windjammer or Tribute After Shave 6oz $6* **MP $20**

1969 *Wise Choice in Leather or Excalibur After Shave Lotion 4oz $4* **MP $5**

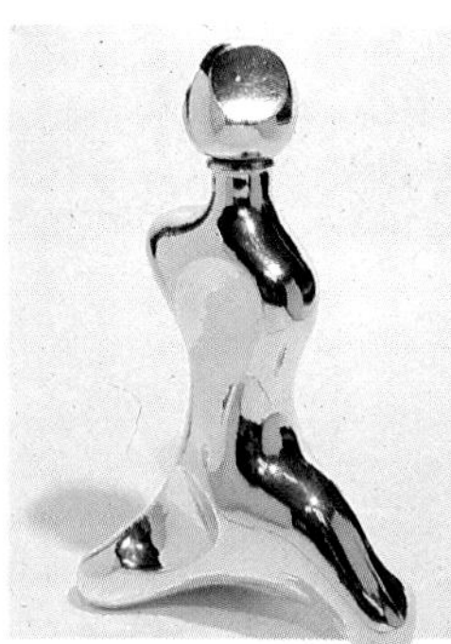

1969 *Futura in Excalibur or Wild Country Cologne 5oz $7* **MP $26**

Classics (After Shave Lotion) –
1969 *Windjammer 6oz $3.50* **MP $9**
1969 *Tribute 6oz $3.50* **MP $8**
1969 *Leather 6oz $3.50* **MP $9**
1969 *Wild Country 6oz $3.50* **MP $8**

**Available from Avon at time of publication*

1969 *Avon Calling. Wild Country or Leather Cologne in phone 6oz. Talc in receiver 1¼oz $8* **MP $12, $15 boxed**

1969 *Weather-Or-Not in Leather, Tribute or Wild Country After Shave 5oz $5* **MP $6**

1977 *Weather Vane in Wild Country or Deep Woods After Shave 4oz $6.50* **MP $4**

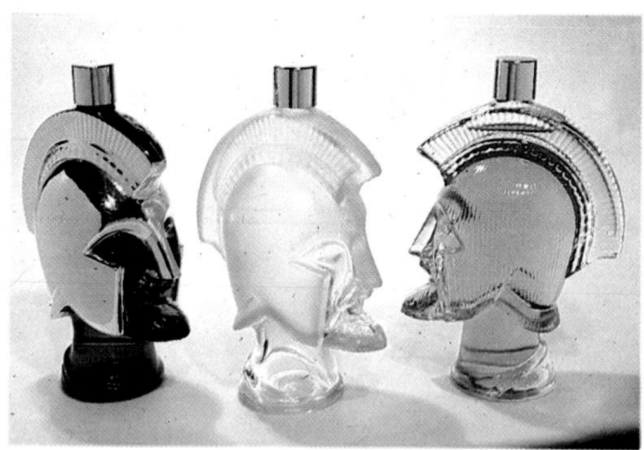

Warrior (in Tribute fragrance only):
1967 *After Shave Lotion 6oz $4.50* **MP $18**
1968 *Cologne, frosted 6oz $4* **MP $7**
1971 *Cologne, clear 6oz $4* **MP $6**

1970 *Stamp Decanter in Spicy or Windjammer After Shave Lotion 4oz $4* **MP $6**
1969 *Inkwell Decanter, Windjammer or Spicy After Shave Lotion 6oz $6* **MP $9, $11 boxed**

1967 *Gavel in Spicy, Original or Island Lime After Shave $4* **MP $17**
1979 *Super Sleuth Magnifier in Wild Country or Everest After Shave 2oz $9.50* **MP $8**

1968 *After Shave Caddy in Leather or Island Lime 6oz $7* **MP $20**
1977 *Desk Caddy in Clint or Wild Country Cologne 4oz $10* **MP $8**

1973 *Avon Calling 1905 in Spicy or Wild Country After Shave 7oz and Talc ¾oz $10* **MP $10**

1969 *Snoopy Surprise Package. Excalibur or Wild Country After Shave or Sports Rally Lotion 5oz $4* **MP $7**
1975 *On the Air in Spicy, Wild Country or Deep Woods After Shave Lotion 3oz $5* **MP $4**

1972 *Remember When Radio in Wild Country or Spicy After Shave or Hair Lotion 5oz $4* **MP $5**
1972 *Piano Decanter in Tai Winds or Tribute After Shave 4oz $4* **MP $5**

1974 *Electric Guitar in Wild Country After Shave or Sure Winner Lotion 6oz $5* **MP $5, $6 boxed**

1970 *Captain's Pride in Windjammer or Oland After Shave 6oz $5* **MP $7 with stand**

1966 *Defender (Cannon) in Leather, Island Lime or Tribute After Shave 6oz $5* **MP $21**

1975 *Revolutionary Cannon in Spicy or Blend 7 After Shave 2oz $5.50* **MP $3, $4 boxed**

Leather –
1965 *All-Purpose Lotion for Men, silver cap 8oz $5* **MP $12**
1966 *All-Purpose Cologne, gold cap 8oz $5* **MP $6**
1966 *Spray Cologne 3oz $4* **MP $4.50**
1971 *Cologne, no strap 8oz $5* **MP $4**

1968 *Pump Decanter in Wild Country, Windjammer or Leather After Shave 6oz $5* **MP $7**
1980 *Boots 'N Saddle After Shave in Wild Country or Week-end 7oz $11* **MP $9**

1972 *Indian Chieftain in Spicy After Shave or Hair Lotion 4oz $3.50* **MP $3, $4 boxed**

1974 *Indian Tepee in Wild Country or Spicy A/S 4oz $4* **MP $3, $4 boxed**
1975 *Totem Pole in Wild Country, Deep Woods or Spicy After Shave 6oz $6.50* **MP $5.50**

AVON AMERICANA

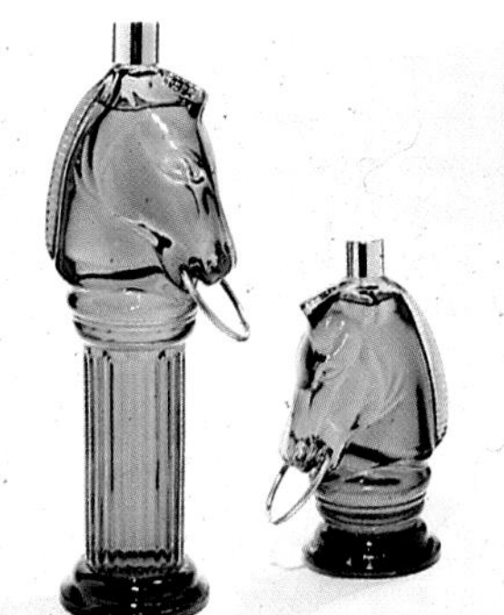

Pony Post After Shave Lotion:
1966 *(Green) Leather, Island Lime or Tribute 8oz $4* **MP $10**
1968 *(Green) Choice of 3 frag. or Pre-Electric Shave 4oz $3.50* **MP $5**
1972 *(Gold) Tai Winds or Leather 5oz $5* **MP $7**
1973 *Miniature in Spicy or Oland 1½oz $4* **MP $3**

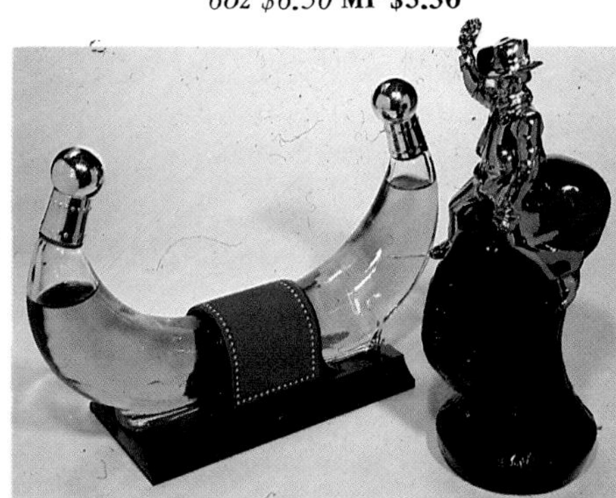

1967 *Western Choice. 1 each Wild Country and Leather After Shave 3oz each $6* **MP $22**
1971 *Bucking Bronco, Oland or Excalibur After Shave Lotion 6oz $6* **MP $8**

1974 *After Shave on Tap (gold) in Wild Country or Oland 5oz $4* **MP $5**
1978 *Little Brown Jug in Deep Woods or Tai Winds After Shave 2oz $4.50* **MP $3**
1976 *After Shave on Tap in Wild Country or Spicy 5oz $4* **MP $2**

1979 *On Tap Mug After Shave in Wild Country or Deep Woods 4oz $8* **MP $7**
1979 *Bath Brew, Wild Country Bubble Bath 4oz $5* **MP $4**

1980 *By The Barrel with Wild Country Shampoo or Bubble Bath 8oz $6* **MP $5***
1980 *Avon's Finest Cologne in Trazarra or Clint $6* **MP $4**

1971 *Western Saddle in Wild Country or Leather After Shave 5oz $7.50* **MP $7**
1971 *Pony Express. Leather or Wild Country After Shave 5oz $6* **MP $7** *(one of the "Transportation" group of figurals)*
1973 *Western Boot in Wild Country or Leather After Shave 5oz $5* **MP $4**

1972 *Blacksmith's Anvil in Deep Woods or Leather After Shave 4oz $5* **MP $6**
1973 *Homestead Decanter in Electric Pre-Shave or Wild Country After Shave 4oz $4* **MP $4**

1970 *Pot Belly Stove. Bravo or Excalibur After Shave 5oz $4* **MP $5, $7 boxed**

**Available from Avon at time of publication*

1978 *No Cause for Alarm in Tai Winds or Deep Woods After Shave 4oz $9* **MP $8***
1968 *Daylight Shaving Time in Spicy, Leather or Wild Country After Shave 6oz $5* **MP $8**

1963 *Close Harmony A/S in 3 frag. or After Shower Lotion 8oz $2.25* **MP $25**

1973 *Bottled by Avon. Oland or Windjammer A/S 5oz $4* **MP $5**
1971 *World's Greatest Dad, Electric Pre-Shave Spicy or Tribute A/S 4oz $3.50* **MP $5**

1974 *Barber Pole in Wild Country A/S or Hair Cond. 3oz $4* **MP $4**

1976 *Barber Shop Brush (left) Cologne in Tai Winds or Wild Country 1½oz $4* **MP $3**
1973 *Super Shaver in Bracing Lotion or Spicy A/S 4oz $4* **MP $4**
1974 *Ironhorse Shaving Mug in Blend 7, Deep Woods or Leather A/S $7.50* **MP $8**

1980 *Casey At The Bat Tankard. Glass tankard holds plastic bottle of Weekend or Wild Country After Shave 4oz $17.50* **MP $18***

1966 *Casey's Lantern in Island Lime, Leather or Tribute After Shave 10oz $6 each. Red* **MP $48, $55 boxed.** *Green and Amber* **MP $58, $65 boxed**

1974 *Whale Oil Lantern in Wild Country, Tai Winds or Oland After Shave 5oz $7* **MP $7**

1975 *Captain's Lantern 1864 in Wild Country or Oland After Shave 7oz $7.50* **MP $6**

1977 *Coleman Lantern in Wild Country or Deep Woods Cologne 5oz $8.50* **MP $6**

1979 *Country Lantern in Deep Woods or Wild Country After Shave 4oz $8* **MP $5**

LANTERNS AND STEINS

1965 *Stein in 4 frag. A/S 8oz $3.50 to $4* **MP $12**
1968 *Stein in Spicy, Windjammer or Tribute After Shave 6oz $4.50* **MP $10**
1972 *Hunter's Stein in Deep Woods or Wild Country After Shave 8oz $10* **MP $13**

1976 *Collector's Stein of Stoneware, 16oz cap. ind. numbered, holds plastic bottle of Cologne in 8oz Everest or Wild Country $30* **MP $35**

1977 *Tall Ships Ceramic Stein ind. numbered. Holds plastic bottle of Cologne in Wild Country or Clint 8oz $30* **MP $35**
1978 *Sporting Stein, ind. numbered. Holds plastic bottle of Cologne in Trazarra or Wild Country 8oz $30* **MP $35**

1979 *Car Classics Ceramic Stein, ind. numbered. Holds plastic bottle of Trazarra Cologne 8oz $37.50* **MP $33**
1980 *Western Round-Up Ceramic Stein, ind. numbered. Holds plastic bottle of Wild Country or Trazarra Cologne 8oz $45* **MP $38***

MINI-COLLECTIONS

A magnificent series of replicas to bridge the excitement of the future with the nostalgia of the past.

Whether he's an antique car buff, a train enthusiast, a collector of Americana, a chess player, lover of sports or a gun collector, there's an Avon mini-collection tailored to his interests.

Many who have saved an Avon replica of the past did not realize they would become an Avon collector of the future.

** Available from Avon at time of publication*

1967 *Twenty Paces Set. Wild Country or Leather All Purpose Cologne and After Shave 3oz 3ach $11.95, box lined in red* **MP $50,** *in black* **MP $120,** *in blue* **MP $150**

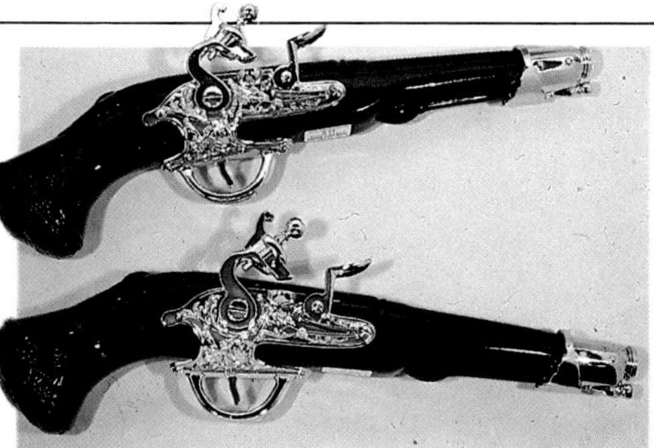

1973 *Dueling Pistol 1760 in Deep Woods or Tai Winds After Shave 4oz $10* **MP $11**
1974 *Dueling Pistol II (black glass) in Wild Country or Tai Winds After Shave 4oz $10* **MP $10**

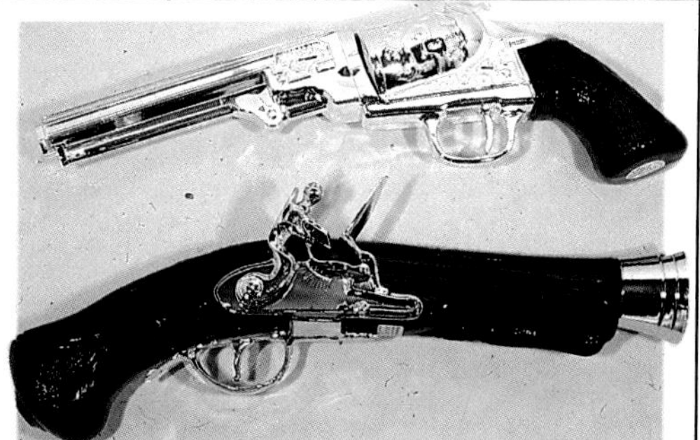

1975 *Colt Revolver 1851. Wild Country or Deep Woods After Shave 3oz $12* **MP $9**
1976 *Blunderbuss Pistol 1780. After Shave in Everest or Wild Country 5½oz $12* **MP $9**

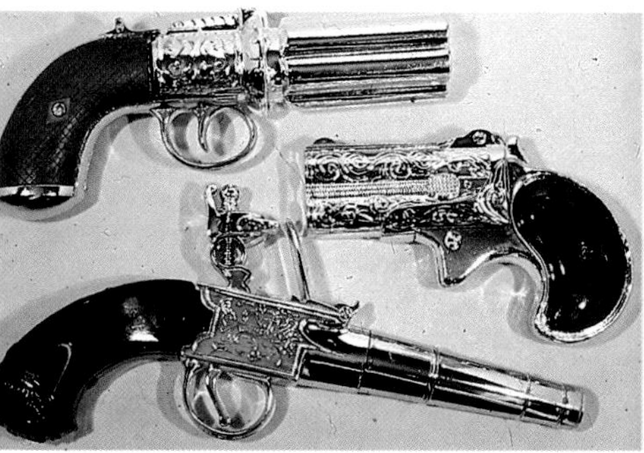

1976 *Pepperbox Pistol 1950. Everest or Tai Winds Cologne 3oz $12* **MP $9**
1977 *Derringer in Deep Woods or Wild Country Cologne 2oz $8* **MP $5**
1978 *Thomas Jefferson Handgun in Everest or Deep Woods Cologne 2¼oz $12.50* **MP $9**

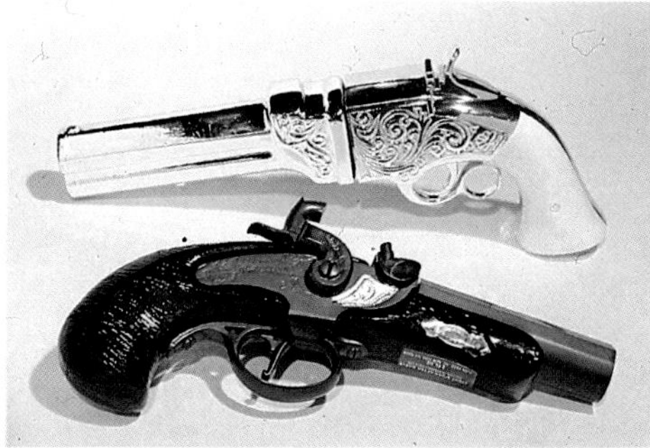

1979 *Volcanic Repeating Pistol in Wild Country or Brisk Spice Cologne 2oz $14* **MP $11**
1980 *Philadelphia Derringer in Light Musk or Brisk Spice After Shave 3oz $12* **MP $9**

GUNSHOP

1976 *Good Shot! Deep Woods (yellow) or Wild Country (red) After Shave 2oz $4 each* **MP $2**
1977 *Wild West. Everest or Wild Country After Shave 1½oz $5* **MP $2**

1970 *George Washington. Spicy or Tribute After Shave 4oz $3.50* **MP $4**
1971 *Abraham Lincoln. Leather or Wild Country After Shave 4oz $3.50* **MP $4**

1970 *Capitol Decanter. Leather or Tribute After Shave 5oz $5* **MP $6**
1976 *Capitol Decanter. Wild Country or Spicy After Shave 4½oz $7* **MP $4**

1966 *Dollars 'N' Scents. Spicy After Shave Lotion 8oz $2.50* **MP $27**
1970 *First Class Male. Wild Country or Bravo After Shave or Liquid Hair Lotion 4oz each $3* **MP $5**

PATRIOTIC REPLICAS

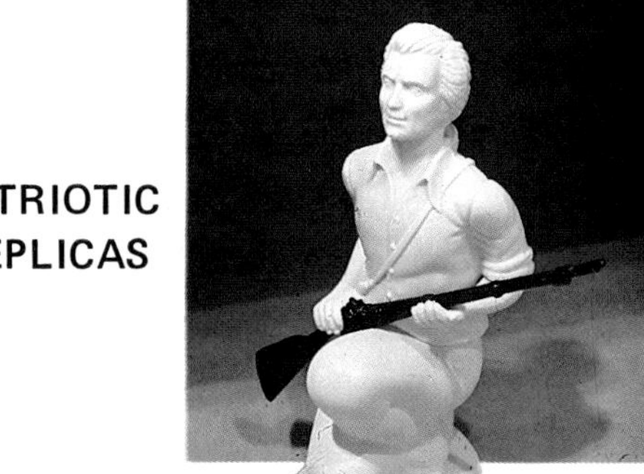

1975 *Minuteman. Wild Country or Tai Winds After Shave 4oz $8.50* **MP $7**

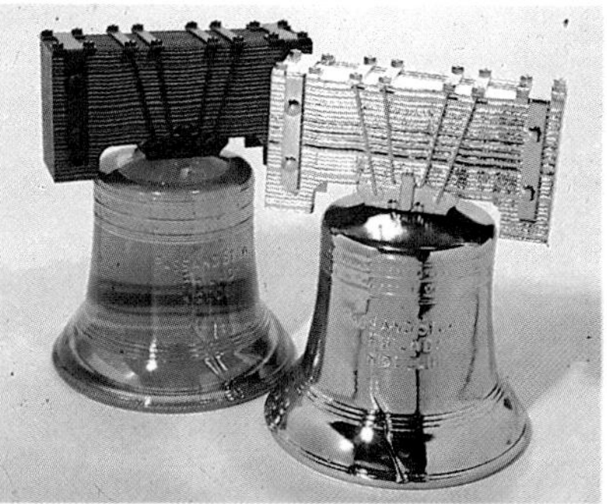

1971 *Liberty Bell in Tribute or Oland After Shave or Cologne 5oz $5 & $6* **MP $6**
1976 *Liberty Bell. Oland or Deep Woods After Shave 5oz $7* **MP $5**

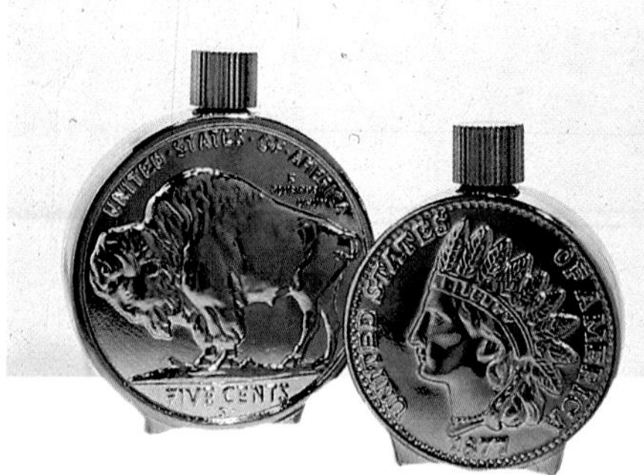

1971 *Buffalo Nickel in Wild Country, Spicy After Shave or Hair Lotion 5oz $5* **MP $9**
1970 *Indian Head Penny. Excalibur, Tribute or Bravo After Shave 4oz $4* **MP $9**

1971 *$20 Gold Piece in Windjammer After Shave or Electric Pre-Shave 6oz $5* **MP $9**
1970 *Liberty Dollar. Oland or Tribute After Shave 6oz $5* **MP $9**

1979 *President Lincoln, dated 1979, in Deep Woods or Everest After Shave 6oz $13* **MP $11**

1973 *President Lincoln in Tai Winds or Wild Country After Shave 6oz $6* **MP $8**
1979 *President Washington, dated 1979, in Wild Country or Tai Winds After Shave 6oz $13* **MP $11**
1974 *President Washington in Tai Winds or Deep Woods After Shave 6oz $8* **MP $8**

1974 *Benjamin Franklin in Wild Country or Tai Winds After Shave 6oz $8* **MP $8**
1975 *Theodore Roosevelt in Wild Country or Tai Winds After Shave 5oz $9* **MP $8**
1977 *Thomas Jefferson in Wild Country or Everest After Shave 5oz $10* **MP $7**

ORIGINAL SET – *3oz $4 each, raised to $5 in 1975. Unless noted,* **MP $5 each, $5.50 boxed**
1971 only *Smart Move (above, left) in Tribute or Oland* **Cologne MP $10, $13 boxed**
1974-78 *in Wild Country A/S or Hair Cond.*
1972-73 *King in Tai Winds or Oland* **MP $7, $10 boxed (MP $8 with Tai Winds, $11 boxed)**
1974-78 *King in Wild Country or Oland (Add $3 for 1974 box)*
1973-74 *Queen in Oland or Tai Winds After Shave* **MP $7, $10 boxed**
1974-78 *Queen in Wild Country or Deep Woods (add $3 for 1974 box)*
1973-74 *Rook in Oland or Spicy A/S* **MP $7 with Oland label, $10 boxed. Spicy boxed MP $1**
1974-78 *Rook in Spicy or Wild Country (add $3 for 1974 box)*
1974-78 *Pawn in Wild Country or Electric Pre-Shave (add $3 for 1974 box)*
1974-76 *Bishop in Wild Country, Blend 7 After Shave or Hair Lotion* **MP $6 with Hair Lotion label, $7 boxed**
1977-78 *Bishop in Wild Country or Blend 7 A/S*
OPPOSING SET –
(Chess Pieces II) 3oz $5 each, **MP $5, $5.50 boxed**
1975-78 *King II in Spicy A/S or Hair Lotion*
1975 *Smart Move II in Wild Country After Shave, Hair Lotion or Hair Conditioner*
1975 *Bishop II in Spicy A/S or Hair Lotion*
1975 *Rook II in Wild Country A/S or Hair Lotion*
1975 *Queen II in Spicy A/S or Hair Cond.*
1975 *Pawn II in Spicy A/S or Hair Cond.*

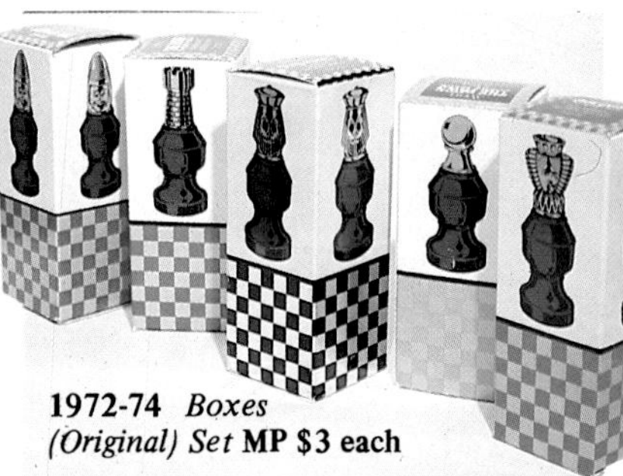

1972-74 *Boxes (Original) Set* **MP $3 each**

1975-78 *Boxes (Chess Pieces II)* **MP 50¢ each**

THE CHESSMEN from AVON

1973 *Eight Ball in Spicy After Shave, Electric Pre-Shave or Hair Lotion 3oz $4* **MP $4**
1978 *Domino After Shave Decanter in Tai Winds or Everest 1½oz $5* **MP $4**
1978 *Weekend Decision Maker in Tai Winds or Wild Country After Shave 3oz $9* **MP $6**

1974 *Just for Kicks in Spicy After Shave or Sure Winner Lotion 7oz $4.50* **MP $5**
1974 *Super Shoe. Sure Winner Bracing Lotion or Hair Trainer 6oz $4* **MP $4**
1976 *Motocross Helmet 6oz Wild Country After Shave or Protein Hair Lotion with Decals $5.50* **MP $4**

1960 *Bowling Pins. 5 of 10, each a different 4oz Men's product $1.19 each* **MP $14**

1969 *King Pin. Wild Country or Bravo After Shave Lotion 4oz $3* **MP $4**

1973 *Marine Binoculars in Tai Winds or Tribute After Shave & Cologne 4oz each $10* **MP $8**

1974 *Triple Crown in Spicy After Shave or Hair Conditioner 4oz $4* **MP $3**
1975 *Sport of Kings, 5oz Wild Country, Spicy or Leather After Shave $7.50* **MP $6**

1975 *Perfect Drive. Spicy After Shave or Hair/Scalp Conditioner 4oz $7.50* **MP $8**
1969 *The Swinger. Bravo or Wild Country After Shave Lotion 5oz $5* **MP $7**

WORLD OF SPORTS

1973 *Pass Play Decanter in Sure Winner Lotion or Wild Country After Shave 5oz $5.75* **MP $7**

Opening Play (Sports Rally Bracing Lotion, Wild Country or Spicy After Shave) –
1968 *Gold without stripe 6oz $4* **MP $16**
1968 *Clear glass* **MP $100**
1969 *Shiny gold without stripe* **MP $27**
1968 *Gold with stripe $4* **MP $13**

1973 *Tee-Off Decanter in Spicy After Shave, Electric Pre-Shave or Hair Lotion 3oz $4* **MP $5**
1973 *Long Drive Decanter in Deep Woods After Shave or Electric Pre-Shave 4oz $5* **MP $5**

1971 *Fielder's Choice Hair Trainer, After Shave or Bracing Lotion 5oz $4* **MP $5**
1970 *First Down Decanter Wild Country After Shave or Sports Rally Bracing Lotion 5oz $4* **MP $6**

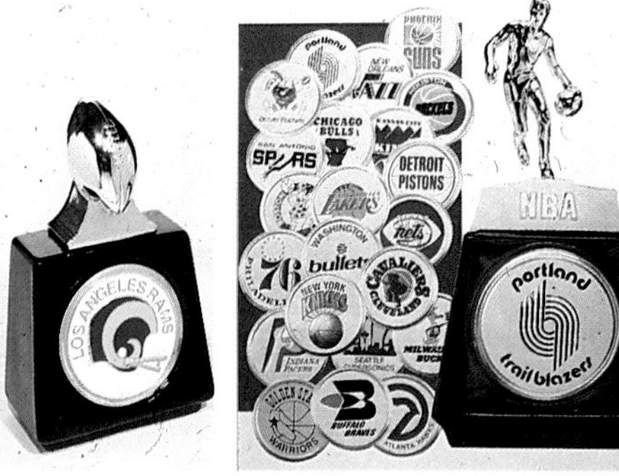

1976 *NFL Decanter. Wild Country After Shave or Sure Winner Bracing Lotion 6oz choice of 28 embossed metal insignia emblems $8* **MP $6**
1977 *NBA Decanter in Wild Country After Shave or Sure Winner Lotion 6oz $9.50* **MP $7** *Choice of 22 embossed emblems* **MP 75¢ each**

1974 *Golf Ball Soaps, Spicy scented, three 1½oz each $3.50* **MP $6**

1970 *The Angler. Windjammer or Wild Country After Shave 5oz $5* **MP $6**
1977 *Sure Catch. Spicy or Wild Country After Shave 1oz $5* **MP $3**

1973 *Gone Fishing in Tai Winds or Spicy After Shave 5oz $7* **MP $7, $8 boxed** *(Also one of the "Transportation" figurals)*

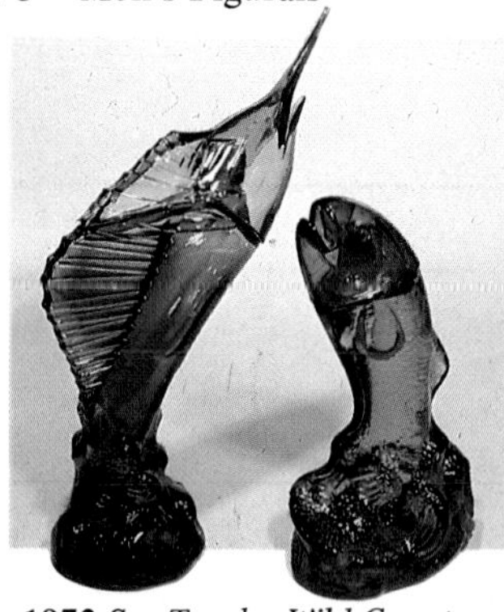

NATURE SERIES BY AVON

1972 *Sea Trophy Wild Country or Windjammer After Shave Lotion 5½oz $6* **MP $7**
1973 *Rainbow Trout in Deep Woods or Tai Winds After Shave 5oz $6* **MP $6**

1974 *Wild Turkey in Deep Woods or Wild Country After Shave 6oz $7.50* **MP $6**
1976 *Bold Eagle After Shave in Tai Winds or Wild Country 3oz $11* **MP $8**

1973 *Quail in Blend 7, Deep Woods or Wild Country After Shave 5½oz $7* **MP $7**
1973 *Canada Goose in Deep Woods or Wild Country After Shave or Cologne 5oz $7 & $8* **MP $6**

1967 *Mallard in Blue Blazer, Tribute or Spicy After Shave 6oz $5* **MP $12**
1978 *Wild Mallard Ceramic Organizer and Clint Soap 4oz $25* **MP $20** *Those ind. numbered and dated May 1978 sold for 2 campaigns only* **MP $25**

American Eagle After Shave in Oland or Windjammer 5oz $5
1971 *(amber)* **MP $7**
1973 *(black)* **MP $5**

1974 *Mallard-in-Flight in Wild Country or Tai Winds After Shave or Cologne 5oz $8 & $9* **MP $7**
1972 *Pheasant Decanter in Oland or Leather After Shave 5oz $7* **MP $9**
1977 *Pheasant in Deep Woods or Wild Country After Shave 5oz $9* **MP $6**

1975 *Noble Prince 4oz Wild Country After Shave or Electric Pre-Shave Lotion $6.50* **MP $5**
1977 *Faithful Laddie in Wild Country or Deep Woods After Shave 4oz $7* **MP $4**

1972 *Old Faithful Wild Country or Spicy After Shave Lotion 5oz $6* **MP $9**
1973 *"At Point" in Deep Woods or Tribute After Shave 5oz $5* **MP $5**

1975 *Longhorn Steer. Wild Country or Tai Winds After Shave 5oz $9* **MP $7**
1975 *American Buffalo Wild Country or Deep Woods After Shave 5oz $7.50* **MP $6**

1972 *Big Game Rhino, Spicy or Tai Winds After Shave 4oz $5* **MP $7**
1977 *Majestic Elephant in Wild Country or Deep Woods After Shave 5½oz $11* **MP $7**
1976 *Artic King 5oz Everest After Shave $7* **MP $4**

1973 *Classic Lion in Wild Country, Tribute or Deep Woods After Shave 8oz $7.50* **MP $7**
1973 *Ten Point Buck in Wild Country or Leather After Shave 6oz $8.25* **MP $8**

1977 *Kodiak Bear 6oz Wild Country or Deep Woods After Shave $8* **MP $6**
1975 *Ram's Head Decanter in Blend 7 or Wild Country After Shave 5oz $6.50* **MP $6**
1974 *Alaskan Moose in Wild Country or Deep Woods After Shave 8oz $8* **MP $8**

1967 *Pipe Dream in Spicy, Tribute or Leather After Shave 6oz $5* **MP $18, $23 boxed**

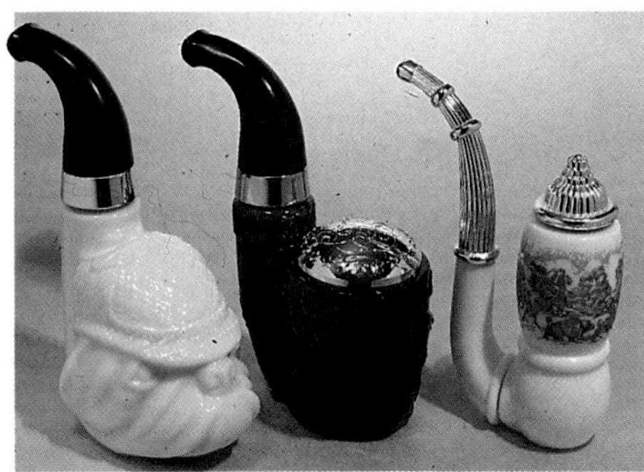
1972 *Bulldog Pipe in Wild Country or Oland After Shave $5 or Cologne $6* **MP $7**
1974 *American Eagle Pipe in Tai Winds or Wild Country Cologne $7.50* **MP $7**
1973 *Dutch Pipe in Tai Winds or Tribute Cologne 2oz $8* **MP $9**

1974 *Calabash Pipe. Wild Country or Deep Woods After Shave 3oz $9* **MP $10**
1974 *Corncob Pipe. Spicy or Wild Country After Shave 3oz $4* **MP $4**

AVON PIPES

1971 *Pipe Full. After Shave Lotion in 4 frag., amber glass 2oz $3.50* **MP $6, $7 boxed**
1972 *Pipe Full (green) in Tai Winds or Spicy After Shave 2oz $3.50* **MP $5**

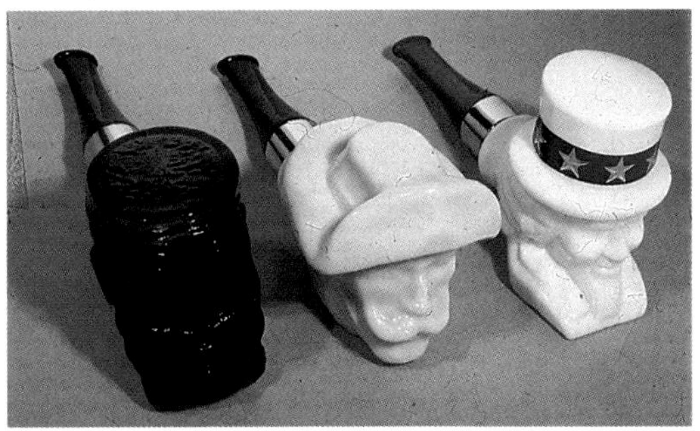
1973 *Collector's Pipe in Windjammer or Deep Woods After Shave 3oz $4* **MP $5**
1975 *Pony Express Rider Pipe 3oz Wild Country or Tai Winds Cologne $6.50* **MP $6**
1975 *Uncle Sam Pipe 3oz Wild Country or Deep Woods After Shave $6.50* **MP $6**

1976 *Bloodhound Pipe. 5oz Wild Country or Deep Woods After Shave $7* **MP $6**
1976 *Wild Mustang Pipe, 3oz Wild Country or Deep Woods Cologne $7* **MP $6**

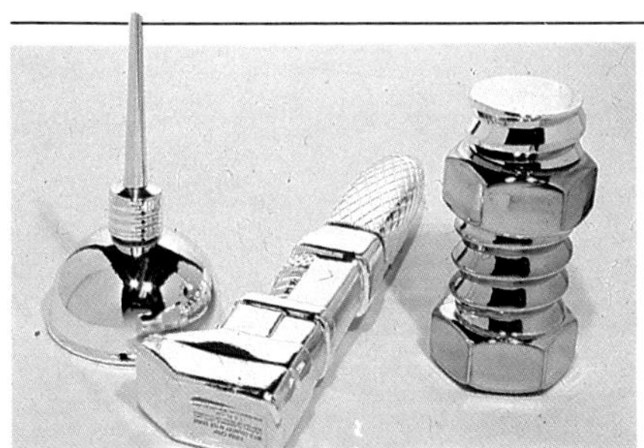
1978 *Smooth Going After Shave in Deep Woods or Everest 1½oz $5* **MP $3** *(left)*
1977 *Firm Grip After Shave in Wild Country or Everest 1½ $5* **MP $3**
1976 *Big Bolt After Shave in Deep Woods or Wild Country 2oz $4* **MP $2**

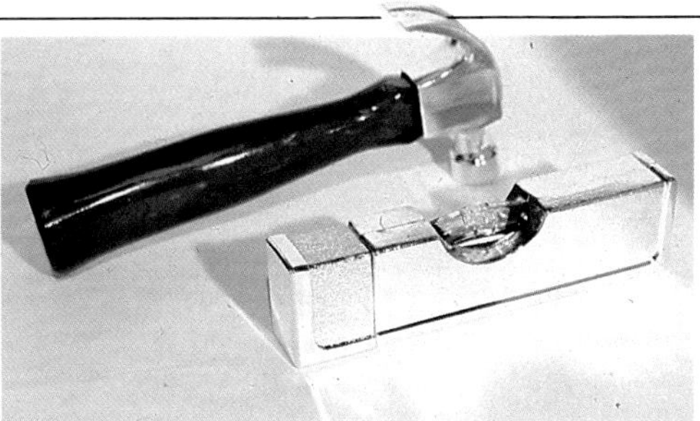
1978 *On The Mark After Shave in Wild Country or Everest 2½oz $7.50* **MP $5**
1978 *On The Level After Shave in Deep Woods or Everest 3oz $6* **MP $4**

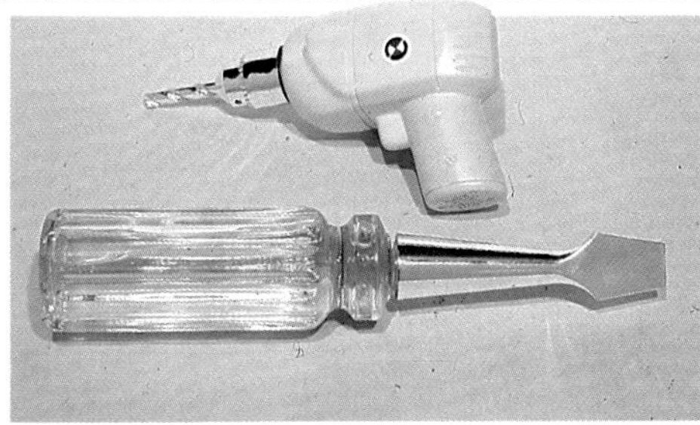
1979 *Power Drill in Wild Country After Shave or Pre-Electric Shave 5oz $7.50* **MP $5**
1976 *One Good Turn After Shave in Deep Woods or Everest 3oz $6* **MP $4**

1977 *Hard Hat After Shave in Deep Woods or Everest 4oz $6.50* **MP $4**
1976 *Super Charge. Spicy or Everest After Shave 1½oz $4* **MP $3**
1977 *Right Connection in Oland or Wild Country After Shave 1½oz $4* **MP $2**

1978 *Quaker State Heavy Duty Powdered Hand Cleanser 12oz $4.50* **MP $3**
1979 *Dutch Boy Heavy Duty Powdered Hand Cleanser 12oz $5* **MP $3**
1980 *Turtle Wax Heavy Duty Powdered Hand Cleanser 10oz $6.50* **MP $3**

1980 *Wilson Championship Stepping Out Foot Powder 5oz $3.50* **MP $3***
1980 *Heavy Duty Care Deeply Lotion 10oz $6.50* **MP $3**

* *Available from Avon at time of publication*

1970 *It's a Blast in Oland or Windjammer After Shave 5oz $7* **MP $11**
1973 *Auto Lantern in Deep Woods or Oland After Shave 5oz and 1¼oz Talc $14* **MP $15**

1968 *Greeting Card given with Father's Day Purchase* **MP $5**
1969 *Father's Day Card. With Purchase of Sterling Six or Straight 8 Car Decanter* **MP $5**

1968 *Sterling Six. Tribute, Spicy or Leather After Shave 7oz Smooth top $4* **MP $35**
Ribbed top (not shown) $4 **MP $8**
1978 *Sterling Six (Silver) "May 1978" in Tai Winds or Deep Woods After Shave 7oz $13* **MP $11**
1973 *Sterling Six II. Wild Country or Tai Winds After Shave 7oz $5* **MP $6**

1974 *Fire Alarm Box in Spicy After Shave, Electric Pre-Shave or Hair Lotion 4oz $4* **MP $3.50**
1974 *Stop 'n Go. Wild Country or Spicy After Shave 4oz $5* **MP $5, $6 boxed**
1975 *No Parking. Wild Country After Shave or Electric Pre-Shave 6oz $6* **MP $4**

1969 *Solid Gold Cadillac. Excalibur, Wild Country or Leather After Shave 6oz $5* **MP $10**
1970 *Silver Duesenberg. Olander or Wild Country After Shave 6oz $6* **MP $10**

1969 *Straight Eight. Windjammer, Wild Country or Island Lime After Shave 5oz $3.50* **MP $8**

AVON CARS

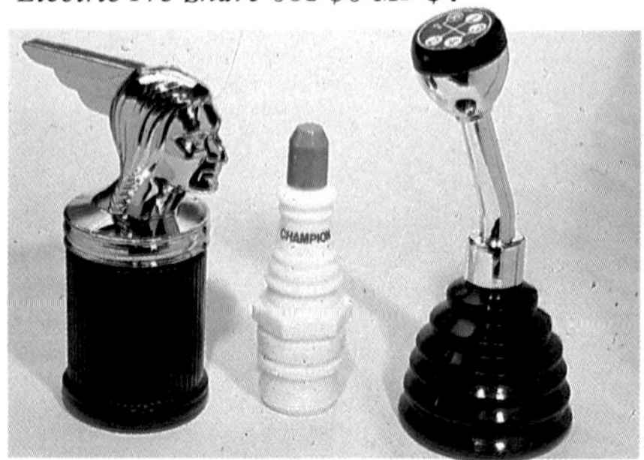

1976 *Chief Pontiac in Tai Winds or Deep Woods After Shave 4oz $8* **MP $8**
1975 *Spark Plug. After Shave in 3 frag. 1½oz $3* **MP $2**
1978 *Super Shift in Sure Winner Lotion or Everest Cologne 4oz $9* **MP $5**

1974 *Thomas Flyer 1908. Oland or Wild Country After Shave 6oz $7.50* **MP $7**
1974 *1936 M.G. Tai Winds, Wild Country or Blend 7 After Shave 5oz $7* **MP $7**

1972 *The Camper. Deep Woods or Oland After Shave 4oz and Talc 5oz $9* **MP $10**
1973 *Country Vendor. Wild Country or Spicy After Shave 5oz $7* **MP $10**

1972 *Big Whistle, Tai Winds or Spicy After Shave or Electric Pre-Shave 4oz $4.25* **MP $5**

1976 *Remember When Gas Pump (red) After Shave in Deep Woods or Wild Country 4oz $7* **MP $7**
1979 *Remember When Gas Pump After Shave in Cool Sage or Light Musk 4oz $9* **MP $6**

1978 *Stanley Steamer (Silver) "May 1978" in Tai Winds or Deep Woods After Shave 5oz $13* **MP $11**
1971 *Stanley Steamer. Windjammer or Wild Country After Shave or Cologne 5oz $5 and $6* **MP $8**

1969 *Touring T. Excalibur or Tribute After Shave 6oz $6* **MP $10**
1978 *Touring T (Silver) "May 1978" in Deep Woods or Everest After Shave 6oz $13* **MP $11**

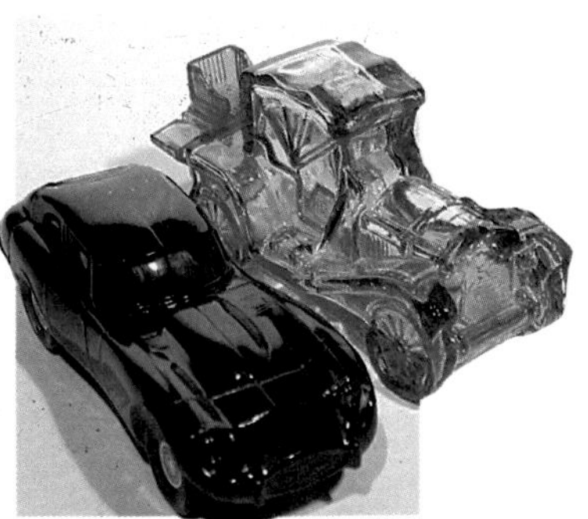

1973 *Jaguar. Deep Woods or Wild Country After Shave 5oz $6* **MP $7**
1970 *Packard Roadster. Oland or Leather Cologne 6oz $6* **MP $8**

1970 *Electric Charger. Leather, Wild Country or Spicy After Shave 5oz $4* **MP $6**
1971 *Dune Buggy. Sports Rally Lotion or Hair Lotion 5oz $5* **MP $7**

1973 *Hayes-Apperson 1902. Blend 7 or Tai Winds After Shave 4½oz $6* **MP $7**
1974 *Army Jeep. Wild Country or Spicy After Shave 4oz $6* **MP $7**
1976 *'64 Mustang. 2oz Spicy or Tai Winds After Shave $5* **MP $4**

1972 *Sure Winner Racing Car. Sure Winner Bracing Lotion or Wild Country After Shave 5½oz $6* **MP $8**
1972 *Model "A". Wild Country or Leather After Shave 4oz $6* **MP $8**

1973 *Blue Volkswagen. Oland or Windjammer After Shave 4oz $4* **MP $6**
1970 *Black Volkswagen. Elec. Pre-Shave Wild Country or Spicy After Shave 4oz $4* **MP $6**
1972 *Red Volkswagen. Sports Rally, Oland or Wild Country After Shave 4oz $4* **MP $10**

1974 *Thunderbird '55. Wild Country or Deep Woods After Shave 2oz $4* **MP $5**
1975 *Corvette Stingray '65. Spicy, Deep Woods or Wild Country After Shave 2oz $4* **MP $7**
1975 *Ferrari '53. Wild Country After Shave or Protein Hair Lotion 2oz $4* **MP $7**

1971 *Station Wagon. Tai Winds or Wild Country After Shave 6oz $6* **MP $8**
1972 *1906 Reo Depot Wagon. Oland or Tai Winds After Shave 5oz $6* **MP $8**

1972 *Rolls-Royce. Deep Woods or Tai Winds After Shave 6oz $8* **MP $9**
1972 *Maxwell '23. Deep Woods or Tribute After Shave or Cologne 6oz $6 & $7* **MP $8**

1975 *'55 Chevy. Wild Country After Shave or Electric Pre-Shave Lotion 5oz $8.50* **MP $10**
1975 *Pierce Arrow '33. Wild Country or Deep Woods After Shave 5oz $7.50* **MP $7**

1974 *Stutz Bearcat 1914. Oland or Blend 7 After Shave 6oz $7* **MP $7**
1974 *Cord '37. Tai Winds or Wild Country After Shave 7oz $8* **MP $8**

1974 *Bugatti '27. Wild Country or Deep Woods After Shave or Cologne 6½oz $8 and $9* **MP $10**
1974 *Stock Car Racer. Wild Country After Shave or Electric Pre-Shave Lotion 5oz $7* **MP $7**

1976 *'36 Ford After Shave in Tai Winds or Oland 5oz $8* **MP $7**
1976 *'48 Chrysler Town and Country. Everest or Wild Country After Shave 4½oz $9* **MP $8**

1975 *'51 Studebaker Wild Country or Spicy After Shave 2oz $5* **MP $7**
1975 *Triumph TR3 '56. Wild Country or Spicy After Shave 2oz $5* **MP $7**
1976 *'68 Porsche Spicy or Wild Country After Shave 2oz $5* **MP $5**

1978 *Winnebago Motor Home After Shave in Wild Country or Deep Woods 5oz $10.50* **MP $10**
1975 *Volkswagen Bus with 4 peel-off decals. Tai Winds After Shave or Sure Winner Bracing Lotion 5oz $6.50* **MP $7**

1977 *1926 Checker Cab. 5oz Wild Country or Everest After Shave $8* **MP $7**
1978 *Ford Ranger Pickup. After Shave in Wild Country or Deep Woods 5oz $10.50* **MP $9**

1979 *'53 Buick Skylark in Clint or Everest After Shave 4oz $14* **MP $11**
1980 *Volkswagen Rabbit in Light Musk Cologne or Sure Winner Lotion $9.50* **MP $7**

1979 *Vantastic After Shave in Everest or Wild Country and Decals 5oz $9.50* **MP $7**

1977 *Extra Special Male After Shave in Deep Woods or Everest 3oz $6.50* **MP $6**

TRANSPORTATION

1970 *Covered Wagon, Wild Country or Spicy After Shave 6oz $5* **MP $8**
1970 *Stagecoach Decanter. Wild Country or Oland After Shave 5oz $5* **MP $8**
1977 *Re-issue with "R" embossed on bottom Wild Country or Tai Winds 5oz $6* **MP $4**

1970 *Spirit of St. Louis. Windjammer or Excalibur After Shave 6oz $8.50* **MP $15**

1977 *Viking Discoverer After Shave in Wild Country or Everest 4oz $12.50* **MP $11**
1972 *American Schooner in Oland or Spicy After Shave 4½oz $6* **MP $8**

1973 *The Harvester in Wild Country After Shave or Hair Lotion 5½oz $6* **MP $6**
1973 *Big Mack in Windjammer or Oland After Shave 6oz $6* **MP $8**

1974 *Cable Car in Wild Country or Leather After Shave 6oz $8* **MP $9**
1976 *'31 Greyhound. 5oz Spicy or Everest After Shave $9* **MP $7**

1978 *Goodyear Blimp After Shave in Wild Country or Everest 2oz $7.50* **MP $6**
1971 *Side Wheeler. Wild Country or Spicy After Shave Lotion 5oz $6* **MP $6**

1971 *First Volunteer in Oland or Tai Winds Cologne 6oz $8.50* **MP $11**
1975 *Fire Fighter 1910 in Wild Country or Tai Winds After Shave 6oz $8* **MP $8**

1974 *Golden Rocket 0-0-2 in Tai Winds or Deep Woods After Shave 6oz $8* **MP $9**
1971 *The General 4-4-0 in Tai Winds or Wild Country After Shave 5½oz $7.50* **MP $10**

1973 *Atlantic 4-4-2 in Deep Woods or Leather After Shave or Cologne 5oz $9 and $10* **MP $12**
1976 *Cannonball Express 4-6-0 in Deep Woods or Wild Country Cologne or After Shave 3¼oz $9 and $8* **MP $8**

1978 *Red Sentinel Fire Truck After Shave 3.5oz and Talc 6oz in Wild Country or Deep Woods $14.50* **MP $13**
1978 *1876 Centennial Express After Shave in Wild Country or Everest 5oz $10.50* **MP $9**

1977 *Highway King After Shave 4oz & Talc 6.5oz in Wild Country or Everest $12.50* **MP $10**
1975 *Big Rig. 3½oz After Shave and 6oz Talc in Wild Country or Deep Woods $12.50* **MP $11**

1979 *Cement Mixer After Shave 3oz and Talc 6oz in Wild Country or Everest. With decorative decals $15* **MP $13**

1974 *Super Cycle (blue) After Shave in Wild Country or Spicy 4oz $6* **MP $6**
1971 *Super Cycle in Island Lime or Wild Country After Shave 4oz $6* **MP $7**

1973 *Road Runner in Wild Country After Shave or Sure Winner Lotion 5½oz $7* **MP $7**
1973 *Snowmobile in Oland or Windjammer After Shave 4oz $7* **MP $7**

1972 *Mini-Bike. Wild Country After Shave or Sure Winner Bracing Lotion or Avon Protein Hair Lotion 4oz $6* **MP $6**
1972 *The Avon Open in Wild Country or Windjammer After Shave 5oz $6* **MP $9**

MEN'S FRAGRANCE LINES

Fragrance-matched toiletries, each in its own unique packaging design.

Dorothy Bernard's FRAGRANCE DATING GUIDE —For Men and Boys

1929 *Bay Rum (formerly Aromatic Bay Rum and California Bay Rum)*
1931 *After Shaving Lotion (renamed Original 1965)*
1959 *After Shower*
'Vigorate
1961 *Deluxe*
Spice (later Spicy)
1963 *Tribute*
1964 *Blue Blazer (for Young Men)*
"4-A"
1965 *Leather*
Original
1966 *Island Lime*
Sport Rally (for Boys)
1967 *Wild Country*
1968 *Windjammer*
1969 *Bravo*
Excalibur
1970 *Oland*
1971 *Tai Winds*
1972 *Deep Woods*
Sure Winner (for Boys-Tai Winds fragrance)
1973 *Blend 7*
1975 *Everest*
1976 *Clint*
1978 *Trazarra*
1979 *Weekend*
Avon Naturals:
Brisk Spice
Cool Sage
Crisp Lime
Light Musk
1980 *Black Suede*
Lover Boy
Rookie (for Boys)
1981 *Rugger*

(See page 7 for CPC Fragrance Dating Guide, page 34 for Women's and Girls' Fragrance Line Dating)

1979 *Light Musk After Shave (plastic) 3oz $3* **MP $3***
1979 *Light Musk Cologne 2oz $4* **MP $4***
1979 *Brisk Spice Cologne 2oz $4* **MP $4***

AVON NATURALS

1979 *Cool Sage After Shave (plastic) 3oz $3* **MP $3***
1979 *Cool Sage Cologne 2oz $4* **MP $4***
1979 *Crisp Lime After Shave (plastic) 3oz $3* **MP $3***
1979 *Crisp Lime Cologne 2oz $4* **MP $3***

1979 *Fragrance Gift Set, 1.5oz Talc and 3oz After Shave in Brisk Spice, Cool Sage or Light Musk $5* **MP $5**
1979 *Above Set with Talc and 2oz Cologne $6* **MP $6**

1980 *Avon Naturals After Shave Sampler Set. Three 3oz After Shave in Brisk Spice, Cool Sage and Light Musk $10.50* **MP $10**

Bay Rum

A he-man aroma reminiscent of West Indies spices and the tang of salt spray. It was this traditional favorite that was issued in Avon's first figural for men. . . the Bay Rum Jug!

1936 *Bay Rum After Shave 4oz 52¢, 8oz 89¢, 16oz $1.51* **MP $35**

1964 *Bay Rum Gift Set. After Shave Lotion and Talc 4oz each $2.50* **MP $40**
1964 *Talc only $1.25* **MP $15**
1964 *After Shave Lotion only $1.25* **MP $15**

1965 *Bay Rum Keg. After Shave Lotion 8oz $2.50* **MP $22**

1964 *Bay Rum Boxed Soaps, two 3oz cakes $1.25* **MP $30**
1962 *Bay Rum Jug After Shave Lotion 8oz $2.50* **MP $20**

1981 *Spray Talc 4oz $5* **MP $3**
1980 *Cologne Spray 3oz $9.50* **MP $7***
1981 *Bar Soap 3oz $2.25* **MP $1.25***

1980 *After Shave 4oz $7* **MP $6***
1980 *Cologne 4oz $9.50* **MP $7***
1980 *Gift Soap with Case 3oz (Sold only for 2 campaigns) $6.50* **MP $6.50, $5.25 Case only**

1969 *Santa's Helper After Shave 4oz with Santa decals to decorate box $1.98* **MP $10**
1969 *Talc 3½oz $1.25* **MP $3**
1969 *After Shave 4oz $2* **MP $4**

1969 *After Shave Towelettes, 100 Student Samples* **MP $15¢ each, $20 full box**

* *Available from Avon at time of publication*

1973 *Cologne 5oz $5* **MP $4**
1973 *Shower Soap 5oz $2.50* **MP $10**
1973 *Emollient After Shave 5oz $5* **MP $4**
1974 *Spray Talc 7oz $3* **MP $2**

1965 *Blue Blazer Deluxe Set. After Shave Lotion 6oz, Deodorant 1¾oz and Tie Tac $5.50* **MP $75, Tie Tac MP $18**

1976 *Travel Kit. Canvas with vinyl interior 8x5" $14* **MP $16**
1976 *Wrist Chain $12* **MP $10**
1977 *Travel Set for Men. After Shave 3oz and Talc 1½oz $5* **MP $5, $2 each**

1964 *After Shave Spray 5½oz $1.95* **MP $13, $16 boxed**
1964 *Talc 3½oz $1.25 ("For Young Men" omitted)* **MP $15**
1964 *Foam Shave Cream 6oz $1.25* **MP $13**

1967 *Spray Deodorant (2¾oz on front, short issue) $1.25* **MP $15**
1964 *Talc 3½oz $1.25* **MP $10**

1964 *Shower Soap-On-a-Rope 5oz $1.50* **MP $18**
1964 *Hair Dress 4oz $1.25* **MP $12, $15 boxed**
European Talc **MP $15**

1976 *Shower Soap 5oz $4.50* **MP $5***
1977 *Spray Talc (short issue) $4* **MP $2**
1977 *Talc 3½oz $2.50* **MP $2.50***

1966 *Soap and Sponge 3oz $2.50* **MP $22, $25 boxed**
1964 *After Shave Lotion 6oz $1.95* **MP $22, $26 boxed**

1964 *Blue Blazer Set No. 1. After Shave 6oz and Shower Soap 5oz $3.45* **MP $55**
1964 *Set No. II. Talc 3½oz and Spray Deodorant 2¾oz $2.50* **MP $32**

1980 *Spray Cologne 3oz $8.50* **MP $7***
1977 *Spray Talc 7oz $4* **MP $2**
1979 *Spray Talc 4oz (not shown) $4.50* **MP $1**
1979 *Roll-On Deodorant 2oz $1.69* **MP $1.50***

1973 *Emollient After Shave 5oz $5* **MP $4**
1972 *Cologne 5oz $5* **MP $3**
1973 *Cologne Spray 3oz $5* **MP $4**
1976 *Bar Soap 3oz $1.25* **MP $1.50**

1972 *Shower Soap-On-a-Rope 5oz $2.50* **MP $7**
1975 *Shower Soap-On-a-Rope 5oz $4.50* **MP $6**
1977 *Talc 3.5oz $2.50* **MP 75¢**
1972 *Spray Talc 7oz $3* **MP 75¢**

1976 *Cologne 5oz $6.50* **MP $7***
1976 *Bar Soap 3oz $1.25* **MP $1.50***

1977 *Gift Set. Cologne and Shower Soap 5oz each $12.50* **MP $15**

* *Available from Avon at time of publication*

DELUXE

1962 *Deluxe Set for Men. Choice of Foam Shave Cream, Stick Deodorant and After Shave-After Shower Spray $4.98* **MP $45**

1962 *Foam Shave (Regular or Mentholated) 6oz $1.35* **MP $11**
1962 *After Shower Spray-A/S 5½oz $1.98* **MP $11**
1962 *Talc for Men 4oz $1.35* **MP $10**
1961 *Stick Deodorant 2¾oz $1.35* **MP $12**
1962 *After Shave Lotion 6oz $1.79* **MP $27**
1962 *Electric Pre-Shave Lotion 6oz $1.79* **MP $27**

EVEREST

1975 *Shower Soap-On-a-Rope 5oz $4.50* **MP $5**
1976 *Bar Soap 3oz $1.25* **MP $1.50**
1975 *Spray Talc 7oz $4* **MP $1**
1977 *Talc 3.5oz $2.50* **MP 75¢**
1975 *Cologne 5oz $6.50* **MP $1**
1975 *After Shave 5oz $5* **MP $1**

1970 *Spray Talc 7oz $3* **MP $3**
1970 *Soap-On-a-Rope 5oz $2.50* **MP $9, $11 boxed**
1969 *Cologne 6oz $5* **MP $7**

ISLAND LIME

1969 *After Shave 6oz $4* **MP $5 boxed**
1973 *After Shave (gold cap) 6oz $4* **MP $7**
1972 *Spray Talc 7oz $3* **MP $1**
1966 *Soap-On-a-Rope 6oz $2* **MP $20**

1967 *Clear Glass, light yellow weave 6oz $3* **MP $13, $16 boxed**
1966 *Clear Glass, dark yellow weave 6oz $3* **MP $16, $19 boxed**
1969 *Green Glass 6oz $4* **MP $22, $25 boxed**

öland

1970 *Spray Talc 7oz $3* **MP $1**
1975 *After Shave 5oz $5* **MP $2**

1970 *Gift Set. Cologne 6oz, Talc 3½oz and Soap 5oz $8* **MP $17**

1970 *Cologne Spray 4oz $5* **MP $10**
1970 *Talc 3½oz Shaker top (from Set)* **MP $5**
1970 *Cologne 6oz $5* **MP $3**
1970 *Shower Soap-On-a-Rope 5oz $2.50* **MP $8**
1970 *Soap 5oz (from Set only)* **MP $5**

Avon ORIGINAL

1956 *After Shave Lotion 2oz (Sets only)* **MP $8**
1949 *After Shave Lotion 4oz 49¢* **MP $10**
1949 *Talc for Men 2.6oz 43¢* **MP $8**
1949 *Cologne for Men 6oz $1.50* **MP $18**
(2oz 69¢ **MP $10;** *4oz in Sets only* **MP $15**
Not Shown: Deodorant 2oz **MP $8,**
4oz in Sets only **MP $10***)*

1949 *After Shave Lotion 4oz 49¢* **MP $10**
1965 *Original After Shave (no Avon on label or box) 4oz 98¢* **MP $8, $10 boxed**
1954 *Cologne 4oz (issued in Personal Note Set)* **MP $18**
1949 *After Shave Sample ½oz* **MP $10,** *Cologne Sample (not shown)* **MP $15**

1965 *After Shave 4oz 98¢* **MP $6, $8 boxed**
1966 *Soap-On-a-Rope 5oz $1.75* **MP $18, $22 boxed**
1965 *After Shave Spray 5½oz $1.50* **MP $10**

LEATHER

1966 *Aerosol Deodorant 4oz $1.50* **MP $6**
1969 *Spray Talc 7oz $3* **MP $3**
1966 *Bath Soap 5oz $1.75* **MP $18**
(See Cologne, Boots pg. 171)

(Deluxe Men's Gifts in 1961 contained a Spicy fragrance. The same packaging in 1962 was used for "Deluxe" a Forest-Fresh fragrance. See pg. 184)

1961 *Deluxe After Shower Powder 4oz $1.35* **MP $15**

1961 *Deluxe Electric Pre-Shave Lotion 6oz $1.79* **MP $28**
1961 *Deluxe After Shave Lotion 6oz $1.79* **MP $28**

1961 *Deluxe Foam Shave-Reg. 6oz $1.35* **MP $11**
1961 *Deluxe After Shave-After Shower Spray 5½oz $1.98* **MP $15**
1961 *Deluxe Foam Shave Cream-Mentholated 6oz $1.79* **MP $11**
1961 *Deluxe Oatmeal Soap for Men, two 4oz cakes $1.35* **MP $30**

LOVER BOY

1980 *Lover Boy After Shave 3oz $5* **MP $4***
1980 *Lover Boy Cologne 3oz $6* **MP $5***

ROOKIE

1980 *Rookie Cologne 2.5oz $3.50* **MP $3.75***

1965 *Soap Miniatures 1½oz each $2* **MP $25**

1965 *Holiday Spice. Talc and After Shave Lotion $1.85* **MP $25**

RUGGER

1981 *Cologne Plus 4oz $9* **MP $7***
1981 *After Shave Soother 4oz $6* **MP $5***
1981 *Shaker Talc 3.5oz $3.50* **MP $2.50***
1981 *All-Over Moisture Rub 5oz $5* **MP $4***

AVON Spicy

1965 *Talc 3½oz 89¢* **MP $6**
1965 *After Shave 4oz 98¢* **MP $8**
1965 *After Shave Spray 5½oz $1.50* **MP $6**

1966 *Spice O' Life Set. 3½oz Talc and 4oz After Shave Lotion $1.96* **MP $25**
1965 *Overnighter Set. 4oz After Shave Lotion, 3½oz Talc and 3oz Soap, all in Spicy $7.50* **MP $45; Soap MP $7**

1965 *First Edition Father's Day Gift Set. After Shave 4oz and Talc 3½oz $1.87* **MP $32** *(Left, inside cover of box)*

1965 *Christmas Wreath. Two 4oz After Shave $1.95* **MP $25**

1967 *After Shave Lotion, clear 4oz $1.25* **MP $4**
1967 *After Shave Lotion, amber 4oz $1.25* **MP $6**

** Available from Avon at time of publication*

. . . AVON **Spicy**

1967 *Oatmeal Soap 3oz 98¢* **MP $6**
1967 *After Shave for Dry/Sensitive Skin 2oz 98¢* **MP $4**
1967 *Talc 3½oz 98¢* **MP $1**

1967 *Twice Spice Set. 3½oz Talc and 4oz After Shave Lotion $2.23* **MP $15**

1968 *Spicy Treasure Set. After Shave Lotion 4oz and 3½oz Talc $2.23* **MP $13**

1966 *Bracing Lotion Towelettes (not shown) 12 per box $1.25* **MP $10 each box**

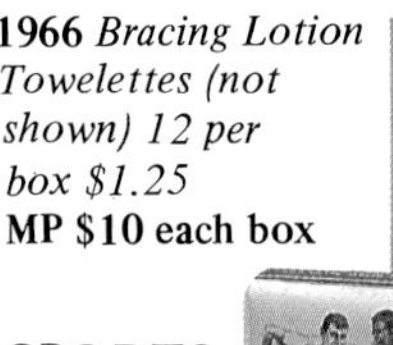

SPORTS RALLY

1966 *Deodorant Soap 4oz $1.50* **MP $15, $19 boxed**
1966 *Hair Dress 4oz $1* **MP $8**
1966 *Bracing Lotion 4oz $1.50* **MP $11**
1966 *Talc 3½oz $1* **MP $6**
1966 *Aerosol Deodorant (not shown) 4oz $1.25* **MP $6**

1966 *Sports Rally Clear Skin Soap 3oz $1* **MP $6**
1966 *Sports Rally Clear Skin Lotion, plastic 4oz $1.25* **MP $5**

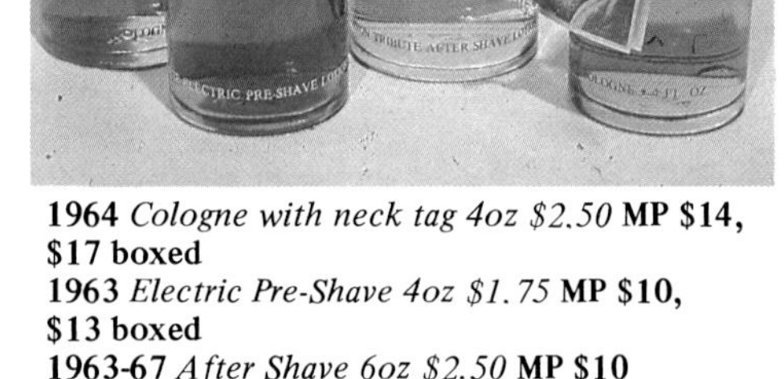

1964 *Cologne with neck tag 4oz $2.50* **MP $14, $17 boxed**
1963 *Electric Pre-Shave 4oz $1.75* **MP $10, $13 boxed**
1963-67 *After Shave 6oz $2.50* **MP $10**
1967-68 *All Purpose Cologne with neck tag 4oz $3* **MP $16, $19 boxed**

1971 *Spray Talc 7oz $3* **MP $1**
1971 *Soap with rope 5oz $2.50* **MP $5**
1971 *Cologne 5oz $5* **MP $7**
1975 *After Shave 5oz $5* **MP $2**

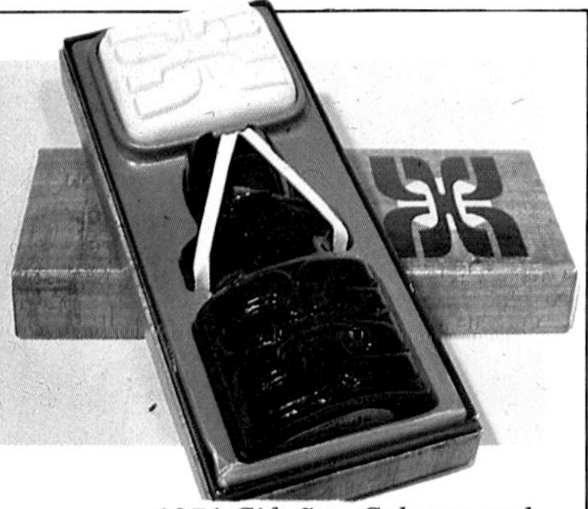

1971 *Gift Set. Cologne and Soap $8* **MP $16**

Tai winds

1963 *Soap, boxed, 1 round bar 4oz $1.75* **MP $25**
1963 *Cream Hair Dress 4oz tube $1.75* **MP $8, $12 boxed**
1964 *Shampoo 4oz tube $1.75* **MP $8, $12 boxed**
1967 *After Shave 4oz $2.25* **MP $6**

TRIBUTE

1978 *Shower Soap 5oz $5.50* **MP $5***
1978 *Talc 3½oz $2.50* **MP $2.50***
1978 *After Shave Lotion 4oz $6* **MP $1**
1978 *Cologne 4oz $8.50* **MP $7***

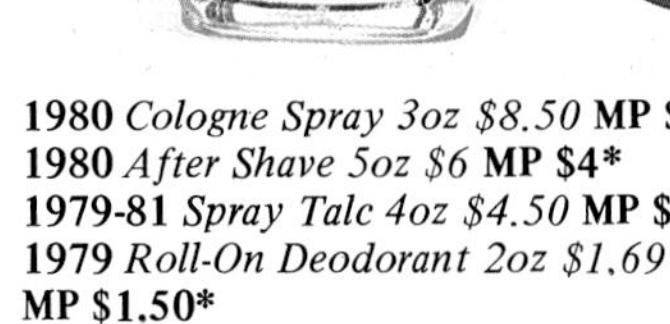

1980 *Cologne Spray 3oz $8.50* **MP $7***
1980 *After Shave 5oz $6* **MP $4***
1979-81 *Spray Talc 4oz $4.50* **MP $1**
1979 *Roll-On Deodorant 2oz $1.69* **MP $1.50***

1963-67 *Aerosol Deodorant 3oz $1.75* **MP $8**
1963-67 *After Shave-After Shower Spray 5½oz $2.50* **MP $8**
1969 *Spray Talc 7oz $3* **MP $7**
1963 *Talc 4oz $1.75* **MP $5**
1963 *Foam Shave Cream, Regular or Mentholated 6oz $1.75* **MP $7**

** Available from Avon at time of publication*

WINDJAMMER

1969 *Cologne, paper label 5oz $4* **MP $5**
1968 *Cologne, painted label 5oz $4* **MP $10**
1968 *Spray Talc 7oz $2.50* **MP $3**
1969 *Rubdown Cooler (plastic) 10oz $3* **MP $3**

1979 *Get-Away nylon Duffle Bag, with $8.50 purchase, $4.99* **MP $15**
1980 *Cologne Spray 3oz $8.50* **MP $7***
1979-80 *After Shave 4oz $6* **MP $3 (short issue)**
1980 *After Shave (not shown) 5oz $6* **MP $4***
1979 *Cologne 4oz $8.50* **MP $7***

WEEKEND

1979-81 *Spray Talc 4oz $4.50* **MP $2**
1979 *Shower Soap 5oz $5* **MP $5***
1979 *Roll-On Deodorant 2oz $1.69* **MP $1.50***
1979 *Bar Soap 3oz $1.50* **MP $1.50***

1963 *Tribute Gift Set No. 1. 5½oz After Shave-After Shower Spray, 4oz Talc and choice of 6oz Regular or Mentholated Foam Shaving Cream $6.50* **MP $40**

1968 *Cologne Spray 2½oz $4* **MP $6**
1968-81 *Cologne 6oz $4* **MP $2**
1976 *Belt Buckle with any Wild Country purchase $1.99* **MP $4**

1970 *Foam Shave Cream 11oz $1.75* **MP $1**
1969 *Aerosol Spray Talc 7oz $3* **MP $1**
1975 *Aerosol Deo. 4oz $1.79* **MP $1**
1978 *Roll-On Deo. 2oz $1.59* **MP $1.50***

1977 *Travel Set. Talc 1.5oz and After Shave 3oz $5* **MP $5, $2 each container**

1963 *Tribute Gift Set No. 2. Gift card attached. 6oz After Shave Lotion, 4oz Talc and 3oz Aerosol Deodorant $6.50* **MP $40**

1967 *Body Powder 6oz $4* **MP $15**
1967 *Shower Soap-On-a-Rope 6oz $2* **MP $6**
1971 *Talc 3½oz $1.50* **MP $2.50***
1968 *Cologne Spray 2½oz $4* **MP $6**
1971 *After Shave Lotion 4oz $3* **MP $1.50**

1970 *Saddle Kit. Foam Shave Cream 6oz, Spray Talc 7oz and Cologne 6oz $16* **MP $16, $11 kit only**

WILD COUNTRY

1964 *Tribute Shave Set. 6oz After Shave and 6oz Regular or Mentholated Foam Shaving Cream $4.25* **MP $27**
1966 *Boxed Soap, 2 round bars 3oz each $1.75* **MP $22**
(See Tribute "Warriors" pg. 170)

1980 *Spray Cologne 3oz $8.50* **MP $7***
1975 *After Shave 5oz $5* **MP $5***
1979-81 *Spray Talc 4oz $4.50* **MP $1**
1981 *Cologne (new size) 4oz $9* **MP $7***

1972 *Protective Hand Cream 3oz $1.75* **MP $3**

1977 *Gift Soap 5oz in metal embossed container $4* **MP $6**
1975 *Soap-On-a-Rope 5oz $4* **MP $5***
1976 *Bar Soap 3oz $1.25* **MP $1.50***

** Available from Avon at time of publication*

MEN'S TOILETRIES

1930-36 *Talc for Men 35¢* **MP $40, $50 boxed**
1930-36 *After Shaving Lotion 4oz 35¢* **MP $50, $60 boxed**

1930 *Styptic Pencil 10¢* **MP $10**
1930-36 *Shaving Soap* **MP $45**

1930-35 *Hair Dress, tube 50¢* **MP $25**

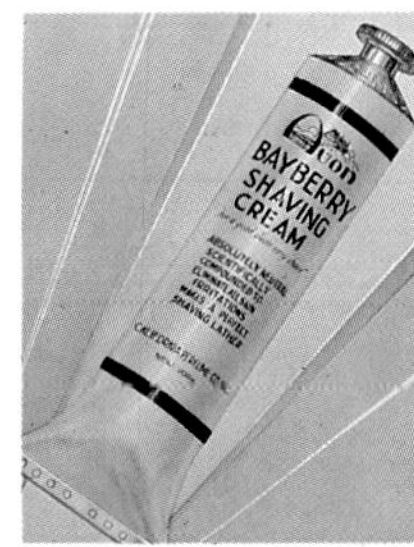

1930-35 *Bayberry Shaving Cream 35¢* **MP $25**

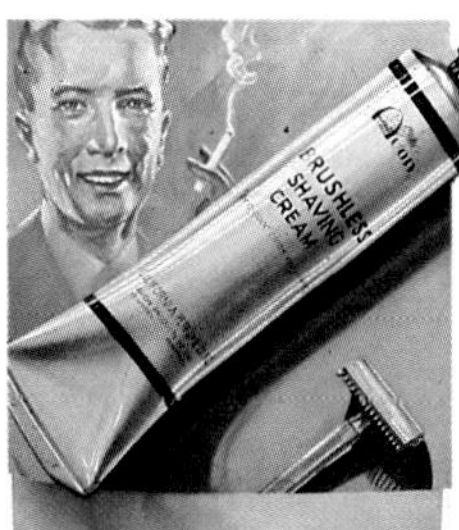

1934-35 *Brushless Shaving Cream 50¢* **MP $25**

1936-44 *Menthol Witch Hazel Cream, tube 37¢* **MP $9, $13 boxed**
1944-49 *Styptic Cream 17¢* **MP $18, $22 boxed**

1936-48 *Shaving Stick in bakelite holder 36¢* **MP $15**
1936-43 *Styptic Cream 15¢* **MP $25**

1936-49 *Brushless Shaving Cream 41¢* **MP $15**

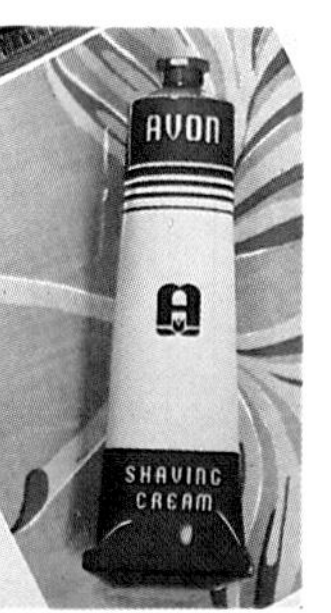

1936-49 *Shaving Cream 36¢* **MP $15**

1941 *Smoker's Tooth Paste 39¢* **MP $15**

1936-49 *Hair Dress 37¢* **MP $15, $18 boxed**

1938-39 *Hair Tonic 6oz 52¢* **MP $45, $55 boxed**

1938-43 *Smoker's Tooth Powder, issued only in Men's Sets* **MP $15**
1943 only *Talc for Men 43¢* **MP $45**
1945 only *Talc for Men 43¢* **MP $45**
1944-45 *Elite Powder (with hexagon cap) 43¢* **MP $45**

1944-45 *Tooth Powder 57¢* **MP $22**
1946 *Smoker's Tooth Powder, issued in Men's Sets* **MP $15**

1944 only *Talc for Men, cardboard with hexagon lid 2-5/8oz 43¢* **MP $45**
1936-42, then 1946-49 *Talc for Men 37¢ & 39¢* **MP $18**

1942-49 *After Shaving Lotion 4oz 43¢* **MP $25**
1936-41 *After Shaving Lotion 4oz 37¢* **MP $35**
1939-40 *Hair Lotion 6oz (shown) 52¢* **MP $40**
(1941-49 *Hair Lotion as above with Good Housekeeping Seal on front label* **MP $35**
1939-43 *Hair Lotion 16oz $1.35* **MP $50)**
1946-49 *Cologne for Men 6oz $1.50* **MP $80**

1939 *Hair Tonic Sample ¼oz* **MP $50**
1937 *After Shaving Lotion Sample ½oz* **MP $40**
1947-49 *Deodorant for Men 2oz 59¢* **MP $22**
1948 *Cologne for Men 2oz (issued in Men's Sets)* **MP $30**

1949-59 *Lather Shaving Cream 3-7/8oz 49¢* **MP $10**
1949-59 *Brushless Shaving Cream 4-1/8oz 49¢* **MP $10**
1949-57 *Cream Hair Dress 2¼oz 49¢* **MP $10**
1954-57 *Deodorant for Men 4oz (Sets only)* **MP $10**
1949-58 *Deodorant for Men 2oz 63¢* **MP $9, $11 boxed**

For Men –

1949-58 *Liquid Hair Lotion 4oz 59¢* **MP $15**
1949-58 *Cream Hair Lotion 4oz 59¢* **MP $15**
1953 *Cologne for Men 4oz (Before and After Set only)* **MP $25**
1950's *Liquid and Cream Hair Lotion Samples 1oz each* **MP $25**
1953 *Liquid Shampoo 1oz (Parade Dress Set only)* **MP $25**

For Men –
1949-58 *Cologne 6oz $1.50* **MP $15**
1949-57 *Cologne 4oz (Sets only)* **MP $15**
1952-58 *Cologne 2oz 69¢* **MP $12**
1950's *Cologne ½oz Sample* **MP $25**

For Men –
1958-62 *After Shaving Lotion 4oz 79¢* **MP $8**
1958-62 *After Shaving Sample ½oz* **MP $12**
1958-62 *Deodorant 2oz 69¢* **MP $9, $10 boxed**
1958 *Cologne 2oz (Happy Hours Set only)* **MP $15**
1959 *After Shower Sample ½oz* **MP $15**

1958-59 *Cologne for Men 4oz $1.25* **MP $15, $19 boxed**
1959-62 *After Shower for Men 4oz $1.25* **MP $12, $15 boxed**
1959-62 *After Shower Powder for Men 3oz 89¢* **MP $8**
(1958-59 only *Talc for Men, not shown, same can as above 69¢* **MP $15)**
1958-62 *Liquid Hair Lotion 4oz 89¢* **MP $10**
1959-61 *Stick Deodorant for Men 2½oz $1* **MP $12**

1958 *Deodorant for Men 2oz in Christmas Box 69¢* **MP $15**
1958 *Cream Lotion 4oz in Christmas Box 89¢* **MP $14**

1960-61 *Deodorant for Men 2oz (issued in First Prize & Gold Medallion Sets)* **MP $12, $20 boxed**

1958 *Liquid Hair Lotion 4oz 89¢* **MP $10**
1958-62 *Cream Hair Lotion 4oz 89¢* **MP $8**
1959 *Attention Hair Dress 4oz 89¢* **MP $10**

1960-62 *Spice After Shaving Lotion 8oz $1.89* **MP $18, $25 boxed**
1960-61 *After Shower for Men 2oz (issued in First Prize & Gold Medallion Sets)* **MP $12, $20 boxed**
1961-62 *'Vigorate After Shaving Lotion 8oz $2.50* **MP $20, $28 boxed**
1961-62 *Spice After Shaving Lotion 4oz $1.25* **MP $10, $15 boxed**

1960-61 *Electric Pre-Shave 2oz (issued in First Prize & Gold Medallion Sets)* **MP $12, $20 boxed**
1961-62 *After Shower for Men 8oz $2.50* **MP $20, $28 boxed**
1960-61 *Cream Hair Lotion 2oz (issued in First Prize & Gold Medallion Sets)* **MP $10, $18 boxed**

1962-65 *After Shower Cologne for Men 4oz $1* **MP $8, $10 boxed**
1962-65 *Electric Pre-Shave–Spicy 4oz 89¢* **MP $8, $10 boxed**
1962-65 *After Shave Lotion–Spicy 4oz 89¢* **MP $8, $10 boxed**

1965-66 *Original After Shave Spray 5½oz $1.50* **MP $11**
1959-62 *Brushless (shown) or Lather Shaving Cream 5oz 79¢* **MP $9, $12 boxed**

1962-65 *Cream Hair Lotion 4oz 89¢* **MP $6**
1962-65 *Liquid Hair Lotion 4oz 89¢* **MP $7, $9 boxed**

For Men –
1962-65 *Spray Deodorant 2¾oz 89¢* **MP $4**
1963-65 *Roll-On Deodorant 1¾oz 89¢* **MP $5**
1962-65 *Liquid Deodorant 2oz 79¢* **MP $4**
1960-63 *Roll-On Deodorant (plastic) 1¾oz 89¢* **MP $4**
1959 *Spray Deodorant 2¾oz 89¢* **MP $6**
1963-65 *Oatmeal Soap 3oz 39¢* **MP $12**

1962-65 *Brushless Shave Cream–Spicy 4oz 89¢* **MP $6**

1962-65 *Lather Shave Cream –Spicy 4oz 89¢* **MP $6**
1962-65 *After Shave for Dry or Sensitive Skin–Spicy 2oz 89¢* **MP $7**
1962-65 *Talc for Men–Spicy 3oz 89¢* **MP $12**
1960-61 *After Shave for Dry or Sensitive Skin 2oz 89¢* **MP $10**

1963-65 *Plastic bottles 2oz issued only in 1963 Jolly Holly Day, 1964 Christmas Trio and 1965 King For a Day in choice of 9 daily-use products* **MP $4 each**

1963-65 *After Shower Cologne Spray 5.5oz $1.75* **MP $4**
1963-65 *Original After Shave-After Shower Spray 5.5oz $1.50* **MP $4**
1962-65 *After Shave-After Shower Spray 5.5oz $1.50* **MP $4**
1963-65 *'Vigorate After Shave-After Shower Spray 5.5oz $1.75* **MP $4**

1963-65 *Stand Up Hair Stick 1½oz 89¢* **MP $6**
1962-65 *Hair Trainer 4oz 89¢* **MP $10**

1959 *Cream Hair Lotion 4oz in Christmas Box 89¢* **MP $14**
1959 *Stick Deodorant for Men 2½oz $1* **MP $12, $18 in Xmas box**
1959 *Hair Trainer 4oz 89¢* **MP $3, $8 in Xmas box**

1958 *Hair Trainer 4oz 89¢* **MP $3, $10 in Xmas box**
1959 *Hair Trainer 4oz 89¢* **MP $3. $10 in Xmas box**

1960-61 *Hair Trainer 4oz 89¢* **MP $3, $9 in Gift box**
1958-63 *Stand Up Hair Stick 79¢* **MP $5**
1960-61 *Above in Gift box shown* **MP $9**

1966 *All-Purpose Skin Conditioner 5oz $2.50* **MP $7**
1969 *Skin Conditioner 5oz $2.50* **MP $4**
1968 *Bath Oil 4oz $2.50* **MP $5**
1969 *Hand Cream, tube 3oz $1.50* **MP $2**
1968 *After Shave Soother 4oz $2.50* **MP $4**

. . . MEN'S TOILETRIES

1966 *Electric Pre-Shave Lotion 4oz 89¢* **MP $2**

1965-67 *Bath Oil for Men 4oz $2.50* **MP $20**
1965-67 *After Shower Foam for Men 4oz $2.50* **MP $15**

1966-67 *Bath Soap for Men, two 5oz cakes $2.50* **MP $25**

1972 *Men's Shampoo/Shower Soap-On-a-Rope 5oz $2.50* **MP $8**

1966 *Liquid Deodorant for Men 2oz 79¢* **MP $3**
1970 *Spray Deodorant for Men 4oz $1.25* **MP $3**
1971 *Stick Deodorant for Men 2¼oz $2.25* **MP $3**

1967 *Body Powder for Men 6oz $4* **MP $12**

Protein Hair Products –
1972 *Hair Spray 7oz $1.75* **MP $1.50**
1972 *Hair Lotion 6oz $1.75* **MP $1.50**
1973 *Hair Managing Control $1.75* **MP $1.50**
1972 *Cream Hair Dress 4oz $1.59* **MP $1.50**

1978 *Foam Shave Cream 11oz $1.79* **MP $1.50***
1976 *Electric Pre-Shave Lotion 4oz $1.49* **MP 50¢**
1971 *Foam Shave Cream 11oz $1.50* **MP 50¢**

1979 *Full Control Aerosol Hair Spray 6oz $2.39* **MP $2 (short issue)**
1980 *Full Control Pump Hair Spray 6oz $2.99* **MP $2.50***

** Available from Avon at time of publication*

1953-56 *First Class Male gift box holds Cologne for Men 6oz $1.50* **MP $25 boxed**
1957 *Royal Order gift box holds Cologne for Men 6oz $1.50* **MP $25 boxed**

1956 *Triumph gift box holds Cologne for Men 6oz $1.50* **MP $25**

1959 *'Vigorate Lotion 8oz $2.50* **MP $50, $75 boxed**
1960 *'Vigorate Lotion 4oz $1.25* **MP $13**

1964 *"4-A" After Shave Lotion 6oz $2* **MP $20, $25 boxed**

A GENTLEMAN'S CHOICE

1959 *After Shower for Men 8oz $2.50* **MP $62 with neck cord, $70 boxed**

1970 *Cologne Spray for Men 4oz in Oland, Wild Country and Leather $5* **MP $6**

1979 *Gentlemen's Talc, Tin holds Wild Country, Clint or Trazarra Talc 3.75oz $5* **MP $2**

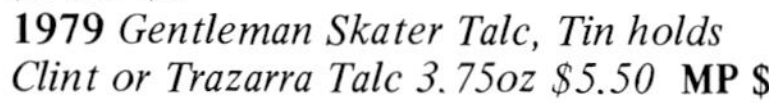

1979 *Gentleman Skater Talc, Tin holds Clint or Trazarra Talc 3.75oz $5.50* **MP $1**

1980 *Travel Case, all vinyl, fully lined. Sold in U.S. only with $7.50 purchase in C-23. $5.99* **MP $11 value**

GIFT COLOGNES

1969 *Gentlemen's Choice in 5 frag. 2oz $1.75* **MP $4**
1970 *Gift Cologne in 4 frag. 2oz $3* **MP $3**
1977 *Cologne Miniature in 3 frag. ½oz $2* **MP $1**
1978 *Cologne Miniature in 4 frag. ½oz $2.50* **MP $1**
1979 *Cologne Accent for Men in 7 fragrances .5oz $2.50* **MP $1**
1980 *Gift Cologne for Men in 8 frag. .5oz $3* **MP $1.50***

1974 *Gift Cologne in 4 frag. 2oz $2.50* **MP $2**
1975 *Gift Cologne in 4 frag. 2oz $3* **MP $2**
1976 *Gift Cologne in 5 frag. 2oz $3* **MP $1**
1977 *Gift Cologne in 4 frag. 2oz $3* **MP $1**
1978 *Gift Cologne in 4 frag. 2oz $3* **MP $1**

1960-62 *Shower Soap-On-a-Rope 6oz $1.35* **MP $34**

SOAPS FOR MEN

1936 *Shaving Soap, two cakes 31¢* **MP $50**

1964 *Most Valuable. Three 3oz Soaps $1.35* **MP $30 boxed**

1061-63 *Oatmeal Soap for Men. Two 4oz cakes $1.35* **MP $30**

1966-67 *Lonesome Pine Soap. Two 2oz cakes $2* **MP $25**

* *Available from Avon at time of publication*

(See Golf Ball Soaps pg. 175)

1977 *M.C.P. Soap 8oz $5* **MP $6**
1967 *Light of My Life, Light Bulb shaped Soap-On-a-Rope 5oz $1.50* **MP $20**
1960 *Bowl 'em Over, Avonlite Bowling Ball shaped soap on a cord 6.4oz $1.19* **MP $45 with box, $30 Soap only**

1978 *Buffalo Nickel Soap Dish and Clint Soap 4oz $10.50* **MP $9**
1966 *Top Dollar Spicy scented Soap-On-a-Rope $1.75* **MP $22, $35 boxed**

1978 *Barber Shop Duet. 5oz Wild Country molded soap and Mustache Comb $5* **MP $4 boxe**
1978 *Safe Combination Change Bank with two 3oz Tai Winds scented soap in the shape of gold bars. Embossed metal bank made in England $9.50* **MP $8**

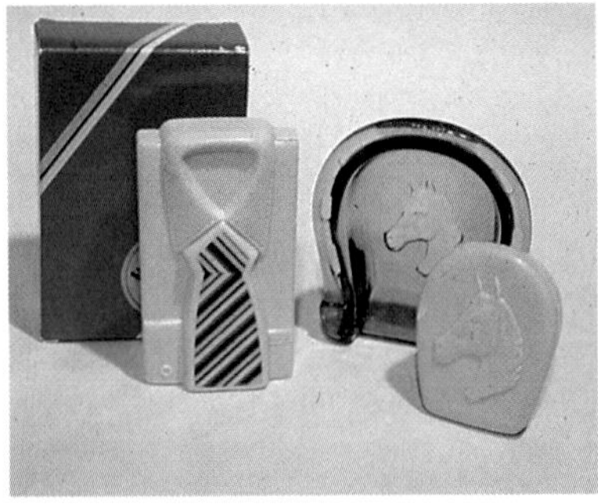

1978 *Suitably Gifted Soap with necktie decal. Deep Woods fragrance 6oz $6.50* **MP $6**
1979 *Lucky Horseshoe Soap Dish and Soap 3.5oz $9.50* **MP $9**

1979 *Farmer's Almanac Thermometer and two 3oz Gentleman's Blend scented soaps. A 1980 Farmer's Almanac with purchase $10.50* **MP $10**
1980 *Perpetual Calendar Container and 5oz Classic Blend scented soap. Metal container made in England $10* **MP $9**

1980 *Birds of Flight Ceramic Box with Trazarra scented soap 5oz. Box made in Brazil $25* **MP $15 box only**

(See also Men's Fragrance Lines pgs. 182-186 and Men's Sets pg. 203)

1972 *Sure Winner Brush and Comb $3.50* **MP $7**
1972 *Sure Winner Soap-On-a-Rope $2.25* **MP $12**

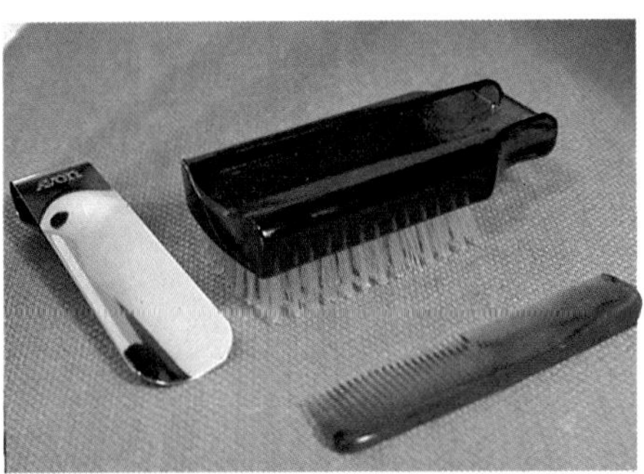

1972 *Trio Valet. Brush, Comb & Shoehorn $5* **MP $7**

1974 *Model "A" Soap Set in Tai Winds or Wild Country 3oz each $3* **MP $8**
1974 *Outdoorsman Brush and Comb Valet $5* **MP $7**

BRUSHES AND BRUSH SETS

1969 *Brush and Comb Valet $5* **MP $8**
1975 *Brush and Comb Valet $6.50* **MP $7**
1978 *Brush and Comb Valet $9* **MP $7**

1970 *Brush and Comb Valet $4* **MP $8**
1970 *Club Brush $4* **MP $6**

1978 *Men's Deluxe Hair Brush $9* **MP $8**

1930 *Hair Treatment Set for Men. Liquid Shampoo 6oz, Pre-Shampoo Oil 2oz, Hair Tonic (for dry or oily hair) 6oz and Hair Dress $2.75* **MP $200**

1931 *Men's Traveling Kit, 7¼x6½x2" contains Bayberry Shaving Cream, After Shaving Lotion 4oz, Styptic Pencil and Talc $1.95* **MP $155**

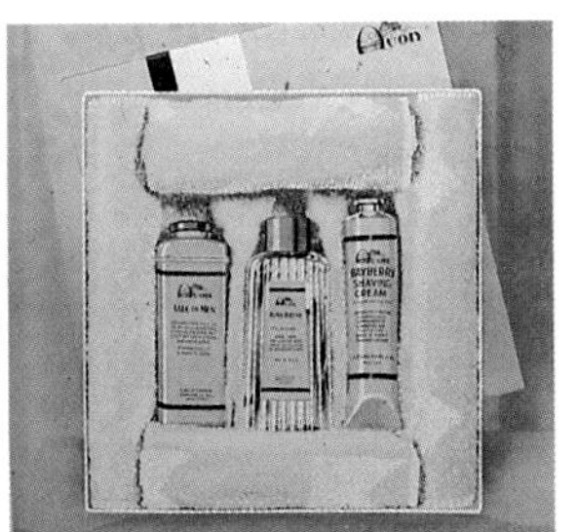

1930-32 *Humidor Shaving Set. Bay Rum 4oz Lilac Vegetal 2oz, Styptic Pencil, Menthol Witch Hazel Cream, Bayberry Shaving Cream, Talc for Men $2.60* **MP $230**

1932 *Assortment No. 7 Talc, Bay Rum 4oz, Bayberry Shaving Cream, Cannon Towel 13½x19", 2 Wash-cloths $2* **MP $160**

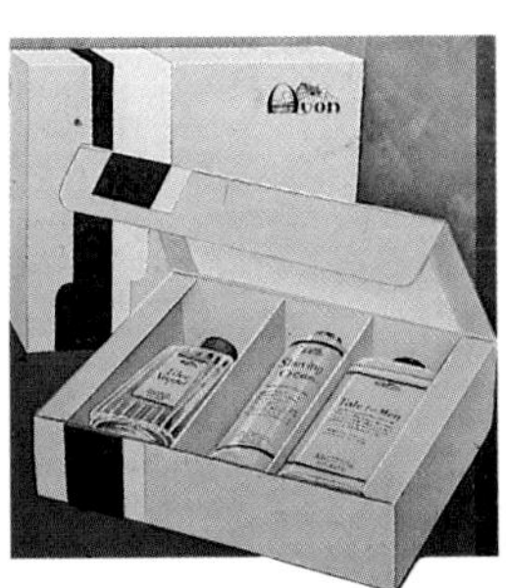

1932 *Assortment No. 2. Lilac Vegetal 2oz, Shaving Cream, Talc $1.40* **MP $115**

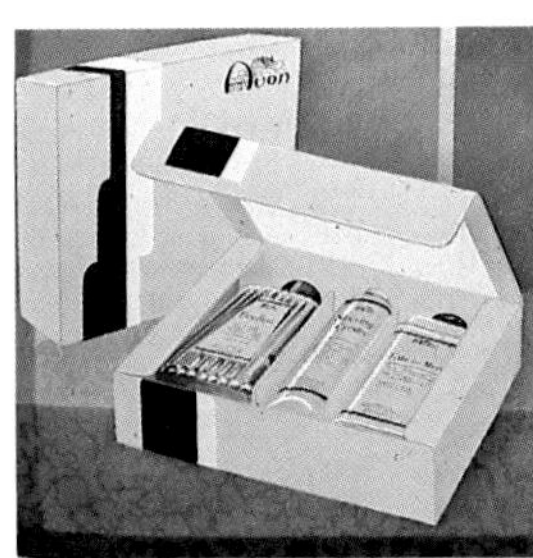

1931 *Assortment No. 1. Bay Rum 4oz, Shaving Cream, Talc $1.20* **MP $115**

1934-35 *Men's Package. (Div. on label, rare) After Shaving Lotion 4oz, Smoker's Tooth Powder, Talc and Bayberry Shaving Cream $1.61* **MP $200 with rare labels**

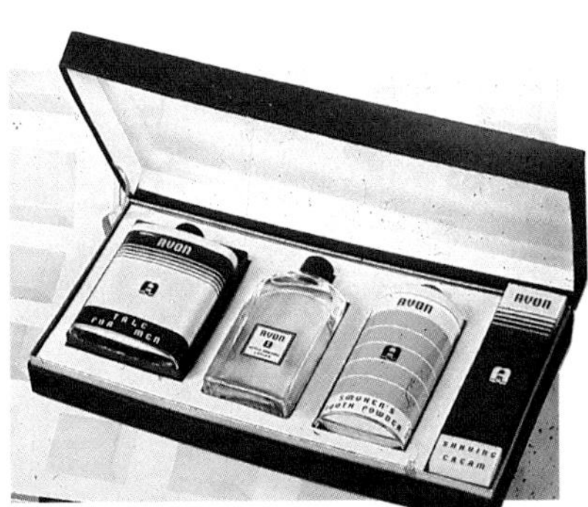

1936-37 *Avon Men's Package. Talc, After Shaving Lotion, Smoker's Tooth Powder and Shaving Cream $1.65* **MP $115**

1938 *Smoker Trio. Antiseptic, Toothbrush and Smoker's Tooth Powder $1.39* **MP $85**

1938 *Headliner for Boys. Hair Dress, Toothbrush and Toothpaste $1.10* **MP $45**

1936-38 *Assortment No. 2. Brushless Shaving Cream, After Shaving Lotion 4oz and Talc $1.10* **MP $80**

1939-46 *Olympic Set. Hair Lotion, Shaving Cream and After Shaving Lotion $1.29* **MP $105**

1939 *Esquire Set. Shaving Cream, Bay Rum 4oz, Talc $1.15* **MP $85**
(1936-38 *Same set called Assortment No. 1* **MP $90)**

1939 *Brushless Shave Set. Brushless Shaving Cream, After Shaving Lotion and Talc $1.10* **MP $85**

1938-39 *The Valet. Talc, After Shaving Lotion, Smoker's Tooth Powder and Shaving Cream $1.65* **MP $100**

1940-42 *The Valet. Smoker's Tooth Powder, After Shaving Lotion, Shaving Cream and Talc $1.69* **MP $100**

... SETS OF THE 1930's

1938 *Men's Traveling Kit. Shaving Cream, Talc, After Shaving Lotion and Styptic Cream $2.16* **MP $115**

1940 *Country Club. Shaving Cream, After Shaving Lotion 4oz and Talc $1* **MP $85**

1940 *Brushless Shave Set. After Shaving Lotion, Brushless Shaving Cream and Talc $1.10* **MP $85**

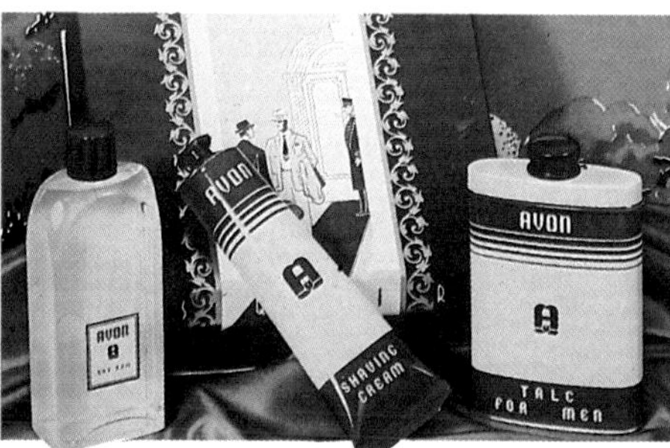

1940 *Esquire. Bay Rum 4oz, Shaving Cream and Talc $1.15* **MP $85**

SETS OF THE 1940's . . .

1940 *Commodore Set. After Shaving Lotion, Talc and 2 cotton Handkerchiefs $1.39* **MP $85**

1943 *Country Club. Shaving Cream 3-1/8oz, After Shaving Lotion 4oz and Talc 2-5/8oz $1.15* **MP $100**

1944 *Men's Traveling Set. Styptic Cream, After Shaving Lotion, Talc and Shaving Cream $2.57, with Brushless Shaving Cream $2.65* **MP $135, $165 boxed**

Wartime Cardboard Packaging – **1944-45** *Army & Navy Set. Brushless Shaving Cream, Tooth Powder and Elite Foot Powder $1.46* **MP $105 (1940-42** *Set, as above, held After Shaving Lotion, Shaving Cream and Elite Powder $1.35* **MP $110)**

1945 *Country Club. Shaving Cream, After Shaving Lotion, Talc $1.13* **MP $100**

1946 *Country Club. Talc, After Shaving Lotion and choice of Shaving Cream $1.35* **MP $73**

1946 *Valet Set. Smoker's Tooth Powder, Talc, After Shaving Lotion and Brushless or Lather Shaving Cream $2* **MP $85**

1947 *Modern Knight Set. After Shave Lotion 4oz, Deodorant 2oz and Talc $1.75* **MP $80**

1948 *Pleasure Cast. Cologne, Deodorant for Men 2oz each and Lather or Brushless Shaving Cream 3oz $1.69* **MP $70**

1949-51 *Pleasure Shave. Talc, Shaving Bowl and After Shave Lotion 4oz $2.25* **MP $80, $40 Shaving Bowl only**

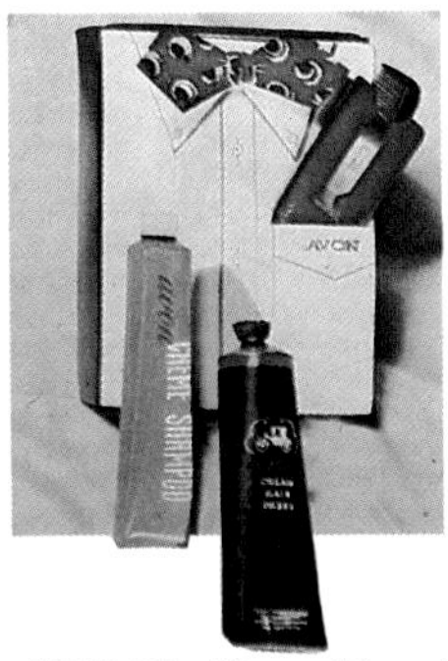

1949 *The Young Man. Creme Shampoo, Cream Hair Dress, Comb and Nail File in pocket case $1.50* **MP $45**

1949-51 *Commodore. Cologne, Deodorant 2oz each and choice of Brushless or Lather Shaving Cream $1.90* **MP $45**

1949-51 *Deluxe Trio. Cologne, Deodorant 2oz each and choice of Liquid or Creme Hair Lotion 4oz $2* **MP $50**
(1952 *Deluxe Trio, not shown. Same as above, but box had removable lid* **MP $45)**

1949-51 *Country Club. After Shave Lotion 4oz, choice of Brushless or Lather Shaving Cream and Talc $1.75* **MP $45**

1949 *Men's Traveling Kit. After Shave Lotion 4oz, choice of Shaving Cream, Styptic Cream and Talc $4.66* **MP $80**

1950-51 *Classic Set. Cream or Liquid Hair Lotion 4oz, Deodorant 2oz and Men's Toilet Soap $1.75* **MP $60**

1950 *Hi Podner. Red leatherette Cuffs hold choice of Cream Hair Dress or Creme Shampoo, Toothbrush and Ammoniated or Dental Cream Toothpaste $2.39* **MP $60**

1949 *Valet Set. Cologne 4oz with choice of Talc (shown) or Shaving Soap $1.65* **MP $40, $50 with Shaving Soap**

1950 *Valet Set. Cologne 4oz with choice of Shaving Soap (shown) or Talc $1.65* **MP $50, $40 with Talc**

1951 *Valet Set. Deodorant 2oz, choice of Brushless or Lather Shaving Cream and Liquid or Cream Hair Lotion 4oz $2* **MP $48**

1951 *Avon Service Kit. Military Waist Pocket Apron holds Brushless Shaving Cream, Toothpaste, Comb, Toothbrush, Dr. Zabriskie's Soap and unbreakable bottle of After Shave Lotion $3.90* **MP $100**

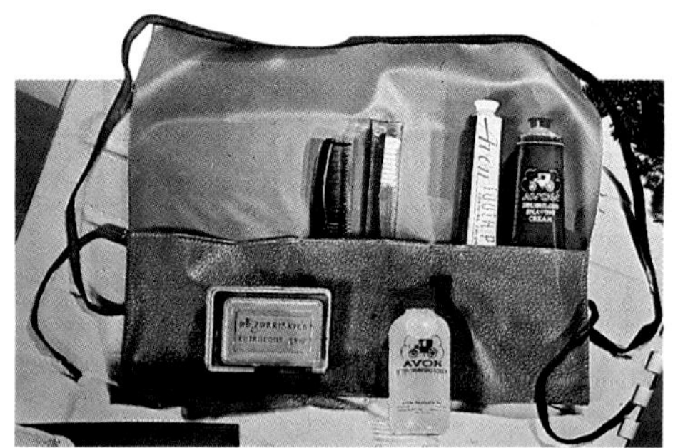

1953 *Avon Service Kit. Military Waist Pocket Apron holds Comb, Toothbrush, Brushless Shaving Cream, Dr. Zabriskie's Soap, Toothpaste and unbreakable bottle of After Shave Lotion $3.95* **MP $100**

1952 *U.S. Male. Choice of 2 bottles After Shave, Cologne or Deodorant 4oz each $1.22* **MP $35**

1957 *Cuff Links Set. Cologne and Deodorant 4oz each and 2 gold-plated Cuff Links $3.50* **MP $50**

1952 *Country Club. After Shave Lotion 4oz, choice of Brushless or Lather Shaving Cream and Talc $1.85* **MP $48**

1952 *Pleasure Shave. 2 tubes of Brushless or Lather Shaving Cream 98¢* **MP $28**

1952 *Changing of The Guard. Hand Guard and Hair Guard 2oz each $1* **MP $55, $20 each bottle**

1953 *Rough 'n' Ready. Cream Hair Lotion, Chap Check and Dr. Zabriskie's Soap $1.25* **MP $55**

1952 *Avon Classic. Cologne 4oz, Deodorant 2oz and Talc $2.25* **MP $48**

1953 *Quartet. After Shave Lotion 4oz, Deodorant 2oz and choice of 2, Brushless or Lather Shaving Creams $2.20* **MP $60**

1953 *King Pin. Two bottles After Shave Lotion 4oz each $1.18* **MP $50**

1953 *Space Ship. Plastic ship holds Chlorophyll Toothpaste, Toothbrush and Creme Shampoo $2.10* **MP $50**

SETS OF THE 1950's . . .

1953 *Before and After. Cologne 4oz and choice of Cream or Liquid Hair Lotion 4oz $1.69* **MP $50**

1953 *Deluxe Trio. Toilet Kit contains choice of Liquid or Cream Hair Lotion 4oz, Cologne and Deodorant 2oz each $2.25* **MP $55**

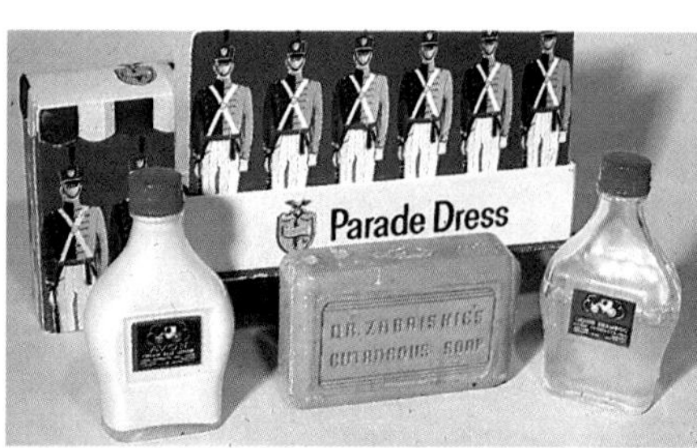

1953 *Parade Dress. Cream Hair Lotion and Liquid Shampoo 1oz each and Dr. Zabriskie's Soap $1.19* **MP $80, $25 each bottle**

1953-55 *Men's Traveling Kit, Plaid or pigskin Leatherette holds Talc, Deodorant 2oz, Shaving Cream, Styptic Cream and After Shaving Lotion 4oz $7.50* **MP $85**
(1950-52 *Traveling Kit in Leatherette only, contents as above $6.50* **MP $85)**

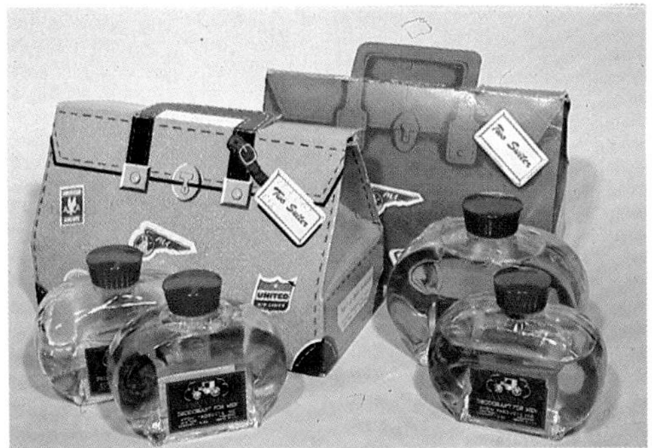

1953 & 1954 *Two Suiter Sets. Holds choice of two 2oz Deodorant or one Deodorant and After Shave 4oz or Deodorant and Cologne 2oz $1.26*
MP $50 Set

1954 *Sport-wise. Two bottles After Shaving Lotion 4oz each $1.18*
MP $50

1954 *Classic Set. Talc, Deodorant 2oz and Cologne 4oz $2.25* **MP $55**

1954-56 *Personal Note. After-use box that looks like memo pad holds 4oz Cologne, 4oz Deodorant and gold Ball Point Pen $2.95* **MP $50**

1954-56 *Black Sheep Set. Deodorant and Cologne for Men 4oz each and a black sheep made of Soap $2.50* **MP $100 complete**

1954 *Pleasure Cast No. 2 After Shaving Lotion 4oz and Talc $1.25* **MP $40**

1955 *'Round the Corner. Kwick Foaming Shaving Cream and 2oz Deodorant $1.59* **MP $35**

1954 *Backfield Set. Two 2oz bottles of Hair Guard and Hand Guard and Football shaped Soap $1.95* **MP $65,**
$20 each bottle

1955 *Pigskin Parade. Creme Shampoo, Hair Guard, Toothbrush and Chap Check $1.95* **MP $50**

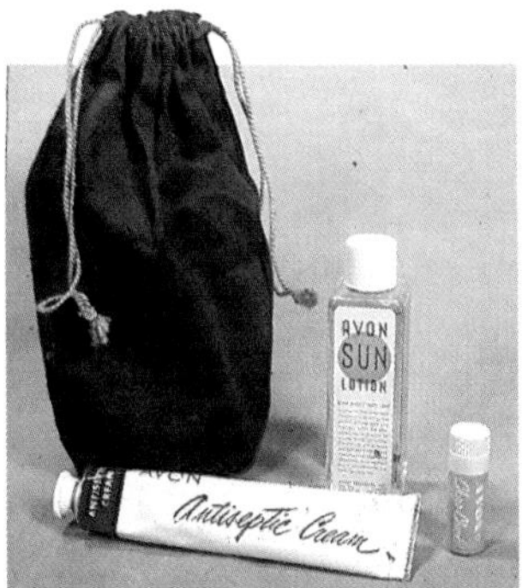

1954 only *Camping Kit for Boys or Girls. 2oz Sun Lotion, Antiseptic Cream, Chap Check and Cream Hair Dress or Creme Shampoo $1.95*
MP $75, $25 Sun Lotion only

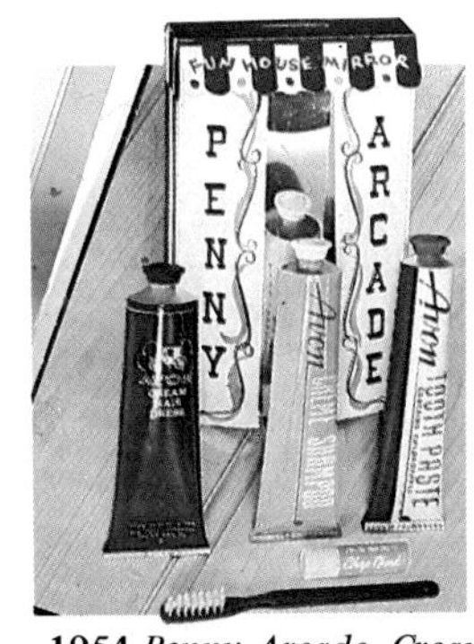

1954 *Penny Arcade. Cream Hair Dress, Creme Shampoo, Toothpaste, Youth's Toothbrush and Chap Check $2.25*
MP $65

1955 *Penny Arcade. Toothpaste, Cream Hair Dress, Creme Shampoo, Toothbrush and Chap Check $2.25*
MP $60

1955 *Space Scout. Toothbrush, White Toothpaste, Hair Guard, Antiseptic Cream and Chap Check $2.25* **MP $60**

1955 *Flying High Set No. 2. (left) Deodorant and Talc 4oz each $1.49* **MP $35**
No. 1 (right) After Shaving Lotion and Deodorant 4oz each $1.49 **MP $45**
1956 *Happy Hours. Above box held same items as No. 1 Set (above right) $1.59* **MP $45**

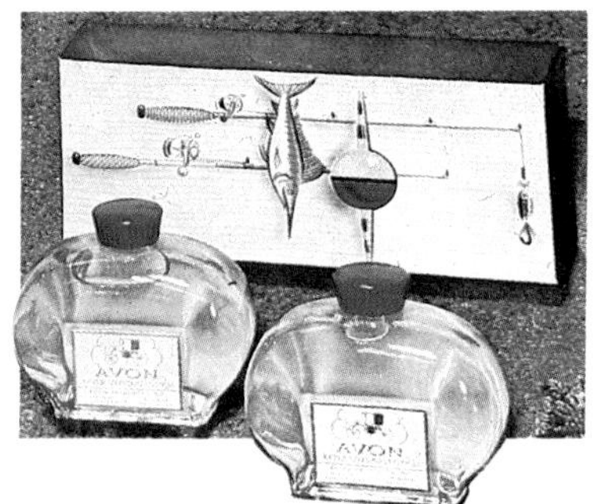

1955 *Pleasure Cast. Two 4oz bottles After Shaving Lotion $1.25* **MP $50**

. . . SETS OF THE 1950's . . .

1956 *More Love Than Money. 4oz Cologne and After Shave Lotion, 2oz Deodorant, Wallet and* **1956** *penny $5.95* **MP $80**

1955 *Saturday Knight. Choice of Cream or Liquid Lotion and 4oz Deodorant and Bow Tie $2.69* **MP $55**
(1956 *Same set re-named Varsity $2.19* **MP $55)**

1955 & 1956 *Father's Day Set. Holds two 4oz After Shaving Lotion or 1 After Shaving Lotion and choice of Deodorant 4oz or Talc $1.29* **MP $50**

1956 *Sailing, Sailing. Two 4oz After Shaving Lotion $1.29* **MP $50**

1956 *Hair Trainer Set. 6oz bottle Hair Trainer and pocket comb 79¢* **MP $30, $18 Hair Trainer only**

1956-57 *Touchdown Set. Soap in football shape. Hair Guard and Hand Guard $1.29* **MP $55**

1956 *Shave Bowl Set. Shaving Bowl and choice of 4oz Deodorant or After Shave Lotion $2.50* **MP $60, $40 Shaving Bowl only**

1956 *Holiday Holly. Talc and 4oz After Shave Lotion $1.29* **MP $35**

1956 *Top O' The Mornin' Set. Kwick Foaming Shave Cream and 2oz After Shaving Lotion $1.59* **MP $45, $18 Shave Cream only**

1956 *Overniter. Zippered case holds choice of 4oz Hair Lotions, 2oz Deodorant and 2oz Cologne $2.50* **MP $47**

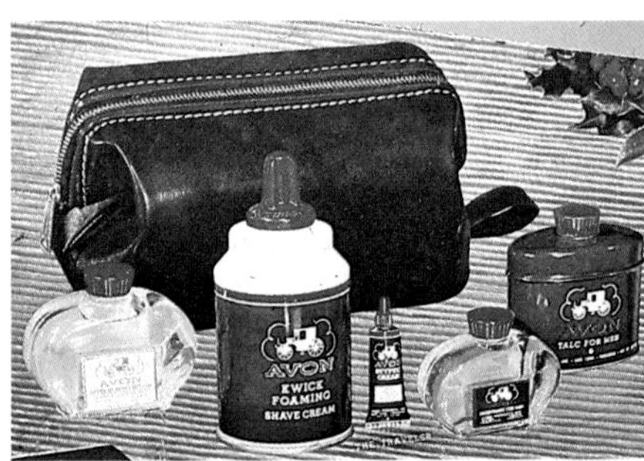

1956-57 *The Traveler. Travel Kit holds choice of Shaving Creams (Kwick, Lather, Brushless) 4oz, After Shave Lotion, 2oz Deodorant, Talc and Styptic Cream $7.95* **MP $70**

1956 *Smooth Shaving. Two tubes Brushless or Lather Shaving Cream $1.29* **MP $28**

1956-57 *Country Club Set. Talc, 4oz After Shave Lotion and choice of Brushless or Lather Shaving Cream $2.* **MP $45**

1956 *Good Morning. Two 4oz Hair Lotions, choice of Liquid or Cream $1.29* **MP $38**

1957 *Attention Set. After Shave and choice of Liquid or Cream Hair Lotion $1.49* **MP $38**

1957 *Trading Post. Hair Trainer and Foamy Bath 2oz each 98¢* **MP $60, $22 each bottle**
1958 *Stage Coach. Hair Trainer and Foamy Bath 2oz each 98¢* **MP $60, $22 each bottle**

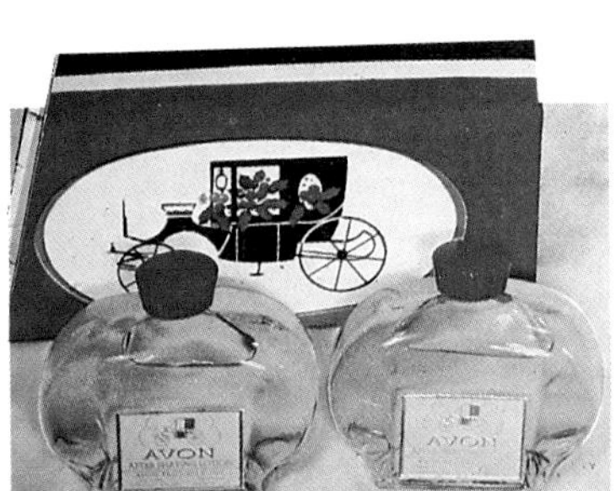

1957 *Send Off. Two 4oz bottles of After Shave Lotion $1.49* **MP $50**

1957 *Refreshing Hours. 4oz After Shave Lotion and 4oz Deodorant $1.69* **MP $35**

1957 *Merrily. Kwick Foaming Shave Cream and 2oz bottles of A/S & Deodorant $1.98* **MP $40, $12 Shave Cream only**

1957 *On The Go. Travel case holds Talc, 2oz Deodorant, 4oz After Shave Lotion and choice of Shaving Creams $8.95* **MP $65**

1957 *Man's World. Two 4oz Cream or Liquid Hair Lotions $1.49* **MP $38**

1957 *New Day. 4oz bottles of After Shave and Pre-Electric Shave Lotion $1.59* **MP $35, $15 Pre-Electric Shave only**

1957 *Money Isn't Everything. 4oz bottles of Cologne and After Shave, 2oz Deodorant and Cowhide Wallet $5.95* **MP $75**

Avon sets for Men came on the collecting scene during the 30's with only a few wartime sets issued from 1942 thru 1945. The 50's proved to be a popular decade for Men's Sets, and the 60's, too provided numbers of fine collectibles in this important category. Fewer sets in the 70's, and only one in the early 80's indicate heightened value for the sets that remain in private collections.

1957 *Good Cheer. After Shaving Lotion, Deodorant and Cologne 2oz each $1.98* **MP $50**

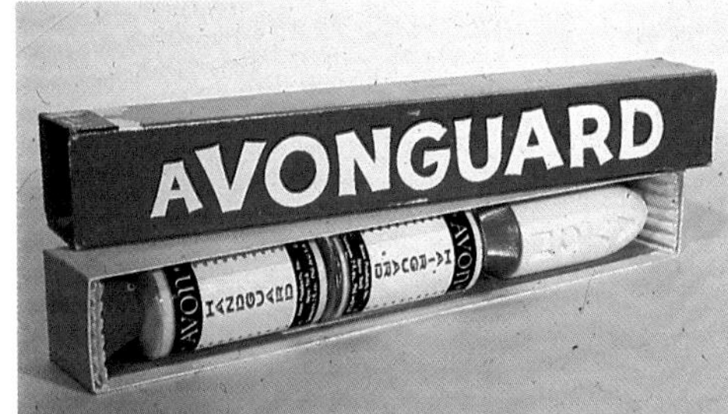

1958 *AvonGuard Set. 2oz Hairguard and Handguard and rocket shaped Soap $1.39* **MP $65, $15 each bottle, $20 Soap**

1958 *Coat of Arms. 2oz bottles After Shave Lotion and Deodorant and 6oz Kwick Foaming Shave Cream $1.98* **MP $40**

1958 *Modern Decoy. 4oz Cologne and Hair Lotion for Men and gold Papermate Pen $4.50* **MP $45**

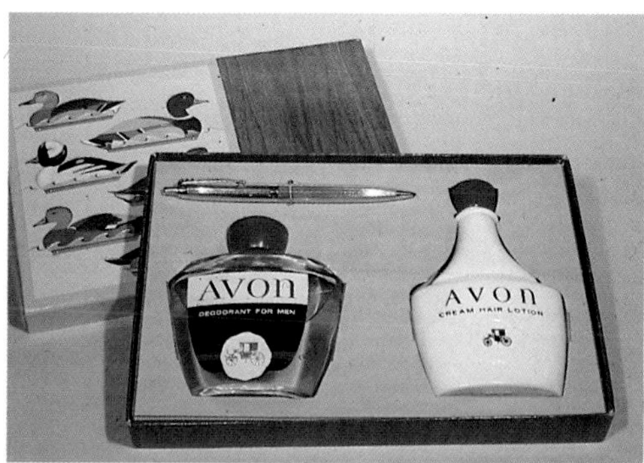

1958 *Modern Decoy with 4oz Deodorant and Cream Hair Lotion and gold Papermate Pen $4.50* **MP $35**

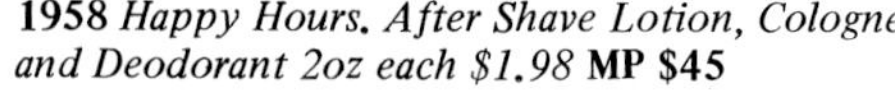

1958 *Happy Hours. After Shave Lotion, Cologne and Deodorant 2oz each $1.98* **MP $45**

1958 *Overniter. Italian-Luggage design case holds a choice of Cream or Liquid Hair Lotion and 2oz Deodorant and After Shave Lotion $2.98* **MP $50**

1958 *Neat Traveler. Glove leather case, moisture proof lining, holds 2oz Deodorant, 4oz After Shave Lotion, choice of Shaving Cream or Pre-Electric Shave and choice of Hair Lotion $8.95* **MP $55**

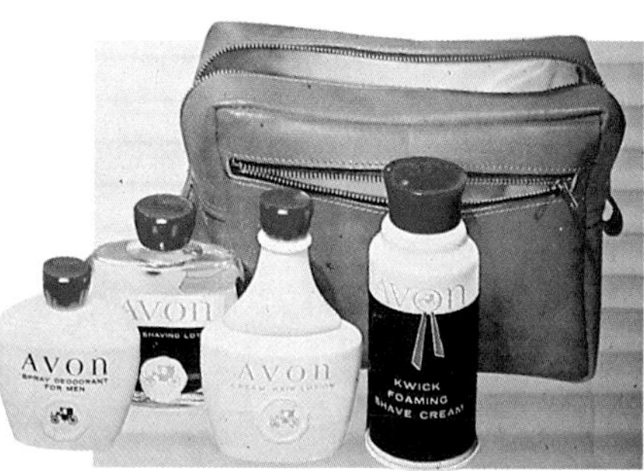

1959 *Travel Deluxe. Spray Deodorant, After Shaving Lotion 4oz, Hair Dress (Cream, Liquid or Attention) and choice of Shaving Cream (Kwick, Lather, Brushless or Electric Pre-Shave Lotion) $8.95* **MP $50**

1960 *Travel Deluxe, as above, but with Roll-On Deodorant (see Deodorant below) $9.95* **MP $50**

. . . SETS OF THE 1950's

1959 *Captain of The Guard. Tube of Cream Hair Dress and Spray Deodorant $1.98* **MP $35**

1959 *Out in Front. 2¾oz Spray Deodorant and choice of Cream or Liquid Hair Lotion $1.98* **MP $35**

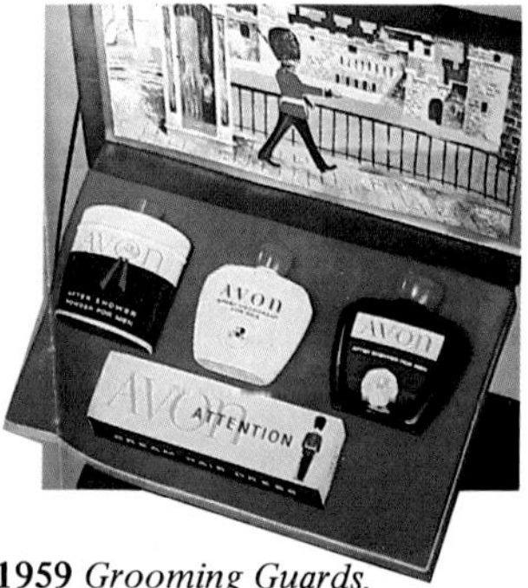

1959 *Grooming Guards. Attention Cream Hair Dress, After Shower Powder, Spray Deodorant and choice of After Shower or After Shave Lotion 4oz $4.95* **MP $50**

1960 *Dashing Sleighs. Cream Hair Lotion, After Shower Powder, Roll-On Deodorant and choice of 'Vigorate or After Shower for Men 8oz $4.98* **MP $60**

1959 *Lamplighter. 2oz After Shaving and After Shower Lotions and 1½oz Deodorant $2.98* **MP $50**

1959 *Carollers Set. After Shower for Men, Stick Deodorant and Talc $3.10* **MP $50**

1959 *Triumph Set. Choice of 2 products in combination of After Shave Lotion, Electric Pre-Shave or After Shower Powder 4oz each $1.79* **MP $30**

1960 *Overniter. Travel Case holds Roll-On Deodorant, After Shaving Lotion 3.5oz and Cream Hair Lotion $3.98* **MP $32**

1960 *First Prize. Combination of any three 2oz bottles from a choice of 8. After Shave for Dry or Sensitive Skin and Cream Hair Lotion are plastic, all others glass. $2.50* **MP $12 glass bottle, $20 boxed; $10 plastic bottle, $18 boxed; $6 sleeve only**

1961 *For Gentlemen. 4oz Cream Hair Lotion, Roll-On Deodorant, choice of Kwick Foaming Shave Cream or Electric Pre-Shave and choice of After Shower or 'Vigorate Lotion 8oz $5.17* **MP $65**

1961 *Gold Medallion. Combination of any three bottles from a choice of 10. After Shave for Dry or Sensitive Skin and Cream Hair Lotion are plastic, all others glass. $2.50* **MP same as the First Prize Set, above center**

1962 *Holly Time Set. 2 Cream Hair Lotions 4oz each $1.78* **MP $25**

1962 *Holly Time. 2 Liquid Hair Lotions 4oz each $1.78* **MP $30**

SETS OF THE 1960's . . .

1962 *Christmas Classic. Choice of 2 Spicy or 2 Original After Shave Lotions $1.78* **MP $22,** *or 2 'Vigorate or 2 After Shower Colognes $2* **MP $25**

1962 *Under The Mistletoe. Electric Pre-Shave and Spicy After Shave Lotions $1.78* **MP $22**

1963 *Jolly Holly Day Set shows 3 lotions from a choice of 9, plastic 2oz each $1.98* **MP $20 set**

1962 *Good Cheer Set. 4oz Spicy or Original After Shave Lotion and 3oz Spicy Talc $1.78* **MP $25**
1964 *Holly Star Set. 4oz Spicy After Shave and 3oz Spicy Talc $1.78* **MP $25**

1962 *Christmas Day Set. 4oz Spicy or Original After Shave and 4oz Liquid Deodorant $1.78* **MP $22**
1964 *Christmas Morning Set. 2 bottles Spicy After Shave Lotion 4oz each $1.78* **MP $22**

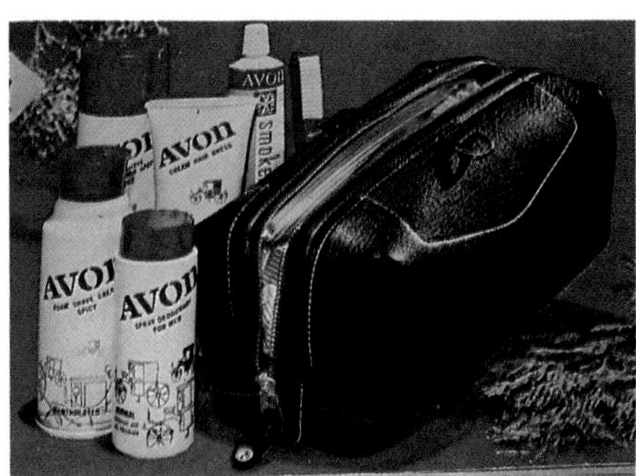

1963 *Men's Travel Kit. Vinyl kit by Amity with Foam Shave Cream (Regular or Mentholated), After Shave-After Shower Spray in Spicy, Cream Hair Dress, Smoker's Tooth Paste, Tooth Brush and Spray Deodorant (Gentle or Normal) $11.95* **MP $65**

1964 *Holiday Greetings Set. Electric Pre-Shave and After Shave Lotion, both Spicy 4oz each $1.78* **MP $22**
1964 *Santa's Team Set. Spicy After Shave and Liquid Deodorant 4oz each $1.78* **MP $22**

1964 *Christmas Trio. Three 2oz bottles with a choice of any 3 of 9 different products $1.98* **MP $20**

1965 *Original Set. (Father's Day Only) Two 4oz Original After Shave Lotions $1.96* **MP $22, $6 each bottle**

1965 *Christmas Call. Two 4oz Original After Shave Lotions $1.95* **MP $20**

1965 *(Father's Day Only) King for A Day. Three 2oz bottles in choice of 5 assortments $1.98* **MP $25**

1966 *Protective Hand Cream for Men, two 2oz $2.50* **MP $12**

1966 *(Father's Day) Fox Hunt Set. 2 Avon Leather All-Purpose Lotion for Men $4* **MP $40, $15 each bottle**

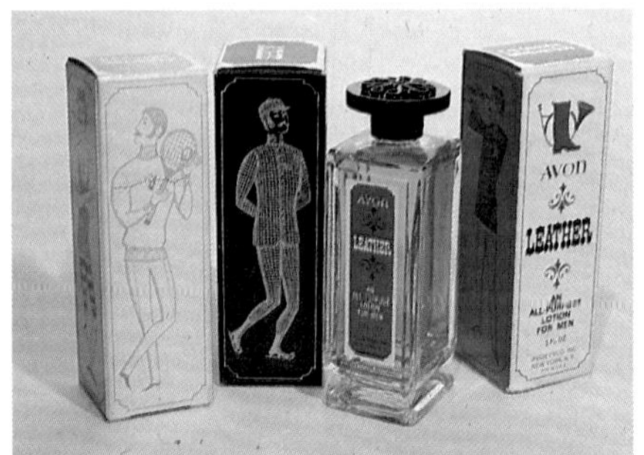

1965 *Fragrance Wardrobe. Three 2oz bottles in choice of 4 assortments fit into sleeve (not shown) $3.50 each set* **MP $45 with sleeve**

1966 *After Shave Selection in Father's Day Gift Box. Three 2oz bottles in a choice of 3 combinations $2.98* **MP $40, $9 each bottle**

1966 *Bureau Organizer. 2oz Tribute, Spicy, Blue Blazer After Shave and Leather All Purpose Cologne $11.95* **MP $60, $20 tray**

. . . SETS OF THE 1960's . . .

1966 *Fragrance Chest. After Shave Lotion in 4 frag. 1oz each $4* **MP $48, $9 each bottle**

1966 *Fore 'N' After Set. Spicy Pre-Shave and After Shave Lotion 4oz each $1.96* **MP $25, $10 each bottle**

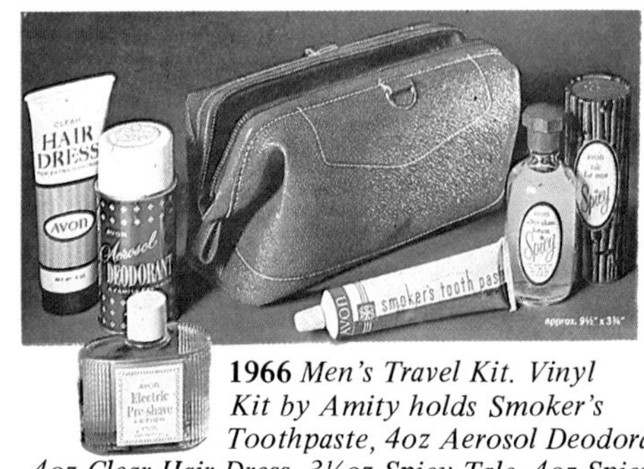

1966 *Men's Travel Kit. Vinyl Kit by Amity holds Smoker's Toothpaste, 4oz Aerosol Deodorant 4oz Clear Hair Dress, 3½oz Spicy Talc, 4oz Spicy After Shave Lotion, plus choice of Electric Pre-Shave Lotion or 6oz Foam Shave Cream $12.95* **MP $55**

1967 *Smart Move. Spicy, Tribute and Original After Shave Lotion 2oz $4* **MP $50, $12 each bottle**

1967 *Men's After Shave Choice. Tribute, Leather and Wild Country Lotion 2oz each $5* **MP $25, $6 each bottle**

1968 *Gentleman's Collection. 1 each of Leather, Wild Country and Windjammer Cologne 2oz each $8* **MP $30, $13 box only**

1967 *Tag-Alongs. 3oz Spicy After Shave Lotion & 3oz Squeeze Spray Deodorant $2.50* **MP $16**
1968 *Overnighter. Squeeze-Spray Deodorant 3oz and Spicy After Shave Lotion $2.50* **MP $14**

1968 *Boots and Saddle (glass) Leather and Wild Country After Shave Lotion 3oz each $3* **MP $20**
1969 *Traveler Set. Bravo or Spicy After Shave 3½oz and 3oz Squeeze-Spray Deodorant $2.50* **MP $13**

1974 *Travel Set for Men. Talc 1.5oz and After Shave 3oz in Wild Country, Deep Woods, Oland or Spicy $4* **MP $6**

1980 *Fragrance Duo. Talc 1.5oz and After Shave 5oz in Wild Country, Trazarra, Weekend or Clint $8.50* **MP $7**

1969 *Structured for Man: Glass, Wood and Steel Colognes 3oz each $8.50* **MP $25**
1969 *Cologne Trilogy. Windjammer, Wild Country and Excalibur Cologne 1½oz each $8* **MP $25, $6 each bottle**

1970 *Master Organizer. Oland or Excalibur Cologne and After Shave 3½oz each and 6oz Soap. Set $25* **MP $45**

1971 *Collector's Organizer in Tai Winds or Wild Country After Shave and Cologne 3oz each with Soap, 5oz $25* **MP $50**

SETS OF THE 1970's AND 1980's

1981 *Club Collection Decanter 4oz in Black Suede or Wild Country Cologne $8* **MP $7*** *or After Shave $7* **MP $6***

1981 *Club Collection Hair Brush $8.50* **MP $7***
1981 *Club Collection Caddy, 4x6" glass tray $9.50* **MP $8***

1972 *American Eagle Bureau Organizer in Deep Woods or Tai Winds Cologne and After Shave 3oz each with 5oz Soap $25* **MP $40**

1973 *Whale Bureau Organizer. Blend 7 or Deep Woods Cologne and After Shave 3oz each and 5oz Soap $30* **MP $40**

** Available from Avon at time of publication*

(See also Men's Fragrance Lines pgs. 182-187)

MEN'S JEWELRY

In 1971 and 1972 the men's jewelry line consisted of cuff links, tie bars and button covers. In 1976 the first piece of men's body jewelry was introduced – the Clint Wrist Chain. In 1977 men wore their first Avon neckchain, the Ankh Pendant. All handsome designs, each piece is crafted in a masculine style.

1978 *Infinity Symbol Neckchain $10.50* **MP $9**
1977 *Arrowhead Pendant $12.50* **MP $10***
1977 *Ropetwist Neckchain Gold-filled or Sterling Silver $19.50* **MP $18**
1977 *Ankh Pendant Neckchain $10* **MP $9**

1978 *Wild Country Pendant Neckchain $11.50* **MP $10**
1978 *Anchor Pendant Neckchain $11.50* **MP $10**
1978 *Eagle Pendant Neckchain, Pewter or Goldtone $11.50* **MP $10**
1978 *Tomahawk Pendant Neckchain $12.50* **MP $10**

1976 *Clint Wrist Chain $12* **MP $11**
1977 *Regent Street Wristband $15.50* **MP $14**

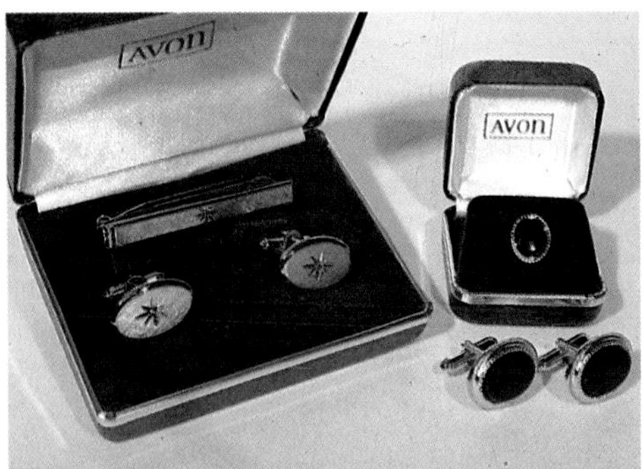

1971 *Starburst Cuff Links and Tie Bar Set $10* **MP $16**
1971 *Classic Accent Tie Tack $4* **MP $8**
1971 *Classic Black Cuff Links $8* **MP $11**

1971 *Convertible Cuff Links $12* **MP $14**
1971 *Brushed Oval Cuff Links $7* **MP $10**
1971 *Geometric Cuff Links $8* **MP $10, $11 boxed**

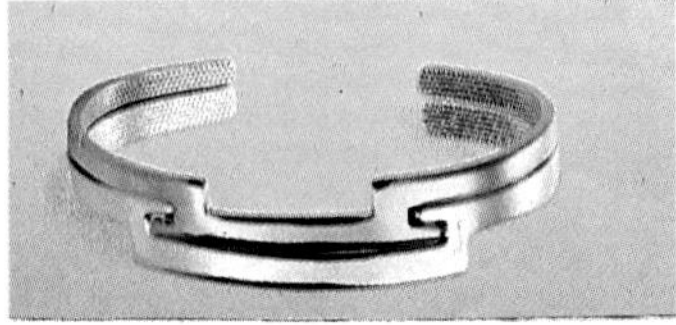

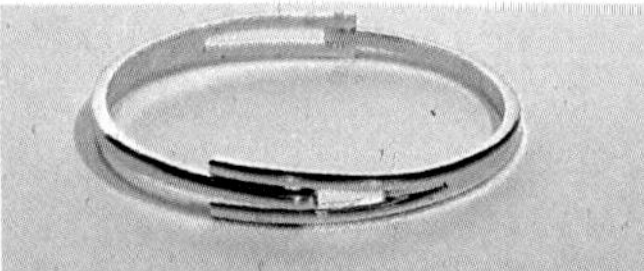

1977 *Counterparts Interlocking Bracelets $9.50* **MP $9**
1978 *Interlock Wristband $13* **MP $11**

1978 *Trazarra Wrist Chain $12.50* **MP $10**
1977 *Polished Bar Wrist Chain $10.50* **MP $9**

A Jewelry Mood for every man to set him apart with style and flair – adornments for every occasion.

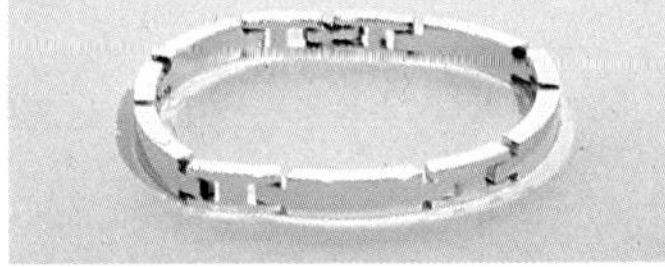

1979 *Bold Stroke Wrist Chain $9.50* **MP $8**
1978 *Jet Stream Wrist Chain $17.50* **MP $15**

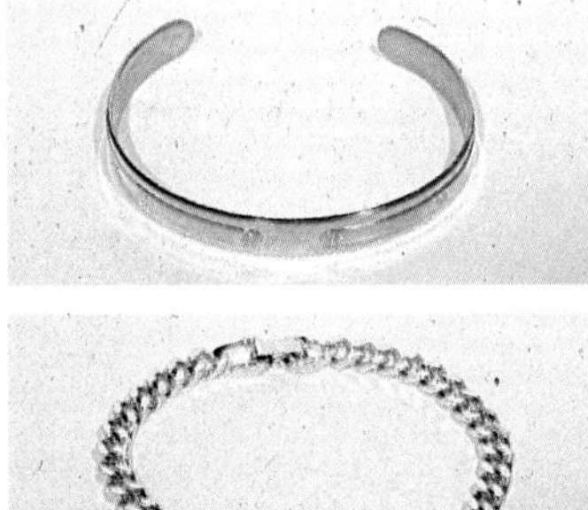

1979 *Copper Cuff Bracelet $10* **MP $8**
1979 *Classic Style Wristchain $10.50* **MP $8**

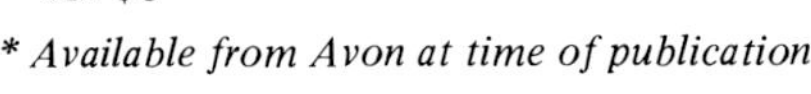

* *Available from Avon at time of publication*

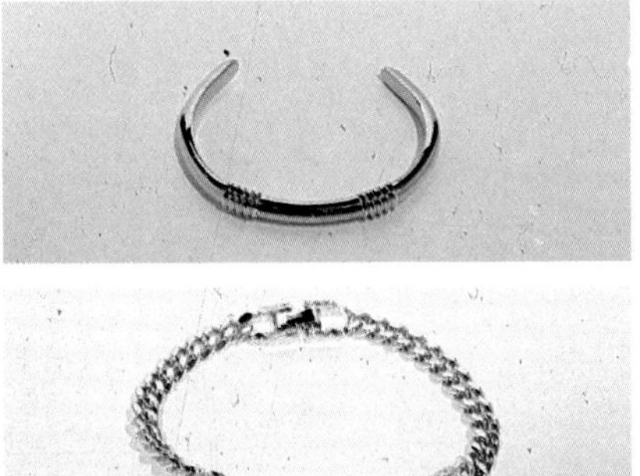

1980 *Marlboro Wristcuff $14.50* **MP $12**
1980 *Personally His Wristchain $16.50* **MP $14**

1979 *Bold Stallion Tie Tac $8* **MP $6**
1980 *Western Saddle Belt Buckle $14.50* **MP $11***
1981 *U.S.Flag Money Clip $15* **MP $12***

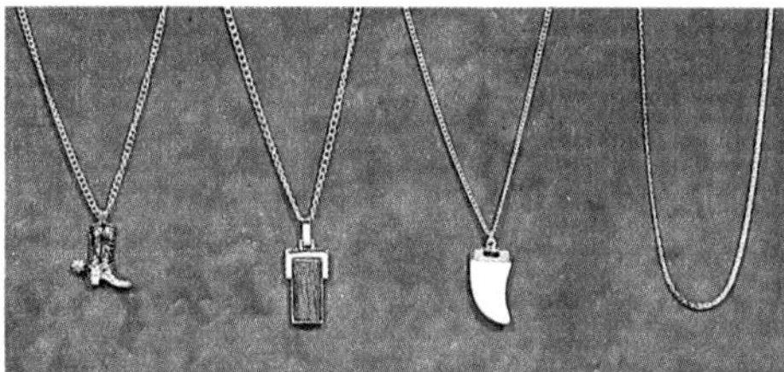

1979 *Western Boot Pendant, Goldtone or Silvertone $12.50* **MP $10**

1979 *Natural Wood Pendant Neckchain $13.50* **MP $11**

1979 *Adventure Pendant $10.50* **MP $8**

1979 *Sterling Silver Neckchain $21.50* **MP $20**

1979 *Bengal Tiger Neckchain $15.50* **MP $13**

1980 *Wild Mustang Neckchain $9.50* **MP $7**

1980 *Star Signs Pendant Neckchain in 12 Zodiac signs (Aries shown) $16.50* **MP $13***

1980 *Roman Coin Pendant $14.50* **MP $12**

1980 *American Buffalo Neckchain $10.50* **MP $8**

1981 *Lucky Horn Pendant Neckchain $11.50* **MP $10***

1972 *Station Wagon Cuff Links $9* **MP $15**
1971 *Rope Twist Tie Bar $5* **MP $9**
1972 *Rolls Royce Cuff Links $9* **MP $15**

1972 *Button Style Button Covers $5* **MP $9**
1972 *Blue Enamel Button Covers $5.50* **MP $10**

1980 *Men's Jewelry Valet 8x5" $18* **MP $16***

The precious look of jewelry, with a secret cache of Perfume Glace –

FRAGRANCE JEWELS BY AVON

(rear)
1969 *Patterns Perfume Glace Ring $6* **MP $10**
1969 *Ring of Pearls. Charisma, Brocade or Regence Perfume Glace $7.50* **MP $10**
1970 *Cameo Pin Perfume Glace in Bird of Paradise, Elusive, Charisma, Brocade or Regence $10* **MP $15**
(front)
1970 *Cameo Ring Perfume Glace in Elusive, Charisma, Brocade or Regence $10* **MP $15**
1970 *Bird of Paradise Ring, Perfume Glace Bird of Paradise only $10* **MP $10**

(See Table Top Glace Jewelry pg. 144)

1969 *Golden Leaf Pin. Perfume Glace in 11 frag. $6.50 to $7* **MP $10**

1965 *Solid Perfume Jewel Locket. Choice of 9 frag. $5.25, $5.50 and $6* **MP $18**
1969 *Daisy Pin. Perfume Glace in 9 frag. $5.75, $6 and $6.50* **MP $9**
1970 *Flower Basket Pin. Perfume Glace in 5 frag. $7* **MP $9**

(below left)
1968 *Golden Charmer Necklace/Bracelet in 9 frag. $9.25 $9.50 & $10* **MP $15**

1966 *Solid Perfume Locket/Pin. 1½gr in 9 frag. $8, $8.25 and $8.50* **MP $18**
1966 *Solid Perfume Locket/Pin. 1½gr $8, $8.25 and $8.50* **MP $18**
1965 *Jewel Locket Chain. Solid Perfume in 9 frag. $5.25, $5.50 & $6* **MP $18**

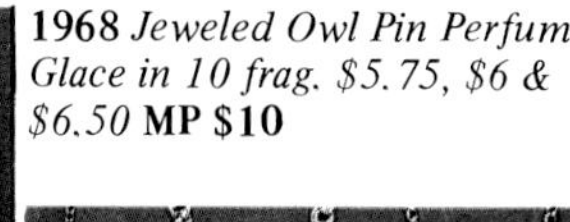

1968 *Jeweled Owl Pin Perfume Glace in 10 frag. $5.75, $6 & $6.50* **MP $10**

1970 *Perfume Pendant in Elusive, Charisma, Brocade or Regence 1/8oz $14* **MP $16**
1971 *Golden Moments Pendant Perfume in 5 frag. 1/8oz $14 and $15* **MP $15**
1972 *Perfume Pendant in Moonwind or Sonnet 1/8oz $12.50* **MP $16**

** Available from Avon at time of publication*

1973 *Classic Charm Bracelet, 7" long, 14k gold-electroplated $5* **MP $10**

Classic Charms inspired by famous Avon decanters, 14k gold-electroplated.
1973 *Sweet Shoppe $4* **MP $8**
1973 *Victoriana Pitcher and Bowl $4* **MP $8**
1973 *Fashion Boot $4* **MP $8**
1973 *Precious Owl $4* **MP $8**
1973 *Country Store Coffee Mill $4* **MP $8**
1973 *French Telephone $4* **MP $5**

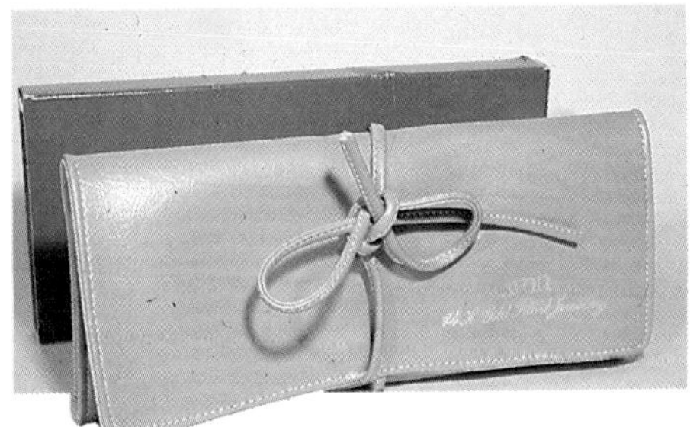

1977 *Jewelry Wrap demo to hold 14k Gold Jewelry $2.50* **MP $6**

WOMEN'S JEWELRY

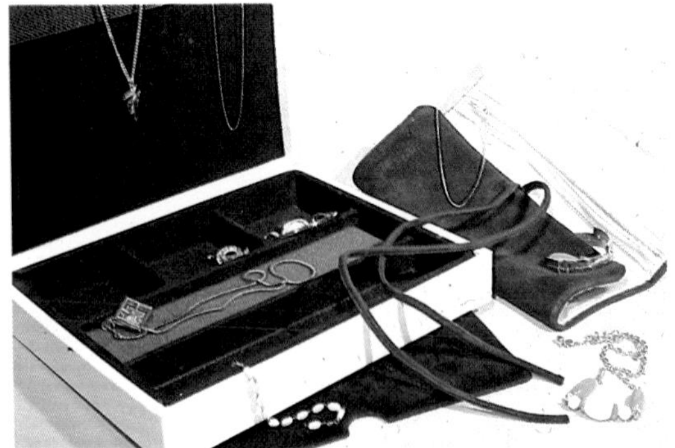

1977 *Jewelry Case, sim. leather. Approx. 10x8" with removable velvety pad. $5 with a $10 purchase, one Campaign only* **MP $11**
1977 *Jewelry Wrap, sim. suede. $3.50 with purchase of 2 jewelry items in C-14 only* **MP $6**

1978 *Decorator's Jewelry Chest, wood, dated for collectors. $6 with $10 order in C-15 only (because Avon rejected the entire shipment, only those sold to Reps as demos were issued.* **MP $40**

1981 *Women's Jewelry Pouch, sold only in U.S. $3.99 with jewelry purchase only in C-3* **MP $10 retail value**

1971 *Precious Pretenders (4 & 8) $10* **MP $20**
1971 *Evening Creation (7 & 8) $14* **MP $22**
1972 *Love Blossoms Convertible Necklace/Pin (1) $10* **MP $16**
1972 *Blue Teardrop (1) $9* **MP $15**

1972 *Contempora Convertible Necklace/Pin $12* **MP $16**
1972 *Rope Twist $12* **MP $19**
1972 *Royal Tassle (1) $10* **MP $15**

1972 *Multi-Strand Convertible Necklace/ Bracelet $12* **MP $16**
1972 *Purple Pendant $10* **MP $15**
1972 *Convertible Creation Necklace/Bracelet/ Belt $14* **MP $15**
1972 *Creation-In-Blue Convertible Necklace/ Pin (5) $12* **MP $20**

(below left)
1973 *Sweet Violets Locket $9* **MP $12**

1972 *Romanesque $8* **MP $12**
1973 *Sierra (6) $9* **MP $11**
1973 *Royal Occasion (5) $6* **MP $9**
1973 *Ming Green Adjustable $9* **MP $11**

1973 *Serena Rose Mirrored Pendant (3) $10* **MP $18**
1973 *Black Cabochon (5) $7* **MP $10**
1973 *Ovalesque $9* **MP $11**

1973 *Sonnet Convertible Necklace/Bracelet $10* **MP $18**
1973 *Autumn Glory Convertible Necklace/ Pin $10* **MP $18**
1973 *Baroness (7) $8* **MP $10**
1973 *Granada $9* **MP $11**

Matching jewelry: (1) Earrings (2) Bracelet (3) Ring (4) Earrings & Bracelet (5) Earrings & Ring (6) Bracelet & Ring (7) Bracelet, Earrings & Ring (8) Pin

1973 *Goddess Diana $10* **MP $13**
1974 *Ebony Teardrop $9* **MP $10**
1974 *Dear Heart (1) $8* **MP $11**
1974 *Pale Fire (5) $9* **MP $12**

1974 *Queensbury (5) $8* **MP $10**
1974 *Mayan $7* **MP $8**
1974 *Rosegay Convertible Choker/Bracelet (5) $12* **MP $13**
1974 *Sun Brilliants Convertible Pendant/Pin (5) $9* **MP $11**

1974 *Medallion $9* **MP $10**
1974 *Yesteryear Picture Locket $10* **MP $12**
1974 *Reversible Cameo Pendant (3) $9* **MP $10**
1974 *Owl Pendant $9* **MP $11**

1974 *Castillian (1) $7* **MP $9**
1974 *Glorianna (1) $10* **MP $12**
1974 *Mirabella (5) $10* **MP $11**
1974 *Queen Ann's Lace $12.50* **MP $14**

1974 *Moon Magic (3) $10* **MP $12**
1974 *Florentine Flowers (1) $12* **MP $13**
1974 *Queen's Ransom Pill Box/Charm Necklace $12.50* **MP $12**
1974 *Town and Country $12* **MP $10**

1974 *Abbey Pendant $9* **MP $9**
1975 *Rosamonde Convertible Choker Bracelet (5) $10* **MP $11**
1975 *Burnished Rose Convertible Necklace/Pin (7) $10* **MP $11**
1975 *Victorian Locket $14* **MP $14**

1975 *Silhouette Pendant $12* **MP $11**
1975 *Sea Swirl (1) $9* **MP $9**
1975 *Come Summer (1) $8* **MP $7**
1975 *Lace Medallions $9* **MP $9**

1975 *Desert Stones (1) $9* **MP $10**
1975 *Starblaze $6* **MP $6**
1975 *Plaza IV (7) $10.50* **MP $10**
1975 *Silver Note $9* **MP $9**

1975 *Sunny Star, Gold $8* **MP $7**
1976 *Sunny Star, Silver $8* **MP $7**
1975 *Juliet Cross, Green $11* **MP $9**
1976 *Juliet Cross, Ivory $11* **MP $9**

1975 *Moonspun (1) $9* **MP $10**
1975 *Golden Links (2) $7* **MP $7**
1976 *Key to My Heart $8.50* **MP $8**
1976 *Great Lengths Chains, 28" $6* **MP $6**, *32" $6.50* **MP $5.50**, *36" $7* **MP $6**

1976 *Magnifying Glass Pendant $10.50* **MP $12**
1976 *Versailles (5) $10.50* **MP $9**
1976 *New Dimensions (3) $10.50* **MP $9**
1976 *Contempora Pendant $9.50* **MP $10**

1976 *Windchimes (1) $9.50* **MP $9**
1976 *Crystalique $8.50* **MP $6**
1976 *Crystal Palace (5) $9.50* **MP $8**
1976 *Class of 77 Pendant $7* **MP $9**

Matching jewelry: (1) Earrings (2) Bracelet (3) Ring (4) Earrings & Bracelet (5) Earrings & Ring (6) Bracelet & Ring (7) Bracelet, Earrings & Ring (8) Pin

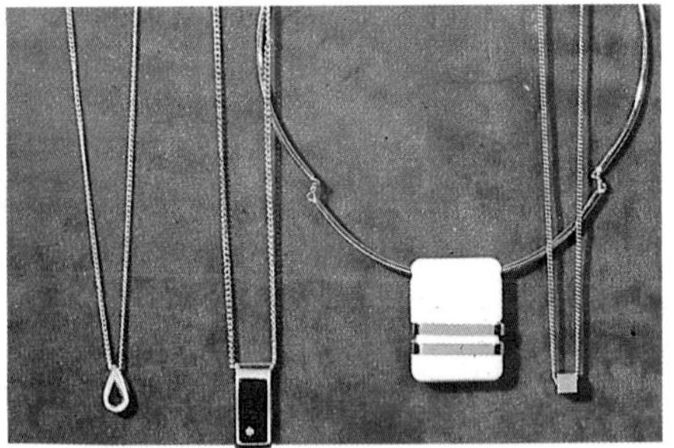

1976 *Birthstone Pendant $9.50* **MP $9**
Garnet, Amethyst, Aquamarine, Diamond, Ruby, Emerald, Alexandrite, Peridot, Topaz, Sapphire, Rose Zircon, Blue Zircon (Austrian glass)
1976 *Del Monico (5) $10.50* **MP $10**
1976 *Variations Reversible Pendant $10.50* **MP $9**
1976 *Single Cube, silver or gold, (1) $9.50* **MP $7**

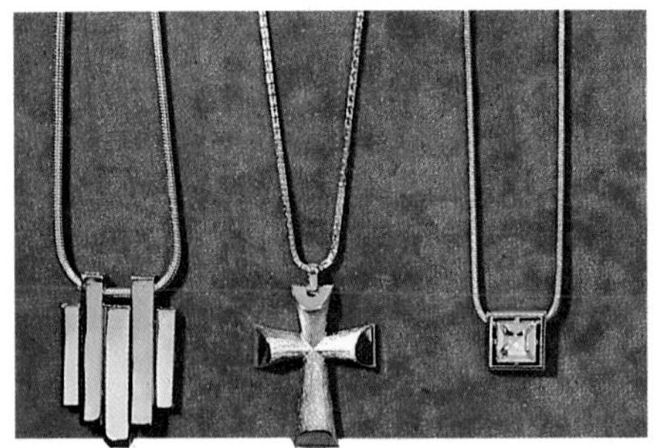

1976 *Geometric (1) $23* **MP $20**
1976 *Florentine Finish Cross $25* **MP $22**
1976 *Square-Cut Lead Crystal (1) $17* **MP $15**

1976 *Viennese (5) $11.50* **MP $9**
1977 *Sculptured Heart (1) $10.50* **MP $9**
1977 *Park East (5) $10.50* **MP $9**
1977 *Tender Blossoms Ceramic $7.50* **MP $6**

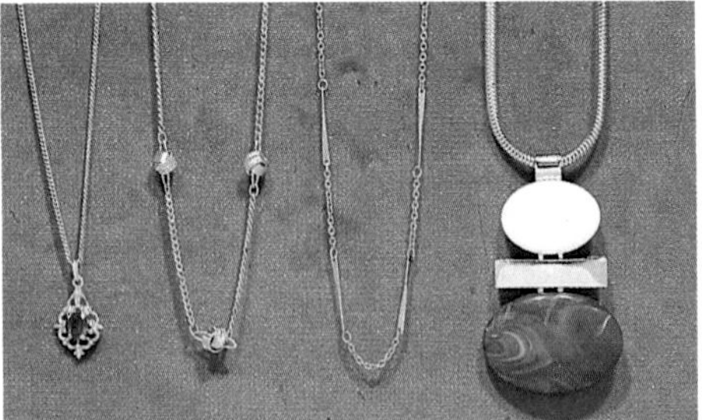

1977 *Venetian Lace (5) $9.50* **MP $8**
1977 *Delicate Knot (1) $8.50* **MP $8**
1977 *Chainfall Necklace in 3 shades: Yellow Goldtone 26", Rose Goldtone 24", Silver 22", $7.50, $7 & $6.50* **MP $7 each**
1977 *Polished Ovals (1) $18* **MP $16**

1977 *Butterfly Pendant $12.50* **MP $10**
1977 *Summerset (1) $10.50* **MP $9**
1977 *Gilded Circles $10.50* **MP $8**

1977 *Floralpoint Locket $16.50* **MP $14**
1977 *Spun Swirls Choker (5) $10.50* **MP $9**
1977 *Class of 78 Pendant $7.50* **MP $9**

1977 *14k Diamond Loop with .01 Diamond $24* **MP $22**
1977 *Frostlights Pendant (3) $11.50* **MP $9**
1977 *Fireflow Teardrop $10.50* **MP $8**
1977 *Delicately Yours $8.50* **MP $7**

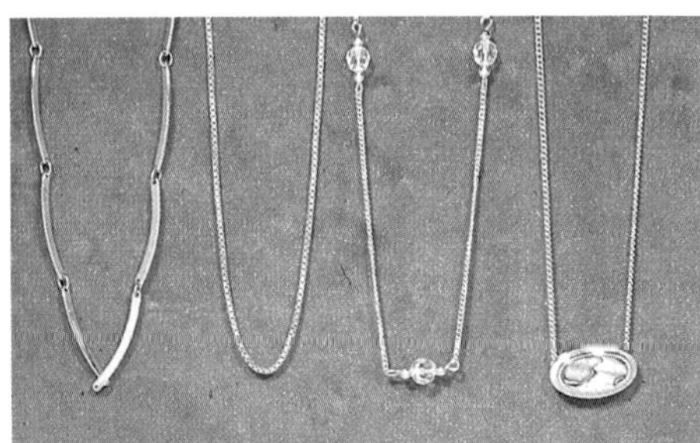

1977 *Scalloped Casual (2) $9.50* **MP $8**
1977 *14k Box Chain $18* **MP $15**
1977 *Lead Crystal Bead $18* **MP $10**
1977 *Abalone Pendant (7) $10.50* **MP $9**

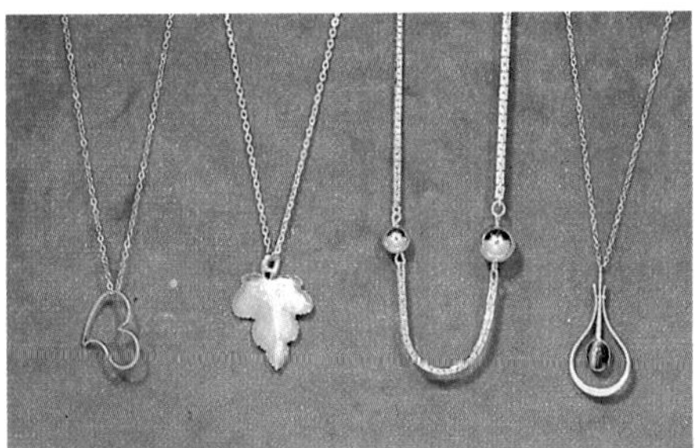

1978 *Carefree Heart Pendant, 14k gold $10.50* **MP $10**
1978 *Radiant Leaf Pendant $7.50* **MP $7**
1978 *Beaded Chain $8.50* **MP $7**
1978 *Tiger Eye Pendant (1) $20* **MP $18**

1978 *Shy Butterfly (3) $9.50* **MP $8**
1978 *Class of 79 Pendant $9.50* **MP $8**
1978 *Initial Attraction Pendant $8.50* **MP $6**
1978 *Lotus Blossom Pendant $8.50* **MP $7**

1978 *Soaring Dove Pendant $8.50* **MP $6**
1978 *Genuine Crystal Apple $10.50* **MP $9**
1978 *Gilded Strands with Mother-of-Pearl Accents $13.50* **MP $11**
1978 *Versatile Links Convertible Necklace/Bracelet $17.50* **MP $13***

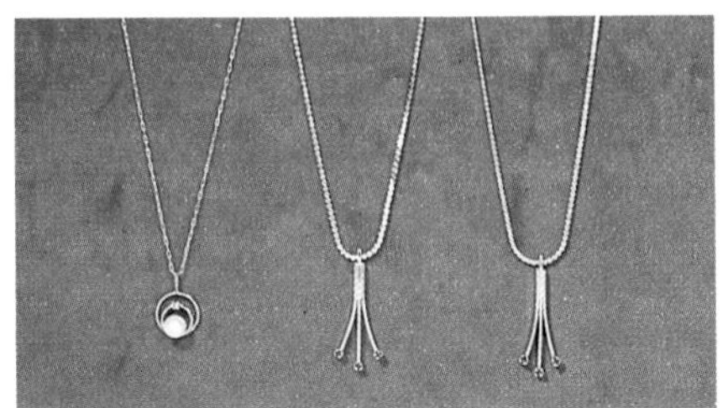

1978 *Cultured Pearl with Diamond Accent (5) $70* **MP $50**
1978 *Precious Sapphire Sterling Silver Pendant $45* **MP $35**
1978 *Precious Ruby 14k gold filled $45* **MP $35**

** Available from Avon at time of publication*

Matching jewelry: (1) Earrings (2) Bracelet (3) Ring (4) Earrings & Bracelet (5) Earrings & Ring (6) Bracelet & Ring (7) Bracelet, Earrings & Ring (8) Pin

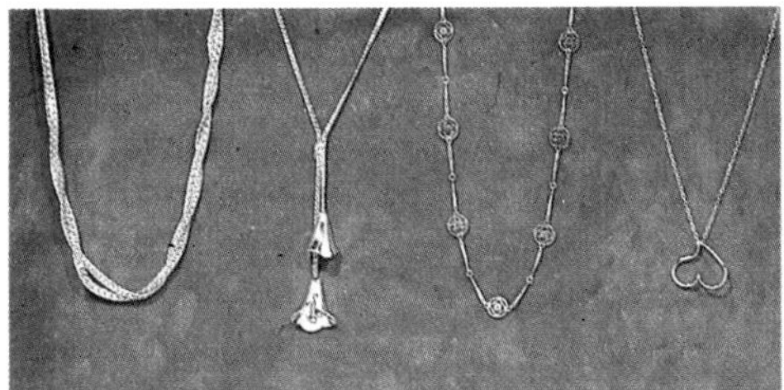

1978 *Interweave $14.50* **MP $13**
1978 *Lily Lariat $13.50* **MP $11**
1979 *Flowerlace, (2) Goldtone or Silvertone $11.50* **MP $10**
1979 *Carefree Heart Sterling Silver Pendant $12.50* **MP $10**

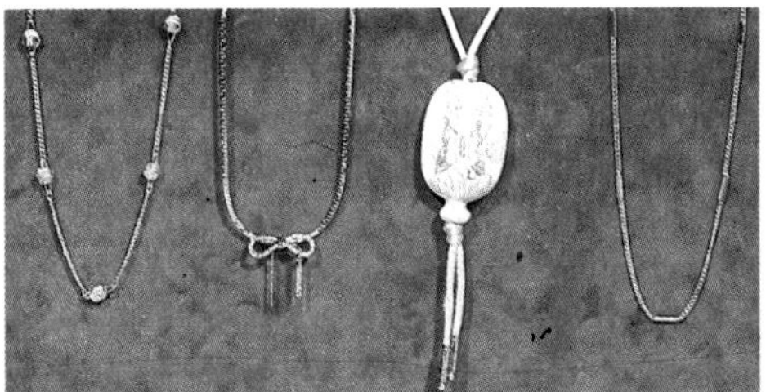

1979 *Delicate Knot, Silvertone (1) $9.50* **MP $7**
1979 *Fashion Bow $14.50* **MP $12**
1979 *Tender Butterfly Ceramic $10.50* **MP $8**
1979 *Delicate Strand, Goldtone or Silvertone $11.50* **MP $9**

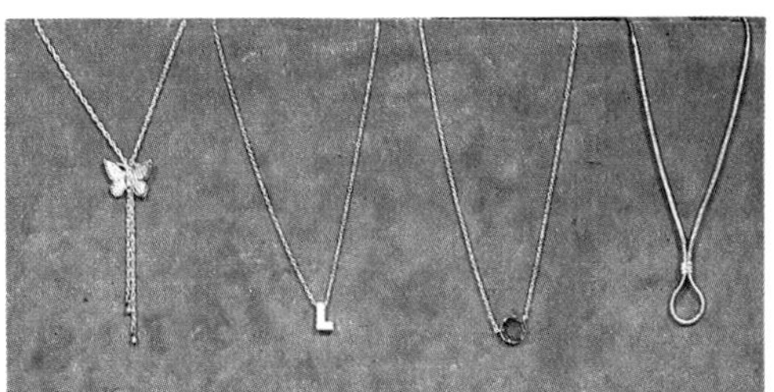

1979 *Butterfly Lariat $13.50* **MP $11**
1979 *Initial Attraction $9.50* **MP $7**
1979 *Burgundy Wine (5) $8.50* **MP $6**
1979 *Shimmering Loop (2) $11.50* **MP $9**

1979 *Crystal Droplets (1) $14.50* **MP $12**
1979 *Florette Lariat $12.50* **MP $10**
1979 *Royal Highlights $12.50* **MP $10**
1979 *Whispering Leaves $12.50* **MP $10**

1980 *Captured Heart $11.50* **MP $9**
1980 *Royal Impression $14.50* **MP $12**
1980 *Seashine Drop (1) $10.50* **MP $8**
1980 *Spectator Style, Black or White (1) $13.50* **MP $11**

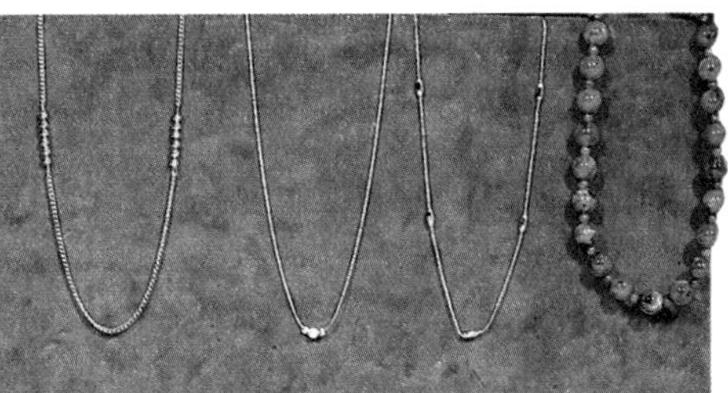

1980 *Gilded Complement (1) $13.50* **MP $11**
1980 *Cultured Pearl Sterling Silver (5) $40* **MP $30**
1980 *Silken Bead, Goldtone or Silvertone (2) $11.50* **MP $9**
1980 *Fashion Lustre Beads, Jade or Ivory (1) $10.50* **MP $8**

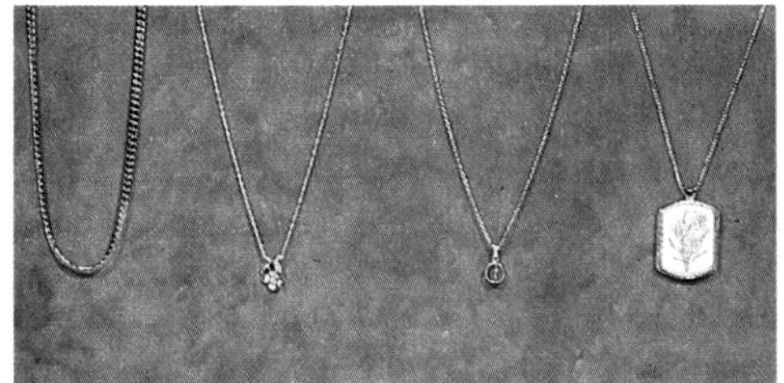

1980 *Perfect Accent (2) $13.50* **MP $11**
1980 *Dogwood Blossom $11.50* **MP $9**
1980 *Captivating Beauty, Carnelian or Blue Agate (short issue) $10.50* **MP $10**
1980 *Floral Heritage $19.50* **MP $17**

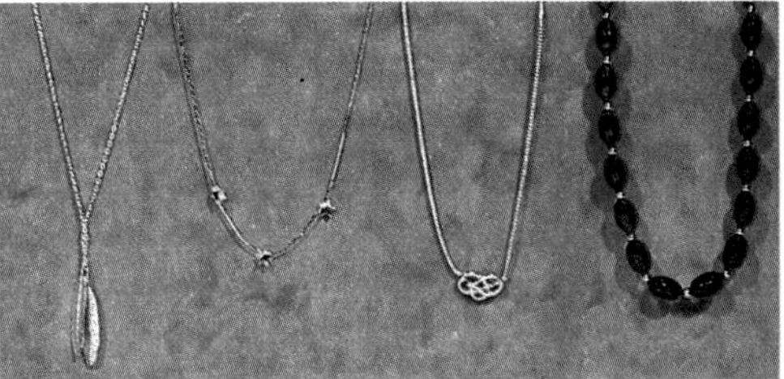

1980 *Feather Flurry Lariat (1) $15.50* **MP $13**
1980 *Tracy Austin Rising Star (1) $16.50* **MP $14**
1980 *Love Knot Choker $14.50* **MP $12**
1980 *Turtle Bay Beaded (1) $13.50* **MP $11**

1980 *Turtle Bay Slide (1) $20.50* **MP $18**
1980 *Essential Accent $10.50* **MP $8**
1980 *14k gold filled Rose Pendant (1) $50* **MP $39***
1980 *Glowing Bells $10.50* **MP $8**

1980 *Pearlessence (1) $49.50* **MP $35**
1980 *Sterling Silver Heart $50* **MP $39***
1980 *Color Essence, Carnelian, Onyx or Lapis Lazuli $14.50* **MP $12**
1980 *14k gold filled Neckchain $45* **MP $35***

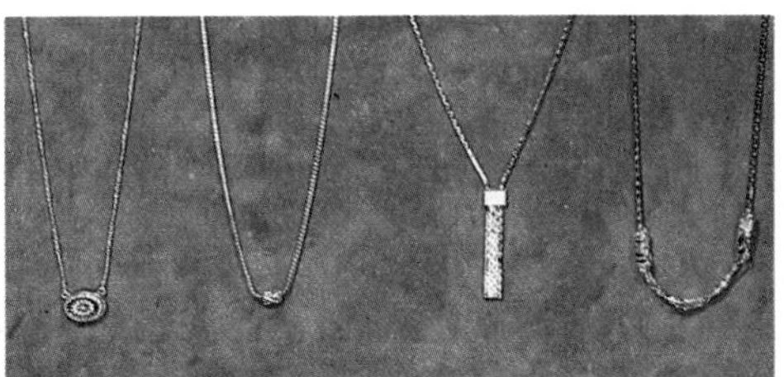

1980 *Snow Fantasy (1) $13.50* **MP $10***
1980 *14k gold filled and Sterling Silver Kiss (2) $55* **MP $45***
1980 *Glimmering Slide $26.50* **MP $23**
1980 *Subtle Shimmer (1) $15.50* **MP $13**

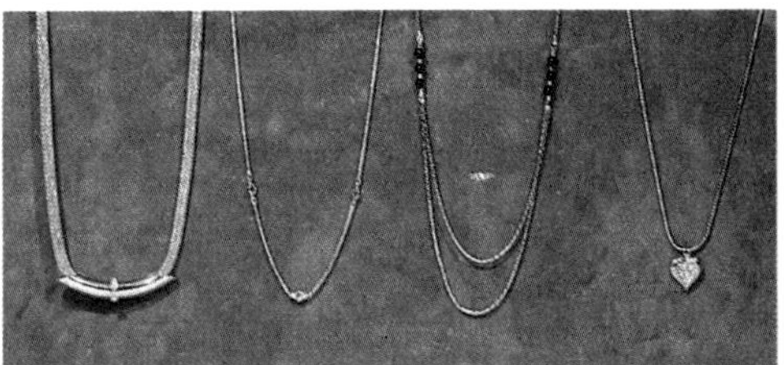

1980 *Woven Beauty Convertible $22.50* **MP $17***
1980 *Birthstone Trio $11.50* **MP $10***
1981 *Personal Style $17.50* **MP $15**
1981 *Pave Heart $17.50* **MP $13***

** Available from Avon at time of publication*

Matching jewelry: (1) Earrings (2) Bracelet (3) Ring (4) Earrings & Bracelet (5) Earrings & Ring (6) Bracelet & Ring (7) Bracelet, Earrings & Ring (8) Pin

1975 *Cameo Princess Necklace (3) $6* **MP $6**
1975 *Secret Garden Necklace (2) $6* **MP $6**
1976 *Flopsy Pendant Necklace $6* **MP $6**

1976 *Secret Heart Locket (2) $7* **MP $7**
1976 *Kelly Star Necklace, Gold or Silver $6* **MP $5**
1977 *Dancing Ballerina $6* **MP $5**

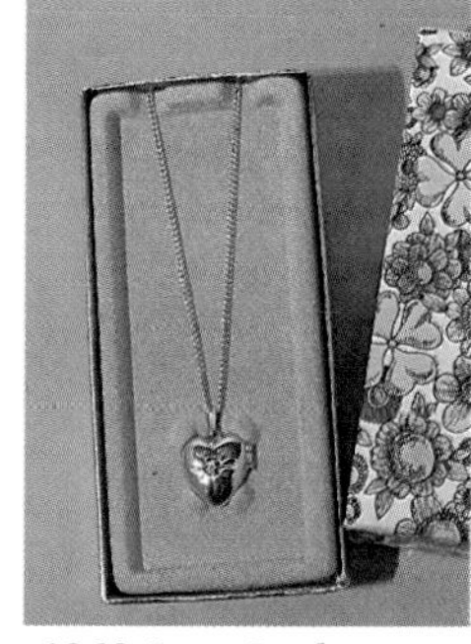

1969 *Love Locket Fragrance Glace $4.50* **MP $12**

1965 *Peach Necklace (from Peach Delight Set)* **MP $25**

GIRL'S JEWELRY

1977 *Tender Heart Birthstone Pendant, choice of 12 colored stones $7.50* **MP $6**
1978 *Swing Sweetly Pendant $7.50* **MP $5**
1978 *Playful Angel $7.50* **MP $6**
1979 *Sweet Hearts, 3 plastic hearts $7.50* **MP $6**

1979 *Darling Ducklings $9* **MP $7**
1979 *Candy Apple (5) $8* **MP $6**
1980 *Love Dove $8.50* **MP $6**
1980 *Tender Memories $11.50* **MP $9**

1972 *Love Locket Perfume Glace, Charisma 1/8oz $4* **MP $13**
1974 *Sunny Fresh Orange Necklace. Plastic holds .04oz orange scented glace $4* **MP $5**

1973 *Genny Giraffe Necklace $1.75* **MP $3**

1976 *Put on the Dog Pendant $6.50* **MP $6**
1979 *Skateboard Pendant $7.50* **MP $6**
1979 *Fast Track Pendant $8.50* **MP $7**

1976 *Class of 77 Pendant $7* **MP $9**
1977 *Class of 78 Pendant $7.50* **MP $9**
1978 *Class of 79 Pendant $9.50* **MP $8**

1981 *Teddy Bear Pin on Card $6.50* **MP $4***

. . . FOR BOYS AND GIRLS

1979 *Winning Combination Pendant $9* **MP $7**
1979 *Galactic Robot Neckchain $8* **MP $6**
1980 *Mr. Snowman Pendant $9.50* **MP $7**

1980 *Command Module I Neckchain $9.50* **MP $7***
1981 *Top Hit Pendant $11.50* **MP $8***
1981 *Perfect Catch Pendant Neckchain $11.50* **MP $8***

1981 *Three Little Dollies Earring Tree $5* **MP $3***

**Available from Avon at time of publication*

Matching jewelry: (1) Earrings (2) Bracelet (3) Ring (4) Earrings & Bracelet (5) Earrings & Ring (6) Bracelet & Ring (7) Bracelet, Earrings & Ring (8) Pin

Pin Pals – Fragrance Glace each .02oz
1973 *Calico Cat $2.50* **MP $4,** *Blue* **MP $4**
1973 *Elphie $2.50* **MP $5**
1973 *Blue Moo $2.50* **MP $4**
1973 *Funny Bunny $2.50* **MP $4**

Here are the bright spots — pin glaces, called . . .

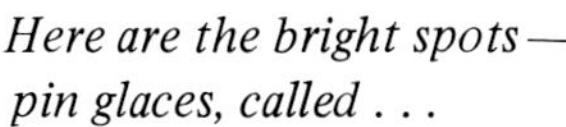

– little girls' jewelry that looks all grown-up. A little girls' fragrance glace hides in a decorative container she will delight in wearing.

Small World –
1970 *Polynesian Pin Pal Perfume Glace $2.50* **MP $7**
1971 *Scandinavian Miss Pin Pal Perfume Glace $2.50* **MP $7**

Pin Pals – Fragrance Glace each .02oz

Pin Pals – Fragrance Glace each .02oz
1972 *Sniffy $2.50* **MP $5**
1971 *Blouse Mouse $2.50* **MP $5** *(pink trim),* **MP $7** *(white trim)*
1972 *Gingerbread Man (white trim) $2.50* **MP $5**
1976 *Gingerbread Man (pink trim) $3.50* **MP $3**

1974 *Wee Willy Winter $3* **MP $4**
1974 *Willy the Worm $3* **MP $4**
1974 *Lickety Stick Mouse Pin (not a Pin Pal Glace) $1.75* **MP $3**
1975 *Chicken Little $3.50* **MP $4**
1975 *Puppy Love $4* **MP $4**

Pins – **1973** *Fly-A-Kite $2.25* **MP $4**
1973 *Luv-A-Ducky $2.50* **MP $4**
1973 *Fuzzy Bug $2.25* **MP $4**
1973 *Perky Parrot $2.25* **MP $4**
1973 *Bumbly Bee $2.25* **MP $4**

1975 *Magic Rabbit Pin $2.50* **MP $3**
1975 *Pedal Pusher Pin $2.25* **MP $3**
1975 *Peter Patches Pin Pal Fragrance Glace .02oz $3.50* **MP $4**
1975 *Bobbin' Robin Pin $2.50* **MP $3**

Pin Pals – Fragrance Glace each .02oz
1975 *Rock-A-Roo $3.50* **MP $3**
1976 *Jack-In-The-Box $3.50* **MP $3**
1976 *Cottontail $3.50* **MP $3**
1977 *Chick-A-Peep $3.50* **MP $3**

1973 *Pandy Bear Pin $2.25* **MP $4**
1974 *Rapid Rabbit Pin Pal Glace .02oz $3* **MP $3.50**
1974 *Minute Mouse Pin $2.50* **MP $3**
1974 *Myrtle Turtle Pin Pal Glace .02oz $2.50* **MP $4**

1946 *Lullabye Baby Set. Baby Soap, Cream, Oil and Talc and Baby Gift Card $3.55* **MP $150** *(Sold individually: Boxed Soap 69¢* **MP $25;** *Baby Oil $1* **MP $50;** *Baby Cream 89¢* **MP $20;** *Talc 65¢* **MP $20)**

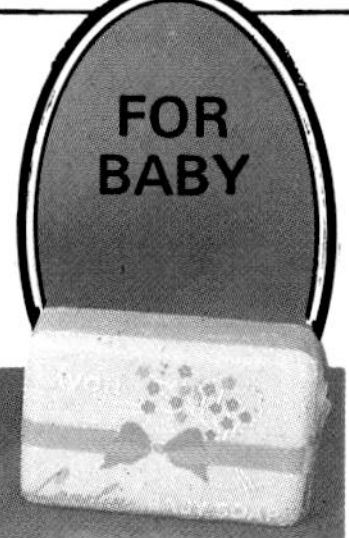

1946 *Lanolin Baby Soap (1 cake shown) 86¢ for box of two cakes* **MP $45 for boxed set of 2 cakes, $18 one cake**

1951 *Baby Soap, Lanolin Two 3¼oz cakes 69¢* **MP $25**
1955 *Baby Soap, Castile with Lanolin 29¢* **MP $14**

1952 *Lullabye Baby Set. Baby Soap 3¼oz, Baby Talc and 4oz Baby Lotion $2.35* **MP $75**

1953 *Bo Peep Soap Set. Three molded lamb Soaps $1* **MP $75**

1954 *Little Lambs Set. 2 molded Soaps and 2oz Baby Powder $1.25* **MP $75,** *Baby Powder Container only* **MP $20**

1955 *Lullabye Set. Baby Oil 8oz and Baby Powder 9oz $1.39* **MP $60**

1958 *Baby Lotion 6oz 98¢* **MP $10**
1955 *Baby Powder 9oz 59¢* **MP $15**
1955 *Baby Oil 8oz 79¢* **MP $20**

1957 *Baby and Me. Baby Lotion 8oz and Cotillion Toilet Water 2oz $1.98* **MP $60**

1962 *Sweetest One. Baby Powder 9oz, Baby Oil 6oz and Soap $2.07* **MP $40 (1961** *Set with same items, but soap wrapper is white with blue center band* **MP $42)**

1962 *Baby Cream 2oz 89¢* **MP $7**
1955 *Baby Soap, Castile with Lanolin 29¢* **MP $15**
1960 only *Tot 'n' Tyke Baby Shampoo 6oz 89¢* **MP $15**
with light blue cap

1966 *Tree Tots. Hair Brush, Nursery Fresh Room Spray, Non-Tear Shampoo and Soap $3.98* **MP $28**

1964 *Lullabye Set. Baby Lotion 6oz, 2 Baby Soaps 3oz each $1.76* **MP $25, Soaps $7 ea.**

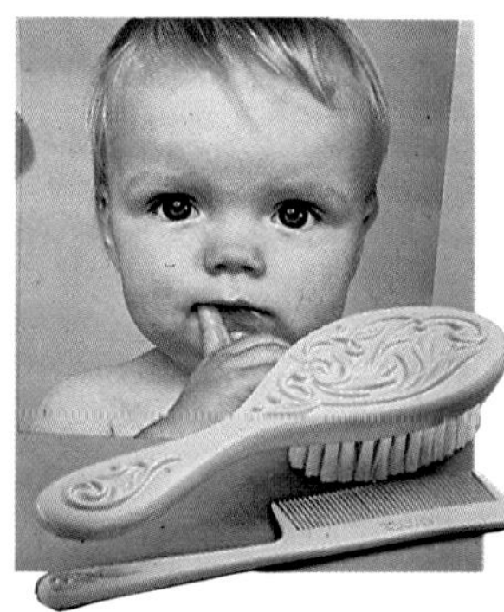

1974 *Baby Brush and Comb Set. Brush 6" long, comb 5" long $3.50* **MP $4**

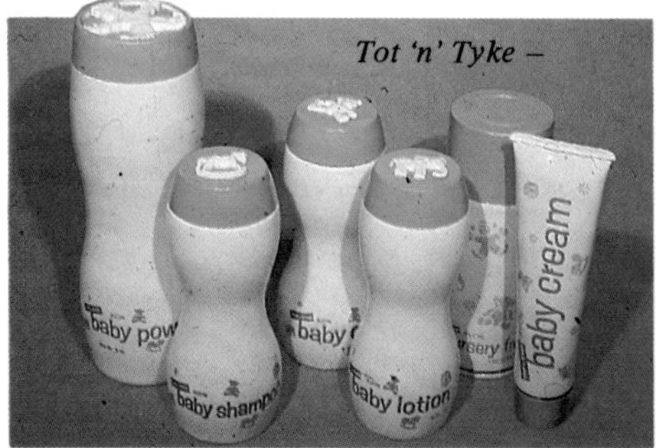

Tot 'n' Tyke –

1964 *Baby Powder 9oz 98¢* **MP $6**
1964 *Baby Shampoo 6oz 98¢* **MP $6**
1964 *Baby Oil 6oz 98¢* **MP $7**
1964 *Baby Lotion 6oz 98¢* **MP $6**
1965 *Nursery Fresh Spray 6oz $1.35* **MP $4**
1964 *Baby Cream 2oz 98¢* **MP $4**

1969 *Baby Powder 9oz 98¢* **MP $2**
1969 *Nursery Fresh Room Spray 6oz $1.50* **MP $2**
1969 *Baby Shampoo 6oz 98¢* **MP $2**
1969 *Baby Lotion 6oz 98¢* **MP $2**
1969 *Baby Cream 2oz 98¢* **MP $2**
1969 *Baby Soap 3oz 59¢* **MP $3**

Clearly Gentle –
1975 *Baby Lotion 10oz $2.50* **MP $1**
1975 *Liquid Cleanser 10oz $2.50* **MP $1**
1975 *Nursery Spray 7oz $1.98* **MP $2**

1973 *Sunny Bunny Baby Pomander 5oz $6* **MP $7**
1973 *Safety Pin Decanter Baby Lotion 8oz $4* **MP $4**
1973 *Baby Shoe Pin Cushion Baby Lotion 7oz $5* **MP $6**

1954 *Three Little Bears, 3 molded castile Soaps $1.19* **MP $65**

1955 *Away in a Manger, 4 molded Soaps $1.49* **MP $80**

CHILDREN'S SOAPS AND SOAP SETS

1974 *Honey Bear Baby Cream Decanter 4oz $5* **MP $5**
1974 *Precious Lamb Baby Lotion 6oz $5* **MP $5**
1980 *Rock-A-Bye Baby hanging pomander. Nursery Fresh fragrance $8.50* **MP $7**

1955 *Kiddie Kennel, 3 molded Soaps $1.49* **MP $65**

1956 *Best Friend molded Soap 59¢* **MP $40**

1974 *Jack-in-the-Box Baby Cream 4oz $5* **MP $5**
1975 *Rock-A-Bye Pony 6oz Clearly Gentle Baby Lotion $5* **MP $4**

1955 *Santa's Helpers, 3 molded Soaps $1.19* **MP $65**

1956 *Santa's Helpers. 3 molded Soaps $1.19* **MP $65**

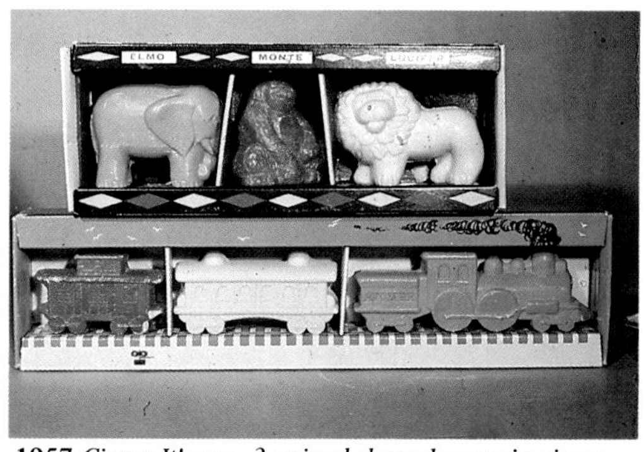

1975 *Non-Tear Shampoo 12oz (deer) $2.49* **MP $1**
1975 *Creme Hair Rinse 12oz (rabbit) $1.69* **MP $1**
1975 *Bubble Bath 12oz (swan) $2.19* **MP $1**

1957 *Circus Wagon. 3 animal shaped soaps in circus wagon box $1.25* **MP $70**
1956 *Casey Jones, Jr., 3 soaps boxed $1.19* **MP $70**

1958 *"Old 99" Train engine Soap 59¢* **MP $40**
1957 *Fire Engine No. 5 Soap 59¢* **MP $40**

1958 *Texas Sheriff. 2 molded soap guns and metal badge $1.19* **MP $55**

1958 *Forward Pass. Football Soap-On-a-Rope 7½oz $1* **MP $35**

1959 *Pool Paddlers, 3 soaps $1.39* **MP $37**

Fun to see and fun to use, are these child-sized novelty soap sculptures. Adorable companions, designed for both child and collector appeal.

1962 *"Watch the Birdie" Soap-On-a-Rope $1.19* **MP $22**
1962 *Sheriff's Badge Soap-On-a-Rope $1.19* **MP $24**

1960 *Frilly Duck Soap 5¾oz 89¢* **MP $21**
1962 *L'il Tom Turtle Soap 5½oz 98¢* **MP $22**
1965 *Mr. Monkey Soap 5½oz $1.35* **MP $15**

1963 *Life Preserver Soap-On-a-Rope 6oz $1.19* **MP $20**
1964 *Sea Biscuit Soap-On-a-Rope $1.25* **MP $18**
1971 *Al E Gator Soap-On-a-Rope 5oz $2* **MP $8**

1965 *First Down Set. Junior size rubber Football and Football Soap-On-a-Rope 6oz $3.95* **MP $45, $15 Soap, $18 Football**

1965 *Gingerbread Soap Twins. Two 2½oz bars and 2 plastic cookie cutters $1.50* **MP $27**
1965 *Hansel and Gretel Soaps in box 3oz each. Set $1.35* **MP $25**

1966 *Papa Bear Baby Oil 3oz $1.25* **MP $11**
1966 *Baby Bear Tot 'n' Tyke Shampoo 3oz $1.25* **MP $10**
1966 *Mama Bear Baby Lotion 3oz* **MP $10**
1966 *Goldilocks molded Baby Soap 5oz* **MP $13**

1962 *A Hit. Baseball Soap on a cord $1.19* **MP $20**
1969 *Mighty Mitt French milled Soap 4oz $2* **MP $8**
1973 *Football Helmet Soap-On-a-Rope 5oz $2.50* **MP $5**

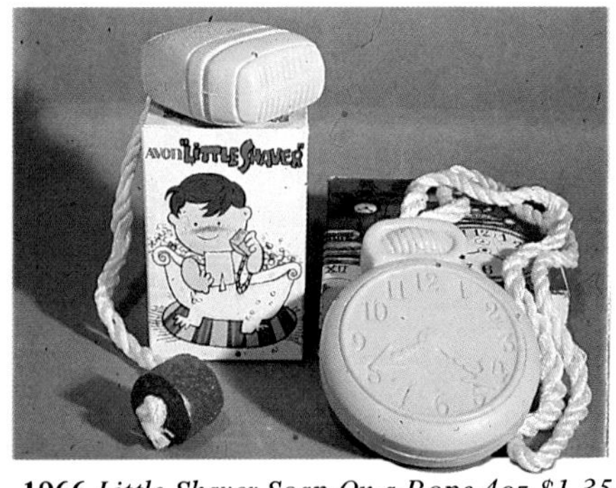

1966 *Little Shaver Soap-On-a-Rope 4oz $1.35* **MP $22**
1961 *Li'l Folks Time Alarm Clock Soap-On-a-Rope 5½oz $1.19* **MP $24**

1966 *Yo Yo Set. Yo Yo and Soap 3oz $1.50* **MP $26, $10 each Yo Yo and Soap**
1966 *Sunny the Sunfish Soap-On-a-Rope $1.35* **MP $16**

1966 *Speedy the Snail Soap-On-a-Rope 4oz $1.35* **MP $18**
1973 *Hooty & Tooty Tugboat Soaps 2oz each $1.75* **MP $6**

1969 *Modeling Soap 6oz $2* **MP $7**
1966 *Chick-A-Dee Soap-On-a-Rope $1.35* **MP $12**

1967 *Bunny Dream Soap-On-a-Rope $1.25* **MP $20**
1969 *Easter Bonnet Bunny Soap 5oz $1.35* **MP $8**
1970 *Peep-A-Boo Soap 5oz $1.35* **MP $8**

1969 *Mitten Kittens, 3 bars Soap 1-7/8oz each $1.50* **MP $10**
1968 *Ruff, Tuff and Muff Soaps in box 1½oz each. Set $1.35* **MP $10**

1973 *Petunia Piglet Soap-On-a-Rope 5oz $2.50* **MP $6**
1968 *Easter Quacker Soap-On-a-Rope 5oz $1.35* **MP $10**
1969 *Yankee Doodle Soap 6oz $2* **MP $10**

1969 *Tub Racers. Three 3oz Soaps $1.75* **MP $10**
1971 *Aristocrat Kittens Soap Trio. Each 1½oz $2* **MP $7**

1971 *Tweetster's Soaps. Three 1½oz Soaps $2* **MP $7**
1970 *Tub Racers. Three 3oz Soaps $2* **MP $6**

1971 *Three Nice Mice. Three Soaps each 2oz $2* **MP $6**
1973 *Sure Winner. Three Snow Buggy Soaps each 2oz $2.25* **MP $5**

1972 *Blue Moo Soap-On-a-Rope 5oz $1.75* **MP $6**
1972 *Percy Pelican Soap-On-a-Rope 5oz $2* **MP $6**
1971 *Honey Lamb Soap-On-a-Rope 5oz 99¢* **MP $6**

1974 *Tubby Tigers Soap Set. 2oz each $3.50* **MP $4**
1974 *Wilbur the Whale Soap-On-a-Rope 5oz $2.50* **MP $4**
1978 *Furry, Purry, Scurry. Three 2oz Soaps $5* **MP $5**

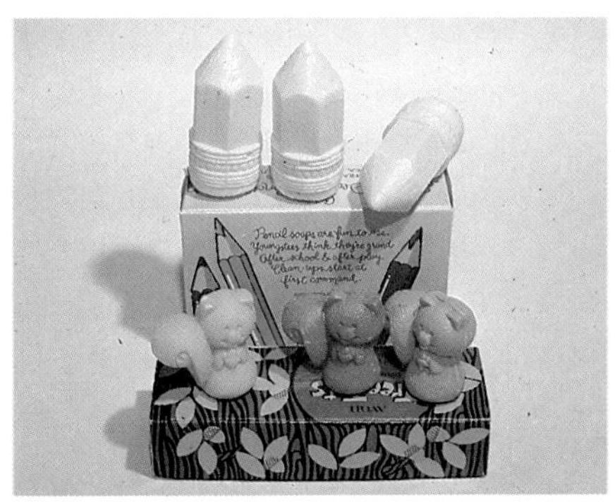

1980 *Scribble Dee-Doo, three 2.5oz pencil-shaped Soaps $6* **MP $5**
1970 *Tree Tots, three 1.5oz squirrel-shaped Soaps $1.75* **MP $8**

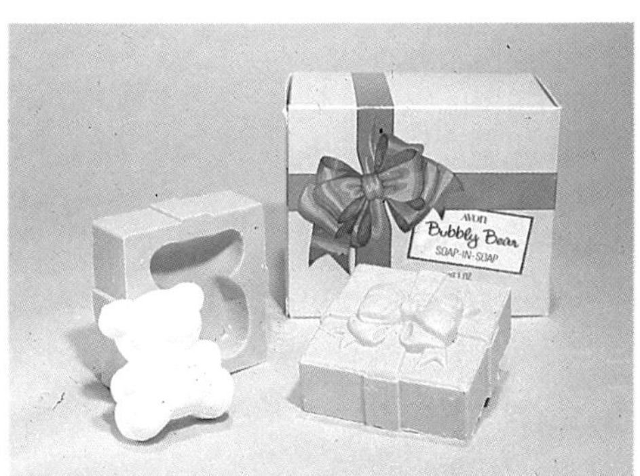

1980 *Bubbly Bear Soap-In-Soap, three 2oz Soaps $7.50* **MP $6**

1966 *Ring-Around-Rosie. Elephant's trunk holds 3oz Soap $2.25* **MP $20**

1973 Clancey the Clown Soap Holder and Soap 3oz $4.50 **MP $6**

1974 *Hooper the Hound Soap Holder and Soap 3oz $5* **MP $6**

1965 *Freddie the Frog Soap 3oz $1.75* **MP $15**
1969 *Freddie the Frog floating Soap Dish and 3oz Soap (right) $2.50* **MP $6**

1966 *Wash Aweigh floating Soap Dish and 3oz anchor-shaped Soap-On-a-Rope $1.98* **MP $20**

1967 *Gaylord Gator. 9½" long, holds 3oz Soap $2.25* **MP $7**
1966 *Perry the Penguin Floating Soap Dish and Soap $1.98* **MP $17, $7 Penguin, $10 Soap**

1970 *Reginald G. Racoon III Soap 3oz and Floating Soap Dish 7" long $2.50* **MP $7**

1972 *Randy Pandy Floating Soap Dish and Soap 3oz $3.50* **MP $6**
1974 *Quack and Doodle Floating Soap Dish and Soap 3oz $4.50* **MP $5**

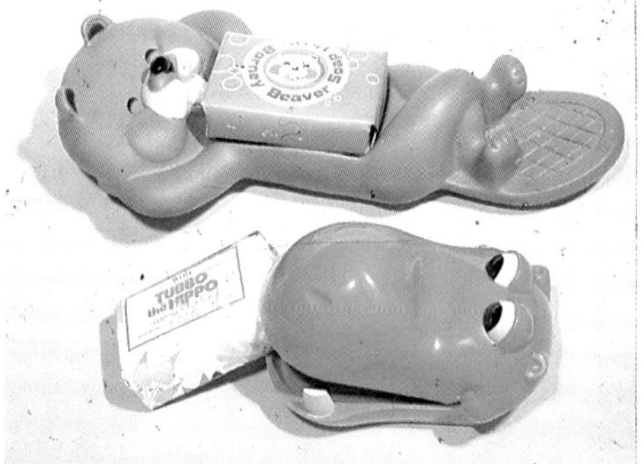

1971 *Barney Beaver Soap Dish and 3oz Soap $3.50* **MP $6**
1979 *Tubbo the Hippo Soap Dish and 3oz Soap $6.50* **MP $5**

1972 *Soap Boat Floating Soap Dish & Soap 3oz $3* **MP $7**

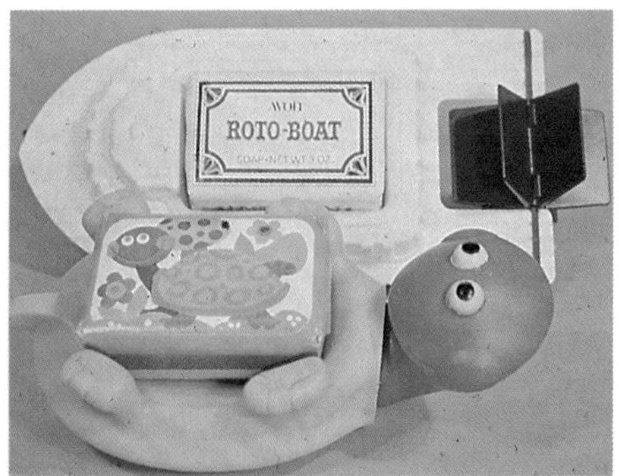

1973 *Roto-Boat Soap Dish and Soap 3oz $3.75* **MP $4**
1973 *Topsy Turtle Floating Soap Dish and Soap 3oz $3.75* **MP $4**

1975 *Paddlewog Frog Floating Soap Dish and 3oz Soap $6* **MP $5**
1977 *Terrible Tubbles 3oz Soap $5.50* **MP $4**

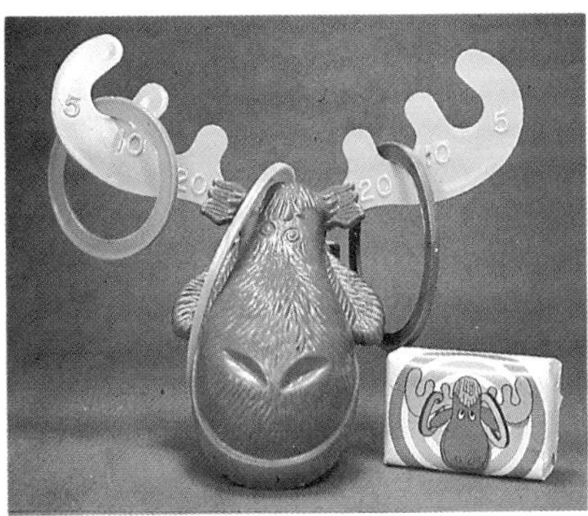

1972 *Loop-A-Moose with Soap 3oz $3.50* **MP $6**

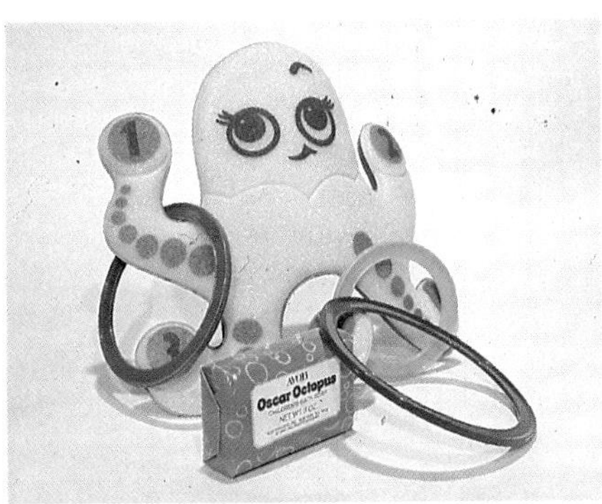

1980 *Oscar Octopus Ring Toss Game with 3 plastic rings and 3oz Soap $7* **MP $5**

1965 *Minnie the Moo Sponge Puppet and Soap 3oz $1.75* **MP $15**
1966 *Little Pro Soap 'n' Sponge. Mitt Sponge and Soap 6oz $2.25* **MP $13**

1967 *Nest Egg Soap 'n' Sponge 3oz $2.25* **MP $13**
1966 *Spongaroo. Kangaroo foam Sponge and Baby Ru Soap 3oz $2.25* **MP $15**

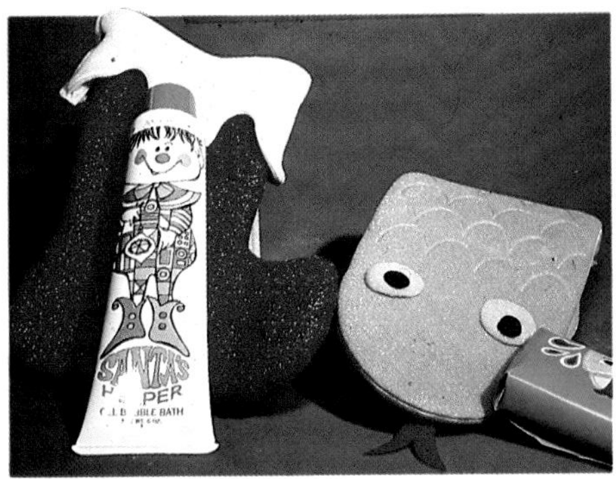

1967 *Santa's Helper Xmas stocking Sponge and tube of Gel Bubble Bath 6oz $2.50* **MP $13**
1968 *Clarence the Sea Serpent Puppet Sponge and 3oz Soap $2.25* **MP $8**

1969 *Parrot Puppet Sponge and Soap 3oz $3* **MP $7**
1969 *Monkey Shines Puppet Sponge and Soap 3oz $3* **MP $7**

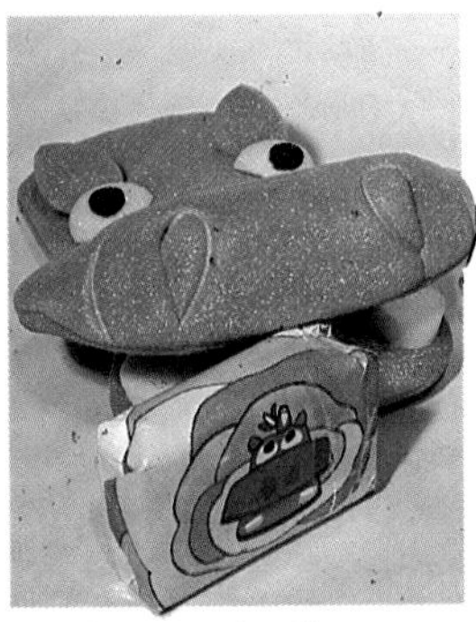

1970 *Hubie the Hippo Sponge and 3oz Soap $4* **MP $7**

1971 *Clean Shot Basketball shaped Sponge and 3oz Soap $4.50* **MP $8**

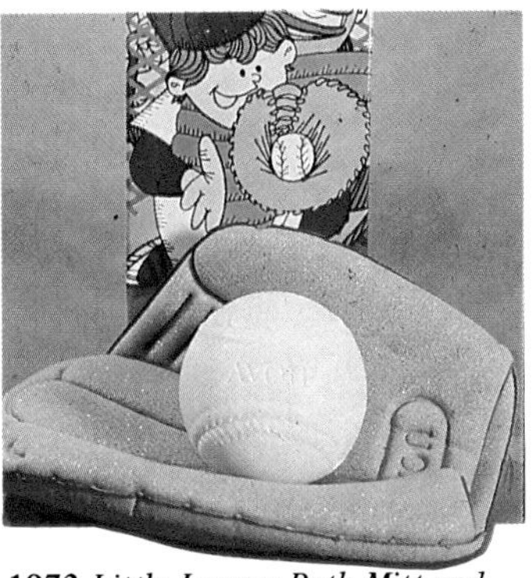

1973 *Little League Bath Mitt and Soap 3oz $3* **MP $6**

1973 *Cedric Sea Serpent Puppet Sponge and Soap 3oz $3* **MP $5**
1973 *Soapy the Whale Bath Mitt and Soap 3oz $3* **MP $5**

1974 *Good Habit Rabbit Bath Mitt and Soap 3oz $3.50* **MP $4**

1978 *Misterjaw Bath Mitt and 3oz Soap $6.50* **MP $5**
1977 *Pink Panther Sponge and Soap 3oz $6* **MP $5**

1980 *Spider-Man Sponge Mitt and 3oz Soap $6.50* **MP $5**

1972 *Happy Hippos Nail Brush and Soap 2oz $3* **MP $4**
1972 *Hydrojet Scrub Brush and Soap 2oz $2.50* **MP $4**
1973 *Pig-In-a-Tub Nail Brush and Soap 2oz $2.75* **MP $4**

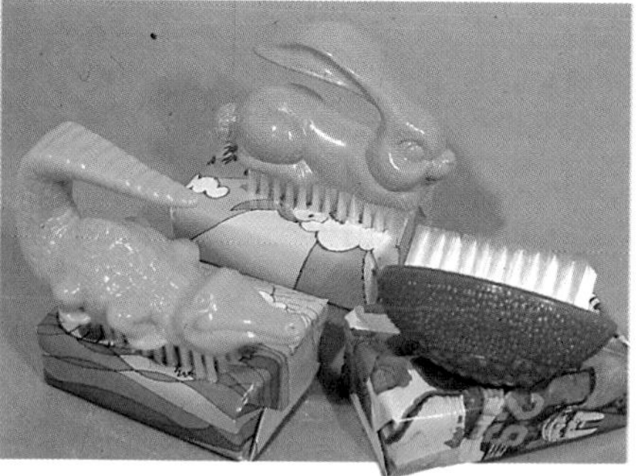

1974 *Gaylord Gator Scrub Brush and Soap 3oz $3.50* **MP $4**
1974 *Good Habit Rabbit Nail Brush and Soap 3oz $3.50* **MP $4**
1975 *Gridiron Scrub Brush and 3oz Soap $4* **MP $4**

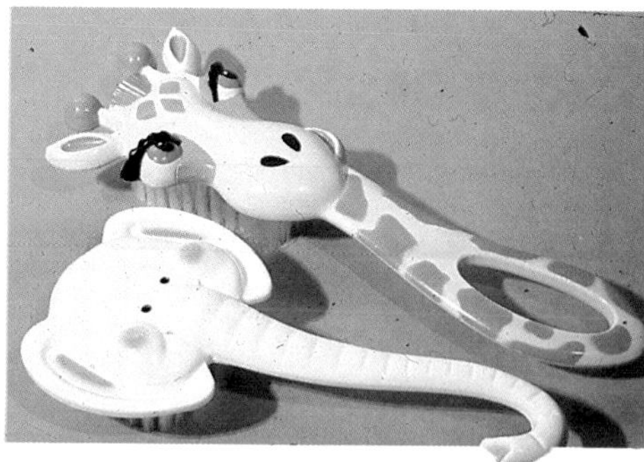

1976 *Giraffabath Bath Brush $6* **MP $5**
1974 *Scrubbo the Elephant Bath Brush $5* **MP $5**

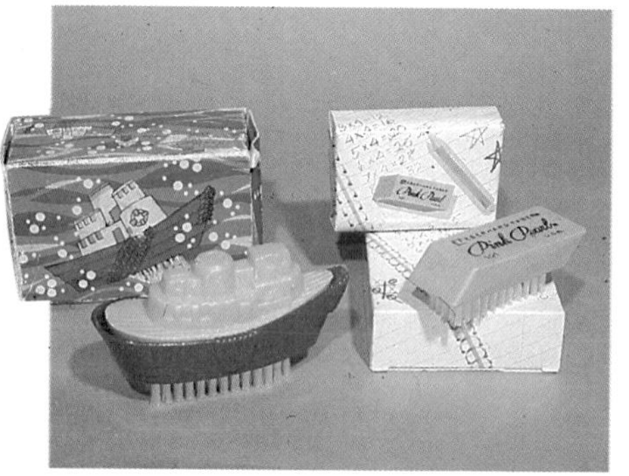

1971 *Scrub Tub Nail Brush and Soap 2oz $2.50* **MP $5**
1977 *Scrub Away Nail Brush and Soap 3oz $4* **MP $4**

1972 *Grid Kid Comb and Brush $3.50* **MP $5**
1972 *Reggie Raccoon Brush and Comb $3.50* **MP $5**

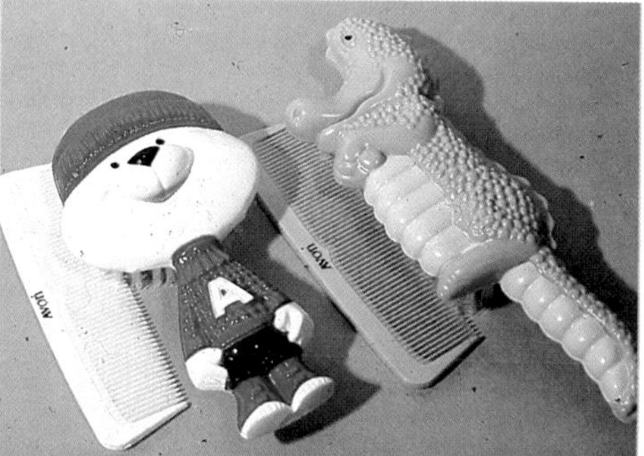

1974 *Arch E. Bear Brush and Comb $4* **MP $4**
1974 *Al E. Gator Brush and Comb $4* **MP $4**

1975 *Hot Dog! Brush and Comb $5* **MP $5**
1976 *Shaggy Dog Comb $2.50* **MP $2.50**
1976 *School Days Ruler Comb $3* **MP $3**

1974 *Slugger Hairbrush 7" long $4* **MP $4**
1975 *Curly Caterpillar Comb 6" long $2* **MP $2**

1977 *Cub Scout Knife Brush and Comb $6* **MP $6**
1973 *Jackknife Brush and Comb $4.50* **MP $5**

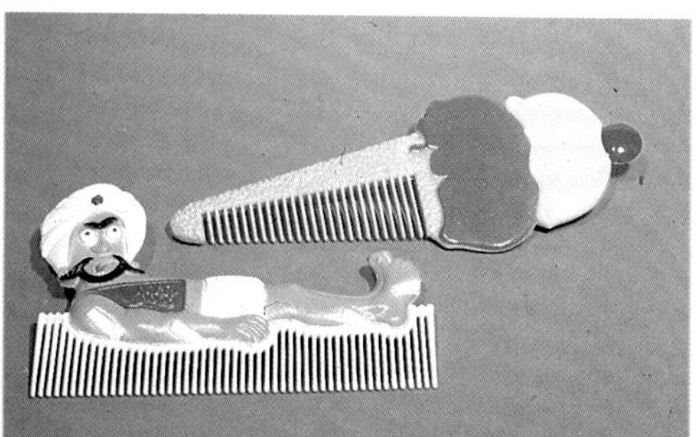

1977 *Ice Cream Comb $3* **MP $3**
1978 *Bed of Nails Comb $3.50* **MP $3**

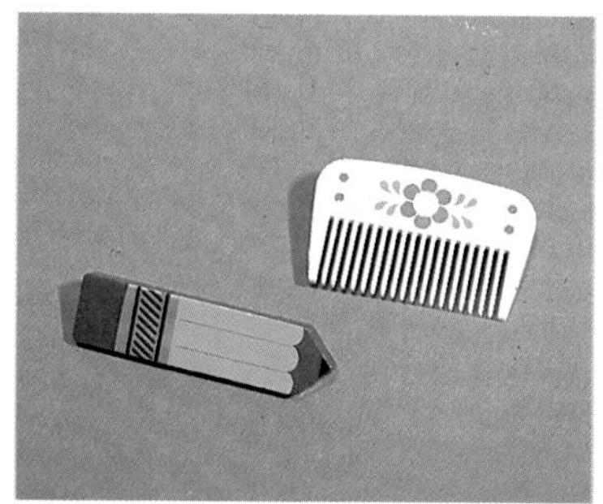

1973 *School Days Barrette $1.50* **MP $2**
1973 *Comb Barrette $2* **MP $2**

1979 *Combsicle Comb $3* **MP $3**
1981 *Good Habit Rabbit Brush and Comb, Both, 5½" long $6.50* **MP $6***

* *Available from Avon at time of publication*

1979 *Imp the Chimp Bath Brush $8.50* **MP $7**

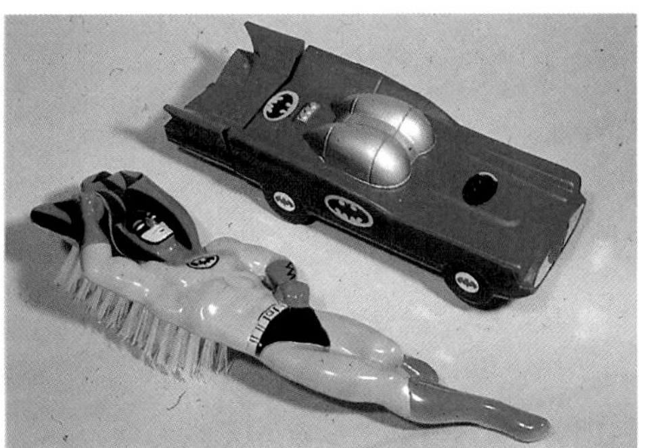

1977 *Batman Styling Brush $6* **MP $5**
1978 *Batmobile Bubble Bath 6oz with decals $6.50* **MP $5**

1976 *Superman Styling Brush 8½" long $6* **MP $5**
1978 *Superman Bubble Bath 6oz $8* **MP $7**
1978 *Wonder Woman Mirror 7½" $7.50* **MP $6**

1973 *I Love Toofie Toothbrush Holder and 2 Brushes $2.75* **MP $5**

1974 *Ted. E. Bear Toothbrush Holder and 2 Brushes $2.75* **MP $4**

1976 *Toofie Tiger Toothbrush Holder and 2 Brushes $3.50* **MP $4**

1974 *Toofie Train, Tube of Toofie Toothpaste, 2 Toothbrushes and a plastic Cup $6* **MP $7**

1973 *Barney Beaver Toothbrush Holder and 2 Brushes $2.75* **MP $5**
1979 *Spider-Man Toothbrush Holder and 2 Brushes $6* **MP $6**

1976 *Spotty to the Rescue Toothbrush Holder and 2 Brushes $3.75* **MP $4**

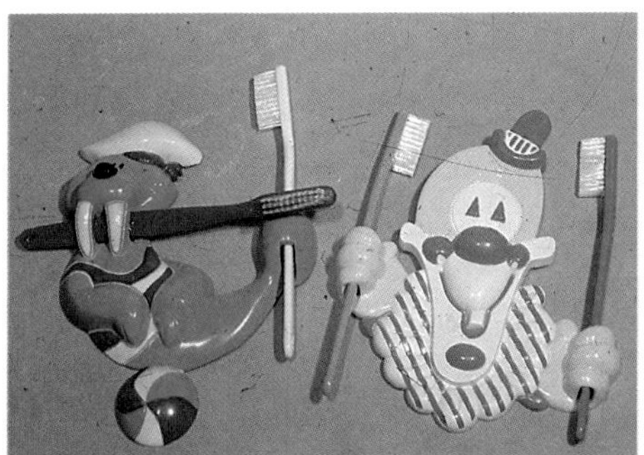

1977 *Wally Walrus Toothbrush Holder and 2 Brushes $4* **MP $4**
1978 *Toofie the Clown Toothbrush Holder and 2 Brushes $4.50* **MP $4**

1980 *Smiley Snail Toothbrush Holder and 2 Brushes $7.50* **MP $6**

1980 *Tuggable Teddy moveable Toothbrush Holder and 2 Brushes $6.50* **MP $5**

1966 *Toofie Tiger Twosome Toothpaste 3.5oz and Brush $1.35* **MP $10**

Toothpaste/Toothbrush Sets 3½oz –
1967 *Toofie (Raccoon design) magenta toothbrush $1.25* **MP $8**
1964 *Toofie Twosome (Clown design) red, blue or green toothbrush $1.25* **MP $12**
1968 *Toofie on Guard, green toothbrush $1.25* **MP $7**
1969 *Toofie (Hi Diddle Diddle design) red toothbrush $1.35* **MP $6**
1970 *Toofie Toothbrush (Giraffe and Bunny design) 3.5oz 89¢* **MP $5**

TOOFIE

1965 *Children's Toothbrush Trio Pak, red, yellow and green toothbrushes $1.25* **MP $8 boxed**

(See also Toofie Duo pg. 222)

SWEET PICKLES†

- each character comes in a "house" carton and the cartons form a Sweet Pickles town.

1978 *Accusing Alligator Bubble Bath 6oz $8* **MP $6**
1978 *Loving Lion Non-Tear Shampoo 6oz $8* **MP $6**

1978 *Fun Books and Records. Each "All About..." book 11x7" with a built-in sing-along record $2.50 each* **MP $3**
Yakety Yak Yak hard cover book **MP $3**
1978 *Pick a Pack Puzzles. Three Sweet Pickles puzzles 25¢ with any Sweet Pickles purchase during C-20-78 only* **MP $1 in sealed package** *(front)*

1978 *Outraged Octopus Toothbrush Holder and 2 Brushes, red and white $5.50* **MP $5**
1978 *Zany Zebra Hair Brush 7½" $6.50* **MP $5**
1979 *Fearless Fish Sponge Mask and Soap 3oz $6.50* **MP $6**

1979 *Worried Walrus Sponge Mitt and Soap 3oz $6.50* **MP $5**
1978 *Yakety Yak Taxi Sponge and Soap 3oz $6.50* **MP $5**

† Characters © Perle/Reinach/Hefter 1979

PEANUTS

Happiness is a complete collection of these loveable little characters from Avon.

© PEANUTS Characters: 1950, 1951, 1952, 1958, 1965 United Features Syndicate, Inc.

1968 *Snoopy Soap Dish and Soap 3oz $3* **MP $6**
1968 *A Colorful Story of Charlie Brown. Coloring Books sold to Representatives only* **MP $3**

1969 *Charlie Brown Bath Mitt & Soap 3oz $3* **MP $7**
1971 *Charlie Brown Brush & Comb $3.50* **MP $6**

1968 *Linus Bubble Bath Holder with Gel Bubble Bath, tube 4oz $3.50* **MP $7**
1969 *Snoopy the Flying Ace Bubble Bath 4oz $3* **MP $6 with goggles**

1968 *Charlie Brown Non-tear Shampoo 4oz $2.50* **MP $6**
1970 *Linus Non-tear Shampoo 4oz $3* **MP $6**
1969 *Lucy Bubble Bath 4oz $2.50* **MP $6**

1969 *Charlie Brown Mug Bubble Bath 5oz $3.50* **MP $10 with lid**
1969 *Snoopy Mug Liquid Soap 5oz $3.50* **MP $10 with lid**
1969 *Lucy Mug Non-tear Shampoo 5oz $3.50* **MP $10 with lid**

1973 *Snoopy Come Home Soap Dish and Soap 3oz $4.50* **MP $7**

1974 *Great Catch. Charlie Brown Soap Holder and Soap 3oz $5* **MP $7**

1975 *Woodstock Brush and Comb $6* **MP $5**

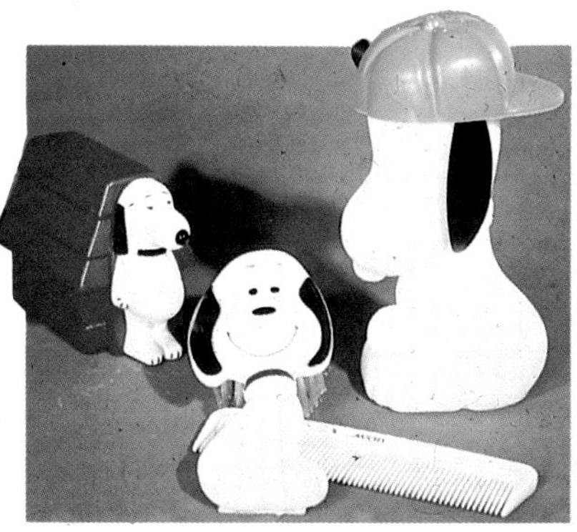

1969 *Snoopy Doghouse Non-tear Shampoo 8oz $3* **MP $6.50**
1970 *Snoopy Brush and Comb $3.50* **MP $6**
1969 *Snoopy Surprise Package. Excalibur or Wild Country After Shave or Sports Rally Lotion (glass) 5oz $4* **MP $7**

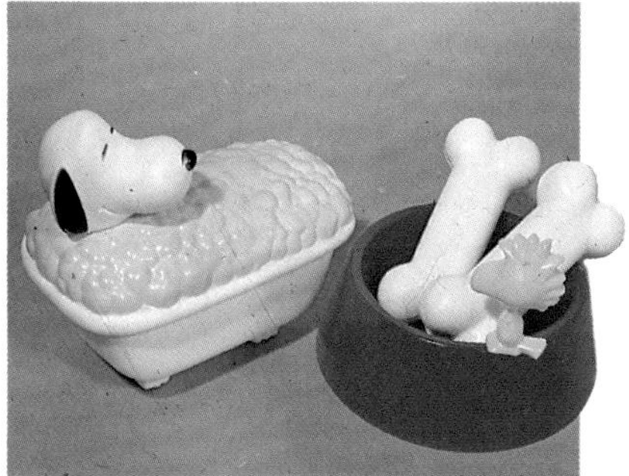

1971 *Snoopy's Bubble Bath Tub $4* **MP $5**
1973 *Snoopy's Pal Soap Dish and 2 Soaps 2oz each $3.75* **MP $6**

1970 *Peanuts Gang Soaps, three 1¾oz cakes $2* **MP $8**
1970 *Schroeder Bubble Bath 6oz $3.50* **MP $7, $10 with piano box**

1974 *Snoopy's Ski Team Bubble Bath 8oz $6* **MP $5**
1972 *Snoopy Snow Flyer Bubble Bath 10oz $5* **MP $5**

1960 *Pig in a Poke Bubble Bath 8oz $1.79* **MP $16**

TOYS FOR TOTS

1960 *A Winner Set. Hair Guard and Hand Guard 4oz each $1.98* **MP $22**
1967 *Little Champion Set. (blue glove) Non-tear Shampoo, (yellow glove) Hair Trainer 4oz each $2* **MP $15**

1961 *Li'l Folks Time Bubble Bath 8oz $1.79* **MP $15**
1965 *Cuckoo Clock Bubble Bath 10oz $2.50* **MP $12**
1967 *Tic Toc Tiger Bubble Bath 8oz $1.75* **MP $10** *(Moveable hands on all clocks)*

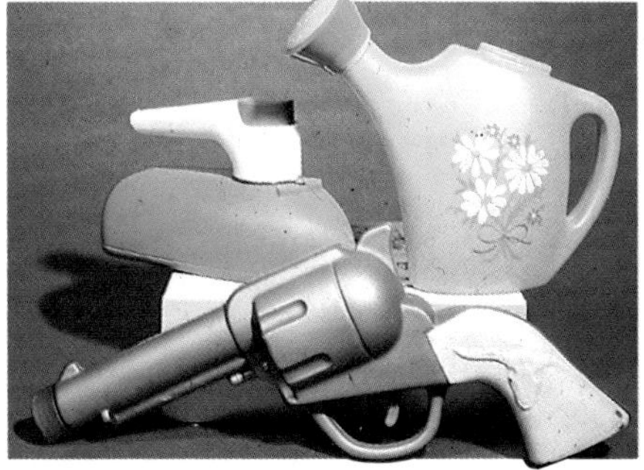

1962 *Little Helper plastic iron Bubble Bath 8oz $1.98* **MP $15**
1962 *Watering Can, plastic Bubble Bath 8oz $1.98* **MP $15**
1962 *Six Shooter, plastic No-tears Shampoo 6oz $1.98* **MP $20**

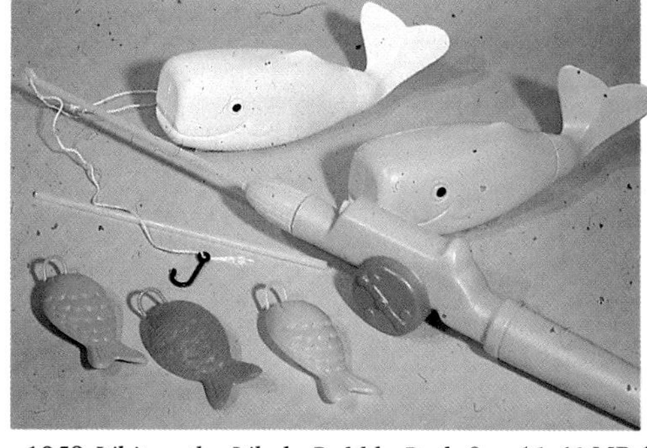

1959 *Whitey the Whale Bubble Bath 8oz $1.69* **MP $15**
1967 *Smiley the Whale Bubble Bath 9oz $1.98* **MP $7**
1968 *Tub Catch Fishing Rod and 3 plastic fish. Rod holds Bubble Bath 6oz $3.50* **MP $11 complete**

1963 *Captain Bubble Bath 8oz $1.79* **MP $12**
1963 *First Mate's Shampoo 8oz $1.98* **MP $12**
1964 *Aqua Car Bubble Bath 8oz $1.98* **MP $15**
1961 *Naughty-Less plastic sub with Bubble Bath 8oz $1.79* **MP $20**

1962 *L'il Tom Turtle, plastic. Green molded Soap 98¢* **MP $22** *Yellow Shampoo, blue Baby Oil, red Baby Lotion 3oz each $1.10* **MP $15 each**

1963 *Humpty Dumpty Bubble Bath 8oz $1.98* **MP $11**
1969 *Yankee Doodle Soap 6oz $2* **MP $10**
1960 *Clean As a Whistle Bubble Bath 8oz $1.79* **MP $16**
1968 *Space Ace Hair Trainer 4oz $1.50* **MP $10**

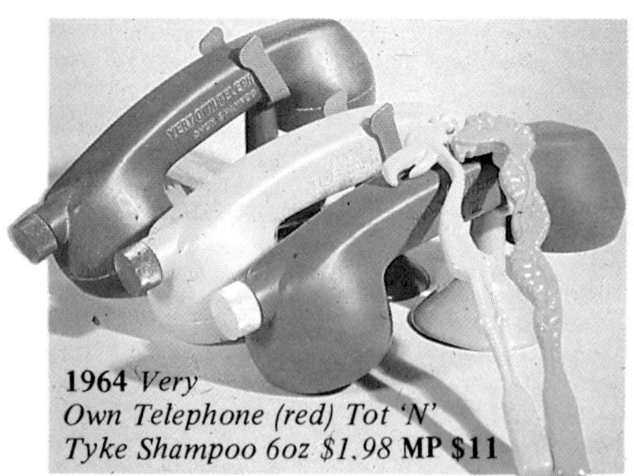
1964 *Very Own Telephone (red) Tot 'N' Tyke Shampoo 6oz $1.98* **MP $11**

1967 *Tub Talk (yellow) Non-tear Shampoo 6oz $1.75* **MP $9**
1969 *Tub Talk (blue) Non-tear Shampoo $2.25* **MP $7**
1972 *Toofie Toothbrush Duo, Bird & Worm $2* **MP $5**

1964 *Santa's Chimney. Powdered Bubble Bath 5oz. Top of box is game $1.98* **MP $18**

1964 *Bubble Bunny Gel Bubble Bath 6oz $1.98* **MP $20 complete**

1964 *Packy Elephant. Blue Baby Oil, yellow Baby Shampoo, red Baby Lotion 3oz each $1.10* **MP $15 each**

1966 *School Days plastic pencil box. Non-tear Shampoo 8oz $1.98* **MP $10**
1965 *Avon Bugle Non-tear Shampoo 6oz $1.98* **MP $13**
1965 *Safe Sam Bubble Bath 8oz $1.98* **MP $13**

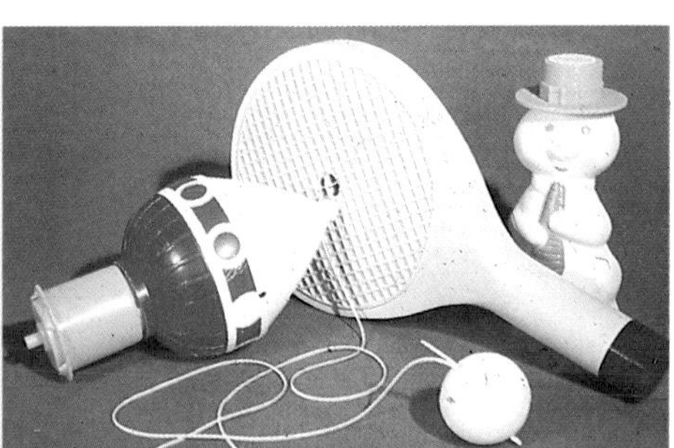
1966 *Spinning Top Bubble Bath 4oz $1.75* **MP $10**
1966 *Paddle Ball Set. Shampoo 6oz $1.98* **MP $14**
1967 *Good Habit Rabbit Tot 'N' Tyke Shampoo 3oz $1.50* **MP $10**

1966 *Little Missy Rolling Pin Shampoo 8oz $2.25* **MP $11**
1965 *Avon Fife Hand Lotion or Hair Trainer 6oz $1.75* **MP $14**
1961 *Land Ho! plastic telescope with Hair Trainer 8oz $1.49* **MP $18**

1964 *Toy Soldiers: Hair Trainer, Shampoo, Hand Lotion and Bubble Bath each 4oz $1.25 each* **MP $13 each**

1965 *Jet Plane Gel Bubble Bath, Gel Shampoo or Hair Trainer 3oz each $1.50* **MP $15**

1966 *Globe Bank Bubble Bath, plastic 10oz $2.50 each* **MP $18 complete**
(3 different colors of snap-on countries)

1966 *Whistle Tots: Fireman Tot 'n' Tyke Shampoo, Policeman Hair Trainer, Clown Bubble Bath 4oz each $1.50* **MP $10 each**

1967 *Tin Man blue Pipe and Non-tear Shampoo 4oz $1.50* **MP $9**
1967 *Mr. Lion red bubble Pipe and Bubble Bath 4oz $1.50* **MP $9**
1967 *Straw Man yellow bubble Pipe and Hand Lotion 4oz $1.50* **MP $9**

1968 *Little Red Riding Hood Bubble Bath 4oz and "Granny" Glasses $1.50* **MP $9**
1968 *The Wolf Non-tear Shampoo 4oz and "Funny Fangs" $1.50* **MP $9**

1965 *Mr. Many Moods with moveable eyes, nose and mouth. Non-tear Shampoo 6oz $1.98* **MP $12**
1965 *Topsy Turvy Clown Bubble Bath 10oz $2.50* **MP $16**

1968 *Mr. Presto-Chango Non-tear Shampoo 6oz $2.25* **MP $9 complete**

1968 *Easter Dec-A-Doo Bubble Bath 8oz $2.50* **MP $6 with decals**

1967 *Little Piggy (yellow) Baby Shampoo 3oz $1.35* **MP $9**
1967 *Little Piggy (blue) Bubble Bath 3oz $1.35* **MP $9**
1967 *Little Piggy (pink) Baby Lotion 3oz $1.35* **MP $9**

1968 *Mary Non-tear Shampoo 3oz $1.35* **MP $9**
1968 *Schoolhouse Bubble Bath 3oz $1.35* **MP $9**
1968 *Little Lamb Baby Lotion 3oz $1.35* **MP $9**

1969 *Jumpin' Jimminy Bubble Bath 8oz $3.50* **MP $6**
1969 *Wrist Wash Bubble Bath 2oz $3* **MP $8**

1967 *Birdfeeder Powdered Bubble Bath 7½oz $3.50* **MP $11**

1969 *Birdhouse Powdered Bubble Bath 8oz $3.75* **MP $10**

1968 *Scrub Mug liquid Soap 6oz $2.50* **MP $6**
1968 *Tic Toc Turtle Bubble Bath 8oz $2.50* **MP $7**
1968 *One, Two. . . Lace My Shoe Bubble Bath 8oz $2.98* **MP $8**

1970 *Gaylord Gator Mug Non-tear Shampoo 5oz $3.50* **MP $8**
1970 *Freddy the Frog Mug Bubble Bath 5oz $3.50* **MP $8**

1970 *Moon Flight Game. Playboard, markers, Lem, Space Capsule Non-tear Shampoo 6oz $4* **MP $10 complete**

1970 *Ring 'Em Up Clean Non-tear Shampoo 8oz $2.50* **MP $5**
1970 *As above (with white lid) $2.50* **MP $8**

1969 *Mickey Mouse© Coloring Book of Avon Toys* **MP $3**
1967 *A Colorful Story of Avon Toys. Coloring Book not for sale, except to Representatives* **MP $4**

1969 *Mickey Mouse© Bubble Bath 4½oz $3.50* **MP $7**
1971 *Aristocat Non-tear Shampoo 4oz $3* **MP $5**
1970 *Pluto© Non-tear Shampoo 4oz $4* **MP $7**

1969 *Chief Scrubbem Liquid Soap 4oz $2.50* **MP $8**

1971 *Hickory Dickory Clock Non-tear Shampoo 8oz* **MP $8**
1970 *Mad Hatter Bubble Bath 6oz $3* **MP $10**

1970 *Bo-Bo the Elephant Non-tear Shampoo 5oz $2.50* **MP $6**
1973 *Bo-Bo the Elephant Baby Shampoo 6oz $4* **MP $5**

1970 *Topsy Turvy Bubble Bath 4oz $2* **MP $6**
1971 *Maze Game Non-tear Shampoo 6oz $2.50* **MP $8**

1970 *Splash Down Bubble Bath 8oz $4* **MP $6 complete**
1971 *Cluck-A-Doo Bubble Bath 8oz $3* **MP $6**

1972 *Ball and Cup Shampoo for Children 4oz $3.50* **MP $8**
1971 *Kanga Winks. Tiddley-Wink Game and Bubble Bath 8oz $4* **MP $8**
1972 *Turn-A-Word Bubble Bath 8oz $3.50* **MP $5**

1971 *Looney Lather Bubble Bath 6oz $2* **MP $6**
1971 *Looney Lather Shampoo 6oz $2* **MP $6**

1972 *Spool-A-Doo Rollette .33oz $3* **MP $6 complete**

1962 *Concertina Bubble Bath 8oz $1.98* **MP $15**

1970 *Concertina Bubble Bath 8oz $2.50* **MP $7**
1971 *Mr. Robottle Bubble Bath 5oz $3.50* **MP $6**

1978 *Hang Ten Skateboard Bubble Bath 5½oz $6.50* **MP $4**
1980 *I.M. Clean II Pump Dispenser Liquid Cleanser 8oz and decals $8* **MP $7**
1980 *Children's Liquid Cleanser Refill 8oz $4* **MP $3***

©Walt Disney Productions

** Available from Avon at time of publication*

1973 *Little Wiggley Game Bubble Bath 8oz $4.50* **MP $6**

1974 *Loveable Leo Children's Shampoo 10oz $4* **MP $3**
1975 *Winkie Blink Clock Bubble Bath 8oz $5* **MP $5**

1971 *Huggy Bear Bubble Bath 8oz $3.50* **MP $5**
1979 *Most Valuable Gorilla Bubble Bath 4oz $7.50* **MP $5**

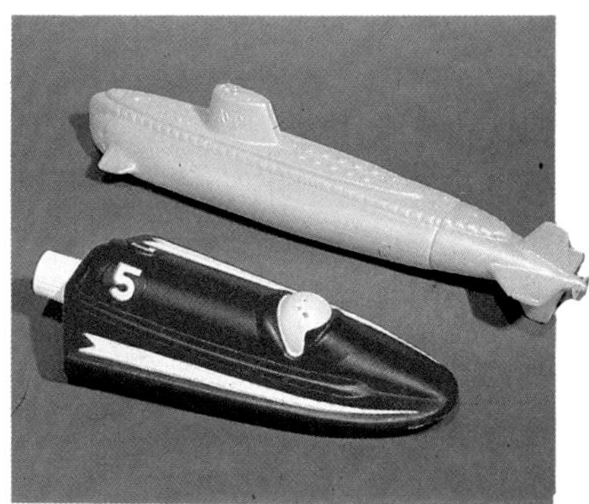

1972 *Red Streak Bubble Bath 5oz $2.50* **MP $6**
1978 *Tub Sub Bubble Bath for Children 6oz $6* **MP $3**

1971 *Puffer Chugger Bubble Bath 4oz, Soap Coach 3oz and Caboose Non-tear Shampoo 4oz each $2.25* **MP $5 each**

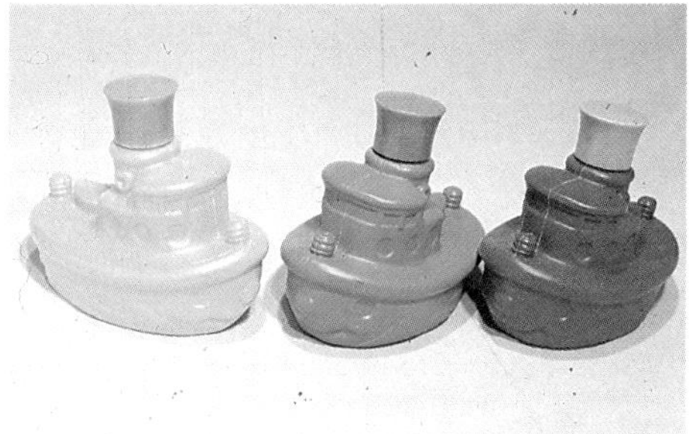

1980 *Tub Tug Non-Tear Shampoo (Yellow), Liquid Cleanser (Blue), Bubble Bath (Red) 5oz each $5* **MP $3 each**

1979 *Red Streak Bubble Bath 7oz and Decals $5.50* **MP $3**
1976 *Custom Car Bubble Bath 7oz and Decals $5* **MP $4**

1978 *Heavy Hitter Non-tear Shampoo 4oz $7* **MP $4**
1979 *Willie Weatherman Non-tear Shampoo 6oz $7.50* **MP $4**
1961 *Avonville Slugger (bat) Non-tear Shampoo 6oz $1.49* **MP $16**

1974 *Grid Kid Hair Trainer 8oz $3* **MP $4**

1974 *Sure Winner Catcher's Mitt Hair Trainer 6oz $3* **MP $4**
1973 *Sure Winner Slugger Decanter. Hair Trainer, Bracing Lotion or Spicy After Shave 6oz $3* **MP $5**
1973 *Sure Winner Baseball Hair Trainer 4oz $2.50* **MP $4**

1975 *Brontosaurus Bubble Bath 10oz $5* **MP $4**
1976 *Tyrannosaurus Rex Bubble Bath 9oz $5.50* **MP $4**
1977 *Triceratops Bubble Bath 8.5oz $5.50* **MP $4**

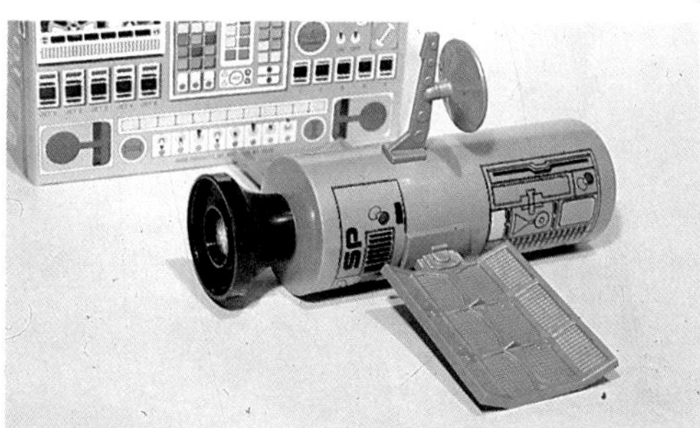

1979 *Space Patroller Bubble Bath 8oz and decals $7* **MP $4**

1978 *3-Ring Circus Talc 5oz $3.50* **MP $1**
1981 *Spongie The Clown Liquid Cleanser 6oz $6* **MP $5***

Playful Pups –
1981 *Wall Hook 3x5" with adhesive backing $4* **MP $3***
1981 *Light Switch Cover with Fragranced Bow 3½x5½", plastic loveable puppy or sheepdog design $5.50* **MP $4.50***

* *Available from Avon at time of publication*

Flavored Lip Pomades –
1974 *Ice Cream Cone in Cherry, Strawberry, Tutti-Frutti $2.50* **MP $3**
1974 *Ice Cream Soda in Cherry, Strawberry, Tutti-Frutti $3* **MP $3**
1973 *Lip Pops in Cola, Cherry or Strawberry $1.75* **MP $3** *Solid red issue in Strawberry* **MP $7**

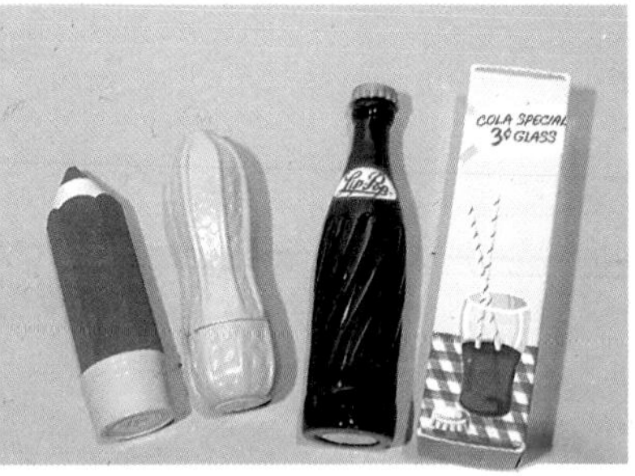

1975 *School Days Lip Pomade in Cherry, Strawberry or Tutti-Frutti Pomade .13oz $3.50* **MP $3**
1974 *In a Nutshell Color Magic Lipstick 2 shades .13oz $3* **MP $3**
1978 *Lip-Pop Pomade Cola-colored and flavored lip balm .13oz $3.75* **MP $3**

1975 *Sunbonnet Sue DemiStik Pink & Pretty .19oz $3.50* **MP $3**
1976 *Gilroy the Ghost Finger Puppet. Care Deeply Lip Balm .19oz $3.50* **MP $3**
1977 *Millicent Mouse Finger Puppet DemiStik. Pink & Pretty .19oz $3.75* **MP $3**
1977 *Glow Worm Finger Puppet. Care Deeply Lip Balm .19oz $3.50* **MP $2**
1977 *Huck L. Berry Finger Puppet Lip Balm .20oz $3.75* **MP $2**

1979 *Flavor Savers, flavored Lip Gloss in Grape, Cherry, Chocolate, Strawberry, Lime and Orange .15oz $2* **MP $1* ea.**

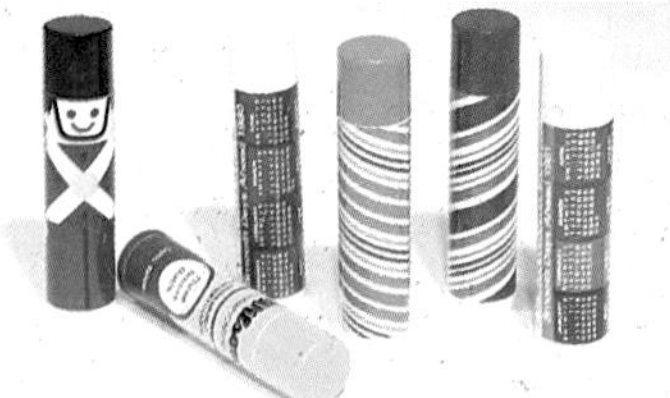

Care Deeply Lip Balm .15oz each –
1979 *Toy Soldier $1.29* **MP $1**
1979 *Wilson Championship $1.29* **MP $1**
1979 *Smooth Days Ahead $1.29* **MP $1**
1980 *Candy Cane, Wintergreen or Peppermint (red) $1.49* **MP 50¢**
1980 *Smooth Days Ahead $1.49* **MP 50¢**

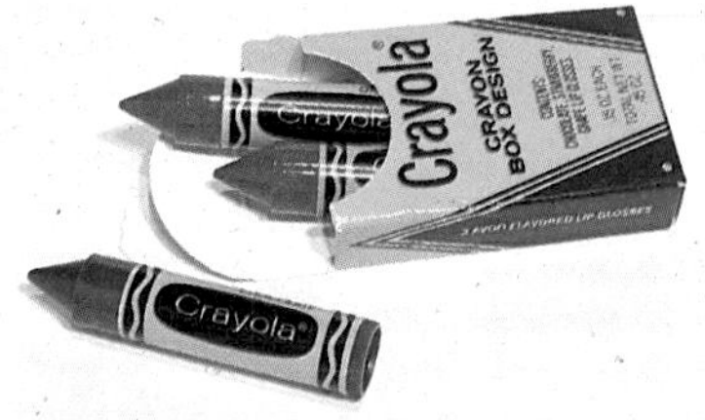

1980 *Crayola Lip Glosses in Grape, Strawberry and Chocolate, each .15oz $6.50* **MP $5***

1980 *Santa's Helpers Care Deeply Hand Cream 1.5oz and Lip Balm $2.79* **MP $1.50**

FOR CHILDREN AND TEENS

1976 *Felina Fluffles Pink & Pretty Cologne 2oz $6* **MP $4**
1978 *Good Fairy Cologne in Delicate Daisies 3oz $8* **MP $4**

1977 *Church Mouse Bride. Delicate Daisies Cologne 2oz $6* **MP $4**
1979 *Church Mouse Groom. Delicate Daisies Cologne .75oz $7* **MP $4**

1979 *Cute Cookie. Hello Sunshine Cologne 1oz $5.50* **MP $4**
1980 *Fluffy Chick. Hello Sunshine Cologne 1oz $7* **MP $6***

1980 *Bundle of Fun in Hello Sunshine Cologne or Sure Winner Lotion .75oz $6.50* **MP $4**

1969 *Bunny Puff. Her Prettiness Perfumed Talc 3½oz $3.75* **MP $6**
1979 *Bunny Fluff Puff with children's Talc 3½oz $8* **MP $5**

1978 *Duster D. Duckling Fluff Puff. Delicate Daisies Talc 3½oz $6.50* **MP $3**

1979 *Mrs. Quackles with fabric bonnet, Delicate Daisies Cologne 2oz $8* **MP $6**

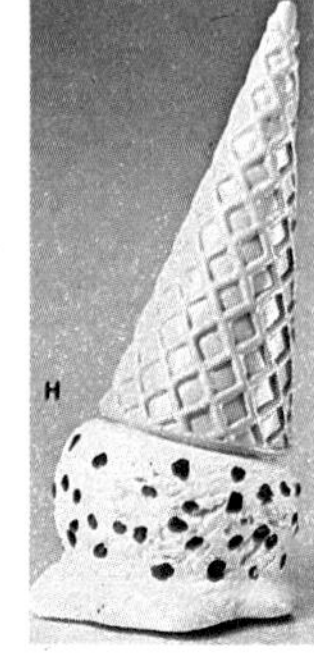

1981 *Oops! Cologne in Country Breeze or Sweet Honesty 1.5oz $7.50* **MP $7***

* *Available from Avon at time of publication*

1929-36 *Sales Catalog* **MP $50**
1929 *Representative's Beauty Case* **MP $55**

1948-52 *Representative's Beauty Case* **MP $28**
1937 *Sales Catalog $2.50* **MP $40**

1948-52 *Sales Catalog* **MP $30**

1953 *Sales Catalog* **MP $40**

1954-57 *Sales Catalog* **MP $20**

1954 only *Sales Catalog imprinted with "Honor Representative President's Award" on cover* **MP $35**

REPRESENTATIVE'S SALES AIDS

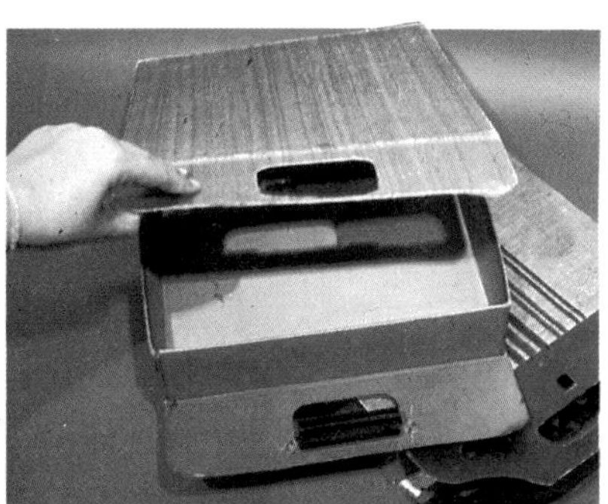

1943-44 *Gift Display Ensemble Boxes (cardboard) to carry Xmas Gift Demos and Sets* **MP $25 each**

1960 *Avon Ad, Engraver's Proof: "199 Cosmetics"* **MP $17**

1952 *Representative's Beauty Case, green plastic lining* **MP $25**

1953 *Xmas Gifts by Avon Book* **MP $25**
1975 *Xmas Gift Book Cover* **MP $4**

1969 *Representative's Summer Beauty Showcase, a "Spring Fever" Recommendation prize* **MP $22**

1950's *Representative's Beauty Case* **MP $22**

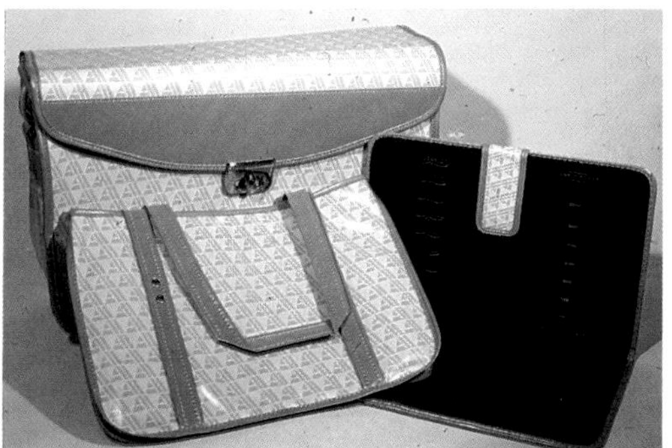

Sales Mates –
1978 *Beauty Showcase, empty $11.50* **MP $11.50***
1978 *Tote Bag, empty $4* **MP $4***
1978 *Jewelry Demonstrator, empty $5* **MP $5***

** Available from Avon at time of publication*

Product and Price List Folders –

top – **1950** *Spring (8 pages)* **MP $5**
1962 *C-8 (4 pgs. shown open)* **MP $4**
1962 *C-2 (6 pgs. shown open)* **MP $4**
bottom – **1955** *Spring (8 pages)* **MP $5**
1962 *C-8 (4 pages)* **MP $4**
1963 *C-2 (4 pages)* **MP $4**

Across top –
1964-65 *Make Yourself Known Cards* **MP $1 ea.**
Across bottom –
1966-68 *Make Yourself Known Cards* **MP $1 ea.**

Across top –
1969-70 *Make Yourself Known Cards* **MP $1 each**
Across bottom –
1971-72-74 *Customer Service Reminders*
MP 75¢ each

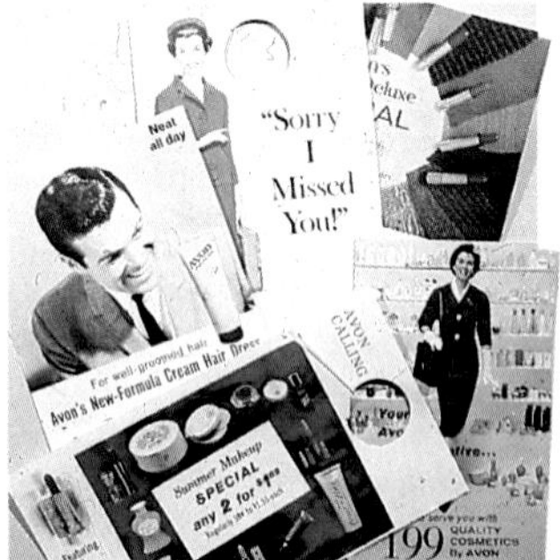

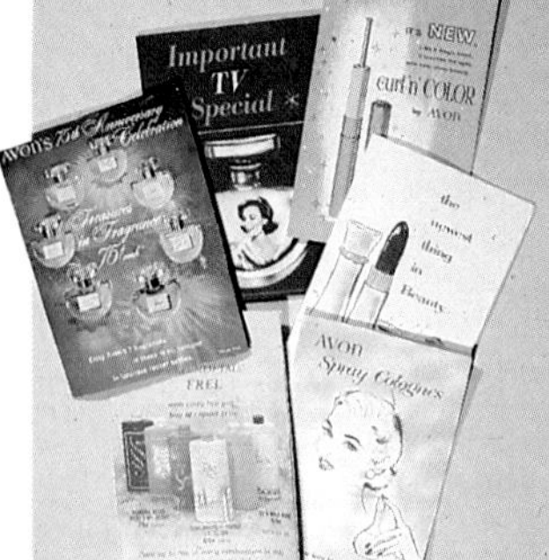

Assortment of "Make Yourself Known" Folders and Door-Hanger "Call-Back" Reminders of the 60's:

4 page special "New Products" Folders **MP $4**

2 page Price Folders **MP $3**

Door Hanger Reminders **MP $1 ea.**

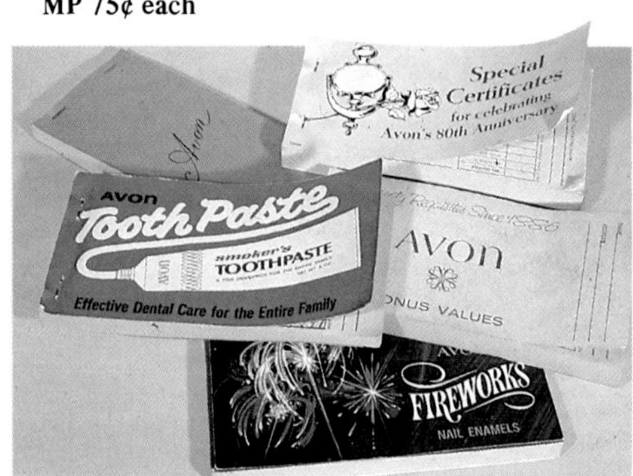

Representative's Order Books –
1940's *Script Avon on cover* **MP $15**
1966 *80th Anniversary cover* **MP $10**
1967 *Toothpaste Promotion cover* **MP $8**
1965 *Contains Bonus Value Coupons* **MP $10**
1967 *Fireworks Nail Enamels Cover* **MP $8**

. . . REPRESENTATIVE'S SALES AIDS

1937 *Order Book and Cover* **MP $15 each**
1940's *Customer Name Book* **MP $10**

1948 *Order Book* **MP $15**
1949 *Order Book* **MP $15**
1950 *Order Book* **MP $15**

1956 *Order Book* **MP $8**
1957 *Order Book* **MP $8**

1971 *Representative's Organizer Showcase holds Order Book, Samples, Color Chart, Pen and Catalog* **MP $20**

Xmas Gift Calendars –

1978 *Floral Calendar (1979) sold only to Representatives to distribute as customer Xmas gifts 25¢ each* **MP $1**
1979 *Nature Calendar (1980) sold only to Representatives to distribute as Xmas gifts 30¢ each* **MP $1**

1980 *How-To Beauty Calendar (1981) sold only to Representives to distribute as customer Xmas gifts 20¢ each* **MP 50¢**

1935 *Demonstration Case. Gardenia and Cotillion Perfumes ¼oz each. Skin Freshener and Astringent 2oz each, Rose Water, Glycerin and Benzoin Lotion 4oz, Lotus Cream 4oz, One jar each of Tissue, Cleansing and Vanishing Cream, Face Powder, Rouge Compact and Lipstick* **MP $1000**

1946 *Skin Care Demonstration Kit. One tube each of Night Cream and Special Dry Skin Cream. Skin Freshener 4oz* **MP $75 complete**

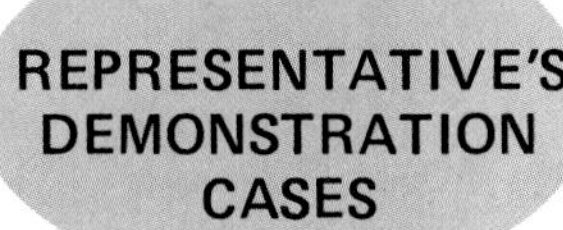

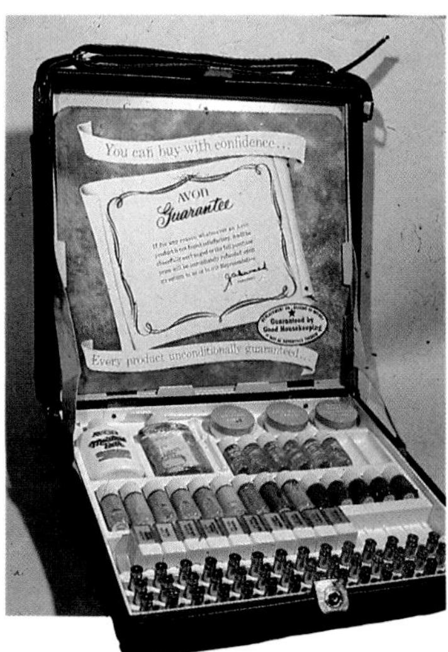

1959 *Beauty Counselor Demonstration Kit. Plastic bottle of Moisture Bath, Skin Freshener 1oz. One plastic jar each of Rich Moisture and Vita Moist Cream and Strawberry Cooler. Demonstrator bottles of Perfumes, Foundations, Rouge, Face Powder and Lipstick Samples* **MP $350 complete**

1941 *Founder's Campaign Special Cream Combination Demonstrator. Large jar of Cleansing Cream, medium jar Night Cream, small jar Foundation Cream and 4oz Skin Freshener* **MP $100**

1947 *Skin Care Demonstration Kit. One tube each of Liquefying Cleansing Cream and Fluffy Cleansing Cream* **MP $75 complete**

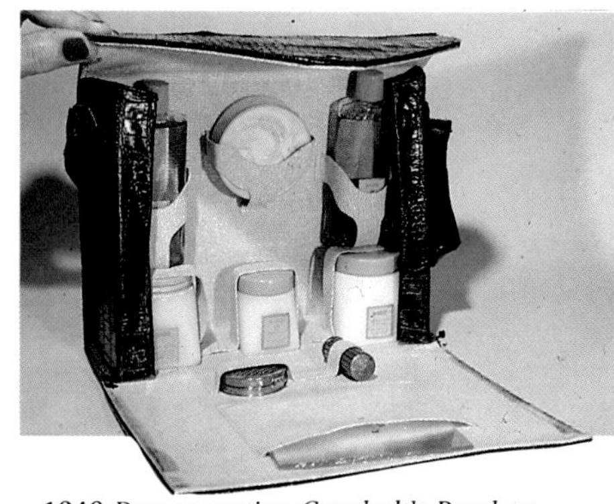

1948 *Demonstration Case holds Bamboo Lipstick and Rouge Compact, Skin Freshener and Astringent, Night Cream, Foundation Cream and Super Rich Cream* **MP $100**

Highly prized collectibles, cherished by both collectors and Representatives.

1953 *Leatherette Kit holds ½oz Brushless Shaving Cream, ¾oz Toothpaste, ½oz each After Shave Lotion, Cologne and Deodorant, 1oz each Liquid Shampoo and Cream Hair Lotion* **MP $200**

1956 *Skin Care Demonstrator holds Deep Clean Cleansing Cream, Skin Freshener, Rich Moisture Cream, Hormone Cream and Spatula* **MP $100**

1963 *77th Anniversary Gift Demonstrator. Compact, 2oz Topaze Cologne Mist, Skin-So-Soft and 1oz Cream Foundation* **MP $40 complete**

(See also Foreign Demonstrators pg. 271)

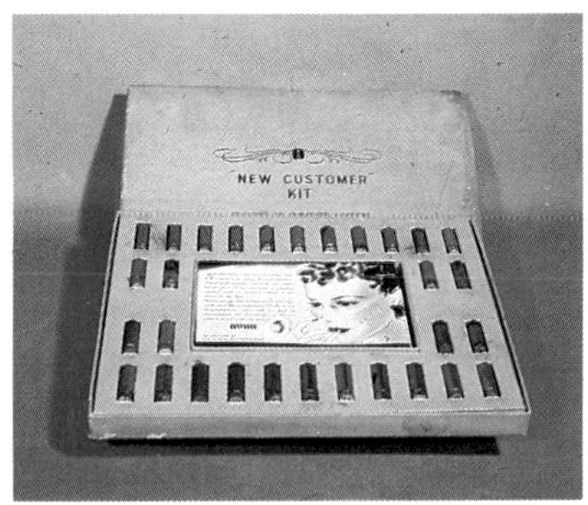

1937-39 *New Customer Kit of 30 Lipstick samples* **MP $55**

1940-42 *Lipstick Demonstrator Case of 30 samples* **MP $45**

1945-47 *Lipstick Demonstrator Case of 30 samples* **MP $35**

1948 *Lipstick Demonstrator Case of 30 samples 4 x 3½"* **MP $35**

1949 *Box of 30 Lipstick Samples and Cards 50¢* **MP $30**

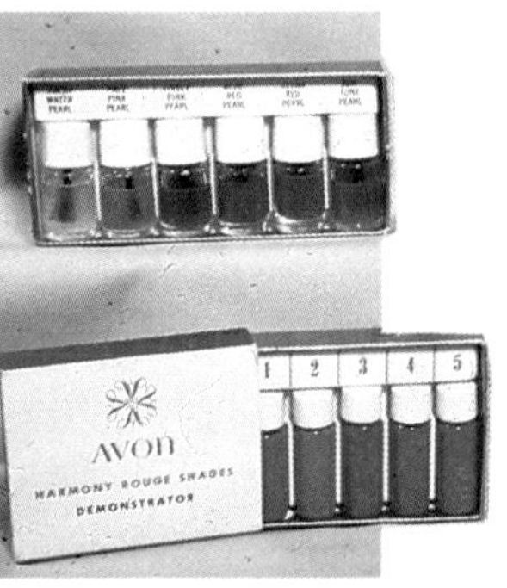

1950 *Nail Polish Demonstrator, six ½ dram bottles* **MP $22**
1956 *Harmony Rouge Demonstrator, 5 bottles* **MP $18**

1952 *Fashion Lipstick Demonstrator Case of 5 colors* **MP $32**

1950 *Lipstick Sample Case, 10 shades* **MP $30**

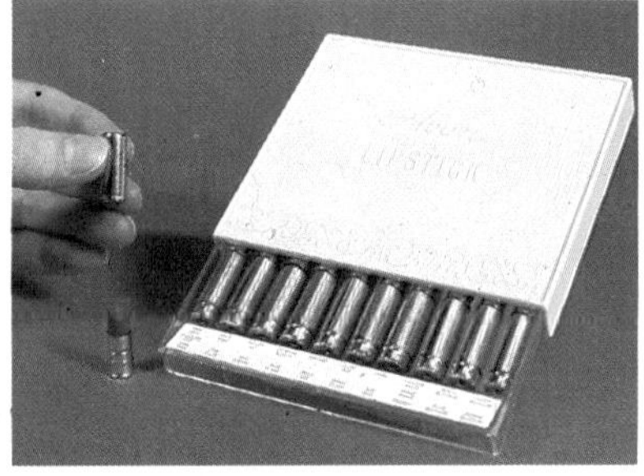

1951 *Jewel-Etched Lipstick Demonstrator* **MP $25**

1952 *Lipstick Demonstrator with 4 regular lipsticks and 1 refill (shown)* **MP $45 complete**

1961 *Introductory Demo of Deluxe Lipstick on black plastic pedestal, topped with lucite dome* **MP $20**

MAKEUP DEMONSTRATORS AND SAMPLES

1950 *Matchstick Eye Shadow Try-Ons* **MP $20**
1960 *Matchsticks Eye Shadow Try-Ons* **MP $15 for 50 sticks**
1961 *Matchstick Eye Shadow Try-Ons* **MP $15 in Violet Mist, 15 sticks**

1960 *New Beauty for Eyes Demonstrator holds Curl 'N' Color Mascara, Eyebrow Pencil, Eye Shadow Stick and Try-On Demos of Eye Shadow* **MP $60**

1963 *Eye Shadow Stick Demonstrator with new shade Eye Shadow Try-Ons* **MP $22**

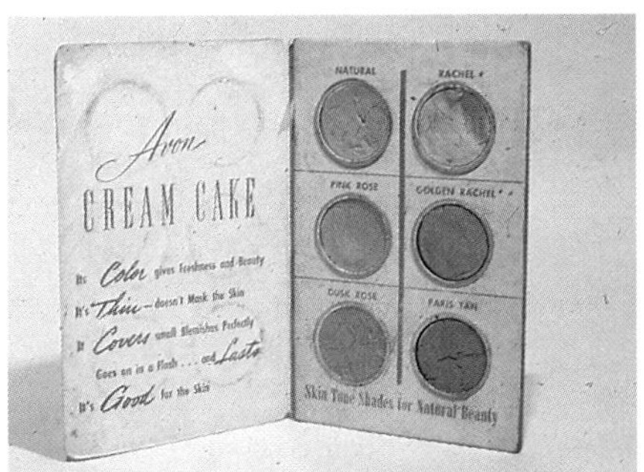

1948 *Cream Cake Demonstrator, 6 shades* **MP $22**

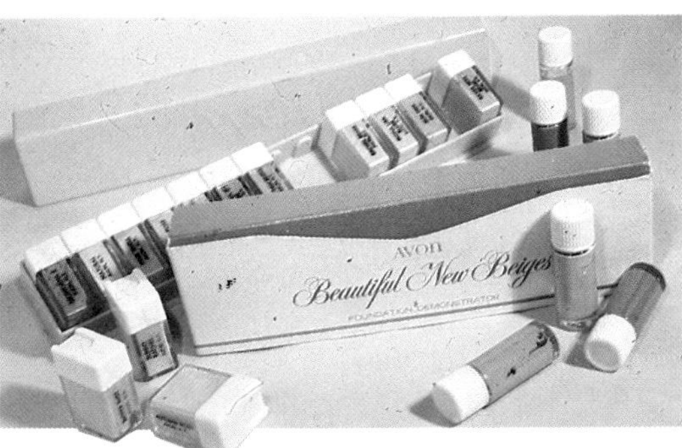

1961 *Face Powder Demonstrator, 13 shades* **MP $15**
1965 *Beautiful New Beiges Demonstrator* **MP $12**

1965 *Manager's Product Case holds Face Powder, Natural Radiance, Tone 'N' Tint, Cream & Luminous Eye Shadows, Cake Eyeliner, Eyeliner Brush, Eyeliner Pencil, Eyebrow Brush-A-Line, Deluxe Lipstick and Deluxe Compact* **MP $75**

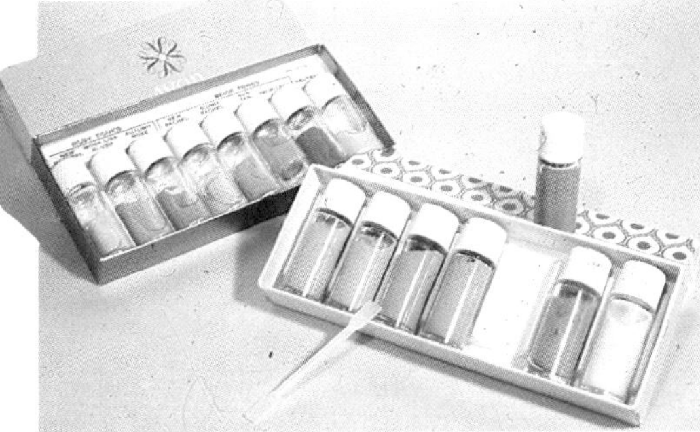

1957 *Makeup Demonstrator holds 8 shades* **MP $18**
1973 *Makeup Demonstrator holds 7 shades $1.75* **MP $6**

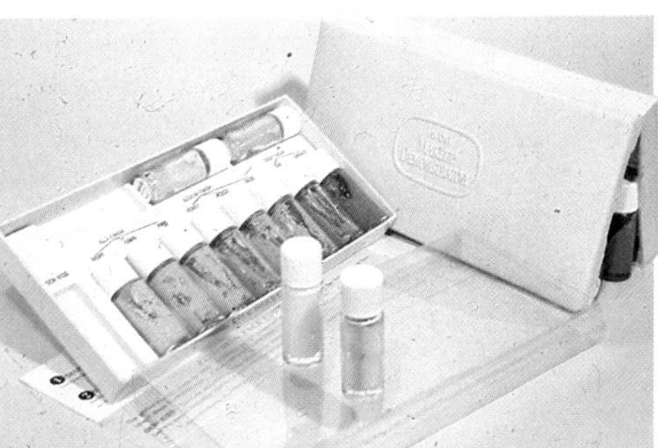

1966 *Makeup Demonstrator holds 3 shades Face Powder, 8 Foundations and 1 Dew Kiss* **MP $9**
1967 *Makeup Demonstrator holds 3 shades Face Powder, 8 shades Foundation and Dew Kiss in covered plastic case* **MP $10**

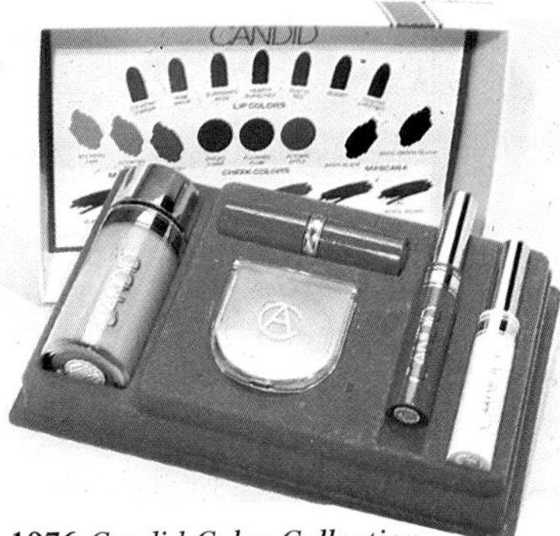

1976 *Candid Color Collection Demonstrator holds Makeup 1.5oz, Lip Color, Cheek Color, Eye Color and Mascara* **MP $16 with Color Chart in lid**

1977 *Colorworks Demo Kit holds 5 products $4.50* **MP $12* contents, $14 boxed**
1977 *"It's Not Your Mother's Makeup" Pin given to Reps at Sales Meetings* **MP $2**

1978 *Colorcreme Lipstick Demonstrator. One Richly Russet full size lipstick and 15 samples given only to Reps attending C-16 Sales Meeting* **MP $5**

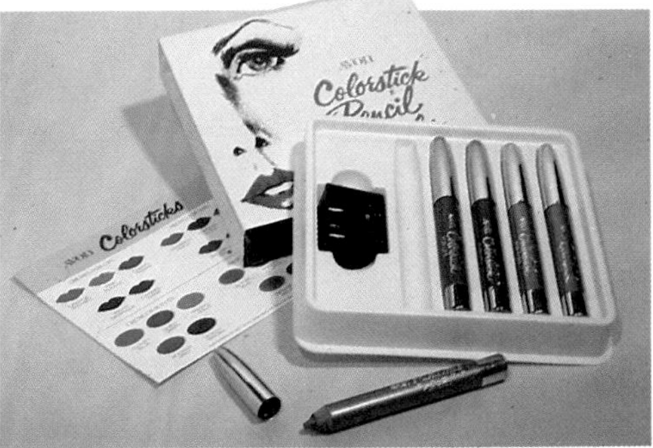

1977 *Colorstick Pencil Sampler holds 2 Colorsticks for Eyes, 2 for Lips and a Twin Sharpener, Color Chart $3.99* **MP $10* contents, $13 boxed**

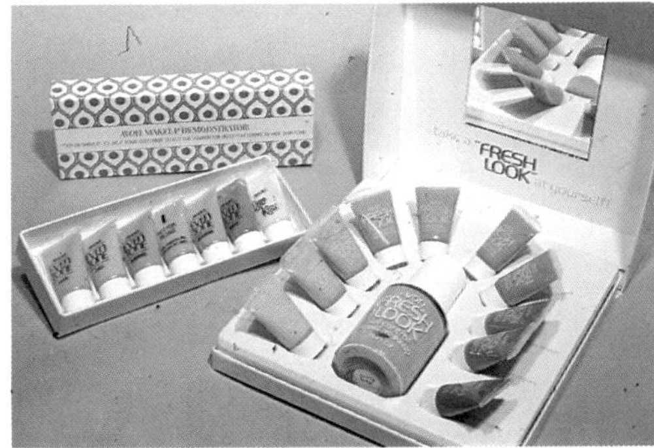

1979 *Makeup Demonstrator Kit with tube of Dew Kiss and all 6 shades of Even Tone Makeup $2* **MP $3 complete, 25¢ each tube**
1979 *Fresh Look Makeup Demonstrator with one full size bottle and 10 demo tubes of makeup. Given only to those attending C-2 Sales Meeting* **MP $6, $3* bottle only**

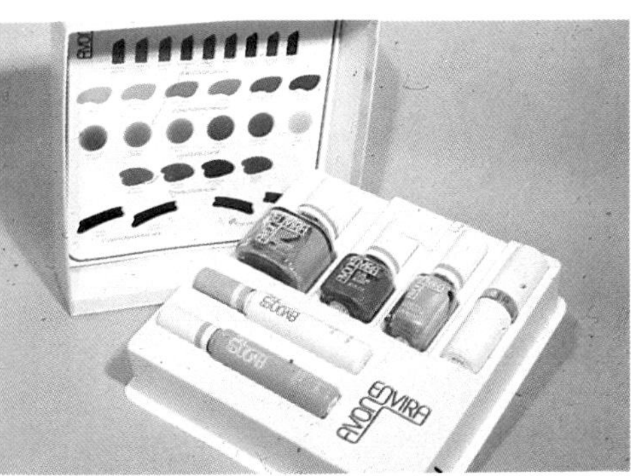

1979 *Envira Makeup Demonstrator holds Conditioning Makeup, Color Blush, Eye Color, Lipstick, Eye Definer, Mascara* **MP $17* contents, $18 boxed**

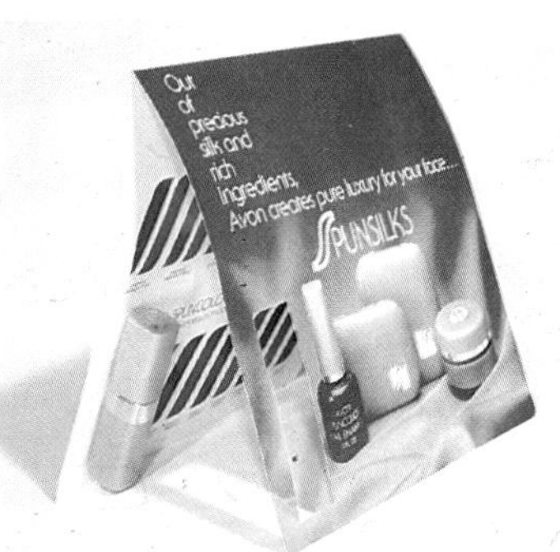

1980 *Spunsilks Color Chart Demonstrator with Spuncolor Lipstick* **MP $3* Lipstick, $3.50 with chart**

* *Available from Avon at time of publication*

1941 *Palette, 8 Face Powder shades 20¢* **MP $40**

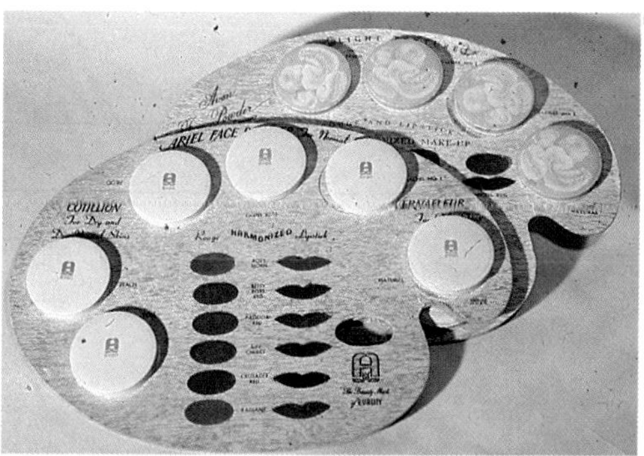

1942 *Palette (top) 8 shades, metal 20¢* **MP $42**
1940 *Palette, 6 shades in Cotillion, Ariel & Vernafleur frag. 20¢* **MP $45**

1946 *Palette (top) 9 shades have Heavenlight printed on lid 20¢* **MP $35**
1944 *Palette, 8 shades in cardboard containers 20¢* **MP $38**

FACE POWDER DEMONSTRATORS AND SAMPLES

1947 *(top) Heavenlight Face Powder, 9 shades, cardboard 20¢* **MP $35**
1948 *Heavenlight Face Powder, 9 shades, metal 30¢* **MP $33**

1949 *Face Powder Palette, 8 shades 30¢* **MP $33**

1957 *Face Powder Selector (top) 10 shades 50¢* **MP $28**
1951 *Face Powder Palette, 9 shades 30¢* **MP $30**

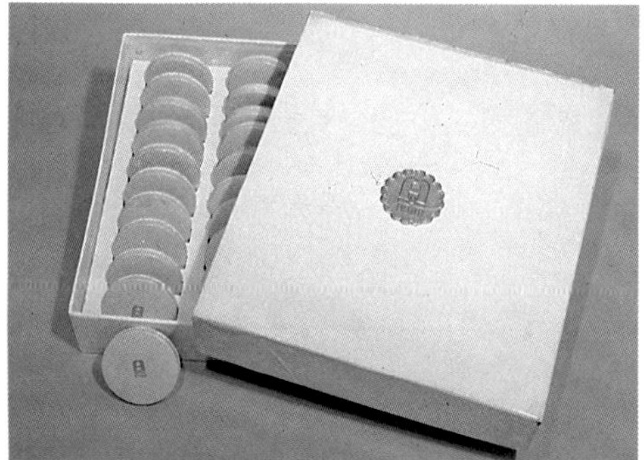

1940 *Face Powder, box of 30 Samples 50¢* **MP $115 complete, $3 each sample**

1943-44 *Face Powder Samples, box of 30 cardboard containers 50¢* **MP $140 complete, $4 each sample**

1944-45 *Face Powder Samples, box of 30 cardboard containers 50¢* **MP $140 complete, $4 each sample**

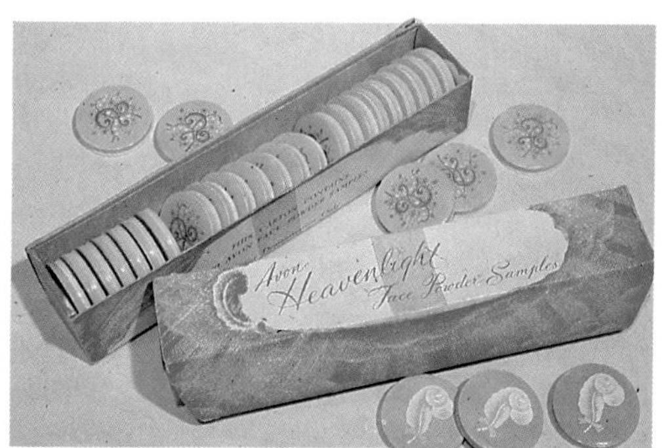

1949-52 *Face Powder, box of 30 samples 50¢* **$90 complete, $2.25 each sample**
1948 *Heavenlight Face Powder, box of 30 samples 50¢* **MP $120, $3 each**

1948-49 *Face Powder, box of 30 samples 50¢* **MP $40 complete, $1 each**

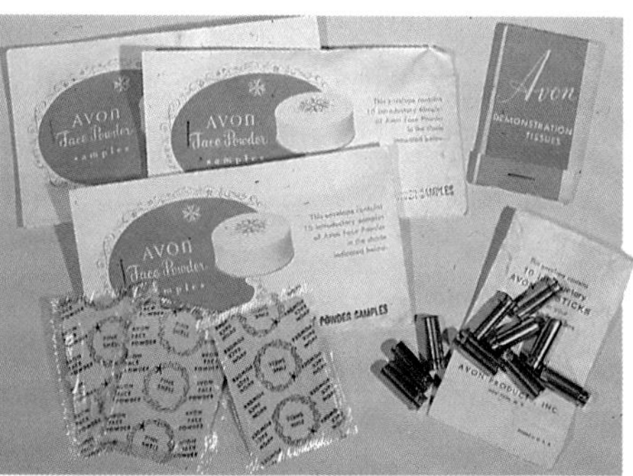

1953-57 *Face Powder Samples, pkg. of 10* **MP $12, $1 each**
1948-49 *Demonstration Tissues by Kleenex, pkg. of 10* **MP $16**
1950's *Lipstick Samples, pkg. of 10* **MP $8**

1937 *Cleansing Cream Sampler Box for new Representatives. Ten ¼oz tubes and "Your Skin Can Be Beautiful" folders* **MP $50 complete**

1937-41 *Cleansing Cream Samples, box of 24, ¼oz 50¢* **MP $95 complete, $3 each**

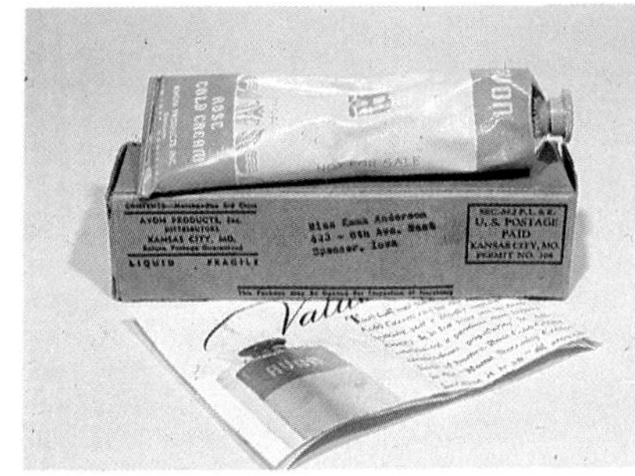

1937 *Rose Cold Cream Demonstrator. Tube reads "Not for Sale"* **MP $35 boxed**

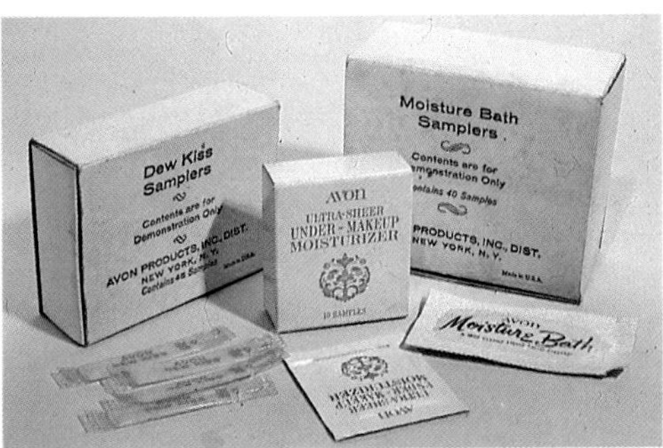

1960 *Dew Kiss Samplers, box of 45* **MP $40, 75¢ each**
1969 *Ultra Sheer Under-Makeup Moisturizer, box of 10* **MP $3, 25¢ each**
1961 *Moisture Bath, box of 40* **MP $40, 75¢ each**

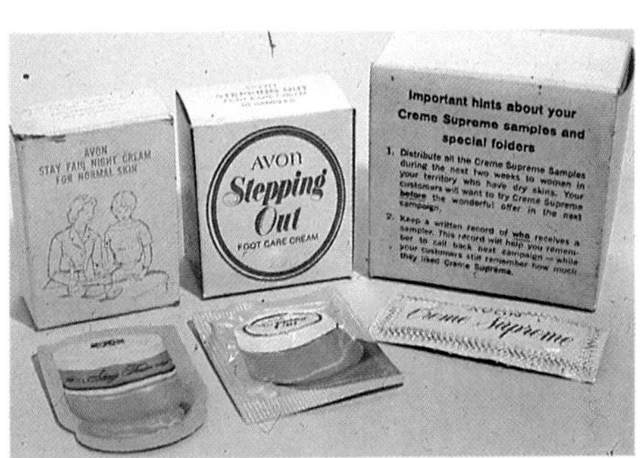

1966 *Stay Fair Night Cream, box of 10, 20¢* **MP $12, $1 each**
1969 *Stepping Out Foot Cream, box of 10, 25¢* **MP $3, 25¢ each**
1961 *Creme Supreme, box of 30* **MP $25, 75¢ each**

1976 *Skin Care Samples, box of 24 given only to those attending C-11 Sales Meetings. 8 each of Perfect Balance, Delicate Beauty & Moisture Secret* **MP $5 complete**

1979 *Nurtura Replenishing Cream Demo* **MP $5*, $6 as shown**

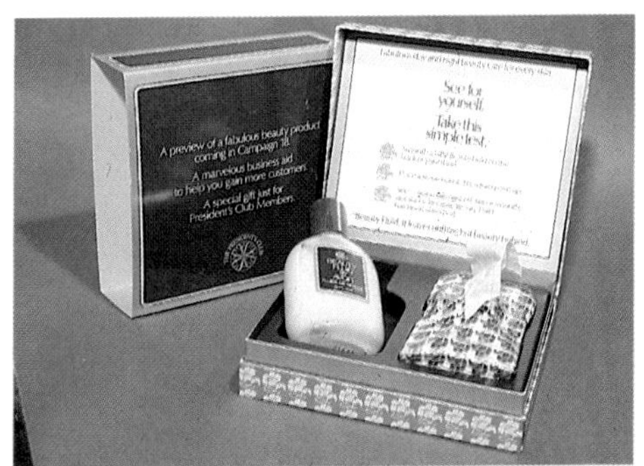

1980 *Beauty Fluid 3oz and package of Tissue, gift to President's Club Members* **MP $4* Beauty Fluid, $7 complete**

1980 *Time Control Temporary Wrinkle Smoother Kit holds 7 bottles Time Control .75oz each and a 5-minute timer. Only to Representatives pre-ordering 6 bottles Time Control at C-14 Sales Meeting* **MP $10**

1961 *Perfumed Soap Demonstrator 8½ x 11", plastic, holds eight 3oz cakes soap in new wrap. Somewhere, Here's My Heart, Rose Geranium, Lemonol, Topaze, To A Wild Rose, Cotillion and Royal Jasmine* **MP $75 complete, $5 each soap**

Little sample treats that make a lasting impression on both Avon customers and Avon collectors . . .

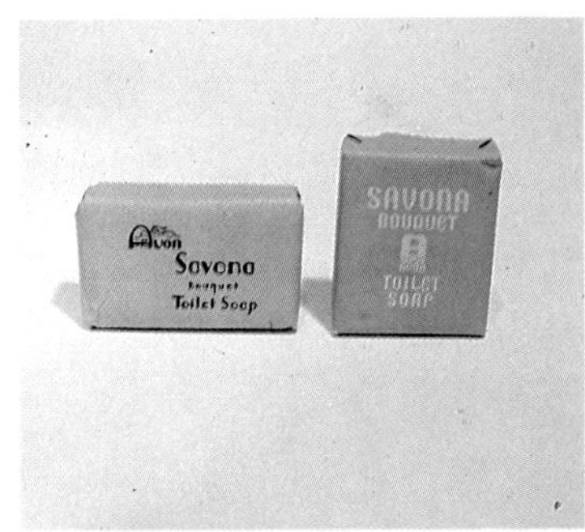

1931 *Savona Bouquet Toilet Soap sample* **MP $20**
1937 *Savona Bouquet Toilet Soap sample* **MP $15**

** Available from Avon at time of publication*

1941 *Fragrance Demonstrator. Cotillion, Garden of Love, Gardenia* **MP $80**
1951 *Fragrance Demonstrator. To A Wild Rose, Cotillion, Quaintance, Golden Promise, Forever Spring* **MP $28**
1952 *Fragrance Demonstrator. Same fragrances as above* **MP $26**

1946-50 *Perfume Samples. Each blue or pink cardboard tube holds 8 glass ampules of perfume (10 frag. available). Bottled for Avon by Nips, Inc. Each tube with 8 ampules* **MP $42, each ampule $4**
Set of 5 tubes in envelope **MP $225**

1937 *Jardin d'Amour Perfume sample and envelope* **MP $26, $20 Perfume only**
1964 *Somewhere Perfume Oil Demonstrator Bottle* **MP $10**
1949 *Demonstration Tissues by Kleenex, pkg. of 10* **MP $15**

1951 *65th Anniversary Demo. Styrofoam birthday cake holds five 1 dram Perfumes in To A Wild Rose, Flowertime, Quaintance, Golden Promise and Cotillion* **MP $150 complete**

1954-58 *Fragrance Demonstrator holds 6 of the 9 fragrances offered between 1954-58* **MP $22**
1959-60 *Fragrance Demonstrator holds Topaze, Here's My Heart, Persian Wood, Cotillion, To A Wild Rose, Bright Night* **MP $20**

1965-66 *Avon for Men Demonstrator, 8 bottles of fragrance* **MP $15**
1970 *Avon for Men Demonstrator, 8 bottles of fragrance* **MP $15**
1972 *Avon for Men Demonstrator, 8 bottles of fragrance* **MP $10**

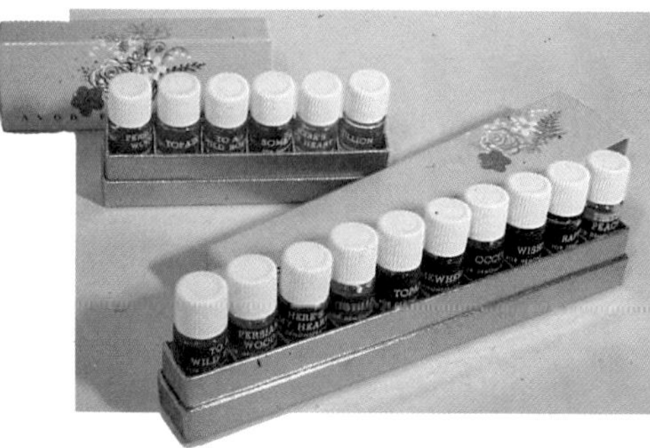

1961 *Fragrance Demonstrator. Persian Wood, Topaze, To A Wild Rose, Somewhere, Here's My Heart, Cotillion* **MP $18**
1964-65 *Fragrance Demonstrator, 10 bottles* **MP $18**

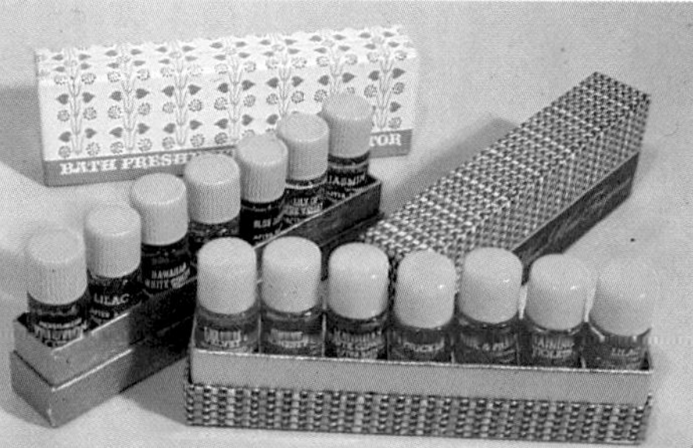

1967 *Bath Freshener Demonstrator. Lemon Friction Lotion, Lilac, Hawaiian White Ginger, Blue Lotus, Lily of the Valley, Jasmine and Honeysuckle* **MP $13**
1974 *Fragrance Demonstrator No. 2 holds Lemon Velvet, Sweet Honesty, Hawaiian White Ginger, Honeysuckle, Pink & Pretty, Raining Violets and Lilac* **MP $8**

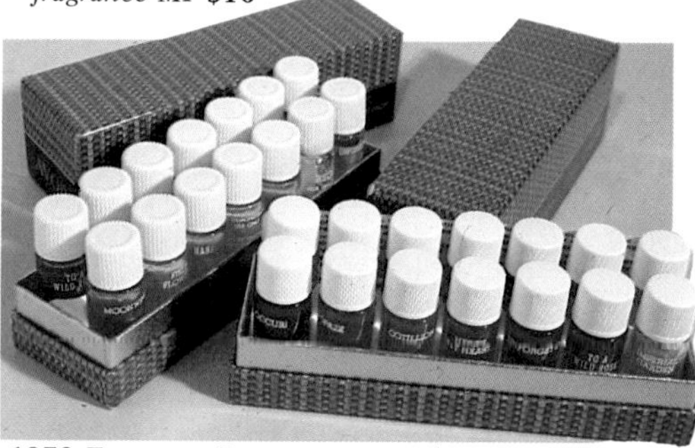

1972 *Fragrance Demonstrator, 14 bottles* **MP $10**
1973 *Fragrance Demonstrator, 14 bottles* **MP $10 (smooth lids)**

FRAGRANCES DEMONSTRATORS AND SAMPLES

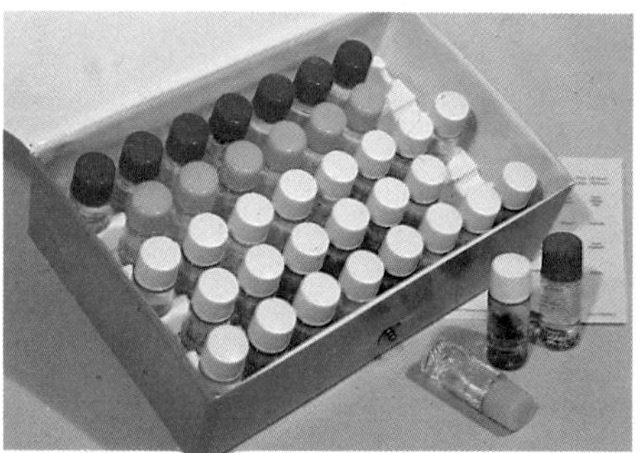

1975 *Fragrance Demonstrator, 38 bottles of Women's, Men's, Girl's and floral fragrances* **MP $15**

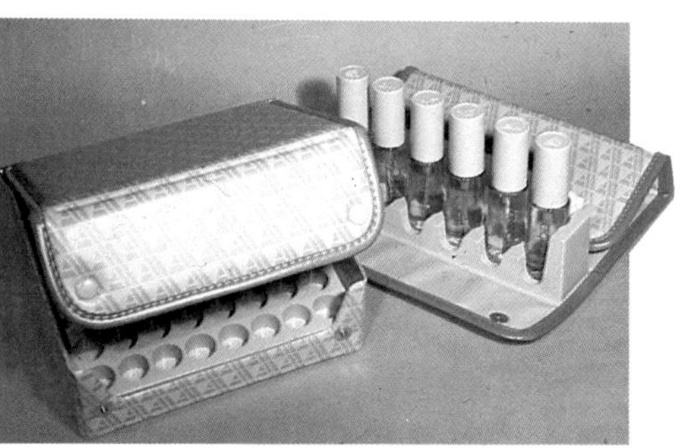

1978 *Sales Mates Sample Kit holds a variety of samples $2 (empty)* **MP $2.25**
1978 *Sales Mates Fragrance Demonstrator with a choice of 6 miniature Sprays $4.50, empty $1.75* **MP $5*, $2* empty**

1980 *Foxfire Fragrance Folio holds 12 samples* **MP $2**

**Available from Avon at time of publication*

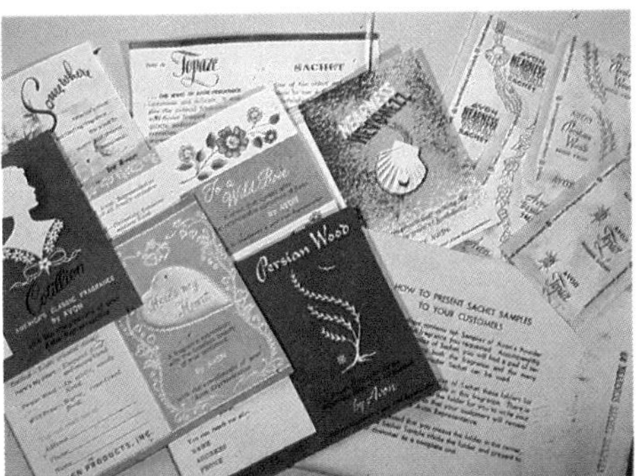

1950's & 1960's *Assortment of Powder Sachet Samples, envelope of 10 with matching Folder* **MP $12, $1 each sachet and folder**

1969 *Bravo Samples, box of 10* **MP $4**
1967 *Spicy Samples, box of 10* **MP $5**

1968 *Windjammer Cologne Samples, box of 10* **MP $6**
1969 *Excalibur Cologne, box of 10* **MP $4**
1964 *"4-A" After Shave, box of 10* **MP $8**
1964 *Tribute After Shave, box of 10* **MP $8**
1961 *Spicy After Shave, box of 30* **MP $20, 50¢ each**

1972 *Mineral Springs Bath Crystals, box of 5* **MP $3, 50¢ each**
1963 *After Bath Freshener in Lilac, Lily of the Valley, box of 10* **MP $15, $1.25 each**
1972 *Skin-So-Soft Bath Oil, box of 10, 40¢* **MP $3, 25¢ each**

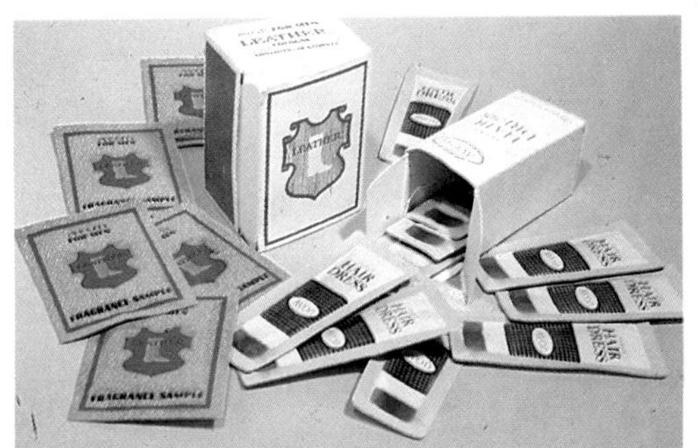

1965 *Leather Samples, box of 10* **MP $5**
1966 *Clear Hair Dress Samples, box of 10* **MP $7**

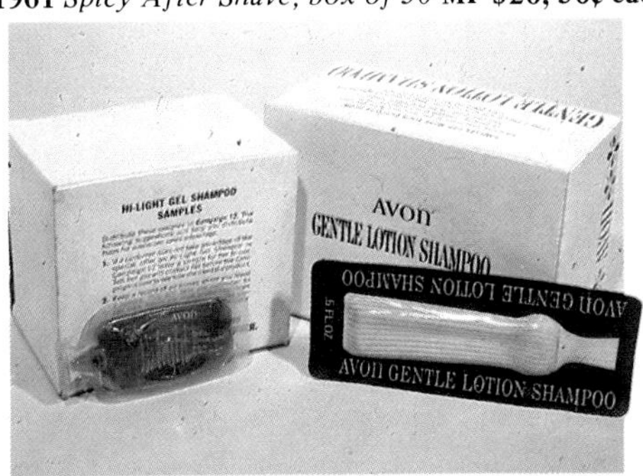

1962 *Hi-Light Gel Shampoo, box of 15* **MP $23, $1.25 each**
1969 *Gentle Lotion Shampoo, box of 10, 60¢* **MP $7, 50¢ each**

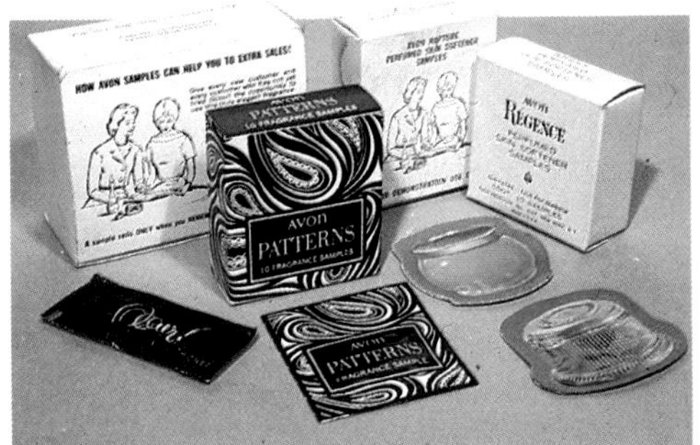

1964 *Occur! Cream Sachet Samples, box of 30 $1* **MP $18, 50¢ each**
1968 *Patterns Fragrance Samples, box of 10* **MP $2**
1965 *Rapture Skin Softener, box of 10* **MP $12, $1 each**
1967 *Regence Skin Softener, box of 10* **MP $9, 75¢ each**

1949 *Shaving Cream Samples in Lather or Brushless ¼oz. Box of 20, 50¢* **MP $120, $5 each**
1958 *After Shave Sample ½oz. Box of 20, 50¢* **MP $250, $12 each**
1959 *After Shower Sample (black) ½oz. Box of 20, 50¢* **MP $310, $15 each**
1949 *After Shave, ½oz. Box of 20, 50¢* **MP $210, $10 each**

1949 *Cream Hair Lotion, 1oz trial size* **MP $25, $35 boxed**

1968 *Mix and Match Beauty Dust Demonstrator* **MP $40 boxed**

1964 *Premium Toothpaste Samples, foil-wrapped, 50 in a box* **MP $15**

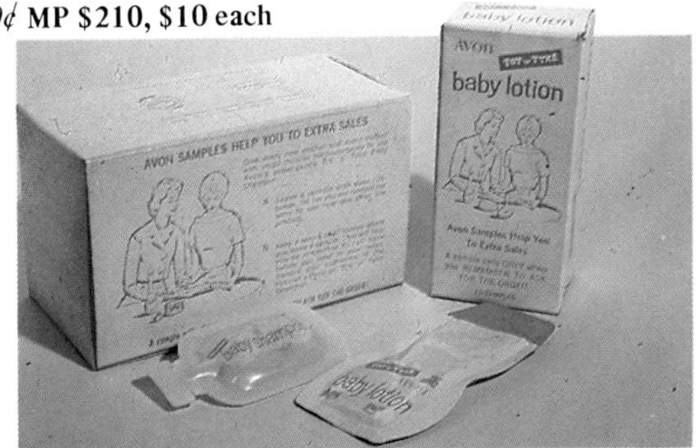

1964 *Baby Shampoo, 20 in a box* **MP $18, 75¢ each**
1964 *Baby Lotion, 10 in a box, 30¢* **MP $9, 75¢ each**

1970 *Stellar Manager Award, 2nd quarter* **MP $100**

1950's *"Woman of the Year" Award given thru 1959 to the top Representative in each District* **MP $125**
1970 *Avon Trophy* **MP $50**

1961 *Woman of Achievement Award, one in each District "Western Germany"* **MP $200**
1969 *"Better Way" Award, one in each Division "Western Germany Dresdner Art". Some have engraved plaque on base (shown without base)* **MP $250**

Over ninety years ago, Mrs. Albee, the California Perfume Company's first Representative, knocked on a door launching Avon's tradition of door-to-door selling and personal service. The legacy of Mrs. Albee lives on with charming statuettes in her image. The Avon "First Ladies" are awarded to Representatives for outstanding achievement – Avon's very best!

1973 *Avon Lady Trophy Award given to approximately 6,000 Representatives of 5 winning Districts in each Branch* **MP $200**

1978 *Albee Trophy Award, 10 in each District* **MP $125**
1979 *Albee Trophy Award, 10 in each District* **MP $125**

1980 *Albee Trophy Award, 10 in each District* **MP $125**
1981 *Albee Trophy Award, to all Representatives attaining President's Club Membership* **MP $50**

1976 *First Avon Lady Porcelain Figurine made in Spain. Anniversary Sales Award to President's Club Members* **MP $50**
1976 *Bicentennial Coin Pendant. Anniversary Sales Award* **MP $30**

Each Precious Moments figurine is a very special limited edition, representing a memorable moment in the Avon experience.

1980 *"Ready for an Avon Day" awarded for sales of $175 each in Campaigns 4, 5 and 6* **MP $25**
1980 *"My First Call" for sales of $250 each in each of three campaigns* **MP $30**
1980 *"Which Shade Do You Prefer?" for sales of $350 in each of three campaigns* **MP $40**

1980 *"The Day I Made President's Club" awarded for membership in President's Club* **MP $40**
1980 *"Merry Christmas Avon '80" awarded for two successful Recommendations, only in C-22, 23 and 24. Limit of 1 per Representative* **MP $50**

1936 *50th Anniversary Gift to Representatives. Quill Pen and Certificate* **MP $55** *Certificate only* **MP $25**

1936 *50th Anniversary Award 24k gold-plated pin.* **MP $55, $65 boxed**

1910 *CPC Identification Pin* **MP $160**
(See also pg. 8 for pre-1910)

1938 *Service-Counsel-Satisfaction Medallion* **MP $58**
1938-45 *Identification Pin* **MP $40**
1938-43 *Honor Award Pin* **MP $45**
1938-45 *Star Representative Medallion 1/20-10k Gold Filled* **MP $55**

1933-35 *Identification Pin (top left) silver plated* **MP $55**
1935-38 *Identification Pin (top right) silver plated* **MP $50**
1930-33 *Identification Pin (bottom left) silver plated (left leg of "A" and "N" intersect lower rim of oval)* **MP $65**
1935-38 *Honor Award Pin, Gold Filled* **MP $60**

(below)
1956-61 *Representative's Highest Award, 5 diamonds on "A" of pin and 5 diamond Star Guard for sales of $26,000 within a year* **MP $300**

1945 *Identification Pin, leaf patterned* **MP $25**
1945-61 *Jeweled Pin Award with 5 seed Pearls, 10k Gold* **MP $30**

1945-56 *Jeweled Pin with Numeral Guards, given for each consecutive $1,000 in sales. Numeral 2 through 5* **MP $15,** *6 through 10* **MP $20,** *11-15* **MP $30,** *16-20* **MP $40,** *21-30* **MP $50,** *31-40* **MP $60,** *41-50* **MP $70,** *51 and up* **MP $85,** *Pin serves as Numeral 1* **MP $30**

1956-61 *Diamond Star Guards replace Numeral Guards #5 and higher. Star Guard with 1 diamond for sales of $6,000 in a year or less* **MP $20 Guard only** *With 2 diamonds for sales of $11,000 in a year or less* **MP $30** *With 3 diamonds for sales of $16,000 in a year or less* **MP $50** *With 4 diamonds for sales of $21,000 in a year or less* **MP $100**

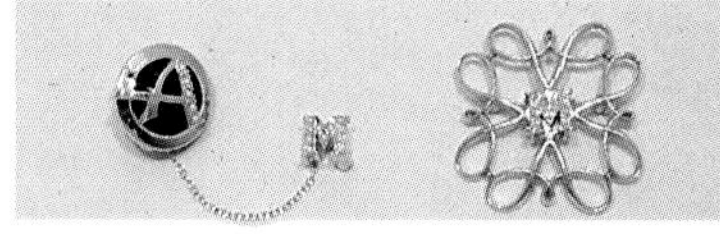

1945 *City Manager's Identification Pin and "M" Guard with 11 seed Pearls* **MP $100**
1961 *Manager's 4-A Pin with 11 diamond "M"* **MP $125**

1961 *Representative's Diamond 4-A Pin Award* **MP $50**
1963 *Sapphire 4-A Pin Award* **MP $35**
1963-70 *Pearl 4-A Pin Award* **MP $28**
1973 *Ruby 4-A President's Club Membership Pin* **MP $18**

1971 *Manager's diamond and pearls Circle of Excellence Ring* **MP $300**

JEWELRY AWARDS

Recognition of superior sales achievement is an Avon tradition. The Award Pin Program, introduced in 1928, continues to this day.

1964 *Manager's Sterling Silver Doorknocker Pin* **MP $40**
1964 *Representative's Gold-plated Doorknocker Pin on green card* **MP $12, $10 on white card**

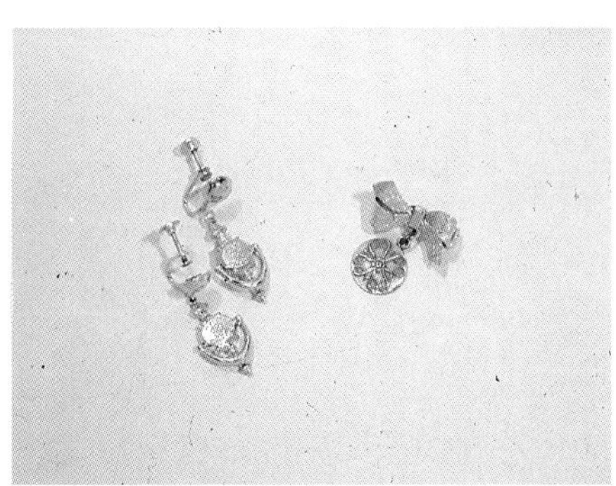

1967 *Representative's Doorknocker Earrings awarded to Championship Teams from each Branch* **MP $25**
1967 *Ten year Service Pin awarded to Representatives on retirement, engraved on back and rare* **MP $100**

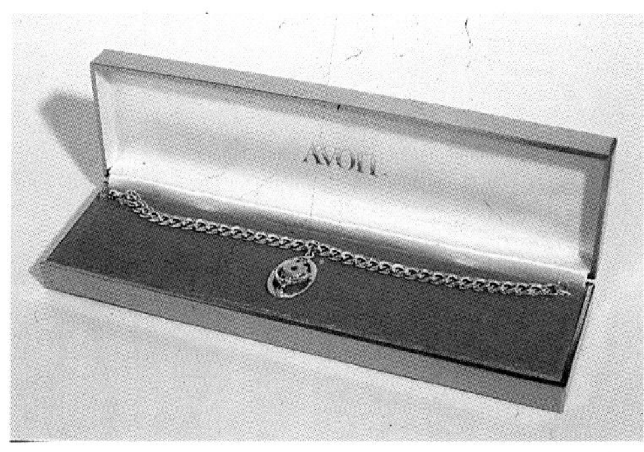

1974 *Silver Doorknocker Bracelet awarded to only 40 Managers in each Branch* **MP $150**

1968 *Anniversary Team Champions Key Chain* **MP $30**

1962 *Service Award Key Chain* **MP $30**

1964 *Crown Pin Award for top sales* **MP $20**
1969 *President's 22k Court Charm & Bracelet* **MP $30, $20 charm only**

1962 *Manager's Christmas Gift. Pearl & Diamond Bracelet & Earrings* **MP $300**
1966 *Regence Crown Performance Pendant/Pin Combo & Earrings to winning team in General Manager's Branch contest* **MP $100, $125 boxed**
1967 *Pin/Pendant incentive Award to Managers* **MP $50, $65 boxed**
1975 *Avon Lady Pendant to top 15 Reps in each district* **MP $40**
1968 *Shell Pin and Earrings recommendation prizes* **MP $7 each**

1966 *Cameo Glace Brooch Locket, Honor Award* **MP $30**
1965 *Avon Lady Award Pin* **MP $20**
1951 *Three-Leaf Clover Pin by Coro, Award for Customer Service* **MP $30**

1960 *Golf League Tournament Charm to Pasadena Branch employees* **MP $50**
1961 *Star Award Earrings Representative incentive Award* **MP $15**

The President's Club – an elite group of special Representatives who share the pride of being Avon's very best . . .

1968 *Manager's 14k gold Bracelet awarded for high achievement in the General Manager's Contest* **MP $100 with certificate**
1969 *Manager's diamond and pearls Circle of Excellence Pin* **MP $300**
1976 *Diamond Sterling Silver Necklace, engraved "1976 #1" on back* **MP $75**

1964 *Christmas Bells Earrings to winning team in each Division, General Manager's Contest* **MP $35**
1964 *Four Leaf Clover Pin, simulated pearl, by Coro. To Reps in "Lucky 7" contest* **MP $10**
1970 *Five year Avon Employees Service Pin* **MP $25, $35 boxed**
1976 *Manager's Xmas Conference Name Badge* **MP $7**

1966 *Cuff Links worn by Avon Executives in 10k gold* **MP $450** *(in other metals awarded to employees* **MP $35)**
1973 *Branch Tour Guide's Jacket Guard* **MP $30**

1974 *Sterling Silver Doorknocker Cuff Links with Sapphire, incentive Award to Manager's, only 200 to 300 made* **MP $250**

1971 *Manager's Valentine Gift of Precious Pretenders Bracelet & Earrings* **MP $45 boxed with letter, $15 letter only**

1976 *Sterling Silver Doorknocker Circle Pin (left) with Sapphire. Awarded top 100 Representatives in Excelsior Division, Rye Branch only* **MP $130 boxed with letter, $50 without letter**
1976 *Team Leader Christmas Gift* **MP $25**
1976 *Double "e" Necklace, gift to Team Leaders for Emprise Survey* **MP $25**

1968 *Sweater Guard, General Manager's Honor Award, given to winning teams in each Branch* **MP $25**
1973 *Key Ring, Representative's Prize, "What's In It For You" Program* **MP $10**

1974 *Curio Box. Red lined with embossed Rose and engraved "President's Celebration '74". To Reps in winning districts* **MP $55**
1974 *Diamond Necklace. Given to top ten Reps of each winning District during President's Campaign. 14k pendant with 3pt diamond* **MP $85**

1976 *District Manager Panelist Identification Pin* **MP $35**
1967 *Distinguished Management Award, Key Chain and Fob* **MP $35**
1968 *Manager's Award, "G" Clef Pin 14k for "Making Beautiful Music with Avon"* **MP $50, $60 boxed**
1975 *Manager's Sunny Star Necklace, engraved on back "August 1975"* **MP $15 boxed**

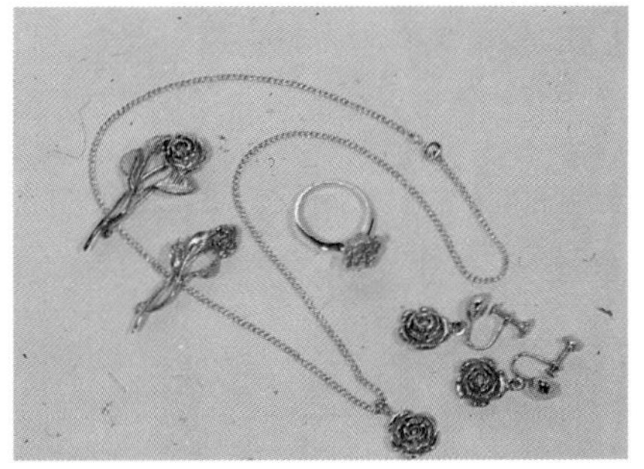

1971 *85th Anniversary Awards of 22k gold-plated sterling silver in shape of rose with diamond, large Pin (President's Club Members)* **MP $35,** *small Pin* **$25,** *Pendant* **$35,** *Ring (2 awarded per District)* **$80,** *Earrings* **$25**

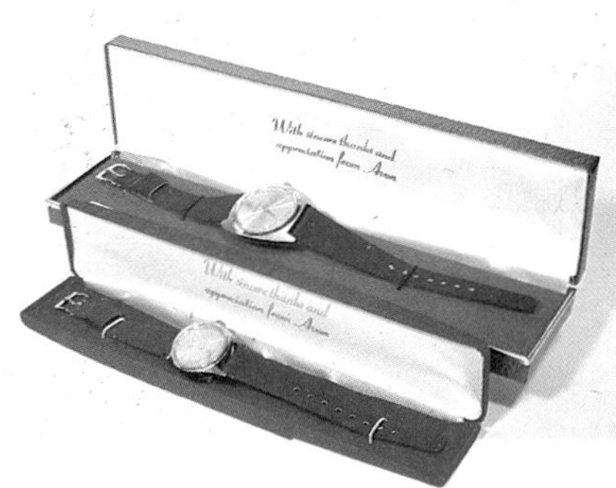

1977 *Male Manager's Wrist Watch* **MP $200**
1977 *Manager's Wrist Watch* **MP $125**

1970 *Sheffield Pendant Watch awarded to 6 Representatives from each District for superior sales achievement* **MP $50**

Manager's Stick Pin Watch **MP $50**

The **"Jeweled A"** *honors Representatives' Achievement.*

1976 *Step Up to Stardom "A" Pin Award for Sales Achievements* **MP $7**
1976 *As above, first issued in white box* **MP $9**

1977 *Team Leader Mirror, Appreciation Day gift* **MP $8**
1977 *Team Leader Christmas Gift, Jeweled Wrist Watch with floating "Avon" second hand* **MP $70**

Women's President's Club Membership Pin (top row) **1979 MP $20, 1980 MP $15, 1981 MP $15**
Men's President's Club Membership Tie Tac **1979 MP $30, 1980 MP $25, 1981 MP $25**

1981 *President's Club Membership Stickpin* **MP $15**

1980 *Men's President's Club Pocket Watches, both engraved "President's Club 1981"* **MP $100 each**

1969 *Male Executive Tie Tac with blue Sapphire* **MP $200**
1976 *Male Manager #1 Cuff Links* **MP $125**
1978 *Male Team Leader Christmas Gift, 10k gold and diamond Tie Tac* **MP $150**
1980 *Manager's Shooting Star Pin. Box sleeve reads "We're Going To Be Stronger and Better Than Ever"* **MP $40**

1978 *President's Club Members 4-A designed ruby Ring* **MP $50**
1978 *Men's President's Club Members ruby Ring* **MP $200**

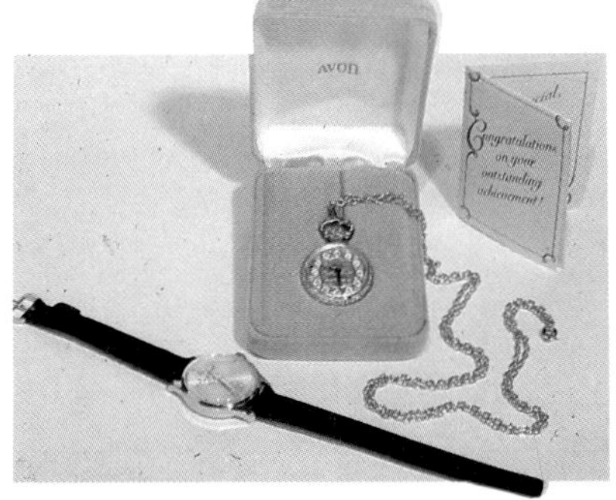

1974 *President's Club Wrist Watch. "The President's Club" and 4-A symbol on face.* **MP $55**
1980 *President's Club 17-jewel Pendant Watch with "Albee" engraved on back* **MP $55**

1978 *Team Leader Xmas Gift, 10k gold and diamond Earrings* **MP $55**
1979 *Manager's Xmas Gift, 10k gold with 2 diamonds. Engraved "District Manager 1979 Avon 10K" on back of Pendant* **MP $150**
1979 *Team Leaders Xmas Gift (not shown) as above* **MP $90**

President's Club Highest Award, Charm Bracelet and Charms (in box) complete **MP $280**
- 1971 *Bracelet and "4-A" Charm* **MP $30**
- 1972 *Avon Rose* **MP $20**
- 1972 *First Lady Charm with topaze* **MP $30**
- 1973 *World of Avon with aquamarine* **MP $35**
- 1973 *Doorknocker with amethyst* **MP $35**
- 1974 *Jeweled A with sapphire* **MP $40**
- 1974 *Key with garnet* **MP $40**
- 1975 *Great Oak* **MP $50**

1963-65 *Manager's Circle of Leadership Bracelet with 10k gold filled Charms and genuine jewels. (Listed in Achievement sequence)*

1. *Circle of Leadership, 4 diamonds & Bracelet* **MP $65**
2. *Heart Locket, ruby* **MP $40**
3. *Cotillion Cologne* **MP $45**
4. *Great Oak Book* **MP $50**
5. *Women of Achievement* **MP $55**
6. *Emerald Charm (square)* **MP $60**
7. *Acorn* **MP $65**
8. *Door Charm Locket* **MP $70**
9. *Oval with star and 4 sapphires* **MP $75**
10. *10, 11 & 12, not shown, are same shape as Charm 9, but set with rubies, emeralds and diamonds, consecutively* **MP $85, $100 and $150**

Avon's Exclusive Symbols –
The **"4-A"** *design is the world-wide Avon corporate symbol.*
Avon Rose *symbolizes beauty made possible by Avon products.*
First Avon Lady *represents Mrs. P. F. E. Albee, mother of the California Perfume Company.*
The **"World of Avon"** *is the symbol of the 31 countries Avon served in 1981.*
Doorknocker *is the symbol of personal and loyal service.*
The **"Jeweled A"** *honors Representative's Achievement.*
Avon Key *is the symbol of "key" to success.*
The Great Oak *signifies the growing success and solid foundation on which Avon is based.*

1980 *Manager's Royal Ribbons Award Pin* **MP $25**
1980 *Manager's Royal Ribbons Award Pin* **MP $50**

1965 *Representative's Golden Circle of Service Charm Bracelet (top) 22k gold finish and 5 charms* **MP $75 complete, $10 each charm**

Charms awarded in following sequence –
- **Avon Lady**
- **The Door,** *inscribed "Avon Calling. . . Guaranteed to Please"*
- **Heart,** *inscribed "Quality and Service Are the Heart of Avon"*
- **Clock,** *inscribed "Avon Hours. . . Time for Opportunity"*
- **Rose Locket,** *inscribed "Avon. . . a History of Beauty Since 1886"*

1969 *Representative's Charm Bracelet, with Doorknocker, Bell, Avon Rose, Spinner and Acorn charms.* **MP $50 complete, $8 each charm**

Recognition of outstanding performance has long been important to Avon. It began more than 95 years ago with personal letters of commendation to outstanding Representatives from Avon's founder and first president, Mr. David H. McConnell.

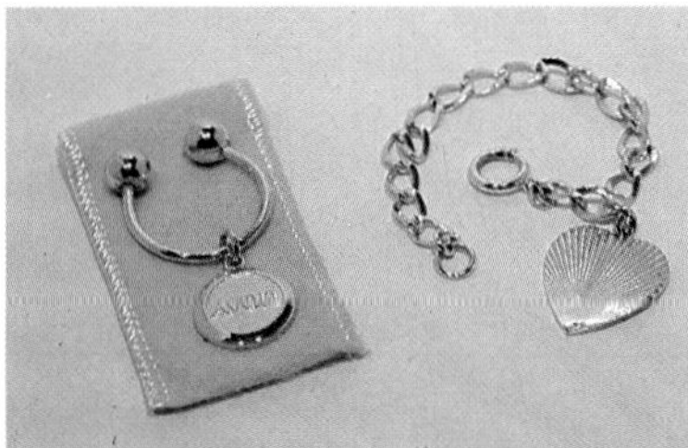

1971 *Key Ring, gift to employees. Medallion reads "Avon" on one side and "You're In Demand" on reverse* **MP $30**
1953 *Valentine's Gift to Representatives, Sterling Silver Bracelet and Heart charm inscribed "1953"* **MP $65**

1974 *Team Leader Bookmark* **MP $18**
1979 *Team Leader Key Ring & Heart Medallion inscribed "Thanks for Making Us No. 1"* **MP $15**

1975 *Manager's Boca or Bust Key Ring with 4-A design* **MP $20**

1980 *Manager's Sales Achievement, President's Celebration Award* **MP $200**
1979 *Male Manager's 10k gold and 2-diamond Money Clip engraved DM* **MP $175**
1979 *Male Team Leader Xmas Gift (not shown) as above* **MP $130**

Avon, the world's largest cosmetic company, presents these symbols of success to those who helped the company to greatness.

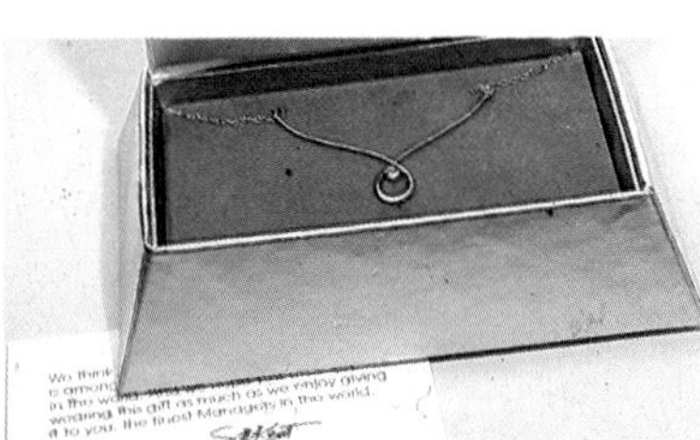

1977 *Manager's Diamond Loop Necklace in gold presentation box* **MP $40**

1978 *Manager's specially boxed Cultured Pearl Necklace* **MP $75 boxed with card**

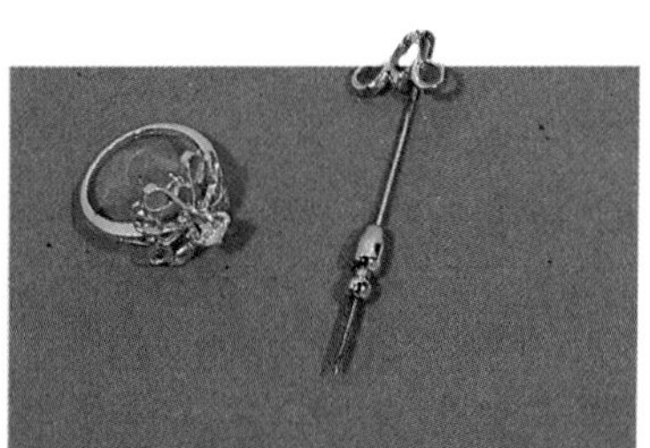

1968 *Manager's ¼ carat Diamond Ring* **MP $425**
1978 *President's Celebration Award. Sterling Silver Stickpin to top ten Reps in each District* **MP $25**

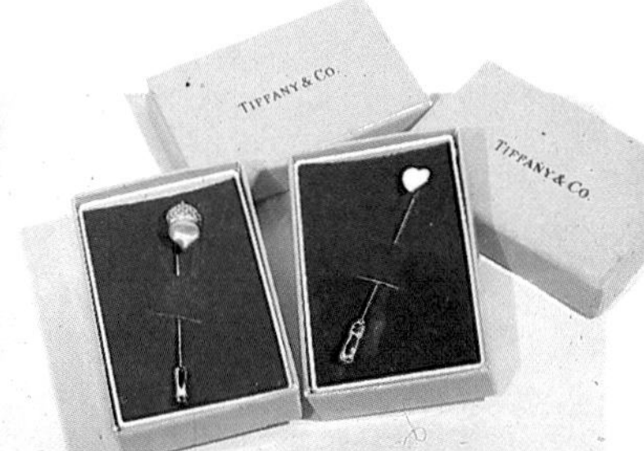

1978 *Manager's Appreciation Gifts. Sterling Silver Acorn and Heart Stickpins by Tiffany.* **MP $50 each, boxed with card.**

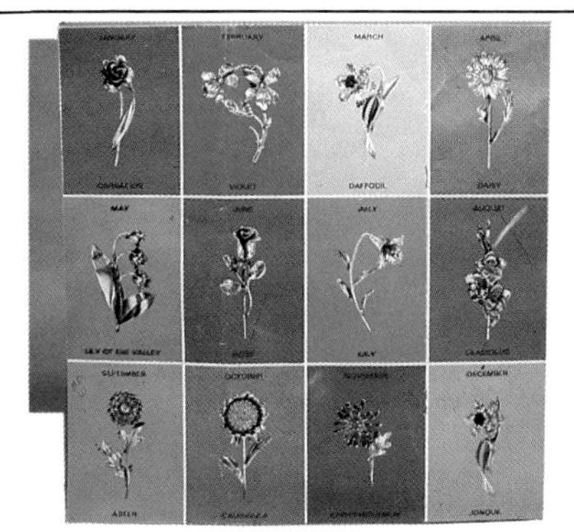

January – Carnation
February – Violet
March – Daffodil
April – Daisy
May – Lily of the Valley
June – Rose
July – Lily
August – Gladiolus
September – Aster
October – Calendula
November – Chrysanthemum
December – Jonquil

1967 *81st Anniversary Sterling Silver Pins. Winning Reps could choose 1 of 12 exclusive flower-of-the-month designs* **MP $25, $35 boxed**

The grace and fragrance of a Year of Flowers, each one a favorite in someone's collection. . .

1968 *Spring Fever Pins. Representative's recommendation prizes* **MP $6 each pin, $50 with card**

1979 *Division Manager's Tac Pin with red enamel heart* **MP $35**
1979 *Manager's Tac Pin, "Thanks America" promotion, engraved DM on back* **MP $25**
1979 *Representative's Pin, as above, not engraved* **MP $15**

1977 *Gold and 12-diamond Pin, Sales Achievement Award to Representative with highest yearly sales in each Division* **MP $1000**

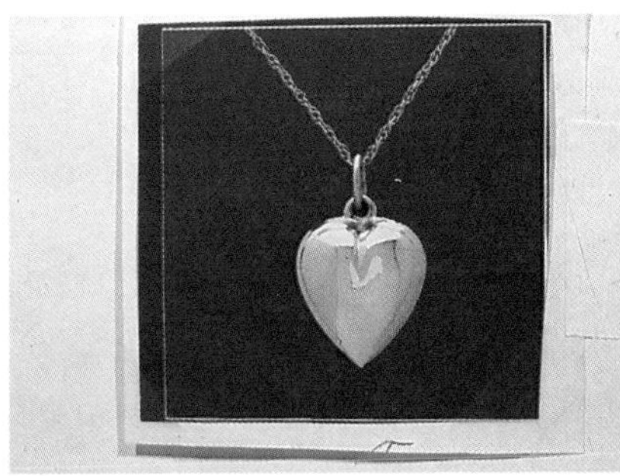

1978 *Valentine Sweepstakes 14k gold Pendant and chain. A winning Rep in each District, 2500 total. Retail value $50* **MP $70 boxed**

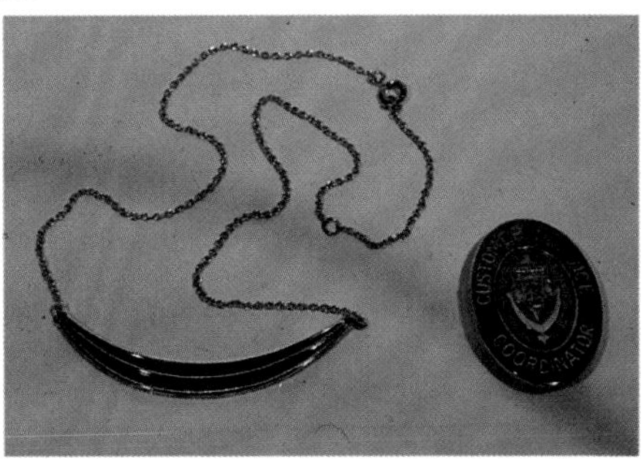

1978 *Smile Necklace, engraved "Team Leader March 1978"* **MP $15,** *Manager's engraved "D.M."* **MP $20**
1977 *Division Manager's Award, Pasadena Branch* **MP $15**

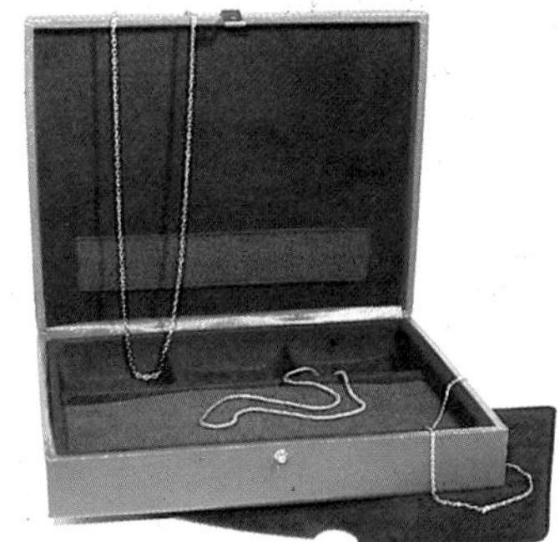

1975 *Representative's Jewelry Display Case for reaching sales goal* **MP $7**

1977 *Representative's Sales Achievement Award Pendant to top 10% in each Division* **MP $25**

1980 *President's Celebration goldtone Oak Tree Pendant awarded to 20 Representative's in each District* **MP $20**
1980 *Silvertone Oak Tree Pendant Representatives of Number One District in each Division* **MP $50**

1980 *Team Leader Cologne Atomizer, embossed "TL" on bottom* **MP $10, Manager's emb. DM MP $20**
1980 *Manager's Sterling Silver Bracelet by Tiffany with heart Charm engraved "DM"* **MP $110**

1977 *Sterling Silver Star Necklace with diamond, President's Celebration Award to 1 Manager in each Division* **MP $250**
1979 *Manager's Sterling Silver Tiffany Shell Award inscribed "1979 Sales Leader"* **MP $150**

1981 *Manager Silver Acorn Necklace by Tiffany* **MP $125**
1976 *Manager's Necklace Award* **MP $75**

1955 *Sterling Silver Robin Pins, given in pairs to Representatives for reaching customer goals in "Red Robin" Campaign 7* **MP $28 pair**
1967 *Representative's Sterling Silver Bracelet by Tiffany with Bell and clapper* **MP $40**
1964 *Rapture Dove Pin, antique silver finish awarded in General Manager's Contest* **MP $35**

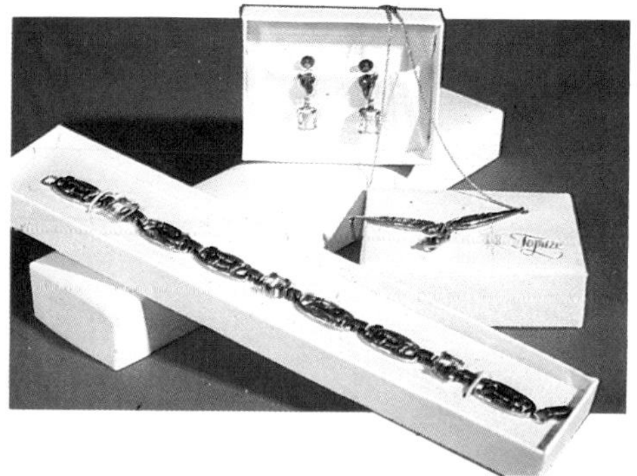
1960 *Topaze Jewelry Awards 12k gold filled with Topaze stones. Earrings & Necklace* **MP $40 each**
14k solid gold Bracelet, highest level **MP $100**

1976 *Cross 14k gold filled Pen engraved "Avon Calling" with Rose embossed case. Recommendation gift* **MP $22**

1968 *Sales Achievement Award, Charisma Pin* **MP $25**

1968 *Charisma Jewelry Awards – Convertible Necklace/Pin* **MP $15**
Bracelet **MP $15**
Earrings **MP $15**

1970 *Avon employees 15 year Award, 14k gold Cross Pen and Pencil set, engraved "Avon 15 years" and initials. Case has ruby in 4-A.* **MP $50**
1969 *14k gold Cross Pen with 4-A symbol on clip* **MP $20**

1970 *Hana Gasa Jewelry. Enameled Pin and Earrings, Recommendation Prize* **MP $20 set**

1977 *Silvery Pendant Necklaces hold "Inch of Ariane" fragrance –*
Manager's Bouquet with Silvery Pendant engraved "August Conference 1977" in bag with red drawstrings **MP $50**
Representative's Pendant in bag with black drawstrings **MP $15**
President's Club Members Pendant engraved "P.C." in bag with silver drawstrings **MP $25**

1980 *Representative's Gold Pen and Pencil Set engraved "President's Club Candidate" awarded to new Representative's for sales of $250 in 4 consecutive campaigns* **MP $25 with pen refill**

1979 *Manager's Tasha Necklace, 18k gold over Sterling Silver with flower, butterfly and seashell Charms. Satin-like drawstring bag serves as box* **MP $35 in bag**

1940's *Valentine's Day Gift Perfume 1/8oz* **MP $80**

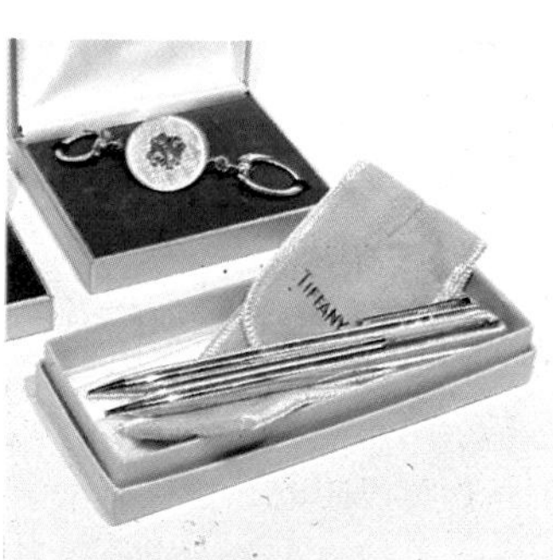
1974 *Five Year Service Award to employees, come-apart Key Ring with 4-A design* **MP $35 boxed**
1979 *Ten Year Service Award to employees, gold Pen and Pencil Set by Tiffany. Personalized with initials* **MP $50 boxed**

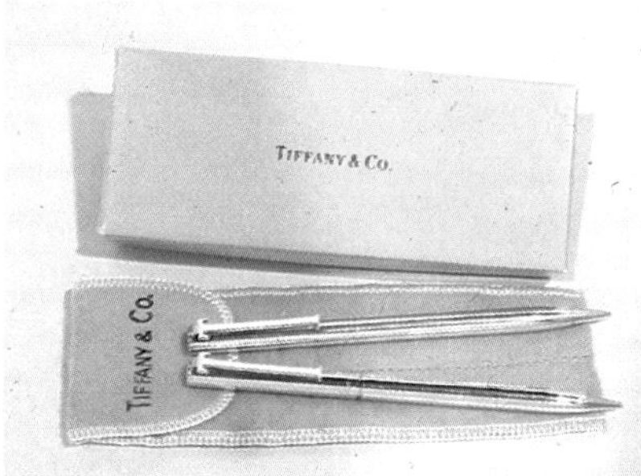

Manager's Sterling Silver Pen and Pencil Set by Tiffany, letter "T" serves as pocket clip **MP $125**

1977 *Manager's Recruiting Award, Quill Pen and Pen Holder* **MP $55**
1972 *Manager Award Desk Set, by Cross. Gold plaque on marble base has manager's name and 4-A* **MP $50**

1953 *67th Anniversary Celebration letter from Irene Nunemaker, Editor of the Avon Outlook, to Representatives. Envelope postmarked 5/22/53, London, England* **MP $65**

1970 *Memento Alarm Clock by Seth Thomas. Recommendation Gift. (No engraving on back)* **MP $35**
1968 *Distinguished Management Award. Brushed gold paperweight – clock in one end, engraved on other end and a 3 minute timer in center* **MP $175**

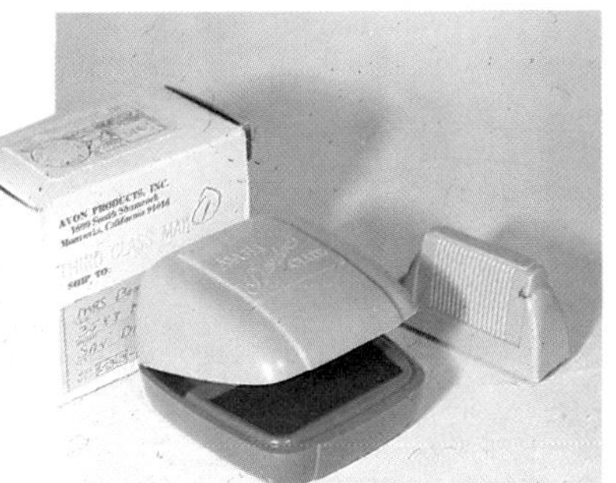

1972 *Name Stamp, President's Club Members Award* **MP $8**

1974 *88th Anniversary Award. Marble Pen Stand and Pen for $125 order* **MP $25**

1976 *Recommendation Gift. George Washington's acceptance letter to Office of President, April 14, 1789. Reproduced especially for Avon Representatives by permission of the Lilly Library, Indiana University* **MP $8**

1971 *"Tole-Alarm" Solid Wood, Hand Painted Clock by Seth Thomas, Recommendation Prize* **MP $30**
1970 *"Picture Yourself" two-sided mirror with Florentine Handle Representative's Prize for selling 7 Body Lotions* **MP $7**

1970 *Calling Cards with Carrying Case awarded to President's Club Members* **MP $10**

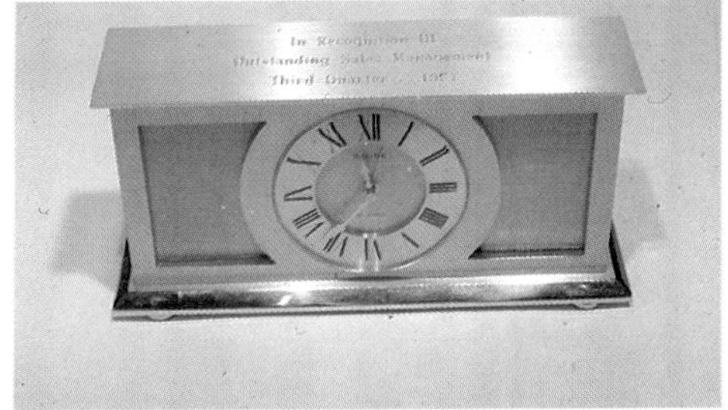

1977 *Manager's 15-jewel Clock Award engraved "Outstanding Sales Management Third Quarter 1977"* **MP $90**

1977 *Million Dollar Baby Clock by Bulova awarded only to 40 Managers for outstanding sales increase* **MP $150**

1979 *Manager's Sales Achievement Award 2nd Quarter* **MP $25**

1979 *Manager's Panasonic Pencil Sharpener with engraved nameplate, Xmas Conference gift* **MP $40**

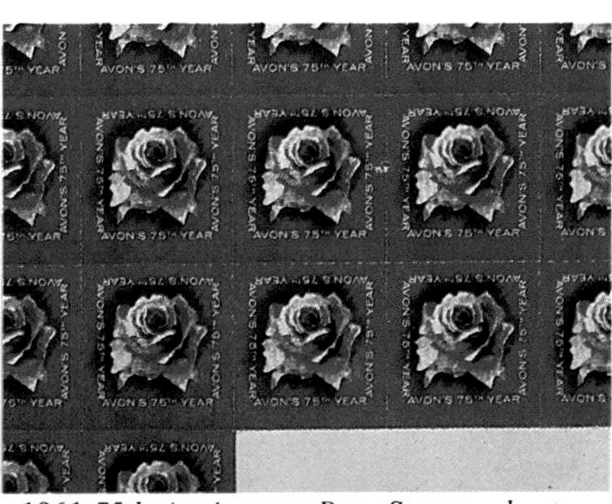

1961 *75th Anniversary Rose Stamps, sheet of 75* **MP $20 sheet, 50¢ each stamp**

FRAGRANCE AND PRODUCT INTRODUCTION AWARDS AND GIFTS

A fantastic array of specially designed and packaged gifts – each one a unique and prized collectible . . .

1924 *CPC American Beauty Fragrance Jar, painted. Representative's Gift* **MP $300**

1942 *56th Anniversary Gift. The Album holds pictures and messages from Avon personnel and two sachet pillowettes. Gold imprinted on back "From your Friends at the Avon Laboratories . . . 56th Anniversary 1942."* **MP $125 complete, $30 each pillowette**

1943 *57th Anniversary Gift Avon Cologne 6oz* **MP $100, $135 boxed**
1945 *59th Anniversary Gift, Violet Bouquet Cologne 16oz* **MP $150, $180 boxed**

1948 *62nd Anniversary Gift, Quaintance Cologne 4oz* **MP $85 boxed**
1963 *Gift Perfume Award, Occur!* **MP $200**

1949 *Representative's 63rd Anniversary Gift. Quaintance Perfume 3 dram for selling 63 products during Anniversary campaign* **MP $75, $110 boxed**

1947 *61st Anniversary Gift, Wishing Cologne* **MP $85, $110 boxed**

1950 *Luscious Perfume Award 3 drams* **MP $165 boxed**

1951 *Oct. 8 Gift. 1 dram Forever Spring, introduced October 8th* **MP $45 boxed**

1960 *Representative's Gift, styrofoam Nosegay of Blossom Colors holds 4 new lipsticks in Peach, Cherry, Plum and Orange Blossom shades* **MP $65 as shown**

1959 *Golden Slipper Award, Topaze Perfume 1oz to one winning District of each Branch in Avon's 73rd Anniversary contest. Slipper and perfume* **MP $200, $250 boxed**

1961 *Christmas Gift. Specially designed Cream Sachet Decanter for Representatives, Somewhere 1½oz* **MP $15, $20 boxed**
1961 *75th Anniversary Gift, Perfume Mist in Somewhere* **MP $16 as shown**

1960 *Representative's Xmas Gift, Deluxe Lipstick* **MP $15 boxed**

1962 *Perfume Creme Rollette, Xmas Gift to Representatives* **MP $15 boxed as shown**

1964 *78th Anniversary Gift (not a Xmas gift) tree ornament holds .4oz Rapture Cologne, Avon's major pre-Christmas fragrance introduction* **MP $65 complete with card, $45 ornament and bottle**

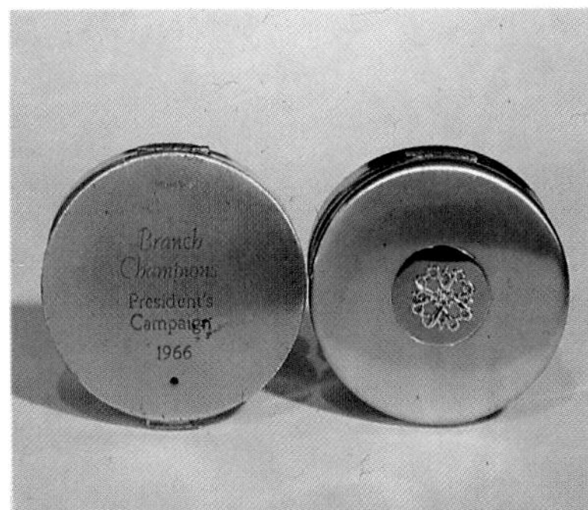

1966 *Deluxe Compact, engraved to Branch Champions, President's Campaign* **MP $25**

1969 *Patterns designed plastic carry-all bag. For submitting recommendation names* **MP $6**

1969 *Elusive Awards: Mini Bag lettered "An S. M. Kent exclusive for Avon by Enger Kress" Scarf with S. M. Kent signature and Avon embossed Cuff Links. Cuff Links* **MP $12,** *Purse* **$15,** *Scarf* **MP $10.** *Blouse (not shown)* **MP $20**

1969 *Elusive Record sent to Representatives at time of Elusive introduction* **MP $10**

1969 *Bird of Paradise Prize Awards, Scarf* **MP $10,** *Order Book Cover and Pen* **MP $7,** *Bracelet and Earrings* **MP $20 each,** *Pin* **MP $15,** *Robe (not shown)* **MP $35**

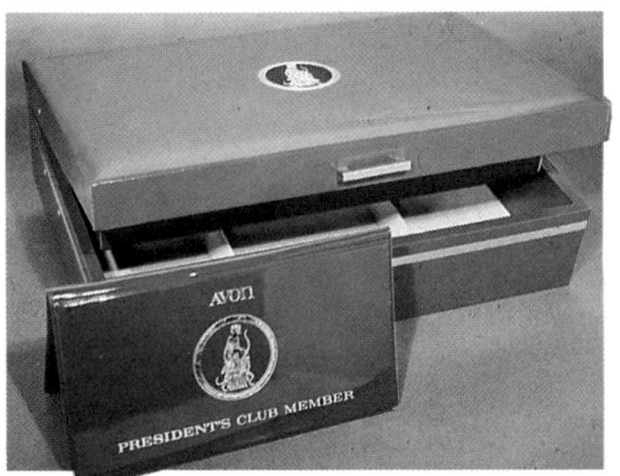

1971 *Moonwind Prizes. Order Book Cover and Pen* **MP $7**
Jewelry Box **MP $25**
Robe (not shown) **MP $35**

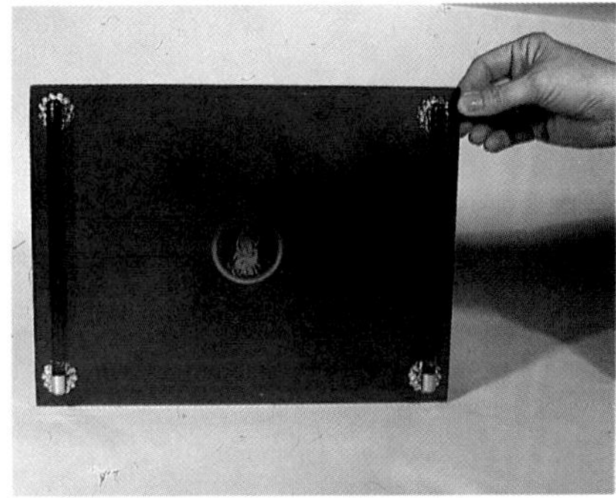

1971 *Moonwind Tray, Award for selling Cologne Mists* **MP $25**

1971 *Field Flowers Awards: Tote Bag* **MP $12,** *Umbrella* **MP $10,** *Cape (not shown) with Sash* **MP $20**

1970 *Hana Gasa 33-1/3 rpm Record with emblem. Given to all Representatives prior to fragrance introduction* **MP $16**
1970 *Hana Gasa Manager's Letter, from Japanese Manager, relating story of "Hana Gasa"* **MP $30 with envelope**

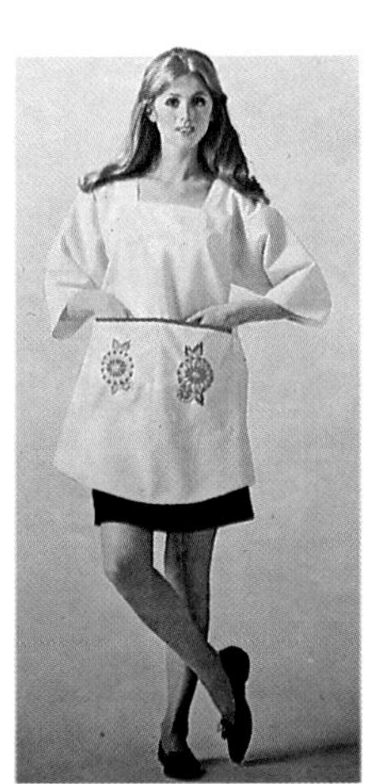

1970 *Hana Gasa Happi-Coat Recommendation gift* **MP $28**

1970 *Hana Gasa Umbrella given to managers for use at Sales Meeting introducing Hana Gasa* **MP $125**

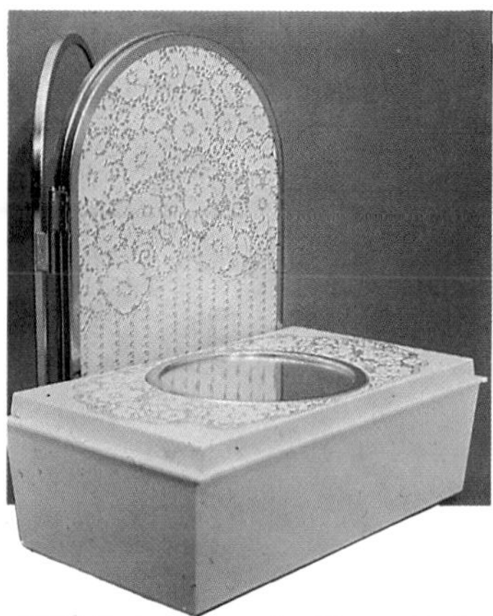

1972 *Sonnet Awards: Three sided mirror* **MP $28** *Vanity Box* **MP $18**

1972 *Sonnet Robe, President's Club Prize* **MP $38**
1972 *Vanity Tray (not shown)* **MP $12**

1975 *Moisture Secret Gift Set to Managers. 4oz Cremegel Cleanser, 5oz Freshener, 3oz Night Concentrate* **MP $25**
1975 *Moisture Secret Night Cream Concentrate 3oz. President's Club Members Gift* **MP $9 boxed with sleeve**

1974 *Perfect Balance Manager's Gift. Freshener and Astringent 6oz each, Cleansing Cream and Lotion 4oz each, Night Cream 2½oz, Moisturizer 3oz* **MP $40**

1974 *President's Club Members Gift. Collector's Edition of Ultra Timeless Cologne Mist 2oz. Embossed 4-A on base of bottle* **MP $15 with card**
1974 *Manager's Timeless Gift Set. 2oz Cologne Mist, .66oz Creme Perfume and Perfume Rollette* **MP $37**

1975 *Vial of Unspoken to Managers only* **MP $15 boxed**

1975 *Manager's California Perfume Co. Anniversary Keepsake Bottle. Limited edition carries the 4-A design on base beneath the label* **MP $17**

1975 *Gift Sample of Queen's Gold Foaming Bath Oil given to President's Club Members, with "Pamper You. . ." Card* **MP $10**

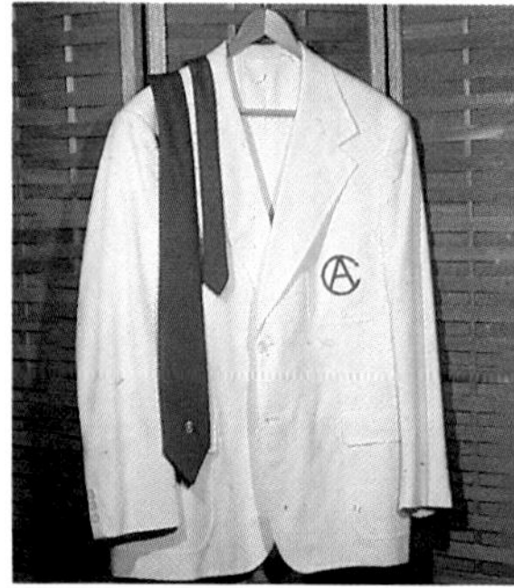

1977 *Candid Blazer and Tie* **MP $100**

1975 *Unspoken, Manager's Gift. Blue velour drawstring bag holds 3oz Cologne Spray, silver outer box* **MP $25 with box**

1976 *Emprise Evening Bag. Awarded for highest Emprise sales* **MP $20**

1977 *Candid Prize Awards. Tote Bag* **MP $10,** *Purse Organizer for highest Candid sales* **MP $8,** *Scarf, a gift to President's Club members* **MP $7**

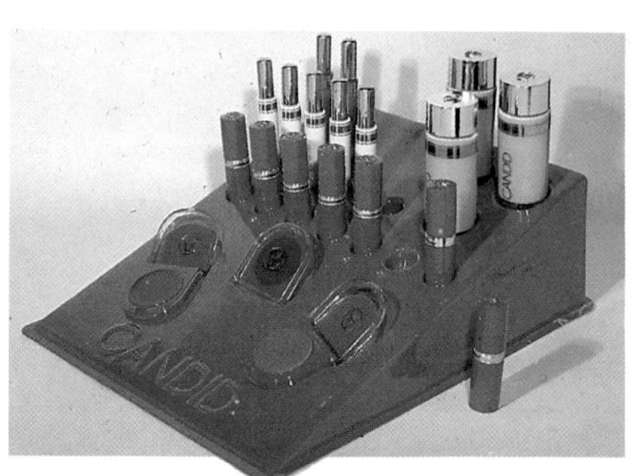

1977 *Manager's Display Tray used at Sales Meetings to hold Candid makeup products* **MP $9 empty**

1978 *Quaker State Hand Cleanser, empty container used by Managers as demo at Sales Meeting. Note different lid* **MP $10**
1978 *Manager's Tempo Cologne Portable in drawstring bag* **MP $20**

1978 *Tempo Cologne Spray in drawstring bag, designed for Reps only at C-20 Meeting* **MP $12**
1975 *President's Club Members blue velvet drawstring Bag with silver plastic medallion (to carry Unspoken Cologne Spray demo not included)* **MP $5 Bag only**

1978 *Feelin' Fresh Insulated Bag, free to Reps with purchase of C-14 demonstration product assortment* **MP $10**

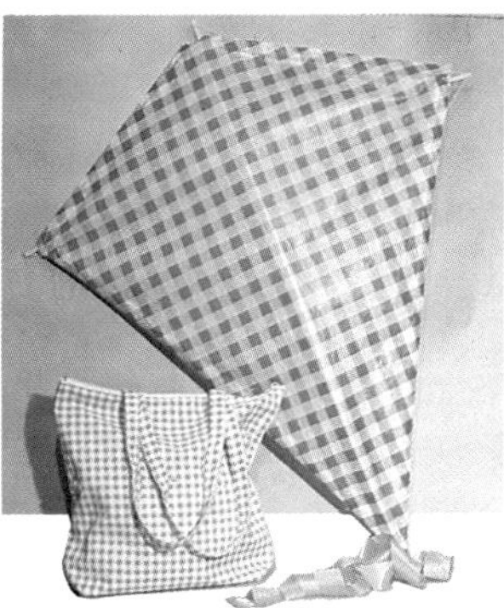

1980 *Country Breeze Kite* **MP $5**
1980 *Country Breeze Tote to Representatives selling 10 bottles Cologne Spray in C-12* **MP $8**

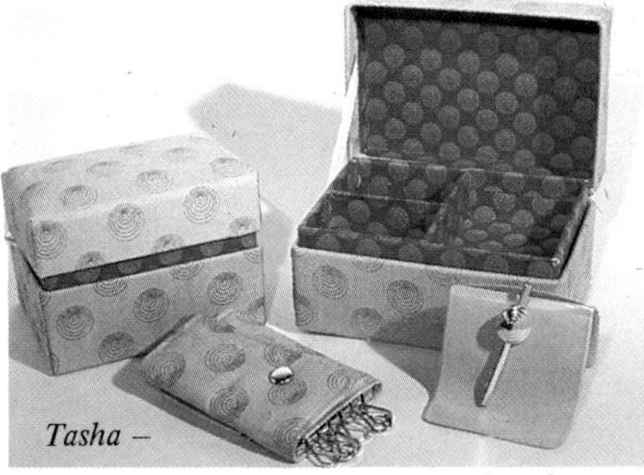

Tasha –
1979 *Wishing Box to Representatives for Cologne Spray pre-order of 10 bottles* **MP $8**
1979 *Dream Box and Fantasy Pin to President's Club Members, 20 bottle order* **MP $25, $7 pin only**
1979 *Key Case Award to Representatives with a 40-customer list in Name Book* **MP $6**

Tasha –
1979 *Manager's Gift Cologne Spray in ribboned box* **MP $15**
1979 *Manager's Tasha-designed Conference Folder* **MP $4**

Tasha – Gifts to "Flight to Fantasy" Monte Carlo winners:
1979 *Gift Scarf from Princess Grace Boutique* **MP $35 with card**
1979 *Tasha Flight to Fantasy Vase* **MP $40 with card**

Tasha –
1979 *Flight to Fantasy Passport in suede case* **MP $15 with folder**
1979 *Flight to Fantasy suede Luggage Tag* **MP $10**
1979 *Dream Diary to Representatives at Sales Meeting* **MP $1**

Tasha –
1979 *Stowaway Bag won in Fantasy Sweepstakes by 7 finalists from each District* **MP $30**
1979 *Fantasy Fan to Representatives at C-22 Sales Meeting* **MP $2**

1979 *Zany Sweepstakes AM Transistor Radio and Disco Bag to 25,000 customer Sweepstakes winners* **MP $45, $35 radio only**

Tasha –
1979 *Manager's Conference Gifts: Tote Bag* **MP $4**, *Basket with Nail Polish and packet of sand from Hawaii* **MP $6**, *Butterflies and Gift Cards* **MP $1 each**

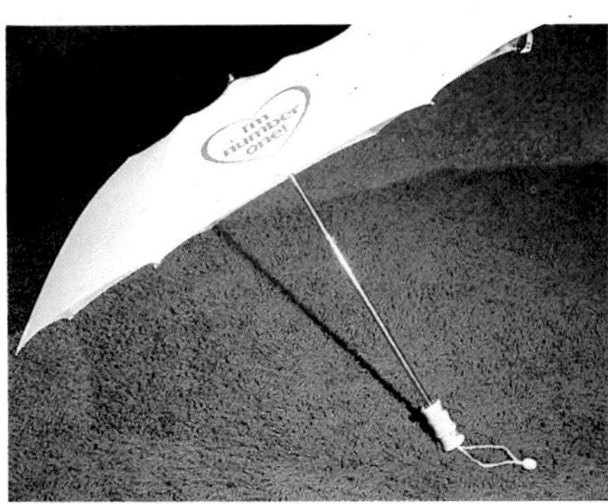

1979 *"I'm Number One!" Umbrella, a gift to Flight to Fantasy winners* **MP $15**

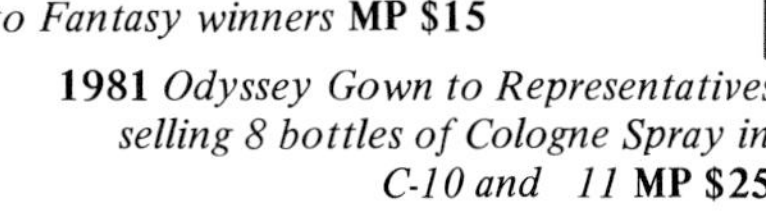

1981 *Odyssey Gown to Representatives selling 8 bottles of Cologne Spray in C-10 and 11* **MP $25**

1981 *Robe for selling 15 bottles of Cologne Spray in C-10 and 11* **MP $35**

1980 *Avon Rose 94th Anniversary Collection –*
3rd Level: Pitcher, 64oz capacity **MP $20**
2nd Level: Four 8" diam. Luncheon Plates with rose motif **MP $8 each**
1st Level: Four 8½oz Goblets with rose motif **MP $6 each**

1972 *Roses, Roses Prizes: Clock* **MP $22,** *Corningware Trivet* **MP $12,** *Bowl of Roses* **MP $15**

THE AVON ROSE
—symbol of beauty and fragrance

Throughout the years, the rose has had special significance for Avon. The Queen of Flowers symbolizes 95 years of bringing beauty and fragrance to the American woman.

The loveliness of the Rose is captured in these exclusive Avon creations, designed especially for Representatives as a reward for superior sales achievement.

The living "Avon Rose", developed by Jackson & Perkins, world's largest rose growers, has one of the most intense and persistent fragrances to be found in any rose variety. It was introduced in 1961 in honor of Avon's 75th Anniversary and made its debut at the Annual International Flower Show in New York.

The Avon Rose has a family history that can be traced back 136 years! Its earliest recorded ancestor was a rose called Gloire des Rosomanes that flourished in 1825. Its nearest "kin" are the famous roses Nocturne and Chrysler Imperial. It is also a very close relative of the popular Crimson Glory, another gorgeous rose.

The Avon Rose is a brilliant, scarlet-red hybrid tea rose, particularly noted for its amazing fragrance. It is tall and elegant and keeps its color and perfume as long as it lives. (The Avon Rose is presently grown by Kimbrew-Walter, rose growers of Wills Point, Texas)

1978 *Manager's Hudson Manor silverplated Bud Vase. Bottom inscription "Avon August Conference"* **MP $30**

1976 *Porcelain Treasure Box, awarded to each Representative in 252 winning Districts. Bottom inscription "Avon President's Club 1976. Made in Spain"* **MP $45**

1972 *Mikasa "April Roses" Dinnerware, 65 piece set. One winner in each District in Roses, Roses Spring Sweepstakes, total 1900* **MP $200 complete set**

1972 *Mikasa Montclair China. Eight cups and saucers, President's Club Members only* **MP $10 per Cup/Saucer**

1971 *Desk Folio Calendar and Phone Index Gifts for sending in C-1 & 2 orders* **MP $13 set**
1972 *Roses, Roses Order Book Cover & Pen* **MP $7**

1972 *Roses, Roses Robe. Representative's Prize Award* **MP $35**

1972 *Mikasa Montclair China. Representatives Sales Achievement Prizes. Candleholders* **MP $8 each,** *Sugar & Creamer* **MP $9 each,** *Beverage Server* **MP $18**

CHINA AND CERAMICS

1964 *78th Anniversary Prize. Lenox China Swan* **MP $75**

1942 *Representative's Sugar Bowl Award* **MP $60**

1972 *Patchwork Prize Awards. Patchwork Cookie Jar* **MP $20,** *Canister Set, 3 pieces* **MP $22**

Imperial Garden Prizes

1973 *Melamine Serving Tray* **MP $12**
1973 *Ginger Jar, hand-blown Italian glass 10¾"h.* **MP $25**
1973 *Mikasa Garden Bud Vase* **MP $12**
1973 *Coasters, gifts at Meeting* **MP $7 each**
1973 *Robe (not shown)* **MP $35**

1973 *English Bone China Tea Set with Imperial Garden Motif by Crown Staffordshire, Ltd. of England. Teapot, 4 cups and saucers won by 1 Representative in each District, 2067* **MP $150** *(Rare, limited edition)*

1971 *Patchwork Prize Awards. Crock-Pot Cooker* **MP $35** *Two regrigerator containers* **MP $6 each**

1975 *Pitcher and Bowl, an exclusive Avon Recommendation Prize* **MP $50**

Currier & Ives

Currier & Ives Porcelain, trimmed in 22k gold. Each piece is marked "Awarded exclusively to Avon Representatives"
1978 *Pitcher, 1 qt.* **MP $20**
1977 *Sugar & Creamer* **MP $15**
1978 *Butter Dish* **MP $15**

1978 *Pedestal Cake Plate* **MP $35**
1977 *Sweets Plate 8"* **MP $6**
1978 *Dinner Bell* **MP $8**
1978 *Set of 6 Coasters for submitting two Recommendation names* **MP $8 set**

1977 *Pitcher and Bowl, an exclusive Avon Recommendation Prize* **MP $40**

1977 *Four Teacups & Saucers* **MP $35**
1977 *Teapot, 5 cup* **MP $15**

1977 *Manager's Currier & Ives Porcelain marked with "M" on base. Add* **MP $10** *to each piece with "M"*

Second Anniversary, "The Avon Doorknocker" **MP $15**

Fifth Anniversary, "The Great Oak" **MP $18**

Tenth Anniversary "The California Perfume Co." **MP $30**

1973 *Anniversary Commemorative Award Plates, created to honor Representatives on their Avon Anniversaries.*

Fifteenth Anniversary, "Avon Roses" **MP $40**

Twentieth Anniversary, "The First Avon Lady" **MP $60**

Twenty-Fifth Anniversary, "A Message from Avon's President" Sterling Silver Plate accompanied by a letter suitable for framing **MP $110**

Produced by Enoch Wedgwood (Tunstall) Ltd., England

1975 *Representative's Sales Achievement Award Plates. Bluebird* **MP $22,** *Yellow Breasted Chat* **MP $30**

1975 *Representative's Sales Achievement Award Plate. Baltimore Oriole* **MP $37**

1976 *Independence Hall Plate. Representative's Sales Achievement Prize* **MP $30**

1976 *American Wildflower Plates – Exclusive Avon Sales Awards by Wedgwood*

Southern Wildflower Plate **MP $22**
Eastern Plate **MP $22**

Northern Plate **MP $28**
Western Plate **MP $28**

1976 *Liberty Bell Plate, Representative's Sales Achievement Prize* **MP $40**

(See Tenderness Commemorative Plate, pg. 166)

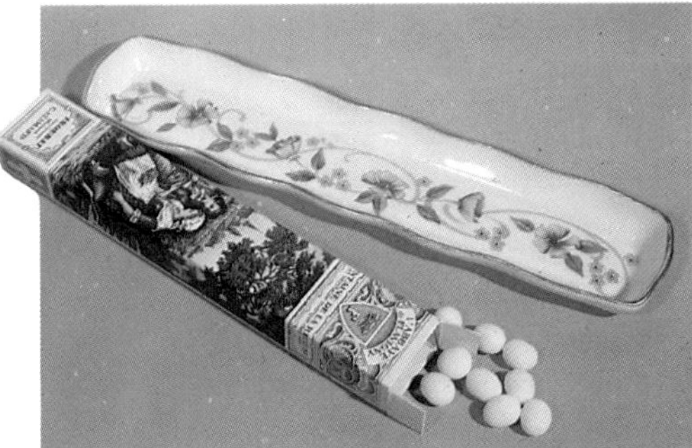

1977 *Port O'Call Pasadena Candy Dish and candy* **MP $20**

1930's *Covered Vegetable Dish with CPC-Avon printed on bottom of bowl. One of several prizes offered for submitting an order of $35 to $49.99* **MP $100**

1967 *Hawaiian White Ginger Glace Compact, Representative's Honor Award in President's Campaign* **MP $22**
1968 *Cartier Crystal Bell awarded to 1 Rep in each District for most Recommendation appointments* **MP $50, $65 boxed**

1978 *Stoneware Pitcher and Bowl by Pfaltzgraff, Recommendation Prize* **MP $35**

1975 *Posset Pot made in Brazil exclusively for Avon as a Recommendation Prize* **MP $40**

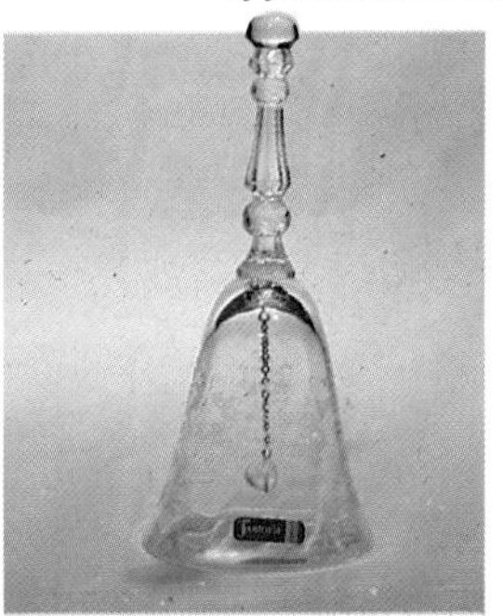

1980 *Recruit-A-Thon Fostoria Glass Bell Award to Team Leaders* **MP $40**

1980 *Candlestick Holders and Candles engraved "The President's Celebration 1980"* **MP $40 pair**

1977 *Yorktowne stoneware soup tureen 3½qt with ladle and 10" serving plate (not shown) Recommendation Prize* **MP $35 boxed**
1978 *Set of four handcrafted Coffee Mugs, Recommendation Prize* **MP $20 boxed**

1980 *Lenox Bowl awarded to each member of the 1980 President's Club* **MP $40**

1977 *Team Achievement Awards, First and Third Quarters* **MP $22 each**

1973 *Nelson McCoy's Pottery Prizes (in Avon boxes only) Bean Pot* **MP $15,** *Pitcher* **MP $7,** *Cookie Jar* **MP $20**

1980 *Candy Jar and Candy gift to President's Club Members* **MP $15 boxed**
1980 *Covered Crystal Dish, Valentine's Gift to Team Leaders* **MP $18 with card**

1978 *Team Achievement Award, First Quarter. Coffee Mug* **MP $15**

1970 *84th Anniversary Monogrammed Awards. President's Club Members won 6 5½oz and 6 11oz goblets* **MP $5 each.** *Non-PC Members won 6 6oz and 6 12oz glasses* **MP $4 each.** *Representatives who won both sets received six coaster-ash trays* **MP $3**

1975 *Avon Lady Stemware, set of six 6oz and six 10oz glasses awarded to winning District in each Branch* **MP $60**

1971 *Antique Car Glasses, set of 8, for selling Avon Car Decanters* **MP $7 each**
1971 *Antique Car Pitcher, prize program and gift of recommendation* **MP $20**

Circle of Excellence Managers
1975 *Madrid, Spain, Gift of Osborne Cream Sherry and 2 engraved wine glasses* **MP $150, $50 each**

1974 *Circle of Excellence etched Champagne Glass* **MP $50**

1976 *Circle of Excellence Champagne Glass* **MP $50**
1977 *Circle of Excellence Champagne Glass* **MP $50**

1978 *"Big Apple" Glass Paperweight etched "Dick Kovac You Made New York Smile" Sales Achievement Award* **MP $100**

1974 *Manager's Wine Glass, etched "Avon 1974 Pasadena Branch 1"* **MP $25**

1971 *Eight 14oz Front Page Tumblers headlined with Representative's name and "Top Avon Sales Lady", Recommendation gift* **MP $2 ea.**

1978 *Smile Glasses, six 15oz by Anchor Hocking. Bonus Recommendation prize* **MP $20 boxed set, $3 each**
1978 *Smile Buttons* **MP $1 each**

1977 August *Xmas Conference, Rye Branch Managers only –*
Miniature of Christian Brothers Brandy **MP $2,** *Brandy Snifter* **MP $25,** *and Card* **MP $3** *(card reads "The Magic of Avon has just begun. Sleep well.")*

1980 *Six Avon Fashion History Glasses, 12oz, Bonus Recommendation gift in C-8 and 9 only* **MP $45 boxed set, $7 each**

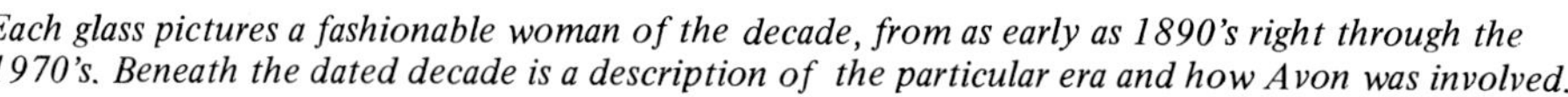

Each glass pictures a fashionable woman of the decade, from as early as 1890's right through the 1970's. Beneath the dated decade is a description of the particular era and how Avon was involved.

1977 *Silver-plated Bowl engraved "President's Celebration 1977" awarded to Representatives in the two winning Districts from each Division* **MP $20**

1971 *Representative's Sweepstakes Prize. Glass Sauce Dish and silver-plated spoon* **MP $15**

1962 *Silver-plated bowl awarded to Representatives from winning Districts in President's Campaign* **MP $45**

1973 *Tic-Tac-Toe Prize Program Award. 10" apple shaped, clear glass bowl and silver-plated fork and spoon, Grand Elegance pattern by Wm. Rogers* **MP $20**

President's Club Members only could win 6" divided Apple Relish Dish with silver-plated fork and spoon by William Rogers **MP $25**

1977 *Pasadena Branch silver-plated Tray engraved "Top Ariane Spray Cologne Sales 1977 Award"* **MP $15**

1972 *"People Who Like People" Prize Program Awards*

1st Level:
6oz crystal and silver bowls in walnut base **MP $15**

2nd Level:
Chip 'n Dip Serving Set, crystal and silver tray and bowl **MP $20**

3rd Level:
Eight 10oz crystal and sterling silver faceted glasses **MP $5 each**

4th Level:
Footed crystal and sterling silver Fruit Bowl **MP $25**

1974 *88th Anniversary Award. Silver-plated Paul Revere Bowl by Oneida. Ten per District* **MP $20 with plain insignia, $25 with President's Club insignia**

1976 *Pasadena Branch Sales Award* **MP $20**

1963 *77th Anniversary Queen's Award, to 10 Reps in each District. Fostoria Serving Dish* **MP $60.** *Rhinestone Tiara, Certificate and Ribbon* **MP $60**

1965 *79th Anniversary Award to winning team of Representatives. Fostoria Bowl with Rapture dove motif. 12"* **MP $40**

1961 *Fostoria Coin Glass – Representative's Prize Awards dated 1886: Wedding Bowl and Cover, 7" bowl*
MP $35 with Avon box
Pair Candleholders **MP $30 with Avon box**
Oval Bowl **MP $25 with Avon box**

1964 *78th Anniversary Queen's Award to 10 Reps in each District. Wm. A. Rogers gold lined, silver plated bowl with Queen's Certificate, Crown Award Pin and colorful cardboard Tiara (not shown)* **MP $45 Bowl, $30 Certificate, Pin and Tiara**

1965 *Honor Award General Manager's Campaign. Silver plated tray 9¾" diam. to Representatives in 1 winning District from each Branch* **MP $60**

1964 *78th Anniversary Representative's Prize. Fostoria Condiment Set.*
MP $50 with Avon box

FOSTORIA AWARDS . . .

1965 *79th Anniversary Queen's Award to 10 Reps in each District. Silver plated bowl with Queen's Certificate, cardboard Tiara* **MP $40 Bowl, $30 Certificate, Pin and Tiara**

1967 *Manager's Distinguished Management Award* **MP $50**

1971 *President's Campaign Fostoria Coin Glass Awards –*
Salt & Pepper Shakers **MP $10**
Creamer **MP $10**
Nappy Serving Dish **MP $10 boxed**

1977 *Silver plated Tray, sales award C-23-76 to C-9-77 to Top 50 in El Camino Division, Pasadena Branch* **MP $20**

1978 *Commemorative Silver plated Tray 12" diam. engraved "President's Celebration 1978" awarded to Representatives in the two winning Districts from each Branch (3000)* **MP $40**

1969 *Fostoria Coin Glass Punch Set. Eight Cups and 1½ gallon capacity Bowl. Coin motif inscribed with "1886" date (see left). A selection from "Avon in Wonderland" prize program* **MP $40 boxed**

1971 *Fostoria Coin Glass Plate, with 1886 Coin design* **MP $15 boxed**
1970 *American Beauty Vase, carved crystalward by Abilities, Inc. Recommendation Gift 11"* **MP $30**

1971 *Fostoria Coin Glass Jelly Dish with 1886 Coin design* **MP $10 boxed**

1971 *Fostoria Coin Glass Sugar Bowl with 1886 Coin design* **MP $15 boxed**
1971 *Fostoria Coin Glass Covered Candy Jar with 1886 Coin design* **MP $18 boxed**

Jewelled "A" Plate **MP $15**

First Representative Plate **MP $15**

Doorknocker Plate **MP $15**

Great Oak Plate **MP $15**

1978 *92nd Anniversary Fostoria Lead Crystal Plates. A different Avon symbol in the center of each plate. First 4 plates awarded for sales of $250 in C-12, 13 and 14. Last 4 to President's Club Members only for sales of $300 in each of 3 campaigns.*

The "4-A" Plate **MP $20**

Avon Key Plate **MP $20**

World of Avon Plate **MP $20**

Avon Rose Plate **MP $20**

91st Anniversary Fostoria Coin Glass Awards (Avon symbol motifs in coins) –
1977 *Centerpiece Bowl* **MP $30**
1977 *Footed Compote* **MP $20**

1977 *President's Club only, set of Candleholders* **MP $30**

1975 *Fostoria Coin Glass Cake Salver, 1 in a choice of 3 Xmas gifts to Team Leaders* **MP $50 with card**

REPRESENTATIVE'S XMAS GIFTS

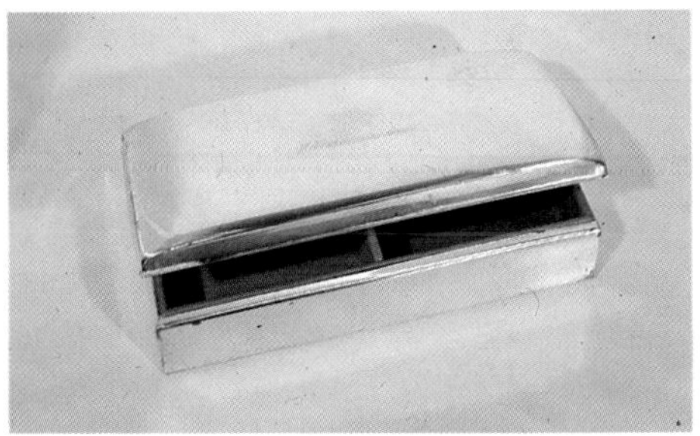

1961 *Representative's Christmas gift. Cigarette Case, lid engraved with 4-A design and Christmas 1961* **MP $45**

1969 *Christmas Gift, Longine's Xmas music recorded for Avon* **MP $15**

1970 *Christmas Gift, Nelson Riddle Xmas music recorded for Avon* **MP $15**

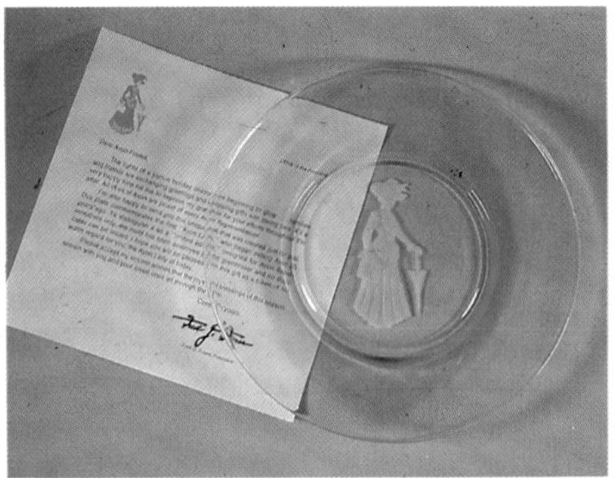

1971 *Representative's Christmas gift. Fostoria Plate 8" diam. "limited edition".* **MP $30 boxed with letter**

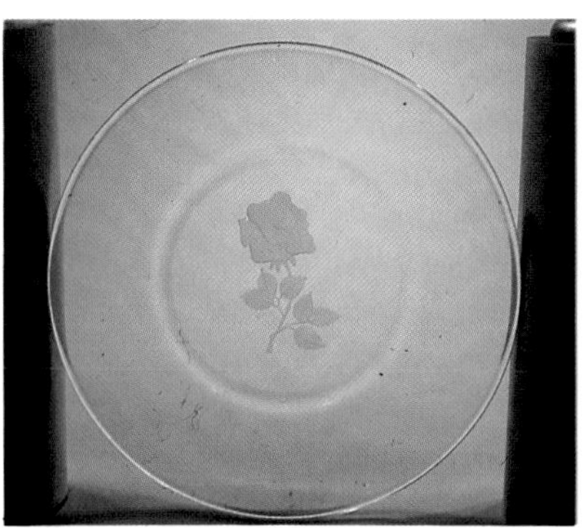

1972 *Representative's Christmas gift. Fostoria Plate 8" diam. "limited edition".* **MP $25 boxed with letter**

1973 *Christmas Gift. Mikasa China Bell (only to Representatives with Avon for less than two years)* **MP $20**

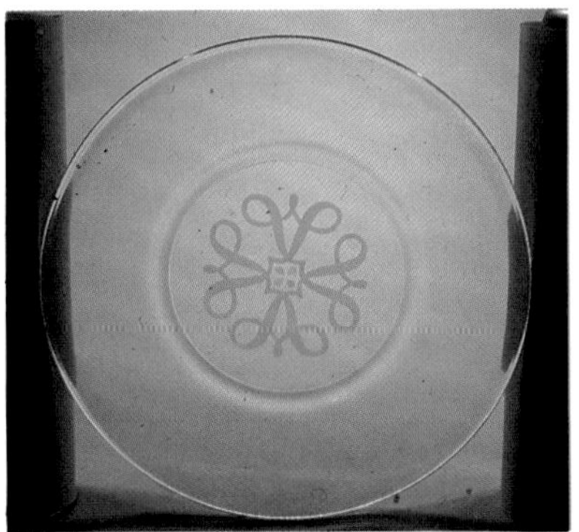

1973 *Representative's Christmas gift Fostoria Plate 8" diam. "limited edition"* **MP $20 boxed with letter**

1974 *Representative's Christmas gift. Fostoria Plate 8" diam. "limited edition"* **MP $20 boxed with letter**

1975 *Representative's Christmas Gift. 1oz Trailing Arbutus Powder Sachet* **MP $15 boxed**

1976 *Representative's Christmas Gift* **MP $20**

Representative's Xmas Gifts by Fostoria, inscribed with date and "4-A" symbol
1977 *Cut-crystal Bud Vase* **MP $18, $25 boxed**
1978 *Lead Crystal Candy Dish* **MP $18, $25 boxed**

1979 *Representative's Christmas Gift. Ceramic Picture Frame 5" square with message from William Chaney* **MP $15**
1980 *Representative's Christmas Gift. Matching Note Paper Holder with note from Mr. Chaney* **MP $12**

1966 *"Sound of the Seasons" Music Box by Cartier, with Key and jingle bell, plays Sound of Music. To managers for reaching 4th quarter sales projections. (No pin included)* **MP $90 with felt bag, $70 bag only**

1978 *Sterling Silver Basket of Roses by Cartier. Increased Sales Award to one Manager in each Division* **MP $125 boxed**
1968 *Beehive Bank, Manager's Gift introducing Silk & Honey* **MP $18**

1980 *Team Leader Gift. Wicker Basket of Silk Flowers* **MP $20**

1980 *Jewelry Box engraved "Avon Team Leader President's Celebration 1980"* **MP $22**

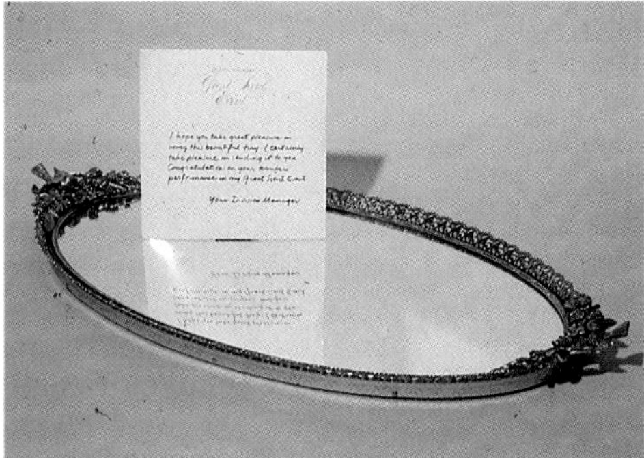

1980 *Scent Event Vanity Tray to 15 Representatives per District for top sales of Cologne Sprays in C-9* **MP $25 with letter**

1979 *President's Celebration Commemorative Lucite Heart Bud Vase to Representatives in winning Districts* **MP $25 boxed**
1979 *Manager's Lucite Heart Bud Vase in suede-like drawstring bag* **MP $35**

1958 *Merry Moods of Christmas Ornament, given to Managers at Christmas Conference* **MP $50 each**

1974 *Christmas Ornament Music Boxes. Representative Recommendation Prizes* **MP $25 each**

1980 *President's Club Members token gift, Box of 25 Note Cards and matching Envelopes* **MP $8**
1980 *Avon Christmas Card given to Managers to send to Representatives* **MP $2 each**

1977 *Manager's Christmas Ornament, first in a series* **MP $30**

1978 *Manager's Christmas Ornament, hand-crafted by renowned metal sculptor, Bijan* **MP $30**

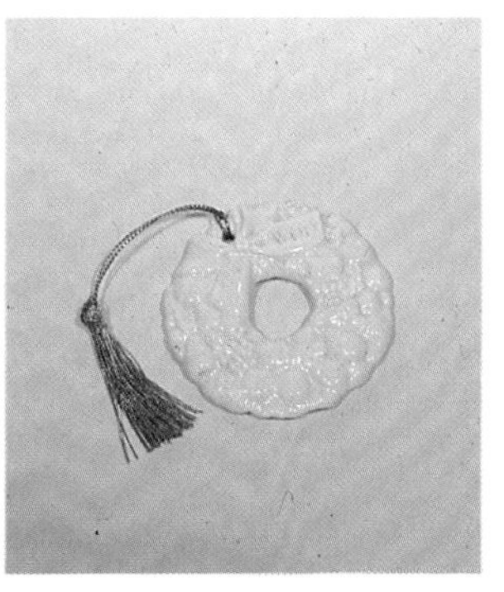

1980 *Manager's Ceramic Wreath Xmas Ornament, Personalized with gold initials* **MP $30**

1980 *President's Club Members Birthday Gift. Bouquet of fabric Flowers, boxed* **MP $15**

1981 *Electric Warm-O-Tray personalized with a California Perfume Company picture* **MP $25**

1936 *CPC Souvenir Spoon, stamped "50th Anniversary of Mr. and Mrs. D. H. McConnell". Gold wash Argyle silver plate* **MP $75,** *in Hammer tone box* **MP $110**

1915 *CPC Panama Pacific Exposition Spoon awarded to Representatives selling 12 cans of Bath Powder during May and June.* **Not** *sold or given away at the Exposition. (Reference: April 1915 Outlook)* **MP $125**

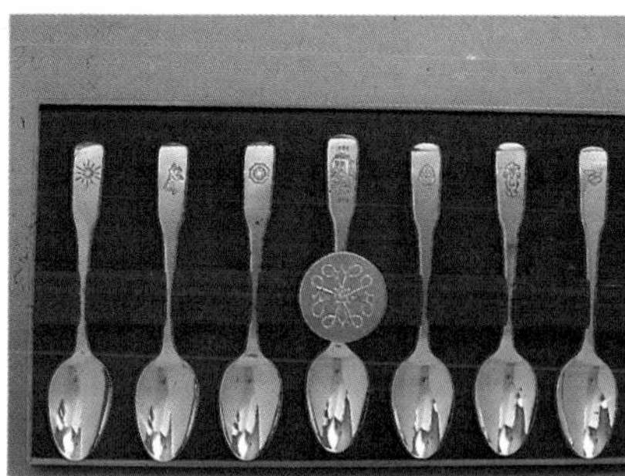

1969 *83rd Anniversary silver-plated demitasse spoons, fragrance symbol on handles. Center spoon only to reps in winning District each Branch* **MP $75 boxed set, $7 each, $20 center spoon**

1967 *Customer Service Award Placemat* **MP $8**

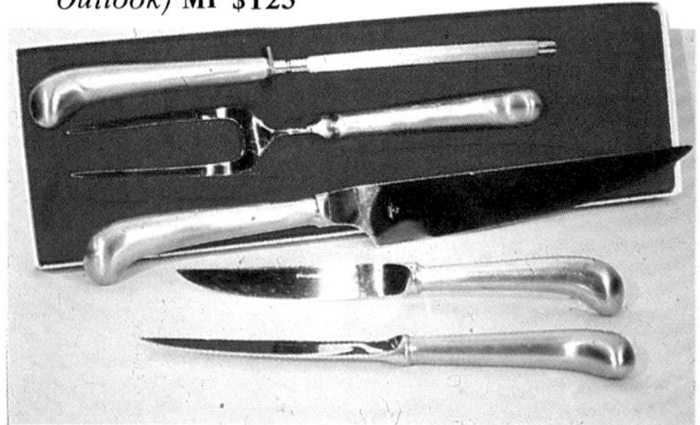

1972 *Six Steak Knives in Avon Award Box* **MP $20** *President's Club also received Oneida Carving Set in Award box* **MP $20**

1978 *92nd Anniversary Cake Server Award by International Silver to all President's Club Members* **MP $20, $25 boxed with card**

1970 *Representative's Gift for sending in a C-1-70 order. 15½ x 28½" linen wall calendar* **MP $8**

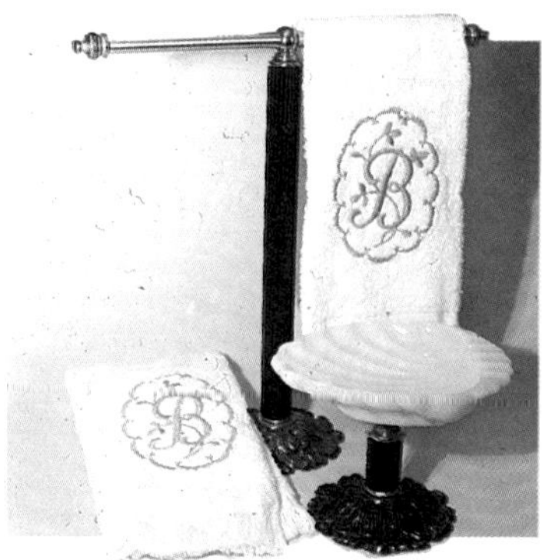

1972 *Towel Rack Prize and Milk Glass Soap Dish, an exclusive Avon prize. Rack* **MP $10,** *Soap Dish* **MP $15,** *Towels* **MP $7**

1970 *Six Initialed Placemats and Napkins, President's Club sales achievement prize* **MP $25**

1970 *Personalized Business Cards (150) and Carrying Case, President's Club Member sales achievement prize* **MP $10**

1980 *Nice Krispies Box, served as gift box for Team Leader cash award* **MP $3**

1980 *Grandma Wheaton's Blue Ribbon Gift Sets with Gift Card from National Sales Manager of each Avon Branch. District Manager prizes for reaching appointment goals in "Beat the Clock Program"*

Kitchen Canister Set, 3 glass canisters hold Apron, Hot Mitt & Towel **MP $25 with card**
Sun Tea Set, 2 glass canisters hold loose Tea and Tea Bags **MP $20**
Relish Set, 2 jars relish, glass Kettle and Spoon **MP $15 with card**

Jams and Jellies, set of 12 small jars **MP $15**
Cheese Kettle Set, 2 handled kettles of cheese & cheese spreader **MP $15**
Honey Set, 3 jars Clover, Wild Flower and Orange flavored honey **MP $20 with card**

1974 *What's Cooking Recipe Box, metal* **MP $8**

1974 *What's Cooking Plasticware by Geni, Div. of Avon. Scoop, strainer, measurer, funnel and egg separator, gifts to Representatives for Sales Meeting Attendance* **MP $3 each**

1974 *"What's Cooking Apron, Recommendation Prize* **MP $15**

1969 *"4-A" Quilt by Barclay, tape-bound edges, in gold, avocado or pink, Recommendation prize* **MP $45**

1971 *"4-A" Quilt by Barclay, reversible, ruffle-edged comforter 76 x 86" in gold, avocado or blue. Recommendation prize* **MP $45**

(back) *(front)*

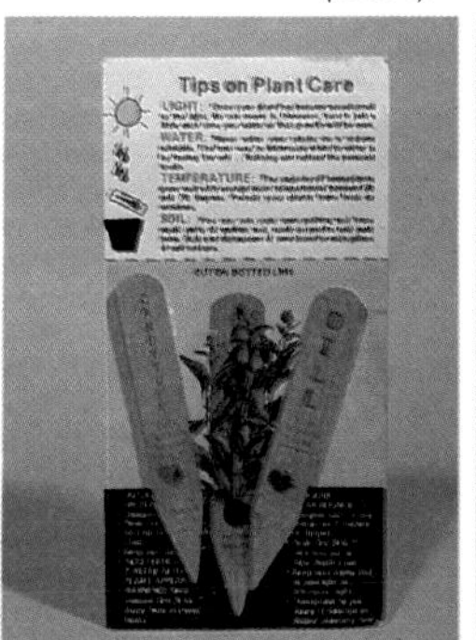

1974-75 *Grow with Avon Plant Spikes with herb, flower or vegetable seed, ready to plant. To Representatives attending Sales Meetings* **MP $3**

1978 *Cookbook, created exclusively for Team Leaders, dated July 4, 1978* **MP $20**

1981 *Director's Chair, "Avon Proudly Presents" used at Conference and then sent to Managers* **MP $35**

1980 *Director's Chair, "You Never Looked So Good" by Domestic Industries with 2 slip-on backs, one plain* **MP $35**

1975 *Reflections of Success. Purse Mirror awarded to Representatives of Enterprise Division, Pasadena Branch, approx. 3500* **MP $13**
1971 *No More Tears for You, Representatives Sweepstakes Gift Handkerchief* **MP $8 with card**

1980 *Manager's Xmas Card and Calico drawstring bag held Xmas bonus check, Xmas Conference Invitation, Place Card and Napkin* **MP $7**

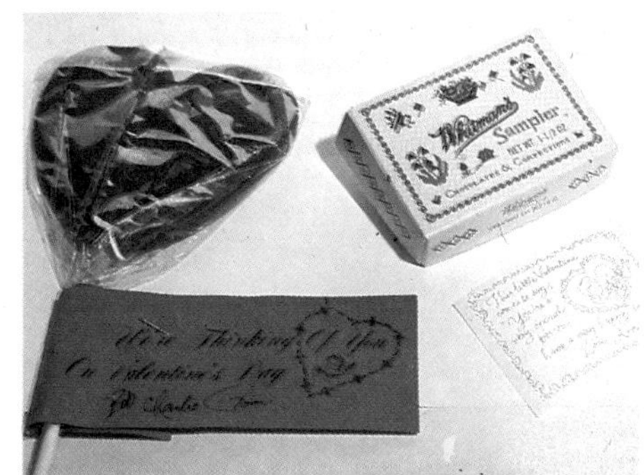

1981 *Manager's Valentine Heart-shaped Sucker* **MP $10 with card**
1976 *Representative's Valentine gift, Whitman's Sampler Candy* **MP $12**

1978 *President's Club Members luncheon gift. Heart-shaped box of Barton's Candy 4½oz* **MP $3 box only** *(candy can be replaced)*

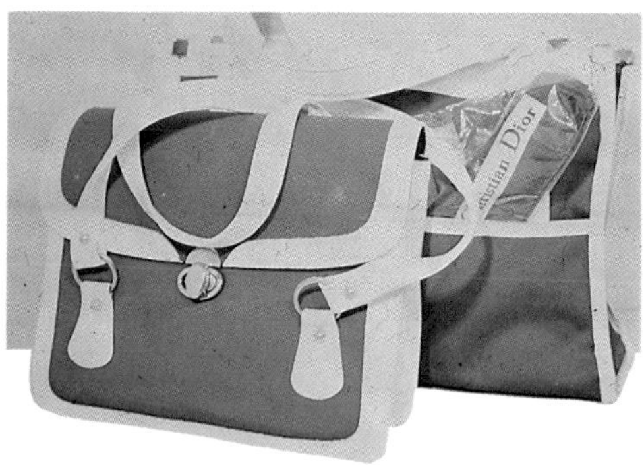

1974 *Representative's Prizes: President's Club Kadin Handbag* **MP $20**
Exclusive Christian Dior Scarf **MP $10**
Tote Bag **MP $15**

1973 *Representative's Prizes of suede by St. Thomas.*
1st level: Key Case **MP $10**
2nd level: French Purse **MP $15**
3rd level: Clutch Bag **MP $20**

1973 *President's Club Members 4th level prize. Suede Shoulder Handbag by Kadin* **MP $30**

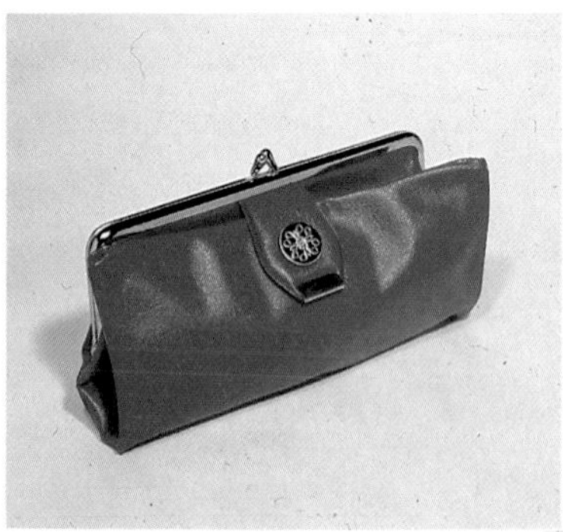

1967 *Representative's Pursette Award for sales achievement* **MP $20**

1980 *Sales-Aid-on-Wheels to carry orders and demos. C-16 Sales Meeting prize* **MP $25**

1976 *Sunny Griffin Make-Up Case. Representative's Sales Prize*
MP $15 with certificate

1978 *Pasadena Manager's Conference Gifts –*
Tote Bag **MP $20**, *Portfolio* **MP $18**, *Invitation* **MP $3**

1976 *Avon Umbrella. Recommendation Prize* **MP $25**

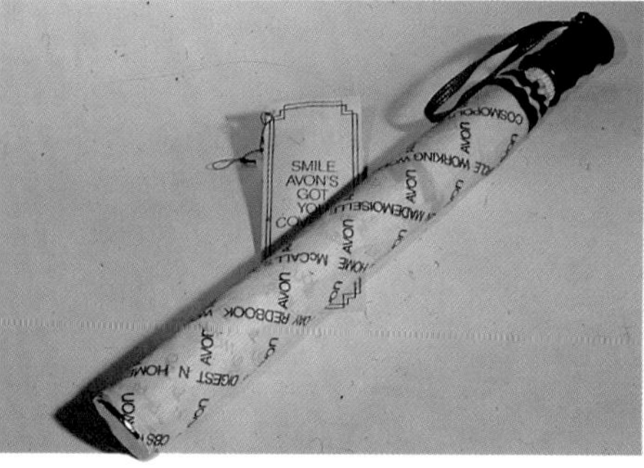

1977 *Manager's Advertising Media Umbrella. Imprinted with names of TV shows and magazines that carry the Avon commercials and ads* **MP $25**

1977 *Circle of Excellence Manager gift. Leather-like Garment Bag to use on New York-Bermuda trip* **MP $60**

1978 *Manager's Conference Gifts –*
Sweet Pickles Tote Bag **MP $15**
Sweet Pickles Cooky **MP $5**
Sweet Pickles Napkin (not shown) **MP $1**

1978 *Manager's "It's Not Your Mother's Makeup" Apron* **MP $8**
1979 *Zany Tote Bag. With pre-order of 10 Zany Cologne Sprays at Sales Meetings* **MP $6**
"I've Gone Zany" buttons (not shown)
MP 75¢ each

1980 *Avon Bag 'n Brella, President's Club Members incentive prize* **MP $40**

1979 *Manager's Circle of Excellence contender gift, Pasadena Branch. Hard Hat, plastic* **MP $10**
1975 *Manager's Circle of Excellence Trivet* **MP $25**

Circle of Excellence Managers –
1977 *New York-Bermuda, Plastic Photo Cube* **MP $10**
1976 *Hawaii, Wood Tiki God* **MP $35**
1975 *Florida, Ceramic Planter* **MP $40**

Circle of Excellence Manager's Awards, Hawaii –
1976 *Stationery and Imprinted Notebook* **MP $15**
1976 *Pocket Organizer and Matching Key Case* **MP $40 set with card signed by Pat Neighbors**

Manager's Circle of Excellence Awards – with C of E monogram
1977 *New York-Bermuda. Robe* **MP $45,** *Tote Bag* **MP $15,** *Hat* **MP $15**

1976 *Circle of Excellence Manager Awards, Hawaii –*
1976 *Beach Towel* **MP $20**
1976 *Tote Bag* **MP $15**
1976 *Hat* **MP $15**

1977 *Manager's Circle of Excellence Memorabilia, Honor Banquet in New York City. Invitation and Matchbooks* **MP $3 each,** *Match Holders* **MP $4 each,** *Notebook and Pen with penlight* **MP $13 set**

Circle of Excellence Manager Gifts, Paris –
1979 *Tote Bag* **MP $15**
1979 *French Cap* **MP $10**
1979 *Shawl* **MP $15**

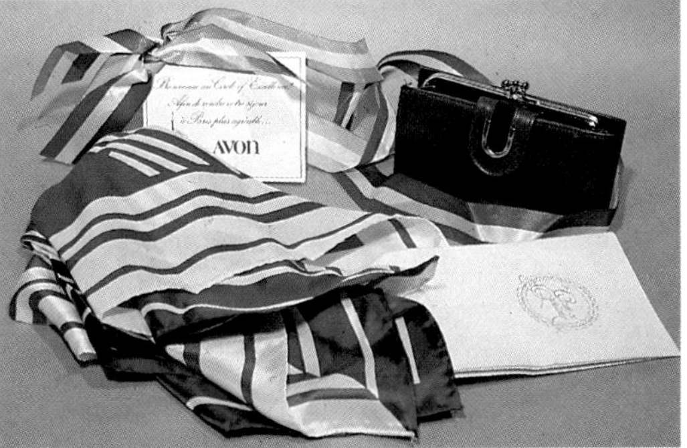

Circle of Excellence Manager Gifts, Paris –
1979 *Banner* **MP $8**
1979 *Scarf* **MP $12**
1979 *French Purse* **MP $20**
1979 *Menu* **MP $3**

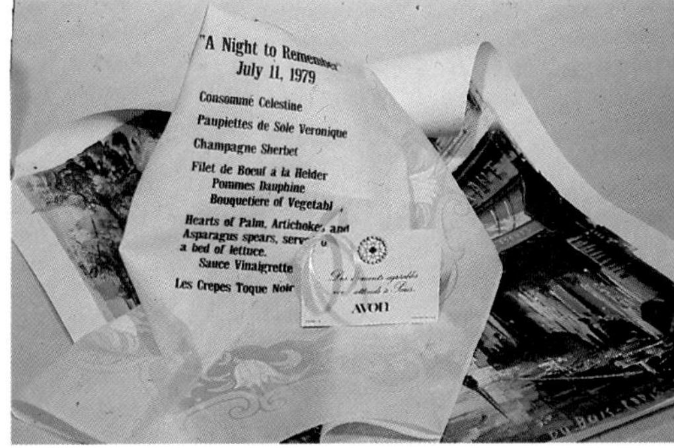

Circle of Excellence Manager Gifts, Paris –
1979 *Napkin Menu* **MP $20**
1979 *French Print Poster* **MP $12 with card**

Circle of Excellence contender gifts, Paris –
1979 *Envira Lipstick, 4 shades* **MP $6 each**
1979 *Matchbox* **MP $3 each**

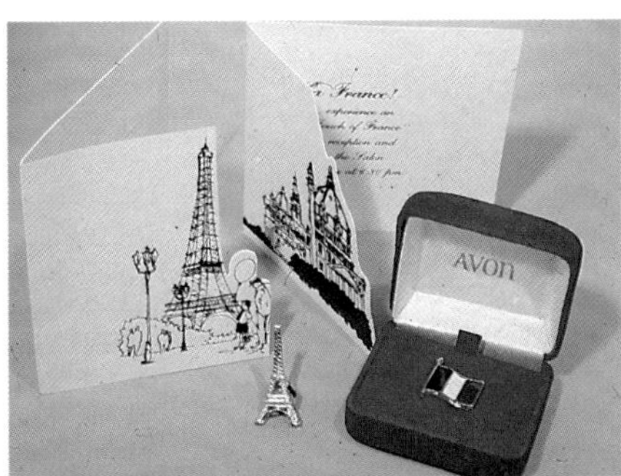

Circle of Excellence Manager Gifts, Paris –
1979 *Eiffel Tower Pin* **MP $25**
1979 *French Flag Pin* **MP $20**

1980 *Circle of Excellence Pin* **MP $25**

Circle of Excellence contender gifts, Monte Carlo –
1981 *French Beret with Monte Carlo button* **MP $15**
1981 *Handled vinyl organizer* **MP $5**

1979 *"Avon Number One" Scarf* **MP $8**
1980 *Sportif Signature Scarf for Representative's order of 10 bottles Cologne Spray in C-6* **MP $6**

1979 *"Color Never Looked So Good" glasses, set of 6. Prize at C-11 Sales Meeting* **MP $24 set**
1979 *Color-Up Tablecloth used at Manager's kick-off Color Up America Luncheon* **MP $20**
1979 *Color-Up Luncheon Napkin, Manager's* **MP $5 each**
1979 *Color-Up Banner* **MP $4**

1980 *Avon Transistor Radio* **MP $75**

1980 *Customized Casio Calculator in wallet cover with Avon crest. Recommendation prize* **MP $22**

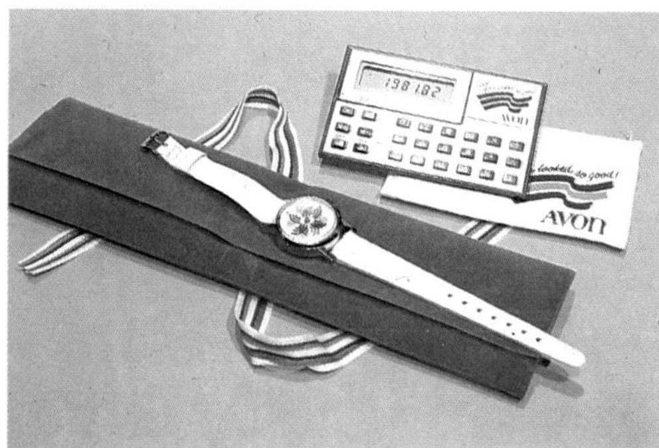

1979 *Color-Up Calculator, auction prize at C-11 Sales Meeting* **MP $30**
1979 *Color-Up Watch, 15 per District for customer service* **MP $50**

1980 *Canvas Bag, only to 61 Managers in 4 H.E.A.T. (High Energy Advertising Test) areas* **MP $25**
1980 *Canvas Hat only to 600 Team Leaders in H.E.A.T. areas* **MP $15**

1977 *President's Celebration Order Book Cover* **MP $5**
1977 *Purse Mirror, exclusively for Representatives attending C-12 Sales Meeting* **MP $6**

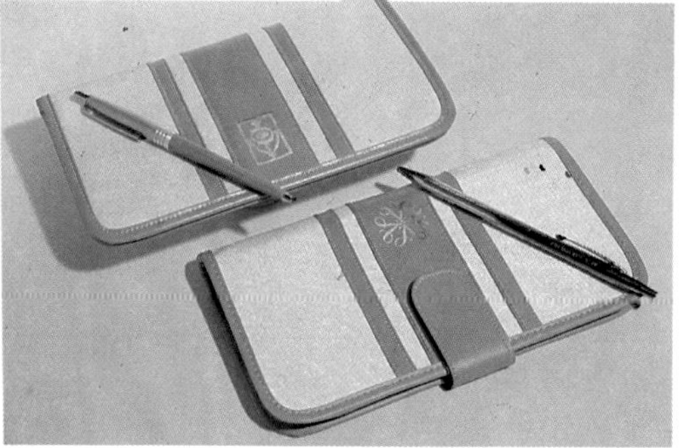

1980 *"Opportunity Knocks" Order Book Cover and Pen to new Representatives for meeting territory coverage goal* **MP $8**
1980 *Customized "President's Club" Pen and fabric Money Organizer with 4-A symbol, incentive prize to President's Club Members* **MP $18**

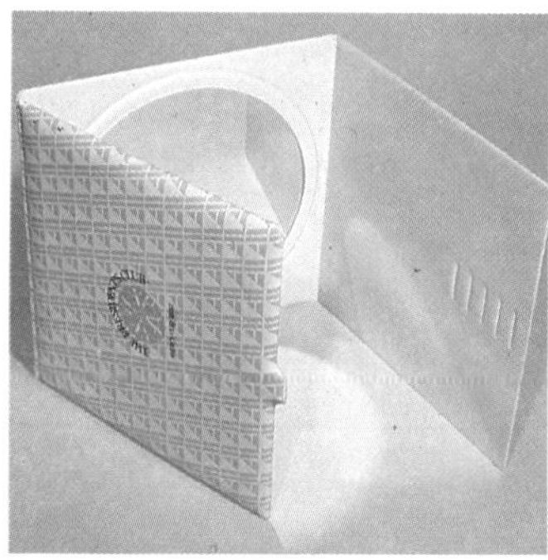

1979 *President's Club Mirror Award, box has message from Sunny Griffin* **MP $15, $18 boxed**

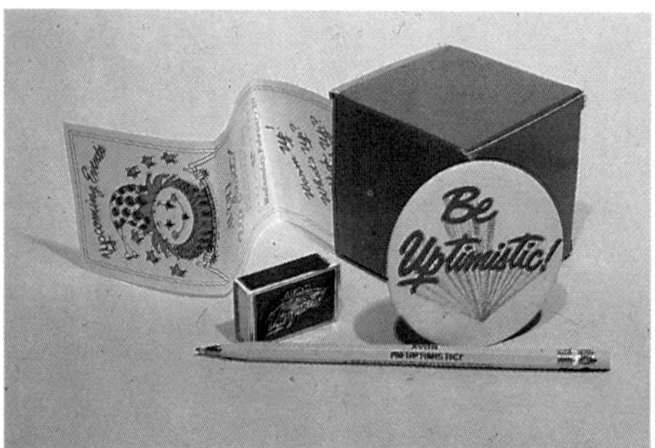

1979 *Manager's Workshop "Uptimistic" gifts. Upcoming Events, Matchbox, Button and Pen* **MP $3 each**

1978 *Mirror in "You Make Me Smile" plastic case* **MP $3**
1978 *Key Holder, "I'm an Avon Record Breaker"* **MP $3**

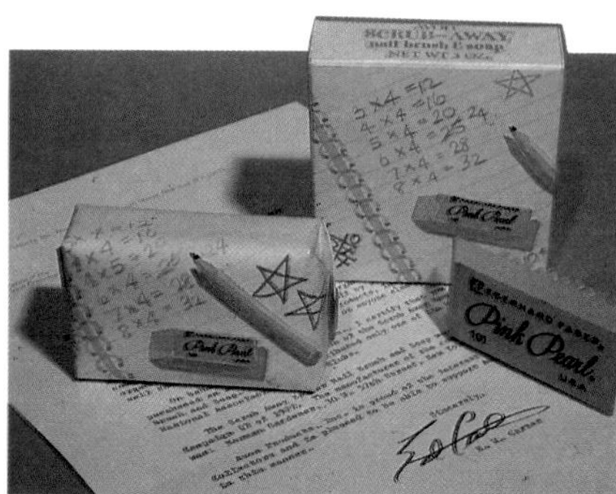

1977 *Scrubaway Nail Brush and Soap Comp (One-of-a-kind comprehensive mock-up used for photography in Avon brochures) with letter of certification from Mr. E. W. Carter, Avon Products, Inc. Owned by Doyle and Faye Darch of California* **MP $350**

1978 *Operation Smile Plaque with Lipstick* **MP $15**

1978 *Smile Music Box awarded to team winners of the Lipstick competition* **MP $40**
1978 *Smile Scarf, only to Representatives attending C-11 Sales Meeting* **MP $7**
1978 *Team Leader Smile Necklace* **MP $15**
1978 *Manager's white duck Hat* **MP $15**

OPERATION SMILE

1978 *Smile T-shirt* **MP $10** *and Frisbee (Not all Branches)* **MP $4**

1978 *Smile Promotional Items used at Sales Meetings. Cardboard Hat* **MP $1,** *Lips* **MP 50¢,** *Balloon* **MP 50¢,** *Name Badge* **MP 50¢**

1980 *Teddy Bear Recruiting Award Plaque* **MP $15**

TEDDY BEAR

1979 *Ceramic Teddy Bear Cookie Jar, Team Leader Gift* **MP $35**
1980 *Chrome Pen by Cross with "Teddy Bear" clip, Team Leader gift* **MP $25**

1978 *Team Leader's Teddy Bear Mascot, Xmas gift* **MP $30**
1978 *Team Leader's Shopping Bag* **MP $2**

1979 *Teddy Bear Cut-Out Table Decoration, Team Leader Appreciation Day* **MP $2**
1980 *Teddy Award to 1 Team Leader per District for recommendation support* **MP $75** *(See also pg. 266)*

SALES MATES

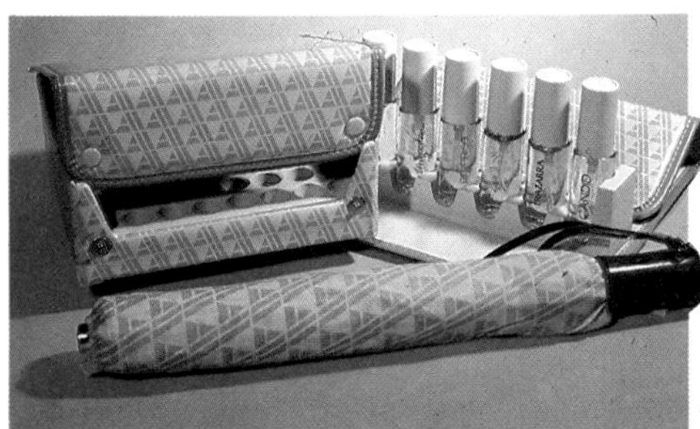

1978 *Sample Kit Recommendation Prize* **MP empty $2.25**
1978 *Fragrance Demonstrator, free for pre-ordering 20 bottles of Ultra Cologne Sprays and Trazarra* **MP $2* empty, $5* full**
1978 *President's Club Prize Umbrella* **MP $20**

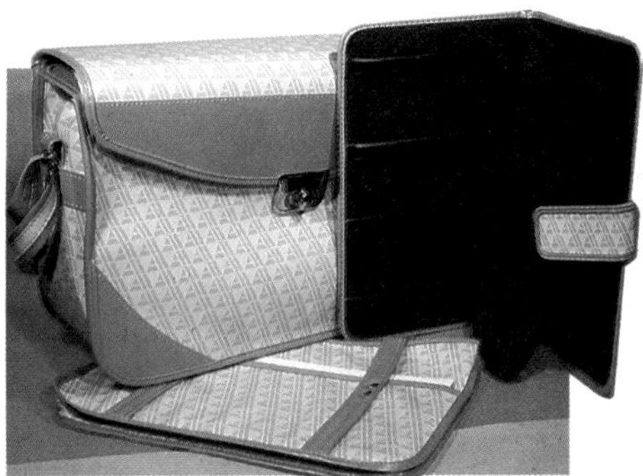

1978 *Beauty Showcase Sales Mate Prize* **MP $9.25***
1978 *Jewelry Demonstrator Sales Mate* **MP $5***
1978 *Tote Bag Recommendation Prize* **MP $4.50***

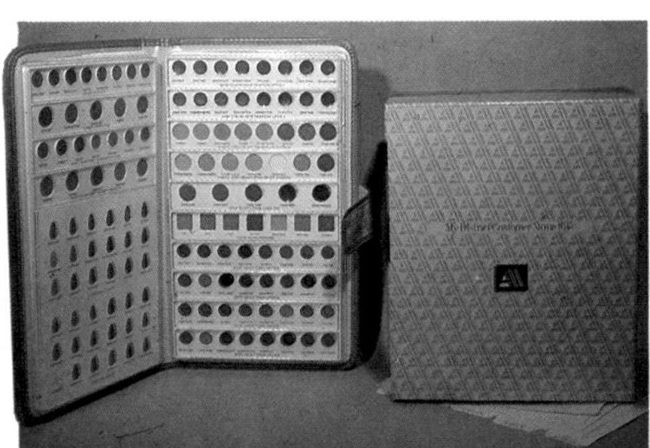

1979 *Makeup Demonstrators Sales Achievement Prize (also available for purchase, 1 to a Rep)* **MP $15**
1978 *Manager's Customer Name File for storage of Representative's Customer Lists* **MP $7 with dividers**

1978 *Avon Territory Coverage Award to new Representatives. Sales Mate Order Book Cover and Pen* **MP $5 complete**

**Available to Representatives at time of publication*

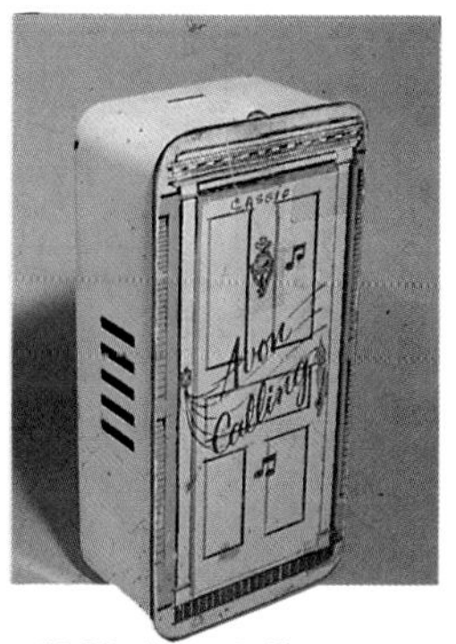

1960 *Avon Calling "Ding Dong" Doorbell used by Managers at Sales Meetings* **MP $100**

1961 *"4-A" Wall Plaque, displayed at Manager's Sales Meetings* **MP $35**

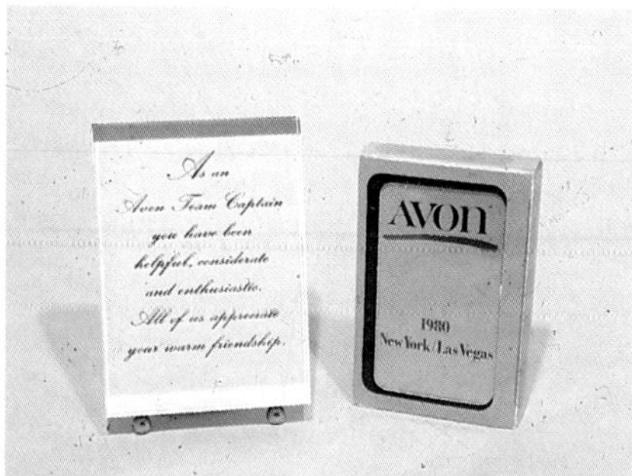

1970 *Frameless Frame 3 x 4" Xmas gift to Team Captains (not called Team Leaders)* **MP $20**
1979 *Boxed deck of Playing Cards. N. Y. to Las Vegas promotional gift to all Division Managers* **MP $30**

1979 *Manager's Koorknocker/ Doorbell Award for reaching appointment goal during 3rd quarter. Full-size brass doorknocker and "Ding-Dong" door chime* **MP $100**

1977 *Pasadena Branch Division Award for highest percent of increased sales in 1977* **MP $20**

1978 *Picture Frame to Team Leaders for soliciting recommendations* **MP $10**

1980 *Manager's Display Ads, with letter, on laminated hardwood 10 x 18". "One to One, That's what makes Avon #1"* **MP $15**

1979 *Manager's Workshop Lucite Clipboards "Up Front" and "Thanks America"* **MP $10 each**

1964 *Paul Gregory Trophy Award to winning District in General Manager's Campaign Contest* **MP $40, 1966** *(right)* **MP $35**

1977 *Distinguished Sales Management Award Plaque* **MP $35**

1980 *President's Celebration wood and ivory plaque* **MP $25**

1977 *Team Leader gift, Address Book with note pad and pen has a suede-like cover* **MP $7**

1968 *Springdale Branch Champions Booklet, Awarded in President's Campaign* **MP $12**

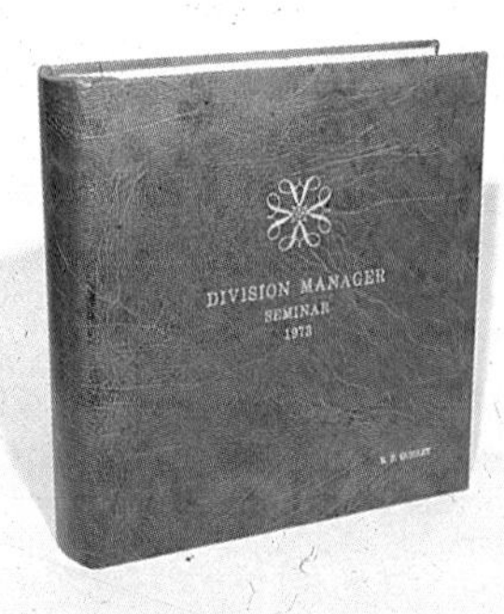

1973 *Division Manager's Seminar loose-leaf Binder* **MP $50**

1979 *Date Book, only to President's Club Members attending annual luncheon* **MP $15**

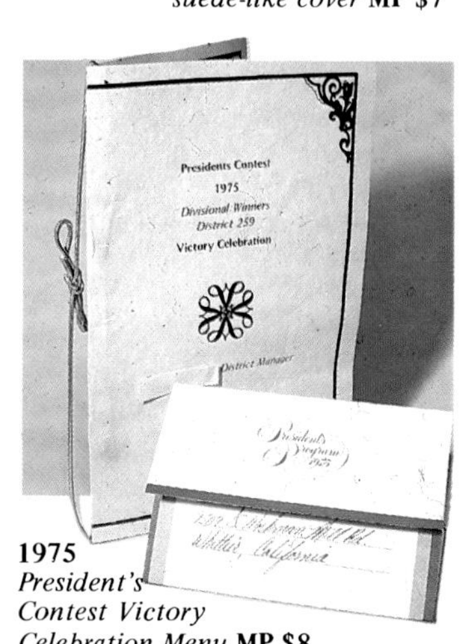

1975 *President's Contest Victory Celebration Menu* **MP $8**
1975 *Invitation to above* **MP $5**

1966 *Divisional Manager's Loving Cup, Pewter* **MP $160**

1974 *Silver Vase awarded to 250-300 Canadian and U.S. Circle of Excellence Managers* **MP $75**

1978 *Additions Award for recruiting Representatives* **MP $20**
1977 *Sales Excellence Award to Representatives in the top 2% of each Division* **MP $50**

1978 *Customer Service Trophy (Pasadena Branch) to Rep in each District who served most customers during the year* **MP $20**

1937 *Key to Success, gold foil on cardboard, serves two purposes –*

((left) With miniature container attached (Face Powder shown). Token gift for "Greater Face Powder Sales", etc. **MP $30** *(with product)*

(right) Representative's Award for writing letters on their success selling a particular Avon product. Only 2 awarded each campaign **MP $20**

1977 *Award Trophy to top 10 Representatives in each Division for highest yearly sales* **MP $75**

1980 *Pasadena Branch Paper Weight Award with Avon crest, inscribed "Pasadena #1" Reverse pictures Oak Tree* **MP $100**

1968 *Field Operations Management Award (unmounted) for participation in the "Better Way Program" initiated in the Pasadena Branch. Reverse side shows blank metal stripping for engraving of name and date* **MP $60**

1943 *Etched Glass Frame shown holding page from Dec. 1943 Outlook that offered frame as prize to Representatives with $75 to $99.99 in customer sales* **MP $200**

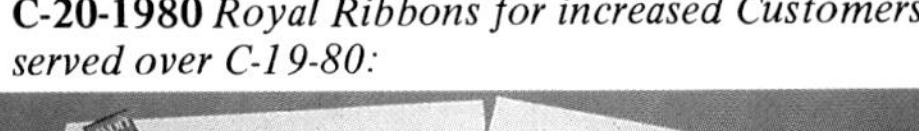

C-20-1980 *Royal Ribbons for increased Customers served over C-19-80:*

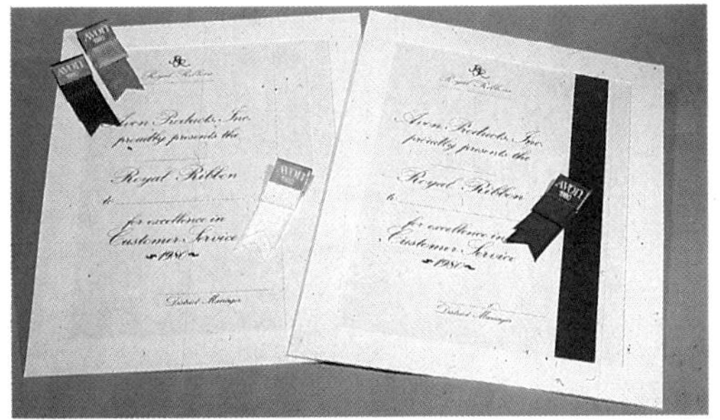

Gold Ribbon, 5-9 customer increase **MP $4**
Red Ribbon, 10-14 increase **MP $5**
White Ribbon, plus White Ribbon Parchment for 15 customer increase **MP $8**
1980 *Blue Ribbon Society Parchment with Blue Ribbon for reaching above goals and serving a total of 80 customers in 1 campaign* **MP $10**

1972 *Team Honor Award to winning team in each District* **MP $35**

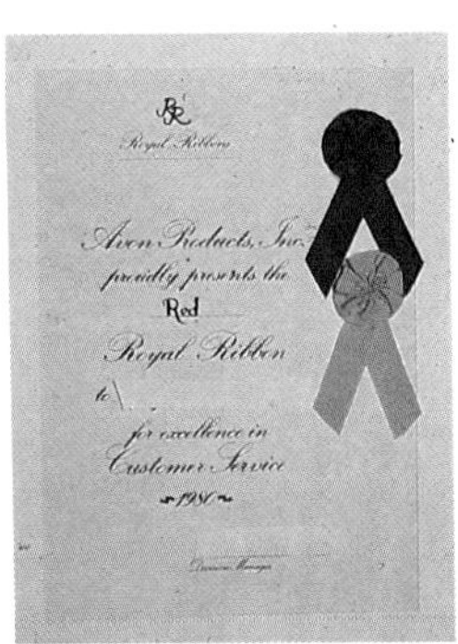

1980 *Red and Gold Ribbons, plus Parchment* **MP $10**

1980 *Royal Ribbons Team Leader Trophy* **MP $15**
1980 *Royal Ribbons Brass District Plaque listing Blue Ribbon Society Membership* **MP $50**

1979 *Team Leader Award Plaque* **MP $20**

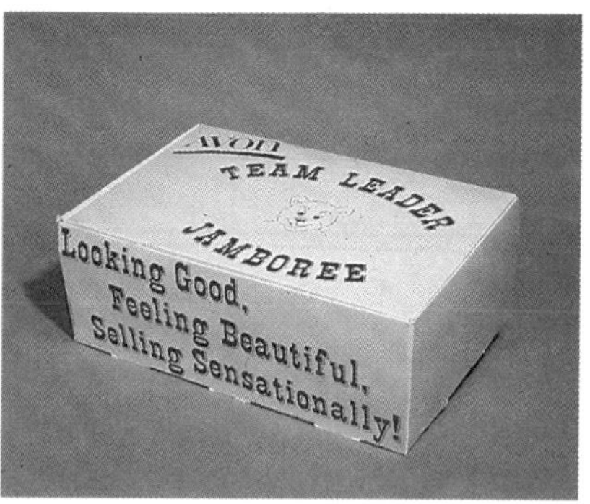

1981 *Team Leader Jamboree Cardboard Lunch Box* **MP $5**

1981 *Looking Good, Feeling Beautiful, The Avon Book of Beauty, hard cover edition* **MP $18**

1981 *Representative's Award, Look A Lite lighted makeup mirror by Schildkraut, made exclusively for Avon, with carrying bag* **MP $32 with bag and boxed**

1981 *Manager's Attache Case* **MP $35**

1980 *Team Leader Teddy Bear Cards, 4 designs. Pasadena Branch* **MP $2 each**

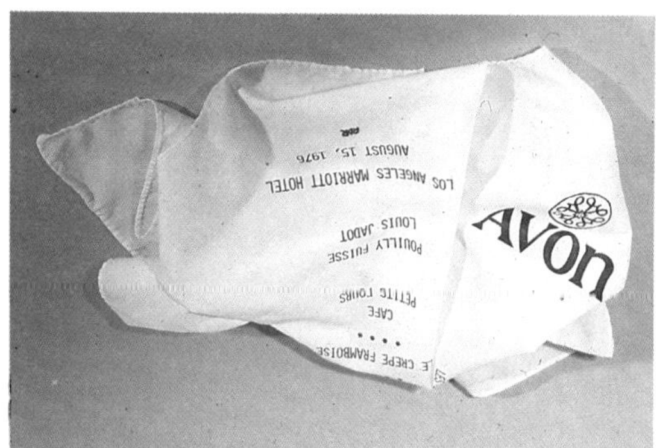

1976 *District Manager Napkin Menu, Pasadena Branch* **MP $15**

1976 *District Manager Panelist Napkin Menu, Pasadena Branch* **MP $25**

1978 *Steppin' Out Hosiery (Knee-Highs shown) by Berkshire, exclusively for Avon Representatives* **MP $4 each package**

1980 *Coin Award, Pasadena Branch, pictures Oak tree. Opposite side, with Avon crest reads "Pasadena #1 1980"* **MP $50 boxed**

1980 *Women's Avon Marathon Championship Medal* **MP $40**

1979 *President's Day Trophy. Golf Championship Silverplate Bowl* **MP $40**

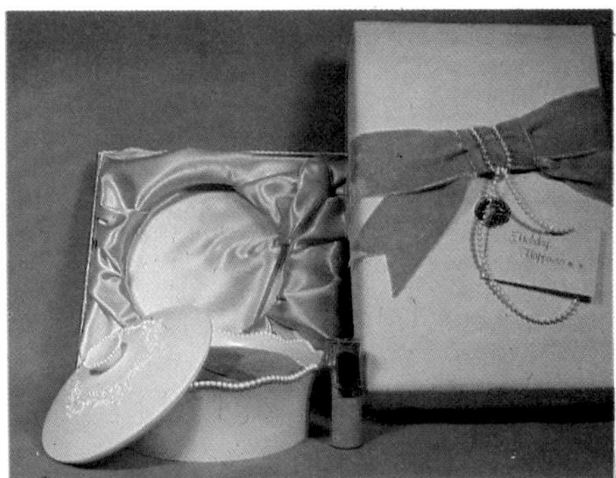

1958 *Here's My Heart Beauty Dust, Lotion Sachet and Top Style Lipstick* **MP $70** *(Spray Perfume shown, not in set)*

1961 *Cotillion Beauty Dust 6oz, Cream Sachet .66oz and Cologne Mist 3oz* **MP $60**

1964 *Rapture Cologne 2oz and 4-A After Shave Lotion 6oz* **MP $55**

1963 *Occur! Cologne Mist 3oz and Tribute Cologne 4oz. One bottle each side* **MP $44**

1966 *Regence Cologne Mist 3oz* **MP $45**

STOCKHOLDER'S GIFTS

1967 *First Edition Wild Country Cologne 6oz and Brocade Cologne 4oz* **MP $45**

1969 *Elusive Cologne Mist 3oz and Rollette .33oz* **MP $38 with card**

1970 *Bird of Paradise Cologne Mist 3oz with card* **MP $35**

1968 *Charisma Cologne Mist 3oz and Pony Post Decanter 4oz Windjammer* **MP $40**

Stockholder's Gifts not shown –

1957 *Persian Wood Perfume Mist and Persian Wood Beauty Dust* **MP $75**

1959 *Topaze Spray Perfume, Topaze Cologne Mist and After Shower Lotion for Men* **MP $70**

1960 *Topaze Treasure Set. Beauty Dust, 3oz Cologne Mist, Cream Sachet and 8oz Spice After Shave Lotion* **MP $60**

1962 *Skin-So-Soft Bud Vase and Bay Rum Jug* **MP $60**

1965 *Just Two Set. 3oz Rapture Cologne and 3oz Tribute After Shave Lotion* **MP $100**

1971 *Moonwind Cologne Mist 3oz* **MP $30**

1972 *Deep Woods Cologne 5oz* **MP $30**

Specially designed Stockholder's Gifts were sent as Christmas Gifts from 1957 through 1973.

FOREIGN AVON AWARDS

UK Avon Branch in Northampton: As it was . . . 1959 . . . As it is today. . . .

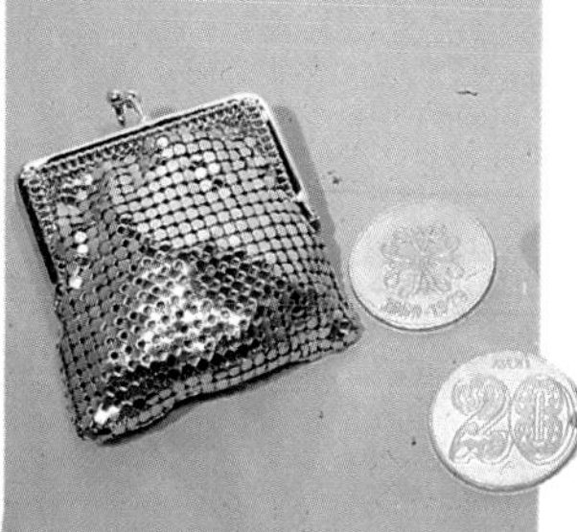
England, 1979 *Gold Purse and Coin Award, 20 year President's Celebration* **MP $50**

England, 1979 *Silver-plated Vase for requalifying membership in 1980 Silver Circle Club* **MP $30**

England, 1978 *Porcelain Albee Anniversary Award to top 10 Reps in each Zone (District)* **MP $400**

England, 1978 *Capodimonte porcelain Candleholders to Reps of the 2 winning Zones in each Division* **MP $50 pair**

England, 1978

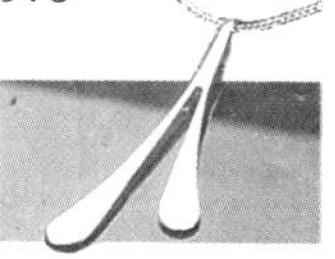
Representatives Silver Circle Awards:

Sterling Silver Ring, 1st level in Silver Circle Club **MP $20**
Silver Pendant Award, 2nd level **MP $25**
First Avon Lady Charm Excellence Award, 2nd level **MP $40**
Sterling Silver Bracelet with Avon "A" Charm, Excellence Award **MP $35**

England, 1980 *Silver-plated Casserole with interior glass dish to top Representative in each Zone* **MP $50**

Canada *Engraved Silver Award. Bracelet, Pin and Earrings* **MP $50**

Canada, 1977 *Golden "A" Key Pin given to Reps for Customer List* **MP $15 boxed**

Cut-lead Crystal Bowl to re-qualifying Members, a one-time award **MP $45 boxed**

SILVER CIRCLE AWARDS

England, 1980 *Silver-plated Gravy Boat to top 5 Representatives in each Zone* **MP $40**

Highly Prized collectibles, cherished by Avon Representatives and collectors alike.

Canada, 1972 *President's Club Plate* **MP $45**

England, 1977 *Awards:*
Silver Jubilee Plate, only 506 awarded. Silver plated **MP $160**
25th Anniversary of Queen Elizabeth's reign. Commemorative Plate (Wedgwood) **MP $70**

England, 1980 *Silver-plated Napkin Rings, boxed set of six awarded to top 10 Representatives in each Zone* **MP $35 boxed**

Mexico, 1980 *Candlestick Holders awarded in Pres. Celebration to 30 Circle of Distinction Winners* **MP $35**

Mexico, 1980 *Candlestick Holders awarded in Pres. Celebration to three Representatives in each Zone with highest C-16 sales* **MP $20**

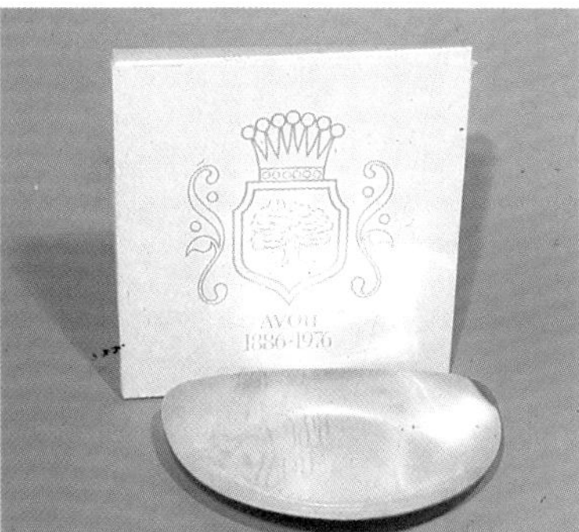

England, 1976 *Anniversary Award, 1886-1976 metal Pin Dish* **MP $25**

Canada, 1980 *Four Seasons Collection Awards, created in Spain. For reaching sales achievement goals,* **Spring Maiden MP $30, Summer Maiden MP $30, Autumn Maiden MP $40, Winter Maiden MP $25**

Germany, *Sterling Silver Napkin Rings Award, boxed set of 4* **MP $50**

England, 1977 *Anniversary Awards, 1886-1977 Trinket Box and Pin Dish* **MP $20, $40 Trinket Box**

England, 1981 *Crystal Champagne Glasses, set of 6 in a satin-lined Presentation Case, awarded to 4 top Representatives from winning Zones in "We're No. 1 Celebration"* **MP $75 in Case**

Makeup Travel Bag **MP $20**

England, 1977 *Chic Prize Collection. Double-sided hand mirror* **MP $10**
Vanity Tray & Jar **MP $15**

England, 1980 *Italian Collection Fashion awards for achieving sales goals in C-6. All are embossed with the Avon motif.*

Scarf made in Italy 32" square, polyester "crepe de chine" **MP $15**
Umbrella, 100% polyamide with adjustable rope strap and real wood shaft and handle **MP $30**
Leather Handbag made in Milan, Italy with detachable shoulder strap **MP $60**

England, 1979 *T-Shirt and Sunhat sold only to Representatives for "Avon No. 1" Event. T-Shirt $2.80* **MP $10** *Sunhat $2.40* **MP $10**

England, 1980 *Banquet Royale Collection, silverplated exclusively for Avon Representatives. Awarded for sales achievement in Campaigns 2, 3 and 4.*

1st level: 6 Teaspoons **MP $2 each** *and Cake Slice* **MP $6**
2nd level: 2 Serving Spoons **MP $5 each** *and 6 Dessert Forks* **MP $3 each**
3rd level: 6 Dessert Knives **MP $4 each** *4th level: 6 Dessert Spoons* **MP $4 each**
5th level: 6 Dinner Knives and Forks complete the 39 piece collection **MP $5 each**
Silver Circle Members who completed the 39-piece Collection were awarded a wood Presentation Case with tarnish-proof inlay **MP $35, $200 for complete Silverware Set and Case**

England, 1979 *Cosmetic Bag to all Representatives attending C-8 "Avon No. 1" Sales Meeting* **MP $7**
England, 1979 *Matching Travelers Bag awarded to ten top customer servers in each Zone* **MP $20**

Canada *Moonwind Tray* **MP $15**
Germany *Moonwind Clock Award* **MP $45**
Canada *Field Flowers Tray* **MP $12**

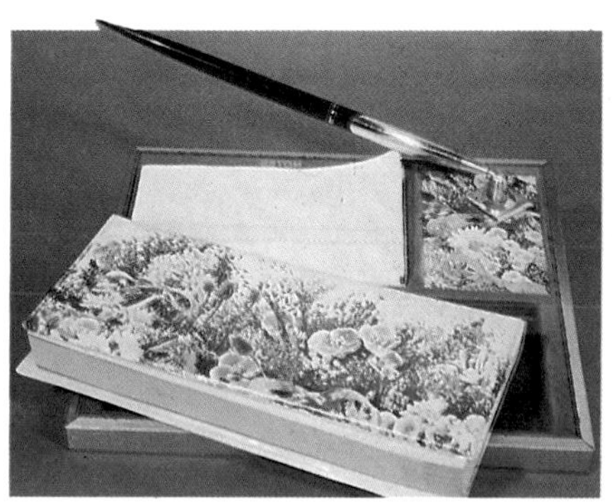

Canada *Desk Set. Note sheets, pen and order book cover* **MP $25**

Canada *Mirror. Roses, Roses Award* **MP $10**

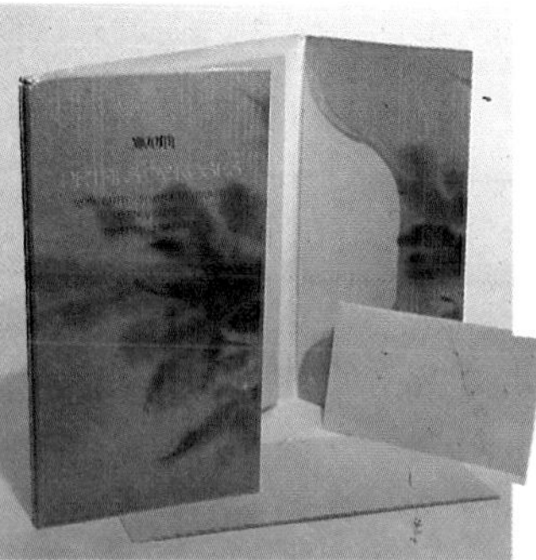

Australia *Petals of Roses Stationery Award* **MP $15**

Canada *Bird of Paradise Tray, blue plastic with bird motif in center* **MP $12**
Canada *Bird of Paradise Order Book Cover with card case* **MP $10**
Canada *Order Book* **MP $5**

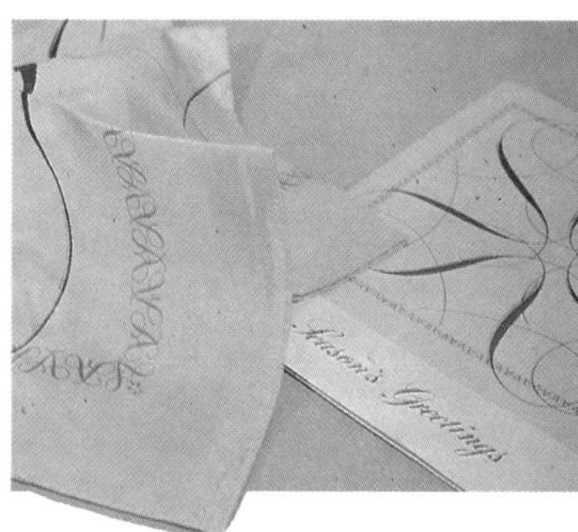

Canada *Christmas Gift. Scarf with 4-A design. R.J. Fairholm, pres.* **MP $15**

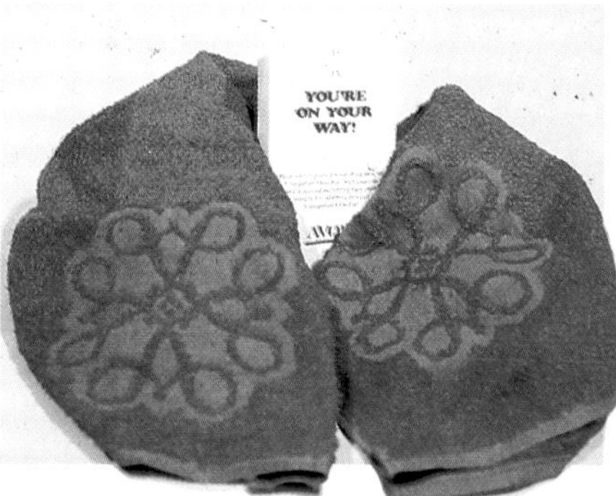

Canada, 1979 *Bath Ensemble, Representative's "Be Good to Yourself" Prize Program* **MP $30**

Japan, 1980 *Sunseekers Customer Sweepstakes Prizes –*
Sunseeker Pendant, 2000 awarded **MP $25**
Sunseeker T-Shirt, 4000 awarded **MP $15**

Canada, 1980 *"Avon with a Heart" Glasses, set of 6. Recommendation prize* **MP $4 each**

Mexico, 1980 *Tempo Glasses awarded to Representatives for selling 8 Tempo Cologne Spray* **MP $5 each**

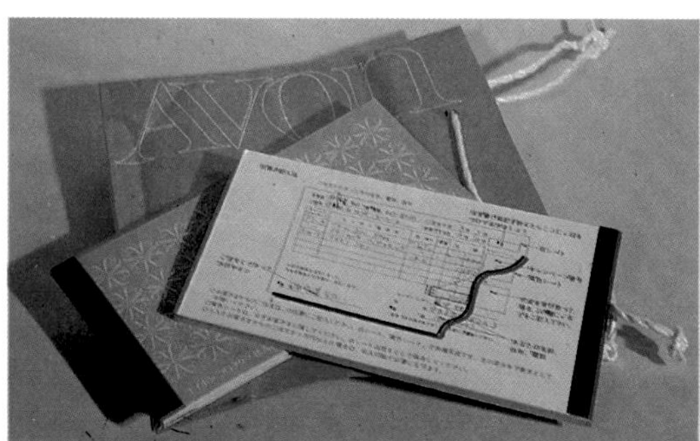

Japan, *Drawstring Bag* **MP $8**
Order Books **MP $4 each**

Japan, 1978 *Pendant Necklace* **MP $25**

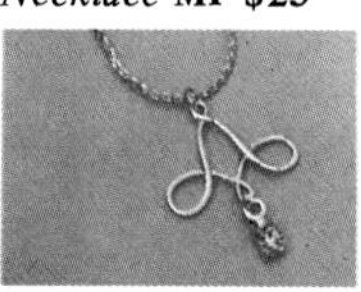

Japan, 1978 *6 Cups and Saucers (Eng.)* **MP $75**

Japanese Awards

1978 *Representative's Sales Awards:*
1st order *Representative's Prize Folding Desk Mirror, 8" square* **MP $7**
2nd order *of 10,000 yen (approx. $50) Skin Silk Milky Lotion and Clutch Purse* **MP $8 Lotion, $15 Purse**
3rd order *of 15,000 yen (approx. $75) Sonnet Soap and Geometric Pendant Necklace* **MP $10 Soap, $20 Necklace**

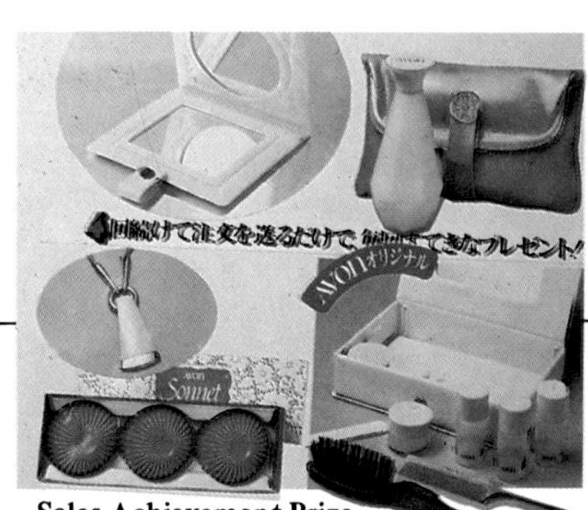

Sales Achievement Prize
Travel Kit. Mirrored Case holds mini-brush and comb, 3 each empty jars, bottles and spatulas **MP $15**

England, 1979 *California Perfume Company Atomiser Eau de Cologne, Lavender, Moonwind or Occur! 45ml $9.50* **MP $30**

England, 1980 *Avon 1886 Perfume-On in 5 fragrances 10 ml $4.25* **MP $6**
England, 1977 *Avon 1886 Eau de Cologne in 100 ml and 60 ml $3* **MP $25**

England, 1978 *Moonwind or Lavender Eau de Cologne 30ml (1oz)* **MP $20**

Europe, 1974 *Thistle Bottle Eau de Cologne, Field Flowers 1oz* **MP $6**
England, 1974 *Promise of Heaven Cream Sachet* **MP $5**

Germany *Clear glass bell* **MP $35**
Scotland *Eau de Cologne* **MP $8**
Germany *Clear glass bell* **MP $30**
Scotland, England *Lavender Eau de Cologne* **MP $15**
England *Clear glass cruet* **MP $20**

1977 *English. Commemoration Crown Eau de Cologne in Charisma or Moonwind $3* **MP $25**

Europe, 1978 *Ultra Eau de Cologne Spray in 3 frag. 25ml $4.80* **MP $6**

Canada *Teardrop Cologne in 3 frag. ½oz $2.50* **MP $4**

Europe *Eau de Parfum in 4 frag. 15ml $3* **MP $5**

Europe *Eau de Cologne in 6 frag. 15ml $2.60* **MP $5**

Europe *Eau de Parfum Purse Spray in 4 frag. 7g. $3.80* **MP $5**
Europe *Parfum Concentre in 3 frag. 15ml $5.80* **MP $7**
Europe *Avon Perfume 4ml in 3 frag. $3.80* **MP $4**

FOREIGN COLLECTIBLES

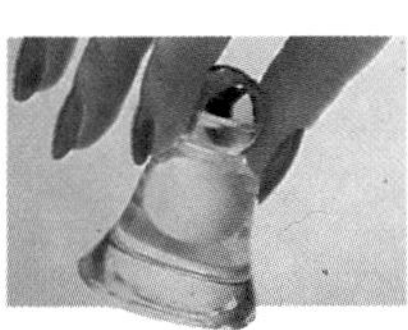

England, 1979 *Fragrance Bell Eau de Cologne in 8 fragrances. 1 Campaign only 15ml $1.86* **MP $5**

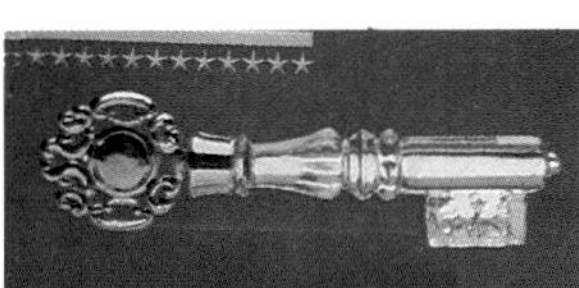

England, 1979 *Fragrant Key Ultra Eau de Cologne in 5 fragrances 7.5ml $5.43* **MP $9**

England, 1980 *Basset Hound Eau de Cologne in Elegance, Moonwind or Sweet Honesty 30ml, with Mother's Day Card $8* **MP $12**

England, 1980 *Precious Rabbit Eau de Cologne in First Flower or Sweet Honesty 30ml $7.08* **MP $10**

Canada, 1972 *Fragrance Ornament* **MP $20**

Canada, 1972 *Small World Hand Cream* **MP $6**
Canada, 1981 *Tender Love*

Glace in 5

France, 1980 *9th Anniversary Recommendation Brochure, Campaign 10-13 and recommendation certificate* **MP $4**

Europe, 1977 *Fragrance Demonstrator 14 vials, approx. 1 dram each* **MP $22**

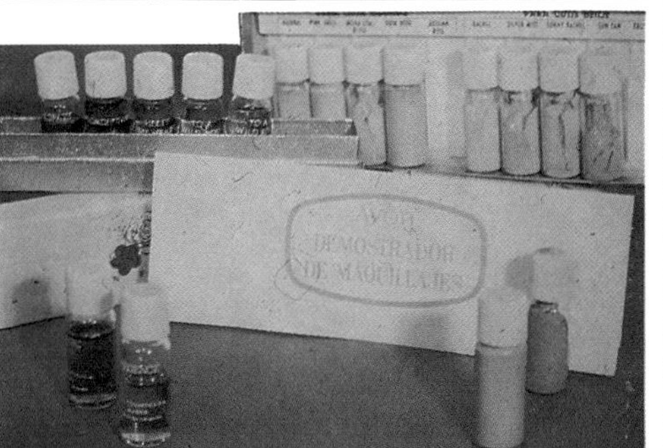

Spain, 1971 *Fragrance and makeup Demonstrators* **MP $22 each**

FOREIGN DEMONSTRATORS

Canada *Skin-So-Soft Decanter 6oz $7.50* **MP $15** *(right)*

Canada, 1972 *Fashion Boot Hostess Soap 4oz $1.95* **MP $12**

Mexico *Grape Bud Vase Locion Refrescante 170ml* **MP $13**
Mexico, 1974 *Swan Lake Colonia in Elegante, Charisma, Elusive, Brocade 88ml* **MP $13**

England *Christmas Ornament. Elegance Perfume* **MP $20**

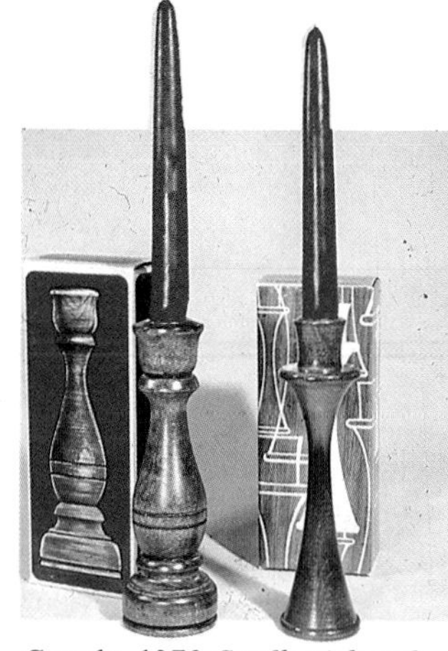

Canada, 1972 *Candlestick and Candle, Wassail scented $6.50* **MP $18**
England, 1972 *Festive Candle, Lavender scented $5* **MP $18**

Canada *Lotion Luxury Decanter 6oz $5* **MP $16**

Europe. *Facets of Light Fragrance Candle in Potpourri (Made in W. Germany) $8* **MP $15**

Mexico *Bostonian Glass with Bayberry Candlette $8.66* **MP $10**

Germany, 1972 *Eau de Parfum. Elegance 15ml* **MP $15**
Germany, 1972 *Courting Lamp. Elegance 150ml* **MP $25**

Mexico, 1976 *Precious Rabbit Cologne* **MP $15**
Mexico *Pretty Peach Solid Perfume Compact* **MP $8**
Mexico, 1976 *Teddy Bear Cologne 50ml. Frosted glass, plastic head* **MP $25**
Mexico, 1975 *Teddy Bear Cologne. Frosted glass, plastic head* **MP $20**

. . . FOREIGN COLLECTIBLES

Canada, 1974 *Campaign Brochures* **MP $2**
Canada, 1974 *Snowman Cologne, 11 frag. 1oz $4* **MP $10**
Canada, 1972 *Pineapple Decanter, 5 frag. 3oz $6* **MP $10**

Canada, 1975 *Emerald Elegance Decanter, Mineral Springs Bath Crystals 6oz $7* **MP $14**
Canada *Mineral Springs Body Soap-On-A-Rope 4oz $4* **MP $7**

Canada, 1971 *Skin-So-Soft 21 Bath Capsules $6.50* **MP $18**
Canada, 1971 *Skin-So-Soft 33 Bath Capsules $7.50* **MP $19**

Canada *Sleigh Mates. Nail Polish .5oz and Lipstick* **MP $20**

England *Bath Oil Set. Three 1oz plastic bottles: Royal Jasmine, Persian Wood and Floral* **MP $35**

Europe, 1974-76 *Perfumed Pair Matching 71g Soap and 78g Talc* **MP $12**

. . . FOREIGN FIGURALS

Canada *Unicorn* **MP $20**
U.S. *Unicorn* **MP $4**

England, 1979 *Enchanted Isles Eau de Cologne in Elegance, Sweet Honesty or Moonwind 60ml $4.72* **MP $7**

England, 1979 *Bath Scape Bubble Bath 400ml $6.25* **MP $10**

Canada, 1974-75 *Little Girl Blue Soap 120g* **MP $18**
Canada *Little Girl Pink Soap 120g* **MP $15**
Canada *Garden Girl Soap* **MP $15**

Europe *Teddy Bear Cologne* **MP $24**
Europe *Christmas Ornament Eau de Cologne* **MP $17**

Canada *St. Bernard Spicy Soap* **MP $18**
Germany, 1975-76 *Persian Kitten Soap 4.25DM* **MP $18**

Japan *Charisma Perfumed Soap* **MP $12**
Canada *Cupid Soap Set* **MP $12**

Germany, 1975-76 *Fragrance Bell Soap (dark pink) 3.95DM* **MP $10**
Canada *Fragrance Bell Soap (light pink)* **MP $8**
Europe *Parisian Belle Soap* **MP $15**

Japan *Love Bird Soaps, 6 cakes* **MP $20**
Europe *Token of Love, 3 heart-shaped soaps* **MP $18**

Canada *Skin-So-Soft Soap, 3 cakes* **MP $18**

England, 1979 *Winter Song Decal Soap Set, 2 2.7oz cakes $6.02* **MP $10**

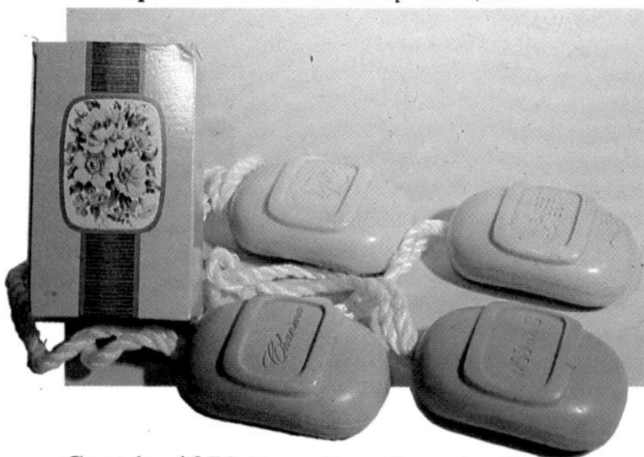

Canada, 1978 *Soap-On-a-Rope in Charisma, Topaze, Moonwind and Sweet Honesty* **MP $8 each**

England, 1979 *Lady Slipper Soap Set, four 1.5oz cakes $7.53* **MP $12**

England, 1980 *Bath Blossom Sponge and Soap $10.62* **MP $20**

Mexico, 1974 *Dutch Shoe Soaps* **MP $18**

England *Elegance –*
a-Perfumed Talc 100g $2.81 **MP $4**
b-Perfume-On $4.72 **MP $6**
c-Spray Eau de Cologne 50ml $8.97 **MP $10**
d-Cream Sachet 19ml $5.07 **MP $8**
e-Deluxe Soap Set, three 78g cakes $7.79 **MP $11**

England *Style –*
a-Luxury Bath Foam 150ml $4.72 **MP $6**
b-Ultra Eau de Cologne Spray 50ml $10.86 **MP $12**
c-Ultra Cream Sachet 19ml $5.55 **MP $6**
d-Perfumed Talc 100g $2.81 **MP $3.50**
e-Ultra Eau de Cologne 60ml $8.97 **MP $10**
f-Ultra Perfume-On 10ml $5.19 **MP $7**
g-Parfum Compact 5.5g $6.37 **MP $8**
h-Ultra Eau de Cologne Spray 30ml $8.50 **MP $10**

Canada, 1974 *Spring Promise –*
Fragrance sample **MP $1**
Cologne Mist 3oz $7.50 **MP $9**
Powder Mist 7oz $5 **MP $7**
Perfumed Skin Softener 5oz $4 **MP $6**
Cream Sachet .66oz $3.75 **MP $5**
Perfumed Rollette .33oz $3.75 **MP $6**

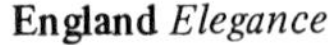

FOREIGN FRAGRANCE LINES

Ireland *Charisma Boxed Soap, 3 cakes* **MP $25**

Curacao (Dutch East Indies), 1975 *Avon Gift Set, Moonwind, glass with plastic caps $15* **MP $50**

England *Cool Eau D'Avon Spray Cologne 50ml $7.55* **MP $9**
Cool Eau D'Avon Roll-On 10ml $3.54 **MP $5**

Mexico *Elegante –*

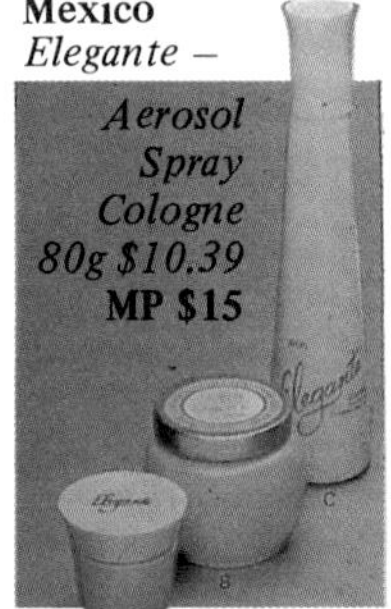

Aerosol Spray Cologne 80g $10.39 **MP $15**
Cream Sachet 17g $4.33 **MP $6**
Perfumed Skin Softener 14g $4.33 **MP $6**

Canada *Flower Talk –*
1973 *Hand Cream* **MP $10**
1973 *Talc* **MP $10**
1976 *Talc, cardboard* **MP $18**
1976 *Soap-On a-Rope* **MP $20**

Europe *Golden Nile Talc 100g $1.60* **MP $4**
Europe *Golden Nile Cream Sachet $2.80* **MP $5**
Europe *Golden Nile Spray Eau de Cologne 85g $7.40* **MP $9**

Europe – *Promise of Heaven*
Spray Eau de Cologne 85g $8 **MP $8**
Parfum Concentre 15ml $5.80 **MP $6**
Talc 100g $1.60 **MP $2**
Perfume-On 10ml $3 **MP $3**
Cream Body Lotion 120ml $2.60 **MP $3**
DemiStik $2.30 **MP $3**
Cream Sachet 19ml $3.50 **MP $4**

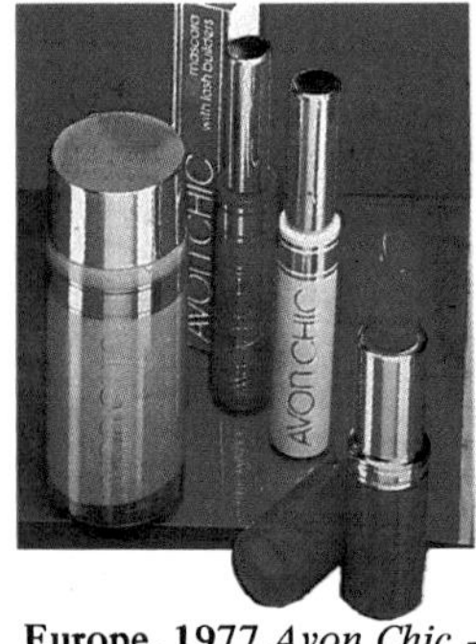

Europe, 1977 *Avon Chic —*
Sheer Makeup $3 **MP $4**
Mascara, 2 shades $3 **MP $4**
Automatic Cream Eyeshadow $3 **MP $4**
Sheer Lipstick $2.40 **MP $3**

Europe, 1978 *Avon Chic Talc 100g $1.60* **MP $2**

Europe, 1978 *Avon Chic Ultra Eau de Cologne Spray 50ml $7.20* **MP $8**

Mexico *Nearness Perfumed Talc 100g $2.60* **MP $5**
Mexico *Nearness Perfumed Skin Softener 140g $5.20* **MP $7**

Mexico *Nearness Cream Perfume 19g $5.20* **MP $7**
Mexico *Nearness Cologne 58ml $7.79* **MP $10**
Mexico *Nearness Cologne with Atomizer 53ml $9.53* **MP $12**

Europe, 1971 *Elegance Spray Cologne 57g* **MP $12**
Bronze Glory 120cc **MP $6**
Protective Hand Cream for Men 85g **MP $6**

Europe, 1972-75 *Fougere Perfumed Bath Oil, plastic 150cc $2.40* **MP $5**

Europe *Blue Bay Bubble Bath 240ml $3.20* **MP $4**

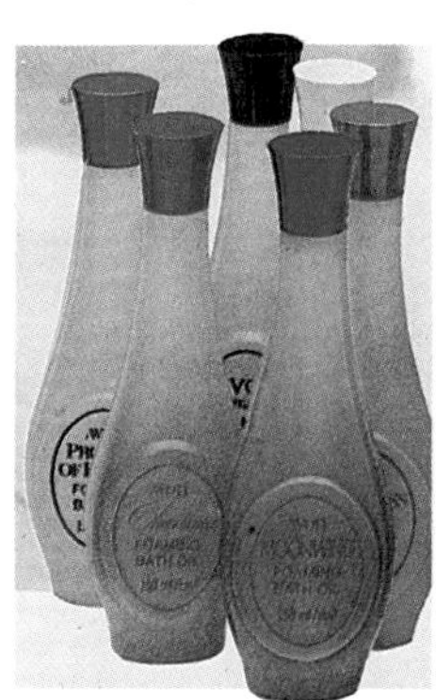

Europe *Foaming Bath Oil in 6 frag. 150ml $4.30* **MP $5**

Europe *Country Strawberry Talc 100g $1.60* **MP $3**
Bubble Bath 180ml $2.50 **MP $3**
Country Peach Talc 100g $1.60 **MP $3**
Bubble Bath 180ml $2.50 **MP $3**

England *Spray Eau de Cologne in Occur!, Elegance, Moonwind, Topaze, Nearness and Charisma 80ml $7.60* **MP $8***

England, 1979 *Ultra Purse Spray 12ml in 5 fragrances $14.99* **MP $9.50***

Europe *Cool Eau d'Avon Spray 57g $5* **MP $6**

Mexico, 1971 *Topaze Cologne 118cc* **MP $12**

Mexico, 1971 *Dew Kiss 103cc* **MP $12**
Mexico, *Avon Cool 60cc* **MP $12**

FOREIGN TOILETRIES

Europe *Perfumed Talc, 100g –*

Come Summer $1.50 **MP $3**
Nearness $1.60 **MP $3**
Timeless $1.60 **MP $3**
Charisma $1.60 **MP $3**

Elegance $1.60 **MP $3**
Moonwind $1.60 **MP $3**
Unspoken $1.60 **MP $3**
Emprise $1.60 **MP $3**
Occur! $1.60 **MP $3**

England *Select 'N' Shadow 4 eyeshadows and 2 sponge-top applicators 3g $10* **MP $8**

Europe, 1977 *Cool Mint Moisturising Facial Mask $2* **MP $2**

Mexico, 1974 *Talco Perfumado (Perfumed Talc) in 12 fragrances* **MP $4**

Europe *Perfume-On roll-on in Lily of the Valley, Honeysuckle, Lilac and Lavender $2.40* **MP $3**
Europe, 1977 *New Look Perfumed Talc 100g (same fragrances as above) $1.50* **MP $2**

England *Aqua –*
Soap 100g 85¢ **MP $2**
Talc 100g $2.10 **MP $1**
Roll-On Deodorant 60ml $1.65 **MP $1**
Freshener 250ml $5.25 **MP $1**
Shower Gel 150ml $3.30 **MP $1**
Bath Foam 500 ml $6 **MP $1**

**Available from Avon at time of publication*

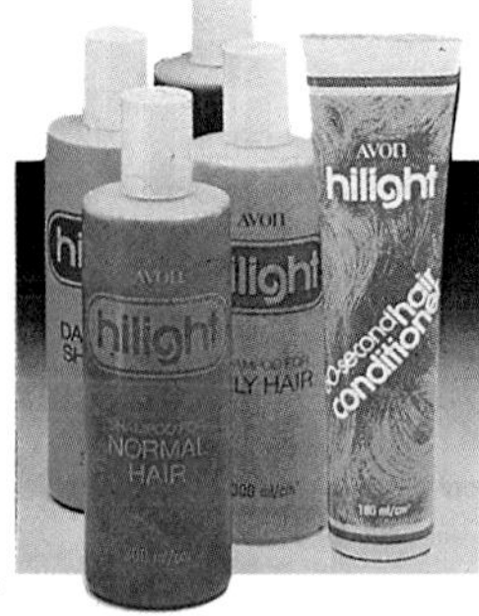

Europe *hilight – Shampoo for Dry, Oily, Normal or Dandruff 300ml $1.58* **MP $3**
60-Second Hair Conditioner 180ml $1.18 **MP $2**

Europe, 1977 *hilight Setting Lotion 100ml $1.18* **MP $2**

England, 1979 *Great Hair – Extra Body Conditioner 240ml $5.50* **MP $4***
Setting Lotion 240ml $5.50 **MP $4***
Conditioning Shampoo 240ml $7.75 **MP $5.75***
Hot Conditioning Treatment, three 20ml tubes per box $6.50 **MP $4.70***

Europe *Rich Moisture Hand Lotion 120ml $2.20* **MP $4**
Europe *Glycerine Hand Lotion 120ml $2* **MP $55**
Europe *Care Deeply Hand Lotion 120ml $2.40* **MP $4**

England *Petal Fresh – Hair Conditioner 240ml $3.75* **MP $1**
Jonquil Shampoo 240ml $3.75 **MP $1**
Hyacinth Shampoo 240ml $3.75 **MP $1**

Europe *Quick Touch Creme Hair Rinse 240ml $1.18* **MP $2,** *480ml $1.58* **MP $2**

England *Avon Creme 200ml $3.52* **MP $2.80***

England *Vita-Moist Creme $4.25* **MP $3***
England, *Skin Beauty Day Cream $2.70* **MP $2***

England, 1979 *Vanity Jar with Rich Moisture, Vita-Moist or Day Cream 150ml $9.50* **MP $6.50***

. . . FOREIGN TOILETRIES

Spain, 1975 *Dr. Zabriskie's Soap $3* **MP $8**
Canada, 1969 *Vita-Moist Cream. Yellow painted glass with white plastic cap 2¼oz $4.50* **MP $10**

Europe *Foot Care Products – Comfort Spray 135g $1.70* **MP $3**
Powder Spray 198g $1.90 **MP $3**
Cream $1 **MP $2**

Scotland, England *Adidas Football Shoe 90ml* **MP $10**
Germany *Avon Invigorate 120cc* **MP $25**
Germany *Gentlemen's Collection After Shave 50ml & Soap Set* **MP $30**

Mexico, 1979 *Baseball Decanter, Shampoo 177ml $3.90* **MP $3***

England *Football Decanter holds Tai Winds or Hud After Shave or Pre-Electric Shave 90ml $3.75* **MP $3***

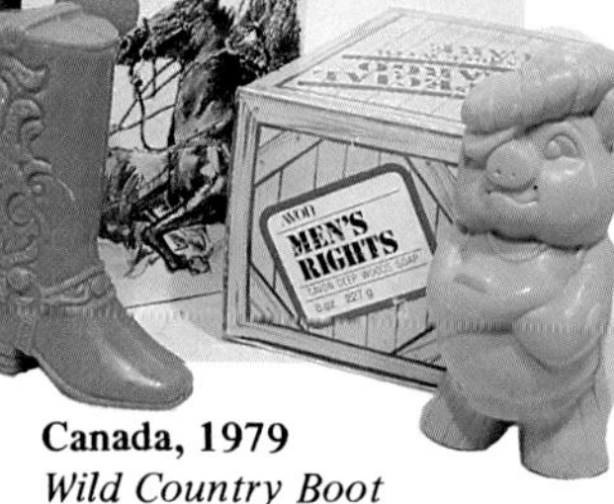

Canada, 1979 *Wild Country Boot Soap 5oz $6* **MP $6**
Canada, 1979 *Men's Rights Soap* **MP $8**

England *Grand Tourer Soap Set, two 2.3oz Windjammer fragranced cakes $5.90* **MP $7**

**Available from Avon at time of publication*

England, 1970 *Andy Capp Blue Blazer Body Powder 100g $3* **MP $200, $250 boxed**

Germany, 1971 *Column Decanter Imperator After Shave Lotion 150cc* **MP $18**

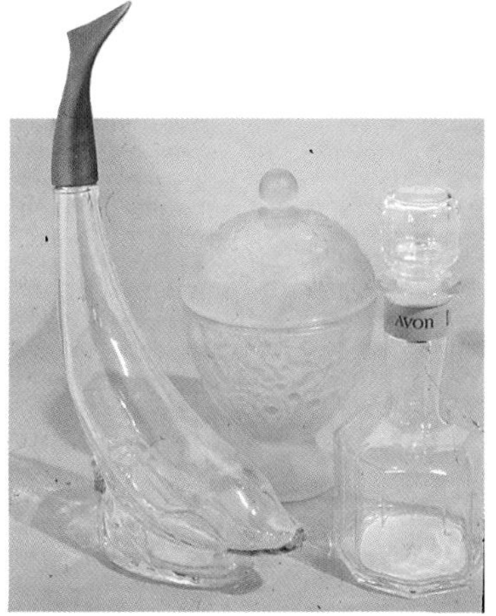

England *Dolphin, clear glass, smaller than U.S. frosted* **MP $35**
Canada *Frosted Candle Container* **MP $22**
Australia *Lotion Luxury Decanter* **MP $10**

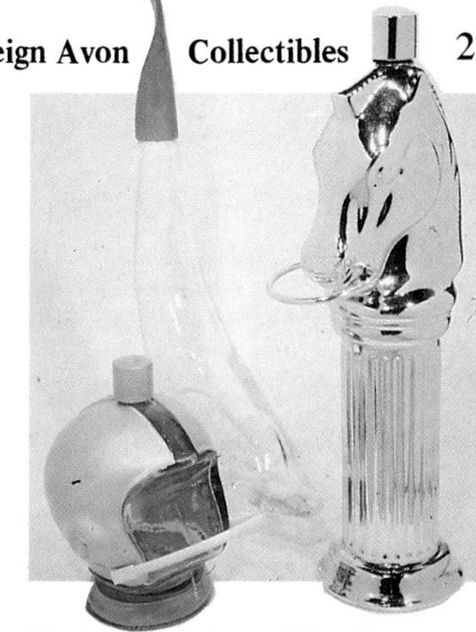

Mexico *Touchdown After Shave* **MP $25**
Mexico *Dolphin. Blue Lotus* **MP $20**
Mexico *Pony Post Cologne (Colonia para Caballeros ASL, 120cc)* **MP $35**

England, 1970 *Red glass candle container (not painted)* **MP $50**
England, 1978 *Grand Prix (shell) After Shave 60ml* **MP $5**
Mexico, 1973 *Boot* **MP $18**

Mexico, 1977 *Leather de Avon 207ml* **MP $8**
Mexico, 1978 *Plumiere After Shave 75ml $6* **MP $10**
Mexico, 1978 *Leather Locion $8* **MP $10**

Mexico, 1979 *El Toro, After Shave Locion 90ml $12* **MP $18**

Mexico, 1971 *Leather Cologne 236cc* **MP $12**

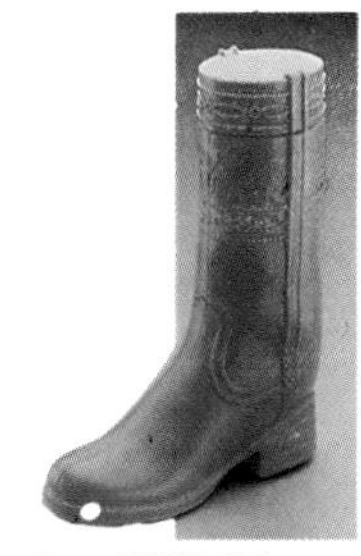

Mexico, 1980 *Dingo Boot After Shave in Wild Country or Spicy 175ml $6.15* **MP $3.75***

Australia, 1973 *Dark amber, large cap and threads (rare)* **MP $125**
Australia, 1976 *Light amber, small cap and threads* **MP $10**

Canada, 1973 *Pony Decanter, amber glass, After Shave or Hair Lotion 4oz $5* **MP $10**
Canada, 1971 *Pony Decanter, green glass, After Shave 4oz $5* **MP $15**

Canada, 1976 *Triumph TR3 '56 (green glass with plastic fitments) $6* **MP $15** *(shown in Wild Country After Shave)*

Germany, 1975 *1936 MG. Green glass, plastic cap (spare tire) 19.50DM* **MP $20** *(shown in Wild Country After Shave Lotion)*

Mexico, 1977 *Super Cycle After Shave 118ml* **MP $20**
Europe, 1977 *Racing Motorbike After Shave 100ml $3* **MP $25** *(black glass)*

England, 1979 *Bugatti '27 After Shave in Nexus or Hud 195ml $14* **MP $9.50***

**Available from Avon at time of publication*

Canada, 1971 *Chess Piece 3½oz $5* **MP $20**

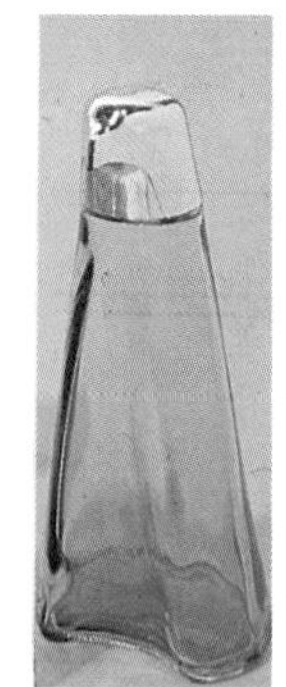

Germany, 1971 *Falcon After Shave 150ml* **MP $40**
Europe, 1975 *named Hawk 150ml* **MP $30**

Germany *Old Barrel After Shave Lotion 180cc* **MP $28**
Germany *St. Bernard 180ml After Shave* **MP $20**
Germany *Silver Candle Container* **MP $20**

Mexico, 1978 *Llama Canon, Tai Winds Cologne 58ml* **MP $8**
Europe *76 Siege Cannon, Windjammer After Shave 60ml* **MP $11**

Mexico, 1979 *Futbolista. After Shave Locion 90ml $11, Cologne 90ml $14* **MP $18 each**

Europe, 1978 *Championship Decanter After Shave with choice of country emblem 120ml.*
Scotland (shown) **MP $15**
England **MP $15** *Brazil* **MP $25**
Sweden **MP $20** *Netherlands* **MP $15**

Japan, 1979 *Book Decanter with Spicy After Shave, Cologne or Hair Tonic* **MP $20**

Mexico, 1976 *Locion Capilar $8* **MP $12**
Australia *Super Shaver* **MP $8**
Mexico, 1974 *New World After Shave* **MP $7**

Italy, 1975 *Tai Winds After Shave 50ml* **MP $11**

Europe, 1976-77 *New Style Eau de Cologne for Men in 4 frag. $2* **MP $4**

Europe, 1977-78 *After Shave Lotion 30ml in 5 frag. $1.50* **MP $4**

Europe, 1976-77 *After Shave Lotion 30ml in 4 frag. $1.80* **MP $4**

England, 1979 *New Design After Shave in Hud, Tai Winds Wild Country or Windjammer 30ml $2.50* **MP $2.10***

Europe *Wild Country After Shave 30ml $1.50* **MP $4**

Germany *Decisions 6oz, 120 cc* **MP $40**

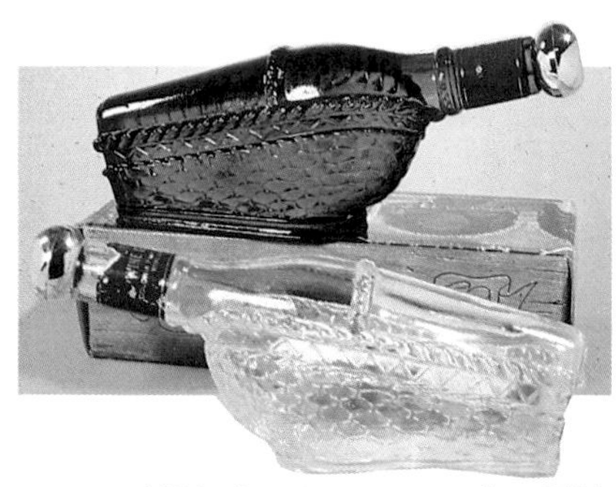

Mexico, 1972 *Wine Server, green glass. Wild Country Cologne 6oz $6.32* **MP $38**
Mexico, 1969 *Wine Server, clear glass. Windjammer Cologne 6oz $6.32* **MP $45**
Canada *Wine Server (not shown) green glass* **MP $30**

England, 1979 *V.S.O.P. After Shave or Eau de Cologne 30ml in 2 frags. each $5* **MP $2.50***

Mexico, 1980 *V.S.O.P. Cologne 28ml $3.90* **MP $2***

Mexico, 1979 *Champagne de Avon for Men in Everest or Lavender Cologne 58ml $4.35* **MP $3***

Europe, 1978 *Chateau D'Avon, 30ml After Shave or Eau de Cologne* **MP $10**

**Available from Avon at time of publication*

Canada, 1955 *Flying High No. 1. After Shave and Deodorant for Men 4oz* **MP $30**

Mexico, 1979 *After Shave Locion* **MP $10**

Canada *Spicy Talc for Men 2.75oz* **MP $5**

Canada *Men's Talc in 6 frag. 2.75oz $2* **MP $3 each**

Mexico *Talcs in New World, Spicy, Wild Country, Leather, Blend 7 and Blue Blazer 100g $2* **MP $1***

Canada *Men's Shower Soap in 6 frag. $5* **MP $8**

Europe, 1976 *After Shave Miniatures 15ml in Endeavour, Windjammer, Tai Winds, Wild Country.* **1977** *Hud and Spicy* **MP $7 each**

Canada *Carte Blanche for Men –*
1971 *Gift Set. After Shave 6oz and Soap-On-a-Rope $7.95* **MP $22**
1971 *Spray Talc 7oz $3.50* **MP $7**
1971 *After Shave Balm 3oz tube $2.50* **MP $4**

Mexico *Aqua de Colonia 300ml and 180ml $3.90 and $3* **MP $2.40* and $2***

Europe, 1978 *Blue Blazer After Shave 175ml $5.10* **MP $8**
Europe *Blue Blazer Talc 100g $1.50* **MP $3**

Europe *Blue Blazer After Shave Lotion 170cc $2.60* **MP $10**
Europe *Blue Blazer Talc 100g* **MP $6**
Europe *Blue Blazer Soap-On-a-Rope* **MP $8**

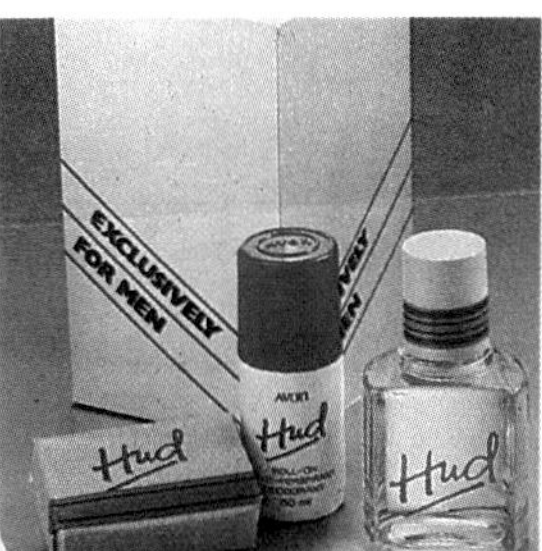

England *Matched Trio Presentation Box holds 2 bars Soap, Roll-On Deodorant and After Shave. $7 each set* **MP $10 boxed**

Europe, 1977 *Hud After Shave Lotion $4.40* **MP $8**
Europe, 1977 *Hud Talc 100g $1.50* **MP $4**

Europe *Endeavour After Shave Lotion 150ml $5.10* **MP $8**
Talc 100g $1.50 **MP $3**

Europe, 1976 *International Men's Set, Soap and After Shave* **MP $18**
Europe, 1977 *Gentlemen's Collection, Soap and After Shave* **MP $15**

Mexico, 1978 *Avon Llama (Travel Set) After Shave and Deodorant $6* **MP $10**

Mexico, 1978 *Llama Sport Talc, tin 100g* **MP $5**
Mexico, 1978 *Llama Sport Lotion Juvenil 120ml* **MP $7**

**Available from Avon at time of publication*

England *Nexus –*

(rear)
Talc 100g $2.80
MP $2.25*
Roll-On Deodorant
60ml $2.35 **MP $2***
Voyager After Shave
75ml $3.75 **MP $2.75***
After Shave (glass)
120ml $9.20
MP $6.50*
(front) Soap-On-a-Rope 14g $6.15 **MP $4.20***
Bar Soap 78g $2.80 **MP $2.25***
Eau de Cologne 50ml $5.20 **MP $2.75***

Europe *International Men's Set shown in Oland After Shave and round bar of Soap* **MP $18**

Cream Hair Lotion 4oz 95¢ **MP $30**
Liquid Hair Lotion 4oz 95¢ **MP $30**

Talc for Men 70g 65¢ **MP $30**

After Shaving Lotion 4oz 85¢ **MP $50**
Cologne for Men 4oz $1.15 **MP $50**
Invigorate 4oz $1.25 **MP $50**

KAVON

Avon entered the German market under the name of KAVON, from 1959 thru 1963.

Persian Wood – Powder Sachet .9oz $1.20 **MP $30**
Lotion Sachet 1.5oz $1.20 **MP $30**

Here's My Heart – Perfumed Talc 3oz 67¢ **MP $25**
Toilet Water 2oz $1.75 **MP $50**
Spray Cologne 3oz $2.95 **MP $30**

White Pearl Hand Lotion 6oz 87¢
MP $20

Hand Cream 3oz 77¢
MP $15

Rich Moisture Sude 6oz $1.17 **MP $20**

. . . MEN'S FOREIGN TOILETRIES

England *Master Plan – Shampoo/Shower Soap with cord 140g $7.03* **MP $6.35***

Protective Hand Cream 90ml $2.50 **MP $2.35***
Lather Shave 120ml $3.10
MP $2.80
Skin Conditioner 150ml $6.25 **MP $4.70***

Mexico, 1979 *After Shave & Talc Set in Oslo or Spicy $5.20* **MP $7**

Mexico *Oslo –*
Talc 100g $2.35 **MP $1**
Deodorant 90ml $1.95 **MP $1**
Cologne 168ml $7.80 **MP $4**
After Shave 168ml $5.65 **MP $3**

Europe *Tai Winds After Shave 150ml $5.80* **MP $9**
Europe *Tai Winds Talc 100g $1.50*
MP $3

England *Imperator –*
Eau de Cologne 120ml $9.45
MP $5
After Shave 120ml $6.85
MP $3

England *Imperator – Boxed Soap for Men* **MP $15**

Europe *Today's Man Shaving Bowl & Soap* **MP $25**
Hand Conditioner 5oz **MP $5**

Mexico, *Today's Man –*

Desodorante Solido 70g $1.92 **MP $3**
Desodorante 60ml $1.60 **MP $4**
Brillantina Liquida 60ml $1.60 **MP $4**
Vrillantina Solida 57g $1.60 **MP $3**
Desodorante 114g $2.80 **MP $5**
Spray para Caballeros (Hair Spray) 198g $3.20 **MP $6**

Europe *Torero Squeeze Spray Deodorant 81cc $1.10* **MP $5**
Europe, *Torero After Shave Lotion 120cc $1.60* **MP $8**

England *Windjammer –*
Voyager After Shave 75ml $3.75
MP $2.75*
After Shave (glass) 120ml $8.25 **MP $6***
Eau de Cologne 50ml $5.20 **MP $3.40***
Bar Soap 78g $2.10 **MP $1.75***
Soap-On-a-Rope 130g $6.15 **MP $4.20***

**Available from Avon at time of publication*

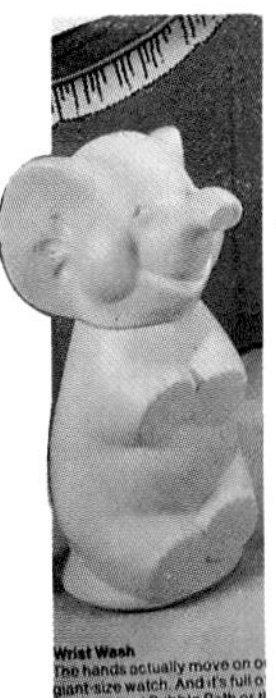

England, 1979 *Jumbo Elephant Bubble Bath or Shampoo 60ml $11.25* **MP $7***

Europe *Little Piggy, Children's Decanter* **MP $8**

Canada *Circus Talc 2.75oz $2* **MP $2**

Mexico, 1971 *Talc $2 (25 pesos)* **MP $8**
Mexico, 1971 *Juanita, Pablito y Pedrito Children's Soap Trio $2 (25 pesos)* **MP $20**

Europe, 1976 *Jumbo Soap Set, each 45g $2.80* **MP $12**
Canada *Jumbo Soap Set (all blue)* **MP $10**

Mexico, 1980 *Set for Baby, Cologne 110ml and Talc 100g and free Baby Book $4.75* **MP $3***

England, 1979 *Toofie Clown Toothbrush Holder and 2 toothbrushes $8.75* **MP $8**

Europe, 1975-76 *High Flyer Soap-On-a-Rope 110g (3.8oz)* **MP $10**

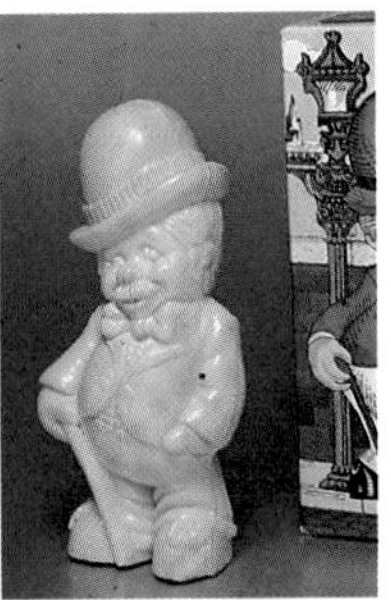

Europe, 1974-75 *Cheeky Chappie Soap-On-a-Rope 130g (4.5oz)* **MP $15**

Europe, 1973-74 *Lord Leo Soap-On-a-Rope 140g (4.9oz)* **MP $15**

Europe, 1972-73 *Top Dog Soap-On-a-Rope 142g (5oz)* **MP $18**

Canada, 1973 *Snowbird Soap Set $3* **MP $12**
Canada, 1973 *Sure Winner Ski Boot Soap-On-a-Rope $2.50* **MP $12**

Germany, 1975-76 *Huggy Bear Soap 4.25DM* **MP $10**
Germany, 1976 *Honey Lamb Soap 3.95DM* **MP $7**

Germany, 1976 *Erik the Brave Soap 4.25DM* **MP $10**

Europe, 1976-77 *Ivor the Diver Soap-On-a-Rope 130g (4.5oz)* **MP $12**

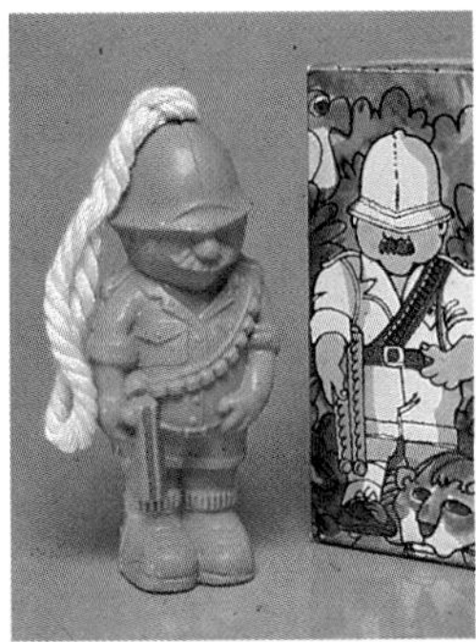

Europe, 1977-78 *Big Shot Soap-On-a-Rope 120g (4.2oz)* **MP $10**

Europe, 1975 *Knight in Armour Soap 115g (4oz)* **MP $15**

Germany, 1976 *Recollections Soap 3.95DM* **MP $8**

Europe *Pretty Peach Set. Talc 71g and Cream Sachet 19g* **MP $25**
Europe *Flower Talk Set. Talc 100g and Cream Sachet* **MP $25**

Europe, 1973 *Brother and Sister Bubble Bath 120cc (cut-out inserts in carton)* **MP $15**

Europe, 1971 *Young Romantics (Teenage Line) –*
Talc 100g $1 **MP $5**
Bath Oil 180cc $3 **MP $8**
Cologne 118cc $3 **MP $12**

**Available from Avon at time of publication*

1969 Avon Handbook *and* **Avon-1,** *the reprinted edition. 96 pages, in black & white and color, with 84 items shown. Only 5,000 of the original edition were produced.* **Avon-1** *was so popular, it was reprinted nine times! Original price $3.95.*

1971 Avon-2, *First of the all-color Western World Avon Collectors Books. 96 pages with hundreds more items. Original price $4.95* **1971 Dorothy May Information Book,** *a premium featuring our Senior Editor's columns from Western World's original magazine, the Western Collector.*

1973 Avon-3, *176 pages with some 2,000 Avon items was the first spiral bound book. Edited by Shirley Mae Onstot, famed Avon collector. Original price $9.95. The* **1917 CPC Catalog** *reproduction, never sold, a premium with purchase of Avon-3.*

1975 Avon-4, *224 pages, all in full color, with over 3,000 Avon collectibles. Original price $12.95. The full-color* **Avon-4 T-Shirt** *was a premium with a purchase of Avon-4 at a 1975 National Avon Show and Sale. Original price $5.95*

1976 Earrings *and* **Open Star Necklace** *in both gold and silver were created and distributed by Western World as a premium for the W'World Newsletter. Sold at $3.95 for the Earrings, and $9.95 for the Necklace. One year only, 1976.*

1977 Avon-5, *320 pages, all color, over 6,000 Avon collectibles shown. Spiral bound. Original price $14.95.* **Avon-5 Deluxe Edition,** *red cloth binding with owner's name imprinted in gold. Original price $21.95.*

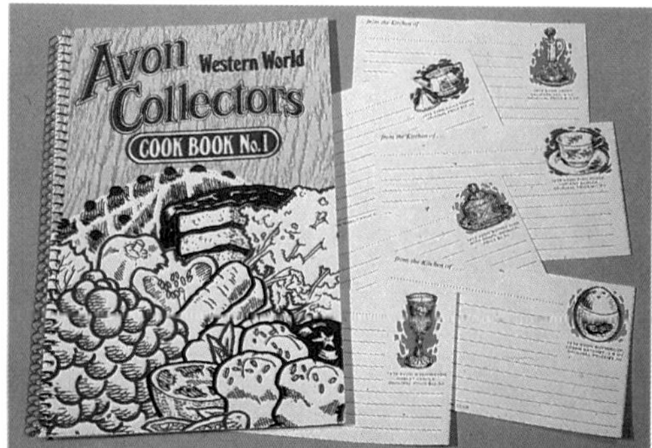

1978 Western World Cook Book No. 1. *96 pages with recipes from W'World Avon Club Members. Original price $4.95.* **1977 Recipe Cards,** *24 to the set featuring Avon collectibles on each card. Given as a premium or a gift. Original price $1.50 per set.*

1979 Avon-6, *448 pages, all in full-color, with more than 9,000 Avon items cataloged. Original price $19.95. The* **Avon-6 Deluxe Edition,** *brown leather grain cover, tabbed index and satin marker. Original price $27.95. Sold by mail only.*

1977-1979 Avon-5 & Avon-6 Jewelry Premiums. *Given to bulk purchasers of Avon-4 and Avon-5 books in recognition of outstanding sales effort. Avon-5 jewelry available as Brooch or Necklace, Avon-6 jewelry as Stickpin or Necklace. Never sol*

1975-77-79 Western World Merchandise Gifts *Felt pens with Avon-4 and Avon-5. Purse or pocket notebooks with Avon-4, -5 and -6. Thank You Notes and Household Hints book given with Avon-6 bulk purchases. Never sold.*

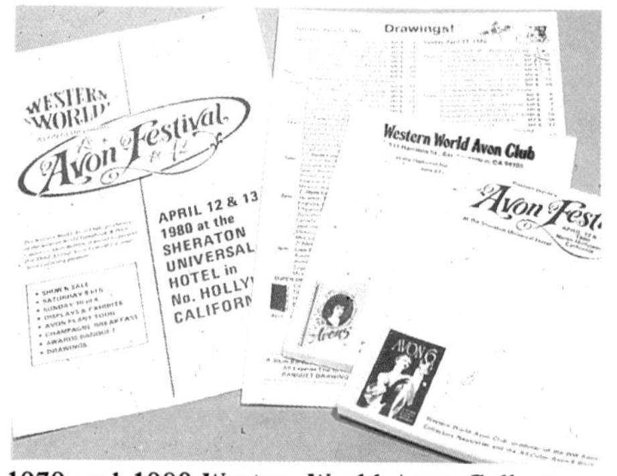

1979 and 1980 Western World Avon Collectors Festival *held at the Sheraton Universal Hotel in Universal City, California. Programs and Souvenir Scratch Pads shown. An Avon Plant Tour, Show & Sale, Dinner Banquet and Displays were featured.*

1981 Avon-7, *all color, in new, larger size. Sewn binding, over 12,000 Avon collectibles, 288 pages. Original price $22.95.* **Avon-7 Deluxe Edition** *with burgundy leather grain, padded cover, gilt edges, satin marker, gold stamped. Original price $29.95*

AVON COLLECTING

There may be an Avon club near you – and if there is – get in touch right away! It's your start on a whole new phase of Avon collecting.

It's picnics and parties, and Shows & Sales – it's Conventions and Festivals and it's a way of getting together with people you'll like – with friends that will last you a lifetime.

To find an Avon Club in your area or to start one, write to Western World at Box 27587 in San Francisco, California 94127 and ask for the Western World Chapter nearest to you. To start a Club and to become a Chapter of Western World, ask for the Free Chapter Kit – there's no cost or obligation and it could be the start of something you and your family can share and enjoy.

The National Association of Avon Collectors also maintains a list of Clubs and they'll be happy to direct you to a Club nearest your town – write to National Association of Avon Collectors, Box 4608, Overland Park, Kansas 66204

And if you like to read – and to write – then the Western World Avon Collector's Newsletter is for you. Inside this book there is a coupon that will bring, free, a sample copy of this most widely read Avon Collector's Newsletter, and with it is a special New Subscriber offer. If the card is not in your book, just write to Western World and ask for your free, New Subscriber, sample Newsletter.

Doyle and Faye Darch of Santa Ana, California, are the Collectors' Collector – their outstanding Avon groupings have been viewed by many hundreds of visitors and is one of the nation's fine Avon exhibits.

Doyle and Faye are part of the WW Photo & Editorial Team and they are seen here at work in their 'Photo Room' where many of the Avon-7 pictures were taken.

All Avons of a *particular fragrance or product line,* with the same in-line design packaging, are found under the proper name unique to the line. For example, each Cotillion item is not individually listed, but can be found under the name COTILLION in the Index. Use the same method for the other specific fragrance or product lines, such as TEMPO, BRONZE GLORY, HI-LIGHT, DELICATE BEAUTY, FASHION MAKEUP and others.

Sub-group listings are found under AWARDS, JEWELRY and PERFECTION.

Where *many fragrances share* the same bottle and packaging design, they may be found under a common title, such as PERFUMES, TALCUM, COLOGNE MINIATURES and other categories.

A

H

I

J

K

L

M

N

T

U

V

W

Y

Z